Also by Christine Rawlins

A Vision of God
A selection from the writings of Elizabeth Goudge

Beyond the Snow

The Life and Faith of Elizabeth Goudge

Christine Rawlins

WESTBOW
PRESS®
A DIVISION OF THOMAS NELSON
& ZONDERVAN

Copyright © 2015 Christine Rawlins.

All rights reserved. No part of this book may be used or reproduced by any means, graphic, electronic, or mechanical, including photocopying, recording, taping or by any information storage retrieval system without the written permission of the publisher except in the case of brief quotations embodied in critical articles and reviews.

WestBow Press books may be ordered through booksellers or by contacting:

WestBow Press
A Division of Thomas Nelson & Zondervan
1663 Liberty Drive
Bloomington, IN 47403
www.westbowpress.com
1 (866) 928-1240

Because of the dynamic nature of the Internet, any web addresses or links contained in this book may have changed since publication and may no longer be valid. The views expressed in this work are solely those of the author and do not necessarily reflect the views of the publisher, and the publisher hereby disclaims any responsibility for them.

Any people depicted in stock imagery provided by Thinkstock are models, and such images are being used for illustrative purposes only.
Certain stock imagery © Thinkstock.

ISBN: 978-1-4908-8618-3 (sc)
ISBN: 978-1-4908-8619-0 (hc)
ISBN: 978-1-4908-8617-6 (e)

Library of Congress Control Number: 2015910288

Print information available on the last page.

WestBow Press rev. date: 8/21/2015

CONTENTS

Wells

The First City Of Bells	3
An Edwardian Family	16
Mother and Child	20
Two Worlds	24
In the Kitchen	31
The Distressed Household	34
Guernsey	38
Bath	45
London and Sussex	46
Uppingham	50
The Unseen Playmate	53
The Hidden Things	56
Childhood Faith	60

Ely

The Second City of Bells	71
Loss	81
Books	83
School	87
Father and Child	90
Fear and Darkness	93
The Great War	98
Choices	100
Painting Pictures	104
First Love	107
Faith and Unbelief	109
Sisters	113
Teaching	115

Oxford and Barton

The Waste Land 121
Tom Quad 124
Oxford Life 129
Barton 132
Academia 136
Time to Write 141
Island Magic 143
Success 150
Getting Away 154
Inner Vision 160
A City of Bells 164
Breakdown 168
Childlessness 174
Lost Love 177
Fears and Burdens 181
Getting Through 185
Towers in the Mist 193
The Dark Tunnel 201
The Secret Discipline - Her Father's Spiritual Legacy 203
Learning to Cope 207

Marldon

Devon 213
Providence Cottage 215
Rebuilding the Waste Land – The Bird in the Tree 217
Work and War 224
The Castle on the Hill 233
Henrietta's House 240
Faith, Myth and Fairytales 244
The Joy to Come 249
Green Dolphin Country 252
The Film 256
The Practice of the Presence of God 257
After the War 262
The Little White Horse 264

A Bleak Winter	270
The White Deer	276
Gentian Hill	282
Mother's Last Illness	287
God So Loved the World	291
The Valley of Song	296
Alone	300
To Make an End Is to Make a Beginning	303

Peppard

Rose Cottage	313
The Heart of the Family	315
The Rosemary Tree	325
Protected	336
Inspiration	339
The White Witch	342
Saint Francis of Assisi	347
Study Always to Have Joy	350
The Dean's Watch	354
Let God Arise	357
Mary Montague	362
Peace of Mind	367
Love of Creation	371
Appleshaw	374
The Scent of Water	377
A New Kind of Heroine	383
Progress	386
The Sixties	388
Pembrokeshire	397
The Child from the Sea	399
The Inward Eye	405
Writing About Herself	408
Neighbours	419
The Little Things	420
Heavenly Music	424
The Three-fold Life	427
Credo	429

The Joy of the Snow 433
Correspondence 439
Willing to Go 451
The Last Two Years 456

The House and Gate of Heaven

"To Die into Your Resurrection" 465
Dreams of Heaven 466
The Last Dream of All 468

Appendix I 471
Appendix II 477

Acknowledgments and Bibliography 487
Endnotes 493
Index 519

For my lovely sister Pam, who gave me *The Joy of the Snow*

> When I began the journey of faith I never dreamed how important a place reading was going to have in it, that it would be quite simply the principal form of the ministry of the word in the Christian life.
> J. Neville Ward: The Following Plough[1]

Dark Moments

'All shall be well' …
She must have said that
Sometimes through gritted teeth.
Surely she knew the moments
When fear gnaws at trust,
The future loses shape,
Gethsemane?

The courage that says
'All shall be well'
Doesn't mean feeling no fear,
But facing it, trusting
God won't let go.

'All shall be well'
Doesn't deny present experience,
But roots it deep
In the faithfulness of God,
Whose will and gift is life.

                      Ann Lewin[2]

'Two strands twisted together, of black and gold'

> But all shall be well,
> and all shall be well,
> and all manner of thing shall be well.
>
> Dame Julian of Norwich
*Revelations of Divine Love*4

Elizabeth Goudge had an extraordinarily long and successful career as a writer of novels, children's books, and hagiography. Although it is now forty years since *The Joy of the Snow* was published, she still has thousands of fans worldwide who love the mixture of honesty, fiction, and faith that they discover in her work. Throughout her career she was generally praised as a writer of charming novels; at times criticized too for the happy endings of her 'escapist' fiction. But at the same time, because she drew on her own life as material for her books, there is a strong seam of reality in them, in which her readers are able to recognize their own life experience and problems, and to find real help and inspiration.

What she did so well – and supremely in her 1960 novel, *The Dean's Watch* – was to weave an almost fairytale thread through the dark reality of human struggle and weakness, and then to lift the whole novel on to a spiritual plane. In fact her bestsellers, that book-shops file under Women's Romantic Fiction, actually progressed into ever-deeper discussion of the Christian faith which was at the heart of her life, and all her work.

The happy endings were deliberate – she wanted to give her readers books filled with light and joy – and yet she also shared with them her personal experiences of loss, depression and nervous breakdown. These coloured her own view of the Christian journey, so that towards the end of her life she described the soul as

a little animal, like a mole, scrabbling with his forepaws to make an upward tunnel, kicking out with his hind-legs at the adversary who tries ceaselessly to drag him back and down. Often he is dragged down, but he recovers himself and goes on and with each fresh beginning he is a little higher up; and always the pull of the sun is far more powerful than that of the adversary.[5]

The Joy of the Snow, her autobiographical book of happy memories, acknowledges but in the main does not dwell upon these experiences of being dragged back and down, for not only did she consider herself to be ridiculously fortunate and even 'spoilt,' but a determined optimism and thankfulness was a central part of her Christian belief. Her clergyman father said in one of his sermons:

> There is a sense in which every Christian must be an optimist. In the very darkest days he can maintain his cheerfulness, because he believes in God and in a great purpose of love which will ultimately be fulfilled.[6]

For most of us, this is much easier said than done in life's "very darkest days." But however difficult it might be, a vital part of the soul's journey as she saw it was to counter the adversary by focusing upon the light above; always struggling to accomplish what Robert Louis Stevenson called his great *task* of happiness. Happiness is therefore central to all her work, even that undertaken at periods of great difficulty in her life. Although the darkness might then, for a while, hold her back:

> *when…the sun showed signs of coming out again I would write as hard as I could, determined that I would write books and that they should be happy ones.*[7]

No doubt it was for this same reason that she left no very detailed account of her dark times in *The Joy of the Snow*. There are only those happy novels… which also deal with loneliness, war, childlessness, mental illness, and breakdown. Her own winter experiences.

A question authors are often asked, she says, is "Do we put ourselves in our books?"

> *Speaking for myself I do not put the woman I am into them but after I had been writing for years I noticed the regular appearance in story after story of a tall graceful woman, well-balanced, intelligent, calm, capable and tactful. She is never flustered, forgetful, frightened, irritable or nervy. She does not drop bricks, say the opposite of what she means, let saucepans boil over or smash her best teapot. She is all I long to be and all I never will be. She is in complete reverse a portrait of myself.*[8]

There appears also, in story after story, at least one character – male or female – who is broken in some way; struggling and suffering but nevertheless trying hard to live their Christian faith; often failing and in their own eyes ineffectual, but still soldiering prayerfully on. Like Jean Anderson in *The Scent of Water*, for whom life is a daily battle. "Many of her fears and burdens would have seemed unreal to another woman, [but] there was nothing unreal about her courage" because she had always "done what she had to do and faced what she had to face."

> *She always did the thing because in obedience lay the integrity that God asked of her. If anyone had asked her what she meant by integrity she would not have been able to tell them, but she had seen it once like a picture in her mind, a root going down into the earth and drinking deeply there. No one was really alive without that root.*[9]

Fiction, of course, can never be assumed to reflect the reality of its author – but as Parson Hawthyn says on receiving the gift of a book in *The White Witch*: "You give me great wealth, for the gift of a book is the gift of a human soul. Men put their souls in their books."[10]

The soul in the books of Elizabeth Goudge reached out to readers worldwide and surely made of her, not merely a romantic novelist but one of the great Christian writers of the twentieth century.

For whatever her life contained, whatever she had to cope with or to live without, she strove to find light in the darkness, and to create comfort and hope for others from her own despair: sharing her winter experiences with her readers, but always taking them beyond the snow, into a place of potential joy. That it was not always easy is apparent from that image of the little, scrabbling animal. But at the end of the struggle she could share with the world a hard-won belief that the light of Christ lies hidden at the heart of all life's darkness, and that indeed All Shall be Well.

Easter 2015

WELLS

❋

1900 - 1911

The First City Of Bells

No child can have lived in lovelier houses than my first two homes, or in a more enchanted city than Wells at the beginning of the century...[11]

Elizabeth de Beauchamp Goudge was born on 24th April 1900 at Tower House, St. Andrew Street, in Wells. It is England's smallest city: set in the West Country, in the green and rural county of Somerset. With still nine months left of Queen Victoria's reign, she was born into a world of petticoats and bonnets, servants and horse-drawn traffic; but her birth came too at the cusp of a new century, when the massive upheaval of two great wars was soon to change the world. Despite the peaceful security of her ecclesiastical childhood, this little girl would have inner battles of her own to fight too: battles which seemed at times as if they might destroy her.

Her work as a writer was never unaffected by her battles - and yet it has always been described, entirely accurately, as enchanting, happy and delightful. They were labels she acquired early on in her career, with novels which largely looked back to childhood – her own and her mother's - or beyond, into history. Much of her autobiographical writing too focuses on the early years and the picture she paints is idyllic – whether writing for her adult readers or, as here in her preface to *A Child's Garden of Verses*, for children. She uses the poetry of Robert Louis Stevenson to enlarge on her own recollections – what *The Joy of the Snow* acknowledges as her gratitude that she was born when she was.

One of my earliest memories of being in a particular place is of being in bed in the night nursery...and looking out of the wide uncurtained window at the sky still full of light...I can see the tree outside the window and my rag doll Violet with the darn on her nose, sitting at the foot of the bed, and outside the window, up in the sky at the top of the hill, there is the steeple of a church silhouetted black against the afterglow, and below it the tumbled uneven roofs of the old houses. The child I remember would watch until the light faded and the walls of the houses were patched with warm squares of lamplight, and then would come the lovely flowering of the lamps as the lamplighter came down the hill. And then presently the stars would come out, "the crowds of the stars...that glittered and winked in the dark," but their light was no lovelier than the light of the lamps that made a double chain of jewels down the street. It must be wonderful, I would think, to be a lamplighter, and then dazzled by the brightness I would turn over and look at the pictures that were "pasted on the wall" beside my bed, Christmas cards and advertisements, and pictures that

Nanny and I had cut out of Pears Annual *and stuck on ourselves with a flour paste that we had made on the kitchen stove.*

> *But the glory kept shining and bright in my eyes,*
> *And the stars going round in my head...*[12]

Her early years were spent in a world that she says had hardly changed for centuries, and she certainly identifies with Stevenson's memories as if they were her own, even though he is looking back to the 1850s.

All the particular joys of those days are here; R.L.S. has captured them all...the barrel organ and the lamplighter, the swing and the hayloft. In our quiet lives the thrill of the lamplighter was followed next in order of thrill by hearing the hurdie-gurdie coming down the street. We would rush to the day nursery window or the garden gate to catch a sight of his little red-coated monkey and to dance to the sound of his tunes. One is sorry for the child of today that he has no lamplighter and no hurdie-gurdie.

He has a swing in the garden perhaps, but...the modern swing is not so wonderful as ours, which was fastened to a very high branch on a very tall tree, in our garden a huge cedar tree, and had long ropes which swung you to such an immense height that you could see right out of your own kingdom into the wider world.

> *Up in the air and over the wall,*
> *Till I can see so wide,*
> *Rivers and trees and cattle and all*
> *Over the countryside.*

There was no joy to be compared with it except the joy of the hayloft. I remember the one where I played as a child, that quiet fragrant place with the bales of hay and the scampering mice, the motes of dust dancing in the golden sunshine that shone through the small window, the Devonshire pony munching in his stall below, beside the old governess cart that took us so many miles through the narrow, dusty white lanes that wound their way up through the high green Somersetshire hills. When we were tired of playing games in the hay we would lie on our fronts, our legs in the air, munching apples and reading.

> *O what a joy to clamber there,*
> *O what a place for play,*
> *With the sweet, the dim, the dusty air,*
> *The happy hills of hay.*[13]

This idyllic picture of a lost England prefaced a new edition of the *Child's Garden* which came out in 1955, seventy years after its first publication. The introduction to an earlier, 1925 reprint had been written by the poet and novelist Laurence Alma Tadema: eldest daughter of the Royal Academician. Curiously, her description of the infant RLS might in many ways be applied to the young Elizabeth too: a "solitary child…more iridescent than other children, beloved yet alone, timorous yet valiant, frail yet strong …a dreamer in action, whose eyes search beyond sight, whose ears are not deaf to silence."[14]

Silence was certainly one feature of Elizabeth's early childhood which she remembered with gratitude:

We are probably better off without the white summer dust, yet I remember it gratefully. It could be so thick in the country lanes about Wells in high summer that the slow trot of the pony's feet, pulling a governess cart full of children to Wookey Hole for a picnic, could hardly be heard. Quietness was complete in the countryside. If you stood and listened in the lanes in those days it was so still that you could hear a dog barking a mile off, and at times it could be complete in the streets of the city. And sound, when it came, was much the same as it had always been; children coming out of school, bells pealing, dogs barking, the baker's boy whistling, someone singing within a house at evening, the sound drifting through an open window. It had hardly changed for centuries.

Even the houses had hardly changed. There must have been a few Victorian villas built here and there on the edge of the old city but I do not remember them. I only remember the changelessness of the place and the sense of safety that it gave, its only contacts with the outside world the few trains that slithered slowly and peacefully as earthworms through the valleys, stopping every ten minutes to pick up milk churns from under the lilac bushes on the station platforms, and to deposit in their place two sleepy passengers and a crate of hens.[15]

❋

Sometimes the grown-ups joined the picnics, and then a dignified Edwardian cavalcade of dogcarts and carriages would wind up the white dusty lanes to the hills above.[16]

Drawing upon this memory at the height of the Second World War, she created a picnic with the grown-ups (in *Henrietta's House*, the last of her Wells-based novels for children) that was particularly splendid.

First the Archdeacon's landau came bowling round the corner, with the coachman very smart upon the box, with a red dahlia in his buttonhole and a little red bow on his whip. The Archdeacon was inside, resplendent in gaiters, with dear old Canon Roderick with his round, rosy face and his two sticks, and Mrs. Roderick dressed in lavender with a lavender parasol, carrying her ear-trumpet and the basket of raspberries, waving their hands to the children.

> *No sooner was Grandmother stowed in with them than Mrs. Jameson and her Pekingese arrived in their victoria, their coachmen also having a flower in his button-hole. Mrs. Jameson was a tall, white-haired old lady who was still very lovely and must once have been staggeringly beautiful. As she was very religious she dressed always in the colours of the Church's seasons, wearing white during festivals, purple in Lent, red at Whitsun and green the rest of the year...Today she was dressed in beautiful shimmering green satin with an enormous green plumed bonnet and a green frilled parasol to match, and lovely diamonds swung in her ears and winked on her fingers and on the front of her dress. Mee-Too, her Pekingese, observed the Church's seasons too. He had a green bow...*
>
> *The Dean's dogcart, with huge wheels, built of yellow varnished wood that shone so brightly in the sun that one blinked when one looked at it...was drawn by a glorious black mare with arched head and floating tail, whose clattering hoofs seemed to spurn the earth they trod on...She champed furiously at her bit when the Dean reined her to a standstill... The Dean was driving his own equipage. He was a fine figure of an aristocratic old gentleman, very upright and stately, wearing a white stock, an eye-glass, and a magnificent glossy top hat tilted forward over a fine aquiline nose...He had a couple of shooting sticks with him in the dogcart; you can quite easily pick out the really aristocratic people at a picnic, because they always have shooting sticks.*[17]

So golden were these memories of life in the early years of the century that she could feel, as she said in the *Child's Garden* preface, "sorry for the modern child."

There is another description of Edwardian life in a small country town in her children's story *The Easter Bunny* – and again she gives many details that, for any reader of *The Joy of the Snow* are recognisably those of her own childhood.

> *In those days the world was peaceful, and clothes were gay. The ladies' spring hats were the size of small cartwheels and had velvet or satin bows on them and bunches of flowers, and sometimes an entire dead bird spreading its wings on the brim. And their spring coats and skirts were of emerald green and royal blue, tight-waisted and flowing to the ground, and the blouses worn with them were lacy and frothed.*

Old gentlemen wore nosegays in their buttonholes and carried gold-headed canes, and little girls had large bright bows on their hair and little boys wore sailor suits complete with lanyards and brass whistles.

And these glories were not hidden in closed cars or crushed up in overcrowded buses, but displayed to advantage in slow-moving dignified victorias or gently jogging governess carts, or upon pavements where pedestrians moved as though they had oceans of time before them and not a trouble in the world.[18]

The Easter Bunny begins with the assertion that "fifty years ago, Easter was a fine time for children" and goes on to list all the wonderful seasonal treats which fortunate youngsters who "were used to a surfeit of good things" had to eat. Elizabeth was certainly one of the fortunate ones, but not just because of the "boiled eggs coloured with cochineal for breakfast, chocolate eggs hidden in the garden…and toy bunnies filled with sweets."[19] From the start, the historic setting for this little girl's childhood ensured that it was both privileged and unusual.

❊

As the daughter of a clergyman, the first half of her life was lived in the shadow of some of England's most glorious cathedrals. The Reverend Henry Leighton Goudge was still in the early days of his eminent teaching career at the time of her birth. He was Vice-Principal of Wells Theological College and his official residence, Tower House, was almost directly across the road from the ancient Cathedral Church of St. Andrew, consecrated in the year 1239 by Bishop Jocelin de Welles. Elizabeth described just such a cathedral in *Sister of the Angels*.

They were standing just inside the west door…and looking up the length of the great nave they could see the…statue of the Virgin and Child that stood high up in the inverted arch that supported the central tower. It was so far away that on many days, gilded though it was, it was almost lost in the darkness, but today a shaft of sunlight, shining through a clerestory window, lit it up with such a golden glory that it seemed like a lamp shining in the heart of the shadowy Cathedral, lighting up a little and no more of this mysterious great building that man had built to the glory of God.[20]

Their home too had centuries of history printed upon its walls... not least, in an arched doorway recognisably the work of William Joy, the King's Mason who was the fourteenth century architect and builder of the cathedral's amazing scissor arches: that "inverted arch that supported the central tower."

Although Elizabeth was born in Tower House, it was her home only until she was two years old. Then Father was promoted to Principal of the College and the little family of three – her mother Ida, the Reverend Goudge and his little Beth, as he called her – moved across the road to the Principal's residence. Another beautiful and historic house, it had "dark corners and passages that were wonderful for hide-and-seek,"[21] she remembered. The move brought them into even closer proximity to the Cathedral - it was now in fact their next-door neighbour, for only a narrow strip of land separates the house from the Cathedral's glorious east windows and Lady Chapel; and its large garden adjoins the Cathedral grounds and the gardens of the moated Bishop's Palace beyond.

I think I am correct in thinking that the garden...was a marvellous one. It was in those days large and as well as the shrubbery it had everything in it that a garden should have; grass and trees, flowers and vegetables, and it had something else in it which few gardens can boast; a cathedral for one of its walls.[22]

When she came to write her novels about Wells, however, it was Tower House that she used as their setting; all except for the bedrooms at the Principal's House, which she remembered "were decorated with carved cherubs of stone or wood."

When I wrote A City of Bells *I placed my family in Tower House but fetched the cherub population from across the road to be with them.*[23]

A City of Bells was published in April 1936. Her third novel, it was nevertheless the first to be set in the city of her childhood – although "Torminster is not an entirely accurate picture of Wells,"[24] she said. One of its young protagonists is named after Bishop Jocelin himself, and this is his introduction to the Fordyce family home:

It was old and grey and solid, its walls half hidden by creepers and its small, diamond-paned windows so withdrawn among them that nothing could be seen of the rooms inside. It would have looked like a farmhouse but for the extraordinary apparition of a tall grey tower that shot up at one side of it.

> *It was an astonishing house. When Jocelyn had walked up the flagged path between the flower-beds, and stooped beneath the branches of an apple-tree, he found himself under the porch in front of the open door looking down a flight of steps into what seemed a dark cellar. The walls of the house, he noticed, were three feet thick and the smell of damp was overpowering... As his eyes grew accustomed to the darkness, he saw that the cellar was a large, stone-paved, vaulted hall.*[25]

It seems that it was not just the cherubs who crossed the road into her fictional Tower House, but the damp as well. For their new house "was not all joy."[26] In its idyllic position near the Palace moat and 'some of the wells that gave Wells its name,'[27] the beautiful Rib, or Bishop's Rib – an ancient name for the mediaeval Principal's House - was damp. It was "a dampness which in those days," Elizabeth remembered, "frequently meant water oozing up through the floors."[28] In a biographical introduction to one of her father's books of sermons, she further explains that the floorboards "were laid on the bare earth with no foundations beneath them" and adds that her father "was the only one whose health was not affected by the damp of that house."[29] But as so often, she turned this darker element of Wells life into fictional light and humour: making Mr. Gotobed observe in *A City of Bells* that "the gentry... don't object to the rheumatics if caused by 'istory."[30]

There was history in plenty at the centre of Elizabeth's earliest memories. The sixteenth-century stone tower at Tower House had "little rooms like monastic cells leading from the spiral stone staircase" and its garden was "enclosed within high stone walls."[31] Immediately behind these walls can be seen the roofs and tall chimneys of the beautiful Vicars' Close, dating from 1348 and believed to be the oldest surviving complete mediaeval street anywhere in Europe.

There is a 1904 Edwardian postcard of the Vicars' Close looking south, one of the 'Oilette' series produced by Raphael Tuck and Sons, "art publishers to their majesties the King and Queen." In this painted image, naturally the picturesque ancient buildings predominate, with the Cathedral towering over all in the background. But the artist has also captured a moment of contemporary time: a man stands at the gate of one of the houses, with an autumnal display of what looks like Virginia creeper tumbling over its garden wall; and a small girl walks down the Close with a female in a grey outfit – what could perhaps be the original, grey uniform of the Norland nanny. The little girl herself wears a long white dress and a large matching hat, rather like the outfit Elizabeth is wearing in *The Joy of the Snow's* earliest photograph of her as a child... Could it have been Elizabeth herself whom the artist sketched that day?

Wells

Hers was indeed an unusual childhood, bearing more than a passing resemblance to the fictional Barsetshire world of Anthony Trollope; for during the first eleven years of her life the canons, bishops and deans of Wells were her family's near neighbours. In fact she shared a birthday with Trollope, who was born eighty-five years earlier on 24th April 1815; and like him, she was to create many delightful and memorable clergymen in her novels. Unlike the divines of Barchester, however, they were drawn from their creator's own memories of life in the cathedral close (called, in Wells, 'the Liberty') and were, she admitted, not always totally fictional.

The Dean made a great impression on my child's mind, unfortunately an impression that was a little too vivid, for as the years passed the originally fine and slightly theatrical figure became in memory no longer awe-inspiring but merely comic... When I came to write A City of Bells *the Dean of that story arrived instantly readymade, tall and handsome with white muttonchop whiskers, a high-pitched voice and a top hat a little on one side, a wealthy man who drove his tall dog-cart in a dashing manner and had an eye for horse-flesh and a pretty woman.*

The Dean was in the book before I knew he was coming but when I did recognise him I am afraid I made no attempt at all to turn him out, and my father when he read the story could hardly forgive me.[32]

Not only did she not turn him out, she used him again in *Henrietta's House* to great comic effect, in the promotion of Grandfather's socialist principles. The Dean reprimands young Hugh Anthony for listening to "the gossip retailed by the Lower Orders..."

"Why do you call the people who don't live in the Close the Lower Orders?" asked Hugh Anthony. "Grandfather calls them God's Poor."
"Eh?" said the Dean, a little startled, and then he adjusted his eyeglass and rubbed his nose in a puzzled sort of way, as though he did not quite know how to answer.
"I suppose," said Hugh Anthony, "that Saint Hugh of Torminster belonged to the Lower Orders?"
"Certainly not," said the Dean indignantly. "The Blessed Saint Hugh was Abbot of Torminster. I hold – I say it in all humility – a position very like his own."
"Before he was Abbot of Torminster, he kept pigs," said Hugh Anthony. "Like Mr. Burton, our butcher."
"Merely legendary pigs," said the Dean.

"And the Apostles were fishmongers," continued the awful child, *"like Mr. Robson in the Market Place... It's a pity, isn't it, that* all *the saints seem to belong to the Lower Orders?"*[33]

For the child Elizabeth, not only the clergy but the ecclesiastical buildings had character, and were numinous presences in her young life. She described their influence not only in *The Joy of the Snow* but in the introduction to an omnibus edition of three of her novels: *Three Cities of Bells*.

[I can remember] leaning against the wall of the cathedral. I must have been very young at the time for it is one of my earliest memories. The cathedral grew up out of our garden like a stone mountain out of a meadow, a vast benign presence brooding over us by night and day, talking to us in bell-music and concerned for our safety.

But I was not in a benign mood as I leaned against its great stone flank, for the devil was in me. It was a warm sunny Good Friday and my request to accompany the adults to the Three Hours' service had been categorically refused; which was not surprising as I was not able at this date to compose myself to orderly behaviour even through the short span of going-out-before-the-sermon matins. But I was furious. I had been denied access to my own cathedral, which grew out of my own garden, and I raged against the wall. And then to my graceless condition grace was mercifully given. Over my head was a stained glass window and it mediated to me the sound of distant music. They were singing far away inside the cathedral. A small thing, perhaps, to leave behind such an indelible impression but the experience was indescribably lovely. To me this was not earthly music. It melted the rage out of me and filled me up instead with awe and longing. It was then, I think, that cathedrals became to me the symbolic presences that they have been ever since...[34]

Beside the Cathedral, under an archway, a gate opened into a small graveyard and from there another archway led into the cloisters... Whenever I liked I could run through the green garth to the cloisters, and I often did. I liked being there alone and gazing out through the arches at the central square of green grass that seemed to breathe out cool quietness as a well does. Years later, when I lived at Oxford, I would escape in the same way to the small cloister at Magdalen College. It had the same sort of stillness.

From the Wells cloisters steps led down to a place of grass and tall trees, and beyond was the outer wall of the Bishop's Palace, and the drawbridge over the moat where the arrogant swans pulled a bell when they were hungry and bread was immediately thrown to them.[35]

In this respect, Torminster in *A City of Bells* is Wells.

If the houses in the Close, hidden behind their high walls, could be seen with the eyes of imagination as fortresses, the Palace was one in actual fact. Grey, battlemented walls, with loopholes for arrows, surrounded it and its gardens, completely hiding them from sight, and a wide moat,

> *brimful of water, surrounded the walls. The portcullis was still there, and the drawbridge that linked this warlike island to the peace of Torminster.*
>
> *As they stood watching, the swans obligingly rounded the curve of the moat and sailed royally towards the drawbridge... The foremost swan...pulled with his beak the bell-rope that hung from the Palace wall. He rang it once, imperiously...and instantly a human menial showered bread from a window. This ringing of the bell was the superb accomplishment of the swans of Torminster, an accomplishment that had made them world-famous.*[36]

Small wonder that Elizabeth said, linking her own childhood experience with that of Robert Louis Stevenson:

> *Looking back from such a different world, through such a length of time, it seems that the sheltered happy childhoods of Victorian and Edwardian days had a very special magic.*[37]

❊

Although she loved stillness and quietness she was "never lonely in those early days," for she was not the only child living in this world of venerable clerics. Her "chief playmates …were a family of boys who lived across the road in the house with the tower."[38] These were the sons of her father's friend Arthur Hollis, afterwards Bishop of Taunton, who had succeeded Canon Goudge as Vice-Principal of the College. She remembered, "Our chief pleasure was in climbing trees. The gardens of Wells abounded in lovely trees, chiefly mulberries and cedars."[39] Some of their play, in the safety of the large walled garden at Tower House, may have been the inspiration behind Henrietta's games with Hugh Anthony in *A City of Bells*.

> *The cedar-tree was glorious. It grew on a patch of grass in the middle of the potatoes and was so big that it was more like a mountain than a tree. Its trunk and branches were a deep red-brown that glowed like fire when the setting sun touched them and the rest of it was a heavenly blue-green, almost the colour of rock-pools when the shadow of night is over them. It was the easiest tree to climb in the world, for the great boughs branched out from the trunk the whole way up it in a series of steps, so that a child could climb to its top in perfect safety...*

And for these children, their theological background informed their play.

> There were shouts and scramblings in the tree and Hugh Anthony bellowed at the full force of his lungs, "Who is on my side? Who? Throw her down!" The Sunday picture-books fell heavily into the potatoes and Henrietta's voice lamented, "So they threw her down, and he trod her under foot, and the dogs ate her."
>
> Grandfather sighed. Not a single word of his Sunday Lesson had sunk in, he supposed, not a single word, but he was to be blamed in that he had allowed them Bibles of their own at too tender an age... Trust the young to fasten instantly upon what you would prefer them not to fasten upon...
>
> Henrietta and Hugh Anthony, having buried what was left of Jezebel, climbed to the top of the tree and were the ark perched on Ararat. Hugh Anthony was Noah and Henrietta was the animals and all round them rolled a waste of waters.
>
> "They're going down!" shouted Hugh Anthony. "Look, you can see the hills poking out... Now where did I put that dove?"
>
> Henrietta, hastily making all the animal noises she could think of, looked and saw how the waters quieted and sank sobbing to sleep while out of them there rose fold after fold of misty hills beneath the arch of a rainbow.
>
> "I'll just go down and tell Ham in the hold," said Noah, and slid downwards, greening the seat of his trousers as he went.[40]

Elizabeth remembered being "not so good at climbing as the boys were" for "I was a fat child and usually stuck at the top, where I would remain shrieking until the gardener came with his ladder and fetched me down."[41]

Another, quieter, pastime as she told a friend[42] in later life, was playing with her hoop in the cathedral close. She also had a friend called Dorothy Pope, to whom she dedicated *Henrietta's House* with these words: "There were once two little girls, one had fair hair and lived in the Cathedral Close of Torminster and the other had dark hair and lived in the blue hills above the city, and they were friends." [The book was published in America under the title *The Blue Hills*.]

And she had her father's companionship, too: "an inveterate walker" who "however busy he was... hardly ever missed his daily tramp."[43] She says, "I can remember how vital he was in those days...he played games hard, he tramped for miles over the Mendip hills, and he bicycled with incredible speed."[44] He also took his daughter for walks, "suiting his pace to mine," she remembered, as soon as she could "stagger."[45]

> *Country walks were his greatest delight... [and] in the country round Wells he had the beauty that he loved spread out all round him in glorious richness. One of my first memories, as a very small child, was his sitting me on top of a gate, with woods and fields around us and Wells Cathedral down below in the valley, and saying, "Now we must thank God for making the world so beautiful."*[46]

But life was not all recreation, of course. Time had to be given to what in *The Joy of the Snow* she called her "non-education."

> *One of these little boys and I did lessons together with a governess, Miss Lavington. To look at she was like the Miss Lavender of* A City of Bells *but she was not like her in her methods of teaching.*[47]

> *Miss Lavender...was tall and thin, with grey hair and a kind, meek face. She always wore grey alpaca, and steel-rimmed glasses, and her beautiful voice was never raised either in reproof or anger... Her method of education was very much ahead of her time, for she employed the modern method of self-government and allowed her pupils to study whatever subject they felt most drawn to at the moment. But in employing this method she was not actuated by a study of child psychology but by a desire for peace and quiet.*[48]

The real Miss Lavington, on the other hand, "was a magnificent, if stern, teacher."

> *I have never had any memory, or any brains, but what little I do know was pounded into my unwilling mind by Miss Lavington. At that time I could actually repeat from memory the dates of the Kings of England from William the Conqueror downwards, and my tables up to twelve times twelve. This intellectual accomplishment was not attained without strenuous and exhausting work on the part of Miss Lavington, and floods of bitter tears on mine.*[49]

The creation of Miss Lavender gave Elizabeth the opportunity to write with humour about the whole process of non-education. In this scene Grandfather has requested that Henrietta and Hugh Anthony be taken to the Tor Woods for Nature study:

> *She loved a country walk with the dear children. She had no clear idea what Nature study was, or how it should be pursued, but she thought they were doing their duty if they took with them a volume called* Wild Life Shown to the Children, *and then when they found any queer-looking fauna or flora they hunted through the book and found they were not there... Which, after all, was not their fault.*[50]

The incompetence of her teacher was pure fiction, but was Henrietta's reaction to a geography lesson at the orphanage perhaps heartfelt enough to be fact?

> *She was sitting with the other children learning about the capes of England, where they stuck out far into the sea and where they did not stick out so far, what towns sat upon them and what towns did not, what counties they stuck out of and what seas they stuck out into, and Henrietta, like Galileo, cared for none of these things.... She was bored.*[51]

Elizabeth may or may not have shared Henrietta's boredom with the capes of England, but they certainly shared a love of art and music, faith and the poetry of words.

> *Henrietta loved words, both the shape and the sound of them...She had discovered through words the symbolism of sound and shape and their relationship, just as in her dreams she had learnt to link colour and movement with music. "Silver" was a word that she especially loved. She thought it was the loveliest of words because it was so cool... she immediately thought of fountains playing and a long, cool drink on a hot day. It was a satisfactory word to write too, with its capital S flowing like a river, its l tall as a silver spear and the v like an arrow-head upside down. Yellow was another good word because of that glorious capital Y that was like a man standing on a mountain-top at dawn praying to God, with his arms stretched out, his figure black against a sky the colour of buttercups.... All her life yellow was her favourite colour and the one that symbolized the divine to her.*[52]

The child Elizabeth used her own love of words to keep her friends entertained – with what she called a re-telling, with "embellishments,"[53] of her mother's stories. She was then still young enough for the physical act of writing to be a chore, for although she and the Hollis boys "wrote a magazine which came out each month," the publication was not long-lived, she remembered. It lasted only "until the labour of writing out my stories palled upon me, which was a very short time indeed."[54] Nevertheless she was still a little girl when she began to write, some time before the age of eleven:

I began to write as a child in the Principal's House at Wells and have scarcely left off since. I began with an interminable story that was intended to be funny but as the only character I can remember is a fat man stuck in a chimney it was probably only vulgar. This work was never finished because I became so absorbed in it that I forgot to feed my caterpillars, and they died. In grief and remorse I abandoned writing for the time being. When I took it up again I kept to short pieces, poems and fairy stories, perhaps feeling they would be less dangerous to the life of others.[55]

An Edwardian Family

However close the bond of love within a family, in an Edwardian middle-class home such as hers there must have been a certain element of distance between parents and their offspring, for children were in the care of a Nanny and lived "behind the green baize door of the nursery wing."[56] They often spent only certain hours of the day with their parents and might not, as would be the norm for many of today's children, have the free run of any room in the house.

One room which was all but out-of-bounds for Elizabeth was Father's special domain, his study - understandably, as much of his work as clergyman, tutor, and author of around thirty published works, would have been carried out at home. He must have spent a good deal of his time closeted there, and greatly valued its privacy, which was largely created by a custom-made double bookcase.

It was about six feet long and five feet high, was lined with bookshelves on each side and placed at right angles to the door. My father had his chair and writing table upon the other side of it and with books at his back and books to right and left sat in a protected nook, unseen by anyone entering the room.

This excellent piece of furniture, she said, was created by "the artist-craftsman of a cabinet-maker who made much of my parents' furniture" and it "accompanied him from study to study wherever he lived."

Its value was greater than may appear at first sight. As a priest my father had to be at any time cheerfully available to anyone who wanted him, but as a writer he hated to be disturbed. At the sound of a knock at the study door exasperation would rise within him, and was sometimes apparent in the tone of his 'come in', but the time it took the visitor to get round to the other side of the bookcase gave him time to compose his features, and take a firmer grip of his Christianity. There was nothing to be seen on his face when the intruder reached him but an expression of angelic patience, and the warmest of welcomes was always apparent in his smile and voice. I know, for I had to intrude myself so many times. But the bookcase had yet another value. To knock at the door, to hear that 'come in' and then have to walk around that bookcase, was intimidating. One did not intrude upon my father on merely trivial matters.[57]

Despite Father's angelic patience and warm welcome, the bookcase which she remembered in such detail sixty years later created a private space for him that was not only intimidating but, for a little girl, at times "most alarming." For she recalled that when in later years they moved to Ely, "one went down steps to the narrow doorway of the study and on entering found a wall to the right…"

It was very dark between that wall and the bookcase. I was only eleven when we went to Ely and if I was entering the study conscious of my misdeeds I found that narrow dim place most alarming; especially with my father dead silent round the corner, no sound to be heard except perhaps the faint scratching of his pen.[58]

> *The next day, with a beating heart, Ermyntrude climbed the steep stone steps which led to her uncle's room…and, standing on tiptoe, knocked at the big iron-bound door.*
>
> *"Come in," said a deep gruff voice.*
>
> *It needed both hands and all Ermyntrude's strength to lift the heavy latch, but she managed it, and the door swung open on creaking hinges. The Baron, his spectacles on the end of his nose, his black skull-cap on the back of his head, was writing with a gigantic quill pen in a huge, leather-bound book. He looked round in surprise as the door opened, and saw little Ermyntrude standing just inside the room, her eyes wide with fright, and her hands clasped together…*
>
> *The Baron was very surprised to see her; he took off his spectacles and rubbed them with an enormous pocket-handkerchief; then he put them on again and held out his hand to her.*

> *Ermyntrude ran across the room, and, her shyness suddenly vanishing, climbed on his knee. The Baron was strangely touched; he had never felt the need of his little niece before, and had never thought that she could need him.*[59]

This is from *The Flower of Happiness*, one of the children's stories Elizabeth published at the age of nineteen in her first book, *The Fairies' Baby and Other Stories*. Although little Ermyntrude's beating heart and fright could have been based on her own experiences, there may perhaps have been a touch of wishful thinking here too - for despite her great love for her father it is doubtful whether the child Elizabeth would ever have had the temerity to climb upon his knee when he was at work in the study. She did just once dare to burst in upon him, in the excitement of being allowed for the first time to choose the fabric for her new summer dressing gown.

> *I chose a material which I think was called delaine. It was white, patterned with little roses of a blinding shade of pink. I thought it beautiful and I could not wait to show it to my father. Perhaps I remember this incident so vividly because it was the only time in my life that I ever approached him in his study without a sense of awe. I did not wait for his intimidating "Come in." I burst the door open, ran to him, shook out the delaine and dropped the appalling pink roses on top of the sermon he was writing. "My dressing-gown," I gasped. "I chose it." He did not fail me. He half-closed his eyes and his face took on the expression of the Bisto kids in the advertisement. "Beautiful." Then disentangling himself and his sermon from the roses he handed them back to me, returned to his work and forgot me. But I was quite satisfied. We had been at one in our admiration of perfect beauty.*[60]

"It was the only time in my life that I ever approached him in his study without a sense of awe." In contrast, she had fond memories of time spent in her grandfather's study.

> *I made a point of standing at his elbow when he was working and if I drove him distracted his serene selflessness let no signs of irritation appear. In memory his little study is full of sunshine, with the scent of the passion flowers rioting over the balcony outside coming in through the open window. It would not even have occurred to me to stand at my father's elbow while he worked; I doubt if he would have tolerated me there. The difference between the two men was that my father did not love children as children, though he did his duty by them when related to him with admirable patience, while my grandfather loved all children, clean or dirty, good or bad, with equal devotion.*
>
> *When he became aware of me he would patiently put down his pen and smile.*[61]

Nevertheless at a time of crisis, when her mother was particularly unwell and went away to Bath for the winter, Father made time for her and for once his study became a place of play.

Somehow he found time to play with me as my mother had done before she became too ill. The playtimes with him were not story-telling sessions for he was not anchored to a sofa... There were big wicker armchairs in the study, for the use of his students when they came to talk to him, and in these marvellous playtimes they were turned upside down and turned into caves inside which my father and I growled and prowled as lions and tigers. Or they became little huts in which such characters as Bruce and Alfred watched spiders and burned cakes.

But on Sundays there were no games. For one thing my father had had a very stern, almost Calvinistic upbringing, with no storybooks or games allowed on Sundays for the children (except Noah's Ark because it came out of the Bible) and though for the rest of his life his mind became steadily broader and more tolerant he was at this time still a little shackled by it.[62]

❄

Elizabeth recounts with some sadness the restrictions of her father's upbringing, by parents who were "stern Protestant Evangelicals."

In that rather sad household fun was suspect; theatres were considered wicked and no stockings might be hung up on Christmas Eve. My father reacted, for gentle though he was he had all his life a streak of the rebel in him. He developed a strong sense of humour, became a champion of the ecumenical cause, a high churchman and a devotee of the theatre.[63]

In contrast to her son, says Elizabeth, "my grandmother's photo shows sadness and resignation."[64] And for Aunt Emma too – her grandmother's sister - "religion was severe." When her husband had taken her to see the celebrations of Queen Victoria's Diamond Jubilee in 1897, they returned "silently with unsmiling faces." The young Ida, who was staying with them at the time, asked, 'Didn't you enjoy it, Auntie?'

"How could I enjoy it, dear? All those thousands of people. It was for me a sight to break my heart..."
"But why?" pursued my puzzled mother.
They looked so unrepentant, dear. I could only ask myself how many of them were lost souls. To think of them in hell, I could hardly bear it."[65]

Much as she loved Aunt Emma, Ida could not forgive her for the sadness and distress this would have brought to Uncle James, in the "total failure" of his attempt to cheer up his wife. In Ida's opinion,

Whatever her private conviction [she] should, for her husband's sake, at least have looked and laughed and smiled as though she thought it was heaven for all. My mother forgot that Aunt Emma was not the excellent actress that she was herself. Though she had a sharply truthful tongue my mother could send any expression she chose rippling over her animated face.[66]

No doubt Ida's acting ability was a factor in Elizabeth's avowal that "my invalid mother was the most wonderful storyteller in the world."[67] But although her story-telling and play-times were missed during that winter she went away to Bath, it seems that the time Elizabeth spent with Mother, too, was generally restricted to certain hours of the day. And as Ida Goudge became "anchored to a sofa"[68] her daughter's memories of maternal contact were, again, connected to a particular room.

In summer [she] told me stories by the open French window of the drawing room, but in winter she had her sofa by the fire and I sat on the white woolly hearthrug to listen to them. The soft wool was as comforting to bare legs as the warmth of the fire.[69]

This soft white rug featured in one of her earliest memories of life with her beloved parents, in which "the three of us were on the same hearthrug together, our arms about each other, and my mother was saying in her clear voice, "A three-fold cord shall not be broken.""[70]

Mother and Child

The quotation is from chapter four of Ecclesiastes. A reflection on the perils of being alone, it includes another phrase which could have had particular resonance in the life of Ida Goudge: "Woe to him that is alone when he falleth, for he hath not another to help him up."[71] For although only twenty-six at the time of her only child's birth, she was already suffering the crippling effects of a bicycle accident, and the two events combined would help to make her an invalid for the rest of her life. Elizabeth describes her young self, indeed, as "this adored child, whom she had nearly died to bring into the world."[72]

From her daughter's description, it seems that Ida had been very much one of the active New Women of the 1890s.

Before the accident...she must have been an extraordinary person.[73] *She... was one of six children, a gay, carefree family who ran wild on the cliffs and by the sea, and in the rambling garden of their country home...*

My mother loved all outdoor things. She could dive and swim and help sail a boat and was an expert...gymnast. When my father met her she was studying at the School of Medicine in London and teaching at the same time, rather a "modern" thing for a girl to do in the eighteen-nineties. She was gay, full of vitality and quite without fear.[74]

Her chosen path of study was indeed very modern, for the London School of Medicine for Women had only been in existence as long as young Ida herself: it opened in 1874. By the turn of the century, twenty-five years later, there were more than three hundred lady doctors - but Ida was not destined to be one of them.

She had doctors on both sides of her ancestry and she wanted to be one herself, the first woman doctor in the family. She scandalised people both by her ideas and the things that she did. Interested in anatomy as she naturally was she carried human bones about in her handbag and tipped them out upon the seats of railway carriages when looking for her ticket. She was an intrepid bicyclist and whirled downhill with her feet up like any errand boy. She was a keen fencer and practised the art in a very masculine costume. She was altogether shockingly modern.[75]

Elizabeth expanded on the story of her mother's high spirits, and their consequences, in a magazine article published a year before *The Joy of the Snow*.

Even as I knew her, in her wheelchair, seldom free of pain, she had an incredible ability to spread cheer and comfort around her. Not just to my father and me: to neighbours, friends, strangers.

In fact, it was her irrepressible high spirits that were in part responsible for the accident. In those days, just at the turn of the century, bicycling was immensely popular. Parties of young people would take their cycles on overnight excursions into the English countryside, spending the night at a farmhouse and returning next day.

My mother and father were enjoying such an outing with a group of friends one fine spring morning when they crested a hill. In front of them was a long, steep grade. With a laugh and a wave of her hand, Mother propped her feet on the handlebars of her bike and sped ahead of the group down the hill, faster and faster, leaving the others far behind.

> *It was too late when she saw the cattle gate, closed across the road round a little bend. The others, hurrying to pick her up, were terrified, but she laughed, wanting to reassure them, as they lifted her back on to the bicycle seat and pushed her to a farmhouse. Indeed, it seemed at first as though not much was wrong. But there were no X-rays in those days and doctors knew less about spinal injuries than they do now. Gradually Mother grew worse...*[76]

And so this "shockingly modern" young woman, so sporty and daring, full of ambition and high spirits, was transformed into that now stereotypical creature: the Victorian invalid wife upon her sofa. Not that this seems to have affected her personality, for "she was never so ill that she could not make other people laugh, and was far too good a fighter to be resigned to anything whatever that she disliked."[77]

However the accident adversely affected her daughter's life as well as her own, for according to the companion of Elizabeth's later years, Jessie Monroe, a thoughtless remark laid a cruel burden of guilt upon her as a little child.

> Poor Elizabeth always had this ailing mother on the couch... She couldn't bear the thought of her mother suffering all the time and I suppose she must have said something to one of the maids, and the maid said, "Well of course it was your fault for being born." And she carried that guilt all her life. But it goes back to the bicycle incident.

She added,

> So there were to be no more children and that was the end of married life for Canon Goudge – he was a saint.

Whether Elizabeth could ever have known this for a fact, or whether it was just surmise on Jessie's part we do not know; nevertheless there were no more children of the marriage, and Elizabeth's first introduction to a baby was at Tower House, in Mrs. Hollis's bedroom.

> *I was taken by her two older sons to visit the third on the day when he was one week old. It was an occasion of great solemnity and I can remember how my heart beat as the three small children approached the door in procession and the eldest knocked. I had not seen the baby yet, indeed I do not think that I had ever seen any very small baby at close quarters before, and the whole thing was fraught with magic and mystery. We were bidden to enter, and went in, and facing us was a nurse seated in a chair with the baby enthroned on her lap. And babies were indeed enthroned in those days. Their lace-trimmed long robes flowed almost to the ground and their royalty was awe-inspiring. The sight of that baby was*

for me one of those moments of dumbfounded astonishment that a child never forgets. He was so small and yet he was so royal. He had not been with us a short while ago and now here he was. What could anyone be expected to make of such an astonishing occurrence? ...Then suddenly I remembered that a person I loved was in some way very much concerned in this and I looked round for Mrs. Hollis. She was also enthroned, in a billowy-white bed only a few feet from me, watching the children at the window. Our eyes met, she smiled at me and I was in heaven...

The event had repercussions when I returned to my own home across the road. Every morning I ran to my mother's room hoping and expecting that she had a small brother for me. He was intensely real to me and I was convinced he would come. I did not ask for him, merely looked around, leaving my poor mother completely mystified as to what I wanted. He did not come...[78]

He never did come, either as brother or son; and the longing for a baby remained, lifelong, one of the harder things that Elizabeth had to struggle with. It even forms the subject matter of her first published story, *The Fairies' Baby* which opens with these words:

> *People are apt to envy fairies, and to think they always have the best of everything. They never have the measles, they never have to go to the dentist, it never rains in Fairyland, and they have endless balls and parties. But what any nice fairy would like to have best of all is a human baby to play with all day long. But, unfortunately for the fairies, there are no human babies in Fairyland. Of course, the fairies can go and play with other people's babies, but that is not at all the same thing.*[79]

Naturally, her situation as an only child meant that there were times in her early years when she was lonely. Worse than this, however, in Elizabeth's own harsh opinion of herself, was that her role as the only child of an invalid mother turned her into "a neurotic selfish little beast."[80]

In my early years no one expected that my mother would live long. She herself was quite sure she would not, and like so many sensitive extroverts her own suffering caused her not only to be acutely aware of illness in others but even to imagine it was there when it was not. She considered me a delicate child who might not live long either...

(Like Isaac in *The Dean's Watch* perhaps, who "had always been a delicate and abnormally sensitive child, prone as the delicate are to seek a little comfort for himself here and there, and dangerously indulged by his equally delicate mother."[81])

And so she, who if she had been a well woman would have been a wise mother of many children, was in illness the reverse. Whenever I sneezed she sent for the doctor. Or if she did not Nanny did, for Nanny well or ill was a congenital spoiler. And so that child was and is a neurotic selfish little beast. I say is for she is with me still. All my life I have been waging war with her.[82]

Two Worlds

Remembering the comfortable warmth of the white woolly hearthrug during her mother's storytelling sessions, Elizabeth recalled that actually she "needed comforting":

because that magic hour with her, between tea and bedtime, often came as the reward and climax of a constantly recurring purgatorial experience endured by all Edwardian children and called 'going to the drawing room'. When nursery tea was over the jam was washed from their faces, the tangles wrenched out of their hair, the comfortable old Holland smocks were removed and starched, frilly horrors took their place. I speak of the little girls. I think the boys wore sailor suits and had the comfort of a whistle.

A good child stood still to be prepared for sacrifice and went bravely downstairs to face the ordeal. Others revolted and had to be dragged downstairs forcibly by Nanny and propelled towards the drawing room door by a vigorous shove between the shoulders. I know I was often guilty of atrocious screaming and kicking behind the green baize door of the nursery wing, but must have calmed down later for what I remember best is standing outside the drawing room door alone in a state of sick misery. On the other side of the hard slab of wood which reared up within an inch of my face was the sound of tinkling teacups and the hum of what Nanny and the servants called 'company'. And I had to turn the handle and go in…[83]

Not to have tea, apparently: that had already been taken in the nursery. It seems that this elaborate ritual of washing and brushing and changing of clothes, and the violent transition from one part of the house to another, had no other aim but that the little girl should briefly take her place in polite company, formally greeting each of her mother's guests in turn. She was always "acutely wretched and embarrassed" and remembered the ordeal as "so awful that it seemed always to take place in semi-darkness." However, she soon realised that there were "two sorts of social intercourse" within her home; this, in the drawing room, and another "behind the study door which faced it across the passage" from whence came "roars of laughter" and "a strong smell of tobacco."

> *I would stand in the passage outside and sniff and I thought it a joyous smell. Part of the joy of course was the bliss of not being of the company. Yet that in there was not 'company', it was just men. I could not solve the riddle. The nearest I could get was to realise one of the undoubted facts of life; 'company' is always predominantly female.*[84]

Like the Reverend John Wentworth in *The Rosemary Tree* who at the sound of company "turned hastily away, for he hated visitors, either his own or other people's."

> *He was aware of inconsistency in loving souls and hating visitors, but the fact was that try as he might he found it hard to realize that the well-clothed body of a visitor was inhabited by an immortal soul. He just could not reconcile the two. His definition of a visitor was narrow. No one lacking this world's goods was a visitor. No one sick, or in any trouble or perplexity, was a visitor, nor anyone below a certain social level. Nothing male was a visitor, nothing holy or humble or unattractive, nothing very old and nothing very young. In fact what it boiled down to was that he was terrified of all well-born, well-dressed, prosperous, good-looking, self-assured females between the ages of twenty and seventy-five.*[85]

But even when there were no visitors, and the time spent in the drawing room with mother was 'delightful' it was still not without its horrors, as the preface to the *Child's Garden* recalls.

> *Though it was delightful to go down to the drawing-room for an hour after tea, dressed in your best dress and coral necklace, and have* A Child's Garden of Verses *read aloud to you, and eat two [no more] sugared almonds out of the silver box, it was not so pleasant to go back again to the nursery afterwards in the semi-dark. It was a long journey and there was no electric light, and the candle in the hall gave only a ghostly glimmer.*

She describes this solitary crossing from one part of her home to another as a "fearful adventure" and remembers "the exquisite joy" of being back in the nursery again, her "own safe, warm kingdom."[86] The family life within the walls of that beautiful mediaeval house in Wells was indeed split into two separate "kingdoms": childhood and adult, divided by a green baize door.

Childhood then was a world to itself. The door which shut off the nursery wing from the rest of the house made a very real dividing line between the life of the child and the adult. Behind it Nanny and her charges lived in their own kingdom, from which they issued out at stated times to shed the light of their countenance upon the outer world. Visitors from this outer world, even mothers and fathers, did not enter the kingdom without hesitating at the portal and saying politely, "May I come in, please, Nanny?" And these same visitors seemed gods and goddesses to the children, revered and wonderful...

This state of things made for magic in both worlds, the same sort of magic that an island holds. There was a concentration of quietness and orderliness within the world, a feeling of adventure in leaving it, that fostered imagination and a sense of beauty. Children did not grow up so quickly in those days but their childhood was perhaps happier and richer.[87]

Richer in one sense, perhaps, because children with a loving Nanny had effectively two mothers. The 1901 Census records that in the Goudge household, the care of the 11-month-old Elizabeth was in the hands of a 21-year-old Nurse Domestic called Ellen Jolliffe. She had been trained at an establishment both new and progressive, not only in its attitudes to the upbringing of children, but in the very fact that – like Ida Goudge's former college - it was preparing young *women* for a career. It was the Norland College, founded by Emily Ward in 1892 as The Training School for Ladies as Children's Nurses, and it was the first college to offer any kind of instruction in childcare.

Nanny...came to us when I was a month old... a plain shy girl, very slow in all she did and with no self-confidence. Yet when my mother's sisters blamed her for choosing such a dull girl as Nanny she replied, "She is the one. She is kind." And how right she was. Shut behind the...door of the nursery wing the children of that period were entirely in the care of their nurse and at her mercy. Nanny was all mercy...[88] *I was with her far more than I was with my mother, and it was she who satisfied the need every child has for a trustworthy experience of security and love.*[89]

> *In from the winter dusk, and the chill air*
> *Of the frost-bound garden, the children come*
> *To Nannie sewing in the nursery chair,*
> *Nannie who to her nurselings is the sum*
> *Of all that makes up warmth and tenderness,*
> *Kind patience and the love that never fails.*
> *In this enchanted fire-lit hour they press*
> *About her, clamouring for the bed-time tales*
> *Of gnomes and fairies, and the angels' wings*
> *That shield the children's beds from midnight fears...*[90]

These are lines from the poem *To Nannie* which she wrote as the dedication to her children's book, *Smoky-House*. And Stevenson's *A Child's Garden of Verses*, too, begins with a similar dedication in verse. RLS was born fifty years before Elizabeth but he had died before she was born, at the age of only forty-four. Like her, he was the only child of an adored semi-invalid mother who was often confined to her bed, and a great deal of childhood love and affection was therefore given to "Cummie," his "dear" Nurse and "second Mother." His dedicatory poem, *To Alison Cunningham from her boy* calls her "the angel of my infant life" and recalls "the long nights you lay awake… all the story-books you read…all the pains you comforted…all you pitied… all you bore…"[91] Elizabeth said:

Thinking of my own Nanny I can echo every word of his dedication to her and greet every mention of her in the verses with an ache of longing. Those wonderful Nannies have gone now with that vanished world, and we are the poorer for their going.[92]

"Of course there were a few flies in the magic ointment," she added. "We were disciplined. A modern child would be horrified at the severity of our training." This is the child Colette in *Island Magic*, confronted by her grandfather's angry housekeeper.

Colette was terrified. Madame Gaboreau's cold grasp sent shivers of fear through her…
"What have you done with your coral necklace? Answer me, child!"

Colette shook her curls. Her obstinacy acerbated Madame Gaboreau's already ruffled temper.
"I can't send you home to your mother without your coral necklace," she snapped. "If you don't tell me what you've done with it I shall slap you. You're a naughty, obstinate child."

But Colette…stood her ground and Madame Gaboreau slapped her hard.

It was the first time she had ever been struck, and the blow was like an earthquake that ripped open the ground at her feet. That morning she had peeped through a little crack and seen horror below, but now horror came leaping up through the great fissure and suffocated her. Cruelty and terror and grief and pain were leaping round the dim room like dancing devils and a pall of darkness was closing down on her and crushing her. Crazy with fright she ran from the room…[93]

And one piece of fictional writing suggests that in those days of 'spare the rod and spoil the child' it was not only naughty children who were slapped. This is poor Ben's experience, in *The Bird in the Tree*.

> *Lucilla retired to bed with a headache, saying she thought she was getting a bit old to be a grandmother; but after dinner she had to get up again for Ben suddenly and unexpectedly had a violent attack of asthma, his first for a year, which was not subdued by the ministrations of the whole household until close on eleven o'clock, when it occurred to Ellen to give him a good hard slapping.*[94]

This is indeed a severity that horrifies; and it cannot be explained away as ignorance of the condition on the author's part, for she knew very well that Canon Goudge's mother had been "an invalid from asthma through almost the whole of her children's memory of her."[95]

Elizabeth's biography is full of love and reverence for her parents, and a deep gratitude for a secure, loved and happy childhood, but as a small child the centre of her world was Nanny. In fact, she admitted that "In my earlier years I think I loved her more than I loved my mother."[96] Lucy, too, in *The Child from the Sea* had similarly divided loyalties.

> *Lucy never took anything home to Nan-Nan without taking something for her mother too. This was because she felt so guilty in loving Nan-Nan more than her mother. Elizabeth had reproached her for this once, saying bitterly, "You love everyone more than your mother." And Lucy had flung herself on her in a passion of tears and cried out, "Oh, madam mother, I love you! But I love Nan-Nan terribly much."*[97]

And sadly, despite her deep love and admiration for him, in those early years she says,

> *I was afraid of my father. He was the very reverse of a harsh man but he was the one who was called upon to administer discipline when my behaviour passed all bounds. Discipline was my chief point of contact with him when I was small and his marvellous tenderness was something I discovered only in later years.*[98]

A marvellously tender clergyman appears in her story of Elizabethan Oxford, *Towers in the Mist*, the last of the novels written before Canon Goudge's death, and the one which she dedicated to him. This fictional Canon lives in a century when the beating of one's children is an obligatory discipline.

Canon Leigh...found himself as he grew older attaching more and more importance to the value of gentleness and less and less to that of discipline... He could no longer bring himself to beat his daughters, and did not beat his sons with any real concentration or enthusiasm... He loathed beating them... This weakness in him was a sin, and he knew it and confessed it during the long hours when he prayed for them, but it was a sin that even with the help of God he could not conquer. He tried to make up for it by lashing them with his tongue instead, but the tongues of learned and holy men are always singularly wanting in lash and at the end of a long scolding his children were sometimes unaware that there had been one... All except Joyeuce, as sensitive as her father and with the same capacity for suffering as his. She always knew when he was trying to scold and gave him all the help she could...

"Yes, Father," she encouraged gently...and, peeping at him out of the corner of her eye, she saw him scratching his bald head in perplexity... She must tell him what to say, as usual.

"I must not talk to young men out of the window," she said. "It was indiscreet and a bad example for the younger girls."
"Thank you, Joyeuce," he said with eager gratitude.
"I entirely forgot myself," said Joyeuce, looking him straight in the eyes. "I have never done it before and I will never do it again: or anything else of an indiscreet nature."
"You are my very good daughter, Joyeuce," he told her, and kissed her three times, on each of her eyelids, that were always a little shadowed with purple because she had too much to do, and on her pointed chin. "I have not hurt you?" he asked anxiously. "I have not said too much?"

"Not a word too much, Father," she comforted him, and she went to fetch the children...from the kitchen for prayers.[99]

Daily prayers were a feature of the Goudges' family life too, although they were not always totally appreciated by every member of his household.

His servants were always devoted to him. "It won't be the Canon's fault if we aren't good," said a young maid rather gloomily, for she found the daily family prayers a slight weariness to the flesh, "I'm sure he tries hard enough to make us what we did ought to be."[100]

They did, however, provide the inspiration for a delightfully humorous episode in *Towers in the Mist*.

> *On most mornings the Lord's Prayer was followed by breakfast, but every now and then Canon Leigh, who did not seem to feel the pangs of hunger like other people...would suddenly be lifted up on the wings of prayer and go on soaring higher and higher, oblivious of the hungry, earth-bound bodies of his wretched family.*
>
> *He did this to-day. He began praying for the suffering, the homeless, the destitute and the sick, above all for the hungry children who had not where to lay their heads. He went on and on. His family were only too pleased to pray for hungry children, provided they were given their own breakfast first, but while they were still themselves among the afflicted they found it difficult...*
>
> *Great-Aunt could stand it no longer... "Gervas," she shouted, "hold your tongue!"*
> *Canon Leigh started and looked up; taken by surprise, bewildered and uncertain of himself, he got to his feet without knowing what he was doing, while Dorothy fled to the kitchen and the children ran to seat themselves round the table before he could change his mind and begin again.*[101]

The "wonderful" servants who were such a part of Elizabeth's childhood "were members of the family, dearly loved and loving" who "never left you except to get married or die." One who did marry was their "incomparably beautiful" parlour-maid Mary, and Elizabeth had the honour to be her bridesmaid at the large and impressive parish church of St. Cuthbert's in Wells. She also describes their housemaid, Araminta, who "came to us as a small girl hardly more than a child" and "had one of those stout hearts that so often go with a very small body, and a loyalty to match her heart."[102] She is perhaps the model for the diminutive, sparkling Polly in *The Dean's Watch*, who was "tough as a pit pony, and a wonderful worker."

> *She did not find drudgery monotonous and was possibly the happiest person in the city. She adored and protected Isaac, she adored Sooty the cat and would have protected him had it been necessary. She pitied Emma. She had never hated anyone, not even those who in the past had cruelly misused her. She was intuitive and looking up now into Isaac's face she knew it was one of his good times. While he soaped his work-soiled hands she darted back into the kitchen and returned with a rough towel which she had been warming in front of the fire.*
>
> *"Ot," she whispered...*[103]

The Goudge family's attitude towards their servants was by no means the norm of course, and much has been written about the hardships of the upstairs-downstairs divide. But for Elizabeth, "something extraordinarily sound and sweet went out of life" when the world changed, and these wonderful, loved and loving servants "disappeared."[104]

In the Kitchen

Another never-to-be-forgotten character in their home was Sarah the cook, the "second storyteller" in their household, who "also reigned supreme beside a fire and a woolly hearthrug."

The rug spread before the kitchen range was black, not white, but just as comforting to bare legs... Going about her work Sarah was a gentle, sweet-voiced little old woman, a marvellous cook, utterly selfless, her only object in life to work for her family, but like my mother she must have had power for when she was enthroned in her rocking chair, a clean white apron tied round her waist over her print frock, she seemed to grow in stature. Her stories were taken from the Old Testament and all the fire packed up within her gentleness flowed out in them. She used her eyes and hands with wonderful dramatic effect and as the story gathered momentum she would rock faster and faster. One day she told me the story of Elijah going up into heaven in his fiery chariot. It grew more and more exciting and when the climax was reached and Elijah was whirled to meet his God she urged the rocker to its utmost speed, crying out loudly, "The chariots of fire and the horsemen thereof!" and flung her apron over her head. I was terrified. I scrambled up from the hearthrug and fled from the lightnings and thunders that filled the big old kitchen.[105]

This memory was used almost wholesale in *The Heart of the Family*. Little Meg, like Henrietta nearly twenty years before her, is impressed by the dramatic stories of the Old Testament.

Meg's religious ideas at this time had been formed more by Mrs. Wilkes than by her mother, and Mrs. Wilkes leaned more to the Old Testament than the New. Sally told Meg shyly and beautifully about the Baby in the manger and little lambs carried in the arms of the Good Shepherd, and Meg listened courteously but was not as yet very deeply impressed, but Mrs. Wilkes's dramatic accounts of the adventures of the Old Testament heroes sent her trembling to her bed and were quite unforgettable.

> *"And up to 'eaven 'e went,"* Mrs. Wilkes would say of Elijah, *"with such a clanging and a banging of that fiery chariot that you could 'ave 'eard it from 'ere to Radford. And all the angels shouted, ducks, and all the archangels blew their trumpets till the sky split right across to let 'im in. Like a thunderstorm it was, ducks. Somethink awful."*
>
> *And then Mrs. Wilkes would fling her apron over her head and herself back in the kitchen chair to demonstrate the awfulness of the noise and light. And that was the way people went to heaven. To Meg it was wondrous strange and deliciously alarming.*[106]

Wonderful Bible stories were not the only thing Elizabeth learnt in the kitchen, however.

> *The moment when I first discovered that crabs and lobsters are boiled alive was what in modern parlance is called a moment of truth. My [Guernsey] grandmother had sent one of the aunts and myself to Town one day to call at the library and to buy a lobster for tomorrow's lunch. This we did and the lobster was placed beneath the library books in the basket. It must have been a very quiescent one for I thought it was dead. After we got home I went to the kitchen to talk to Sophie, my grandmother's maid who did the cooking. I opened the door and saw the lobster frantically trying to climb out of the pan of boiling water. Sophie pushed it down and put the lid on top. I shut the door and ran away. I do not remember where I hid myself and after the fashion of children I kept what I had seen to myself. I did not seek for comfort, not even from my mother when I got back to Wells. I have never been able to eat shell-fish from that day to this.*[107]

She observes that often for a writer "the temptation to alter or improve on the facts…is impossible to resist."[108] Witness, this glorious triumph of Peronelle in *Island Magic*:

> *Those who fancied crab bought him in the market still alive and kicking, carried him home in a basket with the library books on top to keep him in, and plunged him into boiling water still alive and kicking… To Peronelle this seemed a piece of hideous cruelty hard to beat. She could not understand how her family could perpetrate the horror, and above all how they could eat the poor crab after he was dead…It very nearly made Peronelle sick…*
>
> *Only one crab day did she remember with pleasure. They had brought the crab home…placed him on the kitchen table for Sophie to deal with and gone to take off their hats… But Sophie was attending to*

something else... Coming downstairs again Peronelle beheld the crab walking across the hall... Very feeble he was, only just able to drag his poor body over the hard stone floor, but he knew that somewhere, beyond this hideous parching land, was the sea...

Peronelle picked him up and ran... Across the garden she went, across the cliff, down the path that led to the rocks below and there she stood and flung the crab back into the sea. Colin, in this situation, would have concocted a long and wonderful story to account for the disappearance of the crab. Not so Peronelle. She returned home, stood in the middle of the hall and shouted at the top of her voice, "I've put the crab back in the sea. Now there's nothing for supper... Thank God."[109]

The comfortably-off ate far too much but with that kitchen range glowing like an altar at the centre of the house, and the garden packed with food that must not on any account be wasted, it was perhaps not surprising. Yet...though I remember very portly persons I remember too lovely ladies with willowy figures and tiny waists... I would look through the baize door that shut the nurseries off from the rest of the house and see them floating down to dinner in their long dresses.[110]

※

Elizabeth had four aunts: her father's sister Eva, and her mother's sisters Marie, Emily and Irene. There was also an Uncle – Ida's brother William, five years her junior, and his wife Beatrice, the parents of Elizabeth's beloved cousin Hélène. But they lived in Java and *The Joy of the Snow* makes little mention of them as physical presences in her young life – although William must be the model for the delightful Colin du Frocq in *Island Magic*, the novel based on stories of her mother's childhood.

In the preface to *A Child's Garden of Verses* she remembers "the joy of visiting Aunties..."

those very special Aunties who like the Nannies have now entirely vanished, females of grace and elegance who came on long visits and seemed to have nothing to do but play croquet and tell you wonderful stories, who dressed for dinner every evening and came to say good-night to you in the nursery in rustling silk dresses with posies of flowers in their belts. To watch such a creature leave the room was awe-inspiring and you gazed wide-eyed from your bath in front of the day nursery fire.

Whenever Auntie moves around
Her dresses make a curious sound;
They trail behind her up the floor,
And trundle after through the door.[111]

If these aunties seemed to have nothing to do but play then they must have been her mother's sisters, for her paternal aunt Eva was the mother of a young family. In 1894 she had married her brother's fellow Oxford graduate, Clavel Parmiter, at Holy Trinity Church, Marylebone. Uncle James Goodhart signed the register as witness, and her brother himself was the officiating clergyman. By 1903 she had four children – the third, Margaret, born just ten days before Elizabeth. But even the unmarried aunts can only have made their long visits in the school holidays, for both Marie and Emily worked as teachers in English boarding schools. Both, however, were memorable presences in her childhood (Irene was less frequently seen, as she was employed as Nannie in a royal household, abroad) and twenty years after *A Child's Garden* Elizabeth again extolled the virtues of these exemplary women – this time, with memories of visits that were not always so leisured.

There are no aunts today and I sometimes think that is partly what is the matter with us. There are sisters of a child's mother or father, kindly at times but too wrapped up in themselves and their careers to be aunts. An Edwardian aunt was by definition selfless and unattached; or sufficiently loosely attached to get free from what she was doing when wanted. When a crisis blew up, a real tragedy or a minor difficulty, an unmarried aunt was almost at once upon the doorstep. As I remember them they were competent as well as selfless. They came aboard a distressed household like a pilot and brought the ship safe to port.[112]

The Distressed Household

I think our ancestors were not so afraid of death as many people are today. I think it had a kinder face...
In those pre-war days people mostly died in their own homes and a death in the house was as normal as a birth. Even the children knew all about it. You came into the world and you went out again, the children were told. You took off your body as though it were an old coat and went through the door of death into another world. Both birth and death could be painful, and death was hard to bear for the people left behind, but there are other things in life which are hard to bear, we are told; life is not a bed of roses and heartbreak is to be expected.

"*You must expect that,*" *was the constant and lugubrious remark of an old servant of ours. She said it of every disaster, from death to smashing the best teapot.*[113]

As did Sarah in *A City of Bells*:

> *Sarah was tall and gaunt, with grey hair strained back from a grim, determined countenance. She had a heart of gold, though she kept it hidden, and her preference was for the gloomy side of life rather than the sunny one.*
>
> *"Mr. Jocelyn," she exclaimed sepulchrally, but there was a gleam of affection behind her glasses.*
> *"How well you look, Sarah," said Jocelyn cheerfully, shaking hands, "Years younger than when I saw you last." The temptation to annoy Sarah by taking an optimistic view was one he had never been able to resist.*
>
> *"I'm far from well, sir," said Sarah, "the damp of this 'ouse being something cruel, but I keep up for the sake of others... Come this way, sir, tea's ready. You'll find the master and mistress much aged, but you must expect that."*[114]

The invariable remark could rouse hidden laughter in her hearers if the disaster was not too bad, but it represented a serenity of acceptance that took away the dread of death. I think we children grew up with little fear of it.[115]

❋

[I] marvel that [the hive of industry that was an Edwardian home] cost so little to keep going... Light was cheap, consisting of oil lamps and candles. Coal was also cheap but was never used in bedrooms unless you were seriously ill.[116]

From an early age, though, Elizabeth was aware that however cheaply one could live, there were always those who did not have enough; for her parents were very aware of the poverty and hardship existing in Edwardian England.

That past age had many evils that were peculiarly its own and one of the worst was disregard of the misery existing outside the self-centred home, beyond the quiet village or the sleepy country town... My parents were more aware of the suffering of the world beyond the charmed circle than were many of their friends, my father because he had been born in London and as a young priest had worked in a factory town, and my mother because she was deeply compassionate and had made it her business to know.[117]

Socialists as they were, her parents may well have read Fabian Society tracts like "The endowment of motherhood" published in 1910; urging the State to provide financial and medical assistance for mothers in an attempt to reduce the high infant mortality rate amongst the poor. In another 1910 treatise on infant mortality, Helen M. Blagg concluded that "thousands of healthy babies are yearly done to death by preventable diseases;" and thousands more "become mentally and physically deteriorated because they have never had a chance to live a healthy life." It added the sombre statistic that some were "born unfit to live, because of the evils amid which their mothers live."[118]

There was no such poverty in the Goudge household of course. In fact in Elizabeth's opinion her mother, "remembering the austerity of her own childhood, allowed me too many pretty clothes, too many toys, too much spoiling, and ended by having a very nasty little spoilt brat on her hands."[119] But Ida's brother Arnold had died in infancy, as had both her husband's elder brothers, and one can understand why, when her precious only-child did but sneeze, Ida sent for the doctor. Despite the spoiling however – and in addition to the collecting box she kept in the hall for Waifs and Strays - "upon one piece of discipline she did insist."

> *Every Christmas I was forced to choose from my multitude of toys a basketful that must be given away. No matter what the display of tears and temper the basket must be filled. Nanny then took me by the hand and led me to St. Thomas's Street, where lived children poorer than myself, and I had to go from house to house giving away my toys until the basket was empty. I suffered agonies of embarrassment but there was no escape for Nanny was with me and prodded from behind. I can remember only one of the many homes. The kitchen was dark and there seemed nothing in it except too many children. They sat still as statues as they suffered the indignity forced upon them, moving only to put out a hand and take the proffered cast-off toy from the rich little girl who wore a velvet bonnet. That scene of poverty must have burnt itself into my mind for I can see it vividly now, though at the time I think I felt more embarrassed than ashamed.*[120]

When she came to write a fictional account of that scene of poverty, she added a second household where the evils more nearly resembled those in Ms. Blagg's published paper, than the actual scene witnessed by a little girl in St. Thomas' Street, Wells.

> *Henrietta and Hugh Anthony…stood side by side, stiff and miserable, subjected to the unwinking stare of five pairs of eyes; for the tow-headed little girls had now joined the little boys in a group as far removed as possible from their visitors. The whole width of the kitchen separated the well-dressed from the ill-dressed and it was the well-dressed, weighed*

down by numbers, who felt themselves at a disadvantage. What makes one feel uncomfortable, they discovered suddenly, is not what one has got or has not got, but being different...

They went on up the street, giving toys to the children whom they saw and sometimes going inside their homes, and all went well until they turned a corner and came upon a dingy-looking house from which no firelight shone...Inside were dirt and evil smells and dead ashes in the grate. A horrible-looking old woman, the grandmother perhaps, with greasy strands of grey hair escaping from a man's cap, was peeling potatoes and shouting raucously at the children who seemed swarming all over the place. Henrietta, unseen, stood still and stared, for the children had not got faces like the children she was accustomed to. They had old faces and their eyes did not seem to look at anything steadily. When the old woman hit out at two of the little ones they ducked cleverly, and without fear, but their cunning was somehow horrible. Then they saw Henrietta and came boldly crowding up to her, shouting out things that she did not understand, though she knew they were mocking things.[121]

As well as providing material for this scene from *A City of Bells*, the painful sight of people less well off than herself gave the child Elizabeth another kind of inspiration.

The affair was not without its effect upon me, though hardly the one that my mother intended, for I decided to give away the whole of the contents of our apple store, laid out upon slotted shelves in the garden room. It only took me about an hour, filling my basket with apples and running backwards and forwards from the apple room to the garden railings through which I pushed the apples to the delighted children outside.[122]

In 1949 she published *Make-Believe* a book of short stories which, like *Island Magic*, are based on Ida Goudge's early life. The one entitled *Doing Good* however, is based on this childhood scrape of Elizabeth's own. Colette du Frocq, acting upon her mother's scripture teaching during a re-telling (with embellishments) of The Good Samaritan, has given away the entire contents of their apple-room to a poor ragged boy. Later, when the family meet for tea:

[Colette] recounted the afternoon's adventure with placidity and a certainty of approval, touching lightly upon her mother's remarks of the morning and dwelling at length upon the hunger of the little boy. If the silence that

followed her narration was ominous she was too much occupied in not biting over the jam in the middle of her doughnut to notice it.

Rachell, with the ease of long practice, recovered quickly from the shock... "All the apples, darling?" she asked faintly.

"All," said Colette. "You said this morning one must give all," and she gave a little crow of pleasure as she found the jam and bit deep into it.[123]

Rachell's mild reaction does not quite accord with Elizabeth's remembrance of her own escapade: "I could not understand the ensuing row." It made her weep; after which her mother was "mollified and said we would plant an apple tree in my own little patch of garden." But she adds wryly, "the devil saw to it that that tree never bore a single apple." It was her "first depressing realisation that an act of true self-sacrifice is not intended by God to leave you just as comfortable and well off as you were before."[124]

Even without apples, however, and on a clergyman's stipend, Canon Goudge and his household were comparatively comfortable and well-off.

My father had an income of five hundred pounds a year and this supported a medium size house and garden, three maids (though the little one aged about fourteen only earned ten pounds a year) and Nanny and a gardener. There were always many mouths to feed and even when making allowances for what inflation has done to the currency how was it managed? As I think about it I realise that we spent practically nothing outside our home. We seldom went to a theatre and holidays, if taken at all, were a visit to relatives...[125]

Guernsey

In the Goudge family a visit to relatives could actually provide a wonderful holiday, for Ida was a Channel Islander - born in Guernsey in 1874 - and a trip to her family home meant a very exciting journey indeed for a little girl. Elizabeth remembers visiting her grandparents "almost every summer all through my childhood until the outbreak of the First World War." However, as the journey was too much for her mother in her invalid state, they "never went there together." In fact, after the accident that destroyed her health poor Ida, having "left Guernsey for the first time when she was eighteen, was never able to visit her Island again."[126] It was left to the Aunts to make the journey with her child.

> *I was a year old when one of my mother's sisters took me on my first visit, and a grim time she must have had of it for the sea passage from Weymouth to Guernsey in the small boats of those days could be a gruelling experience... Until that great moment came when the cry went up, "We shall be in harbour in half an hour." To climb up out of the stuffy saloon on to the wet deck and see the great waves racing by and be buffeted by the clean cold wind was a great joy. And then came the excitement as the coast of Guernsey came into view and slipped slowly by to starboard...*
>
> *One could see the spire of the town church, and the pier and Castle Cornet on its rock, and there at last was the harbour wall and the waiting people. As the boat drew slowly in to its mooring-place I would try to pick out my grandfather, and perhaps an aunt or even two aunts, who would probably be with him. The moment when I saw him and the moment when he saw me and lifted his hat in greeting were perfect moments...*
>
> *The shouts of sailors and porters, the shrill whistles, the bangs and thuds of cargo being unloaded, the sound of the gangways being run out, the scream of the gulls overhead, the sound of the wind and the slap of the sea all made up a symphony of sound, the music of arrival in a happy haven.*[127]

It must have been such an exciting contrast to life in land-locked Wells, and Elizabeth would reproduce the magic of St. Peter Port harbour again and again in the three books she set in Guernsey: *Island Magic;* the stories collected under the title *Make-Believe;* and later her best-seller *Green Dolphin Country* – the source of this description of a town which is not just magical, but heavenly.

> *He looked at Saint Pierre, and the sight of it under the early morning sun almost took his breath away... [It] looked like a city built of gold and mother-of-pearl. The windows flashed in the sun and there was a flame of light burning in each ripple against the harbour wall. The masts and spars of ships were etched as delicately as the tracery of winter trees... Ramparts of cloud, built up behind and around the furthest climbing roofs of the town, were like a second city in the sky; one could hardly tell where the earthly one ended and the heavenly one began. But both of them were reflected in the water of the harbour, and reality and reflection together made up a perfect circle, a habitable globe in miniature, the city of man completely encircled by the city of God, the flawless shining thing of which God dreamed when He made the world.*[128]

The real thing, on the other hand, was deliciously worldly, foreign, and full of bustle.

Family news was shouted above the babel of noise and the special porter, who always attended our family arrivals and departures with as much interest as though the family were his own, collected the luggage and we pushed our way to where the cabs waited...

Just as there was a special porter who looked after the Collenette family there was a special cabby who drove us. I wish I could remember the names of these two kindly men, I can remember the face of the porter, but not of the cabby; though I remember the smell of horses and straw which pervaded his cab and which I thought a lovely smell... It must be some particular arrival that I remember when I think of clearing skies after rain and wind, and of wet cobbles shining in pale yellow sunlight as the cab rattled us away from the harbour.[129]

To drive through the fictional St. Pierre in *Island Magic* presented greater difficulties, for instead of any cab being able to *rattle* away, "There were only three streets in the whole town which were possible for a carriage, and even then it went up pushed by the whole populace and came down with the horse sitting on its tail."[130] Colin du Frocq's excitement over its steep and foreign streets, however, was modelled on her own.

The streets of Wells slope gently so that St. Peter Port seemed to me strangely exciting, more like a grey stone mountain rent with deep narrow chasms than a town. Here and there the chasms were so steep that instead of streets there were long flights of steps between the houses. In the lower part of the town were the exciting shops, dark and foreign, some of them fronting narrow cobbled lanes where only pedestrians could pass up and down...[131]

> *Past the Town Church Colin took a short cut up a steep, cobbled street that went twisting up the hill like an intoxicated corkscrew. He adored La Rue Clubin and went up it at every possible opportunity; partly because he was forbidden to go near it and partly because its noise and colour fascinated him...*
>
> *On a Saturday evening [it] was particularly attractive, for the whole length of it was lined with booths, lit after dark by flaring gas jets and laden with unimaginable glories; great sticks of striped peppermint rock, boiled sweets of all colours of the rainbow, piles of live lobsters and crabs, fish of every possible variety, vegetables, scarlet petticoats, yellow sunbonnets, more crabs, more sugar sweets, all piled along the gutters in a wealth of smell and colour.*
>
> *Over the stalls the top storeys of the old tumbledown houses jutted out so far that they nearly met overhead, making La Rue Clubin almost like a tunnel, and confining the noise as though in an echoing cavern. And what a noise! The inhabitants of the tumbledown houses, the very poorest inhabitants of the Island, all issued forth of a Saturday*

> *night to buy and sell, to cheat and shout and sing and swear... Now, in this drab twentieth century, [it] has been condemned as a disgrace, rebuilt, cleaned and turned into a respectable thoroughfare, but on the twentieth of August 1888, when Colin du Frocq was eight years old, it was neither respectable nor clean, it was merely a wonder and a glory.*[132]

Although not "pushed by the whole populace," Elizabeth's cab journey did end with "a last slow drag up the hill" to the outskirts of the town.

> *[We] were out in the country, on the flat fields of the hilltop, in sunlight and sparkling air. I believe that hilltop is now completely urban but at the time the row of Victorian villas was lonely and stood out starkly as a sore thumb. But I did not think them ugly. I thought my grandparents' house perfect. The walls were of strong grey granite, and they needed to be for the wind up there could be terrific, and there was nothing but the flat fields between the houses and the cliff edge, and beyond was the sea; and beyond that on clear days one could see a blue smudge against the horizon that was the coast of France.*[133]

This house may have been perfect; but going back a further generation, the former home of her *great*-grandparents seemed to her "to shed a very bright lustre indeed" over her family. ("Children are dreadful little snobs," she says.[134]) In the 1850s her grandmother's father, William Ozanne, had sold his house in Hauteville to Victor Hugo. By the purchase of this home for the sum of 24,000 francs, Hugo – exiled from France - acquired Guernsey citizenship. He wrote prolifically during his Guernsey years - including, in 1862, *Les Misérables* – and although on the advice of his doctor he spent every summer travelling, much of his work was produced in the third-floor study at Hauteville House with its view over St. Peter Port... the house he had bought from Elizabeth's great-grandfather.

Elizabeth must have been an unusually observant child for she remembered her childhood days in remarkable detail, and not just in terms of incident. Given that *Island Magic* was not published until she was thirty-four years old, and *The Joy of the Snow* forty years after that, it is obvious that the beauty encountered on these once-a-year visits to Guernsey made an indelible impact upon her young mind.

> *Michelle could hardly see the bushes in the fog but as she pushed by them they gave out little puffs of scent like hot peaches. She made her way through wet gorse, honeysuckle, foxgloves and tall grasses until she reached the cliff edge, when she dropped cautiously to her hands and knees. Here the cliff sloped downwards to the sea and short turf and wild thyme took the place of the long grass and honeysuckle. On hot days*

> *this slope was as slippery as ice and the unwary one who lost his foothold was in danger of being dashed to pieces on the rocks below. Even today, when the turf was soaking wet and each regal head of purple thyme held a coronet of diamonds, Michelle crept downwards with the utmost caution, digging her toes firmly into crannies and searching with her finger tips for firm bits of rock to cling to.*
>
> *The slope ended in a flat-topped rock and here Michelle lay down, her chin cupped in her lean brown hands... Below was a sheer and terrifying drop to the gull's bay...*
>
> *A sudden rent in the fog told her that the sun was conquering. She watched spellbound. Slowly, very slowly, the tops of jagged rocks appeared, then a stretch of green water, then a patch of early purple heather growing just below her, then a flurry of white wings as two quarrelling gulls flapped the fog away from them... Now trailing white scarves of mist drifted up to her, curled themselves round her rock and disappeared over the foxgloves, and now, quite suddenly, the sun was out and the whole bay below lay bright and clear and sparkling. Each little wet pebble on the beach shone like a diamond and the large flat rocks by the sea's edge were patched with bright green seaweed... The sea, where it lay over beds of seaweed, was wine-dark...while over the sand it was an intense blue-green. Michelle could even see the scarlet anemones in the pools and the yellow lichen staining the rocks below the heather clumps. And everywhere were the gulls. Soaring, dipping, swerving, diving, backwards and forwards, up and down, round and round. Their wings seemed to trace a pattern over the lovely scene, mist it over with a film of white feathers, seemed to gather all the colour together and make of it one lovely gleaming jewel.*[135]

As well as these detailed recollections of landscape, there was the memory of her grandparents' house as a fragrant place, with its "small square of flower garden in front with a bed of mignonette beneath the bay window of the drawing-room."

> *Above was a balcony and a passion flower climbed over it and covered the front of the house. It grew as luxuriantly as the mignonette below and the smell of all those flowers in hot sunshine would drift in through the open windows. There was a larger bit of garden behind the house but this was given over to a green lawn where stood the imposing array of instruments used by my grandfather, who among many other things was a meteorological expert, for measuring rain and foretelling the weather.*[136]

He was, it seems, an expert grandfather too. A "great tease" with a "gift for merry repartee,"[137] he was much beloved by his little granddaughter. She, for all her descriptive powers, was to wonder in later life, "How can I describe what my grandfather was to me as a small child?"[138]

Demonstratively affectionate certainly, for his greeting went beyond the raising of his hat to her as the boat sailed into harbour. She remembers how, having finally disembarked, "I was in my grandfather's arms at last and then standing beside him holding his hand, speechless with the sudden shyness that would come upon me because I had not seen him for a year."[139]

But the shyness cannot have lasted for long. This was the same kindly, tolerant man who would allow the little girl to stand by his desk while he worked. The same man who – in Paris when he heard the news of Elizabeth's birth – had gone "straight out" and bought his new grandchild a beautiful doll, which she described in loving detail in *The Joy of the Snow* and treasured all her life. (Four years before her death she told a friend, with delight: "A dear little girl to whom I showed my 79-year-old doll gazed at me with big blue eyes full of awe and said, 'This must be the oldest doll in the world!'")[140] It had been a generous gift, for "knowing my grandfather I am quite sure he chose for me the most beautiful doll in the whole of Paris. I am also sure that he could not afford it for he never had any money."[141] He was, she says, "the kindest man I have ever known. I cannot believe that he ever had an unkind thought or spoke an unkind word in his life."[142]

There was about him, however, an "inner sadness" which he kept "well hidden,"[143] and one source of this must have been the loss in childhood of Arnold, his firstborn son. Adolphus struggled with health problems too.

Following the family tradition he had chosen medicine for his profession but after only a short period of work he became ill with diabetes. There was no insulin then but with determination and a strict diet he struggled on and lived to be over eighty. But his sight was affected and though he did not go completely blind until he was old, and with strong glasses could continue to read and write, he could not be a doctor. But he wanted to put his medical knowledge to good use and so he opened a chemist's shop. In those days a chemist was almost a doctor; his shop was not flooded with cosmetics and cameras and was almost entirely used in serving those with minor ailments and injuries who could not afford the doctor. My grandfather was expert in help but as he was just as dedicated to those who could not pay as to those who could his business did not thrive financially.[144]

Nevertheless,

He was a man of many interests. One was promoting the teetotal cause. I do not know at what stage of his life he became a purveyor of soft drinks, nor whether they were an adjunct of the chemist's shop or superseded it, but I do know that a large cart full of crates and rattling bottles, drawn by a couple of horses and with A. Collenette inscribed upon it, was a matter of pride to me…It was also a matter of pride to stand outside the library at St Peter Port and read the weather forecast that hung on its wall framed in a glass case, printed in large clear letters and signed A. Collenette. And if a little group of people had gathered and were attentively reading my grandfather's forecast I was in bliss. Weather matters on an island.[145]

Elizabeth called upon memories of Adolphus and his wife Marie-Louise when writing *Island Magic*. They were the patterns for André and Rachell du Frocq; but perhaps because she and her grandmother "loved each other but not I think to any remarkable extent," she deems Rachell to be the better portrait. Her wonderful grandfather on the other hand – he who "was a part of my life from the beginning" is once again beyond description: "the portrait of André," she says "is totally inadequate."[146]

She must have had a lot of fun on these holidays. They went on driving picnics to the beautiful cliff-tops and bays, where the water-lanes ran down to the sea. These were "steep stony paths, green tunnels arched over by trees, with a stream running down the side under a canopy of ferns. It was wonderful for a child to come out at the bottom and see the stream running across the sand, and run with it to the edge of the sea." She remembered her young aunts Emily and Marie playing with her tirelessly on these outings, and also her "furious rages" when they foiled her attempts at too much dangerous rock-climbing.[147] Then all too soon, no doubt,

The last evening came [and] trunks were packed… and I think we all cried a little. The aunts had to survive another term of teaching in English boarding schools before they would see the island again, and I was returning to Wells where there was no bathing; you might not bathe in the moat. My grandfather came with us in the cab to see us off but though I remember the arrivals at the island so clearly I cannot remember any of the departures. Perhaps my grandfather standing alone waving to us as the ship drew away, and then the slow disappearance of St. Peter Port and the ships at anchor and the circling gulls, and then the heading out into the open sea away from it all was too poignant to be remembered. For I would not be back for another year, and a year to a child can seem an eternity.[148]

Bath

Another occasional venue for holidays, much nearer to home, was Bath. Here lived Nanny's parents, and "if there was an aunt handy to be with my mother, Nanny would sometimes take me to stay with them for a short while."

It was almost as good as going to the Island. They were the opposite of my grandparents for it was the old man who was tall and imposing while his wife was tiny, gentle and obedient... I think he must have come from country stock for he had chosen for his retirement an old house that had once been a farmhouse, with a large rambling garden where he spent his days growing superb vegetables and rearing chickens.[149]

Elizabeth remembered that it filled her childhood self with ecstasy, to wake up in the dawn and hear the sound of the cock crowing out in the garden. For this was something completely new to her: "cocks and hens were not kept in the precincts of Wells and I heard the thrilling sound for the first time in Nanny's home."

From visit to visit I looked forward to hearing it again and I shall never hear it without a thrill. When first I made acquaintance with Hamlet *the phrase "The cock that is the trumpet to the morn" went right through me. That was what the triumphant cry was, a trumpet that celebrated the return of light.*[150]

> *The darkness and silence seemed to get heavier and heavier. And then the great black cock, which had been riding all this time silently upon his master's shoulder, suddenly crowed...*
> *It was that triumphant trumpet call with which cocks usher in a new day, and Maria remembered a saying she had heard somewhere, "The night is darkest towards the dawn."*
> *"I believe the night is nearly over," she said.*[151]

This extract from *The Little White Horse* shows not only Elizabeth's love for the birds themselves, but for the symbolic faith-significance of the cockerel - the bird of dawning that heralds the dayspring and the coming of light. One of the reasons she loved the poetry of Gerard Manley Hopkins so much was the discovery of "how often the thought of Christ would be linked with a bird symbol..."

There is "*The Windhover*" dedicated to Christ our Lord, but the best of all to me is the ending of the sonnet on 'Patience'.

> *And where is he who more and more distils*
> *Delicious kindness? He is patient. Patience fills*
> *His crisp combs, and that comes those ways we know.*[152]

London and Sussex

Elizabeth grew up knowing only her maternal grandparents, for her father's parents had both died before she was born; when he was still a young man up at Oxford. However, "I did not feel the loss of paternal grandparents because their place was taken by Uncle James and Aunt Emma, who became father and mother to my father and his sister when their own parents died, and grandparents to their children."

I remember them perhaps too vividly for truth because for me they were figures so august that they took something of a fairy-tale quality, and as soon as the golden glow of a fairy tale starts to gild the facts the latter tend to lose something of their validity. But golden is a correct adjective to apply to Uncle James and Aunt Emma for they had both kinds of gold. They were goldenly good and they were also wealthy. They possessed a town house in Portland Place and a country house in Sussex. When Uncle James, who was a doctor, drove out to visit his patients it was in a smart brougham with his hat poised at an elegant angle.[153]

Did Elizabeth ever have a ride in this smart brougham? Perhaps not, for there is no mention of it in her childhood memories. Nevertheless in *Gentian Hill* she created one little girl who very much enjoyed being driven through the country lanes in the doctor's gig:

> *Dr. Crane's gig seemed to Stella as near flying as made no difference. The seat, suspended from curved springs by leather braces between the two great wheels, swung excitingly, and Aesculapius, the doctor's fine grey gelding, went at a brisk pace. The doctor, in a many-caped brown overcoat, with his tall beaver hat cocked at an angle and his eyeglass in place, drove well, and Stella, sitting very upright beside him in her scarlet cloak, was delightedly conscious of being part of a very smart turn-out indeed.*[154]

Uncle James was in fact such a gifted doctor, notably in the field of paediatrics, that he was made a baronet in the 1911 Coronation Honours List of King George V. His entry in *Who's Who* records that among his many career achievements, Sir James Frederic Goodhart had been one of the "Hon. Staff" of King Edward VII.

We did not stay with Aunt Emma and Uncle James very often; only I think when my father brought my mother to London in search of some relief from her suffering.[155]

Trips to London meant a different kind of suffering for Elizabeth however, to the extent that, looking back, she could not imagine why her parents had included her in these visits, "for my neurotic hatred of all large towns made me nothing but an exasperating incubus. From my babyhood all noise reduced me to an extremity of terror."[156] It was what she called in *The Bird in the Tree* "the strange panting fear awakened by lightning and big bangs." For the child David in this novel, these were on a list of "those terrors of childhood of which no child will ever speak… The horror of a creeping shadow on a wall, the sudden awakening at night to the terrifying dark, the conviction that a nightmare beast is stabled beneath the bed."[157]

I was taken protesting to children's parties and sat through the festive teas cold and shaking in dread of the banging of the crackers. School sports with the pop of pistols terrified me, and so did fireworks, thunderstorms and the noise of London. I think my mind has not often reached such a pitch of terror as was produced by a drive down Regent Street in an open victoria, sitting on the small seat with my back to the horses.[158]

This "would have given delight to any sensible, normal child," she says, but for her "the rush of noise coming from behind me, and the claustrophobia produced by crowds and pressure" was intolerable.[159] Neurotic, exasperating, an incubus… Elizabeth is very hard on her childhood self, when in fact photographs from the early years of the century show that even in the days of horse-drawn vehicles, the London streets were packed with traffic. So very different from the winding streets of St. Peter Port, or the slow pace of life in peaceful Wells, it was no wonder that the sheer volume and noise of London traffic filled her with terror.

The ridiculous terror had no connection with physical danger; what I was afraid of I did not know. And yet driving in a hansom cab brought a sort of trembling bliss; even such a little fool as I was could not help rejoicing in such a magic equipage.[160]

The bliss and the magic are all there for Henrietta, too, when she leaves Torminster for a visit to London in *A City of Bells*.

> *Surely a chariot of the gods, this hansom-cab… The glorious thrill of it, bowling along at a great pace driven by someone you could not even see; the genius shown in the design of the thing, two wheels only, so that you swayed as in a rocking-chair, the graceful curve of the hood over your head, the slanting shutters that were slapped down over your knees, shutting you as firmly in as though you were about to turn a somersault, the trap-door through which you could if you wished hold converse with the god in the sky who drove you. And this god! Always his eyes were blue and twinkling and his nose was red and his hair was ginger; he wore a bowler hat on the side of his head and a flower in his buttonhole and when you peeped at him through the trap-door he winked one eye…*[161]

> *As there was not room for four in a hansom they went to the Firebird Theatre on top of a horse bus. It lacked the excitement of a hansom-cab but had an enchantment all its own, for one felt one was riding over the turbulent sea of London in a golden galleon. It was thrilling to hang over the edge and watch the figures below sway backwards and forwards like weeds under the water.*[162]

Henrietta, here, is enjoying the bus far more than her creator, who says only: "I could bear the top of a horse bus."

> *Perhaps both conveyances gave me a sense of height and of removal from noise, and I have always loved heights; especially if it is quiet up there on top.*[163]

Heights are not only peaceful but again symbolic - like the rock that Nan and Uncle Ambrose climb in *Linnets and Valerians*.

> *Right at the top, looking out over the murmuring sea of green leaves below them, she found that he was as moved as she was by this mounting up and up from floor to floor of one of the mansions of the world.*
>
> *'To have the clouds lapping against one's feet, like the leaves do now, wouldn't it be wonderful?' she said ecstatically.*
> *'I have experienced that on mountain tops,' said Uncle Ambrose. 'These ascents are not only physical, Nan. The world of the spirit too has many mansions. We live upon a staircase.'*[164]

Fortunately, not every visit to Uncle James and Aunt Emma involved the horrors of the London streets. To visit them at Holtye in Sussex brought no experience of "ridiculous terror," for their "lovely country home was a very different kettle of fish. It was bliss." And, like Guernsey, it was a fragrant place.

> *They had a large garden that in my memory basks always in hot sunshine. I have only to think of it to have in my nose the scent of the giant sweet peas that grew there, and the smell of the azaleas and rhododendrons that separated the garden from the open country. By crawling through the bushes I could reach a certain secret place I knew of. There no one could see me from the house and I could sit cross-legged in a bower of apricot and golden azaleas, and see the world stretching away from me in mile after mile of blue shining heat mist.*[165]

Perhaps the glories of this garden were the inspiration behind her description of the grounds of Belmaray in *The Rosemary Tree*.

> *From this terrace the steps lost themselves in the slope of a meadow leading down to the river. This field, and the opposite one on the other side, were planted with rhododendrons and azaleas, and so were the river-banks upon either side until the river was lost to sight beyond the spur of a hill... Upon the other side of the river the rhododendrons climbed the steep field until they reached the edge of a larch-wood. In another two months the larches would wear their heavenly green above a flaming mass of rose and saffron, crimson and gold.*[166]

Such peaceful places were much more suited to Elizabeth's personality – and Henrietta's.

> *Henrietta, at heart a contemplative person, enjoyed alarums and excursions for a short while only. For her a background of quiet was essential to happiness. It had been fun to stay with Felicity...but it had completely upset her equilibrium and she had felt as though she had been turned upside down so that everything that was worthwhile in her mind fell out...*

> *She found herself listening only to the lovely silence and it seemed to her that in it she came right way up again and her dreams, that had deserted her in London, came flocking back, so that with joy she flung open the doors of her mind and welcomed them in. Never again, she vowed, would she live a noisy life that killed her dreams. They were her reason for living, the only thing that she had to give to the world, and she must live in the way that suited them best.*[167]

Uppingham

There was another garden where I was happy. My father's only sister was now living at Uppingham, where her husband Clavel Parmiter was a housemaster and Nanny and I sometimes visited them. There were four children and they had a large sunny nursery in a big house and a Nanny who, like mine, had been trained at the Norland Institute in the arduous business of coping with 'the modern child' of that age. I suppose children always have been and always will be naughty, the rare moments when they trail clouds of glory being for those who look after them mere fitful gleams of sunshine in a long stormy day, but I think we behaved better then than the little demons do now, for I remember the two Nannies reigning very serenely over the five children in that nursery. And I remember these children dressed in their Sunday best, one small boy in a sailor suit and four little girls in white muslin dresses with coloured sashes, sitting good as gold and still as mice in the drawing room after tea while my uncle read aloud to us from (I think) The Child's Book of Saints. *Like my father he read aloud extremely well, trained to it as part of his parental duty, but even so the picture of even temporarily good and quiet children listening to a Sunday story with hands folded in muslin laps is distinctly a period piece.*[168]

The eldest of these cousins, Mary, recalled in old age that theirs was a 'rough and tumble' family and in contrast Elizabeth was rather 'wrapped in cotton wool.' She remembered one visit when the family was playing croquet, which Mary missed as she had to sit on the terrace 'sewing with Elizabeth.' She said:

> We saw very little of her when we were all young. She was so sheltered and such an "only child" – the fact of her mother being an invalid added to her isolation from other children. I remember her coming to stay with us once with her Norland nanny – I can't think she enjoyed the visit![169]

More than one of Elizabeth's novels features a child who is a little different from her peers, like the adopted Edith in *The Scent of Water* or - in this description - Stella in *Gentian Hill*: who again, as a French émigré's child adopted in babyhood by a Devon farmer, does not quite fit in.

She played very little with the other children, for they did not like her. They said, with injustice, that she gave herself airs. This she did not do, but she did not speak their language nor they hers and so she was shy and aloof with them. She grieved and puzzled over this sometimes but try as she would she could not bridge the gulf of their unlikeness. And so she remained, unknown to anyone, a little lonely.[170]

Elizabeth's own shyness was illustrated, in her later years, by a very sad little memory: for she said that her cousins "never shamed their father by the clumsiness and speechlessness of desperate shyness as I shamed mine."

No doubt the "sheltered" little girl did find some aspects of her cousins' rough and tumble family life rather an ordeal, but she did admire them for their skills - one in particular, which she discovered she could share.

They were so clever; they could catch a ball without dropping it and play card games well…and they made fairy houses beautifully…[171] *The roofs and walls of these mansions were constructed of twigs and leaves, and inside were beds for the little creatures made of flower petals and on the floors were carpets made of more flower petals arranged in patterns. We would see who could make the prettiest house but we never knew if they gave pleasure because we never managed to see a fairy inside.*[172]

The fairy houses were recalled in loving detail in her children's story, *The Fairy Queen's Jewels*.

The trunk of the beech tree was thickly covered with ivy, and down at the bottom it was arranged like a curtain and covered a tiny door… The Princess drew the ivy aside and rapped on the door with a little knocker made from a hazel nut…

Presently shuffling footsteps sounded within, and someone shot back the bolts and turned the key in the lock… The Princess, followed by Mr. and Mrs. Gnome, ran joyously forward into the sweetest little room imaginable. It was furnished completely by flower petals and berries. There were the most delicious little armchairs carved out of hips and haws, a soft carpet of red and white rose petals, and lovely soft cushions all stuffed with thistledown. The walls were hung with curtains of rose leaves which matched the carpet. The room was beautifully warm, and Mrs. Gnome, looking round to see where the fire was, saw instead one of the flowers which children call "red hot pokers." It was standing in a corner of the room and sent out a beautiful glow…

While Hannah was getting the tea the Princess took her visitors all over the house. Upstairs there were three bedrooms. The Princess's room was all lined with mauve and white violet petals, and had a little window with curtains of ivy leaves on the outside and rose leaves on the inside, which kept out the damp and wet, but could be drawn aside whenever the Princess wished. Hannah's room was lined with blue cornflowers, she had chosen them because she said they reminded her of her childhood, when she had lived in a cornfield.

But Mr. and Mrs. Gnome thought that their room was the sweetest of all, for the walls and carpet were made of primrose petals.[173]

Fairy houses feature again, some twenty years later, in *Henrietta's House*. As the Old Gentleman muses on the mystery of poetic vision, he reveals the world of faerie to be - not a mere fantasy of childhood - but something much more spiritual. To him, it is just one of "the many worlds of mystery."

"What is a poet but a recorder of visions of another world? To all poets, whether they record with pen and ink, or hammer and chisel, or paintbrush and canvas, I take off my hat, for their recorded visions are vessels into which can flow the wine of another country for the thirsty to drink. But for the poets, my dear sir, we should all perish of thirst."

"Are you a poet yourself, my friend?" asked Grandfather.
"Only of a sort," said the Old Gentleman humbly. "I cannot tell a fairy story with pen or brush or chisel, though the fairy world is my favourite among the many worlds of mystery, but I have continued into a ripe old age the childish pastime of building bowers for the fairy folk out of the flowers and fruits of the earth... Laugh at me if you like."

"I am not laughing," said Grandfather. "Do I laugh at the men who build shrines for the saints and make cribs for the Christ Child at Christmas time? I do not. I take off my hat and quench my thirst for Paradise at those vessels that human hands have made."[174]

But for the child Elizabeth, her visit over:

Somehow, though of course I believed absolutely in fairies, I had never thought of building houses for them in the Wells garden. As an only child I had been more aware of the need for human than for fairy companionship...[175]

The Unseen Playmate

In 1909 the Hollis family had moved on to pastures new, and without her friends "I was lonely for the first time in my life," she said. "I trailed round and round the garden weeping bitterly" – adding self-mockingly, "I was always a watery child."[176] But even this time of desolation had its comforts, the chief of which was "a…pony on whose back I careered through the country lanes."[177]

> *[It was] a Devonshire pony with a long tail borrowed from an old lady who lived in the Liberty. It pulled the governess cart she kept for her grandchildren but it was a gay little pony and could gallop fast and well. I was taught to ride first by our gardener and then by one of my father's students, who took me up to a magic stretch of green turf above the Tor woods and taught me and the pony to go like the wind. At least the pony and I thought we were going like the wind, it felt that way to us, but if I looked up at the tall young man on a tall horse beside me they did not seem to be exerting themselves at all. While we were going at full stretch they were merely cantering easily. I remember I looked up at that young man as though he were one of the gods upon Olympus and I remember gratefully his great kindness to a small child, and the gentleness of his teaching. Never be afraid, he said. If you are afraid you communicate your fear to your horse. Fear is a dreadful thing, so easily communicated that it hurts others as well as yourself. Never be afraid of anything. I wish I had listened to him more attentively.*[178]

If she were not sufficiently fearless herself however she could, in *The Little White Horse* create a fictional child who was.

> *Sir Benjamin had to teach her how to adjust herself to the rhythm of Periwinkle's trotting feet, how to manage reins and crop, how to hold on when Periwinkle broke into a joyous canter over the sweet turf. But she learned in two hours what most girls of her age would only have learned in two weeks, for she was without fear, and after each tumble she was up again, dizzy and bruised yet laughing, and back in the saddle almost before Sir Benjamin had time to draw rein. He was hugely pleased with her. He noted that she had grit and skill, and that sense of oneness with her mount that makes the true horsewoman.*[179]

All Elizabeth's books make plain her great love of animals and birds, and at this lonely time she had the consolation not only of the pony but also, she says, "a dog called Maximilian, a couple of love birds, a guinea pig and sixteen rabbits."[180] Loneliness and the need for human companionship, however, brought another friend into her life.

> *It gave me a deep thrill when I first read [Robert Louis Stevenson's]* The Unseen Playmate *with understanding. For…he came to me, as to all lonely children.*
>
> > *When children are playing alone on the green,*
> > *In comes the playmate that never was seen.*
> > *When children are happy and lonely and good,*
> > *The Friend of the Children comes out of the wood…*[181]

It was not merely to provide a link with Stevenson's poem that she recalled this experience in her Preface; this was a key memory for her. Her unseen playmate had a place in more than one of her novels, and was described by name in *The Joy of the Snow*.

> *[I] found for myself a boy of my own age called Charlie. I do not know if that was his real name because I do not know what sort of boy he was, whether he was the creation of my imagination or whether he really had some mysterious, inexplicable life of his own. He was, in either case, completely real to me, and we played happily together for hours.*[182]

An imaginary playmate was something that adults could understand… but a child with some mysterious, inexplicable *reality* was beyond their ability either to comprehend or to accept, as Caroline discovers in *The Bird in the Tree*.

> *"All alone?"*
> *Caroline, a truthful child, shook her head.*
> *"I invented a dream boy to play with," said David. "Do you invent playmates, Caroline?"*
> *Caroline took her thumb out of her mouth and lifted puzzled eyes to his face. 'Invent' was a word Lucilla had not taught her yet. She did not know what he meant. Then she hung her head and…a tear rolled down her button nose… She was terrified of that word 'invent'. She was afraid that David was going to explain it to her, and that its meaning would be one that she would not be able to bear….*[183]

> *Also he was useful. When I did not want to go to one of the hated parties I said Charlie was coming to tea with me. If I did not want to do my lessons I said Charlie was coming to play with me. The boy became a perfect nuisance to everyone except myself, and finally my*

mother lost patience and spoke terrible words. "Once for all, child, there is no Charlie." It was a death sentence and the boy left me. I cried bitterly but he never came back.[184]

Her mother's attitude becomes Miss Heliotrope's in *The Little White Horse*. Later in the story the object of her unbelief, Maria's "imaginary" friend Robin, does in fact turn out to be a real boy.

> *"You see very odd things," Miss Heliotrope interrupted her... "There was...that peculiar imaginary playmate of yours that you made up for yourself when you were only a little thing, that boy with the feather in his hat who used to play with you in the Square garden."*
> *"But he wasn't imaginary," said Maria hotly. "He was a real boy. He is a real boy. I know he's alive somewhere still, even though he does not come to play with me any more. His name is Robin and he looks like a robin, with bright dark eyes and rosy cheeks and..."*
> *"My dear," interrupted Miss Heliotrope again, somewhat sternly, "you have told me a thousand times what he looks like, or what you imagined at the time that he looked like, and I can only repeat that there was, and is, no such person."*
> *Maria said no more... [She] was very truthful, and when she said a thing was so nothing distressed her more than to hear people say it wasn't.*[185]

Robert too, in *Linnets and Valerians* understands - like Maria - that it is useless to argue with the grown-ups about such matters. And he can see the base reasoning behind their scepticism.

> *Like all children [he] could use exquisite tact when telling a true story to grown-ups. He knew one must not ask too much of their credulity. Things are seen and heard by the keen senses of the young which are not experienced by the failing powers of their elders, but as powers fail pride increases and the elders do not like to admit this. Therefore, when told by the young of some occurrence outside the range of their own now most limited experience, they read them a lecture on the iniquity of telling lies. This can lead to unpleasantness all round, and so the tactful Robert did not tell.*[186]

Despite Miss Heliotrope's scoldings, Maria never ceases to believe.

> *Maria lay for some time between sleeping and waking, thinking of the beautiful park through which she had driven to this lovely house and imagining herself running up one of its glades. And then her fancy*

became a dream and she was in the park, with the scent of flowers about her and spring trees talking to each other over her head. But in her dream she was not alone, Robin was with her, running beside her and laughing. And he was just the same — just as he had been when in her childhood she had been sent to play in the Square garden, and had felt lonely, and he had come running through the trees to companion her loneliness... strong and kind and merry, warm and glowing like the sun, and the best companion in the world...
Maria smiled as she slept.[187]

It seems that Elizabeth too never ceased to believe, for even in her fifties she could say: "We know he is a real person. We may have lost him now but we shall find him again."[188]

❋

It is obvious that Elizabeth did have experience of childhood loneliness which she carried through life, to be worked and reworked in her writing. But the isolation described by her cousin Mary was, perhaps, a very great blessing. Solitude can be immensely creative, and certainly in Elizabeth's case seems to have led her to a heightened awareness that would perhaps not have been possible in a more rough-and-tumble family life. On the one hand, she had a deep awareness of "the joys of childhood that have not changed... the joy in birds and beasts, flowers and stars, water, winds and sunshine." She lists, too, in the *Child's Garden* Preface "the joys of sleep and play," observing that "children of every age are adventurous and their favourite games are always games of adventure."

But she says too, that "there are other games which children delight in, more creative than adventurous, calling for a greater delicacy of imagination and bringing deeper powers of the soul into play...the imaginative escapes of childhood."[189]

The Hidden Things

These escapes were a great joy, known to the young Elizabeth and experienced by several of her fictional children... through an awareness of another plane of existence, which she called "the memory and the foretaste of the hidden things."[190] They involved a mysterious escape into a place beyond the world of mere imaginary play; beyond, for instance, the building of fairy houses in her Aunt Eva's garden: which "seemed a secret, mysterious place to me" she says; where "as I remember it the lawn sloped down to a hollow where narrow paths wound among flowerbeds and under the shade of bushes and low trees."[191] No, this escape was to *another country*.

All of us can dimly remember going to that country

    Where the clover-tops are trees,
    And the rain-pools are the seas,

R.L.S. calls it "The Land of Play," but though the journey there sometimes began as a game, as when…I made a flower house for the fairies at the bottom of the garden and then went inside myself, it could become something much deeper. We did really escape out of this world. We recaptured for the moment something we had nearly lost. It was a gazing back to the coasts of the country that will not be seen again until the voyage is over and our ship comes back to where she started from.[192]

Again, it was something that one did not always share with the grown-ups.

> *"What country?" asked Mary.*
> *"The country," said Winkle "You know." She did not mention her country to grown ups as a rule because she was not sure that they did know, and one didn't like to have one's realities dismissed as idle tales. But Mary was different. Mary was one of those people who made you feel that what you knew she knew too, only better, and where you had been she had been, too, only farther. Winkle suspected that her father was that kind of person, only she did not know her father very well yet; he seemed a bit high up and remote. But Mary was lower down and more accessible. "One goes back there," she said, jogging Mary's memory.*
> *Mary wrinkled her forehead, trying to remember. The shadow of a memory touched her, filling her with sadness, because she could not quite remember; the same sadness that came sometimes with the scent of violets on a cold spring evening, with birds' voices, with the sound of rain on a roof in a summer dawn, with a thousand little things that touched you and stabbed you and were gone. A great symphony or a flaming sunset might fill you with intolerable longing, but it was the longing for something to come and had triumph in it. But this sadness was the ache for something that seemed lost.*[193]

And she continues this passage in *The Rosemary Tree* with words from the final stanza of one of her favourite poems: *Little Gidding* in T.S. Eliot's *Four Quartets*, where he calls this half-remembered place the Source. Her anthology, *A Book of Comfort* has other examples of poets who experienced the memory of this lost heavenly country – R.S. Thomas's *Children's Song*[194] which talks about the Centre that adults can no longer find; and Henry Vaughan's poem *The Retreat*:

> Happy those early days, when I
> Shin'd in my Angel-infancy!
> …When yet I had not walk'd above
> A mile or two from my first Love,
> And looking back – at that short space –
> Could see a glimpse of His bright face…[195]

Even in her first novel, there is a little girl making that journey back into some glory left behind.

> *[Jacqueline] clung to the wall and shut her eyes. The wind that buffeted her was so strong that she gasped for breath, yet so soft in its touch that it was like rose petals falling on her cheeks… She and the storm were one and round them, uniting them, was a ring of pure and endless light; of a depth and height and breadth inconceivable… Clinging to her wall, her eyes tight shut, she slipped back again for a moment, as a child may, into the glory from which she had come, knew what cannot be held in the meshes of the mind and saw from behind closed lids what would have blinded open eyes. The gates of heaven were to shut again and bar her out but who that has seen ever forgets their opening, or ceases to watch for the crack of light under the door?*[196]

She is again quoting from Vaughan's mystical poetry: "I saw eternity the other night / Like a great Ring of pure and endless light."[197] Wordsworth too wrote of a similar experience in his *Intimations of Immortality* - of seeing everything "apparell'd in celestial light" and knowing it to be the result of being born into the world "not in entire forgetfulness" but with a child's remembrance of something known "elsewhere."

> There was a time when meadow, grove, and stream,
> The earth, and every common sight,
> To me did seem
> Apparell'd in celestial light,
> The glory and the freshness of a dream…

> Our birth is but a sleep and a forgetting:
> The Soul that rises with us, our life's Star,
> Hath had elsewhere its setting,
> And cometh from afar:
> Not in entire forgetfulness,
> And not in utter nakedness,
> But trailing clouds of glory do we come
> From God, who is our home:
> Heaven lies about us in our infancy![198]

But to return to the experience of that other small girl, Winkle, in *The Rosemary Tree*:

> *She turned towards the small square high window and saw it framing the branch of a plum-tree with its blossom white against the grey sky. A ringdove alighted on the branch and swung there. She sighed with contentment and her eyes did not leave the flowering branch and the blue-grey wonder of the bird.*
>
> *"Please," she said softly, "could I go there now?"*
>
> *She had a moment of anxiety, wondering if she would be able to go. When she had been very small she had never wondered, the mere flash of a bird's wing, a snowflake looking in at the window or the scent of a flower had been enough to send her back... And she had not exactly gone back, she had been lifted back by the small lovely sights and sounds and scents, as though it were easier for her to be there than here. But now she was five years old it was easier to be here than there. She could not go back without first secluding herself in some hiding-place...without climbing the steps to the door with the least suspicion of an effort, and that little pang of anxiety lest today she might not be able to make the effort. And always at the back of her mind nowadays there was the fear that the day might come when not only would she be unable to make the effort, but that she would not want to go back... Perhaps one day she would have forgotten that she had ever gone back. Nothing would remain of her returns to the other place but a vague longing.*
>
> *But that time was a long way off yet, and meanwhile with relief and unspeakable joy she found herself making the effort and climbing the steps. They were silvery steps and might have been made of light, and they led to the low small door in the rock... A year ago she had been*

small enough to pass through the door without bending her head, but now she had to stoop. If she got much bigger even stooping would not get her through, for it was an exceedingly small door.

She knocked, waited a moment, the door opened and she stepped through into the branch of swaying blossom. Beside her was the dove, and they swung there together in the still grey peace...

Winkle never knew quite what it would be that cradled her. It might be golden praise or the blue of purity or scarlet courage, or just light, or just darkness. It depended on the day and the time. They were all good, but the light was very good because it enabled her to see right to the horizons of the country where the mountains were. The darkness was best of all, even though she saw nothing and did nothing in it, because it loved her.

With invisible sweet airs rocking the fragrance and the light that held her, Winkle gazed at the miracle of a plum blossom that swung above her...The group of long silvery stamens tipped with gold, rising from the delicate green heart of the flower, were like an angel's crown. She could look deep into the heart, down into a green cavern of refreshment. It was like drinking cold water when you are thirsty. Beyond the flowers light shone through the silk curtains of the green leaves, and beyond them was depth beyond depth of peace. It held Winkle, and held the dove too as she leaned back against its warm breast.

She turned her head so that her cheek was against its feathers. She knew it would not fly away. Here, nothing you loved ever flew away.[199]

Childhood Faith

Wordsworth said that we come from our home in God "not in entire forgetfulness," and that "heaven lies about us in our infancy." There are many recorded instances of childhood theophanies which bear witness to this; and Elizabeth's grew out of that difficult winter when her mother went away.

My mother became desperately ill with terrible pains in her head and so paralysed by some form of poisoning that she could hardly drag herself from her bed to her sofa. Our doctor had not the faintest idea what was the matter and was anxious that she should leave home and live in Bath for the winter, in the care of a doctor there who was reputed to be very clever, and of course Nanny had to go too to look after her.[200]

The Joy of the Snow points out that in those days, for "people with adequate homes and families" illness was very much home-based: "and if the illness was serious that made work." A patient would not necessarily be cared for in their own home however: Elizabeth remembered, for example, that "the aunts always came to our home to be ill."[201] It seems possible therefore, even likely, that if Mrs Goudge was spending the winter in Bath, then it would be at Nanny's parents' house - even though Nanny's mother herself was too "frail" to do much more than sit by the fire, even at mealtimes. Bath was not too long a journey from Wells, and Nanny-Daddy's house was on the very outskirts of the city: "there was still country on three sides" with beyond it the "green hills that rolled up to the sky."[202] If this was their venue, it would have been a good source of fresh country air after damp Wells.

The Jolliffe's youngest daughter, Elsie was also a Norland nanny, and it was normally the eldest, Mary, who was the source of all the "superb cooking" in their house. But now Mary made the reverse journey from Bath to look after Elizabeth. The child must have liked her, for she remembered her "at the open front door, smiling a welcome"[203] whenever she was taken to visit them. But "to have both my mother and Nanny disappear at the same moment was for me a very traumatic experience," she says. "Spoilt little horror that I was, I found comfort in resenting Mary and being as naughty as possible."[204]

It would be traumatic for the child of course, but this had surely been a decision based on whose need was the greatest… a healthy little girl, or the mother who was so ill. Elizabeth says that "of course" Nanny had to go too, and this could perhaps be seen as confirmation that they were going to stay at her home. It seems safe to say, though, that although Nanny stood almost in the role of a mother to Elizabeth, she was at least equally important in Mrs. Goudge's life; for "in all her illnesses she never needed a nurse. Nanny did everything for her."[205]

In fact Elizabeth says that "from the time [Nanny] came to us, when I was a month old, her life was centred on my mother. She was like a planet revolving round the sun." She records that "the love of the two women for each other and their reliance upon each other was extraordinary":[206] a relationship which is echoed in the love between Lucilla and her maid Ellen in the Damerosehay novels.

> *Lucilla was a very strong-minded old lady, but in the hands of Ellen she was as wax.*
>
> *It was because she loved Ellen more than anyone else, except perhaps David, that she permitted herself to be domineered over in this way; for even the strongest succumb sometimes to this luxury of yielding love; it is good to have one person upon earth to whom one gives oneself in submission as a child to its mother... Her yielding to Ellen went right down to the depths of her spirit and was one of the sources of her strength. Without Ellen she would have made a poor thing of her life. Unseen, mysteriously, Ellen's spirit had always supported hers...*
>
> *Lucilla was a truthful woman and so she did not mind admitting to herself that she loved Ellen more than any of her children, more than the memory of her dead husband, more than any of her grandchildren... Ellen knew all her secrets... Ellen knew all the heights and all the depths. In such knowledge there was peace.*[207]

Elizabeth describes herself harshly as a "spoilt little horror" - and yet if the trauma surfaced as bad behaviour, who could blame this little girl? If Mother needed Nanny then Elizabeth had to do without her - and at this particular time had to relinquish them both. It was a hard thing for a small child to cope with, and at a time when her mother's illness alone must surely have been a cause of distress. In fact, how much of her mother's actual pain might she have been aware of, from behind the green baize door? It may well be nothing more than fiction, but David in *The Bird in the Tree* remembers how "his mother had not troubled overmuch to keep him out of sight and sound of his father's pain. She had thought he was too little to understand. But he had understood" and he was "terrified by it."[208]

The traumatic experience was not without its reward however. She tells us that one of the facts of life she learned in childhood was that "heaven grows out of doom endured"[209]... and the heaven in this case, was a rare experience of closeness to her father.

> *Quite suddenly my father became for those few months the central figure in my world. He had as it were turned back upon the pathway where he was always in the distance. There would be many of these brief meetings before [the] final turning back, and this was the first of them...*[210]

This was an experience of far more importance than the simple joy of their wonderful games beneath the Study chairs, and she made a detailed record of it in *The Joy of the Snow*.

> *My Sunday scripture lesson, always given me by my mother, was now his task.*
>
> *I think he had not the slightest idea how to set about instructing a small child. My mother had given me carefully prepared instructions which went in at one ear and out at the other. My father took me on his lap, with a cushion placed between his exceptionally bony knees and his child's tender posterior, and turned the pages of a New Testament picture book, commenting briefly on the pictures as we considered them one by one. At the pictures of the passion of Christ I refused to look. I had caught a glimpse of one and that was enough. My father was understanding about this and we turned them over in a lump, leaping straight from Palm Sunday to Easter day and ignoring the crux of the matter altogether. Yet now I think that turning the pages of that picture book with my father was the most important thing that ever happened to me, important because for the first time in my life the man in the picture book came out of it and was alive…*
>
> *The theophanies of children could be the subject of a book in themselves. I am sure most children have an awareness of God in very early childhood, though it can come so early and be so simple that later they forget it; or if they remember they do not wish to speak of it for fear of being laughed at. I am speaking of it now only because I am trying to tell the truth and believe that it was a valid experience and that I am lucky in remembering it so clearly. I owe the clearness perhaps partly to the loneliness of my childhood and to the beauty of my home… And also without doubt to the fact that my father had in some way communicated his own conviction to me. He had made the Christ in the picture book a living person.*[211]

Nor was it an isolated experience. "The winter passed and my mother came home," she continues, "and even though my father receded from me again the spring world was full of joy." It was during this fresh beginning, that the little girl's new awareness of God was reinforced by an even greater experience: first of darkness, then of light.

> *It was in a world of sunshine and birdsong that I had my first conviction of sin. So baldly stated it sounds a comic occurrence but I did not think so at the time. It overwhelmed me. I know the exact spot on a field path where I first knew the vileness of sin in myself; and can recapture the misery I felt because it has been repeated so many times since. What caused this first conviction? Was it because Christ had come alive? Or because I had come to know and love my father better and perhaps subconsciously compared myself to him? Partly perhaps the shock of joy caused by my mother's homecoming, because it was to her I ran when I got home and to her that I poured out the tale of my wickedness; and I hope that the way I had treated Nanny's sister, and also frequently treated my poor daily governess, came first on my list rather than stealing sugar from the nursery cupboard. The shock of*

realising what went on behind the green baize door of the nursery wing must have been a cruel one to my mother but I remember that she stood up to it well and was able to assure me of God's forgiveness.

A little later I was alone in the garden, at a spot where hyacinths and deep red wallflowers were in bloom against a grey stone wall, and God revealed himself in a shining world. Every flower flamed with the glory and every bird sang of it. It would be foolish to try and describe the experience; who can? Only the poets and mystics can capture something of the light, Traherne perhaps even more perfectly than Wordsworth.

> *All things were spotless and pure and glorious; and infinitely mine and joyful and precious… I was entertained like an angel with the works of God in their splendour and glory; I saw all in the peace of Eden; heaven and earth did sing my Creator's praises, and could not make more melody to Adam than to me… Is it not strange that an infant should be heir of the whole world and see those mysteries which the books of the learned never unfold?*[212]

※

She did in fact include an account of a childhood theophany in *Island Magic*. Her comment forty years later about it being "foolish to try" is perhaps an indication that she had felt the attempt to be inadequate. She had certainly admitted in an essay that she "made a bad job" of describing a dream of heaven in *The Bird in the Tree* because "words are poor things with which to try and convey dream impressions;"[213] and perhaps this was no different.

> *It was not until last week that she had really seen God for herself. It had all begun by her wondering about the Canterbury bells. There were great masses of them in the border, pink and blue and white, and she began by wondering whether they ever rang chimes like the church bells did… Sitting on her stool she looked at the coloured world spread out around her and for the first time noticed that it was very beautiful. A carpet of green moss under her feet, a canopy of blue sky over her head, flowers in their hundreds on either side of her, and all apparently let down from heaven, like a bale of coloured silk, for her delight.*
>
> *She had not noticed beauty before. She had taken the gold-dusted whiteness of the lilies as much for granted as eggs for breakfast, but now she looked and looked, and wondered and wondered. The lilies were very tall and their flowers were shaped like bells too…*

God must have made all the bells all the world over to make people happy… It was very kind of Him and it must have taken Him a long time. She felt much obliged. What a lot of bells all round her, and all of them beautiful, white bells of the lilies with gold dust inside, yellow bells of the crown imperials with bulging drops of honey inside, blue and pink and white Canterbury bells, hundreds and hundreds of them. She gazed and gazed and quite suddenly all the bells began to ring. She listened open-mouthed. Yes, they really were. They were swinging slowly from side to side, the lilies, the crown imperials and the Canterbury bells, and chiming away like mad.

Why? It wasn't Christmas night; it wasn't that moment at Mass when the heads are bowed… Then something began to chime inside her and, looking up, she saw God walking down the garden path.

Every day since that Monday morning she had sat herself on her little stool on the mossgrown path, but He did not come again. Every day the lilies and Canterbury bells spread their petals in the sun and shook out little gusts of perfume when the sea wind touched them in passing, but they did not chime again.[214]

One can quite see why some critics would later brand her work as whimsical; nevertheless this had as its inspiration an actual childhood experience which was akin to that of many Christian mystics and poets - and not just those of centuries past, like Traherne and Wordsworth. Dom Bede Griffiths' theophany occurred in his final term at school when, walking alone at sunset, he was suddenly filled with awe and reverence by the sound of the evening birdsong. He became aware of a previously unimagined world of beauty, borrowing Wordsworth's phrase to describe how everything was suddenly transformed, and appeared to him to have 'the glory and the freshness of a dream.' He remembered it ever after as one of the decisive events of his life, of pivotal importance in his spiritual journey. Elizabeth, of her own experience, says:

I do not remember fear, only awed amazement. I picked some of the deep red wallflowers and a small hyacinth, and Nanny let me keep them in a pot of water beside my bed in the night nursery. The scent of wallflowers and hyacinths is now for me irretrievably mixed up with the reading of the Gospels. My godmother had given me a little copy of the New Testament and in the ungrateful way of spoilt children I had not bothered with it and had lost it. But now, I don't remember how, it came to light again and lived under my pillow. I woke up with the birds and read it every morning, not ceasing to read it until I had reached the end of the fourth gospel. I cannot have understood much of what I read but all through that reading time I continued in the amazement of peace and love.[215]

❋

Sometimes in her children's books, she would balance any reference to the spiritual with an immediate lighthearted return to the world, its joys and its humour: As in this extract from *The Little White Horse*, when Maria enquires about the meaning of her family's motto:

> 'The brave soul and the pure spirit shall with a merry and a loving heart inherit the kingdom together,' quoted Sir Benjamin... It refers, I think, to the two sorts of Merryweathers, the sun and the moon... It is also, perhaps, a device for linking together those four qualities that go to make up perfection – courage, purity, love and joy.' Sir Benjamin paused a moment, and then with intense relief suddenly bellowed, 'Sausages!!!'
>
> For a moment Maria thought that Sausage was another thing that one must have to attain perfection, but then a delicious smell told her that her cousin had descended suddenly from the spiritual plane to the material, where she guessed that he was really happier and more at home.[216]

And surely Elizabeth's childhood self must have had, alongside the spiritual side of her nature, a very healthy appreciation of earthly joys... like Henrietta in *A City of Bells*.

> She asked...for some hundreds-and-thousands, which she adored. They were coloured sugar-balls the size of pins' heads and were delicious eaten between slices of bread and butter. First you bit through the soft sponginess of the bread and then your teeth crunched gloriously into the sweet grittiness of the rainbow-coloured balls. The contrast was curiously exhilarating, adding a very special savour to life.[217]

❋

> Henrietta always enjoyed Jocelyn's haphazard teas. Very strong tea out of a black pot, with heaps of sugar, was much nicer than the milk and water with a dash of tea only that she had at home, and nothing is

nicer than a chocolate biscuit held in one hand and a ginger one in the other, with alternate bites taken of each.

"Have you any bullseyes?" she asked, pulling up a chair to sit beside Jocelyn at his table.
"No. Why?"
"They're lovely after ginger biscuits. They cool them down."
"I'll have them next time you come," Jocelyn promised.

Henrietta put her half-eaten biscuits down on his manuscript and had a long pull at her tea, leaving off in the middle of that to show Jocelyn her new clothes.
"Exquisite," said Jocelyn, as she turned slowly round.

She took off her coat so that he could see her dress, green silk smocked by Grandmother, and lifted the skirt a little to show him her new petticoat and frilly knickers. Then she got back into her chair again and finished her biscuits.[218]

ELY

❄

1911 - 1923

The Second City of Bells

Towards the end of their Wells years, she tells us, her father "became a Doctor of Divinity. His men gave him his scarlet hood and great was the pride and rejoicing."[219] Shortly after this, when Elizabeth was eleven, he received the offer of a new appointment: a canonry at Ely Cathedral, combined with the Principalship of the Theological College. Dr. Goudge duly took a trip northwards to the Cambridgeshire fens to inspect what might become his family's new abode. He discovered that in some ways the house that came with the job was a great improvement on their Wells home – even though "the roof was in bad repair and there was no bathroom."[220]

This latter deficiency, of course, was nothing unusual in those days. Elizabeth like all her generation remembered marble-topped washstands in the bedrooms, with basins and water jugs which in cold weather "would be frozen hard by morning" and bath-tubs – "some round, some shaped like armchairs"[221] - in which the adults bathed in their bedrooms, or the children in front of the nursery fire. For Henrietta in *Sister of the Angels*, washing in a cold bedroom presents its own particular problems; (for "a fire in one's bedroom unless one was very ill indeed, was not allowed, however many degrees below zero the thermometer might have fallen.")

> *Henrietta, considering the brass can of warm water that Sarah had placed in her basin while she was still asleep, wrestled with her conscience. In this cold weather she and Hugh Anthony had their twice-weekly baths in tin tubs before the kitchen fire... but on other days they were expected to wash all over, in their rooms, "by bits." It was a process that called for real skill. The technical problem was how to wash a square foot of back, for instance, without uncovering the rest of yourself to the icy air, and it was difficult to solve, but the moral problem was much worse; was it compatible with the Christian religion, which commands its devotees to "endure hardness," to skimp washing on the very iciest of the cold days? Henrietta thought that it was, but found it very hard to decide what days could truthfully be described as the "very iciest," and what portions of the body might be left out upon them.*[222]

Perhaps Elizabeth had wrestled with such moral problems herself after receipt of her tenth-birthday gifts: one of which was John Keble's Victorian poems, *Lyra Innocentium*. Inscribed "with love and every good wish" to her from the Bishop of Bath and Wells, it contained "Thoughts in Verse on Christian Children, Their Ways and their Privileges."[223]

As to Henrietta's conscience about washing... on that very cold morning a tussle with her lower nature ends in the admonition that "If you shirk your middle this morning then you must do it tonight."

> *"Of course," said Henrietta's lower nature rather arrogantly. "But I shan't do my legs at all today, not whatever you say I shan't."*

Not long before the move to Ely, Mrs. Goudge had "lost patience" with the jug-and-basin system and "startled Wells by installing a bathroom."[224] It was not wholly successful - Elizabeth's clearest memory of it being the spectacular display of icicles when all its pipes froze and then burst one cold winter - but with their new home even this somewhat mixed blessing would have to be left behind.

Bathroom or not, the Ely house was "another beautiful old house, part of it Norman, with a glorious garden." It was also airy and dry, although "it had not been modernized at all;"[225] (it was discovered on closer inspection that there was "a well in the middle of the stone-floored apartment called the servants' hall," not to mention "the roots of the grand old garden trees" which had grown into the drains and "hindered them in the performance of their duties.") Her parents made up their minds. After due consideration of their joint needs - "they wanted a climate that would be good for sinusitis and they wanted to do the will of God"[226] - her father accepted the position.

After all, "in those far-off days part of the normal duty of any priest of the Church of England was the upkeep of a large house, and larger garden, upon a salary insufficient for the purpose."[227] (Her father used to say, she remembered, that "laying on water and repairing drains in ecclesiastical houses had been part of his life's work."[228]) There was available, besides - thanks to an endowment by Queen Anne in the eighteenth century - "the bounty from which poor clergymen in financial difficulties could borrow" when faced with such tasks.

> *And so we went to Ely in a state of euphoria and found that what Queen Anne could lend us was insufficient for our needs. She could and did renovate the drainage system and place a modern floor over the stone flags and the well...*

[they also eventually installed a lift for Mrs. Goudge - "a comic thing like a large wardrobe worked by a mechanism of ropes and weights" - which they later took with them to Oxford.[229]]

But she could not mend the roof and my father had to sell his valuable collection of foreign stamps started in his boyhood, and his collection of coins and any other family treasures he could find. But even then he remained in debt for some while.[230]

This experience was adapted for a scene in *The Rosemary Tree*, in which a clergyman invites his young daughter "to come into the study with him." What a joy for the little girl when, alone with her father in his own special room, they shoulder the burden of his financial problem together.

> *"Sweetheart, I'm in such a mess," he said, dropping into his armchair... Margary...stood before her father in a state of grave and sorrowful anxiety. "Whatever have you done?" she asked...*
> *"Promised to buy a house for Miss Giles and Miss O'Hara without having the money to buy it with," said John...They want to start a school together...*
> *Would you like to go there to school...?"*
> *"I'll go," said Margary, "Only you haven't bought it yet. Will it cost much?"*
> *"Not a great deal as houses go, said John. "Only we'll have to sell things to get the money."*
> *Their eyes roved anxiously round the room. One of the stamp albums was lying on John's desk, for he and Margary had been putting some stamps in last night...*
> *"Nothing in this room is worth much except our stamps," said John heavily, "and they're worth a great deal."*
> *"But you like the stamps," said Margary.*
> *"So do you," said John.*
> *There was a silence, and then Margary said, "Do Miss Giles and Miss O'Hara want the little house very badly?"*
> *"Yes, said John. "Very badly."*
> *"All right," said Margary. "I don't mind about selling the stamps if you don't."*
> *"Actually, I do mind," said John. "Only I haven't anything else to sell."*
> *"Will there be enough when you've sold the stamps?" she asked.*
> *"Not quite enough," said John truthfully.*
> *"Then you'd better have my pearl brooch my godmother gave me," said Margary. "There'll be heaps then, for there are real pearls in it."*
> *"But you like your pearl brooch," said John.*
> *"Yes, but I'd like Miss Giles and Miss O'Hara to have the little house."*

Ely

> *"All right," said John. "We'll sell your brooch as well as the stamps. Thank you... But we must know what we've got. We must make a list. It will be hard work. Shall we start now?"*
> *She jumped up in delight. To have work to do with Father was almost worth the pain of parting with the stamps and the brooch. Five minutes later they were happily engrossed.*[231]

How would the eleven-year-old Elizabeth have felt, having to leave behind the "fairyland" of Wells? It seems safe to assume, both from her own memories and from the evidence of the three books about Henrietta in Torminster, that she had loved this "enchanted city."

> *Wells, held in its benign and sheltered cup in the hills felt very safe. Our house too I remember as safe and cosy. Certainly one breathed in Wells the air of a fourth dimension but it was the air of the fairy tales, or of a peaceful book of saints and angels.*[232]

It is now just over a hundred years since the Goudges lived there but Wells is still enchanting, and particularly when — as so often - the air is full of music: be it the joyous pealing of the cathedral bells on the Green; instrumental music drifting through the mullioned windows of the mediaeval Music School; or the voices of the cathedral choir floating on the air from choral evensong, or their practice at the Choir School. Even the music of birdsong seems to have an enhanced ability to "rinse and wring the ear"[233] in the peaceful walled gardens around the cathedral and the beautiful Bishop's Palace.

And yet Elizabeth seems to have been content to move on, for she records no grief at leaving such a beautiful place. Indeed despite the town's "great homeliness in the days of my childhood,"[234] what she recounts of her loneliness and frequent tears - that description of herself as a watery child - suggests that the later years may perhaps have been less happy.

Not only does she express no regret at leaving, she says they went to Ely "in a state of euphoria;"[235] and this surely was, to a large extent, because it promised (and delivered) a time of better health for Mrs. Goudge. There, she was to enjoy "more freedom from the miseries of the body than she knew at any other time between my birth and her death." It took her from the dampness of those wells that gave Wells its name — the damp which had at times brought water seeping through the floorboards — to "a little city built on a hill in the open breezy fen country" and "an airy dry house standing high with bay windows facing south."[236] A great improvement for a young woman (Ida was still only thirty-seven at the time of the move) whose disability would eventually be traced to a dislocated coccyx and "arthritis caused by acute poisoning from sinusitis;"[237] and who had recently undergone a ground-breaking and perilous operation for a sinus abcess pressing on the brain. Elizabeth remembers that during the operation her father "spent the time praying in the chapel of the nursing home," and the severity of the illness had necessitated Ida's spending "a long time away from Wells."[238]

Elizabeth gives no details of her own childhood reaction to this family crisis. It was not the same bout of illness that had precipitated her "spoilt little horror" behaviour - when mother was paralysed by pains in her head as a result of "some form of poisoning" and spent the winter in Bath with Nanny. That long absence had been undertaken on the recommendation of "our doctor [who] had not the faintest idea what was the matter,"[239] whereas this operation was the result of Uncle James sending Ida to a London surgeon, who *knew* what was the matter.[240] There is also an account of a third crisis, presumably pre-dating the operation - of her being taken by her husband, "at the very worst point of her illness in Wells, when no doctor could help her and it seemed she was dying… to see a well-known spiritual healer." She was so ill that they had to travel "in one of those wonderful invalid coaches which were tacked on to trains in those days, complete with bed." But having met the healer she changed her mind about the treatment – "He would have had great power over me. No human being must have that sort of power over another," she said – and Father, who had had "all the anguish of bringing a very sick woman all the way from Somerset to London…had to take her back with nothing accomplished."[241]

The protracted drama of Ida's near-fatal illness would surely have been traumatic for the whole family from start to finish, and beneath the shadow of this crisis – indeed of all the crises - Elizabeth's childhood in Wells cannot have been as idyllic as some of her happier memories might seem to suggest. It must have come like a breath of fresh air to them all in fact: when the danger was passed and Mother had come back to her damp Wells home - "delivered from the worst of her pain…relieved, but…afraid of what would happen when she returned to it"[242] – to find that she could instead make a new life in a very different environment.

※

How can one describe the place? Wells was fairyland, in my memory a diaphanous cathedral and a city so hidden from the world that it seemed to have dropped out of the world, but Ely had the hard strength of reality. The cathedral had nothing diaphanous about it but was a great brooding presence that could at times be terrifying, so much so that at that time there were many people living in Ely who had never dared to go inside it. It leaped on you like a lion, taking you captive beyond hope of escape, but the lion was Aslan the divine lion and once the bondage had been accepted the pursuer became protector. When the winter gales came, or the great thunderstorms of summer roared in a darkening sky, the tall tower looked like a giant's mighty arm held up to keep the storm from falling on the city, and wherever one went on the sea of the fen one could always see the tower standing up like a lighthouse. Without it one might have felt lost and desolate in the vast flatness that lay so helplessly beneath the huge dome of sky, but with it one was safe.[243]

Brooding, terrifying, and yet a guide and protector… the cathedral at Ely is even older than Wells. Go inside it, Elizabeth says, and "the whole of history seems to fall upon you, and because of the great length of the place there is a sense of unendingness."[244]

Completed in 1189, a great part of the building is Norman. However the site has been a centre of Christianity since 673 AD, when St. Etheldreda was installed as Abbess of what is believed to have been, after the fashion of those times, a double monastery of monks and nuns. In the words of the Venerable Bede, "having built a monastery she began to be virgin Mother of very many virgins dedicated to God, both in examples and lessons of heavenly life."[245] When Elizabeth came to write her Ely book, *The Dean's Watch*, she would devote a whole chapter to the history of the cathedral and the city.

Equally historic was the flat fen countryside, which presented a stark contrast to the round green hills of the West Country that the Goudges had left behind.

There were patches of the fen that had purposely been kept in their original wild state; rare butterflies were to be found in them, and rare plants. It was a paradise for the botanically-minded, and for the historically-minded too for everything there was as it had always been. This was the fen as Hereward the Wake had known it, and Etheldreda and the monks of Ely.[246]

This would have been a great joy for her father, for Elizabeth said she did not think anything gave him more joy than "his almost passionate love of the beauty of the world. He was especially fond of birds and butterflies and knew a good deal about them. He would listen for the different bird notes in the spring and watch eagerly for the first appearance of the butterflies on the Michaelmas daisies."[247]

For the children there was the fascination of the water birds. The herons, tall and meditative, had something in common with the windmills and the church towers. They broke the flatness of the grey-green sea of rushes and water with sharp notes of contrast. Something aspired upwards for once, instead of flowing on and on into eternity under the vast dome of the empty burning blue sky.[248]

The fen, like the cathedral itself, was both beautiful and terrifying, for "there was no shade in the fen and if a storm came, no shelter. It was a place of great beauty but sometimes also of fear."[249]

> *The Dean could see a lonely figure coming towards him... In the whole terrible landscape he seemed the only living creature, as though he were the last man left to face alone the doom of all things. As the first flash of lightning lit up the stretch of the fen, so that it seemed for a blinding instant as though every reed and every twig were simultaneously visible, proclaiming aloud the preciousness of its identity before the darkness overwhelmed it, the Dean started forward from the bridge...*[250]

> *The wind and rain came together as [he] stumbled forward over the tussocks of rough grass, driving into his face and nearly blinding him. The windings of the drove hid the other man, he could see nothing but the sheeting rain and the stripped hawthorn boughs tossing in the wind. It was like struggling in a trough of waves.*[251]

It may at times have been a terrible landscape, as in this passage from *The Dean's Watch*, yet Elizabeth loved it. Ely was to her "the home of all homes."[252] The impact the fen countryside had on her in all its moods must have made a great contribution towards her love of the place, for she devotes several pages of her autobiography to describing it in detail, at every season of the year. At the same time she is, perhaps unconsciously, painting a picture of the changes that Ely brought to her lifestyle. It is noticeable that she uses the words 'we' and 'us' in so much of her description of life in the Fens. That often solitary Wells child, now approaching her teens and perhaps, too, a little more independent, seems to have found a very different kind of life. As when, in the joy of springtime, "little girls were riding their ponies along the droves, under the wild crab-apple blossom."[253]

> *The only pony I could get hold of was the milkman's, and he could only be borrowed at hours suitable to the milkman. He was a large stout pony with a very broad back and he could not be persuaded to go faster than he was accustomed to go when he took the milk round... The other little girls rode rather similar mounts, but we were not irked by our leisurely progress because the winding narrow droves in spring were not places where one wished to hurry. They were too beautiful.*
>
> *The droves were the ancient roads through the fen, linking the old farms and hamlets one to another... One could ride or walk along them for hours and never come across another human creature. They were bordered with stunted trees, sloe and hawthorns and wild crab-apple...*

Ely

In the shade of these trees bordering the way grew enormous cowslips. There was much waste ground in the fen in those days and whole fields would be cloth of gold from hedge to hedge...[254]

When I think of summer in the fen I think of the long summer holidays, of water and tall rushes and the sound of oars in the rowlocks. Water picnics were the delight of children in the hot days and we were for ever badgering our elders to take us up the river to the fen waterways, to bathe and picnic and see the swans and the herons. My father was a good oarsman and if he had a free day did not take much persuading. A couple of families would perhaps join together, would hire two or three boats and with sandwiches and bottles of lemonade would go out for the day. There would be a fairly long scull up the river and then we would turn aside up one of the quiet waterways, the fresh smell of water mint in our noses, the tall rushes rearing up like an army of spears on either side, and make our way slowly and peacefully to where we wanted to be.[255]

As far as her father was concerned, "the Fen country could not compare with the Mendip country for beauty, but he loved the glorious sunsets, the splendid stretch of the harvest fields in the autumn" and the droves that "wound for miles through the flat fields. And he loved every stone of the glorious cathedral that could always be seen in the distance towering up on its rock like the city of God itself."[256] The cathedral was a constant, year-round source of joy for his daughter, too.

On sunny days it was warm with colour, for the sun shone through the stained-glass windows and filled it with rainbows...[257]

To enter the nave suddenly on a hot day is like diving into the sea; it is so cool inside, and so amazing, and so utterly another world from the one left behind only a few moments ago.[258]

But it was at the Feast of Saint Etheldreda, in the autumn, that the Cathedral was "at its gentlest and loveliest..."

On the evening of the feast we all stripped our gardens of their flowers and early next morning appeared in the Cathedral with arms full of michaelmas daisies, dahlias, Japanese anemones, the first chrysanthemums and the treasures of the last roses. All the morning we worked in the Cathedral and every tomb was decorated...

I think there was a sort of hierarchy of decorators. The most accomplished ladies did the shrine, those who were gifted but not quite so gifted did the more important of the tombs and the children were given bunches of flowers and greenery and a few jampots and pushed towards obscure tombs and dark corners.[259]

She transferred this memory to Torminster when writing *A City of Bells*:

The Cathedral presented a scene of frantic activity, with all the canons' female dependants scurrying about in overalls with scissors hanging from their waists... There was always a little difficulty as to who should decorate what, all the ladies having the lowest opinion of each other's decorative powers...

It was at moments such as these that Grandfather came in useful. As he came smilingly up the aisle with his arms full of Japanese anemones it suddenly did not seem to matter very much who did what...

Mrs. Elphinstone was not quite sure whether Grandfather and the children could be entrusted with any really important decorating so she handed over to them an obscure chantry whose interior decorations could not be seen from outside... Though aware that he was being poked into a corner Grandfather was not in the least resentful, for he liked to feel that his flowers were honouring the unknown... He sat on one of the praying chairs that stood in a row at the back of the chantry and was full of bright ideas which Henrietta and Hugh Anthony carried out with deft fingers. The chantry looked lovely when they had done... It was sad to think that both the rose and the wreaths on the floor would be dead by night, but the people in the tombs were dead too and Grandfather assured them that death did not really matter at all, what mattered was that life while it lasted should be beautiful.[260]

[The Feast of Saint Etheldreda] was a great occasion and there was nothing to equal it except the festival evensong on Christmas Eve. The choir sang parts of Handel's Messiah under the lantern and I can never hear 'Wonderful, Counsellor, the Prince of Peace', without seeing again the shadowy height of the lantern soaring above our heads with the figure of Christ at its apex.[261]

As part of her Ely chapter in *The Joy of the Snow* she includes the story of the building of this lantern; how, after the central tower collapsed in 1322, a great "stone octagon supported by four Norman columns" was built in its place, "with above it a lantern sixty feet high built of oak wood, the outside covered with lead, suspended in mid air ninety-four feet above the Cathedral floor..."

It is a feat of engineering that takes the breath away. And so does the beauty of it. One looks up and up to where, at the highest point of the lantern, a carving of the triumphant Christ, head and shoulders surrounded by the rays of the sun, looks down with his hand raised in benediction.[262]

Even this breathtaking mediaeval structure proved to be a source of activity in her new life. At the age of seventy-eight she wrote to a friend saying how much she had enjoyed a recent radio programme about Ely Cathedral. "I have climbed the lantern many times," Elizabeth told her.[263]

After Christmas would come the season of the bitter cold... but for the children there could be a wonderful compensation. The floods and the skating. Provided it rained hard enough before Christmas the dykes overflowed, and if the river Ouse... overflowed too that was an added glory. If the floods were very bad indeed the fens could be under water almost as far as you could see...

With intense anxiety we waited for the great freeze-up and it seldom failed us. The children, and grown-ups too, emptied themselves joyously out of the little city and down on to the ice... I have never managed to be proficient at any single outdoor sport but I remember floundering joyously along clinging to the back of a wooden chair, sliding and snowballing all in the glow of a great fen sunset flaming across the ice and snow.[264]

In an autobiographical essay published in 1946 she allowed herself to mention how those fen winters could also be "unspeakably dreary... when the floods were out and the east wind was howling against the windows of our exposed house on the top of the hill."[265] But there is no doubt that – much as she loved the West Country, saying in later life that her roots were there "and nothing now can pull them up"[266] – Ely was a very special place for Elizabeth. Even in her seventies she still described it as the dearest, the "mother figure"[267] of all her five homes. Unusually, she used it as the setting for only one novel, and yet this seems to have been a deliberate act which only underlines its unique and important status, for she says that "the Ely book had always been at the back of my mind, waiting" and on reaching her late fifties – more than thirty years after leaving the place - she at last knew "I was now ready to write that book."[268]

Yet apart from the detailed description of the Fens and the outdoor activities they provided, the picture she has left behind of her family life in Ely seems somehow less clear than that of other homes... perhaps because it does only appear once in the fiction? Perhaps because she was away at school and college for much of the time? Or perhaps she deliberately kept it more private because it was so precious?

Curiously though, of the memories she does share of this home of all homes, many were not happy - starting with one great and terrible experience of loss and grief:

I had to say good-bye to Nanny.[269]

Loss

 This goodbye was the one shadow on the move to Ely. I was to have a daily governess to prepare me for boarding school, my mother was now well enough to manage without a nurse and my father made a terrible decision. A man in debt to Queen Anne was not justified in keeping a Nanny permanently in his household for no reason except that she was beloved, and so Nanny must go. I was told about it but children do not understand the meaning of a grief that they have not as yet experienced, and I received the news with total incomprehension. How can a child understand that someone who has been the foundation of life from the beginning is not going to be there next week? It is the same as being told that the earth itself will not be there on Wednesday. The situation cannot be understood.

 It was not until she said goodbye to me in the hall, and for the first time in my life I saw her weeping, that I realised what was happening to us. I clung to her, but it was no good, she pulled herself away and blind with tears went out to the cab that was waiting at the door, got in and was driven away.

 Then I knew. She was not just going away for a holiday, she was going for good. She might visit us but she would never live with us again. She was going to live with another mother and another child. She would love another mother and child, not us any more. Nanny had gone.[270]

> *Maria was an orphan... Her mother she did not remember, her father, a soldier, who had nearly always been abroad with his regiment, and who did not care for children anyhow, had never had much hold upon her affections; not the hold that Miss Heliotrope had, who had come to her when she was only a few months old, had been first her nurse and then her governess, and had lavished upon her all the love that she had ever known; if she had lost Miss Heliotrope that would have been a different story altogether.*[271]
>
>   The Little White Horse

 Nanny was not her only loss, for Sarah the cook, who used to tell her stories by the kitchen fire, had been left behind when they moved. Now in her sixtieth year, she had felt herself to be "too old to contemplate taking her roots out of Somerset, and she went to live in an almshouse." The maids Lilian and Araminta did make the journey, but "alas we did not keep them very long," Elizabeth remembered, for "their soft West-country voices and their charming ways made havoc of the tough hearts of the Fen men and they both got married."[272]

The unnamed "accomplished cook" who took Sarah's place

was too efficient a person to want children under foot in the kitchen, and the hours I had been used to spend toasting myself in front of the kitchen range at Wells I now spent making toffee with Tortoise.[273]

This was the Tortoise stove, the "peculiar monster" installed by their predecessors in the house - which, she said, despite its light and airy dryness was "remarkably cold, not with the penetrating dampness of Wells but with the east winds from the fen that caught it full blast on its little hill…"

For me personally his chief use was not for warmth for I spent many happy hours making toffee on him… I loved him dearly. He had a distinct personality, hot-tempered but good-natured with it, a friendly sort of dragon, though friendlier when not red-hot. I was with him when I had to say good-bye to Nanny.[274]

She had clung to Nanny before she left, but she makes no mention of clinging to anyone else in her grief. Mrs. Goudge too must have been distraught to lose her beloved Ellen, but she and her daughter did not shed tears together. Elizabeth says, "I wish I could say that my mother and I comforted each other but I cannot remember that we did. My mother was a very proud as well as a very brave woman and in the whole of our life together I never once saw her cry. When she wept she did it alone and no-one would have dared intrude upon her."[275] Out of the whole household, strangely, it was the inanimate Tortoise Stove that Elizabeth remembered and recorded as her companion at this time of painful loss.

They would see Ellen Jolliffe again – she had not actually left their lives for good. But as far as this little girl was concerned her beloved Nanny, who had looked after her all her life, had gone forever, and she was bereft.

I doubt if any of the partings of my life have plunged me into quite such total desolation as this one did. I stayed for a while in the hall…and then went back mechanically to the unfortunate new governess from whom I was careful never to learn one single thing. Not only was my mind closed against her, it was closed in the face of learning for many years to come.[276]

Books

If I had closed my mind to learning in the academic sense I had not closed it to books, for I did not consider that books were education, and if I learned nothing else in my schoolroom I learned to read. Flat on my stomach I read the Andrew Lang fairy books, the Waverley novels and Dickens, and later in an upright position much of Thackeray and Trollope and the Brontës, and last of all Jane Austen. I read them in that order, an order prescribed by my father. I read as children do, by suction... A book just flowed in.[277]

> *Henrietta took books from the shelves with a certainty that quite surprised the Old Gentleman. The Water Babies and Alice in Wonderland, Undine and The Pilgrim's Progress, Jackanapes and Little Women, The Fairchild Family and A Flat Iron for a Farthing, The Back of the North Wind and The Princess and Curdie followed each other into the basket with startling rapidity, followed by Uncle Remus, Hans Andersen, The Swiss Family Robinson, Andrew Lang's Blue Fairy Book, his Red One and his Green One, Mary's Meadow, Lob-lie-by-the Fire, The Wind in the Willows and The Cocky-Olly Bird.*
>
> *"Isn't that enough?" gasped the Old Gentleman.*
> *"Yes, I think that's all," said Henrietta, counting them.*
> *"You seem to know exactly what is required," said the Old Gentleman with much respect.*
>
> *"Yes," said Henrietta. "My father and I have often talked it over. We decided that if a person of my age had a library of twenty books those are just the twenty the person would want."*[278]
>
> Henrietta's House

A children's book entitled *Droll Doings* by The Cockiolly Bird had been published in 1903, when Elizabeth was three years old. It was a lavishly illustrated collection of animal tales in verse - and could well be the one in Henrietta's library. (It is perhaps less likely to be the same bird's *Nursery Book of Science* which describes flora and fauna, and sounds very much like the one that Miss Lavender took on their Nature Walks.) The bird was very much a part of Elizabeth's own childhood, and although "I do not know if I have spelt this bird's name correctly," she says, "yet he is with me today, and is I think the original of a bird who seems to fly in and out of my mind whenever I am writing, and was especially with me when I was writing *The Bird in the Tree*."[279]

He originates in one of her particularly treasured memories of Wells - of Mrs. Hollis reading "*The Cocky Olly Bird*" to them in the panelled drawing room at Tower House.

The sun was warm on the panelling, for it was summer, and there were flowers in the room and a sweet smell. Perhaps they were Mrs. Simpkins pinks, or syringa or Dolly Perkins roses. The children sat on the floor and Mrs. Hollis sat on a low chair, her wide skirts spread about her.[280]

This "small beautiful room half-way up the stairs" (like her Grandfather's study, so fragrant with flowers) may well be the source of all the beautiful little panelled parlours which feature so regularly in Elizabeth's stories.

Although it is not in Henrietta's library list, nor her own, Elizabeth's preface to *A Child's Garden of Verses* says that it was "the best beloved book of my…childhood, the first book I can remember having read to me and the first book from which I remember learning verses by heart."

And judging by certain similarities with *The Dean's Watch*, it seems likely that a popular Victorian novel for children – *The Cuckoo Clock* by Mrs. Molesworth (Mary Louisa Stewart) - was also a childhood favourite. It must have been extremely popular with both children and grown-ups, for the poet Swinburne said of it in 1884, "Any chapter of *The Cuckoo Clock* is worth a shoal of the very best novels dealing with the characters and fortunes of mere adults."[281] In its fifth chapter, *Pictures*, little Griselda tells the Cuckoo, "I would like to see the place where you were born – where that very, very clever man made you and the clock, I mean." And this is what she sees:

> It was not a pretty room – it had more the look of a workshop of some kind; but it was curious and interesting. All round, the walls were hung with clocks… There was one intended to represent the sun, moon, and planets, with one face for the sun and another for the moon, and gold and silver stars slowly circling round them…

> The occupant of the room…was sitting in front of a little table… He was examining, with a magnifying-glass, some small object he held in his hand… He was a very old man, his coat was worn and threadbare in several places… Yet he did not look *poor*, and his face, when at last he lifted it, was mild and intelligent and very earnest…

Said the old man, "The best [clock] of all, the *chef d'oeuvre* of my life, shall not be sold."[282]

It would be hard to believe that Elizabeth did not know and love this book in childhood, given the description of a clockmaker's workshop which forms the opening paragraphs of her beloved Ely book:

The candle flame burned behind the glass globe of water, its light flooding over Isaac Peabody's hands as he sat at work on a high stool before his littered work-table... He was a round-shouldered little man with large feet and a great domed and wrinkled forehead, the forehead of a profound thinker... He dressed in the style of twenty years ago, the style of the eighteen-fifties, because the clothes he had had then were not yet what he called worn out. His peg-topped trousers were intensively repaired across the seat but that did not show beneath his full-skirted bottle-green coat...

Isaac could paint on ivory with the skill of a miniaturist, and his clock face was to be a dial of the heavens. The twelve hours were to be the twelve signs of the zodiac... Within this circle of stars Isaac had planned the sun and moon balancing each other against a blue sky scattered over with tiny points of light that were the humbler stars...[283]

The celestial clock [was] his masterpiece... But he would not sell it.[284]

❋

My new kind governess...had been told not to over-press me, as I was a delicate child, and she certainly did not. She would read lesson books aloud to me in her kind, dreamy voice while I looked out of the window and thought happily of something else.[285]

"Other small girls joined me daily in resistance to education,"[286] she says, and so here is a clue to the 'we' and 'us' of her Ely life. There were other little girls living nearby to take away her loneliness; sharing not only her pony-rides but her lessons too. And having fun in the process, for she adds, "I do not think our poor governess enjoyed herself, but we did." Her memories of her father also record how "in those Ely days he gave a weekly Scripture lesson to me and three of my friends."[287]

The schoolroom was over the drawing room, a big room taking the curve of the roof. I had been allowed to choose the colour scheme and so the walls were white and the door, window and exposed beams were painted the bright cornflower blue which at that period was my favourite colour. [The same colour as the fairy house in *The Fairy Queen's Jewels*, where "Hannah's room was lined with blue cornflowers."[288]]

There was the usual big schoolroom table, uncomfortable chairs, a wooden cupboard, bookcases and an upright piano. There were two windows facing south and east...

The south window looked over the front garden and had a view of the old walnut tree surrounded in spring with hundreds of aconites growing in the grass. But the glory of the room was the east window.[289]

Lovely as the view had been from her Wells bedroom - of the distant church spire, the stars and the lamplighter - now in Ely she could have the glorious beauty of the fen with her, even in the schoolroom.

The tall house was at the summit of the little Isle of Ely and from the east window one looked out as from a tower over the vast stretch of the fen reaching to the distant line of the horizon. The colours of the fen, especially in the days of harvest, were lovely. They changed with every passing cloud and when the floods were out in winter they mirrored the sky. When later I went to boarding school and the schoolroom became my bedroom I had my bed by the east window, and could watch the sun come up over the horizon and paint a huge skyscape of clouds lilac and saffron and crimson and rose.[290]

A love of the dawn sky was something that stayed with her all her life. In 1956, forty years after her school days and by then living in the Oxfordshire countryside, she published *The Rosemary Tree*:

[Harriet] had come to have an almost personal love for her window. She slept with her curtains drawn back, and whenever she woke in the night she looked towards it instantly with eager wonder as to what it had to show her; clouds like galleons crossing the face of the moon, gems of stars set in a pall of blue velvet, Aurora like a golden lamp blazing above the brown rim of a dawn sky. Once she had woken up in the dawn she did not often go to sleep again, for her window faced east and she could not bear to miss a moment of the sun's rising. She loved to see the distant woods, grey and colourless while Aurora still blazed, dressing themselves in colour as the starlight faded. She liked to see the nearer trees catching the light on their plumed crests, and the cattle standing knee deep in the white swathes of mist. Above all she loved the dawn skies with their alternations of bright beauty, flaming so quickly to the penultimate splendour, then passing from glory to glory until the colours were lost in the splendour of the full day. Her eyes could never seem to catch the moment of change; in the span of a breath one

glory had passed and another was passing, and she could not halt the moments as they came; and perhaps only Harriet Martin was awake in Belmaray to tell of what had been.[291]

After publication of this novel Elizabeth was to spend the rest of her life, just over thirty years in total, in the same Oxfordshire cottage. She wrote to a friend just four years before her death, "My room faces east and I look across fields to the woods in the distance, and just lately the sunrises have been amazing... This morning every sheep was outlined in silver and the sun seemed to be hanging behind our pear-tree like a golden shield."[292]

School

The lessons in that cornflower-blue schoolroom came to an end and instead, when she was fourteen she was "sent to boarding school on the South Coast and was there through the years of the First World War."[293]

The outbreak of war and my departure...coincided. Personally, since I had no brothers and the young men I knew had made little impression on my immature and selfish heart, I am afraid I found the latter event the more distressing. In the tumult of...school I found myself no longer the centre of the universe. The knowledge was painfully acquired, and my homesickness, separated from my parents and Ely for the greater part of the year, was terrible...[294] *When immersed in the first torture of boarding school I...developed a shocking stammer, which I did not conquer until late middle life.*[295]

[But] it was a good school and we were happy there. Even I was happy at times, deadly homesick as I was all through every term.[296] [Describing Stephen's home-coming in *The Castle on the Hill*, she would say it recaptured "a faint echo of the joy he had felt when in his schooldays he had come home for the holidays for the first time. There would never be a happiness like that again."[297]] *Miss Lumby, our headmistress...taught us to love God, though how I do not quite know. Not by the daily tramp down the hill, the sea wind in our faces, to the parish church for matins, which was our starting point for the day, and not by [her] divinity lessons. More, I think, by the infection of her own love, which so penetrated and illumined all she did with us and for us.*[298]

Miss Lumby's good school was Grassendale, an old-fashioned establishment where, Elizabeth said, "Jane Austen would have felt at home."[299] Situated at Southbourne in Hampshire, it was "built among windblown pine trees, and from the high garden we could see the lovely tower of

Christchurch Priory down below us, the misty shape of the Isle of Wight and the blue waters of the English Channel."[300]

So she had, at least, another lovely view to help compensate for the loss of home. Grassendale was, too, her introduction to a corner of England that was later to have a great influence on her work, for she used it as the setting for her hugely popular trilogy of novels about the Eliots of Damerosehay. She remembered how, as part of the school's "quiet routine of churchgoing and lessons," she had her "first meeting with the New Forest and the sea marshes of Keyhaven," and she summed up its tremendous impact in one short phrase: "Something important happened to me there."[301]

Once a year on Ascension Day the whole school went to the New Forest but there were also Saturday outings for small groups of older girls, I think as a reward for good marks. It was on one of those expeditions that I discovered the seamarshes; Keyhaven itself I did not discover until many years later.

It was a still, misty day in late autumn, verging on winter. Tired and hungry, three or four girls and a young member of the staff, we had tea in a cottage belonging to an old sailor and his wife... It seemed at the world's end, a small human habitation that had grown up out of the earth, as trees do, almost on the sea strand and raised only slightly above it.[302]

> *Little Village had grown out of the mysterious sea-marshes that linked the peaceful beauty of the green inland pastures to the terror of the sea... [It] had elbowed its way through the exquisite shifting colours of the marshes with the knowledge that they could at any time be swept away like a rainbow by the incoming storm of the sea, and had armoured itself accordingly like some crustacean of the deep.*[303]
>
> The Herb of Grace

[And then] somehow I was by myself at the edge of the sea... It was so still that the half-moons of water from the incoming tide moved as silently as shadows on the sand. The thinning mist half hid, half revealed the sea-marshes to my left. I was so awed that I could not move. I kept listening and watching but I could not hear anything or see anything clearly. It was all hidden in the mist... Keyhaven. The harbour and the old houses, the yachts at anchor and the circling gulls, the rough road through the marshes and the old cornfield that had sprung up by itself after a grain-ship had been wrecked there. Damerosehay and its garden, the oak trees and the ilex tree. It was all there with me in that moment that seemed out of time and all I knew about it was my sense of awe.[304]

❄

Blooming there among the rhododendrons and pines of its high garden[305] *[Grassendale] was a school of a type that has passed away…*[306] *The only examinations were private ones for our school alone; and a child could escape those if she knew how to make her nose bleed…*[307] *Escaping was one of my few skills in those days.*[308]

It was a skill with which she invested Jacqueline in *Island Magic*:

> *How thankful she was for her one great gift – the gift of making her nose bleed at will. It was a wonderful gift and she did not know how she had come by it…it was peculiar to herself. She had only to blow her nose very violently, at the same time closing her mouth and gulping in a particular way, for the blood to gush forth… She did this, and the result was entirely satisfactory. She turned to Miss Brown with a most convincing stain creeping over the handkerchief she had clapped to her nose.*
> *"Please, Miss Brown, my nose is bleeding. Will you excuse me to go to the cloak-room?"*
> *The amiable Miss Brown glanced up over her spectacles.*
> *"Yes, dear, certainly, try cold water and if that won't stop it go to matron."*
> *As Jacqueline left the hall glances of envy and hatred pursued her… The girls knew perfectly well that Jacqueline du Frocq made her nose bleed on purpose… Underhand little beast.*[309]

The school was an anachronism, Elizabeth said, belonging to an era that ended with the First World War… an establishment for young ladies, who among other things were taught how to curtsey, in preparation for their presentation at Court. (Elizabeth's curtsey, she was told, was "distinctly good;" but as she says drily in her autobiographical sketch, "As I have never been presented at Court I have never been able to turn this accomplishment to any profit.")[310] Nevertheless, alongside these social graces "a few subjects were well taught" and these were things that would be of central importance to Elizabeth all her life: music, divinity and English literature. In particular, the English mistress "taught us to love poetry; above all the poetry of Shakespeare." This was Miss Bartlett, "a severe elderly lady with grey hair scraped back in a bun, a dry sense of humour and the sublime faculty of keeping effortless order."[311]

> *She lived to a great old age, and she felt it her duty to read nearly all my books. I do not think that one mistake in grammar or one clumsy sentence escaped her notice. And when it came to the use of a colloquialism, well, it was not in her essentially loving nature to be vituperative, but I will never forget the letter she wrote when I used the phrase 'by and large'.*

Ely

This colloquialism appeared in the children's book, *Smoky-House*, published in 1940:

> *John Treguddick was right to be proud of his children and dogs. Taking them by and large a more attractive family was not to be found in the West Country.*[312]

Such was Miss Bartlett's influence over her forty-year-old ex pupil that, "I have never used it again," said Elizabeth, "and I never will."[313]

Father and Child

During her early childhood Elizabeth had learnt the lesson that heaven grows out of doom endured and sure enough, endurance of the miseries of homesickness and boarding school had now introduced her to the heaven of Keyhaven. Even the travel entailed in being away at school had become a source of happiness too, for it meant some precious time alone with her father.

> *The magic thing happened one winter's day when I was going home for the Christmas holidays, towards the end of my time at school. It was a cold dreary day, the war was going badly…but I was in high spirits as the train pounded towards Waterloo because my father would meet me there. He always had to meet me on every return from school, and convey me across London to Liverpool Street and the train to Ely, because not only was it not de rigueur then for girls to travel alone but my mother was perpetually haunted by a thing called The White Slave Traffic; a menace which I never fully understood but to which I was favourably disposed because it was largely responsible for my father meeting me in his top hat. He hated his top hat but I insisted that he should wear it when meeting me. I was immensely proud of him (no other girl at school had a father as good-looking as mine) and I considered that his charm was increased by his top hat. Looking back now I think I was wrong about this for he was not a top hat man. He looked his best in the cassock with a leather belt that for warmth's sake he always wore at home in our cold house, for that expressed something of what he was in himself.*[314]

So convinced of his superiority was she, that "No-one could have suspected that the scrubby schoolgirl falling joyously from the railway carriage [she must have been about seventeen, if this was "towards the end" of her time at school] was this good-looking man's daughter," she said. In

The Herb of Grace Caroline's beloved father plays an equally important role in her ecstatic homecoming for the school holidays.

> *[Caroline] glanced from the window to her little wrist watch. They were due at Radford in ten minutes. Who would meet her? Mother had said that somebody would come with the car, but not who it would be. It might be Mother herself in her fur coat, smelling of violets; and that would be lovely. Or it might be Malony, which would be very nice. Or it might – perhaps – be Daddy in his rough tweed overcoat that smelt of tobacco and wood smoke. At the thought that it might be Daddy – alone – her ecstasy was so great that she could hardly bear it…*
>
> *Was she tidy? Mother might meet her, and Mother liked her to be tidy. There wasn't a glass in the carriage, but she shook herself, brushing smuts off her grey school overcoat, pulling her long grey woollen stockings straight, settling her grey felt hat more firmly on her shining, smooth gold head. Then she let down the window and hung out. She could see the platform now, with the lights, and the lovely blue dusk behind them, and figures moving about. There was one rather outsize figure, very upright. Was it? It was! She shrieked with delight. It was Daddy in his thick brown overcoat, his hands deep in his pockets, the yellow scarf that she had knitted for his birthday wound round his neck. His felt hat was set jauntily at an angle, as she like him to wear it, and as he always wore it when she was about just to please her, and his eyes were scanning each carriage window as it passed him with an eagerness that almost matched her own.*
>
> *"Daddy!" she shouted… He raised his hat, then strode towards her and held out his arms, and she fell into them as the train glided past.*[315]

Every homecoming was bliss for Elizabeth, but on that one particular winter's day at the start of the Christmas holidays there was an added and never-to-be-forgotten "magic thing." Ironically - but in line with what life was teaching her about the proximity of light and darkness - she discovered this particular bright light at the heart of claustrophobic, noisy London. As she fell into her father's arms she heard his voice saying above her head, "I am going to take you to your first theatre." He had booked tickets for a matinée, and they were to see Shakespeare's *Twelfth Night*. Elizabeth was incredulous with joy - "Shakespeare! And Miss Bartlett had taught me to love him. Could it be true?" It was true, and there was no time to be lost. (And on this particular visit to London, no mention of its horrors, either.)

> *A porter was grabbed (there were always plenty of kind and friendly porters in those days) and my big battered black trunk was trundled along to a taxi. My father strode after him carrying my violin in its case and I ran behind clasping my big black umbrella. The taxi carried us to Liverpool Street where we put the impedimenta into 'the left luggage', swallowed buns and coffee in the refreshment room and raced for a bus.*
>
> *We reached the theatre just in time and sat palpitating in the good seats my father had already booked… The auditorium was full and there was a hushed expectancy before the long rose-red curtains, the light stealing up them from the hidden footlights. Then the curtains parted and the opening words of the play came across to us, "If music be the food of love, play on…"*[316]

As an entire paragraph of her autobiography admits, she was not appropriately dressed for this momentous occasion: for unlike Caroline Eliot returning from school, the teenage Elizabeth was not "tidy."

> *Our school uniform must have been designed to discourage vanity in even the prettiest girl, and I had no beauty except the long hair hidden from sight in a tight pigtail. In summer and winter alike we wore dark blue serge coats and skirts, and the skirt was long for it had to 'cover the fat part of the leg', which was as well, for our thick black woollen stockings were not things of beauty. Tucked into the waist of the skirt was a high-necked white shirt blouse and somehow this always parted company with the skirt at the back, hanging down like a white tail, so the two were generally tethered together by a large black safety-pin. The school tie was thick and cumbersome and when knotted under the collar of the blouse it would maintain its position only for a short while; sooner or later it slipped sideways. The school hat was a hard sailor, tipped forward over the nose and secured with elastic. The elastic used to stretch and we tied knots in it, and somehow the knots always looked black and dirty. And the sailor hats, I don't know how, used to develop a chewed appearance round the edges.*[317]

But what did it matter? The play was "another country, another world." It "flowed on" she said, "funny and lovely and touching," and then too soon no doubt, "it was over, a supreme experience, but I do not remember any desolation because it had ended. Because of course it had not ended, but was a part of me forever. I was now stage-struck."

How could she be anything else, after this watershed of an experience? She had only been to the theatre four times in her whole life, but never until now in London, and never before to Shakespeare. She had seen just two children's plays: *Peter Pan* and an amateur seaside production of *Little Lord Fauntleroy*; plus two performances by the Wells Operatic Society "amidst potted plants on the platform of the Town Hall."[318]

Sitting there with her father in London's Court Theatre, she must have been in heaven. Shakespeare had transported her into another world, and *Twelfth Night* was now a part of her forever. Best of all perhaps, the stimulus of the whole experience had opened up new channels for her own creativity:

From then on, scribbling in my odd moments, I struggled to write plays as well as fairy stories.[319]

Fear and Darkness

For a writer imagination is certainly a blessing, and in addition to my Channel Island heritage I have not far to look for the cause of it. My first two homes were enough to stimulate any child's imagination.[320]

Although she had been aware in Wells of a "fourth dimension" it was a cosy, fairytale dimension, and "in that early garden of Eden the snake was still safely asleep in the sun." (Except perhaps in the shrubbery of the garden at the Principal's House which was "dark and dense as a forest, so much so that when I had been playing there for some while alone a numinous dread would suddenly fall upon me."[321]) Now in Ely, alongside all its beauty and all its joys, her awareness of the dark and frightening things of life was intensified.

Ely, though equally fourth dimensional, gave a sense of safety that was the reverse of cosy. There was strength and power there but it was an embattled power, and there was an equal awareness of the strength of the enemy. For the first time in my life I was aware of these things and afraid of them, and nature in her stormy aspect seemed a warning voice that trumpeted their coming. At evensong in the Cathedral on a dark winter's night when the wind roared round the walls, the candles guttered and the shadows of the great place leaped and shuddered, I used to tremble...though I could not have put what I feared into words. On winter nights I was very afraid, coward that I was and am, of the walk from home to the Cathedral, which when my father was away or ill I had to take alone. If I went out of the front door it was pitch dark and the trees of the park were full of wind and whispers, but if I went out of the back door and down the lane there was a haunted house on my right and another on my left and either ghost might issue out; not to mention our own ghost who had probably walked out of the house behind me and at any moment might lay his hand on my shoulder as we went along...[322]

Ely

It seems there was more to this than just the wildness of the environment acting upon the fears of an imaginative young girl, for she says,

I was not alone in seeing that ghost. Subsequent dwellers in the house have seen him too. I do not know how he appeared to them but to me he appeared as a grey-cowled monk with no face. Where his face should have been there was only darkness. The experience was always the same. I would wake suddenly from sleep as though woken up and alerted, and would find him standing beside me. I would feel fear and revulsion, a sense of struggle as though I fought against something, and then he was gone. He was not a pleasant person.[323]

This unwelcome visitor did not appear in some dark and terrifying place, but in the cornflower-blue schoolroom which, because of its wonderful view, Elizabeth had begun to use as her bedroom after she ceased to be educated at home. After these apparitions she then tried moving to another bedroom, "keeping the old schoolroom as a sitting room," but "the ghost came there just the same." She added, "But it was not as bad as it sounds for as these were my boarding school and college days, I was only at home in the holidays and he was not a very frequent visitor."[324]

Next-door-but-one, Canon and Mrs. Glazebrook too, their servants and their guests, all repeatedly saw a less ghoulish apparition, which their maid dubbed "my angel." The house to the right of the Goudge's was discovered, during alterations, to have the skeleton of a walled-up monk within it – Elizabeth "could seldom walk down the lane without horrible thoughts of what it must feel like to be walled up" - and the one to the left also "had something rather nasty" which was reputed to have once made a male guest rush "headlong from the house in terror."[325]

There were, it seems, drawbacks to the privilege of living in such an historic environment.

❄

Elizabeth devotes a whole chapter of her memoires to extra-sensory perception, whilst admitting she is not qualified to write about it, and has "nothing to go on but my own slight experience and what I have learnt from my astonishing mother who, although she had "remarkable psychic powers… resolutely refused to use them."

It seems that Mrs. Goudge also resolutely refused to help her young daughter when these frightening experiences were reported to her.

When I tried to tell her about my encounters with our Ely ghost, whom I disliked intensely, she made no comment. That she also had her meetings with him I have no doubt, but she would

not say that she did, and when I asked if I might change my haunted bedroom for another she referred the matter to my father, who from first to last of our time in that house remained untroubled by our ghost. He was not a man to see things, hear things or imagine things.[326]

In fact, Elizabeth does not give the impression that either parent, during the Ely days, felt any extraordinary concern about their young daughter's fear of the ghost. All she tells us is that Mother referred the problem to Father; and that Father tried sleeping in the schoolroom himself and pronounced that she "might change it for another" bedroom – but only because "what with the howling of the wind round my high attic and the scuttling of the mice he had scarcely slept all night."[327] The one parent so highly psychic, the other completely unaffected by such things, there is nothing in her memoirs to suggest that either felt the need to investigate further or to give their child any real help with her fears.

She was certainly an imaginative girl, certainly aware of a fourth dimension, and she was by no means the only person to feel fear in those ancient houses around the Cathedral. But she had, too, been parted from Nanny, so abruptly and brutally. She had been sent away from home, to boarding school – an experience traumatic enough (she describes it as *torture*) to have caused her to develop a "shocking stammer."[328] Moreover, although personally unaffected by it, she knew very well that there was a terrible war raging across the Channel. Perhaps these things were completely unconnected with her ghostly encounters, but that young girl must have been, in more ways than one, quite fearful and insecure.

She, looking back, had no complaints however, only a glowing tribute to her wonderful parents.

How difficult some temperaments (mine, for instance) are to live with and how dependent we all are on the love and understanding of those who are with us! Especially the introverts. I think I only realise now how much both my parents always helped me. At the time I took them far too much for granted. If you grow up with wonderful people about you always you do tend to take them for granted. It needs emergence into the world, and contact with the other sort, to know your luck.[329]

Elizabeth continued to have inexplicable experiences into adulthood. They were not always sightings; there was the terrifying, loud double-rap that broke the silence when she was alone on a deserted moor. And not always frightening either - one at least of them was heavenly - when, early one morning, she heard angelic singing in the emptiness of an otherwise silent, snow-covered village lane. It was so beautiful that she said, "I remember that singing every morning of my life and I greet every sunrise with the memory."[330]

Ely

She used this – one of "the memories that are a part of one's immortality"[331]- in *The Rosemary Tree*.

> *And then [John] heard the voice singing. It was like no earthly music that he had ever heard, or ever would hear, though the loveliness of earth was in it. It was not a human voice, though it had something of the clear beauty of a boy's voice singing, neither was it a bird's voice, though it held the liquid note of a nightingale or thrush. He thought of the waterfall, of the running river and the wind in the trees, though it was not like any of these. He felt intense longing as he listened and yet triumph too, for the song was triumphant. The dazzling plumage of the bird was all about him… such light…*[332]

Again, when the singing was reported to her mother "she looked at me and, as usual, made no comment whatever."[333]

❋

She remembered that the Ely days were "hard ones for my father" for he had only "three years of the teaching he loved and then the war broke out."[334]

> *He felt the sin and horror of it acutely and suffered much. His men went to the Front and Ely Theological College became a hospital, while my father himself took up parish work again, taking the place, both at Ely and Wisbech, of younger men who had gone to the Front as chaplains. He was also an extra night orderly at the hospital that had once been his Theological College; a strange change to be in the familiar rooms, not lecturing, but caring for wounded men.*[335]
>
> *His parish work took him down to the poorer parts of Ely, at the foot of the hill and near the river. There was poverty there then, bad housing conditions and the sicknesses and distresses of old age. My father loved people, especially if they were ill or old, and in visiting he was happy and relaxed and able to bring great comfort and help.*[336]

Like Grandfather in *A City of Bells*, perhaps, who

> *sat himself down in a Windsor chair, placed his hat on the floor and talked to the cheerful mother as though he had known her all his life. He felt as though the hard, happy days of his parish work were back with him again, those days when he had not felt conscious, as he was always conscious in the Close, of living a segregated life. He hated segregation, inevitable though he knew it to be. He hated the barriers of time and age and class and language. He longed for the time when all the different lights carried by man in the pageantry of life should glow into one.*[337]

Although Elizabeth was away at school for much of the war, her father made sure that she too was aware of the segregation.

Occasionally he took me with him and it horrified me to find that many old and dying people had no light and airy bedroom of their own, such as we had at home, but had their bed in the downstairs front room into which the front door frequently opened from the noisy street. With the one window filled with geraniums or an aspidistra it could be dark inside, overcrowded with heavy furniture and with a smell of cooking coming in from the kitchen beyond.[338]

John opened the door... The stuffy little room inside was very dark. The lodge was extremely picturesque outside but the creepers hanging over the small diamond-paned windows kept out most of the light. Air was kept out by the fact that old Bob never opened the windows, such as they were, from year's end to year's end. He would have died of asphyxia had it not been that he always kept a fire burning to combat the damp of the rotting boards and mildewed walls of his abode. The one living-room was the shape of a half-circle and behind it was the half-circle of the kitchen. Above were two bedrooms. There was a well in the garden behind, but no water laid on and no drains...

"You there, Bob?" he asked unnecessarily, feeling his way past the circular table with its plush table-cover, and the family photograph album and Bible upon it, to the bamboo stand with the aspidistra that stood near the window, and further assisted the geraniums on the window-sill and the creepers outside to make the room nearly as dark as night...

He lowered himself carefully to [a] slippery armchair. It was the most uncomfortable chair in the world and he could not imagine how Bob, in the grip of the screws, could endure to sit in a similar one hour upon hour. Yet he had been sitting there all day, perfectly still, while the pain waxed and waned, and would continue to sit there until a cousin came up from the village to help him to his bed. "So I can sit here too," thought John. "I can at least do that."[339]

Nearly twenty years after writing that scene from *The Rosemary Tree* she said, "I was distressed for the old people but I think now that they were perhaps happier in the front room, with their own people near them, than they are now in the bright hygienic geriatric wards of today."[340] A further five years down the line, and she had proved the truth of her own words – with

Ely

a harrowing experience of her own hospitalisation recorded in her poem, *Easter in the Ward*.[341]

❋

The poverty and bad housing were the dark patch upon the beauty of Ely. It was that creeping evil that invades all lovely things, as dirt seeps into the corners of rooms and worms wriggle into fine-wrought furniture and perfect moulded fruit.... We know what happens when the worm creeps in. Some work of mercy inspired by love of God and man comes into flower and for a while all is as God wanted it to be. Then there is quarrelling and jealousy and the flower sickens at the root. A war starts as a crusade of liberation and at first a nation can be enriched by it, but somewhere along the way there falls the retribution that waits for those who do evil that good may come and they become as evil as the thing they fight.[342]

Her books contain many images of light at the heart of darkness – but also of darkness within the light, this "creeping evil." Like Nan in *Linnets and Valerians*, who is delighted to be given the use of her very own beautiful panelled parlour – only to discover that it has a terrible book of spells hidden in a dark, secret cupboard.

She pushed the thought of the book away from her... But later, in bed in the dark, she remembered it again, for the sound of the wind and rain were eerie and she was scared. But then she remembered something else and she was no longer afraid. The spells in [the] book might be wicked...but ranged against them was the goodness of Uncle Ambrose...and the bees, and good spirits whom she could not see, but of whom she was aware at this moment, holding over her in the dark a sort of umbrella of safety. She would not be afraid...[343]

The Great War

Elizabeth knew she had been largely sheltered from the horrors of the War: a young girl who had no brothers to lose and whose clergyman father - nearly fifty when hostilities began - was doing his war-work by caring for wounded soldiers in the Ely hospital, and taking over the parish work of younger men. She had passed the war years at Grassendale too, where life had yet to change. There,

in spite of the war raging on the other side of the English Channel it was assumed that we should all go home and help our mothers do the flowers, be presented at court and get married. Yet telegrams arrived now and then telling of the deaths of fathers and brothers and sorrow and dismay would run through the school; and then we would settle back again into our quiet routine of church-going and lessons, with occasional treats of picnics by the sea and in the New Forest.[344]

She cannot have been completely unaware, however, for in later life she recalled that the war had seemed to presage what she called "the end of it all...the horror of a collapsing and disappearing universe."

[When it] had got beyond the cheering and flag-waving stage and had plunged into the ghastliness of the trenches and the shells and the gas we felt very near to that final crash, and the old Christian belief in the end of the world, a belief which the scientists are underlying just now, was very much in our minds.[345]

She also remembered "the influenza that devastated Europe as soon as the fighting ceased."

At least it was called influenza for politeness sake. It was more like some form of plague; so many thousands of dead men and horses all over Europe were not buried deep enough. There was hardly a household that did not have its dead through this illness. I remember the winter as being one of still, dark cold like a pall over the land. No sun, no rain, just a heavy mantle of grey... But probably memory is playing tricks with me and I have spread a few grey days over the whole period.[346]

The world changed so much, so quickly, that looking back sixty years later she would call the Great War a "dividing chasm" - echoing her father, who had said, in the first of a 1935 series of lectures, published as *The Apocalypse and the Present Age*:

> When the Great War came...the old Victorian world had given way beneath our feet; and we had fallen through the chasm... The world of progress in which we had trusted, had become...a world of conflict and disaster of which it was difficult to descry the end. Moreover, when at last Satan seemed to be bound, we did not know how soon he might be loosed out of his prison, to deceive the nations again.[347]

Choices

In 1918 the war had finally come to an end, and so had her schooling. But what was to be her future? That she might marry – up until then the accepted career move for any young lady – was now an unlikely option.

Parents of that era realised that unless their daughters had exceptional beauty and charm they would not marry. The First World War left few young men alive. The phrase used at that time, 'The lost generation' sounds poetical but it was the truth.[348]

And so, "What to do with me when I left school was a problem for my poor parents," she says, "once they had grasped the fact that their daughter knew next to nothing."

She seems to imply that the deficiencies of her education had come as a surprise to them; but this seems unlikely, for she admits that her school reports were "mostly bad"[349] and surely her parents would have been aware of Grassendale's curriculum when they first chose the school? But that was in the pre-war world of course; in this new post-war world Canon Goudge's lazy ignorant daughter – Elizabeth's own words - would have to earn her own living, and it seems that gentle Grassendale had not laid any real foundations for either a career or further education.

That girls as well as men could now go to an Oxford or Cambridge college was still like a dream come true but very few of us who went to that old-fashioned happy school achieved it, and they only the brightest after a long period of intensive coaching.[350]

Women were now not only permitted to study at university, but by 1920 to graduate - at Oxford that is: Cambridge did not allow them full university membership until 1948. One of the first females to obtain an Oxford degree was Dorothy L. Sayers, who had won a place at Somerville in 1912. Her life shared some similarities with Elizabeth's, in that she was brought up in the Fens, in the rectory to which her clergyman father was called, after his post as Headmaster of Christ Church Cathedral School, Oxford; and she too became well known as a bestselling author, of theological works and plays as well as her famous detective stories. But the two young women were very unlike in their academic achievement.

"Academically speaking," said Elizabeth, "there was no hope for me." Except that among those mostly bad school reports "one did make the suggestion that a gift for writing should be encouraged." Occasional compositions had even been read aloud to the "bored" class causing her to sit with "crimson ears sticking out above my pigtail and modestly lowered head; but secretly bursting with pride."[351] Here, perhaps was the answer.

> *I bethought me of my one gift, English composition, and said grandly that I would be a writer. It would be quite easy, I thought, and I set blithely to work on children's stories.*[352]

The result was a slim volume of children's tales, *The Fairies' Baby and Other Stories*, published when she was nineteen. It must have been an extremely attractive little book, gold-tooled as it was on pale sea-green boards like shot-silk. In line with the Victorian tales which she herself would have heard as a child, the final story, *The Flower of Happiness* points a moral for its young readers - the ideal of selfless love for others. More than this however, it introduces a theme which was to recur in several of her later novels and stories –like *The Easter Bunny, Linnets and Valerians* and *The Dean's Watch* - the idea of an older person's life being transformed by love for a child.

Incidentally, around this time a young woman five years Elizabeth's senior was also taking the first steps towards worldwide fame as a maker of children's books. Cecily Mary Barker, although she suffered from epilepsy as a child and was physically delicate all her life, had nevertheless taken a correspondence course in art; and in 1918 the Royal Institute accepted her painting *A Fairy Song* for exhibition, at a sale price of six guineas. Her first Flower Fairies book was published four years later, in 1923; and she created, too, many exquisite illustrations for Christian texts.

Elizabeth was yet to have the benefit of her own Art School training but in 1919, in *The Flower of Happiness*, she nonetheless created this word-picture of a Rose Fairy.

> *As she watched, a dainty pink rose petal fell down on to the window sill, rested there for a minute, and then flew up again and settled into the rose.*
>
> *Ermyntrude opened the window excitedly. A rose petal often falls down, but it seldom falls up; she stretched out her hand and drew the rose towards her. As she did so, the rose petal took a flying jump into her lap, shook itself, and smoothed its frock, and then Ermyntrude saw that it was a fairy.*
>
> *Fairy Rose Petal was a bright, gay little creature. Her hair was golden, like the centre of a wild rose, and her frock was pink and white, with here and there a gleam of green where her petticoat peeped below.*[353]

She was not destined as yet, however, to achieve success in the world of children's literature; unlike Miss Barker, who received £25 for the twenty-four illustrations and verses in *Flower Fairies of the Spring*. For *The Fairies' Baby* did not sell, and it was to be another fifteen years before Elizabeth published another book.

> *I sent more [stories] to the editors of children's magazines. But these editors did not think so highly of my stories as I did myself and sent them back. Throughout this period of strenuous literary labour I earned exactly fifteen shillings.*[354]

Luckily writing was not the only career option. In fact, women's work and education were to undergo massive changes in the years following the First World War. Elizabeth left school just on the cusp of the Sex Disqualification Removal Act of 1919, which changed the law preventing women's entry into the professions. The next decade would see the first female member of the Institute of Marine Engineers in 1929 and, a year later, of the Royal College of Veterinary Surgeons. In 1924 Margaret Bondfield became the first woman minister in Parliament and, five years later, the first woman cabinet member and privy councillor. In 1929 Eleanor Lodge was awarded the first female Oxford doctorate. These and others however were the exceptions, the pioneers, and Elizabeth's horizons were not nearly so wide. At school, they had been "unaware of all the opportunities that would soon open before us and still considered that a girl who must earn her own living had only two choices, to be an actress or a nurse according to temperament."[355]

This, and the telling remark that her future was "a problem for my poor *parents*" seems to indicate that even choice itself was not yet seen as this young woman's prerogative. And so she stayed within the narrow limits prescribed by parents and school. One of the options – acting – was out of the question for Elizabeth, even though she had been stage-struck ever since that first experience of Shakespeare. She might have opted for acting, she says, "had I not been a stammerer… and if by some miracle I had got there and my father had not liked it, that would have been his own fault."[356] Fighting talk! But his "fault," she means, in that he was the one who introduced her to the magic of the London theatre in the first place. Nevertheless, one feels that if the miracle had happened, she might have fought very hard indeed against any opposition in order to be part of the theatre world. But she had the stammer and, after the unsuccessful fairy stories, had also now decided that "literature was no good" either.

> *"I would like to be a nurse," I said. I was merely passing to the second of the two choices, but I had always been obsessed with the thought of suffering, especially the suffering*

of children. It might have come to pass but mercifully for the patients (for I have discovered myself to be the world's worst nurse) providence rescued them by sending me a heart complaint. Could I train at Great Ormond Street? we asked our doctor. "Dead in a week," he replied briefly. So we had to think again.

My mother had an idea. I loved making things with my hands and I loved children. Why not take a training in handicrafts and then, if my stammer subsided with time, teach in a school for crippled children? My father's old friend Professor de Burgh was Vice-Chancellor of Reading College (not yet a university) and a family of dear cousins lived at Reading and had students to live with them. The Art School at the College was a good one. And so I went there a little rebelliously. I lived with my cousins and walking to college every morning I had to pass the hospital. I would look at it longingly and pass on scowling.[357]

The rebellion is not difficult to understand. This college course had after all been her mother's idea. Her own career choice, nursing, had been categorically vetoed by the doctor. Stagestruck as she was, to become an actress was out of the question for a girl with a stammer. Even that most traditional of careers for women, marriage and motherhood, was - thanks to the war - an unlikely option. And of course what Elizabeth really wanted was to write... but the publishers had rejected her stories.

The future cannot have looked particularly rosy. However, despite the scowls, she remembers how "with a flood of other students I would be sucked into the College portal and borne along on the noisy morning tide of hurry and confusion to the haven of the Art School."

At that time, just after the war, there was what amounted to almost a passion for handicrafts. Metal work, leather work, basket making, spinning, weaving, tapestry, embroidery, designing for textiles, we did the lot in the handicraft department.[358]

This "passion" was part of the still-ongoing Arts and Crafts Movement, begun in Britain in the 1880s, whose two most influential figures had been William Morris and John Ruskin. (It was in line with the Movement's principles surely, that Elizabeth's parents, married in 1898, had had much of their furniture made for them by an "artist-craftsman of a cabinet-maker.") A reaction against the dehumanising effects of the industrial revolution, the Arts and Crafts Movement perpetuated the Romantics' belief in the Imagination as the source of all creative power. The Victoria and Albert Museum defined its aims in a recent exhibition, as "a revival of traditional techniques and materials, and the creation of new forms that were both ageless and innovative." The course at Reading certainly seems to have been structured along these lines:

Ely

> *We were never allowed to use any patterns in embroidery or tapestry or leather work that we had not designed ourselves and we had to learn to wield a pencil and paintbrush sufficiently well for the purpose.*

Gradually Elizabeth's scowling rebellion began to subside beneath the power of creative work.

> *As time went on I ceased to look longingly at the hospital as I passed it. The work of creation is hard work, however desperately badly one creates. But it is a joy that gets hold of one more and more.*[359]

Painting Pictures

> *I stayed there for two years, making charcoal sketches of the human form in the life class which were not recognizable as such, painting pictures over which my art master shook his head more in sorrow than in anger, but doing quite well with design and applied art.*[360]

She adds that "during those two years I conceived a passionate attachment for William Morris and all the Pre-Raphaelites." Some of her descriptions of interiors – like this one (a panelled parlour) from her short story 'Sweet Herbs' – are akin to Pre-Raphaelite paintings in their detail of pattern and colour, and follow Morris's ideal of the home as a work of art in itself, containing nothing that was not either useful or beautiful.

> *It was one of those rooms that one never forgets. The parquet floor was black as ebony and the panelled walls, where they showed between the bookshelves, were painted primrose colour. There were a few fine pictures, a few lovely bits of china, several pots of flowers and a rug where the colours were night-blue and old rose, but the crowning glory of the room was an alcove with a glass dome covered with green vine leaves, and the vine tree was growing inside the room, its knotted old trunk rising up out of the dark floor. The sunlight filtered into the room through the green leaves and the pattern of them was etched on the floor.*[361]

Elizabeth loved many of the things that Morris loved - interiors, stained glass, cathedrals, wells, forests. She shared, too his acute sense of place; and his grief at change and redevelopment, for she says she had "a phobia about going back to places where I have lived and that I have loved. I cannot bear to see them changed; an idiotic phobia since change is almost another name for life itself."[362]

One aspect of change to which the Art School perhaps opened her eyes is the Impressionists' awareness of ephemeral beauty. In *Island Magic* she captures a sunset glimpse of St. Pierre harbour that is unique to that particular fleeting moment and will never look quite the same again.

> *There were the Town and the Harbour just as usual, but yet not just as usual. He had not seen them before at just this hour of sunset...*
> *A world of colour and light, transparent and unreal...*
> *A beauty so fragile that it would shiver into nothingness at a touch...*
>
> *Somewhere a door banged and a man shouted... It shivered into a thousand splintered rainbow fragments.*[363]

Perhaps because I loved them so much I could paint flowers passably well but I could draw nothing else. When we were taken out sketching my efforts to capture something of the wider world of nature that I loved also were pitiable. I was mad with frustration. All this beauty and I could not portray it. It was the same with the composition class, where with the future illustrating of books in mind the art students would be told to illustrate a scene from some particular fairy tale or romance...

My contributions were always hilariously bad. Professor Seaby, a kindly man, generally refrained from comment. Yet there was one occasion when he stopped in front of my atrocity and considered it, and it was obvious that he was about to speak. My heart beat hard as the silence lengthened. "The worst drawing of the lot," he said, "but the best evocation of the atmosphere of a fairytale." Then he passed on and again I felt crazy with frustration. What was the use of my...having seen it all so clearly...if I could not say what I had seen?

(In her defence, there would perhaps be few students in the composition class at that time who were not experiencing some degree of frustration over their attempts to illustrate fairytale. This was, after all, the era of Arthur Rackham and Edmund Dulac.)

Yet I was a little comforted. Professor Seaby was a comforting sort of man, probably because he was a humble one... He was certainly a great artist. His passion was for birds and they figured largely in his exquisite woodcuts and colour prints. When he retired he went to live in the New Forest that he might be permanently among the birds. It was from his studio there that he wrote to me twenty years later, after reading one of my books. "Now you have found how to do it," he said. "Now you will be happy."[364]

Elizabeth had developed a love for John Ruskin quite early on in life – she seems to say that it was during her schooldays - "partly because he could paint a skyscape in words as it seemed to me that no one else could do."[365] Now here was her Professor, telling her that she too had learned to paint in words. And Ruskin's own ideas on art can arguably be seen as an influence on her prose; for in *Modern Painters* he had decreed that art should serve a high moral or spiritual purpose, and that minuteness of handling and complete naturalism are essential.

If Professor Seaby had written to Elizabeth after reading a newly-published book, then it may well have been *The Bird in the Tree*. By then (1940) she had indeed discovered "how to do it" and had no need of a paintbrush for this minutely-handled depiction of the first sight of Keyhaven at dawn.

> *The lane that led from Big Village to Little Village was an enchanting place at half-past five on an April morning. The thick high hedges of sloe and briar and hawthorn, blown all one way by the wind from the sea, so that the sea-ward hedges tossed long sprays of emerald green leaves like foam across the lane, were bright and sparkling with sun-shot raindrops, and nestling in the shelter of them were celandines and speedwells that were still asleep.*
>
> *Through gaps in the hedge they could see the east still barred with gold, and the sky curving up through lovely gradations of colour that ended over their heads in a clear deep blue that was reflected on the earth below, by the pools in the lane and the polished surfaces of the wet green leaves…*
>
> *And then the lane topped the crest of a little hill and suddenly, breathlessly, they saw the marshes and the sea. They stood still for a moment, clutching each other, and then quite silently they took hands and ran. They did not stop until they reached the harbour wall, where they sat down very suddenly and looked about them. The gorse was out, flaming under the sun, and all the colours of the dawn were caught in the waters of the harbour and in the pools and channels in the marsh. The gulls were everywhere, and as they watched the swans arrived from the Abbey River, flying one behind the other, their great wings touched with gold. From the old grey cottages behind them a few spirals of blue smoke crept up from the chimneys, and over to their left the sun touched the coral buds of a twisted oak-wood to points of beckoning flame.*[366]

As she said of the child Henrietta in *Sister of the Angels*,

Wherever she went she looked, marvelled and adored, and then stored away in her memory the essential beauty of what she had seen, so that one day she might take it out and make it into pictures.[367]

❄

Although none of William Morris's poetry or prose appears in any of her anthologies, three recurring images in her work can be found in one short verse of his poem, *The Willow and the Red Cliff*. It may be pure coincidence, but with her youthful, passionate attachment to Morris and the Pre-Raphaelites she may well have been influenced, not just by his art, but by his poetry too.

That cliff it rises steep from the sea
On its top a thorn tree stands,
With its branches blown away from the sea
As if praying with outstretched hands.[368]

First Love

Several changes occurred in the late Ely years, as Elizabeth's education came to an end and she moved from girlhood to womanhood. One involved Dr. Goudge's work: for after the war ended the Theological College had reopened, "but it was not the same."

There was the difficulty of getting everything started again, and my father was always worried and irked by business, and there were the two types of men to be dealt with, the older men who had been through the war and the younger who had not. My father was not immune from the exhausted restlessness of those post-war years.[369]

It precipitated a change to their family life. When he had "faced and carried through the difficult task of re-starting the Theological College" and it was at last fully restored, "his vice-principal took his place as principal and he went to King's College, London, to teach theology."

He kept his canonry at Ely Cathedral and we still lived there; indeed I think we hardly contemplated having our home anywhere else. My father lived in his rooms at King's

College during the week and came home to Ely at the weekends. He loved London and he loved Ely and the swing between them was something he enjoyed.[370]

In fact she says he was "very happy and stimulated" there. "On fine afternoons he would tramp for miles on foot through London, re-learning the town he had known so well as a boy and amassing stores of information about it." The teaching itself had a very new and different element too, in that "his pupils at King's included both men and women, and several of the women, working for the Archbishop's Diploma, were brilliant scholars."[371]

What would I not give now to know more about those London adventures, of which he spoke once with a light on his face, but he was a reticent man and with the awful self-centredness of youth (at least my youth) I never asked a single question, for my own affairs at this period were too absorbing.

I was in love for the first time and for a while the world shone... It ended in tears, of course. Does not every first love end in tears? That is if it does end, but sometimes I think that first love is one of the hidden beauties that are a part of us forever. In my case how glad I am that that particular magic was a part of Ely as well as of myself.[372]

Those were Elizabeth's sentiments, writing in her early seventies. Many years earlier, though, her younger self had recorded that during her two years at college: "I fell devastatingly in love, curled my hair with curling tongs and bound it round with coloured ribbons, a different colour for every day in the week... Though I cannot now remember whether those quite unsuccessful efforts to be beautiful were caused by love or the Pre-Raphaelites."[373] The pain of first love's inevitable tears seemingly overlaid with a deliberate flippancy... perhaps it needed the perspective of age to reveal their "hidden beauty."

Dr. Goudge worked at his new London appointment for two years - he was Professor of New Testament Interpretation at King's College from 1921 to 1923. He had a "smoke-grained study"[374] at the college, and lodged during the week in the house of his colleague Dr. Matthews, who later became Dean of St. Paul's. It was thanks to him that Elizabeth had a glimpse of a man and woman very much in love, which was to stay in her memory and be the inspiration for arguably her greatest book.

When I was young my father's friend Dr. Matthews and his wife took me to the Gray's Inn Ball, a most lovely sight in the great lighted hall, with so many men in eighteenth-century splendour, with buckled shoes and lace ruffles. We had not been dancing for long when the loveliness became concentrated for me in a woman who was sitting alone, waiting. I can see her now. She was young but not very young, with the poise of a beautiful woman who is well aware of her beauty, a tall white lily of a woman. She wore a dress of pale, soft orange, a floating dress. The only bright notes of colour were her emerald-green feather fan and her green shoes. I thought I had never seen anyone so exquisite. I felt breathless, looking at her, enchanted as a girl so often is by a lovely woman much older than herself. No one asked her to dance. No one seemed to know her. She did not mind but waited alone in her beauty, serene and still, knowing that he would come.

At last he came… He was much older than she was, tall and rugged, with the saddest, ugliest, but yet I thought the most lovable face I had ever seen. They greeted each other as a man and woman do who are much in love but do not care to show it in a public place. She glanced at him quickly to see that all was well with him, then lowered her eyes. Their hands touched, and a brief smile gleamed on his face, softening his ugliness to tenderness. They moved out together to where the dancers were, and joined them, she very gracefully, her soft dress floating, he, so much older, doing his dignified best. They did not seem to talk to each other; it seemed as though she was afraid to look up at him lest she betray herself; and their faces were not alight but merely quiet. Neither of them danced with anyone else and soon they went away together and were no more seen. But I never forgot them.[375]

There is poignancy in this story of the shy young clergyman's daughter at the glittering London ball, this girl whose own first love had, presumably, already ended in tears, and who was conscious of her own "quite unsuccessful attempts to be beautiful." According to one friend[376] indeed, she had said jokingly of her stammer in later life that "she had only to open her mouth and men would flee."

Faith and Unbelief

Elizabeth makes little mention of individual church services in *The Joy of the Snow*; however one service during her college years was important enough for inclusion – the memorable occasion when she first saw her father's friend Bishop Gore.

He came to preach at St. Giles, Reading, and I went to hear him. His reputation had filled the large church and his sermon on the great crowd of witnesses made them practically visible. The children of the clergy are not generally fond of sermons, for they have had to sit through too many, but this was a sermon to rank with the great discourses that John Donne used to preach at St. Paul's and I listened as though it was the first sermon I had ever heard.[377]

For Elizabeth, who later describes Bishop Gore as "a saint,"[378] the comparison with Donne was highest praise. Not only did she include nine extracts from Donne's prose and poetry in her anthologies, but there was one of his great discourses which she must particularly have loved. Triumphal in its certainty of light emerging out of darkness, it appears in both *A Book of Comfort* and *The White Witch*.

> He brought light out of darkness, not out of a lesser light. He can bring thy summer out of winter though thou have no spring. Though in the ways of fortune, or misunderstanding, or conscience, thou have been benighted till now, wintred and frozen, clouded and eclipsed, damp and benumbed, smothered and stupefied till now, now God comes to thee, not as in the dawning of the day, not as in the bud of the spring, but as the sun at noon, to banish all shadows.[379]

Sadly, however, there was a member of Elizabeth's family for whom the shadows could not be banished. Her Guernsey grandfather was one of the many in his generation for whom scientific discovery had had a devastating effect on faith and belief. Some did manage to adapt and hold on to at least a questioning belief, like the poet laureate Tennyson, in *A Book of Peace*.

> The sun, the moon, the stars, the seas, the hills and the plains –
> Are not these, O Soul, the Vision of Him who reigns?
> ...And the ear of man cannot hear, and the eye of man cannot see;
> But if we could see and hear, this Vision – were it not He?[380]

Others however agreed with the sentiments that Sigmund Freud would later express in *The Future of an Illusion*, that all religious teachings were simply "neurotic relics" and it was high time that they were replaced by the "rational operation of the intellect."[381]

It seems that Mr. Collenette's rational intellect would no longer allow him to believe; nevertheless the loss of his faith left him in darkness and grief – and this was surely a major cause, alongside the death of his firstborn son, of what Elizabeth described as his inner sadness.

> *My grandfather was above all a man of science... He read every scientific book he could get hold of and the amount of knowledge he amassed in a lifetime was very great. Yet if science was his first love it was science that brought him one of the great griefs of his life,*

for while he was still young he completely lost the religious faith that had meant so much to him. The scientific conclusions of his day made it impossible for him to accept the book of Genesis as literal truth. And if Genesis was not true then the Bible, every word of which he had believed to be directly inspired by God, could no longer be the basis for his faith. After an agonising struggle the ground went from under his feet and he fell into the darkness of unbelief, a darkness that shadowed his whole life.[382]

This reached its nadir in the early nineteen-twenties when - over eighty, almost blind, and "totally broken" by the death of his wife – he came to stay with them at Ely for a while. Aunt Emily brought him: "He faced the journey to see my mother again," Elizabeth said. And Emily also took him to London, "to see a famous eye-surgeon, hoping something could be done to save the remnants of his sight. Nothing could be done and despair took hold of him."

Elizabeth had not seen him for some years, as during the Great War "no one might visit the Channel Islands unless they had an urgent reason to do so" and their reunion, which should have brought pure joy, must have been bittersweet for it revealed a great change in him: "I could hardly reconcile this old, broken man sunk in darkness with the laughing grandfather I had known."[383]

❄

The poet Gerard Manley Hopkins was an almost exact contemporary of her beloved grandfather – he was born two years later than Adolphus, in 1844. As Hopkins' sonnets attest, he too knew times of great darkness, but in *God's Grandeur* (which, like Donne's great sermon, made more than one appearance in Elizabeth's work) he affirmed the eternal presence of God. For him, even in a changing and despoiled industrial world it was an everlasting presence, one that can never be diminished by humankind's unbelief.

> The world is charged with the grandeur of God.
> It will flame out, like shining from shook foil;
> It gathers to a greatness, like the ooze of oil
> Crushed. Why do men then now not reck his rod?
> Generations have trod, have trod, have trod;
> And all is seared with trade; bleared, smeared with toil;
> And wears man's smudge and shares man's smell: the soil
> Is bare now, nor can foot feel, being shod.

> And for all this, nature is never spent;
> There lives the dearest freshness deep down things;
> And though the last lights off the black West went
> Oh, morning, at the brown brink eastward, springs –
> Because the Holy Ghost over the bent
> World broods with warm breast and with ah! bright wings.[384]

Hopkins again uses bird imagery to depict the love of God. The poem is in the first of Elizabeth's three anthologies, and in the last of them she included words of Ladislaus Boros, acknowledging that the "abyss of possible doubt"[385] will always be an inescapable part of faith. But equally - as John Donne's sermon said - wherever there is darkness, light can break through; and in this case the light came, not to Adolphus but to his granddaughter. It was a seminal moment in her life.

> *One grey dismal afternoon when we were sitting together…he began to speak; not fumbling for words, voicing his despair quite clearly. "I must die soon," he said, "and go into nothingness… I must die and all that I know will die with me. All that I have and am must die. It is all totally wasted."*
>
> *He sank back into silence and I sat frozen with dismay. I could not speak. But why did I not do as I would have done as a small child, run to him and hug him? Why did I not do something…?*
>
> *I totally failed my grandfather but he did not fail me, though it was years before I realised what it was he had done for me in rooting my faith, that I believe grew up out of his despair… When [he] said that all that he was, all that he knew was going into nothingness I felt at first furious, and then incredulous. What he said was a lie. It was impossible. His knowledge was a closed book to me but I knew what he was in himself, what sort of a man his chosen life of selfless love and struggle had made him. Among living creatures man alone, it appears, is capable of making this deliberate choice, and my grandfather was only one among a great multitude of selfless lovers and seekers. If all this love and struggle and knowledge was to go to waste then not only must God be so crazy that he could not exist but the universe also was crazy and pointless. Yet it did not seem to be. It seemed to bear witness to a marvellous provenance and order. It seemed to bear witness to a God who is not crazy. This is what I worked out later. At the time I simply knew the thing was impossible.*[386]

Sisters

I do not remember the last Ely years in such detail as I remember the early ones, but two events stand out very clearly.[387]

The first of these was her grandfather's visit; the second, the arrival of a new addition to their household – Elizabeth's cousin Hélène. She was the only child of Ida's brother, born a couple of years after the Goudges' move to Ely.

Her parents lived in Java and as was the custom in those days, as soon as she began to wilt in the heat she had to be brought home to England for good… When she arrived [she] had been kept too long in the heat and was a thin delicate child, with great dark eyes in a white face.[388]

The home-loving Elizabeth would have had no difficulty in understanding what a "traumatic experience for a child" this move would be; nor in sympathising with the "dreadful" parting of this little girl from her father. Being an only child, too, must have intensified the trauma - "two children together could perhaps weather it but how one child alone battled through I do not know," she said. And yet Hélène was "perhaps luckier than some children" in similar circumstances for she was greatly loved, not least by the Vice-Principal of her new school: her own Aunt Marie.

And when she came for the holidays to Ely, and later to Oxford, my parents equally loved her… Hélène was a true Channel Islander, brave, vivacious and fascinating. She was very like my mother in temperament and they understood each other completely. My father delighted in her.[389]

Hélène presented a complete contrast to her older cousin, who said of her childhood self: "In nothing did I take after the Collenettes. I was entirely and distressingly English." Distressing, she seems to imply, to her Guernsey grandmother, for she goes on to say that:

When years later [she] had another grand-daughter, the child of her younger son William, she had a grandchild after her own heart, a little creature dark-eyed and vivacious and strongminded as herself, and as brimful of charm.[390]

This might seem to imply that Hélène had a much stronger bond with their grandmother than Elizabeth had herself. However she later says that their grandfather "would have loved Hélène as much as my father did but he never saw her after her first visit to Guernsey when she was a baby."[391] And as his wife pre-deceased him at the end of the war, presumably she too saw just as little of this granddaughter "after her own heart."

Elizabeth says that for the two cousins: "a child, and a much older girl who had hitherto been cock of the walk, reigning with a supremacy that must now be shared," the age gap was initially "difficult to bridge."[392] Records show that the nine-year old Hélène arrived at the Port of London from Singapore in 1922, in their final months at Ely, when Elizabeth was then twenty-two years old and in the early days of her teaching.

She does not expand on that sharing of "supremacy," but it is easy to imagine the potential difficulties of having an unknown cousin suddenly inserted into one's family. For many an only child too, unused to sharing their parents with anyone, the difficulty might be increased by the discovery that the stranger proved to be such a delight to one's beloved father, and had such a bond of mutual understanding with one's mother.

This particular little cousin moreover, thirteen years younger than herself, even appeared to be better-educated. Elizabeth recounts how at her new school Hélène had fallen into "a storm of grief and fury" when she learnt about the death of Socrates, and remembers her father being "utterly delighted" when he heard this story from Marie. The anecdote triggers yet another comment on her father's "severe shock" at her own lack of education, for even though it was now some four years since she had left Grassendale: "he discovered that his own daughter, at her school, had never been told a single word about one of the greatest civilisations the world has ever known, and hardly even knew who Socrates was."

Later, when we were on a short holiday together, we sat in two chairs one on each side of the fire, and I heard the whole story of Socrates. "There," he said when he had finished, "now you know how Hélène felt."[393]

But the difficulties were resolved. Indeed years later, Elizabeth described Hélène in a letter as 'my adopted sister' and always called her much-loved sons 'my nephews.' "If our love was a delicate plant to begin with," she said, "it became with the years a very strong one."[394]

More than thirty-five years later, Elizabeth would publish what must have been for her a very special book: an acclaimed Life of her beloved St. Francis of Assisi. She dedicated it to Hélène.

Teaching

Mrs. Goudge's initial idea had been that, equipped with her college training her daughter should then (when her stammer had been overcome) "teach in a school for crippled children."[395] Not a surprising choice for Ida to make, as teaching was something of a family profession - her husband's, of course, and two of her sisters'; and she herself had also done a little teaching when she was young. Her own mother had started "a little dame's school"[396] in Guernsey in the early, somewhat impoverished days of her married life, and her mother's sister, too, Ida's aunt Rosalie Ozanne, is listed in the 1861 Census as a governess – albeit aged only fifteen. Twenty years later, by then married and with five sons under nine, she was Principal of a Ladies School at St. Peter Port.

And so Elizabeth set out, initially, to follow in their footsteps: "announcing with a confidence that now staggers me that I was capable of teaching design and applied art."[397] She wanted to work from home, because "at college I had been almost as homesick for Ely and my parents as I had been at school... and home again I vowed I would stay there for the present." So she turned the old schoolroom into what she "grandly called a studio," equipping it with a loom and spinning wheel, embroidery frames and "a large table for leather work. And here, "incredibly, I had pupils," she said, adding even more self-deprecatingly, "I can't think I taught them much. I was hopeless as a teacher."[398] Nonetheless, she did admit that "the little studio flourished" and that she and her pupils "had great fun."[399]

> *The ladies of Ely, in the great kindness of their hearts, toiled up the two flights of stairs to my studio, where they dyed themselves as blue as Ancient Britons with my leather stains, pricked their fingers with needles, tangled themselves up in the loom, and actually had the generosity to pay me for their sufferings.*[400]

One of her Goudge ancestors had been a Huguenot weaver, and she herself was always "remarkably happy" when working at her loom: "Weaving was one of my greatest joys when I was young and I know from personal experience that you cannot work at a hand-loom without singing."[401] Years later she would create the character of Froniga in *The White Witch* who "delighted both in weaving and spinning." Elizabeth used her hand-woven fabrics to make clothes, which in line with the fashion of the times were "terrible sack-like garments" that she then embroidered. She did church embroidery too, "with lots of gold thread" and found it "as absorbing as illuminating manuscripts must have been to the monks who once lived at Ely." She and her mother also learned to make lace.[402]

So it seems that these years of change at Ely had both begun and ended in joy, with a great mix of darkness and light in between. She lived there for twelve years in total, and in the first three would surely have enjoyed the improvements to the house, and the happiness of finding new friends and activities. Another great joy would have been her mother's improved health, although even this could be seen as a somewhat mixed blessing; being, as it was, a contributing factor in Nanny's departure. Four years at boarding school meant discovering the magic of Keyhaven and the bliss of Shakespeare, but only being happy "at times" and always homesick for Ely. Even a joyful return for the holidays could be marred by her periodic encounters with the ghost. Post-war, her schooldays over, she published her first book after a happy period of story-writing for children; but then, disappointingly it did not sell. In consequence, at the beginning of the Twenties came her two college years at Reading, and absorption in a very different kind of creativity – yet at the cost of more change, and more homesickness. She fell in love for the first time, and it was a heavenly experience: "for a while the world shone with the same sort of beauty that had lighted the garden at Wells in my childhood."[403] But it ended in tears. Finally, in the last "year or so" came her handicrafts teaching, after the setting-up of the Studio: a "halcyon period" when both she and her pupils had *fun*.

Then the blow fell. Ely, the home of homes, was to be abandoned. My father was offered the appointment of Regius Professor of Divinity at Oxford. It was considered a great honour.

Nevertheless the change seems to have come as a blow to him too: for "he did not want the honour."[404]

If life at King's was stimulating it was also, coming on top of the war years, very exhausting, and he was very tired when in 1923 the office of Regius Professor...was offered to him. Usually, in face of difficulties and anxieties of all sorts, he was very calm, relying utterly upon God's guidance and refusing to be rattled; this was the only time in his life when I have known him to be so worried by indecision that he nearly broke down altogether. He had never held a fellowship, and he felt himself to be out of touch with university life, and he did not feel that his mind was sufficiently academic for him to be acceptable in such a post. Then, too, he was anxious about my mother, who was in no fit state of health for a move, and he was very anxious about the financial side of things; he had very little private money and the big house was an alarming white elephant. But the pressure put upon him, especially by his old friend Dr. Lock, and by Bishop Gore, was very great, and he regarded himself as a soldier does, as a man under orders. Finally, though he would have liked to refuse, he felt that he must accept. And in the end he was happy.[405]

But would his daughter be happy? She had returned from college determined to stay put, because she loved Ely: perhaps with the same kind of love her father had had for their previous home… he, she said, had "loved Somerset so passionately that I am sure he knew that he would leave his heart behind him in its sacred earth."[406]

Now it seems her own heart was to be left behind.

The painful truth was that these years of change had themselves been brought to an end by the greatest change yet. The stability she had planned for was ended. Her periodic homesickness would now become permanent loss: for she must leave Ely and live instead in Tom Quad, Christ Church, in what would prove to be an "old beautiful dark house that we could never learn to love."[407] It was a call to a privileged life, yes; but her father's new and elevated position would bring with it a correspondingly elevated social standing for the whole family – and this was not a change for the better, for someone as shy as the young Elizabeth. Neither was the move to a busy university city, after the peaceful life of the cathedral close at Ely and Wells. In fact, Oxford would be a whole new world.

The Goudges moved into their unloved house in the same spring that brought Elizabeth's twenty-third birthday. She was not to remove from it until she was nearly forty. It was during these years - perhaps not surprisingly - that she had a nervous breakdown. But it was also during her time here that she began seriously to write.

OXFORD AND BARTON

❋

1923 - 1939

The Waste Land

> O God...my soul thirsteth for Thee, my flesh longeth for Thee in a dry and thirsty land, where no water is.[408]
>
> The Psalms: in *A Book of Comfort*

Although life in their quiet cathedral town in the Fens had been pretty much life as Elizabeth had always known it, the post-war world of the nineteen-twenties was now a very different place from the Edwardian England of her childhood. As Canon Goudge said, after the dividing chasm of the Great War even those who had trusted in progress were disillusioned. It had led to tanks and machine guns, mustard gas and aerial warfare, and the young men of Europe lay dead in their millions.

As a result the Goudges would discover, in many of the new generation of students at Oxford, a prevailing mood of pessimism. T.S. Eliot's poem *The Waste Land* had just been published in 1922 and it captured the post-war mood, coining an apt name for a seemingly arid world. Even those too young to have experienced the fighting firsthand could tune in to the mood of despair. In the Michaelmas Term of 1925, only about eighteen months after Henry Leighton Goudge took up his position as Regius Professor, the eighteen-year-old Wystan Hugh Auden went up to Oxford - also to Christ Church. It was there he first read Eliot's poem and realised the truth of its description of his changed world. The England of 1907 when he was born, he said, had been 'Tennysonian' in outlook: now in 1925, its character mirrored *The Waste Land*.[409]

Another new undergraduate of 1925 who shared his generation's disillusionment after the war was Alan Griffiths of Magdalen College. He was aware of the strong and growing interest in both socialism and pacifism in the Oxford of that time, and he himself started out as a keen socialist. However he was soon questioning the nature of a civilisation which was clearly in decay, and lost faith in any kind of political action to change things for the better. For him too, *The Waste Land* was seminal, seeming to capture civilisation's "death knell" and the way the war had fragmented our culture into "chaos."[410]

For many people, Christian faith seemed to be dying too. The religious doubt of the nineteenth century had entered a new and worse phase, for it was no longer just scientific discovery which posed a threat. To many of the generation who had lived through the horrors of the trenches, faith in a loving God had come to seem like a fairytale.

Although things would change again. The author of *The Waste Land* would go on to write some of the greatest Christian poetry of the age. And on 20th December 1932, only a decade after *The Waste Land's* publication, the same Alan Griffiths of Magdalen would be clothed as a novice of the Benedictine order, to become known by his new name in religion: Bede. His Oxford tutor, also an unbeliever in those days, would later become world-famous as a Christian too: his name was Clive Staples Lewis. But just now in the Twenties, such a thing seemed impossible; in fact Bede Griffiths said he would have questioned the sanity of anyone who had told him, during his Oxford years, that he would one day become a monk. Christianity belonged to the vanished pre-war world and no longer had anything to say to their generation.

There is no evidence to suggest that Elizabeth rejected Christianity in the aftermath of the Great War. She was, however, always questioning and searching after her own truth because she believed that "a copy-cat religion… is [not] faith,"[411] and it does seem that at one point she came very close to unbelief, for she describes how during a time of particular suffering during the Oxford years – probably the breakdown:

I could not totally disbelieve in God because during my worst and most despairing nights there had seemed to be something there; some rock down at the bottom… And always my parents' love and faith, the world's beauty and the sound of great music, seemed unexplainable without God… Therefore I had to find a God I could love. I could not love a God who did not stop this suffering therefore I had to have a God who could not, a God who was not Almighty. I was aware of the cosmic struggle since I had experienced the faint echo of it in myself, the spiritual powers of good and evil in conflict. I worked it out that one was not stronger than the other and at the end of it all evil might win. God might again die and this time have no resurrection. But if he was finally defeated it would be our fault, not his, for he would have withstood evil to the utmost limit, as he did on Calvary, and would die only because we are afraid to do the same. Our wounds are in his flesh, always, our griefs in his heart, but he is powerless to stop the evil of sin and pain by himself. He is a God who needs us and cannot do without us. I could love that weak God.

I was happy with this for a while, and then I told my father of my conclusions. The result was disastrous. How unoriginal human beings are! Our great ideas are seldom new. I had thought up the heresy of Manicheism, a faith for which men and women had been willing to be martyred, and which had tempted even Augustine. It was hard to let go of my lovely heresy, but my father had no mercy on it. A God who is not Almighty is not God, and to believe in his possible defeat is not comforting; that way lies despair.[412]

The fact that she gave such a detailed explanation of her "lovely heresy" some forty years or so later seems to confirm how earnestly she had thought it out, and how hard it had been to let it go. But her father had no mercy on it… (nor perhaps on any of the despairing modern ideas that were around at the time. Recalling how he did not read any modern novels or poetry, she gave as the one exception an "earnest but quite unsuccessful effort to understand T.S. Eliot's *Waste Land*."[413]) In his hands, her "carefully constructed explanation was…sent flying like a pack of cards."[414]

I do not remember all he said of his own faith, possibly I did not understand it, but I remember my own conclusions. If our own small intuition, upheld by the experience of the saints and mystics of all religions through all the centuries, persists in murmuring that God exists then there is nothing left for us except the humble acceptance of paradox and mystery. If it is true that God is Almighty, it is also true that he needs us, since he chose that his son should be true man as well as true God, by this choice making Christ and man inseparable. Apart from Christ we have no life; we are merely a dead leaf fallen from the tree. Apart from us he has no body in the world, no hands and feet and heart and voice to bring God's mercy to a suffering world.[415]

It was the anguish of the suffering world - what C.S. Lewis was to call the problem of pain – that caused her so much heart-searching and misery.

I had a little earlier than this fallen in love with the doctrine of reincarnation, since to believe that nothing happens to us that is not the result of our previous actions absolves God from the charge of injustice. But this my father had dismissed with two withering words, "Utter nonsense." I think now that he may have been wrong but at that time I could not believe that my father could be wrong, and I was withered.[416]

These passages are revealing in many ways. They show a young woman who was a Christian and a thinker, but who lived in the shadow of her father's impressive theological scholarship, and could be withered by his opinion. Nevertheless she went on thinking for herself, and drawing conclusions that seemed to her to point to the truth. At her most despairing, the things she could believe in as evidence of God were love and faith, the world's beauty, great music, "our own small intuition" and the saints and mystics of all religions. At Father's insistence she discarded the idea of a weak God whose defeat would be "our fault," but still hung on to the absolute belief that our actions are important. As Christ's body in the world, she concluded – paraphrasing St. Teresa of Avila - what we do as individuals is vital to God.

Tom Quad

Life was not all gloom in the wasteland of course, and nor was all progress destructive. In November 1922, just a few months before their move to Oxford, the words "2LO Calling" had been heard across the nation, marking the beginning of the very first BBC radio broadcast. And just two days after Miss Elizabeth Goudge's twenty-third birthday, the Lady Elizabeth Bowes-Lyon – also shortly to celebrate her twenty-third birthday – married the king's younger son Prince Albert, in Westminster Abbey, on 26th April 1923. For the very first time, this wedding was presented to the nation as a royal public event. Scenes were filmed for the cinema newsreels, and no doubt to the delight of the new "listeners-in" as they were called, it was broadcast on the radio too... although not the actual service itself; the Archbishop of Canterbury, according to the famous anecdote, being afraid that men in pubs might listen to it with their hats on. Through a series of as yet unimaginable circumstances, in a few years' time this young couple would become the country's new King and Queen.

But *The Joy of the Snow* contains no mention of such things; everything seems to have been overshadowed by the loss of her home, and the miseries it ushered in. "On a spring day we left Ely," she says. "I cannot recall a single thing about it."[417] Emily, in Elizabeth's play about the Brontës has a very similar experience.

> *I can't see beyond the present tonight. The fact that we are leaving Haworth towers over me like a great curving wave, ready to crash down on me and drown my happiness. I can hear its roar in my ears... I loathe cities... Four walls always make a prison for me, and what is a city but an endless procession of suffocating walls?*[418]

Elizabeth was not alone in her adverse reaction to the Oxford move, for Mrs. Goudge was immediately ill again.

> *Very vivid, at the other end of a tunnel of forgetfulness, is the memory of my mother's despairing breakdown when we finally landed in our new home, the old beautiful dark house that we could never learn to love...*[419]
>
> *Our new home in Tom Quad, [had] windows looking down on green lawns about the central fountain, Tom Tower and its great bell to the right and the Cathedral to the left. [It] was a strange house, long and narrow. At one end my father's study with the drawing room above it, and at the other the big old-fashioned kitchen with the spare-room and its*

powdering closet over it, spanned the width of the house, but all the other rooms looked north upon the walled garden behind the house and only the long passages enjoyed the sun. In the rather dismal dining room large oil paintings of the previous divines who had died in this house through the centuries (they never looked to me as though they had lived in the house, only died in it), gazed down upon us with disapproval. There was a large and ancient cellar under the house where the gentlemen in the oil paintings must have kept their wine and brandy, but in our day it only contained, in wet winters, several feet of water. The house had a flat roof through which melting snow would seep, encouraging fungus growths in the rooms below. There was a large population of mice, and a smaller one of rats.[420]

This is the house occupied by Gervas Leigh and his family in *Towers in the Mist*:

> *Stone steps led down to the huge dark cellars so thoughtfully provided by Cardinal Wolsey for the beer, the Xeres sack, the skins of Greek wine and the casks of burgundy, to which he had himself been so attached… Only judging others by himself he expected them to have such a lot of it, for the cellars stretched the length of the house and went down into the bowels of the earth.*
>
> *The kitchen, like the hall, was stone-floored, with a large well in the centre…The river ran so near them that there was never any lack of water in the well, and during the rainy winter months there was a further supply of water in the cellars, where it stood two feet deep and gave Canon Leigh the rheumatics.*[421]

The cathedral was…close but [not] dominant. At first sight it looked pushed away in a corner, crowded out by Wolsey's great quadrangle. What dominated us there was Tom Tower, looming up against the sky and looking much taller than it actually is, and its great bell that thundered out the doom of time by day and night, driving sleepless guests to vow they would never visit the place again.[422]

This is not the only mention she makes of the great bell, Tom, telling us also that it tolled the curfew before the college gates were shut for the night. Great Tom, in fact, boomed out one hundred and one strokes every night of term-time at 9 p.m., in representation of the original number of students in the College. And although the cathedral itself might have looked "pushed away", its bells too were only too close.

> *Bells at a distance are a joy but [bells] pealing out almost over your head are not, and on Saturdays bell-ringers from other parts of England would come and peal the Christ Church bells hour after hour.*[423]

This was torture for Ida who "after the [several] sinus operations she had had…could not stand noise of any kind."[424]

It is interesting to compare Elizabeth's descriptions of the three cathedrals beside which she lived for the first half of her life. Wells was her *own* cathedral, growing up out of her back garden; talking to her in bell-music and concerned for her safety. Ely had "possessed" her with its splendour – tremendous, dominant, terrible and beautiful; a constant symbol of eternal life. Christ Church Cathedral at Oxford on the other hand was simply "close, but no longer dominant"… and it was noisy. She says little else about it – not even a mention of what must surely have been of interest to her so soon after her college days: the Pre-Raphaelite stained glass, designed by Burne-Jones and made by the William Morris Company. She does give a description of the cathedral in *Towers in the Mist* however, including a brief mention of its earlier, mediaeval windows … but even so, there is something "strange" about it.

> *For a few moments, as she looked about her, the beauty of the Cathedral lifted the pall from her spirit. The Saxon pillars of the choir, massive and of colossal strength and seemingly as old as time, gave one a glorious feeling of stability, and the perpendicular clerestory that rose above them, and carried the eye up to the fine and graceful pendant roof, seemed like the arches of the years that carry a man's soul from the heavy darkness of the physical earth to the airy regions of heaven. This strange mixture of architecture, that spanned the centuries in one great curve, never failed to affect the mind strangely. One felt cowed by it, a little confused by this leap through time, yet comforted too by a sense of union. Ancient glass, that told the story of Saint Frideswide's life, filled the windows and the sun shone through it to pattern with all the colours of the rainbow pillars and arches and the tombs of the dead that paved the floor.*[425]

❋

Despite all the drawbacks of their new house, it did have its "glories."

> *The oak-panelled study and the high sunny drawing room above it were beautiful rooms, and in my mother's bedroom a carved Adam mantelpiece framed a strange dark oil painting that we loved for its mysteriousness.*[426]

This must have inspired Moonacre Manor's panelled parlour in *The Little White Horse*, which had

> *a lovely graceful Adams fireplace, with the carved woodwork of the mantel sweeping up to form a picture frame, with delicate pillars at the sides... Within the frame was a queer dim oil painting.*[427]

And the one in *The Middle Window* also, with "fluted wooden pillars on each side...surmounted by a carved wooden frame which was of a piece with the panelling."[428]

And although behind the house in Tom Quad was what "to my mother... was a draughty, stuffy town garden"[429] - beyond was the beauty of Christ Church meadows, here described in *The White Witch*.

> *He was strolling with Francis in Christ Church meadows one morning in mid-June. They walked beneath the wall of Merton College and over it roses were climbing. The trees were in their full glory, massive with foliage but with their green still fresh and cool. The grass in the meadows had grown tall, full of moon-daisies and sorrel. Over their heads, as they walked beneath the roses, bees were humming.*[430]

> *Best of all was the wide curving oak staircase that seemed made for the ascending and descending of kings and queens, and upon which one would suddenly feel a sense of joy and a lifting of the heart. But apart from these things it was a house without atmosphere... Never, returning after an absence, did I feel any sense of welcome when I came in at the front door.*[431]

Knowing the significance and importance that houses had for Elizabeth, both in life and in her books, it must have been a strain for her to live in an unwelcoming home – however grand and historic - that she could never learn to love. On top of this, Oxford itself introduced a new and daunting element into her life.

> *A dislike of large towns, even towns as beautiful as Oxford, made me love it less than I should have done,*[432] *[and] after existence in the quiet backwaters of Wells and Ely the life of a big university town seemed to me terrifying.*[433] *At Ely we had lived...quietly and simply [but] in the University life of those days it was very difficult to be either quiet or simple...*[434]
>
> *The two Regius Professors of Divinity, at Oxford and Cambridge respectively, filled the highest teaching posts the Church of England had to offer. They ranked with bishops, [my mother] had been told, and that to her was a pleasing idea. She was told by someone else that my father would now be able to don a court suit and present himself at Buckingham Palace, and during the period when my father refrained from telling her that he intended*

to do no such, to him, useless and silly thing, the thought of the court suit was, to her, very comforting.[435]

Elizabeth, we remember, had been sent to a school where it was assumed that all the girls would go on to be presented at court and which accordingly included the necessary curtsey in its curriculum. But apart from the one mention of a trip to London for the Gray's Inn Ball, there is no suggestion of any kind of social season disrupting the quiet simplicity of their Ely days. She does, however, admit that her mother was always something of a "grande dame"[436] and this is borne out by a recollection of a friend she made at Oxford, Audrey Clark, who was an undergraduate when they met in about 1924. The two young women were about the same age, both daughters of Christ Church academics, and met through their membership of the Girls' Diocesan Association (GDA). Audrey had this memory of Mrs. Goudge.

> In those ancient days mothers used to pay polite calls on each other in between three and four in the afternoon and the Goudges had a very big drawing room in their house at Christ Church, and Mrs. Goudge used to sit in a chair that was as far from the door as it could be, which was by far the best position for her to be in – you know she was rather an invalid, so she couldn't jump up and come to meet anyone, so everybody had to walk the whole length of the room to greet her.

Poor Ida, though, had grown up in a world of class snobbery, and been its victim. She and her sisters, after being taught at home in their mother's little dame's school, were sent to complete their education in Guernsey Ladies' College where they "suffered deeply under the stigma of having a father in trade."

Their father was a chemist and they were made to suffer for it. Life in the Victorian era was less violent and corrupt than ours but at least in this age the distinction between a doctor and a chemist causes no actual suffering.[437]

Oxford Life

Despite the new freedom and opportunity experienced by some women after the first world war, there were still many restrictions placed upon young females in the nineteen-twenties. As E.M. Delafield remarks in her 1930s novel *Thank Heaven Fasting*:

> Much was said in the days of Monica's early youth about being good. Life…was full of young girls who were all being good…never anything but good, since opportunities for being anything else were practically non-existent. One was safeguarded.[438]

When asked for her comment upon Elizabeth's unhappiness at Oxford, Audrey immediately referred to the way young women were hedged about with restrictions.

> She never spoke about it but she obviously wasn't very happy. I think she felt a little bit restricted at home. In those days our mothers used to like to know every detail – of where we were if we were out, and all this sort of thing – and I think some of that worried Elizabeth. She would have loved to have had a while being quite independent, but you see she never could be.

Opportunities for escape may have been restricted, but she did have some fun:

> *That first summer term passed like a pageant; dances and parties, pealing bells and concerts, gardens full of flowers and sunshine on water. I see it now as a kaleidoscope of colour and because I was young enjoyment did break through, even through the distress of my mother's increasing illness.*[439]

A little 1927 volume entitled *Things Seen in Oxford* describes how in the run-up to Commemoration, during "the Eights and subsequent weeks" the river is "the centre of life and gaiety."

Oxford and Barton

> Friends are asked up, and those of the opposite sex are eagerly welcomed. The barges are crowded, white dresses flutter, luncheons are arranged up river, friends are introduced, excursions are arranged, and laughter fills the air.[440]

It was not all to her taste, however.

Life seemed to us a whirl of social gaiety. My mother had all the social graces and had she been well she would have enjoyed it all. My father and I, not being so gifted, knew we ought to be enjoying it more than we did and felt guilty because other people, less fortunate than we, would have thought our life paradise.[441]

Audrey said,

> There were a few years when there were dances given by the senior members of the college and Elizabeth used to always go to those. I don't think she used to go to the Commem Balls very much… you see she was so shy – I think it was largely that. And for anything like the Commem Balls and things it would have been for her to ask a man, as she belonged to Christ Church, and she wouldn't have liked to do that.

※

What brought real joy to Elizabeth was not Oxford's Commemoration Balls but its beauties. Even, occasionally, the opportunity to enjoy the glory in peace and blessed solitude… to escape. "I began to discover Oxford's glories" she said, and used many of them thirty years later as the background for her novel *The White Witch*:

> *Those who were taking the air strolled with slow pleasure down the quiet street and through the East Gate, pausing on Magdalen Bridge, their arms on the parapets, to watch the river winding beneath the willow trees and listen to the music of the water about the piers of the bridge. Over their heads Magdalen tower soared into a tranquil deep blue sky. The rooks in the tall elms in the deer-park were cawing and from all over Oxford, from one tower after another, the hour struck.*
>
> *It was a charmed hour, very still beneath the sound of bells and birds and running water.*[442]

> *I was not, like my mother, a sick woman, I was young and I had a strong pair of legs. Anyone who loves Oxford knows what I discovered, sometimes with my father, sometimes alone. Kingfishers in Christ Church Meadows and bluebells in Bagley Wood. The Library at Merton and the great fan-roofed stone staircase that ascended to the hall at Christ Church, and which echoed at the end of every summer term to the music of Byrd when the Cathedral choir stood there singing in the evening. New College garden...*[443]

> > *It seemed that no one ever came there, except occasionally a few lovers of quietness... It was one of those places that seem to hold a profound and inviolable peace. One could pace up and down on the flagstones under the arcade, or sit on a stone bench looking out at the green garth and the ilex tree, with the Founders Tower above, and hear nothing but the sound of the great pendulum in the Tower, the voices of pigeons and the chime of bells. In this place noise was shut out, and always would be, for it could impose its own peace on all who came...*[444]
> > *[He] turned aside into the cloisters. Though it was now late September it was a warm and golden evening. There was no one there. With relief he sat down on the old stone bench and rested his eyes gratefully on the small green garth, the dark tree and the tower... He shut his eyes and let the peace of the place sink into his very bones.*[445]

And then, not only glorious but essential to her wellbeing, there were the cloisters at Magdalen:

> *These cloisters were for me the heart of Oxford; why I cannot explain. For me it just was so. Through all the years at Oxford, however unhappy I was, however restless and distracted, as soon as I had opened the door in the wall, gone in and shut it behind me, I was at peace. And nearly always alone. It seemed almost as though I was the only person who knew about the door in the wall. Or if there was anyone else there, sitting or strolling quietly, and if one met their eyes, there was the ghost of a smile there, as though they recognised another of a fraternity... Here is our peace...*[446]

Bede Griffiths may even have been of that silent, strolling fraternity, for in his second year at Magdalen, in the autumn of 1926, he moved into rooms in New Buildings which directly overlooked the mediaeval cloisters. He felt it was the "perfect setting"[447] for the kind of life he wanted to live.

For Elizabeth - living in Oxford the kind of life she really did not want to live – here too was her peace. Not to be found apparently - in this third city of bells - within a cathedral... but in her own peaceful cloister, in solitude.

Barton

Amongst Elizabeth's lovely memories of peace and solitude she slips in that phrase, "however unhappy I was, however restless and distracted." For whatever enjoyment might break through, she was not carefree. Within the space of that first summer term her life changed radically yet again, for her mother's illness and Canon Goudge's high-profile appointment combined to place new and very real burdens upon her shoulders.

Towards the end of that first term we realised that my mother could not stay in Oxford any longer… Oxford in the summer might be beautiful but it was airless… My father consulted the map and railway timetable. The easiest seaside place to get to from Oxford was New Milton in Hampshire.[448]

As yet another example of how their young lives at times almost interwove, coincidentally Bede Griffiths, six years her junior, had spent most of his childhood in New Milton. His family moved there when he was a small boy and sent him to a prep school, Furzie Close, at Barton – the same little seaside village that was now, and for the next seventeen years or so, to become Elizabeth's second home. Bede's school was just a few miles from where Elizabeth was being educated at Southbourne; and they are alike in recording how their schooldays in peaceful Hampshire passed largely undisturbed by the Great War.[449]

Elizabeth's father now went down to Hampshire, "found a bungalow he liked and rented it for the rest of the summer."

The one of our maids who was nearest and dearest to my mother, and I, took her down there and in a short time she was reviving. Term ended and Hélène came from boarding school and my father from Oxford to join us and the pendulum once more swung towards well-being. For my mother was so much the Queen Bee of our hive that we all revolved round her. She was our life. We wilted when she did, revived when she did…

In our restored state of well-being we had a look at the new pattern of our life and knew that my mother could not live always in Oxford, and we bought this tiny home, which my mother called Innisfree after Yeats's poem, at Barton-on-Sea, two miles from New Milton.[450]

Presumably the choice of name reflected what Mrs. Goudge felt about her new, non-Oxford home, for *The Lake Isle of Innisfree*[451] is full of images of living alone, in rural peace.

I am quite sure we got into debt to do it for if I remember rightly it cost the whole of five hundred pounds and that was a great deal of money in those days; the whole of my father's total annual income when we lived at Wells. From then on my mother spent only the winter months in Oxford and these she could manage, for she lived only in the two adjoining rooms of her bedroom and the drawing room, with warm fires and closed windows keeping the damp out.[452]

Audrey remembered, "For a lot of the time Mrs. Goudge used to be sitting in an armchair in the sitting room and not moving much – they used to have meals brought on trays to her, and that sort of thing."

For the rest of the year she…lived at Innisfree with her special maid to look after her, and…she went out in her bathchair… My father and Hélène and I joined her for the Easter and summer holidays.[453]

There must have been a deal of stress in the family again now as a result of Mrs. Goudge's ill health, for example the occasion when she was "suddenly taken away from the Barton bungalow for an emergency operation" and was away for "weeks."[454] And of course her illness meant that she was unable to undertake many of the social duties expected of her as the wife of the Regius Professor.

I had to be my father's so-called hostess and housekeeper at Oxford, and how sorry I was for him! Not only was he separated from his adored wife but she was an accomplished hostess and I was the reverse. He and I barely survived; living for the holidays.[455]

Jessie Monroe said of these duties,

> When she had to entertain for her father she was so hamfisted, she said, that things didn't always go very well. I think she apologised once. She said, "I'm sorry I'm not as good as my mother". And, "Oh I wish you *were* like your mother!" he said. So even this marvellous man had to say it once.

In Audrey's recollection,

The entertaining done in College in the Hall, Elizabeth wouldn't have been involved in at all. But there were a lot of occasions when I'm sure the visiting preachers and so on would have been staying with the Goudges.

Because of [my father's] work for Reunion, and also because he was so sympathetically interested in them personally, his house seemed often full of foreigners: Greeks, Rumanians, Russians, Indians, Chinese and Japanese. Language was occasionally a difficulty, for my father was no linguist... [and] it was sometimes necessary to fall back on Latin or Greek. Where there is a will there is a way and a conversation upon the things of God with a Georgian monk, when neither of them knew a word of the other's language, yet gave great joy to both.[456]

Fortunately the most eminent visitors were not always as terrifying as she expected. Not even a bishop whose illustrious career, at the end of Victoria's reign, had included the post of 'Hon. Chaplain to the Queen' - and who had preached one of the greatest sermons Elizabeth had ever heard.

Bishop Gore was a friend of my father's, and what my father felt about him was so compounded of reverence and love that the very thought of him filled me with awe... When we moved to Oxford, [he] came to stay with us for a few days. I expected to be terrified but even though he resembled the Isaiah of my youthful imaginings I was not afraid... One dog-lover [cannot] easily be frightened by another and...upon this visit he lost his heart to our dog...

One day during his visit to us Bishop Gore could not be found. He was discovered with Brownie in the dining room, sharing the sofa, caressing the big dog's wise domed forehead and long silky ears and murmuring over and over again, "I like you, Brownie, Brownie, I like you."[457]

It was not just the many visitors to the house that she had to cope with. Jessie Monroe told how "Mum couldn't take back these appalling calling cards that they had to deliver all round - so Elizabeth had to go." Elizabeth herself, in her autobiographical sketch even put a number on these visits:

I, the shyest person that ever lived, had to return two hundred calls for her; pressing the bell with trembling fingers and praying fervently that they might be out.[458]

There was a curious twanging sound, fumbling and a little eerie...Then light dawned on Mrs. Baker. "Someone trying to ring the bell," she said. "That bell needs seeing to," and she left the room.

Mary followed her, for the weak twanging had almost sounded like a cry for help, and together she and Mrs. Baker dragged the screeching garden door back over the paving stones. Outside on the steps stood the woman whom she had seen coming out of the post office yesterday. She...carried a very large basket in which reposed a very small pot of blackberry jelly, and she was trembling so violently that the pot rattled in the basket. "It's Miss Anderson from the Vicarage, come to see you," said Mrs. Baker in encouraging tones, adding very low for Mary's private enlightenment, "Poor dear."

"Do please come in," said Mary...
She installed Jean by the fire in one of the little gilt chairs...and Mrs. Baker fetched fresh tea. This seemed to revive Jean, though she had to hold her cup with both hands, and presently, while Mary talked about the beauty of Appleshaw, she set her cup down and removed her dark glasses...

The dark glasses, Mary felt, were more of a psychological protection than a physical one. The lack of co-ordination between what she was in herself, and the jarred mechanism of body and nerves, had so deeply shamed her that she must hide. But with Mary she had taken her glasses off. Had she known that she had done it? Mary was afraid to speak lest she frighten them on again.

"My brother," said Jean, "wanted me to bid you welcome. He's the Vicar here, you know. He'll be coming to see you soon. He wanted to know if there's anything we can do." Her face was suffused with crimson but she had got it out...[459]

The Scent of Water

She had got it out." Of course it was not only shyness that Elizabeth had to overcome during these ordeals; there was still, as well, the stammer that she did not conquer until late middle life. The newly-married Prince Albert of York who would later be crowned King George VI had himself a shocking stammer, and publicity surrounding the film *The King's Speech* brought to light the fact that for a number of unenlightened people in those days, stammering was even seen as a sign of 'not being all there' - that is, of being somewhat simple-minded. Even years later when the second world war began, part of Hitler's mendacious propaganda was to sneer at the King as a simpleton.

Elizabeth had been, in her own words, "an inarticulate, frightened child"[460] and in her twenties it seems – hardly surprisingly in light of the above - there was very little improvement in her self-confidence. Even at least ten years later, "when my books began to be read" she said, "there was the terror of parties. I was agonizingly shy and soon formed a vivid image of hell as a roomful of strangers at an endless cocktail party."[461]

How on earth, then, did she cope with the academics of Oxford?

Academia

I also had to go to dinner parties with my father. At one of the first of these I had to sit next to the then Master of Balliol and immediately fell into a coma of sheer terror, but recovered half-way through the fish when I discovered that the Master, with a twinkle in his eye, was quite prepared to do all the talking.[462]

Her reaction can in part be ascribed to an inherited shyness, for she describes a similar ordeal for her father in his youth. When he was ordained by Bishop Creighton, she said,

During his ordination retreat he found himself, during one painful meal, sitting next to Mrs. Creighton. Terror and shyness engulfed him. Mrs. Creighton hopefully tried him with one deeply intellectual subject after the other, but discovered that he apparently knew nothing whatever about any of them.[463]

Nevertheless, however twinkling the Master of Balliol that day, even a young female of much greater self-confidence than Elizabeth might have had problems conversing in such a situation. Here is Humphrey Carpenter's description, in *The Inklings*, of the prevailing attitude at that time towards female dependants of Oxford academics, as exemplified in C.S. Lewis and his contemporaries:

> It would be wrong to say that [Lewis] despised women. He was no misogynist. But he did regard the female mind as inferior to the male, or at least as being incapable of the mental activities which he valued. He told Charles Williams that he thought women's minds 'not really meant for logic or great art.'[464]

"To some extent these attitudes were typical of his social background, and of Oxford in particular," continues Humphrey Carpenter.

> Dons worked in their colleges and took a large proportion of their meals there. Their college was almost invariably the centre of their social life. In the meantime their wives were obliged to remain at home... Added to this was the fact that some of the wives were far less well educated than their husbands, so that even when they were given a chance to talk to those male friends of their husband who came to the house they had very little to say, or at least very little that the men thought worth listening to.[465]

A comment by Lewis in a letter to his brother seems to confirm his belief, at least in 1927, that academia was for men. He wrote that there had been one event of "good omen" during the Term - this was a Statute carried in Congregation, "limiting the number of wimmen [sic] at Oxford."[466]

Elizabeth said even of her father that the best-loved of his Collenette in-laws was Aunt Marie, with her "man's talk." Marie was passionate about mathematics, "yet she understood enough science to be able to talk as an equal with her father, just as she could talk theology with my father." Dr. Goudge maintained that she "had a man's mind." But then Marie was not just clever, she had been educated - at Cheltenham Ladies College, under "the revered Miss Buss and Miss Beale"[467] - whereas many women at that time were given an inferior education as a matter of course. Miss Giles in *The Rosemary Tree* reflects bitterly on how "given a good training she could have done something worth while. But everything had been done for the boys, because they were boys, and nothing for her."[468]

To add insult to injury, the women were then looked down upon for their lack of education. As C.S. Lewis pointed out, men had been educated in the use of "discussion, proof and illustration" and women - who had had mere "school lessons" - could not hope to enter into discussion with them.[469] In his opinion, if women did acquire any "tinge of culture" during their schooling, it was soon discarded after they married. And as they read only women's magazines, their conversation was "almost wholly narrative." Therefore, he said, in mixed company the men had either inexorably to pursue conversations which meant nothing to the females... or if they were "better bred" must attempt to bring the women into their talk – explaining things to them and trying to "sublimate...into some kind of sense" their "irrelevant and blundering observations." As such attempts met with no success, he concluded, talk that in all-male company would have been "real discussion" had to be "deliberately diluted" when women were present, with the result that it soon petered out in "gossip, anecdotes and jokes."[470]

"Cruel," says Humphrey Carpenter, "but true of at least some women at Oxford in the years between the wars; though of course the very fact that Lewis and his contemporaries had this poor opinion of female conversation itself prevented such women from being given any conversational chances. It was a vicious circle…" And he adds that in this respect, Lewis was "typical of his contemporaries."[471]

Poor Elizabeth. It seems she was fully and painfully aware of the academics' attitude to women, as evidenced in this further extract from *The Scent of Water*.

> *"I saw her as I was coming out of the post office," said Jean Anderson timidly.*
>
> *"Who?" snapped the Vicar. His sister started at the sharpness of his question, tears came into her eyes and her tea slopped over into the saucer. They had lived together for ten years now and still she could not get used to the quickness of his speech, his unintentional sarcasm and the pouncing vigour of his mind. And he on his side could not learn to adjust himself to her weakness and incompetence, though he tried hard, and with resolute loyalty always refused to look back to those halcyon days when he had lived alone…*
>
> *All his working life had been passed in Oxford, where he had been Fellow and Tutor at the same college where he had been an undergraduate, with only a few years break as a schoolmaster in between. For many years he had lived in rooms in college in wonderful comfort and seclusion, cared for by an excellent and devoted scout, Arthur Brewster, writing scholarly books, lecturing superbly, dining well, one of the institutions of the place and utterly contented with his mode of life. Then his mother had died and to his intense annoyance and dismay Jean had come upon his hands. But he had not shirked her for he was not a shirker…*
>
> *Jean had been very miserable in Oxford. She…had been terrified of her brother's friends; old men, sarcastic and brilliant, who knew their own abstruse subjects inside out but did occasionally profess ignorance upon other subjects, and even more brilliant young men who knew everything. But young and old they had been alike equally incomprehensible to Jean.*[472]

A mid-twentieth century guide to Oxford informed the world that by then "women and their ways" had become "part and parcel of University life, and as such they are accepted…" It adds, "and not, one suspects, with that masculine reserve and displeasure that tradition dictates."[473]

❋

Amidst all the other stresses of their Oxford life her father, too, was at first not totally happy with his new environment.

The slum districts of the Oxford of those days, some of them existing not far from Cardinal Wolsey's great wealthy College, made [my father] angry and miserable and started him off asking his habitual awkward questions. He was a much-loved man but he was disliked too; he could never leave well alone if in his opinion it was not well.[474]

> *There were a few people in Torminster who did not like [Grandfather]… His life in the slums had implanted in him a slight tendency to think that the well-to-do exaggerated the trials of their existence, and also a tendency to get a little impatient… "Bless my soul!" he would say suddenly in the middle of a Chapter meeting, "what a fuss about nothing! Send 'em all down a coal-mine, dear God, send 'em all down a coal-mine."*[475]
>
> A City of Bells

After all these years I am not sure of my facts here. I am not sure whether Christ Church actually owned some of the slum property or whether my father had been told so and was determined to find out. And if his College was not guilty then who was? And so he had a rather bad start at Oxford. Theologians are expected to stick to theology and not stir up hornets' nests in their odd moments, but my father was hornet-minded and could not help himself. London-born, the contrasts of social existence had bothered him from the beginning.[476]

> *The Dean…reached the North Gate and walked down the dirty steps to the path at the edge of the river, then turned to walk along it behind the Swithins Lane houses… The backs of these houses always made him feel as though he were in a nightmare. The broken windows, stuffed here and there with rags or boarded up to keep out the bitter wind that swept across the fen, looked out on filthy backyards and poor little patches of ground running down to the river path, filled with nettles, cabbage stalks, broken glass and crockery. The path was strewn with rubbish and the river water that lapped against it was always oily and*

> *foul… He picked his way among the cabbage stalks and bits of broken crockery, and his mouth set almost savagely in determination.*[477]

Dr. Goudge was a Socialist of course, and "bothered" by the contrasts of social existence; whereas Christ Church was considered, even thirty years later in the 1950s, to be the most exclusive and aristocratic of Oxford's colleges. There, one's background was of the utmost importance, and to ask people outright for details of their parentage and schooling was quite the norm.[478]

Altogether those early years were "years of strain" for him, "made difficult by self-distrust and by physical exhaustion" although "brightened by his happiness with the friends he worked with."[479]

> *But he did not enjoy, and who does, the endless Oxford committees, many of them quite off his subject and generally held at the sleepiest time of the afternoon. At these latter, he used to confess he "did not suffer from insomnia." The lengthy meetings of the Christ Church governing body were, however, at one time much enlivened for him by the presence of the Common-Room cat, who regularly attended college meetings.*[480]

As this anecdote shows, however hornet-minded her father was at heart a quiet and simple man.

> *Though he loved good talk, and entertaining and being entertained by men and women who were his friends, his shyness made him dislike society as such. And he didn't like being cluttered up "with lots of fings." No man can have had fewer personal possessions.*[481]

In contrast, she said: "My mother…in reaction from the poverty of her childhood, had always veered slightly towards a queenly extravagance."[482] Audrey remembered a time when King George V and Queen Mary, together with the Prime Minister Stanley Baldwin, were entertained at Christ Church on the occasion of its 400th anniversary. (Although originally founded in the 1520s by Cardinal Wolsey, after his fall from power the College was then re-founded by Henry VIII. Being therefore a royal foundation it was, as Elizabeth pointed out, subject to "periodic visits" from royalty.[483]) Mrs. Goudge was a guest at this dinner and had a magnificent dress especially made for the occasion by one of the court dressmakers, which she later gave to Audrey.

The Joy of the Snow can seem to indicate that Ida was an almost permanently housebound invalid, who would never have been well enough to attend such a function; but Audrey said that "she could move about slowly; and naturally she went to these dinners and things, until the last few years when she became more invalidish."

But if the material possessions of life were burdensome to my father he never shirked the responsibilities that they bring. He took far more part than many men do in the domestic life of his household. When things went badly he liked to "do his bit", and when they went well he oiled the wheels by his unfailing gentleness and consideration.[484]

He was amazingly generous with everything that he had, money, time or knowledge, and he loved giving presents, but he never gave them to himself.[485]

Time to Write

Although her mother's absence at Innisfree put great burdens upon Elizabeth, she also benefited from the purchase of the bolt-hole at Barton. It was not only Mrs. Goudge who needed to get away from Oxford. In contrast to the house in Tom Quad, noisy and busy with its "ceaseless comings and goings," there was a simplicity to life in "this tiny home" which both she and her father appreciated.

Innisfree was in a country lane that wound through green fields to the sea. Barton (the name means a hill) was then a flat green plateau that is now a vast bungalow town, but then it was open country. It faced west across the fields, sheltered from the sea winds that swept across them behind a bank crowned by a rampart of hawthorn trees. The bank, separated from the bungalow by a small lawn, was covered with wild primroses in the spring and the trees, a mass of blossom in the spring and jewelled with red berries in autumn, had been twisted by the gales into fantastic and living shapes…I will never forget either the voices or the shapes of those trees. They seemed to fascinate Brownie too, for every evening he would lie at the top of the steps that led to the verandah and the little front door, and watch motionless as the setting sun spread its gold over the sky behind the trees.

And now the trembling light
Glimmers behind the little hills, and corn,
Ling'ring as loth to part

wrote Samuel Palmer. And that was the way the parting sun glimmered behind our trees. When it had nearly gone Brownie and I would walk up the lane to the cliff-top and watch the last lights fade from sea and sky.[486]

Geographically close to Keyhaven, this was familiar territory too. "I owe more than I can say to Barton," she said, for from here "I really discovered the Keyhaven saltmarshes that had caught hold of me in my schooldays, and it was from Barton that I first went to stay...at the house that I have called Damerosehay."[487]

But Damerosehay was still in the future. For now, she had a "long slog" on her hands as she began the serious attempt to become a writer. In part, writing was a practical solution to the problem of how to earn a living... "My handicraft training was not now providing me with what I wanted, a home-based career so that I could be with my mother as much as possible."[488] For it seems that almost from the beginning her attempts at teaching in Oxford were not wholly successful.

When I tried to make a workroom out of a dark north room near the kitchen, [I] found when I had set up my loom that there was scarcely enough light to work by, and who, in a city like Oxford with a fine art school, would even wish to be taught handicrafts by a nobody like myself in a room like this?[489]

At some point she also "tried to teach handicrafts in a school on Boars Hill [but] they had the wisdom to give me the sack with remarkable speed."[490] (In contrast, the very capable Mary Lindsay in *The Scent of Water* is an ex teacher who, like Grassendale's Miss Bartlett, "knew the trick of discipline and taught well."[491]) Elizabeth did do at least some teaching however, for her Autobiographical Sketch states that during this time "life was busy, for I still went on with my teaching." And in trying to chart her time in Oxford, we have to remember that she was there for a total of sixteen years. It was a twenty-three-year-old who moved into the house in Tom Quad and presumably soon after tried to set up her loom, and a woman of thirty-four who - fifteen years after the publication of *The Fairies' Baby* - finally produced her first published novel.

Whatever the level of career necessity however, to become a writer was not just a practical decision. Somewhere in this dualistic swing of life between stressful, high-profile Oxford and retreat to peaceful Barton, writing got a "hold" on her.

In time the Oxford life lost its terrors and the stimulation of it woke up in me the old longing to write.[492] *If it had not been such a happy thing I could have likened it to an octopus, for the stranglehold was growing tighter and tighter.*[493]

Beyond the Snow

It was...at Barton that my private hobby of writing got more and more of a hold on me... Getting up early in the morning and going to bed late at night I had already written my first long and atrocious novel, but not even the partiality of a parent for her first-born could make me think that there was anywhere to put it except the fire and so I put it there and told myself that I was no novelist...

And so my love of the theatre flared up afresh and I started on a long slog of writing plays...[494] the most difficult form of writing possible... Painstakingly I typed them out and anxiously I watched the post as they went the round of the London managers... who remained, like the editors of the children's magazines before them, unimpressed.

I was thirty-two before any success came my way – a Sunday night performance in London of a play about the Brontës. It was a small success, but no bigger one could ever bring me half so much joy again. I saw my play beautifully acted by real live actors...and I had some good notices in the papers. I was in heaven.

I returned home so encouraged that I gathered my plays together into a book and sent it the round of several publishers, with the humble suggestion that it would be nice if it could be published. The publishers, however, did not think so: there was no market for unknown plays. "But," said one kind publisher, "your work shows promise. Why not try to write a novel?" ...Fired with fresh enthusiasm I tried again and wrote Island Magic *about my beloved Guernsey[495] with a speed and ease which will never be mine again.[496]*

Island Magic

Elizabeth says that for most storytellers, a book begins "with a light in the mind,"[497] but added to this light were the several practicalities which, coming together, enabled her to produce her first novel. The Oxford life, no longer terrifying, had provided the stimulation. A kind publisher gave the necessary encouragement. Barton allowed her to escape and find peace - it was actually written, she says, in a corner of Ida's bedroom. Her beloved Guernsey was her inspiration. But in one sense the source of her creativity was still the same as in early childhood - the light in the mind for *Island Magic* had been kindled by her mother's own stories. "It is largely about her childhood," she says, "and has in it many of the stories she told me. Peronelle is my mother as I pictured her at that age."[498]

> *Peronelle, the most practical of the family, was always the one to answer any urgent call for action, and to answer it, too, with a shattering energy. She was thin, small, vital, with fair, curly hair that sprayed*

round her face as though each separate curl had a vivid life of its own. Her tawny eyes and pale pointed little face were the animated sparkling mirrors of every emotion that possessed her. Courageous, quick-tempered, generous, truthful, intolerant and passionately loving, she was a perfect whirlpool of emotion.[499]

Not surprisingly Elizabeth dedicated the finished book to her mother. She then located a copy of the *Writers' and Artists' Yearbook* in the Free Library at Oxford, copied down at random a list of publishers and "sent it out on its rounds." It was a case of only third time lucky. Although, disappointingly, the publisher who had suggested she write a novel "did not like it when it was done" (saying it was "too stilted") and the second on her list pronounced it "not likely to sell," they were both wrong: for when Duckworth and Company then "launched it into the world… it ultimately travelled to America, France and Germany."[500] Gerald Duckworth himself– Virginia Woolf's half-brother, who had founded the publishing house in 1898 - was then still alive. As part of his successful career he had also launched into the world, twenty-one years earlier, D.H. Lawrence's *Sons and Lovers*… and Lawrence's opinion of his new publisher, in a letter to their editor and reader, Edward Garnett, was that "Duckworth is jolly nice."[501] It was Mervyn Horder, however, who was in charge of the company for much of Elizabeth's working life –he was Chairman from 1948 to 1970. When he came to review her autobiography in *The Bookseller* exactly forty years after this first novel, Horder paid tribute to its success - saying that Duckworth had published *Island Magic* in 1934 "and have had it continuously in print ever since."[502]

No wonder, for it received some very favourable criticism. *The Daily Telegraph* said it was "of really remarkable merit;" *The Manchester Guardian*, that it contained "more than one passage" revealing "a rare intuition of spiritual beauty." *Public Opinion* declared: "This is more than a novel of promise; it is an achievement." And Henry Seidel Canby in the *Saturday Review of Literature* pinpointed its "curious charm which is partly style and partly the unusual quality of the background." In this "regional fiction of rather considerable excellence" he found characters worthy of "high praise" and said, "As a first novel, this book deserves attention from connoisseurs."[503]

What the critics collectively found was a depth and intuition far beyond just a retelling of Ida's memories about Guernsey - but then even as a child Elizabeth had retold Mother's stories with embellishments. She had now turned these tales into a novel with a strong spiritual element based on two central themes, the first of which was the nature of freedom. Rachell du Frocq is aware that her little son Colin is longing to grow up and break free, and yet "He did not know what freedom meant… One day she would teach him that only the bound are free... a paradox... a new word he must learn if he would live rightly."[504] How is she to teach him, she wonders, that independence is "a thing of the spirit, and never gained at the expense of integrity?"[505]

Rachell's conclusion echoes a contemporary conversation between Tolkien and Charles Williams, recorded by Humphrey Carpenter in *The Inklings*. On this topic he says, "Williams had much to say, [for] he believed that the only way to find real freedom was to submit oneself to the rule of God. 'The only freedom' he said, 'is a freedom to choose obedience.'"[506]

❉

Was the discussion of freedom in this novel purely academic, or did it relate to struggles of Elizabeth's own? Freedom to lead her own life must have been very much on her mind during the last decade, as she became increasingly bound by the restrictions of the Oxford life and the necessity, as it were, to live much of her mother's life for her. For she had surely never meant to live at home indefinitely. Although her homesickness at college, more than a decade ago, had been not just for Ely but for her parents too, she did say when setting up her home-based Studio that she intended to stay there *for the present*,[507] so it seems that in her early twenties she had had other plans in her head for the future.

But yet she stayed. Perhaps from lack of opportunity, or confidence, or funds? Maybe because it was, despite the frustrations, where she wanted to be? Or perhaps out of obedience to "the rule of God" - because for her, running away was not an option when faced with a duty demanded by love. *Island Magic* tells us that independence is never gained at the expense of integrity; and the young heroine of *Towers in the Mist* five years later, would wonder if even her marriage might be a selfish thing, because it would mean leaving her motherless siblings.

> *She saw them clearly in all their dearness; the people who had until now made up her whole world. Why should she desert them for a stranger? Of what worth was her love for them, if she could not suffer for their sake?*[508]

Elizabeth's upbringing would have left her in no doubt about the shouldering of duty as a tenet of her Christian faith, in which she had before her the example of "the one I wanted to follow"[509] - her father. He had taken on his new position at Oxford "as a man under orders..."[510] Though he would have liked to refuse, he felt he must accept;"[511] and the decision, she says, tormented him. Maybe it had led his daughter into a battlefield too? With on the one side, Duty; and on the other, that yearning in Colin du Frocq: who "wanted independence and he wanted serenity, and to get the two together he would go to any lengths."[512] Her new life, we know, lacked serenity; she was at times restless and distracted, and in desperate need of the peace of those snatched moments in the Magdalen cloisters. There was a dichotomy here, it seems, between who she was, and who she *had to be*.

※

Colin is not the only one in this novel who wants serenity. His sister Michelle is finding it impossible to reconcile the whirlwind of everyday life with the elusive core of peace and beauty which she knows is at its centre.

> *Each scrap and shred of beauty was a feather in wings that bore her soaring up and up towards the lark at heaven's gate… She was getting there… she was going to solve the problem… unity.*[513]

But she cannot get there. Spiritual awareness is too easily blotted out by the mundane; and, the other world's delights being so elusive, the precious inner vision leads her every time, from fleeting joy into agonies of frustration. "One lives in two worlds," she discovers,

> *"And when the…everyday world comes in on top of the other and shuts it out one gets in a frightful temper – at least I do…*
> *What can I do about it…? I can't go through life getting in tempers and making other people miserable and I can't, can't, give up that other world.*[514]

Elizabeth herself had always had a real awareness of another world. There was that shining world of her childhood vision of God in the garden. And at a very young age, being shut out from the worship in the cathedral had put her into a bad temper - which was then soothed by the sound of the heavenly distant music within… in reverse, what Poppet experiences in *The Castle on the Hill*:

> *Poppet never moved. With her lips a little parted and her great blue eyes gazing unseeingly out of the window she seemed to be drawing every note into herself, like a small round bumble bee sucking honey from a flower. When the music had died away into silence she sighed, came back to herself, and smacked Teddy hard. Thus did she express the dissatisfaction of us all when the beauty that has raised us up out of mundane affairs, like a mother lifting her child out of the mud, puts us down again and goes away.*[515]

Michelle knows she cannot go through life "alternating between ecstasy and bad temper" and yet how can she reconcile her interior and outward lives "so that she did not immediately lose her temper when one impinged upon the other?" How can she "live in two worlds at once and be happy in both?"

> *She wondered if her father knew. But if he did know he wouldn't be able to help her very much. Everyone had to find out how to live for themselves – she had discovered that much already. Other people could point the way but one had to tread it for oneself.*[516]

The person who points the way for Michelle is not her father, but his brother Ranulph – ironically the character who in youth did pursue freedom at the expense of integrity. He understands that "in most people you have the soul and body constantly at war with one another and the mind refereeing them and getting battered in the process."

Uncle Ranulph passes on to his niece what he was told by "a German" he once met: that to find unity, "The two worlds must be linked together and you yourself, your spirit, must be linked to what is behind all this… to the whiteness behind colour." Although he has spent his own life "running in the wrong direction" and therefore can only "describe a delectable country at second hand," he can repeat what this unnamed German once told him… that in the process of unity there are three stages:

> *Stage one … irresistible beauty luring you on.*
> *Stage two … tranquillity and acceptance born of storm.*
> *Stage three. Unity. Merged colour. Just the whiteness of light.*[517]

This advice has echoes of the *Theologia Germanica*, one of the ancient texts of mysticism. Thought to have been written in Germany towards the end of the 13th century, it teaches that the pathway to union with God is divided into three stages; and its wisdom, as it appears in Elizabeth's second anthology, seems to offer exactly what Michelle yearns to find.

> Seek only that true peace of the heart, which none can take away from you, that you may overcome all adversity; the peace that breaks through all adversities and crosses, all oppression, suffering, misery, humiliation, and what more there may be of the like, so that a man may be joyful and patient therein. Now if a man were lovingly to give his whole diligence and might thereto, he could very soon come to know that true eternal peace which is God Himself.[518]

Elizabeth said of herself and her prayer life during the Oxford years, "I was not a contemplative sort; I was not even a peaceful person for I lived in a whirl of activity...and the rush of university life seemed to stand between myself and prayer."[519] But from this description of Rachell du Frocq it seems that Elizabeth had at least a deep awareness of where such prayer might lead.

> *She sat quite still with her hands lying in her lap and her eyes closed. Sometimes she would murmur to herself as she sat, "Underneath you are the everlasting arms," and then she would feel her spirit sinking down and down through depths of tranquil light, that grew cooler and sweeter the further she sank, until she felt herself resting serenely against something, drawing in strength and peace through every fibre of her being.*[520]

There had been a great revival of interest in the contemplative way in the early years of the twentieth century, and Evelyn Underhill's *Practical Mysticism* may well have been the source of at least some of Elizabeth's awareness. Certainly one can find echoes of it in *Island Magic*, for Michelle's struggle with the two worlds is what Underhill calls the "unresolved dualism" of one's own personality. Naming them the 'deeper' and the 'surface' selves, Underhill says that between them "no peace is possible: they conflict at every turn."[521] The scene where Ranulph somewhat clumsily tells Michelle about the three stages of Unity is set on a Guernsey beach, where the du Frocq children are prising limpets from the rocks. In *Practical Mysticism* this same activity is used as a metaphor for the battle with the stubborn 'surface' self, which in Underhill's words has "cemented itself like a limpet" and can only be removed by "main force."[522] ("A limpet," said Ranulph, struggling with one, "is nothing but jellified obstinacy."[523]) To begin the new prayerful life, says *Practical Mysticism*, the former "comfortable clinging life, protected by its hard shell from the living waters of the sea, must now come to an end."[524] The living waters of the sea – an image that, some thirty-five years later, would permeate Elizabeth's final novel.

In this first book about the two worlds, and the search for the "true peace of the heart" Elizabeth had laid a foundation stone for the rest of her life's work. In fact, even before *Island Magic*, her play about the Brontës had evidenced a knowledge of the Christian mystics.

> *[CHARLOTTE produces three books from EMILY'S basket and reads out their titles.]*
> CHARLOTTE. *"The Spiritual Espousals" by John Ruysbroeck – "St. Theresa" – "St. John of the Cross" – Popish books! Oh, Emily, how awful! Wherever did you get them from?*

EMILY. *Monsieur Heger gave them to me when he found me reading them in his library at Brussels. They are wonderful books. They have gone through me like wine through water and changed the colour of my mind.*
CHARLOTTE. *[horror-struck] Monsieur Heger! They're Popish. Oh, what would Papa say?*
EMILY. *I can't imagine.*
CHARLOTTE. *And you've read them? Oh, I wonder if I ought to tell Papa?*
EMILY. *If you do he'll take away my books. But it doesn't matter now if he does. I've got there.*
CHARLOTTE. *Got where?*
EMILY. *Down to the cool depths. I've always been wearying to escape and be always there. Not seeing it dimly through tears and yearning for it through the walls of an aching heart, but really in it and of it – and now I am.*
CHARLOTTE. *What are you talking about?*
EMILY. *They call it mysticism. I learnt it in Brussels with the help of those books.*
CHARLOTTE. *Then that explains those strange poems you wrote.*
EMILY. *Yes, I tried to express what I had experienced in those poems. But there are no words.*[525]

Elizabeth loved Emily Brontë's mystical poetry all her life: a fact she revealed at the age of seventy-two in the foreword to *Daffodils in Ice* – a collection of poems by Sister Mary Agnes.

We all have our especially beloved poets who travel with us through our lives, and among their company there is always one who is pre-eminent and lives in the heart. For me that poet has always been Emily Brontë, but now she has been joined by another, the nun who wrote the verses in this book, and the two have become one in my mind... In vision and experience they are strikingly alike. Both are mystics, both identify themselves passionately with the world of nature, where they find God both revealed and glorified; both love night, and the Presence who comes in the stillness of night, and when he appears to leave them for a while they suffer the same agony of loss... "Oh, that I knew where I might find him!" It is the cry of every one of us, the cry of the whole agonized world.[526]

※

It is perhaps no coincidence that *Island Magic* - written when she finally emerged, stimulated to write, from the changes, conflicts and "terrors" of the new Oxford life - contained these lines:

Oxford and Barton

Somehow they battled through, they never quite knew why or how. It was as though they had entered into a whirlwind and after hideous battling had found themselves standing serenely in the core of peace at its centre. Rachell learnt the lesson of withdrawal into her own innermost tranquillity, André learnt that monotonous toil can be so used that it becomes the rhythm of thought, the pulsing background of the accompaniment that sets the notes of the violin winging to height beyond height. And both of them learnt that peace that is not threatened has no value, and thought that is not bought by pain no depth.[527]

Success

The success of her first novel meant that the magazines were now more than happy to accept her short stories for publication.

Duckworth gave me my first stepping stone and Nancy Pearn gave me my second, the beloved old Strand *magazine. Nancy Pearn, when I first knew her, was one third of a new literary agency that had just removed itself from the parent tree of Curtis Brown to start on its own as Pearn, Pollinger and Higham, and Nancy, believing in me on the strength of one insignificant book, took me out to lunch and suggested that I should join their slowly growing family of writers.*[528]

"Kate O'Brien and Stella Gibbons and you, I've had you from the cradle," Nancy Pearn told Elizabeth. (She and L.E. Pollinger had also, like Duckworth, been involved in the early career of D.H. Lawrence, in their Curtis Brown days.)

The first thing she did for me was to get me a commission to write short stories for the Strand *and David Higham settled that stone in place with a piece of good advice. "Write short stories for a living while you build up a reputation with your books. Don't, yet, look to books for a living."*[529]

Her agent's advice was sound, for they were to be an ongoing source of income for many years - her last book of stories would be published in 1971. As examples of both their value to her, and their unchanging popularity with the reading public, one of the early titles taken by *The Strand* in 1935, *A Shepherd and a Shepherdess* was published two years later in her first story collection *A Pedlar's Pack*, and then again in *White Wings* in 1952. And *The Well of the Star*, her delightful tale about a little shepherd boy visiting the stable at Bethlehem, started life in the 1941 collection *The Golden Skylark*, was printed as a hardback novella in its own right, abridged for an advent calendar as *David the Shepherd Boy*, and was still being reprinted in Christmas anthologies in the late Nineties and probably beyond. (Years later however, she self-mockingly told the members of the Romantic Novelists' Association that, at this period in her life she had written "dozens of short stories that were all dreadfully alike, all the same steamed cod but with different sauces – parsley, mayonnaise, chopped egg and onion – disguising the sameness.")[530]

To be working for *The Strand* was to be in illustrious company. In the last three decades or so they had published stories by, among others, H.G. Wells, Jerome K. Jerome, Arthur Conan Doyle, Joseph Conrad, D.H. Lawrence, P.G. Wodehouse, Aldous Huxley, E.M. Delafield and Arnold Bennett. Other magazines bought her work too: *The Passing Show, Good Housekeeping, Woman's Home Companion, Argosy*, and *Woman's Journal* were among the publications, both at home and abroad, that also featured her stories in the late 1930s. In fact, for the next thirty years or so her work would appear again and again in magazines throughout the world.

But plays remained my first love and during these years I had three more produced by Sunday night clubs… They none of them acted well and I realised that I had not sufficient knowledge of the stage to write a good play…[531] *they did not 'come over'. But all the work and disappointment were well worth it because they brought me, for a short while and to a minute degree, inside the theatre world.*[532]

One of these plays was *The Middle Window*, performed on Sunday 18th March 1934 at The Embassy Theatre in Hampstead, by students of the Embassy School of Acting. Its producer was the actress Eileen Thorndike, leader of the Embassy School and younger sister of Dame Sybil. The Thorndikes, incidentally, were also the daughters of a clergyman: their father was a Canon of Rochester Cathedral. Nine years older than Elizabeth, Eileen was one of the friends introduced by that brief entree into the theatre world, and according to Jessie Monroe Elizabeth was very fond of her. (Years later, after her move to Devon, and although by then very tied by her mother's incapacity, Elizabeth may still have been able to see her friend… for during the Second World War Miss Thorndike, now widowed with three daughters, ran a student repertory company whose plays were produced at a small theatre in Bideford. Paul Schofield was one of her students; as was the novelist Elizabeth Jane Howard.)

The Middle Window - the novel - was published a year after the Embassy Theatre production, in 1935. It was dedicated to Miss Thorndike with the explanatory comment that it was she who had "asked that this story, written originally as a play, be made into a novel."[533] Elizabeth later admitted that "it was not a very successful book, and is the one that I care for least myself."[534] Nonetheless, the critical comment shows a real recognition of its author's merits. "There is a talent here" said *The Daily Mail*, and *The Weekly Scotsman* found it "fascinatingly written" and

> Told...with a romantic pen which possesses a wonderful ability to create atmosphere and is not lacking in humour. We expect to hear much in the future of her growing appeal to the public.

"Wonderful sense of atmosphere..." "Keen observation..." "Written with rare charm..." "Some vivid descriptions of Scottish scenery..." The critics were definitely impressed.[535]

The book had, again, a contemporary theme. In the years between the two world wars there was a movement towards a return to rural simplicity, a search for some way to reverse the industrialised "progress" of the post-war world, which was now in Depression and mass unemployment. The Welsh clergyman-poet R.S. Thomas (fifteen of whose poems appear in Elizabeth's anthologies) recognised its appeal: he and his wife Elsi, whom he met in 1937, shared an "inner dissatisfaction" with modern society. They dreamed of breaking away, and going to live in a cottage "on water and a crust."[536] And the idea was not new of course. Yeats, inspired by Thoreau's *Walden*, had written *The Lake Isle of Innisfree* in 1890; and in the 1820s the English painter and poet Samuel Palmer and his friends, dubbed 'The Ancients' had been one of the first groups of artists to turn their back on the modern world. But it was now very much in revival and, yet again prevalent in Oxford, where the old university town and the lovely countryside around it were being slowly swallowed up by the expanding modern city. Bede Griffiths and his friends found themselves longing to live instead in harmony with nature and their first reaction was to flee to the countryside and buy a cottage. Here they planned to live very simply and to support themselves, as far as was possible, by their "own labour."[537]

Ian, the laird in *The Middle Window*, is a doctor who dreams of building Utopia in his Scottish glen, and "I work like a labourer to do it" he says. He tells Judy that

> Utopias are best built in isolation. In the filthy modern world you can't make a thing that's not at once smirched, but here in these glens loveliness can be ringed round and protected by the mountains."
>
> "That's the monastic idea," said Judy, "and I've always thought it rather selfish – a creeping away from life."
>
> "Then you have misunderstood it. The monastic ideal is a core of sanity in a loathsome world, a core of sanity that spreads... If you light a bonfire in a sheltered valley the protection makes such a huge blaze of it that those outside see the whole sky lit up."[538]

The book-of-the-play retains much of its theatricality - there is a lot of drama focused around the centre-stage "middle window" – and in one other sense it is quite different from her other novels: it features the parallel stories of a pair of reincarnated lovers. The four stages of their journey to reunion across the centuries - The Search, Individuality, Union, The Finding – have echoes of the mystical way again, and Ian is perhaps even more aware of life's contrasts than was Michelle; for by trying to build Utopia he is seeking to redeem the "loathsome world." These echoes and Ian's "monastic ideal" however, sit rather uneasily with a melodramatic plot that hinges on reincarnation.

We know that in her attempts to come to terms with world suffering the young Elizabeth had 'fallen in love with the doctrine of reincarnation,' and passages in *The Middle Window* bear witness to her deliberations on this theory.

> [Judith] was a religious woman. She believed in God and in the immortality of all that was worthwhile in life, including the spirit of man at its highest and best, but how the spirit of man lived on she did not pretend to know. She did not see how anyone could know. Perhaps it lived on only in what it had created, perhaps it was absorbed into the great flood of spirit that flowed through the world like blood through the veins of a man, perhaps it had some individual life of its own, coming or going according to the purposes of God, perhaps it did all these things... Who could tell?
>
> All day long she turned the pages of her Bible trying to find something that would give her some leading. "The souls of the righteous are in the hands of God." "Then shall the dust return to the earth as it was, and the spirit shall return unto God who gave it." "The resurrection from the dead." These three trumpet blasts sounded in her room, as

they had sounded down the ages, but they told her nothing definite, they only reiterated the fact of life without telling her the where and the how. And she wanted to know.[539]

And, of course, Elizabeth was withered when, seeking enlightenment from her father, he had dismissed the whole idea as utter nonsense. Perhaps this withering, along with the attempt to turn a theatrical drama into a novel, was to some extent responsible for her own assessment that *The Middle Window* was not a successful book.

For it does not seem to have been unsuccessful in terms of sales. Coward McCann had published it in America, and by 1960 Duckworth were printing their seventh UK impression. There was the Thomas Nelson edition in 1949; the French translation 'L'appel du passé,' the Hodder paperback in 1971, followed by their Coronet edition... etc.

Getting Away

Elizabeth, now an established novelist and short-story writer, had become a woman with her own income who could afford to travel. One restriction of her life so far had at last been lifted.

My good luck delighted my astonished family and opened for me many new doors. Until now my microscopic earnings had not enabled me to go off on my own for holidays; now that I could do that my mother encouraged me and was glad to have Nanny or one of her sisters to look after her while I was away.[540]

This is the first mention of Nanny, well over twenty years since she had been sent away from Ely to "love another mother and child." For how long was she away? Elizabeth does not say; and neither is there any joyful record of subsequent reunion. It seems safe to assume therefore – particularly in view of the close friendship between Nanny and Mrs. Goudge, and that comment of Elizabeth's: "She might visit us but she would never live with us again," that she did indeed visit, and they had kept in regular contact. Happily for both Elizabeth and her mother the bond was not broken, and Nanny was still a part of their lives.

Barton was my point of departure for what, for me was high adventure, for apart from one short visit to France I had never been anywhere except to the Island, to the seaside places nearest to Wells and Ely and to the cottage in the Cotswolds that was the aunts' home after they finally left the Island.[541]

Sadly there were only two Collenette aunts now for one of Ida's sisters had died, aged only 52, some years before this – pretty, dressy Aunt Emily, so clever with her needle, who had bravely taken the one-year old Elizabeth on her first trip to Guernsey, and shared her bedroom there with her little niece. She had given up her work to look after Adolphus in his old age and blindness; but *The Joy of the Snow* tells us that sadly she was the only one in whom the Collenette charm – "a sparkle like light on water" – was lacking, for she "had been born soon after the death of the elder son Arnold and her parents' grief had affected her with a pre-natal sadness… She was never happy."[542] She outlived her father by only half a dozen years or so.

Of the aunts' new home in England Elizabeth said, "Both Hélène and I loved this cottage, high up in the backwoods above Stroud."[543] She word-painted a lofty view of the Cotswolds as the setting for her short story, *A Shepherd and a Shepherdess* – echoing, as she did so, the Romantic vision of both Wordsworth and Ruskin: of houses built to be in harmony with the landscape; homes that, with the weathering-down of the years, would become one with the earth itself.

In front of her the ground fell steeply away into another valley, rising again to a further hill covered with beech trees. The valley and the slope below her were dotted with grey Cotswold cottages, the most delightful cottages in the world, each one apparently not built by man at all but a part of the earth itself. Each had its own garden, gay with spring flowers, and the smoke from the chimneys went straight up into the still air, as though the sun and the clouds of heaven and the fire and the smoke of earth were linked together by fine, tenuous cords.[544]

Elizabeth was now thirty-five years old but that short list of holiday destinations had been the extent of her travelling, she said. Not only this, but the family visits to the Channel Islands had of course come to an end… a 1946 article, *Magic Isles* says, "It is fifteen years since I last sailed away from St. Peter Port on a clear blue summer morning, light-hearted in the certainty that return would come speedily, and dismay and grief would have seized me had I known that it would not."[545] Now however, for a few years, travel would bring delight.

I longed…for high hills, and the first of my adventures was a walking holiday with a friend who lived in the Lake District. The Westmorland and Cumberland hills were the highest I had ever seen and being with them was utter joy… This kind of holiday was repeated again in the highlands of Scotland and in Skye.[546]

Her "utter joy" at being with the hills and mountains manifested itself in the descriptions of Scottish scenery, which *The Morning Post* had praised in *The Middle Window*.

There were no clouds now to hide the top of Judy's mountain; it was outlined in indigo and violet against a golden sky that melted through apricot and primrose yellow to deep blue overhead. Far up the sun's fingers just touched the bog myrtle and bracken to green flame. The wind had dropped now, and beyond the song of the birds and the sound of falling water Judy was conscious of a deep and heavenly silence…

She climbed and climbed, slipping and sliding on the slippery stones, clinging to the trunks of the rowan trees…

High up and facing east, the sun was gloriously warm on her face. There was no breath of wind, no sound at all but the sound of the burn and the delicious, heavenly tinkle of some sheep-bells. But the silence was charged with life… She felt it all around her, running through the visible world like an invisible flame and rising up inside her like a bubbling spring, different in each of its manifestations yet the same in its essence. Out of the silence and the loneliness there came to her a vivid sense of her own individuality… She did not feel dusty now, she felt washed, with her true colours showing; and she could have shouted for joy… She was becoming herself.[547]

When Judy visits Skye, she discovers "a rain-washed island where every leaf and blade of grass seemed sparkling." And here again she begins to climb.

Judy panted on and up, splashing in and out of bogs, sniffing the pungent scent of the bog myrtle and the earthy smell of the orange sphagnum moss that squelched under her feet. She did not care how wet she got. A queer ecstasy possessed her. She felt wild and a little light-headed and now and then she caught herself singing aloud. She did not look behind her, though she knew that the view behind must be one of the loveliest in the world, for she wanted to get to the top.[548]

Elizabeth's autobiography, too, has a definition of this new world of "mountain joy."

The sense of being lifted up into another world, enclosed in its own mystery and belonging to itself alone… The keen air is like wine and we are not our valley selves as we watch the cloud shadows passing along the flanks of the hills, and listen to the sound of falling streams and the crying of the curlews. The whisper of wind stirring the grasses has a distinct voice, insistent at the door of our hearing, and behind it all the vast silence and stillness of this world of the heights seems like the stillness and silence of eternity itself…[549] *the great silence that is always waiting behind the murmuring of these things.*[550]

But joy can turn to terror, and in *The Middle Window* Judy, like Elizabeth herself, hears a sudden frightening noise breaking the silence of the moor.

Before the moor ended she sat down again once more. The sun was out again now and was hot on her back. She was tired and the sound of the burn lulled her almost to sleep.

Suddenly she flung up her head, her eyes dilating with terror. There was a curious, crackling, thudding sound behind her, as though a galloping horseman cracked a whip as he rode at her to drive her away. She jumped to her feet and looked behind her, but there was nothing there, and no sound but the tarn.[551]

Elizabeth had not allowed the 'moor terror' to drive her away from the silence on the heights however, and she went on to discover the mountains of both North Wales and Norway, her continuing travels providing the background for yet more stories. In the fjords, for example, like the ladies in her short story *From Whence?* she must have seen "distant mountains the colour of grapes, tattered clouds clinging to their summits… White torrents foaming down the rocks, and in the far distance the great curve of a glacier dazzling and icy blue beneath the sun…" And then the "small farms beside the fjord, painted amber or egg-shell green, their gardens full of poppies and late roses and their hay crop spread over the fences to dry like tawny rugs."[552]

But of all the holidays of my life the most glorious was a…cruise which took my father, Marie and myself through the Mediterranean to Greece, and on to Constantinople, and home by way of Crete, Sicily and Corsica… We had the advantage that [then] the world was quieter and less populated than it is today. We were alone when we stood by the Lion Gate at Mycenae and saw the hills where the beacons were lit when Troy fell, and looked out over the plain of Argos shimmering in the heat.[553]

This landscape provided the background to *The Strength in the Stone*.

> *The thyme-scented hillside fell steeply away to the great plain of Argos stretching mightily to the far blue distance of the sea. Green and still and shimmering with afternoon heat was the plain of Argos, but the precipitate mountains that sprang from it were white where their great peaks touched the sky, for in April in Greece, though the valleys are green and teeming with new life, the feet of the gods upon Olympus still leave footprints in the snow...*

> *The meadows were full of flowers, scarlet anemone, purple vetch, blue hyacinth, pink asphodel, and...in the orchards about the whitewashed farms there were already golden globes among the green leaves of the lemon trees... At sunrise and sunset, far beyond the plain where the blue sea washed the coast, the rocky cliffs flushed rose-pink at the touch of the sun, so that the water in the shadows of them, where the rose was reflected in the blue, was at morning and evening the colour of purple wine. There was no lovelier land than this in all the world.*[554]

We were blest with perfect weather all the way. We saw the Acropolis honey-coloured against a cloudless blue sky and at Olympia the anemones were red as fire in the green grass. We approached Constantinople in a golden dawn and left it in a flaming sunset, with a school of dolphins playing and leaping around the ship as they escorted us out to sea. San Sophia was still in use as a mosque then and was not the echoing museum which I am told it is today. Holy old men sat there reading the Koran and it was warm with the atmosphere of prayer and gleaming with soft pale gold in the sunlight. Crete was flaming with marigolds and in Corsica I climbed a hill blue with wild lupins, and outside Syracuse there was a hill where wild mignonette smelt like paradise in the sun.[555]

Audrey could remember having occasional holidays with Elizabeth organised by the Girls' Diocesan Association - "*when she was able to, but she was very seldom able to get away on her own.*" And so for her now to be cruising to Greece represented a marked change in her life; her success as a writer had indeed opened new doors.

Her new career also involved at times travelling to London; for example on the memorable occasion when she was first taken out to lunch by her literary agent. And although, lifelong, Elizabeth never had any real love for the capital – as a child she "*was always physically ill*"[556] there as well as being terrified by its noise, and at the age of seventy-eight described it in a letter as "terrible London"[557] – it still did have that one great attraction: the theatre.

She already had plenty of opportunities to see plays in Oxford of course. In February 1933 for instance, Audrey wrote to a friend that she was dining with the Goudges in Tom Quad that evening, after which she and Elizabeth were to see the Oxford University Dramatic Society's production of *King John*. And on a summer night in 1936 they had supper at Audrey's before going on to a play at Keble College. Elizabeth herself recalled how in the early days she saved up her pin-money for visits to The Oxford Playhouse, which "was producing the plays of Ibsen and Shaw and Galsworthy week after week in the dingy little ex-museum in North Oxford that housed its young, great days."[558] But for this young woman who had so adored the theatre world, ever since that first Shakespeare at the Court Theatre, the London stage was sublime.

Occasionally I got to a London matinee to see even greater things. I lay awake all night after seeing the young John Gielgud's Hamlet; it was impossible to sleep after such an experience.[559]

Gielgud played his first Hamlet at the Old Vic theatre in 1930 when he was twenty-six. It was ground-breaking: the first time an actor under the age of forty had played Hamlet in the West End. He then opened in a new production under his own direction, at the New Theatre in 1934. Was it perhaps Gielgud's performance that she was remembering – both his acting and what Olivier called his *voice that wooed the world* - when she described David Eliot's Romeo in *The Herb of Grace*?

> *There was a moment of thrilled expectation... a gasp, and then silence. It was difficult to believe their good fortune. They were to see one of the most famous actors of their generation playing his most famous part... The familiar words floated out into the room like music. The incomparable beauty of the golden voice...the perfect co-ordination of voice and movement, that complete absorption of the artist in his art that gave to it a depth that suggested stillness even while he spoke and moved, the grace and beauty so quietly and unselfconsciously worn, the exciting sense of power held back – those marks of a great actor gave an illusion of perfection that lifted this figure above all human frailty.*[560]

All this theatre-going was in addition to the occasional excitement of seeing her own plays in performance. As well as *The Middle Window* there had been two further performances of *The Brontës of Haworth* - on 2nd and 5th June 1934 at the Taylor Institution, Oxford. (The performance benefited a local good cause, for a collection was taken for the Oxford Diocesan

Church Schools Appeal Fund.) In comparison, however, her everyday home life in Oxford seems to have remained largely uneventful. A diary kept by Mrs. Clark, Audrey's mother, in the Thirties records such mild pleasures as Elizabeth and Audrey visiting each other for tea, and on one occasion a joint visit to a village fete.

Nevertheless holidays and the thrill of the theatre were now able to transport her into another world: as did the fertile inner workings of the writer's Imagination.

Inner Vision

From the first, Elizabeth's novels were always a rather curious mixture - of everyday modern life; happy endings; characters wrestling with problems; a strong sense of place; and often, a thread of history impacting on succeeding generations. Add to these, an awareness of other worlds; a dash of myth, magic and fairytale; and increasingly, a powerful thread of her Christian faith holding the whole thing together, and she had a successful formula that struck a chord with readers young and old, around the world. Nevertheless the elements on that second list, allied to her invariable happy endings, would give some critics the ammunition to label her as a sugar-and-spice writer of romance – particularly when the fashion in novels and plays began to turn increasingly towards gritty realism. What those critics did not see however, was that her work was seeking to convey a truth consistent with her own inner vision: her awareness of what Dr. Alan McGlashan's book, *The Savage and Beautiful Country* called "another world than the everyday."[561]

Near the end of her life she wrote about this book to a friend, saying "I possess it and love it. When I was first reading it I was so excited I could hardly contain myself."[562] A practising psychiatrist who had also been drama critic for the *Observer*, McGlashan writes here about remembering and forgetting; about collective memory… and about an awareness of something beneath the surface appearance of life; something that is lost in concentration on the present alone, or on the merely empirical and pragmatic. He calls it the "translucent quality in all things." If we once catch - even momentarily, he says - this "startled glimpse of another level of being" then our view and our understanding of the world is transformed; our values changed. This is the level one finds in the Parables, he believes; or in the "mysterious golden light" shining through myth and fairytale: it is the level of the kingdom of heaven that St. Luke's Gospel tells us is "within."[563]

A unique feature of Elizabeth Goudge's romantic novels, surely, is that that they give the reader just such a glimpse.

❇

As to that mysterious light shining through the fairytales and ancient myth… Resident in Oxford at that time was an author who became world-famous for his depiction of other worlds, and whose work also contained a golden mixture of myth, magic, fairytale and faith. J.R.R. Tolkien had taken up his appointment as Professor of Anglo-Saxon in 1925, two years after the Goudges moved to Christ Church, and it is interesting to look at his attitude to the power of the Imagination. He believed that anything that was created by the mind had its own truth and reality, and he expounded this theory in discussion with C.S. Lewis, in September 1931. Humphrey Carpenter explains that:

> Lewis had never underestimated the power of myth. Far from it…but he still did not *believe* in the myths that delighted him. Beautiful and moving though such stories might be, they were (he said) ultimately untrue. As he expressed it to Tolkien, myths are 'lies and therefore worthless, even though breathed through silver.'
>
> *No*, said Tolkien. *They are not lies…*
> Man is not ultimately a liar. He may pervert his thoughts into lies, but he comes from God, and it is from God that he draws his ultimate ideals…Therefore, Tolkien continued, not merely the abstract thoughts of man *but also his imaginative inventions* must originate with God, and must in consequence reflect something of eternal truth. In making a myth…and peopling the world with elves and dragons and goblins, a storyteller, or 'sub-creator' as Tolkien liked to call such a person, is actually fulfilling God's purpose, and reflecting a splintered fragment of the true light…
>
> Pagan myths were, in fact, God expressing himself through the mind of poets and using the images of their 'mythopoeia' to express fragments of His eternal truth.[564]

Oxford and Barton

Henrietta, making her first appearance in Elizabeth's next novel, *A City of Bells* seems almost to echo that private conversation of Tolkien's on the products of the imagination, and of the huge responsibility of the story-teller to reflect the true light:

> *Surely that story she had imagined was a real thing? If you created a story with your mind surely it was just as much there as a piece of needlework that you had created with your fingers? You could not see it with your bodily eyes, that was all...*
> *Henrietta realized how the invisible world must be saturated with the stories that men tell both in their minds and by their lives. They must be everywhere, these stories, twisting together, penetrating existence like air breathed into the lungs, and how terrible, how awful thought Henrietta, if the air breathed should be foul.*[565]

Twenty years later, in *The White Witch* Froniga makes a similar comment on the powerful effect of individual human thoughts and imaginings.

> *How little did they know! If they could for one moment close the eyes of their bodies and see with their other eyes, what then? They would see their thoughts alive, passing out from them to stifle or refresh the multitude of human spirits about them, spirits of those whom the world calls living and of those whom the world calls dead, some of them delicate and young and harmed so easily.*[566]

Though not set in the seventeenth century like *The White Witch*, her final children's novel (*Linnets and Valerians*) also features characters who attempt to influence the lives of others through spells and witchcraft. Nan Linnet asks her clergyman uncle for his opinion on these powers, and is given the same message about the power of human thought... but not before receiving a withering setdown, worthy of Canon Goudge himself, perhaps!

> '*Do you believe that witches and warlocks, the black ones and the white ones, can really harm people or help people with their spells?*'
> '*I do not,' said Uncle Ambrose forcibly. 'And I trust that Ezra has not been filling your head with any of his nonsense...*"

She cannot help pointing out that like superstitious old Ezra, her uncle always bows to his bees.

Uncle Ambrose looked at her and then suddenly threw back his head and laughed. 'Yes, Nan, I do. I have the greatest respect for bees.' He paused and then said very seriously, 'And I am very deeply aware of the mystery of things.'

'Do you think Emma Cobley could have harmed Lady Alicia and her husband?' asked Nan.

'Not by her spells, which are nonsense,' said Uncle Ambrose, 'but possibly the thoughts of an unloving mind can have power to do harm if they are not confronted by a corresponding power for good.'[567]

Elizabeth was very much aware of the power of human thought, and of how it could negatively affect oneself too; both in the depression that affected her and her father; and as a possible explanation for the visitations of the Ely ghost who years ago had appeared to follow her from room to room:

Possibly he did not follow me. The first 'seeing' was perhaps a genuine one but the others may have been mere hallucinations caused by my fear and revulsion; for the power of thought is so terrible that there is no doubt we can attract to us what we deeply fear.[568]

But as she knew so well, the imagination is not just about darkness: as Tolkien said, it can also reflect a splintered fragment of the true light. When she was a child at school she had won two book prizes – "for nothing more exciting than good behaviour" she says modestly - and she "loved them both."[569] In one of them, Robert Bridges' *The Spirit of Man*, she would have found John Keats' statement that "the Imagination may be compared to Adam's dream - he awoke and found it truth." Half a century later, writing *The Scent of Water* in her early sixties, she made her own pronouncement on the power of the Imagination in the journey of faith.

He...believed implicitly in his vision. When it was suggested to him that he had imagined what he saw, he said, dream or vision, what did it matter? Whichever it was, his God had by its means lifted him out of his despair.[570]

A City of Bells

A City of Bells, her third novel, was published in April 1936. *The Methodist Recorder* said it was one of "those rare novels whose merits deserve announcing to the world with a trumpet voice." Their critic found the book to be "so perfectly charming that, as one lingers over its pages, the thought that it will have to end is hateful."[571]

Many of her British readers at least must have been in need of a little charm at that time, for 1936 was not the happiest of years. It began with King George V's death in January, and ended in December with his son Edward VIII's abdication – the dénouement of what Audrey's mother described in her diary as the awful tension felt throughout the British Empire on account of the King and his "paramour." This crisis alone would be sufficient to create feelings of instability within society – although it was assuaged by the immediate accession of his younger brother Albert, as George VI - but even greater was the worldwide unrest and suffering caused by the appalling unemployment of the Great Depression.

Whilst their own material security was not under threat of course, the Goudge household would have been very aware of the hardship suffered by the unemployed. At the beginning of his ministry, from 1890 to 1894, Dr. Goudge had served as a curate at St. Mark's Church, Leicester, where "his sister joined him and they made a home together. It was a big working-class parish, with plenty to do, and they both worked indefatigably, my father's gentleness endearing him then, as always, to all the sick and the old."[572] Now, in October 1936, prominent in the Christian Socialist movement, the church served as one of the stopping points for the marchers of the Jarrow Crusade; still with a hundred miles to walk before presenting to Parliament their petition against unemployment in the North East.

❋

A City of Bells is dedicated to M.L.O.C. These were the shared initials of her late Guernsey grandmother Marie-Louise Ozanne Collenette, and her namesake daughter - Elizabeth's aunt Marie, whom *The Joy of the Snow* describes as "the dearest of the aunts."[573] In the eyes of both Elizabeth and her father she was "a wonderful person."[574] She it was who gave them their beloved dog Brownie, and who accompanied Elizabeth and her father on the cruise to Greece: the most glorious holiday of her life.

This was the first book to be written about the safe, sheltered world of her childhood in Wells, that "city so hidden...that it seemed to have dropped out of the world."[575]

> *No words can describe what Henrietta felt about Torminster... If this was not Paradise she would have liked to be told what was. The dreaming city, the west front of the cathedral with the rows of kings and queens and saints, the wooded Tor, the gardens full of flowers, the singing birds and chiming bells, the old house with its carved angels, the humming High Street and the holy well, these things did not belong to the world as Henrietta had hitherto known it...and she felt like one born anew on a different planet.*[576]

It is indeed a perfectly charming book, containing all the elements of what was to become Elizabeth's trademark style. Set in an old and beautiful city built around a magnificent cathedral, it features delightful children and animals, humour, lovable eccentrics, kindly clergyman of all shapes and sizes, and a happy ending. In the depression of the Thirties, it was a piece of imaginative escapism that presented a kind of dream-world.

But the book was not only charming and other-worldly; the critic of *The Sketch* was astute enough to see that it had something else:

> Miss Goudge is a serious as well as an original novelist...
> The two strains of realism and romance are very successfully blended in *A City of Bells*.[577]

The strain of realism comes in the lives of the two male protagonists. The hero Jocelyn, with the legacy of a lame leg from the Boer war, is paying a visit to his grandparents at a time when he has no profession and, it seems, no future.

> *"Have you everything you want?" [enquired Grandfather.]*
> *"Everything but peace of mind," said Jocelyn unexpectedly..." How can a man be peaceful when he has no future?"*

> *"Don't talk nonsense," said Grandfather almost sharply. "We've all a future. You don't know in what direction yours lies, that's all, and you've not the patience to wait and see which way the wind blows."*
> *"The wind?" asked Jocelyn.*

Oxford and Barton

> *"Our destiny is like a wind blowing,"* said Grandfather. *"It carries us along. But now and again the wind seems to drop. We don't know what to do next. Then it may be that a blade of grass growing in the road beside us bends slightly. It is a tiny movement, slight as a whim, but enough to show us which way to take..."*[578]

He advises Jocelyn, while he is waiting for the sign pointing to his future, to "Stay here and do nothing...

> *Stay a year if you like. What does it matter? It's often necessary in life to do nothing, but so few people do it nicely. And as for peace, there's plenty of it in this house and in this town. They are so weighted with age that they have, as it were, fallen below the surface of time, like a buried city below the sea… Fall with them."*[579]

But for another young man, the poet Ferranti, it is a fall into darkness.

> *"I cannot get back…" Now he wanted to get back to the world he had left, but he couldn't. He wanted to get back madly, desperately, but he couldn't… A man who has lived utterly alone for a long time ceases to be normal. A solitary who has cut himself off from human contact comes to have a terror of his fellow humans. A coward who has abandoned all responsibility is afraid to shoulder it again. A failure cannot trust to success. A sufferer who has been broken by life dare not be friends with it again…*
>
> *It was only his own mind that kept him back but a man's mind can be his greatest friend or his greatest enemy, according as it serves or binds his will, and his was his enemy. Its terrors controlled him. He was bound hand and foot by his own weakness. It was no use. He was as good as dead. "I cannot get back."*[580]

One wonders how much of Ferranti's desperation and Jocelyn's lack of inner peace – his inability to see any future for himself - might have been a mirror of Elizabeth's own feelings. Grandfather tells Jocelyn that "peace is as essential to mental health…as light to human life"[581] – and this is something that Elizabeth may well have been discovering for herself. On top of the troubled times in which she was living, we know that around this time the stresses of her own life were intensifying.

It seemed to my father and to me that some doom hung over my mother because she could not stop being ill… During the last years at Oxford and Barton she had one severe illness and two bad operations and from all three she nearly died. The last operation was on her spine, for at last the injury to her back had been discovered, not by a doctor but by our district nurse at Barton, and an Oxford surgeon operated and removed the coccyx. But the years of neglect had done such damage, and she suffered so much for so long after the operation, that it was only just worthwhile. She was reviving at last when my father was for a time devastated by an operation, and then the same thing happened to me.[582]

This seems to have been just over a year after *A City of Bells* came out, for according to Mrs. Clarke's diary, it was in June 1937 that Audrey went down to Barton and stayed in the Goudges' bungalow to cheer 'Eliz' who was in a Home after her operation. And 1937 was the only year of the Thirties, since *Island Magic* when there was no novel published, only a collection of short stories.

There must have been at least a ray of joy for her in the spring though, with the production of yet another of her plays: *Joy Will Come Back* [published as *Fanny Burney*] based on the life of the eighteenth century author. There were two performances at The Arts Theatre, London: Sunday 21st March at 8.15 and a matinee on the following day. Like *Island Magic* and *The Middle Window*, the play has something to say about the need to achieve unity between two worlds. This is Fanny in dialogue with Dr. Johnson:

> JOHNSON. *Take care, Fanny! Because you have written a popular book you will be flattered, feted, ornamented, fed. They will build round your spirit that house of pleasure that is nothing but a prison, and if you are not careful the walls of it will shut you out from life!*
> FANNY. *Oh la! Life?*
> JOHNSON. *[Vehemently] Real life. [Softly] The life that brings back joy again and again… It is a state of union… There is in you and all things that are a something that has no name – call it beauty, call it a flame, call it what you will – and you will live only when the beauty that is in you is in union with all other beauty. When you achieve that union you achieve joy.*
> FANNY. *Surely that kind of life is impossible for the likes of me?*
> JOHNSON. *[Vehemently] It is not! Only shake yourself free of the things that clog and harden, the brutalities and the trivialities of life. Train your perceptions till your spirit is as sensitive to beauty as is a harp string to the plucking fingers. Go out to meet life and its beauty, face it, embrace it, suffer it. Give yourself to the last nerve and the last thought to all that is lovely, whether it be in man or bird or flower or the sky at midnight. Then you will know joy. Then you will live.*

Oxford and Barton

> FANNY. *And suffer. The sensitive suffer.*
> JOHNSON. *The reaction from ecstasy is inevitable. You cannot escape the swinging pendulum but if you are wise you will accept it most gladly as your fate. From the harsh striking of stone on tinder a flame is born; may not the clashing of man and his fate create a soul?*
> FANNY. *Do you believe that it does? A flame that never goes out?*
> JOHNSON. *I have chosen to live my life in the belief that it does.*[583]

The published book of short stories – her first - was *A Pedlar's Pack*. These too were devoted to beauty - and again, what impressed the critic of *The Christian Science Monitor* was that they were full of the joy of living. Each story, "like a different lyric" expressed her "irrepressible gaiety [and] devotion to beauty in all its aspects, tangible or intangible… her wide-eyed wonder in front of the profusion of gifts life offers to those who are receptive."[584]

Irrepressible gaiety - and yet her life was moving to crisis point.

Breakdown

She records that after "the little succession of family disasters"- amongst which she lists her own operation:

> *I fell headlong into what is called a nervous breakdown, a state which as all its victims know can be terrifying. We all feel frightened because we feel that the division between nervous and mental illness is so thin that the thing we all dread more than anything else seems only just round the next corner of the mind… King Lear prays,*
>
>> *O, let me not be mad, not mad, sweet heaven!*
>> *Keep me in temper: I would not be mad!*
>
> *We all feel the same.*[585]

Some twenty-five years after these family disasters she published *The Scent of Water*, a novel about a woman who suffers from mental illness. Cousin Mary Lindsay's diary records,

> *It has happened and I am home again…*

All the crashing ruin, the falling and tumbling, are over, but the dust is horrible. They say it won't happen to me again but I expect they only say it to comfort me. But I must think it won't. I must be like the people who plant gardens and build houses all over again where the earthquake has been.[586]

The imagery of collapse and ruin has echoes of Cardinal Newman's *Dream of Gerontius*, which Edward Elgar had set to music in the year Elizabeth was born: "That sense of ruin, which is worse than pain / That masterful negation and collapse / of all that makes me man."[587] Such an allusion could suggest that Elizabeth's own breakdown had been, at least in part, a spiritual crisis, and indeed she does tell us in *The Joy of the Snow* that "When my mother suffered I was miserable and my faith in God's love was sorely tried. When I suffered myself it was nearly shattered."[588] She was certainly able to write very movingly – in echoes of her grandfather's despairing words at the end of his life - about an experience of loss of faith in *The Dean's Watch*.

She had not believed that such a thing could happen to her. Through the years her faith had grown so strong that she had not believed that she could lose it. The living light that had made love possible had seemed too glorious ever to go out, yet now it had gone and left her in darkness and the loneliness of life without love was to her a horror quite indescribable. It had a stifling nightmare quality. A cold darkness, she thought, would have been easier to bear, but this hot thick darkness brought one near to the breaking of the mind. It had been for nothing, she thought. It was not true, it had been for nothing.[589]

And her friend in later life, Sister Raphael Mary said: "I think Miss Montague is herself in *The Dean's Watch* isn't she? That experience of spiritual darkness described is surely first-hand."[590]

As early as 1935 in *The Middle Window* she had written,

She had not known that misery could be like this. It overwhelmed her so utterly that everything went down before it. She had no faith left and no hope.[591]

The collapse into nervous breakdown was partly a thing of temperament. Having admitted to suffering from the depression that was "the skeleton in our family cupboard"[592] she remarks that to be able to find comedy in the things that happen to us requires an "ability not to take oneself too seriously" - a strength which at this stage in life, she says, she did not have. She describes her depressed self as "mounded up with self-pity and glooming over my fate."[593] But when one looks at her life, there are several possible causes of breakdown above and beyond the inherited tendency to depression. Indeed one could allow this woman a certain amount of self-pity and glooming. Unlike today's thirty-somethings, she probably considered herself by this time to be already middle-aged. She was seventy-four when she published *The Joy of the Snow*, and referred to herself then as having already exceeded the human life-expectation of three score years and ten – "the Bible thinks you have about had it by then" she says wryly.[594] She was thirty-five, exactly half-way through the biblical life-span, when she was writing *A City of Bells*. Its protagonist Gabriel Ferranti, she says,

> *had deep lines scored across his forehead and round his mouth and somehow, for a brief moment, they made [Henrietta] feel sad. She did not know that the man in front of her was living through that difficult moment when the scarred and dying beauty of youth is putting up its last fight before the approach of age, and so she did not know why she felt sad.*[595]

It seems likely, then, that Elizabeth felt her own youth was putting up its last fight. And yet she was still living as a dutiful daughter in her parents' home. Her next novel, *Towers in the Mist*, was to be about the young girl, Joyeuce, whose motherless state forces her to take on the duties of mistress of her father's house. It is a role which in many ways she does not relish.

> *She was a romantic to whom, as yet, the details of practical living brought no joy… She did her duty as housewife with thoroughness, a sense of duty having been whipped into her from babyhood up, but she did not think that doing one's duty was very enjoyable. The life she wanted seemed always to elude her, to be around her and in front of her and above her, but never quite within her reach. She did not quite know what it was that she wanted, she only knew that it was not what she had…*

> *She stood in her house, surrounded by a hundred irksome problems and duties, and she looked out at a loveliness that she could see but could not grasp.… Yet if she left the house and went outside, treading the green grass with her feet and touching the silvery hawthorn with her hands, her worries would go with her, making the grass wet and cold and setting thorns among the flowers…*

Would life always be like that, she wondered? ...Did one go on and on like that, chasing a will-o'-the-wisp until you and he went down together into the darkness of death?... She wanted something nice now.[596]

Later books have characters on both sides of the fence however. Margary in *The Rosemary Tree* is "one of those children who cannot detach themselves from their parents and the shelter of their home. Had she been a fledgling sparrow it would have taken the united efforts of both parents to heave her over the side of the nest" because of her "terror of all that existed beyond her home."[597] Whereas Cousin Mary in *The Scent of Water*, battling with periods of mental illness, longs for the freedom of independence.

I'd like to live in the deep country with my dear Jenny Kennedy... not with Father and Mother and their anxious looks, wondering what next. Jenny doesn't wonder what next, she just loves me and takes what comes.[598]

Coincidentally, when Virginia Woolf's letters began to be published in 1975, they revealed a similar reaction to depression in a 1904 letter to Violet Dickinson:

...the only place I can be quiet and free is in my home, with Nessa: she understands my moods, and lets me alone in them...[599]

Cousin Mary would like to get away from "Father and Mother with their anxious looks." Elizabeth says that her father was a great help to her at this hard time of her life, but it is difficult to gauge how much sympathy her mother might have had for the symptoms of breakdown. On the one hand, Elizabeth said Ida had "the telepathic knowledge of the spiritual needs of others,"[600] but on the other hand she also had her own, physical, pains to deal with. Remembering that Peronelle in *Island Magic* is "my mother as I imagined her"...

Michelle and Jacqueline were always suffering from mysterious griefs that Peronelle could not understand... What there was for anyone to be unhappy about if they hadn't got a pain Peronelle simply could not understand...
Michelle, she supposed, had a pain in her soul. But why? Peronelle never had pains in her soul. They were to her wholly incomprehensible and rather silly.[601]

If this was her mother's attitude however, then Elizabeth knew the value of such astringency. She had recently written this scene in *A City of Bells*, where Grandmother's asperity lifts Henrietta and Grandfather out of their melancholy, as they pick the last flowers of autumn to decorate the cathedral.

> *The Japanese anemones, folded and hanging their heads after a touch of frost, were fairy lanterns of pearl and lilac that might at any moment vanish, and the scarlet leaves of the Virginia-creeper fell at a touch like dead butterflies.*
> *"They'll all come to pieces when we put them on the graves," mourned Henrietta...*
> *"Never mind," said Grandfather, "the fallen petals are as precious in God's sight as the dust of His dead." He spoke sadly for he was always depressed by the disintegration of autumn.*
>
> *"Now don't be morbid, Theobald," said Grandmother, issuing out of the front door in her goloshes. "And don't stand about on that wet grass in those shoes. You've no more sense than a child of two... Here's Bates with the chrysanthemums... Give them to Mrs. Elphinstone with my compliments, Theobald, and if she wants any more she can have them, but you must fetch them, mind. I won't have her running about in my garden without a with-your-leave or a by-your-leave, wife of the senior Canon though she may be."*
>
> *Bates came out from behind the mulberry-tree with a huge bunch of yellow and red chrysanthemums and their colour and sturdiness, together with Grandmother's strong-minded remarks, were somehow exhilarating in this dreamlike, vanishing autumn world.*[602]

On the plus side of life Elizabeth was at last pursuing her chosen career, but writing can be a lonely occupation and this, coupled with the peculiar constraints of her family's life, may have meant that at times she was more solitary than was good for her. Audrey felt that

> The kind of life she lived wasn't very... I was going to say not very *sociable*, because most of us had friends one used to be able to drop in and see without an appointment, but you see her kind of home meant that was rather ruled out, which was rather a pity. Because you see it wouldn't have been at all acceptable in the kind of life she lived – because of the position her father had. I think she would have welcomed

the odd dropper-in if it had been possible. No, we all felt that one had to have an appointment.

Her shyness, too, must have been a barrier, as it was for Margary in *The Rosemary Tree*:

> *She was one of those whose fear and reserve would make it hard for her to have the normal happy traffic with her fellow human beings.*[603]

With her father's high-profile job, and her mother's high-profile illness - a mother whom, ill or well, she described as "the Queen Bee of our hive"[604] - there may perhaps have been little room for this shy woman's own self-esteem to put out roots and flourish. We know that she considered herself to be a very poor substitute for her mother when it came to running the home, and she can only have been further humbled by the awe in which she held her beloved father – not only so far ahead of her on the road of faith but also, she felt, in a very different league as an author.

> *My father was a theologian, and his books were works of scholarship. I had written only four books before he died and though paternity demanded of him that he should read them he found the first three very hard going indeed, but though I begged him not to waste his time he persevered, taking a chapter a day with determined patience. A fourth, a book about sixteenth century Oxford [Towers in the Mist] he liked better, because he was interested to see to what use I had put the historical books he had borrowed for me from the Christ Church library...*
>
> *"You have a wonderful gift," he said, but before my head had time to swell, he went on, "you can make a very little knowledge go such a long way."*[605]

To put this comment on record in *The Joy of the Snow* is typical of her self-deprecating humour; but who knows if perhaps a very little head-swelling might not have gone a long way towards counteracting the shyness and stammering of this middle-aged woman. And the irony of her comparison is that - although not written as works of theological scholarship - her best-selling books, and through them her *faith*, reached a vast worldwide audience. A random check of an Internet bookseller reveals today just over a hundred of her father's books for sale – and four and a half thousand of hers.

❋

For Elizabeth and her contemporaries generally, there may well have been far less of a battle with head-swelling, than with low self-esteem. As they grew to womanhood, they had been dismissed as a superfluous generation, for no other reason than that, thanks to the war, they would not marry. Lord Northcliffe, the proprietor of the *Daily Mail,* had lumped them together as "Britain's problem of two million superfluous women."[606] Marriage was so much the normal goal of a girl's life in those early days, that to have so many single women in society was a *problem*, worthy of discussion in the newspapers. It was even a joke... Currently the *Strand Magazine* was contributing to Elizabeth's income by publishing her short stories; but back then, in 1923, it had carried a cartoon of a lone man with an expression of terror on his face, fleeing at full pelt from a great horde of frantic, pursuing females.[607]

Childlessness

She had brooded so much this last year on the child she had not got...[608]
The Middle Window

Whether or not the "superfluous" women of that generation were so desperate for a man in their lives, they did have to come to terms with the knowledge that they would never have children. This was a painful deprivation indeed for Elizabeth, and one that would likely have become even harder to bear at this time in her life, as the finality of mid-life approached and the door closed for ever on all hope of motherhood. "You have to be fairly old," she said, "before you can recognise and deeply prize the blessings of a single life, for up to that point the deprivation of childlessness is hard to bear."[609] Even for a successful author like herself; or like Fanny Burney in her eponymous play.

> SUSAN. *To my way of thinking 'tis you who live the most fully of us two.*
> FANNY. *Susan, you have children.*
> SUSAN. *You have your books, the children of your mind.*
> FANNY. *Sister, do you think the children of her mind ever make up to a woman for the lack of the children of her body?*[610]

In *The Joy of the Snow* she says of Mrs. Kennion, the bishop's wife at Wells, that perhaps "she loved children in general with that painful love of a childless woman."[611] But in a later chapter she adds: "yet for the childless woman there is no lack of children in the world to love, even if they are not her own,"[612] and this is Froniga's experience, in *The White Witch*.

> *Sometimes at home, looking out from a window of her cottage, she would see a flock of little birds fly out of a bush, as though they were leaves blown by a sudden gale, and drift down upon the thistle seeds lying on the grass in the field. They had been invisible in the bush, and upon the grass they were almost invisible too, until they all flew up again and returned to their bush. In some such magical way, when Froniga came, the gypsy children were suddenly all around her, as though the wind had blown them. She would hear their voices calling like birds in a wood, and see the tall grasses bend and a shimmer of colour along the hedge. Then she would hold out her arms and presently the littlest one would be on her lap, and her arms would encircle two more, and the rest would be strewn over the grass about her, their bright eyes fixed on her face and their fingers pointing to the basket. Then she would open the basket and give them the apples and comfits she had brought them, and they would crowd round her munching, and chattering softly in their own language, just as the birds did, and her heart would be so shaken by maternal passion that if she could she would have fled with them all back to the cottage and hidden them there, behind the ramparts of the sweetbriar hedges. They would have been with her for ever and there would have been no waking from the dream.*
>
> *Would she dream today? Would she once more be the mother of many children? ... She held out her arms and opened her eyes wide, and there they were again. The littlest was in her lap, its thumb in its mouth, its bright beady eyes peering up at her through a thatch of matted hair, and the rest had pressed in as near as they could get. "Rawni! Rawni!" they cried. "Open the basket quick!"*
>
> *She opened her basket and gave them apples, heart-shaped comfits of sugar and rose-water, candied rose-petals and violets and red candied cherries. They opened their mouths like young birds and she rejoiced in them as she fed them... There was about them, somehow, an immortal quality that matched her own immortal longings. In the presence of these children she believed that somehow, somewhere, she would yet be a mother.*[613]

One of the daughters of Elizabeth's cousin Margaret remembered that "she had a great empathy with children, who took to her at once."

> A visit to have tea with Cousin Elizabeth was an eagerly awaited treat, not least for the fine china and wafer-thin sandwiches which they felt went with the grace and charm of her personality. She loved to talk to the children and took a great interest in their lives. She understood them very well, realising that small children seldom like to be kissed by elderly relatives! She would blow them a kiss, saying CYK – consider yourself kissed.[614]

There is evidence for this in one of her early stories, *Little Island Set in a Silver Sea*...

> *Thomas' hair grew quite straight on the nape of his neck, but Benjamin's curled into a little twisty point like a drake's tail. This, of course, was unfortunate for him, because every woman who caught sight of it immediately seized him and kissed him on the place where it met his soft brown flesh. And once they had taken hold of him they usually held on, because Benjamin was nice to hold...*
>
> *He did not, of course, care for these endearments, but no attention was paid to his remark of, "Pleathe, I don't like being kithed," because it was not understood.*[615]

She must have well understood how to communicate with children too. As Henrietta observes in *Sister of the Angels,*

> *Here was one of those sensible grown-ups who was going to treat her as an equal, just as Grandfather and Ferranti did, and not talk down to her as though not having lived so very long in this world made her somehow an inferior being to himself. Henrietta never could see that being grown-up was anything to boast about. One didn't grow oneself, adding to one's inches by one's own skill. God grew one.*[616]

Even love and empathy for other people's children, however, could be a painful thing. As she said in her early forties, writing of Miss Brown in *The Castle on the Hill*:

The quick painful love of a woman who has never borne a son, but who if she had would have had him just like this, went out from her to Stephen. She was going to be happy in this place, but she was going to suffer too.[617]

Lost Love

Of course, women who did not marry were not necessarily women who had never known love, and her friend Freda Green said of Elizabeth, "I understood there was a man in her life that she loved." Audrey too, said:

> Naturally we touched on our emotional involvements with men, but as I always promised to treat such topics in strict confidence I cannot say more... One was sworn to secrecy; that's the trouble. It was an awfully sad story, but I really wouldn't feel I could tell you about it.

A secret it may have been, but over the years Elizabeth created several fictional women who experienced the pain of love relinquished, unrequited, unfulfilled. In *A City of Bells* she had described Felicity's awakening awareness both of the need for love, and the pain of its absence:

> *His look had thrilled her and comforted the lonely place that cries out for help deep inside every human being. Until that moment she had hardly realized that the place existed, but the sudden touch of healing applied to the ache and then withdrawn again had woken her up to awareness... Inside her there was a little room and it was empty and cold.*[618]

Felicity's love is joyfully reciprocated by Jocelyn; but in the same book the poet Ferranti - even though it is his work, not love, that is the cause - is driven to talk of suicide by the anguish of rejection.

> *At rock bottom living is merely a giving of personality in one form or another. If no one wants what you have to give you might as well hang yourself and have done with it.*[619]

Sally in *The Herb of Grace* feels helpless at the prospect of what seems, at that moment, to be a one-sided love.

> *That pang of recognition…had been like a push in the back, saying, "There you are, that's what you were made for, hand yourself over and be quick about it." But you couldn't hand yourself over if you weren't taken.*[620]

If you weren't taken… Jessie Monroe gave away no details, but spoke briefly about one young man in Elizabeth's life: "I don't know if they were engaged or not, but he'd gone to her father and said, I can't go through with it, so that was that."

Very early in her career, Elizabeth had written this rejection scene between Emily Brontë and her father's curate, the Reverend William Weightman.

> EMILY. *Why have you ceased to care for me?*
> WEIGHTMAN. *I have not ceased to care for you, I shall always care for you, but I don't want to marry you…*
> EMILY. *Why don't you want me for your wife? Am I so unpleasant? I want to know the truth about myself…*

He explains what he sees as their incompatibility, and then there is a pause during which Emily holds out her hand to him and "Looking at him steadily, knowing quite well that she will never see him again" says: 'Goodbye, and thank you.'

> WEIGHTMAN. *[Uncomfortably] You've nothing on earth to thank me for. Very much the reverse. If you said you hated me it would be more to the purpose. Good-bye, Emily, and good luck to you…*
> *[Charlotte and Anne come back and stand tentatively by the door, almost afraid to speak]*
> CHARLOTTE. *Emily? …He's gone. Did he – [she pauses]*
> EMILY. *[Defiantly] Pick me up again? No, of course he didn't. He found a flaw in me and threw me away…*
> *[With sudden desperation] What do you do, Charlotte, when you have battered with clenched fists on the doors of Paradise and they have let you in to a dark empty attic?*
> CHARLOTTE. *[Briskly, she knows better than to sympathise with Emily] You grope your way through till you find a door out on the other side, of course.*[621]

Charlotte, with her refusal to sympathise and brisk astringency, sounds rather like Grandmother in *A City of Bells*. Yet her matter-of-fact solution to the problem is easier said than done, as Nadine tells Lucilla in *The Bird in the Tree*:

> *"You say you have proved that what I am setting myself to do can be done... Yet I'm scared, for it really is rather frightening to be so unhappy. I don't know how I'll get through."*[622]

For much of her career, Elizabeth continually put into words the pain of lost love. In *The Middle Window* there is Judith, after her husband's death:

> *And then it began. She had not known that misery could be like this. It overwhelmed her so utterly that everything went down before it. She had no faith left and no hope... She undressed and climbed into the four-poster, lying flat on her back with her arms outstretched. But she could not go to sleep... She did not know that misery could be like this.*[623]

And in *The Bird in the Tree*, after Nadine has come to realise that she must renounce David:

> *She was alone in her darkening room, lying on her face on her bed ... Her whole world seemed tumbling in ruins about her.*
> *One o'clock struck. The hour of a new beginning. She turned over and lay on her back staring at the ceiling. In the faint light of the guttering candles she looked old and haggard. It had happened. Once again... her world had crumbled. She was not going to marry David. Her youth, together with her desperate striving to prolong it, had vanished. Her self-seeking, born of her youthful longing for joy, had gone too. Stripped of it all she lay looking desperately into the empty void ahead, while the candles guttered and went out.*
> *Two o'clock struck. There seemed nothing in that void ahead. Nothing but a dark emptiness.*[624]

Froniga too, in *The White Witch* takes the decision to end her unconsummated relationship with the recusant priest, Yoben, thus setting him free:

> *She...got into the big four-poster bed. Unconsciously she pulled herself into the far corner of it, cowering away from the moonlight like a whipped dog. She lay with her knees drawn up, as though she were in pain, motionless for an hour or more. When she began to weep at last the sobs seemed tearing her in pieces like hands tearing a rotten*

> sheet. The emptiness within her and all round her was appalling. She had said once to Yoben, in her ignorance and foolishness, that there are more ways than one of consummating love, and the hardest way can be the best. But she had not known it was like this. There was nothing grand or inspiring about renunciation. It was just all the years of your life stretching ahead in a long grey dreary emptiness. There was no comfort anywhere.[625]

❋

Twenty years after Emily's rejection in *The Brontës of Haworth* however, we find a rather different account of a jilted woman. Daphne in *The Rosemary Tree* confesses to Harriet that years ago she had received a note from her then fiancé on the night before their wedding: "It was carelessly scrawled and it just said, 'I'm sorry, Daphne, but I can't do it.'"

"Poor girl, poor Daphne," is Harriet's immediate response as she realises that "from the angle of her intolerable humiliation Daphne would have looked askance at everything that had happened to her ever since."

> *"To be taking it to heart like this after all these years,"* thought Harriet. *"Never to have forgiven it. And I don't believe she's ever told a soul."* She felt a little nauseated as she thought of Daphne pushing the memory of her humiliation further and further down, yet never able to get rid of it. The measure of her bitterness was the measure of her failure.[626]

All these may be purely fictional accounts of a universal human experience of course; but if Elizabeth was writing about her own unhappiness then, on the evidence of those thousands of best-selling books, it could not be said that she had never told a soul. As to Daphne's reaction:

> *The tale of her humiliation, never spoken of, had seemed a thing of nightmare proportion in the place where she had buried it, but brought out into the light it looked both paltry and ridiculous. She looked back with contempt to the girl who had stood upon the cliffs in Cornwall and found a sort of self-indulgent pleasure in thinking how easy it would be to throw herself over.*[627]

Despite the heartache and tears, all of her fictional heroines pulled through to the other side of their unhappiness and moved on. In the 1953 novel, Harriet had questioned Daphne about what happened after her jilting – not out of "idle curiosity" but because

> *She wanted to lead Daphne on to the happy ending whose happiness she had never allowed herself either to admit or accept.*[628]

And there was a happy ending for Elizabeth herself. Twenty years after *The Rosemary Tree* she admitted to an interviewer[629] that "her writing would never have got off the ground if a conventional domestic life had been possible." This would surely have been something of a tragedy for herself, as well as for her many readers, for "I…have found great joy in work and in building up a career" says *The Joy of the Snow*. In fact, she had even lived to 'thank Heaven fasting' for the single state.[630]

Fears and Burdens

Elizabeth had lived almost her entire life with the ongoing stress and worry that came from having an invalid in the family - the crises; the operations. That almost rebellious statement of hers about the early Oxford years - "I was not a sick woman, I was young with a strong pair of legs" - shows how she must have had to fight against the constraints imposed at second-hand by someone else's sickness. But even worse than coping with its practicalities, must have been the burden of guilt she had always carried in believing herself – by the effects of her own birth - to be the cause of all the suffering.

She had always struggled with the problem of suffering and had, too, an awareness of the presence of evil that brought frightening nightmares.

> *For years I was pursued by a recurring nightmare. I would be taking part in some happy festivity when a sudden silence would fall and a stillness of horror. Then someone would point and we would see it, sometimes in the middle of the floor where perhaps we had just been dancing, or up in the corner of the ceiling. It was always quite small and in different nightmares it would change its shape. Sometimes it was some foul black creature, very much alive but quite still as it bided its time, but at other times it was merely some queer shape lying there on the floor without movement, a sort of box. Whatever it was the feeling of horror and terror was the same because either symbol spoke of the same thing; the snake that crept into Eden.*[631]

This awareness, alongside what she once worked out for herself about Good and Evil having equal strength, has echoes of what Humphrey Carpenter says of C.S. Lewis.

> By temperament he inclined strongly towards dualism, the belief that God and the Devil are equal powers at war with each other. "I have always gone as near Dualism as Christianity allows," he admitted. Though as an orthodox Christian he had to reject the fully dualist view of the world, he did believe firmly that while the power of evil could create nothing, it could infect everything.[632]

In the novel she had just written, it is not just rejection and disillusionment that drive the Minstrel to despair in Ferranti's poem. He too has a horrific awareness of the constant presence of evil:

> *He tried to find this beauty in his forest, among the trees and the flowers and the nymphs who danced to the music of his flute, but he found that there were snakes coiled on the branches of the trees, and worms and dead bodies under the roots of the flowers, and as the nymphs twisted and turned in the measure of their dance he saw to his horror that there was a satyr prancing about in the middle of them.*[633]

With an inherited tendency to depression, a deep commitment to live a dutiful Christian life, and her anguished attempts to reconcile belief in a loving God with the suffering reality of an evil world, one can see why it might be difficult for this young woman to find comedy in the things that were happening to her. Several of her early books have references to characters of unusual sensitivity, including that remark of Fanny Burney's that "the sensitive suffer." Did Elizabeth class herself among these characters whose sensitivity was verging on the abnormal? In *A City of Bells* she had said that Ferranti

> *wrote the sort of verse that only supersensitives such as himself could have appreciated. You know what I mean. It dealt with problems that are not problems to normal folk, and tortures they would never be likely to feel.*[634]

Even years later she would say of Jean Anderson in *The Scent of Water*, that "many of her fears and burdens would have seemed unreal to another woman."[635] Jacqueline in *Island Magic* too, had been inwardly very different from her "normal" exterior. In fact it is interesting to note how many of her characters are measured with the yardstick of that word, *normal*.

> *No one, not even her father, understood Jacqueline. Outwardly she was the perfect picture of a good, normal little twelve-year-old...but inwardly she was a whirlpool of queer unchildish desires, nightmare terrors, tormenting anxieties.*[636]

And Ferranti, describing the paralysing inactivity of depression to Jocelyn, says

> *I nearly went mad with indecision. It's useless to try and explain. Normal people like yourself could never understand how, under certain circumstances, one's will can become useless. Any sort of action, even the action you want to take, seems impossible...*[637]
> *I was in a queer state, partly physical illness, partly despair at the uselessness of my life and its irreparable mistakes. I meant to kill myself...*[638]

In Ferranti's epic poem his alter-ego The Minstrel - realising that in his rage at its imperfection he has destroyed all the beauty in his life - does commit suicide.

> *Despair seized the Minstrel. The fragments had been there for his taking and what had he done with them? The roses he had trampled underfoot, the statue he had destroyed, the beauty that was in the woman and the child he had driven from him and the stupidity that had caused his bodily weakness had smashed his flute into a hundred pieces. He had destroyed beauty. Beauty was dead and he must follow it, for without it his life was useless to him. His feet carried him through the darkness to the water's edge and the river of death closed over his head.*[639]

Shelley had been Ferranti's inspiration when writing the poem, and it seems that the Minstrel's choice is that of Shelley's Adonais: "Die / If thou wouldst be with that which thou dost seek! / Follow where all is fled!"[640] This had been Judith's aim too, in *The Middle Window*. Having unwittingly caused the death of her husband, she comes to "the breaking point." She decides that Ranald "wanted to take her away to be where he was" but that "she would have to do it herself." She fixes upon the same method of taking her own life.

> *The tarn! She was sobbing with thankfulness when she reached it. Its black, fathomless water looked cool and kind to her hot, aching eyes. Only a little while longer and it would be over…*
>
> *The shock of the water on her heated body brought her to a standstill… It jerked her mind out of the mist of misery that had engulfed and clouded it and for a moment she was herself again… "What am I doing?" she whispered.*[641]

Like Judith before him, Ferranti the poet manages to overcome the temptation to suicide, helped in part by poetry itself. He turns to Shakespeare, knowing that for him there is "nothing so steadying, when you're in pieces, as reading something fine." He recognises, in the poetry, the depressive feelings that had brought him to the brink.

> *It seemed to me that night that Hamlet was myself; all that he felt I felt … the paralysis, the indecision, the torment, the disgust with life, the knowledge that one's misery is caused by one's own mind.*[642]

Finally joy prevails, for he finds in his renewed life not only the success as a poet that had previously eluded him, but the love of his lost daughter Henrietta.

> *Henrietta, gazing at him in adoration he had done nothing whatsoever to deserve, half shy and half eager, did not know yet that he was her father, she knew only that the Pied Piper had come back. He was a magic man, a fairy-tale man, and it seemed to her quite natural that he should have got lost, for fairy-tale people are always easily mislaid, but warm inside her was the certainty that now at last he was found for good.*[643]

A fairytale happy ending for this novel. Nevertheless the temptation to suicide it described was very real: Elizabeth was able draw upon her own experience.

Getting Through

> I was a stricken deer, that left the herd
> Long since; with many an arrow deep infixt
> My panting side was charg'd, when I withdrew
> To seek a tranquil death in distant shades.
>
> There was I found by one who had himself
> Been hurt by th'archers. In his side he bore,
> And in his hands and feet, the cruel scars.
> With gentle force soliciting the darts,
> He drew them forth, and heal'd, and bade me live.[644]

She included these lines from William Cowper's *The Task* in her *Book of Comfort*, giving them the heading *In His Mental Illness, William Cowper Finds He is not Alone*... not alone, that is, because of the compassionate Christ who healed, and bade him live. But in *The Joy of the Snow* she was anxious to give another kind of reassurance to anyone tempted "to seek…death"… the reassurance that they were not alone in their temptation to suicide; she herself had experienced it and it is, she said, "a perfectly normal part of any nervous breakdown."

> *We are frightened of it. If it has been conquered for the time being we dread its return in some time of strain and it possibly will return, like any other temptation, though probably getting weaker every time we get the better of it. I am sure we should try not to be frightened and that the right attitude towards it should be just that – a temptation like any other. Not a dreadful thing at all, perfectly ordinary, and a surprising number of people suffer from it, for we are never alone in what we suffer.*[645]

> *"Fool," he said to himself, lying still in the darkness of his room, stretched tautly by the fear of the pack of nightmare sensations that leaped at him like hounds through the sleepless nights. "This is just what is called a nervous breakdown. No one thinks anything of it. It passes. You don't go crackers and chuck yourself out of the window if you remember that it passes. It passed for ten minutes during dinner. It will pass again when the morning comes. Hilary went through the same thing after the last war and now he praises God through the nights. It passes."*[646]

David, in this extract from *The Herb of Grace*, is saved by the remembrance that he is not alone in what he suffers. For Jo in *The Castle on the Hill*, the saving power is hope.

> *There had been many occasions…when he had been near to ending it but yet had always been held back by the strange hope that he had always had, the hope of the artist in pursuit of beauty, the hope that there was going to be something incredibly lovely round the next corner… a refuge in the wood… something… some sort of rest… some sort of abiding place.*[647]

In the same novel she writes about inner struggle, illustrating it with the story of Cain and Abel.

> *Only a legend, that lost garden, but something of the truth must lie hidden in it, for one had only to look at oneself to see those two men who are the same man, fighting down the ages, the one a rebel for ever, the other straining back always after the lost inheritance.*[648]

At the beginning of her career, in 1934, Elizabeth had a portrait photograph taken by the Bassano studio (now in the National Portrait Gallery collection) which seems to illustrate the struggle inside her in these middle years of her life. Overall, it is not a picture of calm; for there is the suspicion of a frown, and a somewhat wild light in the right eye. But cover that one eye, and her face becomes quite beautifully different: soft, smiling and gentle. It is something like the portrait John Adair is painting in *The Herb of Grace*. When his daughter Sally decides that "It's not quite right," he replies,

> *"No. I've got too far ahead in time. That happens sometimes even in photography, you know…*
> *There's a patient angel in us all, the spirit in the making. And he has two faces. He is the two things that you may be if you do this, or that. Sometimes you see the one looking out of the window, sometimes the other."*[649]

The American photographer Irving Penn acknowledged that in portraiture, although the camera can only record what is "apparent on the outside," nevertheless there is "something more profound we seek inside a person."[650] The Bassano studio seems to have been successful in capturing both faces of this young woman, her two selves. One holding on to belief in an "abiding place" – the other fighting what threatens to be a losing battle with everything the world is throwing at her.

※

In *Sister of the Angels*, Henrietta observes that people need looking after sometimes, and "Some grown-ups can be very tiresome and selfish when they won't let themselves be helped. They give a lot of trouble." For when they are not able to stand on their own feet, she says, "They have to be put there, like tortoises."

> *"Tortoises?"*
> *"Don't you know about tortoises?" asked Henrietta. "If they get on their backs by accident they can't get on their feet again unless someone picks them up and puts them there. And they let themselves be righted. They're only too pleased."*[651]

Whether or not Elizabeth herself had initially been tiresome about letting herself be righted, she must eventually have taken her cue from the tortoises, for she gratefully remembered her father's loving support in getting her back on her feet again: "In a time of trouble for me he turned round and came back to meet me..."[652] He [was] so marvellously good to me in my miseries and problems."[653] His advice and example are recognisable in the novel that deals most overtly with mental breakdown, *The Scent of Water*; for in *My Father* she says,

> *He thought that when one was ill one should not pray to be made well, for if the prayer was not answered it tended to make one beat against the bars in rebellion, and rebellion tended, in his own rather terrible phrase, "to make one hate God."*[654]

In *The Scent of Water* the young Mary's rebellion is countered by a clergyman's deep, quiet faith.

> *He was silent for a long time, rubbing his chin, and then he said, 'You're afraid of it?'*
> *It seemed such a silly question and I spoke sharply I think when I said, 'Of course I am, I'm terrified.'*
> *'Why?' he asked. 'If you lose your reason you lose it into the hands of God.'*

> *I said, 'Why does God let us suffer like this?' and he answered, 'My dear young lady, how should I know? Job didn't know, but he repented in dust and ashes.'*
>
> *He wasn't helping me at all and I said crossly, 'I haven't done anything frightfully wrong. Nothing that calls for dust and ashes.'*
> *He said quietly, 'No?'*
>
> *I said, 'It makes one hate God.'*
> *He said, 'Where you've put him?'*
> *'Where have I put him?'*
> *'On the gallows.'*
>
> *And then suddenly he caught sight of a tortoiseshell butterfly drifting down the path and he gave an exclamation of incredulous joy and ran after it. When I caught up with him he was standing in front of the buddleia tree, which was covered with butterflies like it nearly always is, and he was speechless with wonder, his face absorbed as a child's when the candles have been lit on the Christmas tree.*[655]

(Like her father, who would "stand lost in delight as autumn by autumn he watched the butterflies on the michaelmas daisies."[656])

> *It was almost as though the butterflies shone on him and lit his face. Or else it was the other way round. For a moment there seemed light everywhere, though it was a grey day…*
>
> *He said, 'I will pray for you every day of my life until I die.'…*
>
> *His eyes had the most extraordinary quietness in them. 'My dear,' he said, 'love, your God, is a trinity. There are three necessary prayers and they have three words each. They are these, "Lord have mercy. Thee I adore. Into Thy hands." Not difficult to remember. If in times of distress you hold to these you will do well.*[657]

This old clergyman, Cousin Mary later learns, had been "in and out of asylums for most of his life" and yet, "He hadn't told me. He'd stood aside, speaking only of God and me."[658] Even this "standing aside" is characteristic of her father, for the family skeleton of depression did not only afflict his daughter:

After a period of strain or overwork darkness could fall upon him suddenly out of the blue and last for weeks. My mother and I knew when this happened, for you cannot live in the same house with a soul in darkness and not know it, but not from anything he said or any alteration in his loving manner towards us. I doubt if anyone else knew.[659]

However difficult to achieve, this was the bedrock of his faith - hope, not despair. As his sermon said, every Christian must be an optimist. But by temperament "he was not an optimist," says Elizabeth. "His courage lay in the fact that he could present this gay face to the world whatever his private grief and despair."[660] Courage was the keynote of his character, she says, and remembered him "carrying his recurrent darkness so selflessly that it damaged neither mind nor body." This attitude to his "lifelong anguish" she felt could be "perfectly expressed" in the words of Leslie Weatherhead's prayer, where he asks that "those things which cloud my own way may not darken the path which others have to tread." He prays too for the courage and unselfishness that will make him "ready always to share my bread and wine, yet able to hide my hunger and thirst."[661]

Elizabeth took her father's example so much to heart that this prayer could be seen as a perfect expression of her own striving too – although when it came to her work it was not always by *hiding* her own hunger and thirst that she was best able to share. *The Scent of Water* is marked by a very particular openness and honesty - so much so that its publication generated "a huge correspondence, which afforded exceptional evidence of the rapport established between the author and her readers."[662]

Now it's out. I have said I was sane again and that means that I was not sane before. I have written it down. For I'm to be honest in this diary. That's why I'm writing it. I'm writing this to help myself by speaking out exactly what's in my mind. I can't talk to people because this illness isn't like other illnesses; all that's worst in it you have to hide so as not to spread fear. And anyhow they wouldn't understand...

When did I begin to realize that other people don't wake up every morning in unexplainable misery, don't, as soon as they are ill or exhausted, become sleepless and desperate? People mean different things by desperation. I mean the terror of impending disorder. For disorder, of mind or body, is evil's chance. At least, I think so. It seems to me to be integration that keeps evil out...

I scarcely remember how it happened, after we came back from Paris, for it's all a blur, but I do remember the insomnia and trying to get out of the window to escape from the evil. The time at the Home I only remember as a confused nightmare. But it's odd, I do remember one thing very clearly. I remember who among the nurses was kind to me and who was not. It would be awful to have to go back there...[663]

There is a prayer written especially "For the Nervously Ill" in her *Diary of Prayer.*

Lord of great compassion, we pray to you for those who are nervously ill, and too weak and anxious to lift themselves above the fear and sadness that threaten to overwhelm them. Do you yourself, O Lord, lift them up and deliver them, as you delivered your disciples in the storm at sea, strengthening their faith and banishing their fear. Turning to you, O Lord, may they find you, and finding you may they find also all that you have laid up for them within the safe fortress of your love and peace.[664]

❋

"Weak and anxious" she may have been during this time of illness and breakdown, but if she drew on her own experience in the writing of this prayer, then she was indeed lifted up and delivered - to the extent that she learnt to come to terms with her sorrows, and even to write about them with gratitude and a hint of humour.

For the unmarried women [after the Great War] their fate was mitigated, if not transmuted altogether, by the wonderful fact that they were needed as a labour force. They had proved their worth in the war and now they had the vote and a large and varied field of work was open to them. Women today consider themselves not yet sufficiently free but old women of my age cannot get over the conviction that we were liberated fifty years ago. I am one of many who have found great joy in work and in building up a career. I have even lived to 'thank God fasting' for the single state...[665]

"I hung no more garlands on the tree after I married Jim Heather, the forester," said Mrs. Heather, "I'd not the time. Jim were a proper man, though of a stubborn fashion, an' wooed me beautiful down there in the valley, an' fine I loved him; but after he brought me here I had no peace. Twelve childer us had, some died when they was little 'uns but there's some livin' to-day, though all gone their ways. I was seventeen when I married, an' I took it very hard. But Jim he were a proper man, of a stubborn fashion, an' he couldn't help himself."

> *Her voice ended on a note of matter-of-fact resignation, and Miss Brown tried to put herself in the place of that child of seventeen, the fairy-tale child who had hung garlands on a thorn tree and been wooed in the valley of the singing stream, when her body had been delivered over into the keeping of Jim Heather. Twelve children. She tried to imagine the birth pangs and the weakness, the grief when the babies died, the turmoil when they did not, the noise and overcrowding in the small cottage, the cooking and the mending and the scrubbing, the back-breaking hours over the washtub, the coming and going of the virile husband with his mud-caked boots, his appetite, his incessant demands by night and day, the epidemics, the partings, the tragedy of the forester's death and the final loneliness. But imagination failed her...*
>
> *"You must miss your husband," she said tentatively.*
> *"No, my dear," said Mrs. Heather placidly, "I can't say as I do. Not now."*[666]

In the same novel, *The Castle on the Hill*, Miss Brown's sensible stoicism enables her to find a way through her own experience of love.

> *It is a bitter draught that you love more than you are loved and there are few whose pride lets them face it. But it was Miss Brown's habit to face everything, to get things clear, as she called it...*
>
> *She said to herself...It will be good discipline to hide my love. Nothing is better discipline than letting no one know what you are feeling. And why should I be ashamed of love? I won't be ashamed of it. Requited love gets as much as it gives, but unrequited love gets nothing for itself and so it must be the best sort of love that there is. Perhaps it will teach me how to break away from that circle of myself.*[667]

Perhaps Lucilla's advice to Nadine in *The Bird in the Tree* came from Elizabeth's own realisation that she had not been alone in her suffering – that it was indeed a perfectly normal part of life, and a valuable one.

> *I think a woman's history is very often like one of those old romances.*
>
> *You may laugh at them, but they were truer to life than many of those psychological novels you young people read nowadays. We women don't sit half the day and night analysing our emotions but we do perpetually fall in love out of wedlock, and over and over again we have to fight out the same old battle between love and duty...*

> *My silly little love story isn't really important...but the conclusions one comes to about living are important. They mould our lives, and sometimes other people's lives too.*[668]

By the time she came to write of Sally's love for David in *The Herb of Grace*, pain and despair were countered by a philosophical acceptance.

> *At this point her thoughts would come up against Hamlet's words, "The readiness is all", and cling to them as to a rock. That put it in a nutshell. That was the only possible attitude to life and death, as well as to love. You had to be ready to be used or not used, picked up or cast aside, and it didn't really matter which it was provided you yourself were pliant to fate like a reed to the wind...*
>
> *It was one of the glorious things about life, that for the pliant there was never really any lasting emptiness... If she could manage to welcome sorrow as readily as joy, it would shape her as deftly as joy could have done to whatever beauty of being it was within her power to reach.*[669]

As Elizabeth said of her own life, there is "nothing to prevent a single woman experiencing the richness of falling in love now and again all her life. And indeed it *is* richness, for to every human being the pain of perhaps not having love returned is less important than the blessed fact of loving."[670] And, too, the blessed task of making something out of the pain... as Henrietta realises in *Sister of the Angels*: "life might be terrible sometimes...but it was nice to think how people could comfort themselves by making things."[671] George MacDonald has the last word in *A Book of Faith*. For any "troubled soul," work is the way out of their darkness:

> Fold the arms of thy faith I say, but not of thy action: bethink thee of something that thou oughtest to do, and go to do it, if it be but the sweeping of a room, or the preparing of a meal, or a visit to a friend. Heed not thy feelings: do thy work.[672]

Towers in the Mist

Whatever her feelings in all the turmoil Elizabeth must have followed this advice, for in 1938 *Towers in the Mist* was published. *The Oxford Guide to British Women Writers* says that there was a "hiatus" in her work in the 1930s as a result of the nervous breakdown – but the fact is that she published *Island Magic* in 1934, *The Middle Window* 1935, *A City of Bells* 1936, *A Pedlar's Pack* in 1937, and *Towers in the Mist* 1938. The decade's output would be completed by *Three Plays* and *Sister of the Angels* in 1939. Not only had she continued to "do her work", but amazingly in *Towers in the Mist* she had somehow produced - in the opinion of Jane Spence Southron of *The New York Times* - a book that "breathes the same spirit of joyousness that distinguished *A City of Bells*."[673]

It had needed a fair bit of research, in the books her father borrowed for her from the Christ Church library. Nor had she found it an easy novel to write, and in the Sixties she described the struggle for the members of the Romantic Novelists' Association.

I remember many years ago, when I was a young and struggling writer, that I made up my mind to try and write a story about sixteenth-century Oxford. I thought it would be easy for I was living in twentieth-century Oxford, history was all about me and my home was actually in the Tom Quad that Wolsey built. I tramped about Oxford, I read all the books I could lay hands on, I wrote a few lifeless chapters and they stuck as hopelessly as a fly in treacle. It was no good. I was still in the twentieth century. Then in despair I started going to all the quiet places I knew of and being in them as though I had nothing else in the world to do. I went to Magdalen cloisters and sat there alone. I went to a particular spot by the Cherwell where the kingfishers nested and listened to the sound of the water and watched for the flash of blue. I went to St. Michael's at the North Gate and settled down in one of the pews with only the shadows for company, and the heavy door so firmly shut that the sound of distant traffic faded to a drone of bees. And then at last my mind moved from the living present to the living past as easily as a body walks from one room to another. All writers know the experience well. It makes such words as death, time, past and present, oddly unreal.[674]

Such was her success in overcoming the difficulties that the same reviewer said, "It would be well-nigh impossible to read this book without being caught in the web of enchantment which the writer has woven about the city."[675] But once again, there was more to it than just enchantment.

❋

Teeming with colourful characters from all walks of life, *Towers in the Mist* is set in the Oxford of Elizabeth the First. Principally the story of Gervas Leigh and his family (as we know, domiciled in the Goudges' own house in Tom Quad), it is also the story of the city itself; for the Leighs' exploits, and the love affair of the eldest, motherless daughter Joyeuce, are recounted alongside tales of the history and legends of Oxford. The whole thing culminates in a pageant of what the Goudges had already experienced for themselves – a royal visit from the sovereign.

Curiously, however, there are certain elements in the opening pages of this gentle historical romance which bear an inverse resemblance to another novel about Oxford – a very famous and certainly not a romantic one - Thomas Hardy's *Jude the Obscure*. (Elizabeth tells us that alongside Browning, Dickens and Shakespeare, Hardy was one of her father's favourite authors.) This was published in 1895, only five years before Elizabeth was born, and in her youth therefore it would have been still a fairly modern novel – comparable to a young woman today reading, say, Margaret Atwood's dystopia *The Handmaid's Tale*.[676]

The publication of this, Hardy's final novel, caused a public outcry. His own preface stated that the book was an argument in favour of divorce; a comment on the miseries ensuing from entrapment in an unhappy marriage. But this is not just the story of one man's misery - it is a despairing novel about the future of mankind in a new and godless world; reaching a terrible dénouement when Jude's young children are killed by his eldest little boy, who then hangs himself. An explanation for the horror is put forward by their doctor:

> There are such boys springing up amongst us – boys of a sort unknown in the last generation – the outcome of new views of life. They seem to see all its terrors before they are old enough to have staying power to resist them... It is the beginning of the coming universal wish not to live.[677]

A bleak vision of a terrible life without purpose, unknown in former generations and yet soon to be "universal" - this was Victorian Doubt at its worst. Although he took them to a terrifyingly pessimistic extreme, Hardy was writing about the same new views of life that had engulfed Elizabeth's grandfather in such a dark cloud of despair and unbelief, making him quite sure, on his last visit to her, that life had all been for nothing, and at his death he would go "into nothingness." Elizabeth had been unable to help poor Adolphus at the time... looking back, "Why did I not *do* something?" she agonised. Could it be that this new novel was her attempt, now, to do something – to fire a broadside at all the doubt and despair of his generation? She had so recently come close to sharing his unbelief, grappling with suffering that threatened to shatter her faith. But it had not shattered... and she acknowledged gratefully that it was because of him:

I totally failed my grandfather but he did not fail me, though it was years before I realised what it was he had done for me in rooting my faith, that I believe grew up out of his despair.[678]

In *Towers in the Mist* Elizabeth quite clearly makes the statement of faith that she could not put into words for Adolphus: "There is another country." In the scene when Joyeuce's young brother dies, she finds her grief dispelled by a smile from him that brings to her this "news of a far country. With one brief smile Giles told more of it than a hundred books could have done." As a consequence "her heart within her was like a singing bird," and she attempts to comfort her grieving family with this confident affirmation of hope: "You must not grieve... There is another country."[679] In fact she walks through the house repeating the message, in varying phrases, three times.

❄

There are similarities with *Jude the Obscure*, which are so marked as to suggest that this book really was a deliberate attack on the despairing pessimism of its time. At the beginning of Hardy's novel, Jude makes a vow that he will educate himself in order to be accepted as a student at Christminster (Oxford). A poor boy with only two books to his name, the Latin and Greek grammars, Jude finds himself one day transfixed by a vision of the city that appears out of the dissolving mist, as "points of light" begin to gleam like topaz :

> The air increased in transparency...till the topaz points showed themselves to be...vanes, windows, wet roof slates... It was Christminster... either directly seen, or miraged in the peculiar atmosphere.[680]

But symbolically, as he stares at the golden glory of Christminster it disappears again into mist and darkness, as the sun itself disappears in the west, and it becomes "funereally dark." All the topaz points lose their shine, "going out almost suddenly like extinguished candles. The vague city became veiled in mist...and near objects put on the hues and shapes of chimaeras."[681]

Towers in the Mist (the title itself giving central importance to his vision) starts when a poor boy who has been living with gypsies sets out for Oxford, determined to study there. He has only two books, Virgil and *Foxe's Book of Martyrs*. In contrast to Jude, who shares his name with the patron saint of lost causes, this boy is called Faithful. As he approaches Oxford he stands amazed before his first vision of the city, and then shuts his eyes tight, expecting it to have been a mirage and to disappear. But when he opens them again, unlike Jude's "vague" city, it is still there.

> *He stopped to wait for the sunrise... It came slowly. The mist that had been as thick as sorrow became tenuous and frail. It had been grey like the rain but now it was opal-tinted. The green of the woods was in it, and the blue of the sky, and there was a hint of rose colour that told of the fires of the earth, of the sun and the warmth of daily living... Gradually, with the same mysterious slowness with which night had changed to day, towers rose out of the mist, and he looked down from the heights of Shotover upon the city of Oxford. It could not be real, he thought. It was a fragile city spun out of dreams, so small that he could have held it on the palm of his hand and blown it away into silver mist. It was not real. He had dreamed of it for so long that now, when he looked down at the valley, the mist formed itself into towers and spires that would vanish under the sun the moment he shut his eyes... He shut his eyes, opened them, and the towers were still there.*[682]

Her description, like Hardy's, uses jewel imagery; but in Elizabeth's novel the darkness and light, sunset and sunrise, mirage and reality are directly reversed. Jude's topaz light is extinguished like a candle and becomes funereal darkness, whereas Faithful sees a mist, thick as sorrow, change to opal colours, sunlight and warmth... and what he sees is no chimaera; it is real.

Faithful's two precious books seem to symbolise his upward journey of faith, which will be in direct contrast to Jude's descent into defeat and destruction. *Foxe's Book of Martyrs* tells how this noble army, in the defence of their faith "climbed the steep ascent of heaven mid peril, toil and pain."[683] And in a chapter of Virgil's *Aeneid* dealing with the Descent into the Underworld, Aeneas is told that to descend "is easy; day and night stand open the doors of swarthy Dis; but to recall thy steps and revisit the light of heaven – that is the labour, that is the task."[684] (The quotation is from a translation for the young: *Stories from the Aeneid*, published just before Elizabeth went to Grassendale.)

The message is clear. To be brought low like Jude is easy; the hard thing is to keep climbing and to "revisit the light of heaven." Not surprisingly, as Faithful reaches Oxford and is swept along into a chapel by a crowd of May-day revellers, he finds the assembled congregation singing "I will lift up mine eyes unto the hills.[685]" Nevertheless fear returns to him, in imagery redolent of Jude's unhappy marriage.

> *Faithful's throat grew dry and hard and he stopped singing. The fear he had felt in the night returned, accompanied by a sick rage. Life was a fair-faced cheat… who tempted a man outside the city gates to tread a flowery path under a clear sky, and changed overnight into a devil who betrayed her lover to the shapes of darkness and terror that she set about his path to mock him as he stumbled to his death… Why do we live, O God, why do we live, when the end is death?*[686]

But then he sees Gervas Leigh, who has weathered life's storms and not been destroyed.

> *He reminded Faithful of one of those tall thin trees that grow upon hilltops and are twisted to fantastic shapes by the storms that blow upon them. He could not be called ugly, though he was certainly misshapen, as the trees are misshapen, because his figure, like theirs, had been formed by endurance and the sight of it was as invigorating as a trumpet call… Faithful could have taken his oath that this was a priest and scholar who had suffered persecution for his faith in the reign of the late unlamented Queen Mary; for his body had the angularity of obstinacy, the gauntness of starvation and the bowed shoulders of indefatigable scholarship. His face, seamed by his sorrows, had a keen look, as though the mind behind it were sharp in dealing with muddles and shams, but his blue eyes were gentle and dreamy.*[687]

Faith was under threat too, in a different way, in the sixteenth century, but threat has created in this man a staying power to resist life's terrors; the strength of endurance which Hardy says will be impossible for the new generation. In Elizabeth's novel, though, the new generation is symbolically named: Grace, Joyeuce, Faithful. They will not succumb to any 'universal wish…not to live,' for as Faithful looks at the invigorating evidence of Gervas's endurance his sense of proportion is given back to him, and he too makes that statement of faith: "There is life and there is death, and then there is life again." There *is* another country. The loss of joy is simply part of the cyclical nature of all life; and the novel itself comes full circle too, as Joyeuce's lover Nicolas has his own vision of the city – not in mist, but in the full glory of the dawn light.

> *He paused to look back at the towers and spires so delicately pencilled against the glorious dawn sky that curved above them in the semblance of a great circle. He felt a pang of pain to think that he must so soon leave it all, but yet he had at the same time a glorious feeling of permanence. Raleigh at the last had been quite right. Love was an unchanging thing, not an emotion, but an element in which the whole world had its being. All the lovely things upon earth, beauty and truth and courage, were faint pictures of it, even as the puddles of rainwater at his feet held a faint picture of the fiery sky bending above the earth. And in the mind of man, too, the flame was caught and held; in his own mind whose strength and vigour made it possible for his eyes to see this picture of a fair city and a golden sky, for his soul to face life vowed to integrity and courage, for his heart to feel for Joyeuce an affection so strong that he dared to call it by the name of that eternal and embracing love.*
>
> *Love is a durable fire*
> *In the mind ever burning;*
> *Never sick, never old, never dead,*
> *From itself never turning.*[688]

"I could not totally disbelieve in God," Elizabeth said, "because during my worst and most despairing nights there had seemed to be something there; some rock down at the bottom… And always my parents love and faith, the world's beauty and the sound of great music, seemed unexplainable without God."[689] Whatever unhappiness had brought her to breakdown - to the point where her faith in God was "nearly shattered" - this book is determinedly full of a confident optimism and joy. As George MacDonald tells the "troubled soul":

> That man is perfect in faith who can come to God in the utter dearth of his feelings and desires, without a glow or an aspiration, with the weight of low thoughts, failures, neglects, and wandering forgetfulness, and say to Him, "Thou art my refuge."[690]

Like other clergymen in her books Gervas Leigh has something of her father in his make-up. Canon Goudge's dark times damaged neither his mind nor his body - and neither have life's storms destroyed Gervas. On the contrary, his great faith and spiritual strength have showed Faithful how to climb out of the darkness into light – just as her father had done for Elizabeth. And, too, Gervas looks "like a monk whose background should have been a crucifix upon the wall of a cell..."[691]

My father...had a delightful simplicity and was only able to enjoy things that were simple. It was this I think that made him so uneasy when trapped in elaborate social life. Once, in total exasperation, he cried out, "I wish I possessed nothing but a cell and a crucifix." My mother took this as a personal insult and he had hastily to assure her that after God she was the glory of his life; which indeed she was.[692]

If my father had chosen the monk's cell he would have missed what went so largely to the making of him, and that was his marriage to my mother. His debt to her was incalculable. After his death a great friend of mine described him in a phrase which has remained with me ever since, so perfectly did it catch his charm. "He, so light of step and gentle of spirit, so gay and understanding." Some of that lightness and gaiety would not have been his but for my mother.[693]

But I think he spoke the truth about himself. He would have made a happy monk.[694]

She dedicated *Towers in the Mist* to her father with this slightly adapted quotation from Philip Sidney:

Here now have you, most dear, and most worthy to be most dear Sir, this idle work of mine; which, I fear, like the spider's web, will be thought fitter to be swept away than worn to any other purpose. But you desired me to do it, and your desire to my heart is an absolute commandment.[695]

Gervas Leigh was the last of his daughter's fictional clergyman that Dr. Goudge would encounter. He died the following spring.

But for now, he too had a book coming out: *The Church of England and Reunion*. It was a subject close to his heart, and he had recently attended the 1937 Edinburgh Conference on Faith and Order at which, he said, "it was felt that a real advance towards Reunion was made."[696] (Reunion of the church that had split apart in the sixteenth century, precipitating the burning of martyrs recorded in Faithful's book by John Foxe.) It was a subject both topical and – given the centuries of history behind it – even rather astonishing. A few years later, in a letter to the author Maisie Spens, Evelyn Underhill said that people did not seem to understand how really *remarkable* it was, that representatives of the Roman Catholic, Anglican and Free Churches were increasingly in correspondence with each other, and "acting together in the interests of the Christian life."[697]

Perhaps the book's greatest importance for Elizabeth was that it gave her this treasured memory of her father.

> *Though both of us found the books of the other hard going, he because he had too much intellect for mine and I because I had too little for his, we were in sympathy with each other. I can remember with what joy we sat on the floor together packing up the typescript of his last book for despatch to his publisher. The task completed we sat back on our heels and contemplated the neat parcel...with hearts swelling with thankfulness. Months of dogged perseverance had brought a creative act round full circle to its completion. A book was written. It was going out into the world. Our eyes met and we smiled. "They are our children, aren't they?" said my father. The humility and gentleness with which he spoke seemed to gather his books and mine into one family. I had never felt so close to him or so happy.*[698]

※

Elizabeth had further successes that year. From now on her stories would be published regularly in *Woman's Journal*, and four of them appeared in 1938 — *Midnight in the Stable*, *A Crock of Gold*, *The Well of the Star* and *Nice Man, St. George*. Her association with the magazine — through short stories, articles and the serialisation of several of her novels — was to continue until the nineteen-sixties. Also in 1938 there was a London production of her play about Finland's struggle for independence, *Suomi*.[699] This must have brought a ray of real joy after her troubles. And although the joy would be short-lived, she also found happiness again in a visit to her beloved Hampshire, and a beautiful old house which was to be the inspiration for a new novel.

> *In 1938, trying to recover from the effects of an operation, I went to stay at Keyhaven, in the part of Hampshire I had learned to love in my schooldays, in a quiet, beautiful old hotel which had once been a country house. It had a lovely garden, and beyond the garden were the sea marshes, and just across the estuary was the Isle of Wight. The loveliness of that bit of country completely captured my imagination, and when I went home again I [began to write]* The Bird in the Tree.[700]
>
> *[But] it marked the ending of an epoch, both in my own unimportant life and in the world as well. The years that followed were shadowed years of illness and bereavement and war, one of those periods that come now and again in every life, and which must be passed through like a dark tunnel before one can come out into the light again.*[701]

The Dark Tunnel

Her father died in April 1939 at the age of seventy-two, having been Regius Professor of Divinity for sixteen years.

He had had some plans for life after Oxford; for although he was a Londoner who was fond of London, "his true home was always the West Country. He had hoped, when his working days were over, to live in Dorset, which he thought the loveliest of the western counties. There he had hoped to have leisure to become really knowledgeable about birds and trees and flowers."[702] But, too, Dr. Goudge was a man who loved his work; a man whose spirits would "sink to zero" when he "conscientiously" took a few days' holiday; after which he would "return to work with the delight of a boy let out of school."[703] And so despite his retirement plans, Elizabeth begins her account of his last days by saying that,

> *For some while before his death he had been feeling that the time had come for him to give up his Oxford post and make room for a younger man, but he had been facing retirement with trepidation, sorely afraid of idleness. He never had to endure it. He worked hard up till the last ten days of his life.*
>
> *On Palm Sunday, April 2nd, he preached at St. Peter's Bournemouth…On Good Friday he took the Three Hours at Christ Church, Bristol, returning the same day to our little holiday bungalow in Hampshire. On Sunday he helped our Rector, Mr. Hutchison, through a strenuous Easter Day…*
>
> *A few days later he had a bad fall and on April 24th he died from the injuries he received. Throughout the ten days of his illness, in spite of much pain and a wandering mind, radiance was continually breaking through. The sister who nursed him said, "His gentleness of character showed through like sunshine. The love of God is like that."*[704]
>
> *Then he became unconscious and died in his sleep. The nurses at the nursing home where he died told me I was wasting my time, sitting so many hours by the bed of a dying man who would never regain consciousness. But he did. He appeared to come back from some great distance and said slowly and distinctly, "Dear one, it is loving that matters," and then drifted away again upon the great, peaceful journey.*
>
> *So that is the end of it for these great men. All their accumulated knowledge, all the argument and controversy, seem of little importance. Only love remains important and is immortal.*[705]

When she published *A Diary of Prayer* nearly thirty years later, this prayer from *Hickes' Devotions* about the importance and immortality of loving was her selection for 24th April.

> O God, our heavenly Father, who hast commanded us to love one another as Thy children, and hast ordained the highest friendship in the bond of Thy Spirit, we beseech Thee to maintain and preserve us always in the same bond, to Thy glory, and our mutual comfort, with all those to whom we are bound by any special tie, either of nature or of choice; that we may be perfected together in that love which is from above, and which never faileth when all other things shall fail.[706]

The Monday he died was Elizabeth's 39th birthday.

> *His funeral service was held at New Milton, Hampshire, and the little church was filled with his old pupils and friends, who sang the hymn, "Praise to the Holiest in the Height" with all their hearts in thanksgiving for his life and work. As his coffin was carried out into the bright spring sunshine they formed a guard of honour at the lych gate. His ashes lie now in that country churchyard and on the cross that stands above them this verse from the Psalms is engraved, "He asked life of Thee, and Thou gavest him a long life, even for ever and ever."*[707]

The *Diary* also has this anonymous prayer for "Those who mourn."

> Lord, grant to him light and rest, peace and refreshment, joy and consolation in the nearness of the Saviour, in the companionship of saints, in the ample folds of Thy great love. Grant that he may go from strength to strength until at last he can enjoy the unveiled vision of Thy glory.
> If it may be, tell him, gracious Lord, how much I love him and miss him and long to see him again, and if there be ways in which he may come, grant him to me as a guide and guard, and give me a sense of his nearness in such degree as Thy laws permit.[708]

If these words formed part of her own prayer after Father's death, then they were answered.

We knew that my father still lived and still loved us. So great was his spiritual power that he was able to make that unmistakably clear to both of us after his death...[709] *He appeared to vanish but he was actually only on the other side of the green barrier that separates one mode of living from another. I have heard this described by someone who had entered it, and had been brought back to life again, as 'a green peace.'*[710]

Nevertheless the "shadowed" year of his death plunged her into a dark tunnel, and these words of Archbishop Benson also appear in her *Diary of Prayer*:

> O God, to me who am left to mourn his departure, grant that I may not sorrow as one without hope for my beloved who sleeps in Thee; but that ...I may see him again face to face, in those pastures and beside those waters of comfort where I believe he already walks with Thee. O Shepherd of the sheep, have pity upon this darkened soul of mine.[711]

The Secret Discipline - Her Father's Spiritual Legacy

Audrey said,

> She missed him quite appallingly because they got on so awfully well together and her father had a very light touch about all kinds of things, which was just what was wanted. It was terribly sad when he died.

I had come very near to my father at the end of his life for he had been so marvellously good to me in my miseries and problems. For most of my life...he had always been far on ahead of me...but in the last year of his life it was as though he turned back upon his path to find and be with me on mine. We were close to each other as never before, and part of my sorrow when he died was that our closeness was given no time to mature and grow greater.[712]

It seems that he had been far on ahead of her both intellectually and spiritually, for she described him as "disappearing into countries of the mind and spirit where I could not follow him." And she recognised too the depth of his prayer, when "it seemed to one watching his face that he wrestled and suffered as he prayed…"[713]

With such a man as my father it goes without saying that prayer was the mainspring of his life. He undertook no work or business, great or small, without praying about it, and he prayed always most earnestly for all those with whom he was brought in contact during the day… Sometimes on our walks he would go into village churches and he would kneel down and be instantly and unselfconsciously absorbed in prayer.[714]

Like Lucilla's son, the Reverend Hilary Eliot in her next novel *The Bird in the Tree*, whom David takes to the Chapel of Saint Mary at the Hard.

They lifted the latch and went in and Hilary, happily and unselfconsciously, knelt at once to his prayers.[715]

When he had turned back to be with her in a time of miseries and problems, Dr. Goudge helped his daughter in a way that was to change her life. Many years later, in 1973 she published an article entitled *The All-Day Prayer*, detailing the nature of his gift to her. This essay, like *The Joy of the Snow*, expresses her admiration for the depth of his faith and prayer life, and yet identifies it again as something which separated him from her.

I admired him so much and above all else I longed to have a faith like his. I would watch him sometimes, during the services, kneeling in his stall at the Cathedral, and know that he was far away in a world I had never entered. I longed with all my heart to be able to pray the way he did; as for me, after a few minutes my thoughts always bounced right back to earth – to the dress I was sewing or the poem I was writing.

I was sure that from this deep prayer life Father understood something of the "why" of suffering – he did tell me that he believed it could be "used" but no more than that, for though he would give one guidelines he believed that we learn best what we learn for ourselves. So I kept on grappling with the problem… Prayer, I felt sure, was the answer to using pain.[716]

Then at last one day he did give her the teaching she longed for. She learned from him how to come to terms with the problem of suffering, and at the same time to deepen her own ability to pray.

It was on vacation one year, in the summerhouse of a country cottage, that Father at last gave me the key I had sought so long. I was sitting rather miserably there, thinking of the suffering of the whole world, when he joined me. One cannot, he argued, shoulder too much of the world's pain without going mad. If there is anything one can do, he said, do it; if not, pray, and then put brooding right away.

His eyes roamed for a moment over the green lawn and then he said the words that have changed so much for me.

"As for our own burdens, it is not what we think about them but what we do with them that matters."

I thought of Mother, of what her pain-filled life had meant to so many, and I held my breath, conscious that a great secret lay a step away.

"What do you mean, Father?" I asked.

"When we offer our suffering to God," he said, "He can make of it the most powerful force on earth." Such an offering is an ancient form of intercession, he went on. Roman Catholic theologians called it acting "with an intention" – the intention being to help some person or group or situation for which we were concerned. Usually it was the Mass – Christ's suffering on the Cross – which was offered up in this way, but it could be any sacrificial act.

"When your mother bears a bad day with cheerfulness and courage, she can offer this response with an intention for a small thing, like your writing, or my next Sunday's sermon, or some large thing such as the peace of the world."

I knew at once that I had discovered something wonderful – though it has taken me… years of living "with intention" since that day, to discover just how wonderful. If Mother could make her very pain part of Christ's great reservoir of love, then I could do the same. Not that I then had physical pain to offer, but there were little things over the years, failures, disappointments. Making a home for many years for Mother, after Father died, was a joy to me, but it was not easy through all the dangers and difficulties of the war, and the griefs which we both shared…

"It isn't what we think about our burdens, but what we do with them that matters." Gradually I came to understand that it was not only negative things which could be offered this way; work itself at its best, always has an element of struggle and sacrifice connected with it. If I took time to find exactly the right word instead of the nearly-right one, I offered up this care. When I cooked a special meal, the extra effort became an intention. The writing and the busyness was no longer standing between myself and prayer because work itself was prayer, offered with all my strength and concentration.

Very, very often…the intention of these prayers was for the easing of Mother's pain. Other times it was for a friend, a neighbour, a reader who wrote to share a personal need. For myself the constant offering brought a new peacefulness, and there were glorious answers to many of these prayers. But I knew that many other people were praying too, people who could pray more deeply than I could, and so I could take no credit… only joy. The joy is every Christian's secret: that Christ took the heavy, ugly, hard things in life and turned them, on the Cross, into love.[717]

※

"No longer standing between myself and prayer…" Here at last was an answer to the problem of the two worlds; although it was only a first step - and the journey, as she said, would take years. Maybe this description of Margary in *The Rosemary Tree* tells us something about Elizabeth's own journey.

> *A child still, she knew nothing of herself. She did not understand the reason for the deep alternations of mood that afflicted her, and could not know yet how acceptance of the change from well-being to its opposite, offered for those who suffered, could serve them. That supreme usefulness to which her awareness of the needs of others would eventually lead her was a long way in the future, and before she found the bare cell there would be the desert of ineffectiveness to cross.*[718]

The Rosemary Tree was published some seventeen years after her father's death, and more than twenty since *Island Magic*. Elizabeth was by then in her mid fifties, and it seems that she had travelled a long way since creating Michelle — the girl constantly brought down from well-being to its opposite, as her yearnings to find and dwell in a tantalizing world of beauty are again and again frustrated. Now Elizabeth knew that the cell was bare, and only to be found at the other side of a desert — one of the classic images of the long and difficult journey to union with God. In the same novel she quotes T.S. Eliot's words about worshipping in a desert "somewhere on the other side of despair."[719] Thanks to her father she could now state with quiet confidence that the cell was *there*, and that the discipline of worship in a desert — the secret discipline of turning suffering into prayer - could provide her with a hidden refuge, as secret as the vision of heaven to a young child.

> *There was always the hidden life. For the child the journeys to the little land, the land of the memory and foretaste of paradise, for the man who was truly a man, the secret discipline.*[720]

In *The Rosemary Tree* Margary's father is another clergyman who married and yet would have been very much at home in a monk's cell. It is this cell of peace that will prove to be John Wentworth's greatest legacy to his daughter.

> *He knew the preciousness of the single state... The cell, and the sunlight moving on the bare wall... He had chosen it once, knowing it the life for him, and then...to serve [Daphne] he had shut the door of the cell behind him with himself outside. He had lost his cell, yet, paradoxically, it existed now somewhere within him. He believed that in dying he might leave it to Margary as other men leave their daughter a material house. When she was old she would go in and find peace.*[721]

Learning to Cope

Right now though, in 1939, peace would have been hard to find. Her father's death had precipitated an abrupt change in their circumstances, for their only claim to their home of course had been that it was the official residence of the Regius Professor. Now his widow and daughter had only a comparatively short while in which to pack up and leave.

Once she had mastered her first shock and grief my mother behaved like a phoenix, drove herself back into life and then flamed up into activity and optimism, even into a spurious state of health and strength that amazed Nanny and myself. For Nanny of course had now come to us. Her own parents had died, she was living with her sisters and was free to help us until we had settled into a new home. Hélène was no longer living with us as her parents had come back to England for good and she was with them, and so my mother now only had Nanny and me to galvanise into activity.

We packed up the family treasures to go into store [and] sold the rest of the contents of the big Oxford house to help pay the large sum that was owing to the Inland Revenue.[722]

So there were money problems to sort out too. She says her father had been "too generous a man to be any good at what the Edwardians called 'putting by'..."

In his seventies, if he had to go away, he was still lugging a heavy suitcase to Carfax and catching the bus to the station. Through such economies he had more money to give away...[723] *And he had had to live in large ecclesiastical houses that took a lot of upkeep, so he had been able to leave my mother very little. [But] all my father's pupils, from Wells to Oxford days, with wonderful generosity...joined together to make a gift to my mother in his memory and so she...had a little annuity.*[724]

Our first move was back to Barton, where Innisfree was now home. And we knew how lucky we were. Not many clergy widows, turning out in a hurry, have anywhere to go and we had our bungalow already furnished with the little we needed. Indeed we were lucky for unless I could manage to work much harder and write much better than I was doing at the moment we were going to be very badly off.[725] *I was more than a little scared.*[726]

So she was not only bereft of her beloved father, not only forced to move house almost immediately while still shocked and miserable: she was also now responsible for her invalid mother, with the urgent necessity to augment that small annuity with her own earnings. Yet it was not that long since she herself had had an operation and a nervous breakdown. And as if all this were not enough to make her feel "more than a little scared," the international situation was terrifying. A little over four months after her father's death, on 3rd September 1939, war was declared.

> *Miss Brown was in the grip of fear; not just apprehension or anxiety, but real fear, naked and horrible. Though she looked so serene sitting there in the sunshine her body was ice-cold and she was finding it quite difficult to breathe.*
> *"And yet I'm not worse off than many other people," she said to herself. "I have lost my home and my livelihood, but so have lots of others. This that is happening to me, this sort of chasm opening at my feet, is happening to the whole world. I am not alone. I am not alone. I am not alone."*
>
> *But what she reiterated to herself brought her no conviction. Her loss of everything she had hitherto known was making her feel as solitary as though she were the only human creature alive in the world…*[727]
> *She felt as though she was falling through space…*[728]

This is from *The Castle on the Hill*, the war novel she published two years later. Like Miss Brown, Elizabeth might well have felt that there was a chasm opening at her own feet at this moment. Nevertheless she did manage to have work published that year, even though she says that the shock of her father's death left her temporarily unable to write.

Her *Three Plays* finally appeared in print, dedicated to E.U.P., the initials of her aunt Eva Parmiter, Canon Goudge's sister. They are *Suomi*, *The Brontës of Haworth* and *Fanny Burney*, which had been staged in London two years earlier under the title *Joy Will Come Back*. Elizabeth also tried submitting *Suomi* to the BBC in December 1939 with the recommendation that it had been "produced in London some while ago by a Sunday night society, with the help of the Finnish Embassy,"[729] and with Thea Holme playing a lead part. There was to be no radio broadcast however: the BBC sent it back with a letter of rejection in February 1940.

Her Christmas novella *The Sister of the Angels* was more successful. A sequel to *A City of Bells*, dedicated to "those who love Henrietta," it was published by Duckworth with illustrations by C. Walter Hodges. It also appeared unabridged, complete with some of Hodges' illustrations, in the December edition of *Woman's Journal* under the title *The Constant Heart*. Poignantly, it contains happy scenes between a father and daughter, Ferranti and Henrietta.

> *Her father's face [was] lit by the light that only came upon it when they were going to have one of their glorious secret times.*
>
> *It was only he who gave her these particular glorious times. She had glorious times with Grandfather, and with Hugh Anthony, but they weren't quite the same, not so exciting...*
>
> *Ferranti was a most accomplished story-teller, above all by candlelight, a light which is romantic above all others; a gentle light into which fairies and ghosts are not afraid to step... Henrietta wriggled closer to her father, within the shelter of his arm lest there should be ghosts in the story, and looked with delicious tingling anticipation at the shadows that might presently take shape and form and be one knew not who...*

When the story is finished,

> *"Now you must go to bed," said Ferranti, picking her up... [He] tucked her up in bed with his own hot-water bottle, she only being allowed bedsocks by the rule of the house, and bent down to kiss her... "Good-night, darling daughter."*[730]

It also contains a message that was to appear in more than one of her novels – the idea that what one fails to give in one relationship, one can give in later life to someone else. When Ferranti commissions a portrait from a poor artist, Henrietta can "feel the tingling warmth of his happiness" and says, "You liked telling that man to paint a picture of me." Her father agrees.

> *"Yes... You see I was once in a mess myself, and Grandfather and other people helped me out. I can't repay my debt to the people to whom I really owe it, one seldom can in this world, but I can in a sense repay it to somebody else."*[731]

A decade later, she would say again in *Gentian Hill*: "In this world death has a habit of intervening before we can pay our debts, and the only thing to be done is to pay them to another."[732] It was what she had done in *Towers in the Mist*: she repaid her debt to Adolphus by giving her readers the reassurance she had failed to give to him.

In the same year, four years after its first publication in the UK there was an American edition of *The Middle Window*, again with wrapper design by C. Walter Hodges. Elizabeth also wrote the introduction to a book of poetry: *The Rider of Mendip and other poems* by Alan C. Tarbat. Her published foreword is addressed as from Christ Church Oxford, and dated 12th June 1939. It is - in keeping with the contents of Tarbat's book - a celebration of poetry, legend and the beauties of nature, but it also points to, and reiterates, the insecurity of her world at that time.

> *In the midst of the uncertainty and anxiety of the world today we turn to poetry, as we turn to the unchanging beauty of woods and hills and to all that is lovely in history and legend, for an assurance of security, something to bind us to a sense of permanence. Poetry is the language of insight, a language whose form may change through the centuries, but whose revelation of an unchanging certainty behind the changes and chances of this mortal life is forever the same. Mr. Tarbat's poems give to us a threefold sense of security; they are authentic poetry, and their throne is the loveliness of the countryside and of the inviolable past...*
>
> *At the end of the book we are left giving thanks for two enduring things, "for countryside and common ways" and for the vast scene of legend that stretches behind them and that seems to many of us at times more real than the confused happenings of our modern world.*[733]

She was afraid, but she had the support of her father's way of prayer. She had always understood the impossibility of living in "unchanging beauty," for the hard things of life cannot be avoided; but thanks to his help she knew that the hard things need not plunge us into misery, bad temper or despair; they can instead be *accepted*, and lived, and offered up. With his wisdom to guide her she would be able to write - ten years later, in *Gentian Hill* - about yet another priest giving advice to his daughter in an England at war.

> *"Show no sign of your fear, offer it to God for Zachary, and the costly gift will be a more acceptable prayer than any repetition of mere words," said the Abbé slowly.*
>
> *Stella looked up at him, her eyes suddenly bright with the pleasure of a new idea. He very often now presented her with these new ideas, and always he spoke slowly as though underlining each word, so that she stowed his ideas away very carefully for future use. With a flash of intuition she knew that this one, when put into use, was going to revolutionise the whole of life.*[734]

MARLDON

❋

1939 - 1952

Devon

The turmoil of leaving Oxford over, exhausted by it and with nothing more to do we sank into black misery until my mother was suddenly aware of the first star, the first pointer. "We need a holiday," she said. "We are going to Devon for a month..."

[She] had seen an advertisement in the paper. A small wooden bungalow could be cheaply rented for a summer holiday at a village called Marldon, four miles from Paignton... and she was quite certain that that was where we must go. So Nanny and I dragged ourselves out of the ooze of our exhaustion and we set off, driven by a Barton friend who had a large comfortable car.[735]

They reached their destination late in the afternoon, only to find a bungalow on a hill, enveloped in thick mist. They could see very little, and the next morning the mist was still there... but Elizabeth had been awakened by the sound she loved so well, a sound she had not heard for a long time: "a cock crowing in the garden, across the lane, eastward where the sun would soon be rising." The symbolism cannot have been lost on her.

When later I pulled back my curtains...the morning sun was shining through [the mist] and turning it to gold, and every bush and tree that lined the lane was glistening with diamond drops.

Here, in the morning light that she loved, was a world quite different from the Oxford life of the last sixteen years.

The sun was drawing up the mist and building with it galleons and cities in the air. They drifted across a sky so deeply blue that it was hard to believe it had been dark with rain the day before, and the vastness of the skyscape was almost worthy of the Fen country. Because of the slope of the land the hill seemed higher than it actually was; it seemed high as Ararat, with the wooden bungalow perched like the Ark on its summit. The valley below was even wider and deeper than I had realised the night before and it seemed to hold every beauty that a pastoral Devon valley knows, woods and farms and orchards, green slopes where sheep were grazing, fields of black and white cows, and where there were fields of tilled earth it was the crimson of the earth of South Devon and looked like a field of flowers.[736]

Some years later she published an article entitled *West Country Magic* giving this description of the countryside even closer to her new home.

Just opposite the cottage where I live there is a steep bank covered with periwinkles which bloom all the year round, but in spring are like a cloak of blue over the bank. A very old flight of stone steps leads up the bank to a little stile at the top. When you have climbed the steps and the stile you find yourself in a meadow.[737]

This became one of Elizabeth's very special places: "The field above the periwinkle bank…was to me, in Devon," she said, "what the Magdalen cloisters had been at Oxford." It gave her the selfsame view "that had come through the mist on our first morning at the Ark."[738]

You look west to wild Dartmoor, purple and blue on the horizon, and east to the sea. To the south there is a tall hill called Beacon Hill, where in the days of the Napoleonic wars the sentry stood watching for invasion, and where in 1940 the sentry stood once again watching for invasion. One day I want to write a fairy story about the periwinkle bank, the steps and the little stile. For they have magic in them.[739]

The book she eventually published, in 1964, was not a fairy story but *Linnets and Valerians*. The Black Knight paperback edition contained this Afterword for her young readers.

> *People often ask a writer how a particular book came to be written.* Linnets and Valerians *is the result of leaning on a gate for twelve years. Although I did not lean on the gate all of the day of those 4,380 days I seldom missed leaning on it for part of each day. It was only a short walk from the cottage where I lived and from it, looking across a wide valley, I could see Dartmoor rising up in the distance. Sometimes the hills were grape purple, sometimes blue or silver, and in winter they were often covered with snow. When the gales came they roared over the crests of those hills, and the light warm wind that brought the first white violets and periwinkles into bloom came from the same place, and so they seemed the home of all that was magical.*[740]

Even when writing for adults in *The Joy of the Snow* she stressed the magical quality of the Devon she had known in those days: "before almost the whole county became a holiday playground and the fairies fled." It was to her "an unearthly place."[741]

The round green hills where the sheep grazed, the wooded valleys and the lanes full of wild flowers, the farms and apple orchards were all full of magic, and the birds sang in that long-ago Devon as I have never heard them singing anywhere else in the world; in the spring we used to say it sounded as though the earth itself was singing.[742]

Small wonder, then that she follows up the description of that view, on her first morning at the Ark, by saying "I felt I had come home."

I have never felt so deeply rooted anywhere as I was in the earth of Devon. Or rather I did not so much put roots down as find roots that were already there... I was ashamed that I should not feel one tremor of homesickness for Oxford, or even for Barton. The only tremor was the realisation that in a few weeks' time we should have to leave this earthly paradise and go back to Barton where my father had died. There seemed no death here, only life.[743]

Providence Cottage

Suddenly the war broke out. We could not know then that all through the winter it would be only what we called 'the phoney war'. At the time we expected that bombs would fall instantly on London and parents fell into a state of panic about their children. We had an S.O.S. from a friend...who lived in London and had four small children. Would we let him buy our Barton bungalow exactly as it was, with its contents, that he might send his family to live there immediately? My mother never hesitated. Indeed I think she sent a telegram of acceptance, and then said to me, "We are going to live here – in Devon."[744]

Their landlady, who lived next door, said they could stay on in the Ark - through the winter if necessary – and they began to look for a permanent home.

We made no headway since anything we could afford to pay for, my mother could not ever contemplate as her future home. And she was quite right. It would have been like trying to grow a Guernsey lily in a tin can and she would have wilted and died.[745]

> *'You know, Mother dear,' Hilary said gently... 'I'm afraid your ideas are a bit too large. You can't afford the sort of house you want, darling. You'll just have to put up with the best that we can do.*
>
> *'I will do no such thing, Hilary,' Lucilla said, aggrieved. 'I will have what I want for my children and my grandchildren or I will have nothing...'*[746]

And so it was that the Eliots came to Damerosehay, for Lucilla wanted Damerosehay and Lucilla had to have what she wanted. Her children, worshipping the very ground she trod on, saw this as clearly as she did herself, but what they did not at first see as clearly as Lucilla was how the purchase and restoration of Damerosehay was to be reconciled with the condition in which the family finances unfortunately found themselves. 'I'll sell my diamonds,' said Lucilla happily, and thought she had found the solution of their difficulties. They did not undeceive her. They let her think, since she wanted to think it, that the sale of the diamonds, which just about mended the roof and modernized the drains, but no more, had purchased the whole estate, but secretly they all of them…dived into their pockets.[747]

The Bird in the Tree

What Elizabeth and her mother had the good fortune to find was not a Damerosehay in need of restoration, but a local builder prepared to erect for them a "compact little cottage which had about it an air of charm and originality that suited my mother." The local builder was Mr. Clare, by amazing coincidence the brother of their old friend the draper in the market square at Wells, and as such happy to help them in whatever ways he could. He and her mother, she said,

shared the same sort of sanguine temperament; plus charm and strength of will. If possessed of these three glorious attributes a person does not, I have come to believe, need to do much personally, he or she need only hope and smile and will and other people will do most of it for them.[748]

And so it was that within a short space of time an "ideal plot of land" had been found, plans were drawn up, and the digging of the foundations began. The site that Mr. Clare came up with was "one of the loveliest that could be imagined," in "a small valley that had the lovely name of Westerland." He built the house on a gentle southern slope in one of the orchards there, "a small cider-apple orchard separated from the lane by a hedge of nut trees and a steep bank where primroses grew."[749] During the building, Elizabeth and her mother spent the winter in their wooden holiday bungalow, the Ark, which she said was "a refuge indeed."

During the autumn gales it groaned and creaked and shuddered but stood firm, and during the intense cold of that January, when every twig of every tree was encased in tinkling ice and the poor frozen birds fell dead from the branches, it kept us alive.[750]

But she knew only too well that it was not just a house they needed in order to stay alive.

There was little room in my anxious mind for anything except the necessity for hard work, and I shut myself inside my tiny bedroom and found among my papers the first pages of [the] novel I had begun to write before my father died... The Bird in the Tree. *I did not imagine I could do anything with it for how, now, could I recapture Damerosehay and Keyhaven? I felt I was living in another age and another time and that Keyhaven belonged to a lost century... I have seldom had to struggle so hard over a book.*[751]

Nevertheless, she was writing again and she did finish the book, using Harewood House at Keyhaven, where she had stayed when recovering from her operation, as the model for the home she called Damerosehay. Once again the inspiration came not just from a beloved location but from her mother - for the central character, Lucilla Eliot, has "something of my mother" in her, she says.[752]

Published the following year, it was the first book in what would become the Damerosehay trilogy comprising The Bird in the Tree (1940), The Herb of Grace (1948) and The Heart of the Family (1953).

Rebuilding the Waste Land – The Bird in the Tree

For the background to the story, she looked back to the world of her youth and the aftermath of World War I.

Lucilla, devastated by the loss of her best-beloved son in the war, finds herself in her own private wasteland. But she does not despair. She determines instead to dedicate herself to the well-being of the next generation and buys Damerosehay as a family home, to be a safe haven for her grandchildren. It is to be a place of healing, a bulwark in an otherwise disintegrating world, and a symbol of family unity. It is an historic old house in a dilapidated state, and its restoration symbolises continuity: a resurgence of life in the aftermath of war.

> *And then Lucilla knew what she was going to do with the rest of her life. She was going to build some sort of a refuge, somewhere, to which her children and her grandchildren could escape. Not a permanent escape; even in her grief she still knew that a selfish isolation is the sure road to hell; but that temporary one which is the right of every man. They were talking a lot just now about the war to end war, and a country fit for heroes to live in. She thought they deceived themselves. She had seen now what life could be, and what man could do when the*

> *devil was in him. She had not much hope of any wholesale change; only of the creation of isolated homes of beauty from which, please God, the loveliness should spread. Such a home would she make for her children and her grandchildren. They should come to it weary and sickened and go away made new. They should find peace there, and beauty, and the cleansing of their sins.*[753]

It is similar to the ideal in *The Middle Window* - to create beauty in a kind of monastic isolation, which yet will spread for the good of others. Here at Damerosehay though, the religious imagery is even stronger: the house is to be for the cleansing of sins. As its description continues, it becomes an "altar" and its purchase is almost like the buying of the pearl of great price - they must give all they have and are, to acquire it.

> *They all of them…dived into their pockets and laid the last available halfpenny upon the altar of Damerosehay. The sons suspected that they would be helping to pay for the upkeep of the place until their dying day, and Margaret, facing year after year of struggle with an under-staffed house and garden and ends that could be persuaded to meet only with the greatest difficulty, had felt sometimes that her strength and her courage must surely break. Yet, twenty years later, in this Autumn of 1938, they were all agreed that it had been worth it. Lucilla had been quite right. Damerosehay was their inevitable home. From the very beginning, almost as though it were alive, it had taken them all to its heart and held them there.*[754]

But the world was crumbling into another war as Elizabeth struggled to write this book; and in the same way Damerosehay's power to stabilise and protect the family is now under threat. Lucilla's beloved grandson David has fallen in love with his uncle's ex-wife, the beautiful young divorcée Nadine, and thus begins a struggle between the grandmother's Victorian belief in Duty - the sacrifice of personal happiness for the greater good - and the young man's twentieth-century preoccupation with freedom of the individual.

David's attitude represents the shift towards a new morality that had powerfully influenced the post-war Oxford Elizabeth had known. In reaction against the convention of a moral law, it advocated instead the importance of self-expression, and the freedom to live by one's own lights. Even Bede Griffiths, in *The Golden String*, commented on how powerful a movement it had been: how difficult not to be swept away by it. Earlier still, back in 1900 a modern young female in H.G. Wells' novel *Love and Mr. Lewisham* had endorsed a similar kind of freedom, stating her determination to live her own life, and adding:

> "What a beautiful phrase that is... redolent of honest scorn for moral plagiarism. No *Imitatio Christi* in that..."[755]

For Lucilla, the same phrase is anything but beautiful. It smacks far too much of selfishness to win her approval.

> *It was that declaration of Nadine's, that she wanted "to live her own life," that had exasperated Lucilla beyond anything else... It was a remark frequently on the lips of the modern generation, she knew, and it annoyed her. For whose lives, in the name of heaven, could they live except their own? Everyone must look after something in this world and why were they living their own lives if they looked after antique furniture, petrol pumps or parrots, and not when they looked after husbands, children or aged parents?*[756]

David, on the other hand, revels in the knowledge that this freedom to be oneself involves courage in the pursuit of truth.

> *His love for Nadine was the most shatteringly real thing that had ever happened to him. It was the truth, and it must be served...*
> *Truth. He would have to try to make Lucilla understand how he felt about it, how it was to him the lamp that lit all life. It would be difficult, for her generation and his felt so differently about this truth. Her generation had built from without inwards, had put the reality of law and tradition above the reality of personal feeling, but his built from within outwards, the truth of personal feeling must come first; when there was no longer reality in a union, smash the union; never mind what laws were broken or what lives were crippled; live the truth...*
> *Life, to him, was the fearless facing of reality.*[757]

As the story progresses however, David comes to discover that the truth of personal feeling alone is not enough, and he tells his Uncle Hilary (a man who does live by the rule of *Imitatio Christi*) "I envy you your peace."

> *You men of faith have kept something that the rest of us have lost... singleness of mind. Faith in the value of what you are doing. And... a rule of life that can be used as a touchstone for all your actions. I envy you your faith; I wish I had it.*[758]

Once again Elizabeth had written a novel debating the nature of freedom. Taking up the cudgels against the ideas of the age – which had so recently rocked the stability of even the country itself, through the love affair of that other, royal, David[759] - she placed her emphasis not only on the need for faith, but on the importance of home and family life in an evil and unstable world.

> *Happy homes are very important, I think, far more important than you realize, and God knows how many of them have been built up by the sacrifice of private longings.*[760]

Sometimes stability can only be bought by the sacrifice of personal happiness. As she would still be saying nearly a quarter of a century later in *The Scent of Water* - "love is not some marvellous thing that you feel, but some hard thing you do."[761] Lucilla confesses to the young couple that when young and unhappily married herself, she had also found the "truth" of a new love, but the hard thing she did was to stay with her husband and children, and (as she did in buying Damerosehay) make something creative out of her unhappiness. She hopes to convince David that unselfish action will always be preferable to indulgence of one's own desires. In fact, she argues, unselfishness is in itself a creative force:

> *I am inclined to think that nothing so fosters creative action as the sacrifice of feeling. It's like rain coming down upon the corn.*[762]

※

Corn is a central symbol in all the Damerosehay novels. David has, on the wall above his bed, a reproduction of "Van Gogh's painting of a lark tossing joyously over a wind-blown cornfield."[763] And close by the house, integral to its sense of permanence, there are two cornfields – here described in *The Herb of Grace*.

> *The car swung to the right into the rutted lane, and the cool tang of the sea came to meet them. They were silent while Nadine watched for what to returning Eliots was the first sight of home – the two cornfields that marked the place where the lane swung east towards Little Village; the cultivated one upon the landward side of the lane and the wild one… mysteriously sprung up all by itself in the marsh.*[764]

They are more than simply landscape. Like Damerosehay itself, the corn stands for renewal and continuity; but the fields also have a religious significance, which is underlined by echoes from the Gospels.

> *It was autumn now and the corn was ripe. In the field in the angle of the lane it was cut and standing proudly in golden stooks, waiting to be carried away to make the bread that fed the world; but across the road in the marsh the stunted stalks stood uncut and the pale grains waited only to drop to the earth unwanted. As the wind passed over them they rustled a little desolately, and Ben's heart suddenly ached intolerably for that unwanted, ungarnered gold… He wondered what it was saying. "Except a seed fall into the ground and die…"*[765]

"Except a corn of wheat fall into the ground and die, it abideth alone: but if it die, it bringeth forth much fruit."[766]

> *Every year the queer stunted blades pushed their way up, first the blade, then the ear, then the full corn in the ear. It was never reaped, for it was useless stuff, a mere travesty of what corn should be; so it fell and died and from its death fresh life sprang again, year after year, curiously persistent.*[767]

"For the earth bringeth forth fruit of herself, first the blade, then the ear, after that the full corn in the ear."[768]

The fresh life springing from death is of course a resurrection symbol, and a confirmation of the paradoxical necessity of death so that new life may come. But Damerosehay was created by Lucilla in the aftermath of the Great War; and Elizabeth was writing the book as a second war began, barely a generation later. So the old cornfield also symbolises humankind's dogged struggle against evil throughout the ages; constantly trying and failing, "a mere travesty of what corn should be" and yet "curiously persistent."[769]

The mystery of the old cornfield is that "no one had ever planted it." Once, long ago, a grain ship had been wrecked in the marsh and now the corn just grew by itself… "a strange stunted harvest that could not be reaped, but only reverenced for the mystery of renewal."[770] So, not just biblical echoes here, but a reference to the mystical vision of Thomas Traherne:

> The corn was orient and immortal wheat, which never should be reaped, nor was ever sown. I thought it had stood from everlasting to everlasting.[771]

Traherne died in 1674 but he was not published until the early part of the twentieth century, and so for Elizabeth's generation his words had the impact of the new. Extracts from his *Centuries of Meditation* - including the above verse - were set to music by her contemporary, Gerald Finzi in his great song-cycle *Dies Natalis*.[772] This made its first appearance – like *The Bird in the Tree* – in 1940, its world premiere given at the Wigmore Hall in January of that year. Traherne's work influenced more than one of Elizabeth's books, and can be found too in *A Diary of Prayer* and all three of her anthologies.

It is for the sake of the children that Damerosehay is created, and in the same Traherne extract in *A Book of Comfort* he describes - predating the Romantics –the purity of his own childhood vision.

> All appeared new and strange at first, inexpressibly rare and delightful and beautiful. I was a little stranger which at my entrance into the world was saluted and surrounded with innumerable joys... All things were spotless and pure and glorious; and infinitely mine and joyful and precious...
>
> Is it not strange that an infant should be heir of the whole world, and see those mysteries which the books of the learned never unfold?[773]

All the Traherne quotations she uses are full of reverence for the natural world, which he saw as the expression of God's love and glory...

> I was entertained like an angel with the works of God in their splendour and glory; I saw all in the peace of Eden; heaven and earth did sing my Creator's praises.[774]

Often, Elizabeth's own descriptions of the natural world will personify the landscape in this way too. It no doubt added ammunition to those critics who saw her work as sentimental, but it surely sprang from this same mystical belief that everything is alive with the breath of God. Take Lucilla's first sight of the overgrown garden at Damerosehay, for example. It has reverted to wildness, but it is also – like the house - a symbol of a world fighting back after the evil of war. It is the absolute antithesis of *The Waste Land's* dry rock. Everywhere there are plants refusing to be overcome, holding their heads up high, rampant with "a sort of jubilant madness."

> *What lay within the old red walls…was a wild, crazy garden…*
> *Once it had been planted with orderly care and neatness, but now all the flowers and trees and bushes had gone mad together with a sort of jubilant madness that was one of the loveliest things Lucilla had ever seen. The rose trees, bright with their new green leaves, were running riot everywhere, climbing up over the old wall, festooning themselves over the cherry trees and oak trees…that grew in the tangle of wild grass that had once been lawns and flower-beds, and flinging out greedy suckers over the bushes of silvery lavender and rosemary that were struggling gallantly to keep their heads above the tide of green that threatened to wash over them completely. The cherry trees were out already, a foam of white against the blue, and below them daffodils flowed through the grass in drifts of gold.*[775]

It is a kind of enclosed Eden, full of religious symbolism. The rose of course represents Love. It is also an ancient symbol of the Virgin Mary: as in the mediaeval carol, from a 15th century parchment roll in the library of Trinity College, Cambridge, which calls her "the rose that bare Jesu."[776] Her Son, too, is the "spotless rose" of a 14th century carol; a Rose that sprang from its "sweet root…in Mary, purest Maid." (Another contemporary English composer, Herbert Howells, set this carol to music just after the end of the First World War: it was published in the same year as *The Fairies' Baby*, 1919.) An enclosed garden can, too, symbolise God's people living within his protection, as in the words of the Song of Solomon: "A garden inclosed is my sister, my spouse."[777]

And the dominant feature of Damerosehay's walled garden is the ilex tree,

> *standing up sturdy and strong above the general riot, its stiff little leaves like blobs of dark green paint against the bright sky.*[778]

This was no fiction; there actually was an ilex tree at Harewood House - as there is still in the garden of the Bishop's Palace in Wells. Lover of legend that she was, however, Elizabeth must have known that one member of the ilex family - the holly tree - is a symbol not only of Christmas, the beginning of Christ's life on earth, but of its ending too in the Passion. Its stiff, prickly leaves represent the crown of thorns, and an old legend says that the holly allowed itself to be used for the cross, being the only tree whose wood did not splinter under the axe. And so, symbolically, it could be seen as the cross which is standing up sturdy and strong in the enclosed rose-garden at Damerosehay, this paradise where the children will be safe and protected.

Marldon

> *"Grandmother," said David, "could I go out into the garden..?"*
>
> *"Of course, darling," said Lucilla, and she lifted him over the sill, setting his feet down among the daffodils below the window. In a minute he was gone, running quickly, hidden from sight by the green sea of grass and the swelling waves of the rosemary and lavender. Lucilla did not fear for him. No harm could come to him in a walled garden. House and garden, oak-wood, marshes and sea, it was all of it a children's paradise, and a paradise that would not lose its glory as the children grew older... She had found what she wanted.*[779]

Elizabeth said she had seldom had to struggle so hard over a book. But the result of her struggles was one of her best and most enduringly popular novels - and one that took the faith content of her work to a new level of mystical symbolism and allegory. Did she now begin, perhaps, to shoulder a new responsibility - to take on her father's role not only in earning their keep, but in writing books worthy of his great faith and teaching?

Certainly the author Rosemary Sutcliff, who knew Elizabeth and was a great admirer of her books, felt that her writing seemed to "take off" after her father died.[780] And perhaps it is just coincidence, but the prayer of Archbishop Benson in *A Diary of Prayer* could be read as a pointer towards a new sense of purpose in her work.

> O God, to me who am left to mourn his departure, grant that...always remembering his courage, and the love that united us on earth, I may begin again with new courage to serve Thee more fervently...[781]

Work and War

A new year is at hand. We cannot tell what it will bring. If it brings peace, how thankful we shall be. If it brings us continued struggle we shall remain undaunted.

In the meantime I feel that we may all find a message of encouragement in the lines which in my closing words I would like to say to you..."Go out into the darkness and

put your hand into the Hand of God. That shall be to you better than light and safer than a known way."
May that Almighty Hand guide and uphold us all.
King George VI: *Christmas Broadcast, 1939*

The cottage was finished by the time the apple blossom was in bud. We moved in and almost at once, her task accomplished, my mother broke down and was very ill.[782]

Still in the aftermath of Elizabeth's own ill health and grief came this third house move within the space of a year: Oxford to Barton, Barton to the Ark, and now the Ark to their new home in Providence Cottage, Marldon. Her mother's intuitive plan to go to Devon, sweeping all before her, had come to satisfactory fruition; but as with the transfer from Ely to Oxford, her health broke down as she moved into her new home. She was once again very ill, and the same spring that brought the apple blossom and the move, brought with it also Elizabeth's fortieth birthday. Thus began what must have been the most gruelling period of her life.

Nevertheless, she knew her good fortune.

All times of devastation…leave the survivors with a feeling of amazement. Is it possible that such weak creatures as we know ourselves to be have coped with this? Done what had to be done, borne what had to be borne, picked up the pieces and become ready to begin again and go on living. It took more than a year, moves to three different houses, and the outbreak of a war to bring my mother and myself to this condition of amazement, followed by humble gratitude…

"Providence Cottage" was of course considered a sentimental name by a number of friends ("What have you called the place? Tranquillity Lodge? Serenity Mansion? Peace Villa?") but our feelings were not hurt for we knew what we knew.[783]

Elizabeth was also experiencing something completely new and - despite all the fear and devastation - very satisfying: having only ever lived in Father's official ecclesiastical residences, she and her mother were now acquiring their own home. During the building of the house she had gone out in the winter cold to look down on the orchard and see "the skeleton of the growing cottage."

[The workmen's] cheery voices would come faintly up to me through the still air. I was one of them, I felt, for I had worked hard too to build that twiggy thing down there, looking at the moment more like a nest than a house, and I felt awed as I looked down, as though the building of a home was something entirely new in the world.

Marldon

Having lived always in old houses that were only on loan for as long as the temporary owner could do the job of work they represented, I had no conception of what it feels like to make a home that is yours for as long as you wish it to be.[784]

Much as she owed to her cathedral-close background, much as she loved her father and mourned him and missed him, she was now free, at the age of forty, to be settled in her own home for the first time in her life. It was the start of "the interweaving joy and woe…of all the years that my mother and I spent in Devon. The loveliness lightened the sorrow and the sorrow shadowed the loveliness and the mind was in a state of perpetual confusion."[785]

❋

Perhaps not too much imagination was required, twenty years later, to create the character of Miss Montague in *The Dean's Watch*, who looks back on herself in her middle years as a "toiling drone." Looking back on her own life Elizabeth observed that, for someone brought up in an Edwardian household of cooks and housemaids, domestic life had changed enormously by the time the war began. It certainly had. As an example, as late as 1930 the author Mary Wesley had been sent to domestic science college at the age of eighteen - not to learn any practical skills for herself, but to be taught how to supervise servants. Now, just ten years down the line, life was very different and there was much to learn.

The war years meant not only air raids, sorrow and anxiety, but the total disappearance of the servants who used to make our lives so leisured. We…had to learn to cook and do housework.[786]

> *Miss Brown, coming downstairs to help Fanny with the washing up, marvelled for the hundredth time at the horrid appearance of things that have been emptied of their virtue… Tomato skin without tomato is a revolting sight, while as for a whiting's head and backbone minus the whiting – Miss Brown shuddered and looked the other way… She could never get used to the grease of it, the smell of it, the exhaustion of it and its heartbreaking monotony… But she did not allow the slight discouragement of these thoughts to become visible; that would have been against her principles.*

"Isn't it a nice day, Mr. Boulder?" she said brightly, as she buttoned a chintz overall over her green linen dress.[787]

The Castle on the Hill

At Ely they had had her mother's "three beloved maids, Phyllis, Muriel and Florence," all born in the Fens, who had then moved with them to Oxford;[788] and the household there had been further augmented by their charwoman, Mrs. Rogers, who said to Elizabeth one day "with absolute sincerity and much love,"

"I'm so sorry for ladies. Poor dears, they're so helpless." How ashamed I was! At this period of my life I hardly knew how to peel a potato.[789]

But she learnt.

My alarm clock drags me grumbling out of bed at 7 o'clock on a dark cold winter's morning to wrestle with a kitchen stove that has probably gone out in the night and the problem of war-time breakfast when the bacon ration for the week was finished long ago, the hens aren't laying and the grocer is temporarily "out" of cereal. It is a black moment and while it lasts (that is, until I get the stove going again and have imbibed the first cup of glorious hot coffee which is really all any sensible person needs for breakfast) I consider myself the most ill-used woman ever made...[790]

The alarm clock has dragged her not just from sleep, but from a beautiful dream – she was, she said, a "copious dreamer" - and whatever she had to cope with in these dark years, her dreams, her faith and the beauty of the natural world would come to her rescue: the loveliness would lighten the sorrow.

...But it is after all only a moment. There was wonder behind and there is wonder before. I have emerged from the loveliness of my waking dream and when the light comes I shall unlock the front door, wrap myself in a thick coat and go out into the garden and watch the birds flying across the dawn sky...

It is a glorious moment when the front door of the cottage bangs shut behind me and I am out in the tingling cold of a fine frosty winter's dawn. There is a group of pine trees in one corner of the garden, standing up black and noble against the pale green sky, and I have arrived at the right moment, for the moon is entangled in their branches. To the east the sky is barred with rose over the sea and so I have that especial light of my dreams, that is a mingling of moonlight and sunshine... In its shining the glitter of the hoar frost, though it is flung over the grass like a veil of living light, does not hurt the eyes...

There is a moment of hushed expectancy and then they come, long black lines of them moving across the rosy east, flying from north to south in slow rhythmical ecstasy.[791]

This is from *Dreams*, an essay published in the 1947 anthology *At the Sign of the Dolphin*. She seems to be drawing upon the same memory ten years later, in this extract from *The Rosemary Tree*.

Her eyes followed their flight, the long sweeping curves, the slow beat of the great wings, and then a more gentle rise and fall, as though the still air had unseen waves whose rhythm rocked them. There was a great spaciousness about their movements. Both the sea and the sky were theirs. They were content now in this valley between the hills because their wings could carry them where they would whenever they wished. Birds were more satisfactory symbols of the heavenly spirits, Harriet thought, than any of those sentimental angels that one saw in the children's picture books. There was nothing so swift and free as a bird. Yet, crippled though she was, she felt nothing but joy in watching them. She had always known how to wait.[792]

Harriet, who takes such delight in the morning flight of the gulls, is the parsonage's indispensable old nanny - and Elizabeth owed much to her own Nanny during this period of her life. Ellen was now living with her two sisters in Bath, and therefore "free to help us until we had settled into a new home" - and she seems to have done just that, from the packing up at Oxford, through Barton and into The Ark and Providence Cottage. Thanks to her, despite all the upheaval Elizabeth had time to write.

By the time spring came [The Bird in the Tree] was finished and in sheer relief I wrote [Smoky-House] for Nanny who had been toiling in the Ark's kitchen while I toiled in my bedroom. Now, using part of my mother's...gift from my father's pupils, my own savings, and with two books written, there would be enough...to pay for the cottage.[793]

Nanny, though, was only there to help them until they were settled in, and in the *Dreams* essay Elizabeth said that it was "difficult sometimes to find enough time for writing with so much to do in one's home."[794] But she was now the breadwinner of the family, and her output in this decade of hard work was, after *The Bird in the Tree* and *Smoky-House* in 1940, *The Golden Skylark* and *The Well of the Star* in 1941; *The Castle on the Hill* and *Henrietta's House* in 1942; *The Ikon on the Wall* 1943; *Green Dolphin Country* in 1944. After the war, *The Little White Horse* was published in 1946, *Songs and Verses* 1947, her second book about Damerosehay, *The Herb of Grace* in 1948; *Make-Believe* and *Gentian*

Hill in 1949. Four of these were books of stories, one of collected verses; but nevertheless this was a total of thirteen books published in ten years.

Smoky-House (not hyphenated in the American edition) is a story of smuggling and adventure in which the five Treguddick children save the adults of the village from the dangers of their free-trading life. The book has a delightfully cavalier attitude to smuggling... possibly influenced by Kipling's *Puck of Pook's Hill,* in which a local magistrate turns a blind eye to the misdeeds of his community: "We can't have half Sussex hanged for a little gun-running," he says.[795] The children's rescue attempt only succeeds because they have the assistance of the animals – their dogs Spot and Sausage, and Mathilda the donkey – and the help of the Good People (the fairies) too. This was her first novel written specifically for children, but like *Towers in the Mist* its heroine is a girl who is motherless and in consequence has too many responsibilities on her young shoulders. Circumstances and duty dictate that she has to be "mistress of Smoky-House" and that requires stoicism because "it was not an easy thing to be..."

> *She never had time to pick wild flowers in the lanes, or paddle on the sea-shore, as the others did, and sometimes she was so tired that she cried in the night. But she never told anyone that she was tired and cried in the night, and on the morning after she had cried she always laughed and joked more than usual.*[796]

Two more stories appeared in *Woman's Journal* that year: *The Birthday Party,* a short story about the du Frocq family in the February issue, and in April, *Little Island Set in a Silver Sea.* Its setting was Damerosehay country – the New Forest. The title describes the view of the Isle of Wight from the coast ...but it could also be read, in patriotic echoes of Shakespeare's *Richard II,* as a reference to England itself[797]. A posthumous collection of twenty-two of her father's sermons was also published in 1940 under the title *Glorying in the Cross,* for which Elizabeth wrote her biographical preface *My Father,* comprising twenty-six pages of loving tribute to his life and work.

Nanny too had her tribute from Elizabeth, in the poem written as the dedication for *Smoky-House.* Its final four lines, after the outpouring of happy memories of childhood love and security, speak of a life that has not changed for the better.

> *Clearer the picture of those gentle things*
> *Than harsher memories of later years.*
> *Easy to grope back through the shadowed ways*
> *To Nannie and the love of nursery days.*[798]

For of course at the time of the move into Providence Cottage, and overshadowing her own memories and everyday worries, the phoney war was over and the Second World War frighteningly under way – with, had they but known it, more than five more years yet to be lived through and endured.

❋

The BBC's 9 o'clock news became required listening for everyone; and on the 18th June 1940, Winston Churchill broadcast to the nation:

> The Battle of Britain is about to begin. Upon this battle depends the survival of Christian civilisation. Upon it depends our own British life…
> The whole fury and might of the enemy must very soon be turned on us. Hitler knows that he will have to break us in this island or lose the war. If we can stand up to him all Europe may be freed and the life of the world may move forward into broad sunlit uplands. But if we fail then the whole world, including the United States, including all that we have known and cared for, will sink into the abyss of a new dark age… Let us therefore brace ourselves to our duty, and so bear ourselves that if the British Empire and its commonwealths last for a thousand years, men will still say "This was their finest hour."[799]

> *It was June nineteen forty. Yesterday was gone, burnt up in the blazing inferno of its suffering. There was today, a tiny patch of foothold, but there was no tomorrow. The abyss at whose edge she seemed to herself to be standing was filled with swirling mist. Down below the mist were lightnings and thunders and great voices, and out beyond it presumably the sun still shone, but what shape the things below would take, and whether one would ever win out into the sunlight again, one could not know. Today was one step at a time in the mist, a step taken quite alone because if there were other people there she could not see them, and tomorrow was so uncertain that it did not exist. Memory of the past and hope for the future are companionable things. Now that they seemed to have vanished the loneliness made her very afraid. I can't bear it, she thought abruptly, and for the first time in her life. I just can't bear it…*

Then, almost overnight so it had seemed to Miss Brown, there had been…the drone of enemy planes overhead and the crashing and vibration of their bombs. Stunned and bewildered [she] had listened to grim yet stirring speeches over the wireless, and gradually, in company with all her countrymen, had been dragged by the genius of the man who stood at the head of the nation from bewilderment to resolution, from horror to hope, until at last, though there was no tomorrow, today had given her firm ground beneath her feet and a courage in her soul like beating and ascending wings.[800]

The Castle on the Hill

On the 28th June the Germans bombed Elizabeth's beloved Guernsey, and invaded the Island two days later. The occupation of the Channel Islands was to last for nearly five years, until liberation on 9 May 1945. It was an event that so deeply distressed Ida Goudge that it provoked the only "outburst of passion" Elizabeth ever witnessed from her. Although her mother was "a woman of strong feelings" she said, she usually kept them "wonderfully controlled," but

When England was forced to abandon the islands to German occupation, my mother burst into a storm of grief and fury which shocked me speechless. "I will hate England till I die," she said. And she did.[801]

In August 1940 the Blitz began, and Britain's major cities were relentlessly bombed. Plymouth in their own locality, with its important dockyard, suffered many bombings throughout the war with 1,200 people killed and thousands injured.

❈

In February of that year *Word from England*, a patriotic anthology of prose and poetry, had been published by Lieutenant-General Sir Tom Bridges. In the same way, twenty-four years earlier, his uncle Robert Bridges had compiled Elizabeth's beloved school prize *The Spirit of Man* during the Great War, lamenting in its preface how "the progress of mankind on the path of liberty and humanity had been suddenly arrested" by the hostilities.[802] Compiled for "the King's forces," this new anthology was intended to "sustain and hearten them during moments of crisis and peril." But Elizabeth knew of it too. It featured many of her favourite poets, and in September of that year she inscribed a copy "with love from Elizabeth Goudge" for Beverley Githens, the "American who loved England" to whom she would dedicate

The Golden Skylark the following year. An anecdote in the new anthology's morale-boosting foreword recorded how its author, Ian Hay, had shared a train carriage with some newly-arrived American soldiers during the First World War. One young officer spent most of the journey gazing out of the window at the English countryside, and eventually turned to his fellow-travellers with the affirmation that, having had a good look at this "little island" he had decided it was worth fighting for.[803]

A railway journey through beautiful scenery had always been a great joy for Canon Goudge, who used to say, "If you don't look out of the window at the scenery, it is an insult to God who put it there for your pleasure."[804] And from now on, despite the war, contemplation of the English countryside could again sustain his daughter too, and inspire her. For amid all the recent sorrow and upheaval, loss and fear, there had been one great change for the better in her life: she had left noisy town life behind and returned to her beloved West Country. *The Castle on the Hill* describes just such a transition for Miss Brown, as she too is driven down to Devon.

> *They seemed to slip very abruptly from the bustle of the big town into the leafy stillness of the lanes. Modern villas seemed to change places quite suddenly with white-washed cottages smiling from the depths of gardens that were ablaze with flowers. Gasometers and cinemas were gone and, instead, an ancient grey church towered up above a jumble of old roofs. Hay scented the air, and when the car slowed down the call of a wood pigeon sounded peacefully above the ripple of a stream.*[805]

What a contrast. If Elizabeth had found Oxford too towny in 1923, what was it like in 1939 when she left… after Morris Motors, on its outskirts, had become the largest integrated car plant in Europe? Now it was left behind, and she was living instead this village life in rural Devon, whose glories would provide the inspiration for a total of seven novels. As she said in *West Country Magic*: "Everything I see makes me want to write a story… In our village there is an old smuggling inn called Smoky House that demanded I should write a children's book about it… Not far from my home there is an old castle crowning a hill in the lonely woods and after I had seen it I had no peace until I had written *The Castle on the Hill*."[806]

The Castle on the Hill

This, her war novel, was published in May 1942, reprinted in the same year and again reprinted – twice - in 1943. It is the only one of her books that does not carry a dedication to a friend or family member; instead the novel begins with a fourteen-stanza poem: "Dedicated to The Castle." And yet this is perhaps the most personal dedication of them all – filled with her own awareness of the impact of history, and the fact that all the wars the ancient castle has witnessed throughout the centuries are actually one and the same: the ongoing battle between good and evil.

> *For this is the rock that for all time man defends,*
> *The rock of his soul against which all evil spends*
> *Its fury in vain in the warfare that never ends.*
>
> *And these the embattled walls that the heroes trod,*
> *Swift-winged with flame, their feet with the gospel shod,*
> *For this is the house of all life, the house of God…*

Mr. Birley, the owner of the Castle, has this same awareness of the never-ending battle.

> *Hitler's contemptuous sneer at "the bourgeois virtues of peace and order" was typical of all the anarchists through the ages. Always the perpetual struggle forward of the sane men, the good-hearted, decent, stupid, blundering lovers of God, always the perpetual reeling back as yet another onslaught of the furious men swept in from the sea of darkness. Why so slow and blundering, you children of light? Why so swift and brilliant in dark power, Apollyon? It is easier to be angry than to pity, he thought, to destroy than create, to hate than love. Yet the children of light picked themselves up and went on again, dogged, obstinate, stumbling along after a lost inheritance, blinking stupidly at a half-seen vision of a Holy City far away.*[807]

"Easier to be angry…" She is half-quoting here from *The Uncelestial City* by Humbert Wolfe: a poet she had only recently discovered during the difficult days following her father's death. The passage has a similar message to the opening chapters of *Towers in the Mist*: that for the lovers of God the way forward is a perpetual struggle; the *uncelestial* city is much easier to find than the Holy Land's "dim counties."[808]

Mr. Birley is a writer, and the description of his struggle to work suggests that for Elizabeth too, despite the inspiration of her new surroundings, working in wartime was not proving easy.

> *He found it quite absurdly difficult to write during these days of intense and anxious waiting, these rickety tumbling days when the structure of life as one knew it rocked beneath one. It was only his conviction that those, like himself, who could take little active part in service to their country, must bend their whole strength to keep life running as far as possible in the normal channels, that caused him to keep his unwilling nose resolutely to the familiar grindstone.*[809]

Writing, nevertheless, was probably her only option - unlike cousin Hélène, who had joined the Wrens. Elizabeth was forty-two when *The Castle on the Hill* was published, and did she perhaps have herself in mind as she described Miss Brown?

> *She could not get any war work to do; at present they wanted only strong young women and she was forty-two and looked fragile.*[810]

As her contribution to the war effort it seems likely that Elizabeth too bent her whole strength to the task of counteracting the dark power of Apollyon that was threatening to destroy the world. As Mr. Birley says,

> *Orderliness of life and thought must be maintained as far as possible. When these chaotic days were passed what was left of it would form the scaffolding upon which the new order could be built.*[811]

Here was another novel reiterating the central importance of a stable home. At the castle where the Birley family live, London children are evacuated to safety and Miss Brown too finds refuge in her homelessness. But this was written in the heart of the war, and so there is no cosy stability. Ultimately this castle home that seemed so secure, that had been so carefully preserved and rebuilt over the centuries, is all but destroyed in a bombing raid, and it is then young Stephen Birley's turn to survey the wreckage of his former life… which is now a lost way of life.

> *Then — that was the end. The end of life as he had always known it, the end of this particular pattern that he had loved... Whatever sort of world we have when this [war] is over it won't have landed gentry in it. That's all over. There'll be more important building to be done than the repairing of old castles.*[812]

Yet the human spirit is not destroyed, and he realises that he must pick up the pieces of his life and carry on. "'Go on, go on,' he said to himself. "For some reason or other you're important, necessary, vital to something new."'[813] And he returns to London to continue his pacifist war work of helping victims of the Blitz. The refugee Jewish violinist too, Jo Isaacson, comes to the same conclusion when despair has turned his thoughts to suicide: not only that it "was almost always the choice of his race; to go on;" but that he himself is of some use in the world – "he was still an instrument."[814]

At the end of the novel, Jo recalls words of D.H. Lawrence, written about the outcome of the First World War: "Let the leaves perish, but let the tree stand, living and bare. Let the leaves fall, and many branches. But the quick of the tree must not perish."[815]

> *Nor would it... The end was not yet. Soon would be the time for the turning of the tide and the rising of the sap. The buds would break again and the trees be misted with the living green...*
>
> *Life, he suddenly knew in a flash that struck like lightning, was the glorious eternal God in whom until now he had not believed. A man's life was his own, he had thought once. That was a lie. It was not his own, but God's. It was God...*
> *This quickening divine power that he had experienced could not be confined to this world, for cruel, sordid, ugly, devilish can be this world, and by the nature of things that power could have neither source nor ending in it; only flow through it, around it, over it, under it, gathering up the gold into its eternal shining and burning the dross in its fire.*[816]

As with Damerosehay, there is one important way to rebuild after war – by remaking homes where the lost will find stability, love and care. And so the novel ends with the Castle's homeless ones – Miss Brown, now deprived of home and employment for a second time, Mr. Isaacson and two evacuated, now orphaned, children – coming together to make a new family unit in the cottage at the castle gate.

> *Father and Mother and children. Miss Brown, wielding the brown teapot, marvelled at the powerlessness of evil to destroy that everlasting pattern. It might strike at it, wounding and mutilating, but the severed parts only sought their complement again in a new trinity.*[817]

❋

If the strain of wartime writing ascribed to Mr. Birley was a mirror of Elizabeth's own – as well as his determination to use all his strength in counteracting the evils of war – then the result is a novel with probably too many topics under discussion: the plight of refugees, the homeless, the evacuees, the orphaned; the horrors of the Blitz; the plight of young lovers; the breakdown of an old way of life; and a lengthy discussion of the pacifist stance - a subject on which her father had publicly expressed a view,[818] as she recalled in the introduction to *Glorying in the Cross*.

> *All that he felt about war he expressed most clearly in a university sermon on pacifism preached at Oxford in 1937, and later published by request. It had a wide circulation and helped many people, tormented by this most difficult of all questions in these terrible days, to the clear sane thinking that was his own.*[819]

Nevertheless Elizabeth managed once again to handle all this potentially weighty material in such a way that the overriding impression of the book – as the *Sunday Times'* reviewer said - was of charm…for she is "an author who can invest anything she writes with a distinct charm, and the children she draws – there are two here – are always a delight to meet."[820]

> *She saw two little girls standing hand in hand. They seemed to have no mother or teacher to hold on to, so they held on to each other. They were perhaps six and eight years old, typical* London *children with straight tow-coloured hair, raggedly bobbed, pale blue eyes and pale pointed little faces. They came evidently from a good if poor home, for the scanty blue and pink cotton frocks and carefully darned little knitted jackets that clothed their undernourished bodies were very clean, and so were the white socks above their well-polished and clod-hopping shoes. Two shabby cardboard suitcases stood beside them on the platform and their gas-masks were slung across their shoulders.*[821]

They are Moppet and Poppet, the two evacuees, apprehensively leaving their home and parents in bomb-damaged London for a new and safer life in Devon. Marldon itself had been selected, in fact, as an evacuee village and so Elizabeth must have witnessed similar arrivals at first hand. The plight of all evacuated children was such that the King's young daughters, Elizabeth and Margaret Rose, had made a special, heartening broadcast to them on the BBC's *Children's Hour* in October 1940. Moving children out of the cities did not always keep them safe, however.

> *[We] were anxious about the children now living in the Barton bungalow, but they remained safe through the raids there, while near us in Devon there was a direct hit on a church packed full of children for a children's service.*[822]

This was the tragedy at St. Marychurch in Torquay, when on 30th May 1943 twenty-one children and three teachers were killed while attending Sunday School. Another local air-attack, as she reported to Audrey in a letter, was when "On Bank Holiday they sent over ten planes and bombed and machine-gunned the holiday makers on the beaches."[823] Elizabeth herself was fortunate in being spared direct involvement in such horrors: "Though I often went to Torquay and Paignton I never actually saw the immediate aftermath of an air-raid. I did not have to carry through the rest of my life the memory of sights almost too terrible to bear..."[824] But she made herself imagine them, in Stephen's description of "the grotesque dead bodies, the injured, the filth and stench of it all...

> *The kind of death one sees in peace time, a body decently laid out, with flowers about it and the eyes closed, is one thing, but death in battle is quite another, it's hideous and horrible, and when the dead are little children it drives you mad; you can't forget it.'*[825]

His uncle, listening to this, says, "Somehow I was expecting the London Blitz to smash your pacifism."

> *"But why, Uncle Charles?" asked Stephen. "I was still undecided when I went to London. I went there to see war at first-hand and really make up my mind about it, and after a few days of digging the dead and the dying out of the ruins of their homes I made it up quite easily. War is the most hideous evil that ever existed and I'll fight it with every ounce of strength I have until I die.'*[826]

This hideous element of war very soon impacted on Elizabeth's own life, for just before *The Castle on the Hill* was published, Nanny and her two sisters were killed in an air-raid in the last days of April 1942. Ellen Jolliffe was sixty-two.

> *I suppose that my mother and I suffered less in the war than most people did, and we often felt ashamed of our comparative immunity. We suffered two bereavements that hit us hard. The death in the early days of the war of a cousin to whom we were both devoted, to me more a brother than a cousin, and later on Nanny's death during a raid on Bath. Upon her and her two sisters, and the lovely young daughter of a friend of mine who was staying with them, their house fell, burying them beneath the ruins… But two bereavements were not many. Parents would lose every one of their sons. Men would come home on leave to find their wives and children dead after a raid…*[827]

It was a hard loss, but they did not have to bear it quite alone. Elizabeth always remembered how the Edwardian aunts of her childhood had come aboard a distressed household "like a pilot and brought the ship safe to port,"[828] and sure enough after Nanny's death her mother's sister Irene came "with her strong common sense." She must have been a formidable lady. She it was who had worked as a nanny in royal families abroad and Elizabeth, who said that her mother had "iron determination," yet described Aunt Irene as "the most determined woman I have ever known in my whole life."[829]

> *It seemed strange that Nanny was no longer in the world to come and be with us in this grief, but Irene came with her strong common sense. "Never think how they died," she said. "In war that must be a thing you do not think about." Easier said than done. For some while neither my mother nor I could go to bed at night without feeling the weight of the house falling on us, and wondering, for how long did they live in the suffocating dark before they died?*[830]

As to the finality of death itself, Ida and Irene were the only ones to inherit the "strong streak of extra-sensory perception" that ran in the Ozanne family – the only ones to whom, at the end of the Great War, "my grandmother [had been] able to communicate after her death her discovery of the fact that 'it is all true.'"[831] Nevertheless, although Elizabeth does not reveal any further details of her own reaction, she says that when "Nanny was killed something broke in my mother. She was not defeated but she carried on for the rest of the way without gaiety."[832]

Later, it seems, Aunt Marie came to visit too:

> *We are going to have a busy August as Mother's sister (70 and nearly blind) is coming to stay with us, and four different friends are coming into rooms near. I shall be relieved when they all go away again without having had bombs dropped on them.*[833]

The war brought other, lesser, dangers to the locality. After a reference to her garden in the same 1942 letter to Audrey she said,

We are so thankful for the vegetables, for now that Torquay and Paignton are crowded out with munitions workers having holidays it is quite difficult to get one's rations, and there have been free fights in the streets for food, between residents and holiday makers.

But soon she and Ida were to be holidaymakers themselves. She added that "Mummie has not been at all well…"

So at the beginning of September we are going away for a week to Stoke Gabriel, on the Dart, four miles away. I have found a little hotel there that has a downstairs bedroom, and a lovely garden. It will make a little break and do us both good I think.[834]

And so the support of family and friends was helping her through, and she was even able to make a mild joke for Audrey in the midst of all their misery:

I'm so glad you like The Castle on the Hill. *It is my favourite child because I somehow feel I have put more into it than into my other books. I'm glad you like the bits about washing up and unrequited love!*[835]

Nor was it all misery that Spring, for there was a new baby in the family… Hélène was now married, and had given birth to a son. Small wonder then, that Elizabeth spoke of the interweaving joy and woe of the Devon years. But bombs did fall, even in the comparative safety of their little village, and although they were safe from the destruction the event only worsened Ida's ill-health.

The first two bombs to fall on our parish were the two that fell on the sloping green field opposite our cottage, jettisoned early in the morning by a German plane flying home. They exploded almost together with shattering noise and the cottage seemed to shake and buckle and totter as though nothing could save it. But…it righted itself, with only superficial damage done. That was not the case with my mother. I had been up and on my feet but she had been in bed, lying flat on her back. The very worst position, our doctor told us, in which the human body can suffer earthquake, and she had a severe concussion.[836]

Wartime hardships made it more difficult to juggle the caring, the domestic tasks and the prodigious output of her work, but everything was underpinned by her faith and prayer life, for she still remembered her father's advice about prayer.

Marldon

>When there was a lot of washing up to do or when I had to keep at my typewriter when I ached to stop I would offer these small things to God "for John whose work is so hard," or "for Mary who looks so tired..."[837]

A *Diary of Prayer* has this intercession, written by Elizabeth, asking for Patience and Long-suffering:

> O God, whose glorious power is ever present to strengthen our weakness, help us to lean in faith upon the might of that power whenever the sorrow and toils of life threaten to overwhelm us. Grant us patience in the small trials of everyday, and endurance in the storms of pain and grief.[838]

※

The Castle on the Hill had stoically faced the toils and sorrow of wartime life, its storms of pain and grief which had then come painfully true in her own experience. In complete contrast she now turned away from the grim realities of war for her next book, to revisit her Wells childhood and the almost fairytale stories of Henrietta.

> *Easy to grope back through the shadowed ways*
> *To Nannie and the love of nursery days.*[839]

Easy perhaps, but this book was so much more than just an escape into childhood fantasy.

Henrietta's House

> Well, if I put my neck out, I put my neck out – this is the best book written...for unstuffy, ageless adults and for imaginative children, since Kenneth Grahame wrote "The Wind in the Willows."[840]

It was six months later, and in the *Saturday Review* Richard Ellis was praising Elizabeth's new novel *Henrietta's House* - her third and final book about Henrietta, published in America as *The Blue Hills*. After a novel about war, here was a book beginning "Once upon a time..." whose adventures start with one of the Edwardian driving-picnics of Elizabeth's childhood, and end in a little white house straight out of her dreams.

Sister of the Angels had already told the world that Henrietta, like Elizabeth, was a dreamer. Henrietta "was attached to her sleep…because in it she visited wonderful places, saw lovely sights and heard wonderful sounds."[841] And after the war Elizabeth would publish the essay describing two of her own dreams that recurred "again and again" – dreams which she had combined to form the basis of this new book. One involved a moss-grown path where "the moss is so thick that it is like walking on velvet…"

I know that at the end of the path I am coming to something wonderful and the depth of the happiness that I feel is something I have never known in my waking hours…

In the other I am a little girl again, jogging along in the old-fashioned cab that in my childhood we used to hire to take us to parties. Again I am gloriously happy, for that sense of expectancy is with me again, and looking out of the window of the cab I see a lovely landscape of green hills bathed in that especial light… The ground rises gently to thick beech woods, and with its back to the woods and facing the stream there is a long low white house.[842]

In this last Torminster novel, Henrietta discovers her dream house after driving along a track "thick with moss."

It swept round a little heather-covered hillock, crowned with the shivering loveliness of silver birches, and there before them was a low white house shining like a pearl against the background of the wood.[843]

As in other stories, the house of Elizabeth and Henrietta's dreams conforms to the Romantic ideal of a home that is not so much man-made, as an organic growth within the landscape.

It was an old house. For years it had been elbowing itself comfortable in the rich, deep old garden that surrounded it. Now it was settled to its satisfaction and was no longer an alien growth among birds and flowers and trees, but a living creature that they had taken to their heart.[844]

Apart from Henrietta and Hugh Anthony all the characters in this novel are adults, and yet *Henrietta's House* is a fairytale mix - made up of the giant who kept his heart in a paper bag, wise animals who lead the humans into the right paths, and more than one fairy bower. In fact, compared to the other Henrietta books it is a fantasy novel. Yet at the same time it is also a curiously adult moral tale which preaches, among other things, the necessity to laugh at oneself – and to listen to the inner imp within us all, who mocks at our insincerities. This develops what she had already said, in *Sister of the Angels* - that there was "another part of Henrietta, that curious second self whom we seem to carry about with us; that self that criticizes, observes and admonishes."[845] In this novel it is the Dean of Torminster, in particular, who benefits from hearing its voice.

The Old Man hears no inner voice however. He, like the giant in the fairytale, must first find his heart, and with it the virtues of generosity, kindness, love, and forgiveness. He is a non-believer – for him, neither Fairyland nor Paradise exists - and to help him requires a great deal of courage on Grandfather's part. He enquires,

> *"Is there nothing, my dear sir, in which you believe?"*
> *"The devil," said the Old Man nastily.*
>
> *"And what do you mean by the devil?" asked Grandfather. "Not a hairy gentleman with horns and hoofs, surely? He's a fairy tale, and you don't hold with them."*
>
> *"The devil," said the Old Man, leaning forward with his flashing eyes fixed upon Grandfather, "do be the power in a man's mind that do make 'im able to do 'is will on others. That do be the real power i' the world, that be, not fairy tales an' such rubbish, but power i' the mind. If you 'ave it, there ain't nothin' you can't do…"*
>
> *It was an awful moment… But Grandfather remained calm, his eyes fixed upon the Old Man's face with as piercing a gaze as the Old Man's own.*
> *"And now I'll tell you something," said Grandfather. "It's this. There's a power even stronger than the evil will in your mind, and that's the goodwill in mine."*[846]

Evil and goodwill are thus shown locked in battle, as the book attains to yet another level – that of Christian allegory. As the various journeys to the picnic continue it becomes a kind of pilgrim's progress, with the Dean, Hugh Anthony and Grandfather all losing themselves on rocky roads that lead to dark caves. They go on courageously, with a childlike sense of adventure, only to find themselves plunged into black underground rivers. A similar scene had already appeared in *Smoky-House* but that was Spot the dog, swimming in a cavern and finding a world under the roots of the trees, where dwell "the Good People who are always kind."[847] Here it is adult human beings - eminent clergymen, no less - who have to ship their oars and let go. They courageously choose just to trust, and allow themselves to be carried along by the frightening, rushing water.

> *The Dean looked at the swiftly flowing river, and he looked at the dark cavern into which it flowed...*
> *"Come along, then," he said.*
>
> *So they climbed into the boat and, picking up the oars, they pushed themselves down over the stones and slid with a plop into the river. And at once the current seized them, just as though they had no more weight than a dead leaf, and they slid swiftly through the beautiful green twilight where they had been so long into a deeper twilight of running water, and then once again into the pitch darkness of the depth of the earth, a roaring tumultuous blackness this time, full of sound and fury, that caused them to be suddenly seized by a worse fear than any they had ever known...*
>
> *Still they raced on in the pitch darkness. On and on and on...until with a sudden thud they struck a rock in mid-stream, turning right round and then swirling sideways in a terrifying sort of way. They clutched each other, but the boat did not capsize, and presently they found they were going on again, but not travelling so fast and with the noise of the water not so loud. And then they were drifting quite slowly with the noise faint in the distance. And then they were not moving at all, but lying still upon the surface of some pool in the depths of the earth...*[848]

It is an image that was to be repeated time and again in her subsequent books: a courageous plunge through fear into some kind of darkness, a plunge that is necessary in order to find the light and peace at its centre... just as Grandfather discovers at the heart of his own underground journey.

> *It was a small cave hardly larger than a church porch, and out of it a narrow rock passage dripping with water led downwards into the depths of the earth. A lesser man than Grandfather might have been turned back from the adventure by the cold, wet darkness of this passage, but Grandfather was never turned back by anything when he wanted to go anywhere. He groped his way down it with the help of lighted matches, and when he had finished the matches in his box he still went on, following a faint golden glow, as of fire, that shone from somewhere far down below him...*

Marldon

The light was very beautiful. As he drew nearer to it a strange awed expectancy grew upon him, so that his heart beat fast and he almost stumbled in his eagerness to get to the place where the light was shining.[849]

It is the same experience for them all. When they face the darkness with courage and "go on" in faith, they discover that – amazingly – at the centre of the turmoil is peace, and at the heart of the darkness is light. The allegory is complete when at the end of their journey the house of Henrietta's dreams is awaiting them, light shining from every window. After all their difficulties, her loved ones will be reunited under its roof. She has gone on ahead to make all ready for them; and a feast has been prepared.

Adrian Hastings, in his *History of English Christianity* says that when the Second World War was at its most critical phase, there was a flowering of some "very considerable Christian literary creativity."[850] He highlights 1942, when Archbishop William Temple published *Christianity and Social Order*. But he points out that it was not only the theologians who were writing about faith. Among the laity also, this was the year that Dorothy L. Sayers' series of plays *The Man Born to be King* was broadcast, at four-weekly intervals, by the BBC; the year that C.S. Lewis published *The Screwtape Letters* and T.S. Eliot, *Little Gidding*.

She does not appear on his list, unsurprisingly; but it was also the year that Elizabeth Goudge published a beautiful Christian allegory for children, in which two elderly clergymen and a little boy find light and peace at the heart of darkness… and, somewhat curiously, a Canon of the Church of England insists on a belief in Fairyland.

Faith, Myth and Fairytales

"I think in my heart I have always believed in fairies,"[851] says Elizabeth in *The Joy of the Snow*, and it will strike many people as a strange statement - particularly in today's world, where many now regard even the idea of God as a fairytale, let alone fairies themselves. A strange statement, and one with a childish quality that seems inconsistent with her deep and mature Christian faith.

These are not the fairies "seen in the picture books" however; not the Tinkerbells of the nursery tales "but nature spirits whose life is part of the wind and the flowers and the trees." Believing, she felt, had something to do with her background – "Born in the West-country …how could I do anything else?"[852] And her Channel Island inheritance too, for she said in an interview that she did feel there was a psychic "extra dimension" in the lives of the Islanders in her mother's day. When they were children, she said, their little island was "so cut off they never left it" and she felt that their psychic gifts were the result of "living on an island, alone with their own legends and stories."[853]

Belief in fairies was partly a characteristic of Place, then, but also perhaps of Time – not so much the times in which she herself lived as the Victorian inheritance of the parents whose life she so closely shared. Nowadays, except perhaps for Shakespeare and classical ballet, fairies are a thing of childhood, but in the nineteenth century adults were fascinated by them. In her parents' generation, fairies both good and malicious were an important feature in contemporary art – as too were angels. One celebrated fairy painter was Richard Doyle, whose nephew was one of the most famous and perhaps unlikely believers in fairies - Sir Arthur Conan Doyle, creator of Sherlock Holmes. Queen Victoria herself delighted in fairyland, particularly her favourite Undine whose portrait she gave to Prince Albert.

A late-twentieth century exhibition of Victorian Fairy Painting at the Royal Academy pointed out that not only were fairytales read by adults, but they were in fact central to the movement against the pragmatism and mechanisation of the Industrial Revolution. Dickens wrote that "in a utilitarian age, of all other times, it is a matter of grave importance that fairy tales should be respected."[854] And there were plenty of them around in the nineteenth century: original tales written by the likes of Thackeray, Ruskin, Charles Kingsley, George MacDonald and Dickens himself contributed to what the catalogue called "the rich vein of British fairy literature." *The Dymchurch Flit* however, in one of Elizabeth's schoolroom favourites, Kipling's *Puck of Pook's Hill*, tells how all the fairies left England at the time of the Reformation; and the RA exhibition concluded that, similarly, the horror of the Great War had "banished" the fairies from the world of adults, into their new role in the nursery.[855]

Most of the great Victorian painters and writers of fairy-lore were not only adults but men – clergymen even. Lewis Carroll was fascinated by Sir Joseph Noel Paton's painting of *The Reconciliation of Oberon and Titania*: standing before it and meticulously counting the number of fairies it portrayed (he made it one hundred and sixty-five.) Carroll incidentally, the Reverend Charles Lutwidge Dodgson, studied and later taught mathematics at Christ Church Oxford, and he too lived in Tom Quad. He died just two years before Elizabeth was born.

Fairies, trees with hands and faces, mythical goblins and dragons… they were still very much around in the early twentieth century as Elizabeth grew up, for by then the artist Arthur Rackham was approaching the height of his career. C.S. Lewis, with his deep love of northern mythology, said the 'sky turned round' when, at the age of fifteen he first set eyes on Rackham's illustrations for *Siegfried and the Twilight of the Gods*.[856] And Lewis was fifty-six when he wrote about fairies to his 'American lady' correspondent.[857] These fairies though were alarming creatures: still, in the 1950s, believed in and feared in parts of Ireland, he said. His letter informs her about their size relative to human beings – he has never found anyone who believed in the tiny creatures of Shakespeare - and even describes for her a leprechaun's shoe, shown to him by the doctor who owned it.

Elizabeth loved the work of the Victorian novelist and clergyman George MacDonald. An eminent man, he was a friend of Ruskin and Lewis Carroll, father-in-law of Pre-Raphaelite artist Edward Burne-Jones, and Edward Poynter, President of the Royal Academy; and grandfather to prime minister Stanley Baldwin and Rudyard Kipling. MacDonald was not only an eminent man of the church, but the author of several fantasy novels. His *Phantastes: A Faerie Romance*, published in 1858, was not a children's book but one read and much loved by adults – C.S. Lewis said reading it had 'baptized' his imagination; he described its author simply as his *master*, acknowledging that he had probably quoted MacDonald in every book he had ever written.[858] Side by side with the deeply Christian message of *Phantastes* is a description of the fairy world which, alongside the words of William Blake, might have endorsed Elizabeth's own belief.

> The conclusion I arrived at from the observations I was afterwards able to make, was, that the flowers die because the fairies go away...The flowers seem a sort of houses for them, or outer bodies, which they can put on or off when they please... Whether all the flowers have fairies, I cannot determine, any more than I can be sure whether all men and women have souls.[859]

In those days then, it seems an interest in the world of faerie was not childish or ludicrous – nor was it incongruous in a person of deep Christian faith. The nature spirits Elizabeth believed in, "whose life is part of the wind and the flowers and the trees," sound very like the angels in William Blake's poem in *A Book of Comfort*.

> Where lambs have nibbled, silent move
> The feet of angels bright;
> Unseen they pour blessing,

> And joy without ceasing,
> On each bud and blossom,
> And each sleeping bosom.[860]

And even more like those described by Blake's near-contemporary Christopher Smart in his *Jubilate Agno*.

> For the flowers have their angels even the words of God's Creation,
> For the warp and woof of flowers are worked by perpetual moving spirits.[861]

This, although an eighteenth-century work, was not published until 1939. Four years later Benjamin Britten would set it to music,[862] and in 1976 Elizabeth included it in *A Book of Faith*. Its author Christopher Smart was a "radiantly happy Christian" but also what the contemporary world called mad, and at the age of thirty-four he was admitted to the Bedlam. Samuel Johnson who visited him there, said, "He insisted on people praying with him – also falling on his knees and saying his prayers in the street." Dr. Johnson felt that as such, his behaviour was "not noxious to society." In fact, "I'd as lief pray with Kit Smart as anyone else," he said.[863]

❋

Fairies... Angels... Spirits... Although Shakespeare assures us through *Hamlet* that "there are more things in heaven and earth..." the pragmatic will still reject such ideas. But where exactly does fantasy end and *faith* begin? The awareness of a living Spirit in creation is something very much alive today in the revived Celtic tradition. For the Celts, the visible and the invisible worlds were one, and they revered as sacred those places where the divide between the two was 'thin' - like hill-tops, wells, groves and springs, all of which feature strongly in Elizabeth's work. Canon Anthony Duncan, in his *Elements of Celtic Christianity*, points up the Celtic belief that in a sense there are no inanimate things, for it would be unlikely for a personal God to create anything that "was not – in some sense – a person." He adds,

> The insights of a Teilhard de Chardin, that consciousness is inherent in the hydrogen atom, is wholly consistent with the Celtic vision of things.[864]

Bede Griffiths seems to say too, that whatever name we might give to it in our ignorance, there is a Something there to be named. Writing on mysticism in 1989 he refers back to the early Christian philosopher, Origen, whose understanding was that the world and everything in Nature was watched over by angels, and under their direction.[865] "Fairies, elves, spirits and elementals" are not an invention of the imagination, Bede says, but a human attempt to understand something unseen and yet very real – the "subtle psychic world" beyond our physical existence, which only our "subtle senses" can perceive. Despite what St. Paul says about the spiritual powers,[866] the number of people who have ever experienced angels, or gods, or "any other presences" in our modern, western world is very few however; and therefore any talk about such things is dismissed as fairy stories. In fact, Bede adds, people think that "fairies are only stories…"[867]

"Don't you dare to disparage fairy tales!" says Canon Fordyce sternly to the Old Man.

> *"A fairy tale, dear sir, in relating miraculous happenings as though they were the normal events of every day, is a humble acknowledgment of the fact that this universe is a box packed full of mysteries of which we understand absolutely nothing at all."*[868]

And Elizabeth includes in *A Book of Comfort* Barbara Euphan Todd's delightful poem *Fairy Story*[869] which lists some elements in the box of mysteries – all normal and everyday to the pragmatic mind – which nevertheless are as unbelievably miraculous and seemingly impossible as fairies themselves. Caterpillars becoming butterflies, worms spinning silk, tiny birds-eggs holding the glories of the dawn chorus, grass turning to milk, and ice to water… Where, the poem asks, is the dividing line between such magical miracles and the everyday? Henrietta's Grandfather, can see none.

> *"There ain't no fairyland," said the Old Man obstinately.*

> *"You dare to make a statement like that in a wood like this!" thundered Grandfather in ever-growing indignation. "If this wood is not fairyland, then I don't know what is. Fairyland and Paradise, they're the same place, and always with us. And to dare to say that a thing is not there because you're too much of a fool to see it is the height of arrogance. You must be taken down a peg or two, my friend…"*

> *"An' as for the Garden of Paradise – there ain't no Paradise."*

"What?" cried out Grandfather in horror and indignation. "My dear sir! My dear sir! ...No Paradise? Have you no eyes, no nose, no ears? Have you not seen flowers growing, heard birds singing, smelt wet earth? Have you no heart to feel the beauty of these things...?

Good heavens! Dear me! Did you not realise that these things are green shoots pushing through winter earth, shouting out aloud the promise of the joy to come? And how they shout! No deafness, not even yours, my dear sir, is an excuse for not hearing. They shout so loud about it that one might almost say they are the joy to come. Paradise is already present in these things, my dear sir, even as March daffodils dancing in the wind are present in the green shoots of February.'[870]

The Joy to Come

Elizabeth's belief in the ultimate triumph of the light was reiterated in a wartime short story about the fall of Greece. It was *The Strength in the Stone*, published in 1943 in *The Ikon on the Wall*, and again in *White Wings*, 1952. Twenty-five years later, when Elizabeth was seventy-seven, she was asked if there were any stories in *White Wings* that she was especially fond of, and this was one of only two she named.[871] It ends as an old shepherd on a hillside wakes from a dream of his country's ancient triumphs to watch, from afar, the final battle for Greece in the Second World War. Once again she writes of all humankind as engaged, throughout history, in the same ongoing battle against evil. In this oneness of human experience, the past has the power to teach. Courage is the ultimately invincible weapon.

From out of the past he had now the knowledge that valour, though it might seem to fling itself uselessly against the rock of evil, was yet a thing unconquerable; it sank back sobbing into the deep, but it had more life in it than the rock, it gathered and came again, growing as great waves grow to break at last in the heart of sunshine... The answer to the riddle of life is somehow in the rhythm of it; the scales must swing this way and that, but in the last incline of the balance it is not evil that soars to the sky.

❄

A happier period came to our village. The coastal raids came to an end and no more children were killed. At night we no longer lay awake listening to the German planes streaming over us to Plymouth, and then to the dull distant boom that meant death and agony in the city only a few miles from us, while we lay safe in the shame of our security. The return of the planes meant jettisoned bombs and then some slight shadow of danger did lie over us for a short time as my mother and I shared her bed, determined to be together whatever happened. My mother was never afraid but she liked to have her jewel-case passed to her, for she loved her few pieces of lovely old jewellery and wanted to keep them safe herself. Animated by the same feminine desire to sit upon the eggs I never got into bed beside her without putting the manuscript of the book I was writing, Green Dolphin Country, *on the bedside table. Women are not very logical creatures at the best of times but in times of crisis their reasoning powers tend to fade out altogether. What, if anything, were we thinking? A bomb falling on a little house like ours would have totally destroyed everything in it. Perhaps, like the Egyptians of old, we subconsciously thought that what was close to our bodies in death would accompany our spirits as they entered a new life.*

I do not remember what we thought, but eventually Plymouth was left in ruins and peace, Marldon was once more a safe place for children and joy raised its golden head, for Hélène came to live with us for a while with her small son.[872]

It was a wish come true, for she had already told Audrey, "I wish I could see my godson Mark… I have sent him two adorable little silk smocks with knickers to match."[873] Two poems in the 1947 *Songs and Verses* record some of the joys of having a small child in the house. *Trains* describes games of make-believe railway engines, during which "you must be careful / where you plant your feet /And before you seat yourself / look what's on the seat"… because "every chair's a station / full of steam and din." And there are the delights of bedtime too, in *Amen*.

Young Mark has had his supper,
His apple and his bun,
And now in blue pyjamas,
His evening toilet done,

His bathrobe pulled in tightly
With plaited scarlet cord,
He says his prayers devoutly
To his most loving Lord.

He prays for all his dearest,
He prays to be made good,
He thanks God for the sunshine
And all his lovely food.

He thinks about the angels
And wonders how they fly,
And if they get to heaven
Through holes poked in the sky.

And is a star an angel-hole,
And if not, what's it for?
And do they let down ladders?
And is the moon a door?

Then Mark says "Ah Men" loudly,
And wonders who they are?
And then he thinks, how many men,
And have They come from far?

And are They white or black men,
And have They had their tea?
And if They've come to stay with us,
Wherever can They be…?[874]

The American army, that was later to turn much of Devon into a training ground, had not yet appeared and Westerland was as peaceful as it was beautiful. My mother and Hélène, who so greatly loved each other, were overjoyed to be together again. And Hélène's two-year-old son laughed all day and sang for much of the night; and if his gift of song was less appreciated than his gift of laughter it was none the less joyous.[875]

Another joy for Ida - in fact "the greatest joy of her Devon days" - was that old Bob Patey of Marldon, who worked on the garden at Providence Cottage, would take her out "in her bathchair through the unfrequented loveliness of the lanes." He was a sailor, an ex navy man who "walked with a slow, steady, rolling gait." This meant that "the bathchair rolled too," to such comical effect that anyone walking behind it "was consumed with mirth." During this happy visit, Elizabeth remembered, "The cavalcade looked funnier than ever when Hélène pushed her small son in his minute conveyance alongside the swaying ship" of her mother's chair.[876]

Green Dolphin Country

We laughed a great deal, but I am afraid I laughed less than the others because I was caught in the terrible coils of the most marvellous piece of material good fortune. Overnight I had become a best-seller.[877]

It was 1944. The book she had been writing – finished at last - was published in September, and it turned her world upside down. *Green Dolphin Country*, also known as *Green Dolphin Street, Le Pays du Dauphin Vert, Der Grune Delphin, Il Delfino Verde, El Pais del Delfin Verde, Het land van de Groene Dolfijn, U Zeleneho Delfina*… It was a phenomenal worldwide bestseller, and according to her obituary in *The Daily Telegraph* sold more than a million copies.

The *Dictionary of National Biography* says that to finish the book required "exceptional determination" in view of its author's deep commitment to "nursing her ailing mother;"[878] and in her *Autobiographical Sketch* in *The Elizabeth Goudge Reader*, Elizabeth confirms that "It took me four years to write." (This essay - the anthology's concluding chapter - did not appear in the UK version of the book, *At the Sign of the Dolphin*.)

It was written with many interruptions and in every possible adverse circumstance, some of it even coming into being in the middle of the night during an air raid. Its many words were to me a sort of anti-war dope, but the number of them appalled me when the book was finally finished, and it says much for the courage of publishers that two brave men, one in England and one in America, were willing to take the risk of launching the Dolphin upon the seas of a turbulent and very nearly paperless world.[879]

Anti-war dope? An incongruous phrase, but in translation still very much what Charlotte had said years earlier, in *The Brontës of Haworth* - "I just wrote to drug myself. I was a poor girl who tried to escape from life by dreaming dreams."[880] *Green Dolphin Country* did provide an escape for Elizabeth and for her readers too, from the grim world at war into an age of crinolines and sailing ships, pioneering adventures in New Zealand, and a sunlit Guernsey with no occupying troops. Pure escapist literature - but in true Goudge fashion it also looked squarely in the face of unhappiness, and as always she stitched the whole thing together with a strong thread of faith.

As to the two brave publishers, in America this was Coward McCann who had produced all the US editions of her books so far. In England her publisher was, for the first time, Hodder and Stoughton. Until *The Castle on the Hill* all her books had been in the hands of Duckworth. *Henrietta's House* was then published by the University of London Press, and now in this "very nearly paperless world" she had been strongly advised by her agent that she must place the new book where it could be launched profitably. And so she signed a new contract with Hodders and they also took the paperback rights in all the Duckworth novels.

Mervyn Horder, soon to be Chairman, would succeed to his father's title in 1955. (Coincidentally the first Baron Horder had been, like Elizabeth's Uncle James, a physician to the royal family. Elizabeth once quoted, as an example of the "most wonderful intuitions" doctors used to have, a fact she had gleaned from his son's 1966 biography: that "when he didn't know what was the matter with a patient he used to sit beside them and hold their hand until he did know."[881]) Jessie Monroe described Lord Horder as "a friend of a publisher" – and necessary as it was in the circumstances, Elizabeth never really ceased to feel guilty at having deserted Duckworth. As late as 1968 an article in the *RNA News*, the journal of the Romantic Novelists' Association, reported that "She still feels a slight guilt about the move to Hodders at the instigation of her agent but admits they have done very well for her."[882]

She owed all her success so far to Duckworth who had effectively launched her career. Perhaps her guilt was not helped by the fact that according to Lord Horder, Hodders had been one of the publishers who originally turned down *Island Magic*. However, he said, the new contract was just for fiction and so his company were still able to publish some of her later books, notably *Saint Francis of Assisi* in 1959 and in the early postwar years, *Songs and Verses* and the collected short stories published as *Make-Believe*, *White Wings*, and *The Reward of Faith*. Elizabeth said,

Of the three publishers who for so many years have helped and advised me, and to whom I owe more than I can express, the deepest love and gratitude go to Duckworth.[883]

※

The shortage of paper in the book-publishing world seems to have been responsible for another new element in her career – for during the war years not only stories but her novels too began to appear in magazines, in abridged or serial format. *The Castle on the Hill* had been abridged for the July 1942 edition of *Omnibook* magazine, and now *Green Dolphin Country* was serialised in *Woman's Journal*. The blurb announcing the novel's merits calls them "reasons in plenty for us to publish it for the benefit of those readers who have been unable to obtain a copy." Illustrated by Francis Marshall, the first of the six instalments appeared in January 1945, spread across sixteen pages of the magazine. However paperless the world when the Green Dolphin first appeared, by the time of the tenth UK edition just four and a half years later, it had already sold over half a million copies. The critics praised it. *Punch* described it as "A curiously luminous book which leaves a strong impression of sunshine and windy skies." George Bishop of *The Daily Telegraph* found it "breathtaking…a long vista of undulating story, with here and there peaks of volcanic excitement…" and said that "the heroine, Marianne, is a magnificent achievement."[884]

And it won a prestigious prize. Already the September selection of the Literary Guild in America, who also awarded it Book of the Year, it was chosen out of ninety-nine novels as the winner of the first Louis B. Mayer fiction award of $125,000.

> *[There] came a cable from America telling me that my American publisher had sent the book in as a candidate for a Metro Goldwyn Mayer film prize of £30,000 and the old Dolphin had won it. It was hilarious news for everyone. I was not the type of woman to have this sort of thing happen to me and my unsuitability for the role struck everyone as extremely funny.*[885]

It seems from a letter to Audrey that Elizabeth also was aware of her own unsuitability, although her reaction was not hilarity. "Aren't I a lucky woman about the film!" she wrote. "I am so grateful for this good fortune, but I do feel that I don't deserve such luck. I just don't deserve it. It makes me feel sort of ashamed!"[886]

> *For the village it was a happy nine-days'-wonder in the midst of a horrible war. I remember the laughing faces and the kindness of people who were themselves badly off and yet could rejoice whole-heartedly at the success of someone else. And then came a damper in the person of a Jewish gentleman who with his family had taken refuge in the village from air-raids. He had considerable knowledge of finance, and travelling in the bus from Paignton, our shopping town, in the company of half the village, he told the bus that he doubted if taxation would leave much out of the £30,000. A second financier in the village agreed with him. According to his calculations the American aliens tax, English super tax, agency fees, lawyers' fees and the share in the prize that would go to the publishers of the book, would leave me £3,000. I was so relieved that it was like waking up from a nightmare. £3,000 was a large sum but I felt I could cope with that; the load of £30,000 was enough to crush any poor woman to death. In the end our village financiers were wrong; it was £4,000.*[887]

She was relieved; but the situation highlighted the unfair nature of the tax laws in such circumstances and according to Jessie, as a direct result of her experiences H.E. Bates and other writers took on the Inland Revenue and managed to get the law changed.

That small explosion of private excitement died away, a storm in a teacup. Hélène and her son also went away and once more the war was in the forefront of our living. The American army was now everywhere and gradually all of us in the village began to realise that some hidden undertaking was going on around us...

And then there came an unforgettable night...filled through all its hours by a low, ceaseless rumble... The morning brought a clear, cool, windless day filled with the most extraordinary silence. When I opened the door in the morning there was not a soul in sight...

It was the invasion of Europe, so long planned, hoped for, expected and yet never coming. It was here at last. If it succeeded the end would be in sight; the end of the concentration camps, the end of all the agony and horror. But what if it failed? The queer, unaccustomed, lasting silence made it easier to pray, but individual prayer seemed a feeble, fleeting thing in the face of what was happening over there.[888]

The war memoires of David Best, a schoolboy who also lived in the Westerland area of Marldon, gives a more detailed account of the long preparations for the D-Day landings - and a good understanding of why the silence that morning was queer and "unaccustomed."

> In 1943 there was a steady build-up of American troops and vehicles in and around the camps at Marldon and by 1944 the vast accumulation could not be bottled up any longer. There was an urgent need for additional training space, so almost without notice pieces of land were considered and the army moved in... At school we were horrified as the American soldiers took over our playing field at Cricketfield Road and surrounded the encampment with barbed wire...
>
> In the early months of 1944 when the air was crisp and the ground hard with frost, the bulldozers and cranes arrived... One day, a convoy of amphibious vehicles arrived from the docks at Plymouth to add to the clutter of transport already in the village... The vehicles were cumbersome and in the narrow country lanes the handling qualities left a lot to be desired. It was not surprising therefore that more than one villager had a nasty fright when the monsters returned each night from their daily paddle in the sea...

One of the last arrivals to complete this huge army was the American 7th Field Hospital. All available places had been taken, so a few cuttings were hastily made into the field opposite the Vicarage, and it was here alongside the roadway that the medics erected their tents and set up their hospital…

1944 was also the year of the aeroplane. No longer antiquated relics crawling across the sky, but squadrons of Lancasters from the many Coastal Command stations in Cornwall hedgehopping over the Marldon rooftops and sending cows galloping in all directions. Hurricanes from Bolt Head and Spitfires from Exeter screaming in from the sea as they would do on the day, and all but clipping the chimneys at the highest bit of land at Marldon Cross.[889]

So began, at last, the beginning of the end of the war. Even so,

There was still much more to come, the doodle-bugs and the shattering horror of the dropping of the atomic bombs. People have grown used to the thought of atomic warfare now, the present generation have grown up with the bomb, and so it is hard for them to realise how appalled we were then. And the dropping of the bombs seemed to tarnish victory. When it came at last most of us felt almost more shame than joy.[890]

The Film

Meanwhile in Hollywood casting was under way. Katharine Hepburn and Gregory Peck were among those considered for the starring roles in *Green Dolphin Street* but it was Lana Turner who eventually topped the bill, playing Marianne to Van Heflin's Tai Haruru, with Donna Reed as Marguerite and a new star, Richard Hart as William.

Elizabeth had written to Audrey in the first excitement of winning the prize, "I wonder how long it takes to make a film, and then how long before it gets over here? Some while yet I expect…"[891] She was right: it was 5th November 1947 when the film went on release. The trailer itself boasted that it had been two years in the making, and there had not been a movie of this epic quality since *Gone with the Wind* and *Mutiny on the Bounty*. It added the staggering statistic that twenty million people had read the story – perfectly possible no doubt, given the serialisations across the world in the likes of *Woman's Journal*, *Omnibook* and *Liberty* magazine.

"The film came to Paignton not long ago and was much enjoyed by the village, which went practically in a body!" she reported to Audrey, "and of course loved the earthquake."[892] In fact the special effects were so good that they won an Oscar in 1948, in addition to the film's nominations for Best Cinematography, Best Film Editing and Best Sound Recording. The theme music too - by Bronislau Kaper and Ned Washington - eventually became a jazz classic after Miles Davis recorded it a decade later. (This track, incidentally, inspired the title of another novel in 2001 - Sebastian Faulks' *On Green Dolphin Street*.)

But Elizabeth herself did not love the film. According to Jessie, "Elizabeth was very disappointed in it– dismayed beyond words! Appalling!" The article in the *RNA News* reported that "Miss Goudge had not liked the film"[893] and a friend from Elizabeth's later years, Kathleen Millington, said "She had a special viewing for the film and was absolutely disgusted; she said 'It's not my book at all.'"

The Practice of the Presence of God

Why such disappointment and dismay? Well, she had told Audrey at the outset that the novel was "terribly long… I can't imagine how it's to be made into a film, but no doubt they will just dig out the purple passages and leave the rest alone!"[894]

In fact much of the storyline was used, but as so often in film adaptations, with alterations. It was presented primarily as Marianne's love story and had as its focus, therefore, the kind of feisty heroine so beloved of 1940s Hollywood. But this focus caused an imbalance between the three characters of William, Marianne and Marguerite who in the novel have equal importance and are intended to be, not simply three sides of a love triangle, but a trinity representing "three deep cravings of the self…which only mystic truth can fully satisfy." These are the words of Evelyn Underhill, quoted as the book's epigraph, in which she illustrates the restlessness of the human spirit as a three-fold search: to discover new horizons; to find the perfect love; and to strive for the inner perfection attained by the saints. To be true to its source, therefore, the film would need to have this central element of a trinity and "mystic truth."

Of at least equal importance in the book was a second source of spiritual inspiration - a 17th century text that Elizabeth had only recently discovered. In August 1942, after all her deep sorrow about Nanny, she'd told Audrey that she had "been reading so many good books lately." As one daughter of Oxford to another, she listed "two books by Clive Lewis of Magdalen" - *The Screwtape Letters* and *The Problem of Pain* - and then added:

Also I've discovered (for the first time in my life, to my shame be it said!) Brother Lawrence's Practice of the Presence of God. *Isn't it lovely. I'd like to learn it by heart from the first page to the last.*[895]

The book was so important to Elizabeth that she gave it a central role in the plot of *Green Dolphin Country*. Marguerite is given a copy as a child and years later, at a time of devastating sorrow, its teaching brings about a great reversal in her life. Under its influence, she discovers her vocation to enter a convent and grows into a woman of deep and prayerful faith, eventually becoming Mother Superior. Reading Brother Lawrence had been the beginning of Marguerite's part in the trinity: the journey towards inner purity and perfection. By the end of the story, her progress is such that her face has "the indefinable stamp of spiritual power... young as only the reborn are young, wearing the serenity of her spiritual acceptance like a light about her."[896]

Hollywood paid lip-service to this potential transformation with a shot of Donna Reed as a white-clad novice about to take her vows, carrying a lighted candle and with her eyes raised piously to heaven. But what the film could not portray was that Marguerite's vocation was not simply a case of taking the veil because she was disappointed in love: her faith had involved a life-long journey, a "path of spiritual discipline...that had been the cause of so much torment and so much joy."

> *She knew that in the eyes of the world her life must seem a very trivial thing... but she knew also that what the world sees of the life of any human creature is not the real life...*
>
> *And Marguerite believed that her real life was of value, besides being an immense joy to herself. She assured herself that the practice of the presence of God, that she had learned with such self-discipline of thought and will, was not a selfish thing but something absolutely essential if one's soul was ever to be of the slightest use in this world or the next.*

> *This faith had come to her from the book Reverend Mother had given her... It was a very short book, but that was perhaps an advantage, for its brevity had enabled Marguerite to get it by heart. When she was alone she did not...gossip with herself about this, that or the other, for like Brother Lawrence she had learned by bitter experience that "useless thoughts spoil all", and that nothing so thoroughly ousts the sense of the presence of God as talking to oneself.*
>
> *Through years of hard mental discipline, carried on with homely unseen heroism, she had learned to silence the chatter of self, to focus her mind in meditation, until the beauty dwelt upon became not a picture but an opening door and then with sealed lips but open ears to go away through it by her secret stair to God.*[897]

More than thirty years later, the poet Muriel Grainger quoted from this passage in an article she wrote in praise of Elizabeth's work, and received this response from its now 77-year-old author:

> *It fills me with shame! How far away I am from practising what I write. Marguerite may have silenced self, but I haven't, and I have not much time left in which to do it.*[898]

However that may be, it was not only Marguerite for whom she described the experience of silencing the self in contemplative prayer. For the old nun Mère Madeleine, too:

> *At last the will triumphed, the soul shook herself free of the body's pain and mounted like a bird into that clear air of contemplation where words are caught away by the wind, where the soul listens, hovering with spread wings.*[899]

The great crisis of Marguerite's young life had been caused by a letter to her father – asking that her sister Marianne, not herself, should sail to New Zealand and marry her beloved William. She is devastated. However, in the years that follow she slowly discovers, by the practice of the presence of God, that life's sorrow and loss are more than just tests of endurance; they can be the positive means of grace and spiritual growth. She finds this passage in Brother Lawrence's letters:

> *"I always thought that He would reduce you to extremity...But those who have the gale of the Holy Spirit go forward even in sleep. If the*

vessel of our soul is still tossed with winds and storms let us awake the Lord who reposes in it, and he will quickly calm the sea."

She put the book back, and smiled. Even in sleep, even through the night, the vessel had been carried forward by no virtue of her own; and God had been within it all the time.[900]

Similarly, William's mistake involves him in a test of endurance. Having unknowingly muddled the names of the two sisters in his letter of proposal, his joyous anticipation collapses as he watches the wrong woman step from the sailing ship. Heartbroken and appalled, he nevertheless takes the deliberate decision to keep the secret – to welcome, not reject, Marianne on the quayside. After a disastrously unhappy start to the marriage he then sets himself to follow the advice of his parson friend, Samuel, and "pierce through to the other side"[901] of their unhappiness; and he more than succeeds. The long-term consequence of his noble and loving action is that his mistake in asking for the wrong girl becomes the means of grace for them all.

This muddling of names was a mistake actually made by Elizabeth's great-uncle, her Guernsey grandfather's brother, and she deeply admired his heroism and the hard decision he had made in order to ensure someone else's happiness; for he had written to Adolphus "and told him what an agony it was to meet the unwanted bride with a smiling face."

It had been grand of William, I thought, never to tell his wife of his mistake, and to succeed in making a fine thing of his marriage, and I had always wanted to write his story.[902]

In the film, unfortunately, the grandness of William's decision is simply erased from the plot. It is not his own integrity which prompts him to do the right thing… he goes through with the marriage because his friend Tai Haruru bullies him into it.

As she said, "It's just not my book."

❋

It seems that at least one critic failed to plumb the depths of the novel, too. Although the book was sold with Vita Sackville-West's laudatory words on the dust-wrapper: "packed with ingredients, rich as a plum pudding but far too wholesome to be indigestible,"[903] in fact her review in *The Spectator* is not as complimentary as the quotation suggests. For a start, in her opinion the reader's "credulity is a bit strained" by the muddle over Christian names.

As Elizabeth said ruefully,

I wrote a note at the beginning of the book to say that [the] mistaking of names was true, but as no one ever reads a writer's notes I was reprimanded by several reviewers for cooking up such a fantastic story.[904]

Ms Sackville-West's faint praise admits that the author has skilfully mixed the "sentimental" and the "picaresque" and she credits her with "gusto, facility and invention" (crushingly observing that there is a "rich supply of readers demanding nothing beyond this.") But she says that one look at John Morton-Sale's cover illustration, of Marianne and Marguerite in their tight-waisted green and pink crinolines, sums up what one may expect from the book in the way of "period values."[905]

It is arguable however that anyone reading the opening quotation from Evelyn Underhill would have expected an exploration of something much deeper than mere Victorian values; and on discovering Brother Lawrence at the heart of the plot would have had their expectations fulfilled.

❄

Not only did Elizabeth not like the film, but the new-found wealth - when it finally arrived - proved to be a burden. It did however enable her to have the joy of being generous to her friends, as this letter to Audrey shows.

All the people I love best in the world must share in my luck this Christmas, otherwise I can't be happy! So for my sake I know you won't mind having the enclosed and spending it on something frivolous.[906]

She also had the joy of spending something on herself, although this further letter to Audrey suggests that the expenditure was modest...

Your blue dress and hat sound lovely. I had quite an orgy of shopping the other day. I got a "new look" dress, brown with a little blue trimming, and a...coat which I got for half coupons and half price because it was such a small size that nobody would buy it. There are sometimes advantages in being skinny![907]

The New Look was Christian Dior's collection of 1947, introducing the luxury of long full skirts after the skimpy clothes of wartime austerity. Elizabeth's quotation marks however tell us that her dress was no doubt only influenced, rather than made by Dior - as do her opinions on extravagance and self-indulgence generally. For example, *The Joy of the Snow* records a memory of how "When I began to succeed as a writer I was seized with an absurd longing for a fourposter bed." But, she says, she "fought the addiction" because her politics were "anti-four-poster... to spend so much money on oneself would have been a crime of the worst order for a socialist."[908]

And it was a lifelong persuasion, for when recounting this story at the age of 74 she added, "My politics remain what they were."[909] It is an attitude - even for socialists - very much at odds with the consumerist values of our modern world, where many people would perhaps find it hard to understand her response to this burdensome windfall: "I did not want to be a rich woman, and hoped I would succeed in never living as one."[910] Nevertheless, the prize money was now hers and had to be dealt with:

I had to learn how to administer what came to me and the mistakes I made in learning were at times catastrophic... and to think that I had at one time, at our leanest period, actually prayed for money! Desiring, of course, only a modest competence.

Of the letters, the begging letters were the worst because the machinations of lawyers in both countries delayed the arrival of the filthy lucre for a long time, there was little in the bank and therefore little I could do immediately to help. One night, trying to cope with the letters of every sort and kind, I reached despair, picked up the whole bundle and dumped it in the fire. That is something that will haunt me till my dying day, for although among the writers of begging letters there are many who are only "trying it on" there are also some who are in genuine need.[911]

After the War

We had to have some work done on the cottage, and to get my mother away from the noise we rented a bungalow on the coast, a few miles away, and stayed there a month. It was a modern bungalow with a pretty garden looking over the sea, the war was over, the summer weather was perfect and we took with us a friend whom my mother and I loved dearly.[912]

This all sounds ideal, for it seems fair to assume that Elizabeth would be in need of a little peace and rest by now, just after the turmoil of the war and the consequences of even that positive event, the film prize. But she says that what "should have been a wonderful holiday...was one of the longest months of my life." What she actually found there was not rest but "sleepless misery. The moment I was in bed and had put the light out it fell on me, black and hopeless." It was another unpleasant experience of extra-sensory perception.

About half-way through our time I went to bed for a day with some minor ailment. My mother had not been in my room until then because though it was next to her own even the short distance was a bit too much for her walking powers. But that day she came, though she got no farther than a few steps inside the door. Then she stopped and there was silence as the room made its impact upon her. "Nothing would induce me to sleep here," she said vehemently and went out and shut the door.[13]

As Elizabeth soon discovered, it had been the room occupied by the owner's late husband during his long illness and "I had picked up something of his misery, and so had my mother when she briefly visited his room."

Around this time Elizabeth wrote a short foreword to a little book called *Haunted Borley*. Written by the Rector, A.C. Henning, it records the history and "strange happenings" of a famously haunted church in Essex. Although she occasionally had these inexplicable experiences herself, when writing this foreword Elizabeth very firmly directed its focus away from fear and negativity, towards love and peace, beauty and faith.

What really matters is Borley, and not the strange things which may have momentarily disturbed, but cannot destroy, its peace and beauty. Mr. Henning loves his beautiful church, the villages of Borley and Liston and the quiet countryside about them very deeply, and is able to communicate to the reader both his love and his sense of the great value of village life to England. He has made patient research into the history of the church and…tells us of the strange experiences that have come to him and to others. But these do not seem important. What shines out is the church itself among the tall trees, with the avenue of yew trees leading to the brick porch, and the door that admits you to "the security of home, where all the cares of the world outside drop from you."[14]

❄

By 1946 - despite the amount of time taken up by the Green Dolphin, and well before the film was released - she had published another prize-winning novel. This was *The Little White Horse* which she dedicated to its illustrator, "Walter Hodges with my thanks." The talented C. Walter Hodges had already designed the dust-wrappers for several of her novels, plus the delightful illustrations in the text of *Sister of the Angels* and *Smoky-House*. A graphic artist for most of his professional life, he was himself the author of children's novels as well as being a designer of exhibitions. And he was involved in Elizabeth's beloved theatre world. One of the original designers of the Mermaid Theatre in London and a recognized authority on the structure of Shakespeare's Globe, he also designed scenery and costumes for theatre and films.

His colour-plate *The View from Paradise Hill* must have particularly captured the essence of this book for Elizabeth's friend, Father Louis Bouyer, who according to Jessie could always discern the spirituality in her work, "even in the children's stories." She said that he "adored" this illustration – what she called "the view of the far country" - and that Elizabeth left it to him in her will.

The inspiration behind the book, according to *West Country Magic* was the glorious landscape of Devon and, once again, a dream: "Not far away there is a beautiful cove where the white horses from the sea come galloping in," she wrote; "One night I dreamed that one of them galloped inland and did not go back."[915] But there was another, unacknowledged inspiration behind it too; for the book is quite clearly influenced by Francis of Assisi, perhaps Elizabeth's favourite saint whose life-story she would publish in 1959. And shortly before *The Little White Horse* there had been yet another work influenced by him: in January 1946 a short story, *Our Brother the Sun* was published in *Woman's Journal*. In the story's opening words, "Brother Clement, the old Franciscan, lifted up his voice and sang aloud for joy..." and his song is the canticle of praise written by Francis himself, beginning "Praised be my Lord God, with all His creatures, and especially our brother the Sun."[916] By the end of the tale the friar has sung the whole canticle, verse by verse: "Praised be my Lord," he continues as he tramps along, "for our sister the moon..."[917]

The same beloved canticle of St. Francis appears in *A Book of Comfort*[918] and is sung in *The Little White Horse* too – but this time paraphrased for her young readers as the Spring Song written by Old Parson:

> *Praised be our Lord for our brother the sun,*
> *Most comely is he, and bright.*
> *Praised be our Lord for our sister the moon,*
> *With her pure and lovely light...*[919]

The Little White Horse

And I saw heaven opened, and behold a white horse...[920]
The Revelation

To the east, where was the sunrise and the sea, light was stealing into the woods, like a milk-white mist, and as the light grew so did the sound of the sea grow too. And then it seemed as though the light was taking form.

It was still light, but within the light there were shapes moving that were made of yet brighter light; and the shapes were those of hundreds of galloping white horses with flowing manes and poised curved necks like the necks of the chessmen in the parlour, and bodies whose speed was the speed of light and whose substance seemed no more solid than that of the rainbow; and yet one could see their outline clear-cut against the night-dark background of the tree... They were the sea-horses galloping inland, as Old Parson had told Maria that they did, in that joyful earth-scamper of theirs that ushered in the dawn.

They were nearly upon them now, and there was the roaring of the sea in their ears and blinding light in their eyes. Monsieur Cocq de Noir gave a cry of fear and shielded his head with his arm, but Maria, though she had to shut her eyes because of the brightness of the light, laughed aloud in delight. For she knew the galloping horses would not hurt them; they would just wash over them like light, or like the rainbow when one stands in the fields in the sun and the rain.

And it happened like that. There was a moment of indescribable freshness and exhilaration, like a wave breaking over one's head, and then the sea-sound died away in the distance and, opening their eyes, they saw again only the faint grey ghostly light that showed them no more than just the faint shapes of the trees and the outline of each other's faces. The white horses had all gone... all except one.

They saw him at the same moment, standing beneath the giant pine-tree to their right, with neck proudly arched, one delicate silver hoof raised, half turned away as though arrested in mid-flight. And then he, too, was gone, and there was nothing in the woods except the normal growing light of dawn.'[21]

The Little White Horse is a classic tale of good versus evil. Life at Moonacre Manor and its neighbouring village of Silverydew is adversely affected by an age-old feud, but as in all the best stories the brave children tackle the evil and bring peace to the land, at the same time managing to teach the grown-ups the error of their ways. However in this book, the influence of St. Francis is everywhere. There are Sun and Moon types in the Merryweather family – just as the little white horse is all moonlight and the great tawny lion,

Wrolf, is golden like the sun. Animals are of tremendous importance - to an even higher degree than in *Smoky-House* and *Henrietta's House* in fact, for the humans are dependent upon them for help, protection and wisdom. And Loveday reveals that Old Parson has Franciscan ideals too: for he "does not mind animals inside the church.

> *He says that dogs and cats and horses are much the best-behaved of God's children, much better behaved, as a general rule, than men and women, and he never can see why they should be kept out of God's house."*[922]

"Nor can I see either," agrees Maria, who has already had her own vision of all Creation joining in with the Old Hundredth during morning service, in response to the enthusiastic gallery music, and the superb fiddling of Old Parson himself:

> *It seemed to Maria, her imagination running riot to a shocking extent, that beyond the walls of the church she could hear all the birds in the valley singing, and the flowers singing, and the sheep and deer and rabbits singing in the park and woods and fields and up on the slopes of the great hills. And somewhere the waves of the sea that she had not seen yet were rolling into Merryweather Bay, and crying Amen as they broke upon the shore.*[923]

If the ancient Moonacre feud is ever to be finally resolved then the rule of Francis must be observed, in that wealth has to be given to God, and pride must be humbled. Unity is vital too: past evils cannot be destroyed until the Sun and Moon Merryweathers have ceased their quarrelling. Their family motto tells them, indeed, that God's kingdom is not to be found in either isolation or division: "The brave soul and the pure spirit shall with a merry and a loving heart inherit the kingdom together." Amazingly, the plot of this delightful children's novel even echoes St. Francis' words on the death of the body. "Woe to him who dieth in mortal sin," says his *Canticle of the Sun*:

> *Maria gathered her green cloak about her, knelt down upon the paving-stones, folded her hands and shut her eyes and said a prayer. For this, she remembered, had been a holy place, and her wicked ancestor Sir Wrolf had taken it away from God to have it for himself. And now, they said, his ghost haunted this place and could not enter Paradise because of his sins. "O God," she prayed, "please forgive Sir Wrolf*

for being so greedy. And please show me how to give this place back to You. And then please let him go to Paradise.'[24]

Maria is not disappointed, for there is a fairytale happy ending for all. Except that of course it is not a fairytale, but the answer to prayer and courageous faith in action. Happiness has come to Moonacre not by the waving of a magic wand, but because Maria's pure spirit and Robin's brave soul have come together to challenge and end the long-standing estrangement and wickedness. Their efforts bring forgiveness and reconciliation all round. In the words of the *Canticle,*

> Praised be my Lord for all those who pardon one another
> for love's sake, and who endure weakness and tribulation:
> blessed are they who peacefully shall endure, for Thou, Oh
> Most High, will give them a crown.[25]

Nor is the white horse itself just a fairytale, even though Maria discovers that he is not a real horse but that mythical beast, a unicorn. He is a revelation, a vision of pure unearthly light that is the antithesis of all evil and doubt. And here perhaps is an echo of yet another great spiritual work - included, like the poem of St. Francis, in Elizabeth's *Book of Comfort - The Spiritual Canticle of St. John of the Cross*:

> Rare gifts he scattered
> As through these woods and groves he pass'd apace,
> Turning, as on he sped,
> And clothing every place
> With loveliest reflection of his face.[26]

The silvery light grew even stronger, and was in itself so lovely that she knew no evil thing could live within it. 'It must be moonlight,' she thought, but yet she knew that no moonlight could get through the canopy of darkness overhead, and that not even the moon had quite so wonderful a radiance.

And then she saw him. A little white horse was cantering ahead of them, leading the way, and from his perfect milk-white body, as from a lamp, there shone the light. He was some way ahead of them, but for one flashing moment she saw him perfectly, clear-cut as a cameo against the darkness, and the proud curve of the neck, the flowing white mane and tail, the flash of the silver hoofs, were utterly strange and yet utterly familiar to her, as though eyes that had seen him often before looked through her eyes that had not until now looked steadily upon his beauty; she was not even surprised when he turned his lovely head a little and looked back at her and she saw a strange little silver horn sticking out of his forehead... Her little white horse was a unicorn.

After that they travelled with speed, Wrolf managing to keep the little white horse in sight. But they never caught up with him, and Maria didn't again see him so clearly as she had in that first moment of vision; for the rest of the way he was just a steady shining, a moving shape of light whose outline was not again clear-cut against the darkness. Yet she was content with what she saw, content even when the trees thinned out and the darkness faded, and against the growing splendour of moonlight beyond, the radiance of the little white horse slowly dimmed; content even when it vanished... For now she had seen him...and the fact of him was a thing that she would not doubt again.[927]

Famously praised in recent years by J.K. Rowling who we are told absolutely adored the book as a child, *The Little White Horse* can now be said to have attained classic status. Its timeless appeal in the seven decades since first publication is evident in the ongoing BBC adaptations: including a radio serialisation in *Children's Hour* during August/September 1958; and for television, a five-part reading on *Jackanory* in early 1967 and a six-episode dramatisation under the title *Moonacre* in the spring of 1994. The BBC also produced an unabridged audio book on cassette in 2003, read by Miriam Margolyes, and in 2008 an abridged version on CD by Juliet Stevenson, who played Miss Heliotrope when in 2009 it became the second Goudge novel to be made into a film. Adapted under the title *The Secret of Moonacre*, it is directed by Gabor Csupo and stars Dakota Blue Richards as Maria.

It is a good children's film - the scene where the white horses gallop in from the sea is superb - but who can say if Elizabeth would have liked it any more than its predecessor? There are certainly, again, some rigorous changes. (Why? Perhaps to emphasize how alone in the world Maria is, and in consequence – like Marianne in *Green Dolphin Street* - how feisty?) Whatever the reason, her beloved Robin is for at least half of the film inexplicably her enemy, and actually attacks her carriage when she first arrives at Moonacre Manor. Nor does the originally kindly, hospitable Sir Benjamin seem to be her friend either, for much of the film. The protective, loving Miss Heliotrope is transposed into a comic figure, quite out of character with her original Victorian gentility... and Old Parson and his church are written out of the plot altogether.

Because once again, the deep spiritual message of the book is missing. The film remains true to the novel in that Pride is recognised as the cause of all the hatred between the two families, and all is forgiven and happily resolved by Maria's courageous action; but the things wrought by faith in the book become, in the film, transposed into magic. There is a "spell" on the valley which is broken only when the lost pearls are returned; and in the film it is Nature who wants the pearls back; no-one gives anything to God.

※

Elizabeth experienced a spell of a very different kind when in the summer of 1946 she was able to revisit Keyhaven to take another holiday at Harewood House. She wondered if its impact would be the same as on her first visit, when "that lovely old house and garden, set in the shining beauty of the sea and the Solent and the rainbow-coloured marshes, put a spell upon me..."

It was exactly the same. Between my two visits the war had come and gone, and it had put its scars upon the lovely countryside, and upon the house and garden; yet the spell was just the same.[928]

The sight of the historic Hampshire countryside inspired in her, too, a feeling of renewal; and confirmed her awareness of the continuity of history. In a similar focus to the *Haunted Borley* foreword, she says here that the evils of war are only a passing shadow compared with the everlasting refreshment of nature, and the undying impact of human goodness. Indeed the landscape seemed to her to contain the very spirit of the people who had lived in it.

For so many centuries the natural loveliness has perpetually renewed itself in sea and woods and marshes, lanes and fields; if it is shadowed for a little while it only seems waiting to renew itself again. And the same with the life of the men and women. The monks of Beaulieu who toiled and prayed in the great Abbey, tilled the ground, nursed the sick, taught the ignorant, and set the great bell of the Abbey pealing so loudly that it was heard by the sailors out at sea, were not men whose influence upon the country where they lived can be rubbed out by the passing of just a few centuries. And it is the same with the shipbuilders of Buckler's Hard...and with the men and women who lived in the old stone farms and the thatched cob cottages in the inland valleys, and in the wind-swept fishing hamlets by the sea. The heroism of this human life, the effort, the order and peace, is only waiting to renew itself at the appointed time. It is all there still.[929]

So powerful was its spell that the visit inspired the second novel of the Damerosehay trilogy – although it was not just pure inspiration that made her begin another book. She had contracts to fulfil, as Mrs. Goudge pointed out in a 1946 letter to Audrey from Providence Cottage:

> She is working very hard as she has to get her novel finished this winter. She still has one other novel to finish her contract with U.S.A. and Hodder & Stoughton. Then when this is done I hope she need not sign again, but only work for pleasure not against time. That would be another two years I expect.[930]

Audrey must have suggested a visit; but Ida said that Elizabeth was too busy for visitors. She "would only really enjoy having you when she has finished her book," she wrote, "so that would, I hope, be about April. She is about one-third through." She softened the rejection by adding that they had already had to refuse a visit from another friend... "even though we have not seen her since Leighton died."[931]

Apart from *The Little White Horse* there was one other book that year, from her American publishers Coward McCann. A sure measure of her phenomenal success and popularity since the appearance of the Green Dolphin, *The Elizabeth Goudge Reader*, compiled and arranged by Rose Dobbs, was an anthology of her work which included some previously unpublished material: not only the *Dreams* essay and the *Autobiographical Sketch*, but a short story, *The Three Grey Men* which was later reprinted in both *The Reward of Faith* and *A Christmas Book*. The blurb on the dust-wrapper observes that "It is unusual to find an anthology compiled from the writings of a contemporary novelist, but Elizabeth Goudge is an unusual novelist, and stands apart from other writers in the affection of her readers." So much so, that this was only the first of five anthologies of her work that would be published between 1946 and 1990.

A Bleak Winter

Somewhat ironically, as it turned out, her new story *The Three Grey Men* described the beauty of winters in Devon.

> *When the sun shines in the West Country it seems to shine more brilliantly than in other parts of England. Especially is this so on clear frosty December days, when the deep blue sky, the clear crystal light, the*

> *brief glow of warmth and the powdering of snow on the hedges give the illusion that Maytime has suddenly blossomed in midwinter. The three Grey Men, not natives of this country, found themselves queerly dazzled by the shining splendour as they rode down the hill to the village. Every rut in the road had its slither of sparkling ice, every humblest weed its diamond crown, every bush its exquisite flowery burden of purest white, and the blue air was shot through with silver, and the stillness and the silence held the land so entranced in beauty that time stopped.*[932]

The actual West Country winter that followed publication of this story was appalling, for the winter of 1946/7 was one of the coldest on record. The south-west of England was hit by a blizzard, its worst since 1891, and many Devon villages were isolated. For about seven weeks, from January to mid March snow fell, somewhere in the UK, every day and the temperature seldom rose more than a degree or so above freezing. It was the snowiest winter since 1814. Then in March the temperature abruptly rose, bringing rapid thaw and floods.

To make matters worse in all this misery, there were still fuel and food shortages in the aftermath of the war, as this meal at Damerosehay illustrates.

> *Margaret had made a special effort tonight. She had grilled the sardines and mashed some potatoes, and stewed a few prunes that were so very withered that she had surely been hoarding them for a very long time as a special treat for an honoured guest.*[933]

The opening paragraphs of a short story in the December 1947 *Woman's Journal* gives a further picture of that grim, cold winter of post-war austerity. *The Gap in the Hedge* begins as the heroine lies ill in bed, grumbling about the "beastly cold" and feeling "as though buckets of water were being emptied over me." Although she has a hot bottle, it is a stone one and "You can't cuddle it in your arms like you can a rubber one. What's the good of the war being over if it's still so difficult to get rubber bottles?" She complains too that "There is no warmth in this eiderdown" and she can't light a fire either because "there isn't any coal. We finished it last week and the coal lorry can't possibly get here in this weather. The drifts are four feet deep."[934]

When in 1948 the new Damerosehay novel was abridged in *Omnibook* magazine, the editors reported that it "took a year to do, most of it during the coldest winter in a century. At one point the author says she ran out of fuel for heating and did her writing wrapped in [an] eiderdown."[935] Such were the conditions in which Elizabeth wrote much of *The Herb of Grace*.

In July 1947 Hodders published the Rose Dobbs' anthology in the UK under the title *At the Sign of the Dolphin* and Duckworth produced another, quite different kind of anthology in the same year. *Songs and Verses* was a collection of all the songs and poems – thirty-two in all - that had appeared in her books so far, together with several new poems that were being printed for the first time. It includes this, from the opening pages of *The Little White Horse*, and interestingly, in contrast to all the happiness and reconciliation of the novel itself, her poem is full of darkness, regret and uncertainty.

It was under the white moon that I saw him,
The little white horse, with neck arched high in pride.
Lovely his pride, delicate, no taint of self
Staining the unconscious innocence denied
Knowledge of good and evil, burden of days
Of shame crouched beneath the flail of memory.
No past for you, little white horse, no regret,
No future of fear in this silver forest –
Only the perfect now in the white moon-dappled ride.

A flower-like body fashioned all of light,
For the speed of light, yet momently at rest,
Balanced on the sheer knife-edge of perfection;
Perfection of grass silver upon the crest
Of the hill, before the scythe falls, snow in sun,
Of the shaken human spirit when God speaks
In His still small voice and for a breath of time
All is hushed; gone in a sigh, that perfection,
Leaving the sharp knife-edge turning slowly in the breast.

The raised hoof, the proud poised head, the flowing mane,
The supreme moment of stillness before the flight,
The moment of farewell, of wordless pleading
For remembrance of things lost to earthly sight –
Then the half-turn under the trees, a motion
Fluid as the movement of light on water...
Stay, oh stay in the forest, little white horse!...
He is lost and gone and now I do not know
If it was a little white horse that I saw
Or only a moonbeam astray in the silver night.[936]

There is great unhappiness in this somewhat complex poem – too great, perhaps, for it to have been written merely as the epigraph to a children's book. Here is the "flail of memory" exposing remembered "days of shame;" the whole burden of regret and fear like a "sharp knife-edge turning slowly in the breast." Can it really be no more than a poetic representation of the plight of Moonacre, where lives are tainted and restricted by the sins of a past generation? It all sounds too painfully personal.

Nevertheless it had been the preface to a wonderful book. In 1947 *The Little White Horse* won the Carnegie Medal, the prestigious annual award for the most outstanding contribution to children's literature in the preceding year. The Medal gave her a place among the most respected writers of children's fiction: in its first three years it had been awarded to Arthur Ransome's *Pigeon Post*, followed by Eve Garnett's *The Family from One End Street* and Noel Streatfield's *The Circus is Coming*. The following year, 1948, it would go to Walter de la Mare for his *Collected Stories for Children*; a decade later, to C.S. Lewis for *The Last Battle*.

That would be Lewis's seventh and final Narnia book, but when Elizabeth earned her Carnegie Medal the first of the series was still to come: *The Lion, the Witch and the Wardrobe* was published in the autumn of 1950, four years after *The Little White Horse*. The two books share one important feature... the children, in their battle against evil, have the protection of a lion. And it seems when it came to novel-writing their authors too had a shared characteristic: Lewis, like Elizabeth, owed something to his dreams. He had been having a "good many dreams" about lions, according to George Sayer's biography, and after a good deal of the book had already been written, suddenly had the idea of Aslan the lion, who "came bounding into it."[937]

In each case, the lion is a protector who is at the same time rather terrible. At Moonacre Manor, Maria hears "a rumble like thunder from the hearth of the great log fire..."

> *An animal of sorts, a rather alarmingly large animal, whose body seemed to stretch the length of the hearth, had raised a huge shaggy head from his forepaws... Through the cascade of reddish hair that fell over them eyes like yellow lamps shone disconcertingly upon the assembled company; disconcertingly because they were so terribly penetrating...*[938]

"Robin!" [Maria] whispered suddenly, "I don't believe Wrolf is a dog at all; I believe he's a lion!"
"Of course," said Robin.
"But Sir Benjamin always calls him a dog!"
"It wouldn't do to alarm people," explained Robin.

> "Well!" marvelled Maria. "Well – I – never! I'm glad I got to know him before I realised what he was."[939]

Aslan too, of course, is awe-inspiring.

> As for Aslan himself...the children didn't know what to do or say when they saw him. People who have not been in Narnia sometimes think that a thing cannot be good and terrible at the same time. If the children had ever thought so, they were cured of it now. For when they tried to look at Aslan's face they just caught a glimpse of the golden mane and the great, royal, solemn, overwhelming eyes; and then they found they couldn't look at him and went all trembly.[940]

But neither lion is so alarming that the children cannot climb upon his back for protection and help.

> *Without giving herself time to feel afraid, [Maria] climbed out of her window and on to the great friendly branch beneath it, and so steadily down from branch to branch, until at last her groping right foot felt beneath it not hard wood but the soft strength of Wrolf's back. With a sigh of content she settled herself there and took firm hold of his furry ruff. "I'm ready, Wrolf," she said.*
>
> *He was off at once at a steady pace through the black-and-white magic of the moonlit formal garden...Yet in spite of the peace of the night, when they had left the park behind them and passed into the pine-wood she suddenly felt desperately afraid...The moonlight could not penetrate the thick canopy of the pine branches overhead, and the inky blackness was like a pall muffling not only movement and sight but breath too...*
>
> *She found herself riding with one arm raised to protect her face and her mouth suddenly dry with fear...she felt that hands were trying to pull her off Wrolf's back, and she had hard work not to cry out. And then she had a feeling, just because she could not see him, that Wrolf had left her. It was not Wrolf she was riding, but some horrible nightmare beast who was carrying her deeper and deeper into fear. "If there's never any light, I don't think I can bear it," she thought. And then she said to herself that she* must *bear it. All things come to an end, even the night. Resolutely she lowered the arm she had raised to protect herself, straightened her shoulders and smiled into the darkness.*

And then, almost as though her smile had been a flame that set a lantern shining, she found that she could see a little. She could distinguish the shaggy head of her mount, and he was her own dear Wrolf…[941]

And now she and Wrolf were out in the clearing looking up at the Black Men's castle, and over the top of it the moon hung in the sky like a great shield.[942]

And in Narnia:

> [Aslan] crouched down and the children climbed on to his warm, golden back, and Susan sat first, holding on tightly to his mane…
>
> That ride was perhaps the most wonderful thing that happened to them in Narnia. Have you ever had a gallop on a horse? Think of that; and then take away the heavy noise of the hoofs and…imagine instead the almost noiseless padding of the great paws. Then imagine…the soft roughness of golden fur, and the mane flying back in the wind…
>
> It was nearly midday when they found themselves looking down a steep hillside at a castle – a little toy castle it looked from where they stood – which seemed to be all pointed towers. But the Lion was rushing down at such a speed that it grew larger every moment…And now it no longer looked like a toy castle but rose frowning in front of them…[943]

Elizabeth read C.S. Lewis and told Louis Bouyer, "I learned so much from his books as they came out one by one when I was young."[944] And, "apparently C.S. Lewis used to read her," said Jessie Monroe, "Father Louis said he did."

❋

When Lewis's novel *Out of the Silent Planet* came out in 1938 it had been largely received as pure science fiction. Only two reviewers recognised the Christian theology on which the book was based; and, says George Sayer, Lewis realised that this "great ignorance," gave him the power to "evangelize through the writing of popular books in which Christianity was implicit." It meant that theology could be "smuggled" into his unwitting readers' minds, disguised as romance.[945]

Elizabeth's work too is a successful combination of theology and romance, but for her there was no smuggling involved: she said quite categorically that deliberate evangelizing was never her intention when she set out to write. She wrote firstly to please herself, "because basically we all write because we must," and secondly in gratitude to her readers, "because without them we are lost and we love them more than they know..."

> *I think it is a part of our gratitude that, perhaps unconsciously, and without knowing it, we want to share our faith and what it has done for us and to make contact with those who think as we do. I say unconsciously because in my own case when a book comes into my mind it comes simply as a story; personal belief is something that comes in apparently without my knowledge or contriving. But I think it is this latter unintended thing that makes the strongest link between reader and writer. We all hold our faith with a certain amount of fear and trembling (even Blake wrote, "My hand trembles exceedingly upon the Rock of Ages,") and to find that others share our faith has a steadying influence.*[946]

The White Deer

When Lewis came to write the final chapter of *The Lion, the Witch and the Wardrobe*, he would use the sighting of a white stag as the means to lead the children back from Narnia to their home. He wrote a poem too, inspired by the legend of the white deer, which Elizabeth selected for her second anthology, *A Book of Peace*. Published posthumously in 1964, the poem describes how the stag is pursued through the forest in vain; at times no more than a "mere white gleam."[947]

In *The Herb of Grace* Elizabeth moved on from Maria's pursuit of the elusive little white horse, to the legend of Placidus hunting the white deer in the forest. In April 1948 *Wings*, the Literary Guild Review, printed an article by her about the writing of *Pilgrim's Inn* – the book's American title.

> *And so we come to the symbolic figure of the White Deer, who is an important character in the story. But you know all about him. He has moved as a figure of heavenly loveliness through the imagination of men and women for so long. Poets have written about him, artists have painted him, sculptors have carved him, down the centuries. His likeness by Pisanello hangs in the National Gallery and greets you in several of the cathedrals of England and*

France. I possess a box from Germany with his picture painted upon it, and a little carved statue of him, no bigger than a walnut, that is one of my greatest treasures. He has been so loved by great craftsmen all down the ages that I know it was presumptuous of me to try and write about him. But I could not help it. I did not mean to write about him when I started the book. There was no White Deer in the synopsis that I worked out before I started. He just walked in, upset my plans, made me start the book all over again to accommodate him, and arranged the story about himself just as he wished.[48]

In this second Damerosehay novel, Nadine – swayed by the story of Lucilla's own struggles - has ended her relationship with David Eliot and remarried her ex-husband George. They now have mischievous little twins, who tear the wallpaper in the old store-room of their new home, an historic pilgrim's inn called The Herb of Grace, and discover beneath it some wonderful old frescoes with an image of the White Deer. The room, the Eliots discover, had once been a chapel, and under their careful restoration it becomes a chapel again. A little ancient statue of the deer, too, is discovered buried in the garden. They clean it and place it in an alcove in the cross-shaped central staircase, where it shines a welcome to all comers.

The symbolism is plain. In this novel where people are scarred and damaged in the aftermath of the war, the ancient symbol of the stricken Christ has been rediscovered and restored to its rightful place. It has spent much time in the darkness - behind the wallpaper; lying unseen beneath the soil - but it was never lost, only hidden from sight.

The finding of the glorious frescoes prompts Sally to recount the story of Placidus and his encounter with the deer.

And then, at last, he saw it: a white deer, the most perfect creature he had ever seen, with great branching antlers, the magnificent head reared proudly, the splendid body poised for flight. For a moment the flashing eyes met his, commanding him, and then the creature was off, silver hoofs spurning the ground, the perfect body a white flash of speed, the antlers swaying this way and that, yet never entangled in the branches, beckoning, challenging, defying. One clear call did Placidus sound upon his horn, and then he, too, was off…bent low in the saddle…knowing only that he must follow that deer until the end… But he could not catch up with the creature; it was always a little ahead. The horse was near foundering, his own breath came in gasps, some of the dogs had fallen behind, but still he went on. And then the ground rose steeply and the rocks of a mighty mountain towered up before the failing sight of horse and rider. The deer bounded up it, swift yet unhurried, as though winged. But Placidus could not follow. He reined in his horse…

and bowed his head in shame. He, the unconquerable huntsman, was beaten at last.

And at that moment of his shame the miracle happened. The deer stopped and swung round to face him, lifting its proud head, and the antlers formed themselves into a gleaming cross, with a crucified Figure upon it – that strange symbol of the Christians which he had seen many times, and wondered at for a moment or two; and then had turned aside and gone on his way... But now he could not turn aside, for the deer, the vision sent to him, had led him directly to this end. His way was blocked by this impassable mountain and the challenge of this cross. There was only one thing he could do, and he did it. He leaped from his horse and fell upon his knees. And a voice cried out loudly, echoing through the forest, 'Placidus, why dost thou attempt to injure me? I am Jesus Christ, whom thou hast long served in ignorance. Dost thou believe in Me?' And Placidus answered, 'Lord, I believe.' The voice came again, the words spoken this time very low in his own soul, as though in warning, 'Many sorrows shalt thou endure for My sake, many temptations will assail thee; but be of good courage, I will always be with thee.' A thrill of dismay went through Placidus, yet he did not hesitate, for he knew that he was not yet at his journey's end; as he had followed the vision of the deer to the vision of the cross, so he must follow the vision of the cross to something beyond again. What it was he still did not know, but, in spite of the fear, he did know that to attain at last he would give all that he had, down to the last drop of his blood. 'Lord, I am content,' he said. 'Only give me patience to endure all things for Thee.'"[49]

At The Herb of Grace it is not just the chapel and the statue which are restored. In the hands of the Eliot family the house itself - originally a *maison dieu* - becomes once again a place of refuge for pilgrims, and all who stay there find healing.

Despite the book's deep spiritual symbolism however, Elizabeth still felt the need to make an apology in the *Wings* article for its happy ending.

Like all my books it has a happy ending, for I love these people too much to let them be unhappy for long. I know that happy endings are sometimes inartistic, and certainly not always true to life, but I can't write any other kind. I am not a serious chronicler of the very terrible contemporary scene, but just a storyteller, and there is so much tragedy about us everywhere today that we surely don't want it in the story books to which we turn when we are ill or unhappy, or can't go to sleep at night. We must escape somewhere. I had some happy hours of escape when I was writing this book, and I hope very much that perhaps a few readers may have them when they read it.[950]

Alexander McCall Smith, when interviewed about his favourite music for the *BBC Music Magazine*, did not denigrate happy endings. This twenty-first century author gives them another name: resolution. He believes they are important, in music and in all art, and cites the heavenly *In Paradisum* - the final movement of Fauré's *Requiem* - as a sublime example with its "promise of resolution" in both one's own life and the world.

> Resolution in any artistic work is important as that's what we're striving for in life. We want reassurance that there's some order, that some of the values we want to believe in will work. In a narrative people want, not in simplistic terms a happy ending, but resolution.[951]

Elizabeth's happy endings, too, brought the reassurance that faith values "work" - although the resolution is never simplistic, and happiness is only attained after some form of long-term struggle, pain or sacrifice.

Perhaps she was right, though, to pre-empt what she knew would come from the critics. On 24th April 1948 (her birthday) *The Saturday Review* responded to this "disarmingly honest statement" of hers. The book is flawed, their critic said, by its "sweet side, the Pollyanna note, that fatal emphasis on the happy ending," and the reviewer agrees that she is right to promise some hours of escape, for her readers will enjoy its "complete respite from both trouble and reality."[952]

The respite however is not "complete." This is David Eliot's reaction to his first meeting with his new love, Sally.

> *It was extraordinary how restful it was to be with someone who knew nothing whatever about war, who had not, it seemed, even heard a bomb exploding; someone who was not nerve-racked or tired to death, who had taken no part in the torture and death of the innocent, who was not trying to forget, or alternatively taking a ghoulish or vain-glorious delight in remembering. He was sick of the war, he never wanted to think of it again, he wanted to thrust the whole damnable business out of his mind for ever; and yet he couldn't, because in every face he looked into...he saw the memory of it as a tightness about the mouth and a shadow in the eyes.*[953]

In fact David's experiences as a bomber pilot have brought him to the point of nervous breakdown.

> *Desolation swept in upon David once more. The iron band clamped down upon his head...He was lost again in the darkness of his own futility, of the apparent futility of everything that they had all of them done and suffered during these last years...*[954]

And was this book which emphasised the importance of a secure and happy home life really an "escape to unreality?" It was certainly a reiteration of the ideas in her earlier fiction - the first Eliot novel eight years earlier - but it was also the unmistakably concrete message that King George VI had been urging upon the nation in his post-war Christmas broadcasts: that the security of everyday home life was key to the re-stabilisation of the world. He had ended his 1945 address with these words:

> The same dauntless resolve which you have shown so abundantly in the years of danger, that the power of darkness shall not prevail, must now be turned to a happier purpose, to making the light shine more brightly everywhere. The light of joy can be most surely kindled by the fireside, where most of you are listening.
>
> Home life, as we all remember at Christmas, is life at its best. There, in the trust and love of parents and children, brothers and sisters, we learn how men and nations too may live together in unity and peace.[955]

A month before the first printing of *The Herb of Grace* - on Christmas Day 1947 - the King said, "May God grant that the spirit of goodwill which brightens homes today may spread from them in ever-widening circles until in the fullness of time it changes the face of the world."[956] This idea, of small amounts of goodness having the power to spread and change the world, sounds very like the Laird's vision in *The Middle Window* twelve years earlier. He had wanted to establish "a core of sanity that spreads." He believed that "If you light a bonfire in a sheltered valley the protection makes such a huge blaze of it that those outside see the whole sky lit up."[957]

The King's Speech for Christmas Day 1946 was markedly focused on the spiritual.

Our task of today is to mobilize the Christmas spirit and to apply its power and healing to our daily life. The devastation and suffering everywhere, and especially in stricken Europe, must move the hearts of all of us; but the reconstruction so urgently needed is quite as much spiritual as material; it is necessary not merely to feed hungry people and to rebuild ruined cities, but also to restore the very soul of civilization.[958]

Spiritual and material reconstruction is precisely what is going on at The Herb of Grace. This book may have a happy ending but it is no escape into unreality: it is a part of the post-war aspiration, promoted by the King himself, to reinstate home and family as the centre of national life. Like Lucilla's restoration of Damerosehay after 1914-18, in this novel it is once again the continuation of stable family life that will bring healing, and recovery from the horrors of World War II.

Lucilla knew…that it was homemaking that mattered. Every home was a brick in the great wall of decent living that men erected over and over again as a bulwark against the perpetual flooding in of evil. But women made the bricks, and the durableness of each civilization depended upon their quality.[959]

"Our task of today is to mobilize the Christmas spirit," said the King. Elizabeth's efforts in this direction were so successful that the book's final Christmas chapter was published separately by St. Hugh's Press, London, under the title *Christmas at the Herb of Grace*, its brown front cover bearing a gilt-embossed image of the white deer.

❄

During these years two of her stories were featured in a series of anthologies compiled by Hannen Foss. In 1944 his *Come Home with Me* had also promoted the importance of rebuilding home and family life after the war, and he followed it up with two post-war books, in 1947 and 1951: one focusing on the "family festival" of Christmas, the other on marriage.[960] In both of these, Goudge stories appeared alongside speeches by members of the royal family, and work by, among others, Daphne du Maurier, T.S. Eliot, Hilaire Belloc and Sir Walter Scott.

In 1948 Elizabeth's story *The Easter Bunny* featured in *The Modern Gift Book for Children*, published by Odham's Press. The story's illustrator was John S.

Goodall, who some thirty years later would create an enormously successful series of beautiful picture-books depicting Edwardian life - presumably drawn from his own early memories, for he was born in 1907. They were published in the Seventies, within a few years of *The Joy of the Snow*, and capture that same spirit of another world. Several of the scenes – like the Edwardian kitchen, or skating on the frozen pond - could almost double as illustrations of Elizabeth's own childhood.

In February 1949 she received another rejection letter from the BBC, this time for a play about Thomas More entitled *The King's Servant*. In contrast, her short story about More's last days, bearing the same title, was much more successful: having been published in the US edition of *The Golden Skylark* back in 1941, then again in the 1943 collection, *The Ikon on the Wall* and in *The Elizabeth Goudge Reader*. It was also to appear in *White Wings* in 1952. Ever hopeful, she had also sent them her play about Fanny Burney for possible radio broadcast, but that had been rejected two months earlier, in December 1948. There was, however, a production of it by the Oldham Repertory Theatre Club in the following March. It ran for a week at the Coliseum, with five evening performances and two matinees.

Whatever the BBC's opinion of her plays, they were more than happy with dramatizations of her novels: *Henrietta's House* was broadcast on *Children's Hour* in 1949 with Norman Shelley and Joan Littlewood cast as Grandfather and Grandmother. Thea Holme, who had appeared in the Sunday-night London production of *Suomi* over a decade ago, played Mrs. Jameson. Elizabeth had her usual success with stories and novels that year too, with the publication in 1949 of both *Make-Believe* - a collection of eight tales about the du Frocq family, all of which had previously been published separately in other short-story collections and magazines - and *Gentian Hill*.

Gentian Hill

Its setting was her own village of Marldon, whose ancient name Mergheldon, says a note on the title page, translates as 'the hill where the gentians grow.' Elizabeth later amended this to 'the blue hill' in *The Joy of the Snow*; and the village map produced by Marldon Parish Council in 2008 has yet another version of its original name, simply translated into Elizabeth's book title: "Meargelle Dun, meaning Gentian Hill."

Beyond the Snow

The novel came out in November 1949, and was simultaneously serialised - in four instalments illustrated by Francis Marshall - in *Woman's Journal*. "We are delighted to announce," said the blurb, "that we have once again secured first publication of a new novel by Elizabeth Goudge."[961] The book's popularity was such that it went into a second printing two months later; there was a Book Club edition, also in 1950, and it was condensed for *Omnibook* magazine in May of the same year. It received plenty of favourable criticism, including the *Leicester Mail*'s description of it as "that rare prize these days, a piece of literature and a fine story in one."[962]

Less sympathetic was the review in *Time* magazine on 2nd January 1950, describing her as a writer with "almost nothing to say" and *Gentian Hill* as a novel where "standard breeds of characters" populate a "hollow old stump of a plot." It quotes Elizabeth's weaving-inspired image of life's *carefully woven pattern, where every tightly stretched warp thread of pain laid the foundation for a woof thread of joy* as an example of her "sonorous Victorian style," and notes that the book is "aclog" with fairies and the supernatural, old legends and an "ark" of animals. Nevertheless, the reviewer concedes that her books are always *pulled through* by a combination of her happy endings, "simple optimism" and her "soufflé of fairies and folklore," and concludes that this book "should do it again."

To get a review like this must have been painful – it's possible that she "minded dreadfully" at the time.

Do I mind when the critics give me hard knocks or, as is more often the case, dismiss me with contempt? When I was younger I minded dreadfully, now that I am older and I hope more humble I think they are probably quite right and so I mind less; though I am still almost overcome by joy at the rare-good criticism and think the critic an extremely intelligent man or woman.[963]

So says *The Joy of the Snow*, which was itself reviewed by one of the rare-good critics, Alan Hull Walton, in *Books and Bookmen*. *Gentian Hill* had been the book that first introduced Walton to her work.

> I sat down to read the book. After the first few pages I became interested. By the end of the third or fourth chapter absolutely fascinated. And then enchanted. I couldn't put the book down. I found myself re-reading various paragraphs and sequences...
> After that, every time I saw a book or novel by Elizabeth Goudge I bought it; new, hardcover, paperback, or even secondhand. Whether adult or for children didn't matter...

the books were read, and read again and again; and in the reading they transformed life. It may sound strange; yet it certainly isn't.[964]

He says that from the very start he sensed in her writing an undercurrent of Eckhart and Lady Julian – "not obvious; but there, and unusually potent." In fact there is at least one very obvious Julian reference in this novel... to one of the most famous passages from her *Revelations of Divine Love*, later included in Elizabeth's *A Book of Comfort*.

> Also in this He shewed me a little thing, the quantity of an hazel-nut, in the palm of my hand; and it was as round as a ball. I looked thereupon with the eye of my understanding, and thought: *What may this be?* And it was answered generally thus: *It is all that is made.* I marvelled how it might last, for methought it might suddenly have fallen to naught for littleness. And I was answered in my understanding: *It lasteth, and ever shall last for that God loveth it.*[965]

In *Gentian Hill*, when Father Sprigg is reading aloud verses from the Old Testament: "Blessed of the Lord be His land, for the precious things of heaven..."[966]

> *The brightness fell all around Stella, streaming from a small round sun in the air, that was that one word "precious"...*

> *The whole universe, the living and the dead, those who dwelt in the lighted places and those in the dark outside, became to her no longer separate entities but one small thing, that round small thing up there in the air, no bigger than a hazel nut but bright as a diamond; and it was held securely in the hand of God, who for its very preciousness would not let it fall.*[967]

Julian of Norwich is only one of the many great Christians whose words underpin Elizabeth's work; and among the innumerable words that inspired her, in fact not all are from the Christian tradition. In *Gentian Hill* she several times repeats a passage from Plato's *The Banquet*... "Love is the divinity who creates peace among men and calm upon the sea, the windless silence of storms, repose and sleep in sadness... Love sings to all things which live and are, soothing the troubled minds of Gods and men."[968]

> *To please his wife Charles had become a practising Catholic, though not a very devout one, and now to please her he read the Christian apologists, while she to please him studied Greek and let him put her through a course of his beloved classics. Each was strangely captured by the books beloved of the other. St. Augustine's glowing love of God, the startling beauty of the sentences in which he daringly confessed it, helped Charles to understand Thérèse's certainty. Thérèse, making acquaintance with the wisdom of the Greeks, could almost understand how this to Charles had seemed enough, and how he had halted here.*
>
> *One night, arguing over Christian and pagan conceptions of love, each had written down sentences they liked on scraps of paper and passed them across to each other.*[969]

Charles's were the lines from *The Banquet*. His wife Thérèse chose the words of St. Augustine:

> Blessed is the man who loves Thee, O God, and his friend in Thee and his enemy for Thee. For he alone loses no one who is dear to him, if all are dear in God, who is never lost.[970]

Stella is very afraid that her friend Zachary might be lost, and her image of those who dwell in the light and those in the outer darkness comes from the advice the old Doctor gives her, when she confesses that she feels powerless to help him.

> *Your own life seems to you like a very small lighted room, with great darkness all round it, and you can't see out into the darkness and know what is happening there. But light and warmth from your room can go out into the darkness if you don't have the windows selfishly curtained, keep a brave fire burning, and light all the happy candles you can.*[971]

Once again the image of a small light spreading… if only this little girl can be brave. Zachary, too, must be brave. Having deserted from the navy to escape the intolerable conditions on board his ship, he comes to the sickening realisation that he must have the courage to return to his duties in the war against Bonaparte:

> *"In defence of everything that is dear to you…" It was there that the triumph lay, in the fact of love… He loved Stella enough to go back… to try to keep her safe. It would probably not be of the slightest use. He*

was not such a fool as to think that the return of one midshipman to his duty was going to hold back that vast army. Over and over again the dark power submerged the small lit lamps of love. Yet in a flash of vision he saw them, as each was submerged, lighting another, and knew that while one still shone total darkness, the ultimate triumph of malignancy, would not descend.[972]

Zachary's decision to go back perhaps owed something to Canon Goudge's attitude to bullying, for as a boy, "being unusually small and delicate" he had been "a very popular victim" at his school. Nevertheless he "apparently took [this] as a matter of course" and, "'Go back and face it' was years later his advice to a young cousin whose courage momentarily failed him in face of schoolboy torture."[973] But Elizabeth must have been in need of courage too; for her world was becoming ever darker at this period of her life: *Gentian Hill* was published about eighteen months before her mother's death. There may be a soufflé of fairies and folklore in this novel, but its theme is endurance; the importance of not running away from conditions which at times seem intolerable.

It links back to the theme she explored in her first novel, when under a different kind of restriction – the paradoxical nature of freedom. Esther de Waal discusses this in her book *Seeking God*, explicating it in terms of the three vows of the Benedictine Rule: to stability, fidelity, and obedience. To follow these, she says, involves a determination "not to run away"… it means "perseverance … holding on even under great strain, without weakening or trying to escape"… and it involves endurance too: "a virtue we do not often talk about today." Paradoxically, she concludes, obedience to these demands brings "freedom, true freedom."[974]

※

As Elizabeth reached fifty, there was still a duality in her world. On the one hand, she was living a quiet and retired village life, and caring for her ageing mother. It could be said, even, that in a sense her life still followed the Edwardian archetype of the unmarried daughter who had never left home… except that Elizabeth was no dependent. She was now, in point of fact, very much a woman of the twentieth century with an established and extremely successful career as an international author. In 1950 – the year before her mother died, and therefore at the height of her duties as a carer – she received prestigious recognition of her career achievement when she was created FRSL, a Fellow of the Royal Society for Literature. Another instance of her status as a writer was the production of a special school edition of *A City of*

Bells in the same year. Mervyn Horder abridged it - Elizabeth told him that although she did not like abridgements, she would agree to it if he did - and it was published by arrangement with Duckworth, in the Thomas Nelson *Teaching of English* series. There were apparently plans afoot for another film, too. Her mother's diary records that a man came "to see E about filming G. Hill" on January 23rd 1950, but the film was never made – according to Jessie Monroe, because money was tight in the years after the war.

Also in 1950, another short story collection was published: *The Reward of Faith*. As usual, most of the stories had appeared previously in other collections, although three of the eight are described as "newly written for this volume." (In fact at least one of them, technically, was not: this was *The Canticle of the Sun*, the same St. Francis-inspired story that had been printed in *Woman's Journal* in 1946.) The publisher's blurb on the dust wrapper, however, was now overtly acknowledging her as a Christian writer, saying that *The Reward of Faith*

> brings Elizabeth Goudge's religious stories, new and old, together for the first time between the covers of one book… Each story tells of some manifestation of the triumph of the Christian faith in all lands and all ages – that grain of mustard-seed which has grown to cover the whole earth.[975]

Mother's Last Illness

Elizabeth and Ida had recently suffered what must have been another very painful bereavement, for beloved Aunt Marie had died in October 1949, just before publication of *Gentian Hill*. That reviewer's gibe about "Miss Goudge's simple optimism" is all the more inapt when one considers what her life must have been like at the time… pretty much a blur of hard work and nursing one assumes, for she says, "There must have been a little space between the ending of the war and the beginning of my mother's last illness but I do not remember it…"

There had always been one thing that I had been quite sure of, and that was that because my mother had suffered so much in her life she would be spared a long and painful illness at the end of it. The very reverse was the case. The last illness was long and hard and through the last year there was the humiliation of mental illness added to the physical suffering.[976]

Marldon

Elizabeth told herself, when she began writing *The Joy of the Snow*, that she wanted to think only of the happy memories… "unless a dark period should lead out into some new and happy knowledge. This one did" she said, "and so I can write of it."

> *My mother and I were never parted, and I owe that to the goodness of a nurse who lived in the village. Our doctor had said it was too difficult a case to nurse at home but she pleaded with him. She promised him she would help me through and would never let me down. Nor did she, though she had a husband and small son to look after at home, and was often making her way through storm and snow between one home and the other.*[977]

Ironically Elizabeth, who as a girl had said, "I would like to be a nurse" and had had her suggestion summarily dismissed by the family doctor on the grounds of her own heart complaint, now found herself coping with one of the most strenuous of nursing tasks. Her Marldon friend Mrs. Freda Green, the vicar's wife, said that Mrs. Goudge "became uncontrollable and from somewhere Elizabeth was given great physical strength to hold her down." Ultimately it was not Elizabeth's heart that was affected by the work however, for according to Jessie Monroe,

> The doctor allowed Elizabeth to look after her mother at home, on the understanding she would not lift her back into bed - Elizabeth being weakly herself. She had wonderful help by day but when she was alone she had to lift her back into bed, and doubly did herself in – she had dropped insides from that, and a twisted spine too, so she was never really free of pain.

It may have been thanks to the pleadings of the nurse that "my mother and I were never parted" but - according to Mrs. Green – it had been Ida herself who insisted on home nursing.

> Mrs. Goudge died [at Providence Cottage] nursed devotedly by Elizabeth and helpers – a long illness after years of being a semi-invalid. Mrs. Goudge had a very strong personality and… dominated Elizabeth. [She] was very Victorian and <u>expected</u> her daughter to look after her… [She] had extracted a promise from E that she would never send her to hospital or nursing home when she was dying.

A hard promise indeed, and one difficult to understand in a mother who had once heard that professional veto, "dead in a week" at the suggestion of a nursing career for her daughter. But Ida was beginning to fail, both bodily and mentally. The surviving fragment of her diary, consisting of very brief daily jottings in an exercise book, covers the eighteen months from November 1949. A few entries in the final weeks appear to be in Elizabeth's handwriting, as if at times Ida were too ill to wield a pen herself. It ends abruptly on July 6th 1950, and it seems likely that this date, ten months before her death, marks the final submission to the mental illness that she suffered "through the last year of her life." Elizabeth only wrote of this, she said, "because of the possibility that it may a little comfort someone who is experiencing the same sense of useless, pointless suffering when someone they care for is mentally ill. It may not be useless."

Anyone who has looked after someone they love through mental illness knows the particular misery of it... Death seems in some way to have already taken place for you feel you have lost the person you love. Physical suffering can ennoble and purify but mental confusion seems pointless and useless, and it is this which causes the particular misery of it.

But this illness taught me that it is only a case of 'seems'. The truth may be otherwise. A few days before her death my mother returned, weak and dying but entirely herself. And much more than herself. It was not my imagination but the truth. She came back peaceful and spiritualised. I do not know how else to describe it because there are no words for these things. She had wanted, before she died, to become fit to be with her husband again, and all through the years that she had had to live without him she had been growing. In some hidden way that literally only God knows about, the mental illness had been the last stage of the purification.

Beneath her name on the family grave there is a text from the Book of Wisdom: "God proved them and found them worthy for himself."[978]

On the morning of the day she died...she said she must put on her prettiest nightdress and have the best counterpane on the bed, "because They are coming today..." In the evening the mysterious 'They', of whom the dying so often speak, came, and my mother drifted away into as peaceful a death as it is possible to have.[979]

She died at the age of seventy-seven on 4th May 1951, a day of "dead grey spring cold." Elizabeth was not alone at the time, for her aunt Irene was with them; and she had had too, during that difficult year, the love and support of her friends in Marldon who would "take turns in giving extra help by day or night when it was needed."

This is typical West-country kindness. Such goodness exists all over the world, I know, but the West-country brand of goodness has a particular gentleness and warmth. I was so buoyed up by it, so exalted by the loveliness of my mother's passing, that I could hardly feel any grief at all. With Irene weeping I was ashamed of my dry-eyed calm and happy state. But perhaps that is the way we ought to feel when a soul goes free.[980]

She had recently written, in *God So Loved the World* of the possibility of death as a joyful thing. When the disciples are taking breakfast with the risen Christ, "warm and comforted and happy, their living Lord there in the midst of them and the spring dawn brightening all about them…"

Did they think to themselves that to die and come home to Paradise would be rather like this? Not frightening at all, just a passing out of night and darkness, weariness and failure, into the light. Nothing strange, but a land that was familiar, and Our Lord standing on the shore to welcome them.[981]

But "we should hold to our joy for the short time that it is with us," she said.

For sinners, it cannot last, and the remorse that follows it as we remember all the failure of inadequate love, all the selfish things done and the sharp words said, all the unthinking cruelties of children (some children) to their parents is one of the hardest, if not the hardest, things that we must endure in this life.[982]

The nursing in that last year must have been very hard at times if, as Freda Green said, Mrs. Goudge became uncontrollable and Elizabeth had to hold her down. She wrote, in *Saint Francis of Assisi*:

However devoted and loving the immortal spirit may be the strain and labour of nursing can reduce the mortal part of a nurse to a state that falls very far behind the spirit's intention, and the heartbreaking part of it is that the more the patient is loved the greater can be the fall from grace. The nursing brothers were tired out and their patience was wearing a little thin.[983]

When asked if Elizabeth kept a diary, Jessie said "No she was cured of that – she used to, when her mother was ill, down in Devon, and one of the helps used to read it and tell the village." A small shadow of darkness at the heart of all that blessed outpouring of good-neighbourly light. For what a relief it must have been for Elizabeth, to privately pour out the bottled-up stress and strain on to paper; and how distressing then to find that the diary had been read by that one person, and gossiped about… how that must have intensified her feelings of remorse.

After Mother's death she wrote, in *The Rosemary Tree*:

> *Madness passes, memory does not… That's what judgement is – memory. You remember every shameful thing you ever did, every cruel word you ever spoke. The hooded figures behind the hedge will keep up with you right to the end, and then crowd in upon you, and you'll see their foul faces at last. You'll be the victim then, for your own words will wound you and your own actions choke you. That's hell, and you'll not endure it and live if there's not a sweetness in the air from another's forgiveness and your own remorse, and hills in the distance touched with this light of beauty recognized, accepted and adored.*[984]

God So Loved the World

Elizabeth must indeed have received, with deep gratitude, a great deal of help in caring for her mother. For even in the year of Ida's death, with all the nursing care, she still managed to publish not one, but two books. She seems to have focused more than ever upon her faith at this time - almost as if, with those hooded figures so close, just behind the hedge, she had to abandon the workings of her own imagination and turn to the words of the Bible itself. For she had been writing *God So Loved the World: A Life of Christ*. It came out in March 1951, two months before her mother died, and was dedicated to her four Godchildren.

In her account of the disciples' reaction on the night of Christ's arrest there are some clues to the dark times she had been living through, in the effects of the nursing:

> *Everyone knows what it is like to be awakened suddenly in the early hours of the night from the first deep sleep of exhaustion. We feel disintegrated, "all to pieces," often physically ill. It takes several moments before we can pull ourselves together…*

> *It must have been after midnight now, that hour of the night when a man's vitality is at its lowest and those who are miserable in any case fall into a veritable abyss of misery.*[985]

... and perhaps too, in her reaction to her mother's suffering:

> *All suffering is a mystery, and when we come near to one who is suffering greatly we feel the mystery of it, and feel too a sense of great love and reverence, so that the one who is suffering becomes for the time being almost holy to us. And we feel too a sense of guilt, because we know that suffering is the result of sin, and that every smallest sin of ours has added to the great weight of pain crushing the world...*
>
> *We know what we feel like when we have sinned; the sense of a weight pressing on us, the wretchedness of feeling that by our own act we have put up a dark curtain between ourselves and God's light. We are utterly miserable until we have repented of our sin, prayed to God for forgiveness and been forgiven by his mercy, until the weight is lifted and the barrier down.*[986]

This has echoes of her childhood experience when, after her first awareness of sin in herself, she had owned up to her bad behaviour. And yet... exhaustion, guilt, a weight pressing down, a dark curtain between ourselves and the light... the fruits of sin perhaps, but these sound very much like the symptoms of depression too. Surely Mrs. Goudge had not been the only one who was unwell at that time.

There is today a recognised treatment for the depressed that involves writing it all down, getting it out of the mind and on to paper, focusing on the good things, however small. No wonder she kept a diary at this particularly bad time, as well as writing the two books. For writing had always helped. *Green Dolphin Country* had been a kind of anti-war drug. Working on *The Herb of Grace* had provided some happy hours of escape. In fact it could even be said that this is how many of her books and happy endings came into being. The reality of the darker things in her life – lack of freedom, loss, war, breakdown, the temptation to suicide – provided the undercurrent, and then as the story unfolded in echoes of the poets and mystics, the darkness was overcome. Her books confirmed what Elizabeth believed in faith to be true: that the little hazelnut of creation is in God's hands and for love of it, he will not let it fall... but it must surely at times have been a case of All Shall Be Well "through gritted teeth"?[987]

Nevertheless somehow she conquered... the light is there in every book.

※

God So Loved the World proved that it was not just so-called escapist fiction with happy endings that attracted her readers, for - astonishingly perhaps for such a work - there was a second printing only a month later, and by 1952 it was into its fourth impression. Even more astonishing - given the very different style of women's magazines today - is that it too was serialised in *Woman's Journal,* reproduced in four instalments beginning with the December 1950 issue. Its illustrations were specially reproduced from the paintings of Carl Bloch in Frederiksborg Castle, Denmark, and Elizabeth said some years later in an article for the magazine: "I shall never forget the beautiful pictures that the editor found to illustrate *God So Loved the World*."[988]

The book received much favourable criticism. Daphne du Maurier called it "a deeply thoughtful and most reverent piece of work." Godfrey Winn congratulated the author "on her scholarship, her humanity and her vision." *The Church Times* said that "the whole book is excellent...it should kindle a new flame of devotion in many hearts" and *The Observer*'s critic even stated that "the author writes anew the Life of Jesus with a simplicity and beauty before which the voice of criticism dies away."[989]

In effect, she had produced a life of Christ which was a readable story for people of all ages, from the Godchildren to whom the book was dedicated, to the readers of women's magazines. One wonders, in fact, how many people read the story through the medium of that serialisation alone – quite apart from the several re-printings of the book itself. Perhaps, people who would buy a magazine but might not normally read a Christian text – would perhaps not have considered buying, for instance, a copy of J.B. Philips' *The Gospels in Modern English* which came out the following year, phenomenally successful as that translation proved to be?

The book was even considered for dramatisation on the radio, but nothing appears to have come of it. A BBC memo pointed out that it might be appropriate for the Light Programme, Elizabeth's handling of the subject being much simpler than Dorothy L. Sayers'. The fact of its reverence perhaps made a difference; for according to production notes written for one of Sayers' radio plays, *He That Should Come,* her aim was an "absolutely natural and realistic" style without any "touch of...ecclesiastical intonation or of 'religious unction'."[990] And Elizabeth's is above all a deeply reverent work - one moreover which draws upon her father's attitude to the scriptures: she gave evidence of his "deep reverence for the Bible... the Old Testament as well as the New" in the fact that "in his daily reading and meditation he read both of them upon his knees."[991]

After the Last Supper,

> *They did not yet leave the upper room for Our Lord had so much that he wanted to say to them. For three years now he had been teaching them with unwearied wisdom and patience, but still they were such children and had understood so little, and now his time was very short. He gathered them about him and spoke as men speak sometimes upon their deathbeds…words of such intensity that they are hardly words at all but a sort of distilling of the soul of the man, a precious essence pressed out drop by drop and word by word, an utmost giving of himself in love to those he leaves…*
>
> *To read the 14th, 15th and 16th chapters of St. John's Gospel for the first time is one of the greatest experiences that can ever come to a man or a woman in this world. To read it for the hundredth time is an experience just as great. One can only read them kneeling. From the words "let not your heart be troubled," to the words "I have overcome the world," we do not know where we are except that we are with Our Lord…*
>
> *When Our Lord had spoken to his children he prayed for them, and not only for them but for all of us who have loved him from then until now, for all who ever will love him…*
> *That, too, one must read upon one's knees.*[992]

The Church Times' reviewer, having said that the whole book was excellent, described it as an "imaginative commentary…with the imagination disciplined by a scrupulous regard for truth."[993] Forty years later, this same aspect of the book was afforded some less favourable criticism. William Hamilton, in *A Quest for the Post-Historical Jesus*, calls it "at once biblical and sentimental" and "very nearly unreadable" due to the "peculiar nature of the novelist's additions and decorations." However although he finds the book to be "over-imaginative" and "hard to like" he adds that it is also "hard not to admire this presentation of a splendid Anglican orthodoxy."[994]

Elizabeth's 'orthodoxy' had nonetheless, throughout her career, a very broad appeal. One of the great Roman Catholic theologians of the twentieth century became her personal friend: introduced through his admiration for her work. Post-war, the Hannen Foss anthologies had placed her stories alongside work by members of the old evangelical Oxford Group, now renamed Moral Rearmament. *The Well of the Star* was chosen for inclusion in a 1966 Christmas anthology edited by the Bruderhof; and critical acclaim regularly appeared not only in the Anglican *Church Times*, but in the *Christian Science Monitor*, the *Methodist Recorder*, the URC's *Reform* magazine, and the *Baptist Times*.

Her father of course, although an Anglican clergyman, started life as the son of "sternly unflinching Protestant Evangelicals."[995]

When a Roman Catholic missal was found in the bedroom of their schoolboy son they were appalled. If my father had shown any inclination towards penitence things might have been better but when he stood upon the mat he was not penitent. "I don't want to be one," he insisted, "I just want to know how other people worship God, and why shouldn't I know?"[996] *He said the subsequent family disturbance was "a fuss about nothing." He wasn't sorry, and he wouldn't say he was. He had enjoyed the missal.*[997]

In later life, as he tells us in *The Church of England and Reunion*, he had "contact with the Orthodox Eastern Church, not only by personal friendships, but also by membership in the Anglo-Russian Fellowship of St. Sergius and St. Alban."[998] In all this he "cared for the cause of Reunion most intensely" and had a deep conviction, according to his friend Professor de Burgh "that sectarian rigidity and narrowness was contrary to the spirit of Christ's religion."[999] Elizabeth remembered that "someone once said to him, 'I have such a great love for the Church of England' to which he replied, 'I don't know that I have – it is the whole church that I love.'"[1000]

❄

As well as her re-telling of the life of Christ, Elizabeth had also written a nativity play, which her friend Mrs. Green produced both at Torquay in St. Luke's Church, and in their own church at Marldon. (Amateur dramatics were very much a part of Marldon life, and the archive of photographs on the History Society's website shows a scene from a production of *The Brontës of Haworth* in the Village Hall.).

The Coming of the King ends with a Bible reading and a tableau; but first the shepherds tell of the three gifts they have given to the child in the manger – gifts representing faith, and song, and grief. Then it is the turn of the three wise men to lay their own gifts at His feet, and they are the same blend of the spiritual and the worldly, of joy and pain.

(Balthasar comes forward, kneels down, lifts his crown from his head and lays it before the Mother and Child.)

Marldon

> BALTHASAR: *My Lord and my God, I give you the gift of my wealth.*
> MELCHIOR: *(Kneeling down and putting his censer beside the crown)*
> *My Lord and my God, I give you the gift of my prayer.*
> GASPAR: *(Kneeling down, taking the casket of myrrh from about his neck and laying it beside the other gifts)*
> *My Lord and my God, I give you the gift of my pain.*[1001]

That there was an even stronger concentration on faith in her work at this time, is consistent with what she said about the little scrabbling mole – that the greater the downward pull into darkness, the harder one has to scrabble upwards into the light. She had been dragged down by grief and pain, but as far as her work was concerned, she was still determinedly fighting back, holding on to the belief that just on the other side of all the darkness, there is a valley of song.

The Valley of Song

> The world is a mirror of Infinite Beauty, yet no man sees it. It is a Temple of Majesty, yet no man regards it. It is a region of Light and Peace, did not men disquiet it. It is the Paradise of God... It is the place of Angels and the Gate of Heaven.[1002]
>
> Thomas Traherne

The second of the 1951 works was *The Valley of Song* which, like all her children's novels so far except *Smoky-House*, was published by the University of London Press. Once again the setting is Hampshire - not Keyhaven this time, but the hamlet of Buckler's Hard. It was one of only three of her novels which Elizabeth would admit to loving, even though it was:

> *A mixed up, confused book liked by a few children (and how I adored those children) but otherwise a quickly vanishing failure. I wrote it very much under the shadow of death, but so much seemed to come through to me from the shadow that I loved the book.*[1003]

What "came through" was the inspiration for a novel about a kind of parallel world, where a little girl discovers The Workshop - the creative source of everything beautiful on earth. Living so close to the shadow of death, Elizabeth yet wrote a beautiful fantasy in which there is almost nothing but joy. Youth is restored; old hurts are healed; dreams come true. There is beauty, colour, light and music everywhere: everything is (literally) heavenly in that place.

> *Never in her life had she longed for anything so much as she longed to come to that country. She could see it clearly now, violet-shadowed golden hills and deep blue valleys, fields of rosy flowers and orchards of silver-leaved trees with golden fruit, and above them the shining snows with the stars among their domes and peaks, and long gleaming slopes of white where surely angels paced. She could smell the flowers now and hear the ringing of birdsong and the chiming of laughter. They came even nearer, and she could see the drifts of bright birds, and the companies of little children running and tumbling upon the hills. Now she knew where she was. Now she knew that the fairytale they had told her was true...*[1004]

> *There is a joy that can never be told, a foretaste of heaven which not even the language of music can do more than hint at. Julie could never say afterwards what it was like to play with that company of heavenly children in the meadows of the sky. All she could say was that she was happy there for a hundred years or for a day, she did not know how long it was, and that she brought her happiness away with her when she returned to earth.*[1005]

Julie has been led to the Valley of Song by ten-year-old Tabitha Silver. All the friends with whom Tabitha shares the valley are, like Julie, adults and before they can enter they must first become small enough and childlike enough to go through its tiny door. ("Verily I say unto you, Whosoever shall not receive the kingdom of God as a little child shall in no wise enter therein.")[1006]

The old shipbuilder Job is the first to visit; and he finds that the entrance is beside a singing stream.

> *Where was the singing stream coming from, he wondered, and where was the singing voice? He turned to follow the stream upwards towards its source, as is the instinct of men who know that a thing is always loveliest at its fresh beginning, and it led him to an outcrop of rock overgrown with honeysuckle...*

Marldon

> *The stream came spurting in a bright fountain out of a fissure in the cliff, and just beside it there was a door in the rock, a very small door made of cedarwood and only the height of a child.*[1007]

Shadows in the Water in *A Book of Faith* reveals the source of this idea, of another world beyond the waters of a purling stream... Thomas Traherne himself had become aware of just such a place in his "unexperienc'd Infancy."

> Thus did I by the Water's brink
> Another World beneath me think...
> 'Twas strange that People there should walk,
> And yet I could not hear them talk:
> That through a little wat'ry Chink,
> Which one dry Ox or Horse might drink,
> We other Worlds should see,
> Yet not admitted be...
>
> ...what can it mean?
> But that below the purling Stream
> Some unknown Joys there be
> Laid up in Store for me;
> To which I shall, when that thin Skin
> Is broken, be admitted in.[1008]

In *The Valley of Song* the thin skin is broken, and Tabitha and her friends "admitted in." They find there what Traherne knew to exist:

> Within the Regions of the Air,
> Compass'd about with Heav'ns fair,
> Great Tracts of Land there may be found
> Enricht with Fields and fertile Ground;
> Where many num'rous Hosts
> In those far distant Coasts,
> For other great and glorious Ends,
> Inhabit, my yet unknown Friends...[1009]

What they have discovered is not heaven itself but an intermediate world that has been half-recognised by humankind throughout the centuries. To their astonished question, "Where in the world are we?" their guide, Silkin replies,

> *"Nowhere in the world... When you went through the door from the quarry you left the world and came into the country you call Fairyland, or the Garden of Eden, or Arcadia, or the Earthly Paradise, or the Elysian Fields, or some such ridiculous name. We just call it the Workshop."*[1010]

This other world resembles the belief of a friend of Elizabeth's, "one of the wisest men I know" who she said "had a dream life even richer than my father's." (Elizabeth too had rare and wonderful "dreams of heaven" - which, she said, were "never forgotten, and the comfort and strength they give is lasting."[1011]) This friend believed

> *that between the material in which we live now, and the spiritual world to which we shall eventually pass after death...there lies an intermediate state, almost a fairyland, built up partly perhaps from our own dreams, longings and memories, into which we pass when we leave our bodies and in which we become progressively more and more aware of the penetrating light of the world beyond.*[1012]

In *The Dean's Watch* nine years later, she would describe that world again:

> *Until now life for [the Dean] had meant the aridity of earthly duty and the dews of God. Now he was aware of something else, a world that was neither earth nor heaven, a heartbreaking, fabulous, lovely world where the conies take refuge in the rainbowed hills and in the deep valleys of the unicorns the songs are sung that men hear in dreams, the world that the poets know and the men who make music...*
> *The autumn song of the robin could let you in, or a shower of rain.*[1013]

At least one visitor to the Valley of Song becomes aware of the 'penetrating light' of yet another world beyond its borders; for Job makes the almost impossible climb to the mysterious heights protected by the Crystal Door.

> *To have climbed for so many miles, for so many years, through so much darkness, and then to find only a shut Crystal Door upon which his humility dared not knock, dared not even try to look through, which did not open to him as the others had done, should have filled him with despair. Yet it did no such thing. It filled him with joy past believing. For the Door was...a living, loving thing, and the glow of its love warmed him through.*

Marldon

> *He dropped down on the doorstep like a little dog curling itself up in front of the fire, and sat there soaking up the light and the warmth, until he had forgotten what it felt like to be cold or tired or frightened or alone. And yet it was only the Door. What could the country beyond be like that could make even of the Door to it a thing of living, loving power? Job did not try to think about that because he knew he couldn't…*[1014]

The book says that the bridge world is there, like a parallel universe, if we will just become small enough to go through the door – Go In. And there is another country still, beyond the mountain, behind the locked door… Just to have reached the threshold fills Job with joy past believing.

What she is describing here is the journey towards union with God, which in Carmelite spirituality, says Mark Davis in *Glimpses of the Carmelite Way*, is deemed to be attainable "even in this life." In this centuries-old monastic tradition, the various images used to describe the way to this "blessed state" include "ascending a mountain, crossing a desert or seeking the centre of a castle made of crystal." It is a journey "both joyous and costly" for the place of surrender to God is reached only through a series of "lesser surrenders" and through "fidelity to prayer and… the daily effort to love unconditionally."[1015]

Unsurprisingly, given the deep spiritual inspiration behind this children's novel, there are clear echoes of the Valley of Song in what we are told of the witness of Carmel…

> That there is a sunlit upland, beyond the darkest of nights, and that this is available even to us. The promise and the invitation hold true and the human person is fulfilled. To people so transformed, the door to eternity is already ajar.[1016]

Alone

> *"This is your growing time, now, when you have no Robert to lean on. The propped never grow. You will grow now. You will have to. You have an immense incentive; nothing less than the growing up towards eternal life like a tree towards the sun."*[1017]

Words from *The White Witch* in 1958. But for now, in the summer of 1951…

I went to Damerosehay. It was a lovely summer and the old house and the garden, the sea and the marshes were shining in the sun and there was healing in the air of the place. One day, I remember, I was sitting under one of the trees in the garden and the wind from the sea was blowing through the leaves. A moment of joy seized me, so sudden and so startling that I could hardly believe it. Yet it was true. Into the middle of my wretchedness at this time dropped this sudden joy. Joy is what life is about, I believed at that moment. It lies, somehow, at the root of every pain.[1018]

This was the same conviction that had evoked the sneers of *Time* magazine's critic, after *Gentian Hill*. But at this moment she not only believed it, but experienced it. She wrote of a similar experience of sudden joy – again, in *The White Witch*:

She knew she had no right to be happy…but she had long ago accepted the fact that happiness is like swallows in spring. It may come and nest under your eaves or it may not. You cannot command it. When you expect to be happy you are not, when you don't expect to be happy there is suddenly Easter in your soul, though it be mid-winter. Something, you do not know what, has broken the seal upon that door in the depths of your being that opens upon eternity. It is not yet time for you yourself to go out of it, but what is beyond comes in and passes into you and through you.[1019]

A Book of Peace has C.S. Lewis's poem about the same kind of joy, *The Day with a White Mark*, when despite everything that is going wrong in his life he finds himself "tossed and whirled in a preposterous happiness;" so much so that he could have "kissed the very scullery taps."[1020]

There was though a "shadow of sadness over Damerosehay… The house was shabby and the garden overgrown."[1021] This was not yet Elizabeth's final visit; nevertheless it was only a few years later that Mrs. Adams left – and her home became a victim to bulldozers and redevelopment. But during that stay its spell for Elizabeth was as potent as ever. The seed was sown for a third and final book about the Eliots.

I came back to Providence Cottage to find it an empty shell… People came in and out, talking and laughing, but their voices echoed as voices do in a house that is unfurnished and deserted. Without my mother's vivid presence the place was dead. But I had to stay there since she had made me promise not to leave in a hurry but to stick it out for a year. She was quite right. Few things hold one up better than familiar surroundings and the routine of a life that goes with them. Both the surroundings and the routine may have gone dead on you, but at least they are there, like a pair of crutches. You may hate them but they keep you upright.[1022]

In her eponymous short story about the disciple John, domestic tasks help him to get through the days immediately following the crucifixion.

> *He stopped and looked down for a moment, in the dim light, at the broom handle and his thin brown hands tautly holding it, clutching at it in a stupid desperate sort of way as though it were a spar of wood that kept him from drowning. Well, so it was. The everyday tasks, chopping the wood, carrying the water from the well, washing the dishes, sweeping the floor, did keep one from drowning in grief, going mad from the shock of what one had seen, what one remembered, what one had done.*[1023]

With their help I could get back to work again, and tried to recapture the peace of Damerosehay by starting the third and last book about the Eliot family, The Heart of the Family. *There is something of my mother in Lucilla Eliot and the company of Lucilla was comforting. But the book was such a struggle that I wondered if my writing days were perhaps ended.*[1024]

It is interesting that in Jessie Monroe's opinion Elizabeth "suffered a good deal from her mother, but she always declared total admiration for her – Lucilla is supposed to be modelled on her." Lord Horder even went so far as to call Ida tyrannical and fierce, saying, "I think Elizabeth was frightened of her." Mrs. Goudge was certainly a strong character, for there is that telling phrase "she had made me promise" which shows that Elizabeth (at the age of fifty-one) was still obeying her - even after her death. And of course there had been that other hard promise Ida had extracted, that whatever happened she should be nursed at home.

Also interesting is the discovery of a random, adverse comment about Lucilla in one of Rosamunde Pilcher's novels - *Under Gemini*. One of the characters dislikes Lucilla, thinking her "possessive and domineering." She even abhors the "snobbery" of her "beautifully cut black frocks,"[1025] although actually it is more likely that Elizabeth used Ida's mother as the model for Lucilla's looks: her Guernsey grandmother was "tall and beautiful" with a "slim figure and upright carriage," and "dressed in long full-skirted graceful black dresses." Elizabeth does say she found her "a little intimidating" though; and tells us that like her daughter, Mrs. Collenette had had "no trouble at all in getting her own way. She did not even have to try."[1026] But as Jessie said, Elizabeth always declared total admiration for her mother. It is true that at various times in *The Joy of the Snow* Ida is described as "a dominant woman"[1027] of "iron determination,"[1028] and "strong will,"[1029] who had "a sharply truthful tongue;"[1030] but Elizabeth also says she possessed "a healing personality"[1031] and was "clever,"[1032] "brave,"[1033] "loving"[1034] and "deeply compassionate."[1035] She says simply, "She was our life."[1036]

> *The weeks dragged by in Devon and kind friends came to visit me, but I lived in a dusty desert. Everything, I felt, had come to a dead end. There seemed no way out or through. Then the autumn came bringing with it what I suppose is the greatest miracle of every human life, the miracle of renewal. It taught me that no apparently dead end is ever a dead end, but a new beginning. Also that perhaps no true new beginning is possible until you seem to be standing with a shut door facing you. Also that when you have passed through the door you cannot expect to be quite yet out of the shadows. New beginnings grow slowly.*[1037]

❄

She had called the years following the outbreak of war, one of those periods that must be passed through like a dark tunnel before one can come out into the light again. It seems that it was only now, in the winter of 1951/2, that she began to come out of the shadows. For at least the last twelve years, following on from her breakdown, she had lived through first her father's death, then six years of world war, the death of her beloved cousin, of Nanny and her sisters; the miseries of post-war shortages, Marie's death and Mrs. Goudge's protracted final illness - which to Elizabeth, looking back, had seemed to follow on from the end of the war almost without a break. She was soon to say in *The White Witch*,

> *These black times go as they come and we do not know how they come or why they go. But we know that God controls them, as He controls the whole vast cobweb of the mystery of things.*[1038]

To Make an End Is to Make a Beginning

His Goodness suffereth us never to be alone, but lastingly He is with us, and tenderly He excuseth us, and ever shieldeth us from blame in His sight... All shall be well, and all shall be well, and all manner of thing shall be well.[1039]
Dame Julian of Norwich: *Revelations of Divine Love*

Marldon

I had intended to live alone that first winter without my mother. Having had no experience of living alone I had not yet discovered that that is a thing I cannot do.[1040]

A few years later she gave a telling description of loneliness in The White Witch. This is the child Jenny, after her twin brother Will has been sent away to school.

> *She became, as never before, aware of time. She must lie in this bed in the dark for nine hours without Will, and then she must get up and dress and go through the hours of the day – and there were fifteen hours in her day – without Will… She would have to live the rest of her life without him.*
>
> *The bed seemed enormous. [The dog] Maria was beside her, but Maria was asleep and dreaming of rabbits and not able to share the misery through which Jenny was passing. No one could share it. The bed got bigger and the room beyond the bed got bigger too, bigger and darker, a cavern of loneliness, and out of it there led that passage of the endless hours. Though she was lying in the bed she could see herself walking down that passage, on and on for ever, and always alone. Time was loneliness. She had not known before that people lived alone, or that they lived for such a long time.*
>
> *And then she was no longer watching herself going along the dark passage, but was actually there, plodding on and on in the cold emptiness, trying to get to the end of time because when time ended loneliness would end too… She must get to the end of time. But a cold wind was blowing against her, and though she fought and struggled she could not prevail against it, and suddenly her feet went from under her and she fell headlong, screaming as she fell.*
>
> *She sat up in the big bed, shivering and drenched with sweat.*[1041]

At the time I thought it was what I needed. My wisest, closest friend at Marldon disagreed with me so heartily that she gave me the name and address of a friend of her own who she thought would spend at least that winter with me…[1042]

Freda Green wrote:

> After her mother died, E simply didn't know what to do and asked my advice. She had very good and loyal domestic help

so I suggested that she get a gardener-companion. She asked me to help her find one and I mentioned Jessie Monroe who I knew was just leaving a job.

When I showed signs of resistance she answered, "Go home and write to Jessie Monroe tonight." I went home and turned the idea over in my mind with growing alarm, but felt compelled to make a start on a letter. That evening my friend rang up and asked, "Have you written?" I said I had partly written the letter. "Finish it," she said, and immediately put the receiver down.

And so I wrote to a total stranger at the address given and at first received no answer. My spirits rose. Then I had an answer from Jessie on holiday in Italy. I felt that my own doubt and dismay were echoed in her letter, and in that at least we were united, but she went so far as to say that when she was back in England again she would come, and would see me through the winter. Thankful that she was not contemplating anything longer I wrote a welcoming letter and awaited her arrival with growing alarm.

The appointed day brought her…I heard the sound of a car door being slammed with great determination, went out into the garden and heard a very clear voice saying the words that are now so delightfully familiar. "I'm sorry I'm late." We looked at each other. I saw an upright, capable-looking young woman with a head of hair like a horse-chestnut on fire, and the white magnolia skin that goes with such hair. Her eyes were very direct. She looked young enough to be my daughter and I doubted if she would stand me for long, yet when I went to bed that night to my astonishment I found myself flooded with happiness, and slept deeply.[1043]

Jessie too remembered seeing a woman with very white skin, but in her case it was the unnatural pallor of exhaustion.

When I went the first night, down to Paignton, Elizabeth went to bed early – she was whiter than a sheet; I'd never seen anything walking about quite so pale.

Flooded with happiness Elizabeth may have been, but she added: "Not that the first months were easy for either of us." Jessie agreed, that "Our birthdays were within a couple of days of each other, but we were very different." But whatever their differences in the beginning, Elizabeth could write in her old age, "Jessie…has been the most wonderful event that ever happened to me."[1044] Her publisher Lord Horder agreed. "Certainly one of her greater pieces of good luck was to find Jessie Monroe," he said. "When Elizabeth took herself too seriously, Jessie was always ready to laugh her out of it."

Marldon

In Mervyn Horder's estimation, the reason she was very happy with her was because Jessie was "such a good woman." Elizabeth's loyal fan Kathleen Millington said that "Jessie was the right person for Elizabeth – very good at coping, very practical, very loving." She added, "And of course Elizabeth was very generous with her fans, and Jessie was very good at keeping them at bay. I realised I'd got to mind my ps and qs with Jessie, but we became great friends and had a lot of fun together." A woman, in her own way, as formidable as Mrs. Goudge perhaps? But Alan Hull Walton summed her up with these words: "That delectable personality gifted with so much wit and humour, Jessie Monroe, who is not "The Joy of the Snow," but "The Joy of the Summer Garden."[1045]

❋

1952 began with the publication, by Duckworth, of a book of short stories. *The Reward of Faith* had already collected together all the stories with a religious theme, and *Make-Believe* in 1949 was the complete set of tales about the du Frocq family. Now came *White Wings* which, says the publicity, "contains all the other short stories that Miss Goudge wishes to preserve. They have been collected from the three volumes of short stories published by Duckworth before the war and which now have been allowed to go out of print – *A Pedlar's Pack*, *The Golden Skylark* and *The Ikon on the Wall*."[1046]

The book had a foreword by Elizabeth entitled *The Entertainment of Story-telling*, which begins with her usual note of self-deprecation.

How wonderful it must be to write stories, say the friends of the story-teller, and there are both admiration and envy in their tone. As for the admiration, the story-teller knows he does not deserve it; he knows perhaps that he turned to woo the lady make-believe because he was too unpractical to manage a business, lacked the courage to become a doctor, was too weak of character to impose discipline on classes of unruly children…[1047]

Later paragraphs, however, may give some indication of the strain she had been under in the years since her father's death.

There is no foundation for the admiration, the story-teller knows, but there may be for the envy. Is he to be envied? Sometimes he resents the envy of his friends. They seem to think the work of the story-teller is all so easy… When he owes money to his dentist he has but to compose a story in his bath, and when they are after him for the rent a few flourishes of his pen will scatter them again… It is all so easy.

So say his friends, and sometimes, with that strange desire of human nature to be thought a martyr, he frets and fumes a little. What do they know of the bad times through which he passes and the problems and fears that hedge him about? Those days of ill-health or worry when both imagination and brain refuse to function; those days when troops of glowing images throng the imagination but the dulled brain can find no words with which to catch them; those other days when words stand all ready to attention like well-drilled soldiers but there is no vision to set them marching. And then the fears. Will the book be finished in time? Will the publisher accept it? If he does, will the critics tear it, this beloved child of the story-teller's mind and soul, into shreds and tatters? Above all will readers be disappointed? And always present with the poor story-teller is the problem of adjustment. How can he live the life of imagination and the life of the world at one and the same time?[1048]

The two worlds again. But this hard-working writer's experience of living "the life of the world" had been extremely restricted for years now. A letter she wrote in the late Forties gives some idea of her housebound state in mid-life.

I had quite an exciting day last week, the biggest outing I have had for years. I went to lunch with some friends in Torquay and then they took me to the theatre to see the Malvern Company do a play of Shaw's, "In Good King Charles's Golden Days." I enjoyed it so much.[1049]

And things would have deteriorated since then, in line with her mother's worsening health. Mrs. Goudge's diary[1050], beginning in the autumn of 1949, records the occasional outing for "E" but they are mostly at intervals of several weeks. The only social ones are a modest tea or very occasional lunch with friends; the rest are to church, hairdresser or dentist.

※

Jessie's task, in what was intended to be a temporary visit, was to get this white-faced and exhausted woman through a crisis, which would mean spending at least the winter of 1951/2 with her in Devon.

We had to search for points of contact… Her passion was gardening and I am no gardener, mine was books, and "I've not read any of your books," she warned me. Well, I thanked God for that. No friendships do I value more than those not founded on my books. To be loved as the faulty person you actually are, rather than as the pleasing personality that people think you are, is an unspeakable relief.[1051]

"I hadn't read a word of course," remembered Jessie with a laugh. She cited the memory of one particular occasion when Elizabeth was entertaining "these old people – they were her mother's contemporaries, and they liked to come up every week and have tea parties and grab all her time, thank you very much! And I said I hadn't read any of the books. Absolute silence! Horror!"

Their religious differences were not so easy, Elizabeth remembered.

> *I was a firmly embedded member of the Church of England, she was a fiery Celtic Presbyterian... "Anyone would think you had been brought up on Foxe's Book of Martyrs," I said at the end of a heated argument. "I was," she replied briefly.*
>
> *We have both mellowed since then and learned that friends who are at one in the basic beliefs of their lives have the one unity that really matters, but at that time our first real point of contact was dogs... We got one... A Dandie-Dinmont puppy, the first of the Hobbits, the never-to-be-forgotten Tiki.*[1052]

It was an inspired idea. Not only did it help to cement their friendship, but Tiki's presence would have been comforting and therapeutic to such a dog-lover as Elizabeth. (Cat-lover too, surely – her fictional cats, like Zachariah in *The Little White Horse* are marvellous creations – but she did once say that the birds in her garden would "know, I think, that it is for their sakes that we do not keep a cat."[1053]) She had had a dog for much of her life - from childhood until just before her father's death. As a child at Wells she had bought Max with her own birthday money, "a darling snow-white puppy with black ears"[1054] and he had moved on with them to become their Ely dog. He proved, however, to be "a killer - five pounds' worth of turkeys killed in twenty minutes was a mere nothing to him, and cats were not safe in his presence." (Canon Goudge seems to have had Max in mind when illustrating the nuances between right and wrong in one of his Lenten sermons. "For some reason, to the dog inscrutable," he said, "his master objects to the destruction of fowls, though not to the destruction of rats; and has made his mind on the subject only too plain."[1055])

Then there was the beloved Brownie, who had made such a friend of Bishop Gore. Gifted to them by Marie at Barton when still "a brown ball of fluff the size of a rolled up hedgehog,"[1056] he was a noble animal who would "howl dismally" at modern music, but "enjoyed classical music, especially Beethoven." (Dog and master would sometimes listen to the radio together; for "he never failed to keep my father company in his study late at night, after all the females had gone to bed," Elizabeth said.) He was with them through the Oxford years, but after he died at Barton it was felt he was "too great a dog, and too greatly loved, for it to be possible to think of having another."[1057] And so it seems she had been without a dog for twelve years or so when they acquired Tiki -so named because Elizabeth was reading *The Kon-Tiki Expedition* at the time.

[Tiki] was not beautiful. She must have had a rough time of it in kennels before she came to us at seven months old because she had an injured leg that could not be put right. She was something of a ragamuffin, a gamin.[1058]

It was Tiki who helped to comfort Elizabeth as her old way of life finally came to an end, when she and Jessie decided to leave Devon and move to Oxfordshire. The train journey seemed interminable, she says, "but I had Tiki on my lap, a solid young dog by this time, honey-coloured, furry and warm…"

I would never have believed that I could have got myself out of Devon. I thought I was there for the rest of my life. [But] so many things combined to show us what we had to do.[1059]

One of the things, according to Mrs. Green, was the arrival of a demand for Income Tax which Elizabeth, having been "very generous to all in need" couldn't pay; "and so she had to sell Providence Cottage." (She was later able to buy Rose Cottage, Mrs. Green added, "with the money from her following books.") Jessie too talked about Elizabeth "being hit by income tax and having to sell her house to pay it." If this is so, then it was history repeating itself, for she and her mother had had to sell most of the contents of the Oxford house "to help pay the large sum that was owing to the Inland Revenue (that detested bogey) when my father died."[1060] It seems that in their generosity, both father and daughter had given away money that ought to have been put aside for the taxman. Mrs. Green said that "Elizabeth was very unbusinesslike." And although her Grandfather Goudge had worked at the Bank of England, when it came to business his clergyman son's "brilliant mind closed down altogether. He hated money…and was scarcely able to ascertain if the right change had been given him when he bought a railway ticket."[1061]

It seemed we had to go, and the obvious place was Oxfordshire within easy reach of old friends and relatives who had been urging me to move nearer to them ever since my mother had died. We packed up. Jessie was to stay with her mother for a while and I was to be with a nobly hospitable cousin near Henley…the dearest of the cousins with whom I had lived in Reading. It should have been a happy prospect but I will never forget my misery as the train pulled out of the station and I watched Devon slipping away. It was only then that the full force of my mother's loss came over me. She had loved Devon and had seemed a part of it. Now, as it passed away from me I felt her totally lost.[1062]

A few years later, in 1956, she would write about learning how to turn the pain of loss into willing relinquishment. Maria Wentworth in *The Rosemary*

Marldon

Tree is already alone after the death of her beloved brother, and must now leave her Devon home, the beautiful Belmaray.

> *"This one thing more." She remembered…how she had lain in bed through the storm thinking how things fell away from you in old age, but that she still had Belmaray. Now she had lost it. The misery she had felt…overwhelmed her again. In the pride of life you stood with your hands full of roses, but in old age the petals turned to dust; and then even the dust fell away through your fingers, leaving you with nothing but your empty hands, stained with dirt… Just your sin, that was all you seemed to have at the end.*
>
> *She had nothing but her empty dirty hands… She sat bemusedly looking at them and slowly her misery turned to a faint glow of inward joy as she began to wonder if perhaps they had more value than all she had possessed. Empty, they could be cleansed. She was humble now, she had nothing and could be cleansed. It might be true that…loss… was the one thing needful.*[1063]

And loss - despite its pain - can be not only the beginning of cleansing and humility, but the start of a new life.

> *Once more it was difficult to find the right home… I was as difficult to please as my mother had been, not liking what I could afford and losing my heart to what I could not afford. I had reached despair one morning when I opened the paper at random and found myself looking not at the leading article but at an advertisement of a seventeenth-century cottage for sale not far from us, and my whole dark mind was suddenly full of light… This was no coincidence… This was it, I believed, and out at the other end of all the legal and financial and structural and human difficulties that surround the buying of a house, it was. Jessie was alerted and travelled down to us at once, arriving late one evening. "I'm sorry I'm late," she said, and all the lights went up in Tiki's world and mine and we were ourselves again.*[1064]

Elizabeth sent a postcard to Audrey, postmarked 27th March 1953 : "Rose Cottage, Peppard Common. Henley-on-Thames. Thank you so much for lovely greetings. Writing soon. Elizabeth."

She had a new home.

PEPPARD

❋

1953 - 1984

Rose Cottage

The birds could scarcely contain themselves in this world where sunshine and warmth had returned... In lives where there had been no change for so long there had suddenly been cataclysmic change, as startling as this change from cold grey rain to brilliant sunshine.[1065]

The Rosemary Tree

How amazing the contrast must have been, after all the years of coping with illness and disability, to now have Jessie's company: a fit and active young woman who was vivacious and full of energy, with "so much wit and humour"[1066] and always ready to laugh. And not least, after years of being a carer herself, for Elizabeth to have someone who would look after her at a time when she was still in a very fragile state. Jessie even called it a breakdown, saying of their early days at Rose Cottage,

> When we came here in 1953 she was still finishing up this nervous breakdown – though I didn't know it, I thought she was just exhausted.

Life was now changing for the better, although she was still worn out and – as people so often are after the death of a loved one – probably still full of remorse:

There is no one harder to forgive than oneself; it can take years. Nevertheless we know inside ourselves that it must be done, for remorse is a sin that rots away the very vitals of the soul.[1067]

She was also, in spite of all the joys which must have come with this move to Oxfordshire, homesick for Devon. Even some little while after she had moved into Rose Cottage she still found herself "trying hard to love it (a difficult process because my roots were still in the earth of Devonshire.)"

At regular intervals I have continually insulted my lovely home by allowing waves of homesickness for Devon to sweep over me. My roots are still there, apparently, and nothing now can pull them up. Several times I have nearly succeeded in taking us back to them, but something always crops up to prevent the exodus, yet this cottage is, after the Ely house, the dearest of all my homes.[1068]

She rated Rose Cottage even higher when *The Times* interviewed her soon after the publication of *The Joy of the Snow*, explaining that it was not the cottage which was the cause of the homesickness, but the countryside around it:

While I have never loved a home so much, I don't love this countryside like I love the West Country and the Fens. I was talking to my next door neighbour the other day (she came here from Norfolk) and we longed for some wildness.[1069]

The autobiography itself says it had "no running streams, no high hills, no *wilderness*." Although it was beautiful, it was "too civilised and park-like."[1070] The artist John Piper, in his revised *Shell Guide* to the county – published in 1953, the year Elizabeth and Jessie arrived - called it one of the "most ordinary" of English counties and added that if England were to be "scheduled as a series of beauty spots," Oxfordshire would not rate many "stars." Nevertheless his Guide found much to praise too, including what would surely have appealed to Elizabeth: "a fragment of a wonderful ancient forest (as wonderful as the New Forest, in many ways) in Wychwood."[1071]

Whatever the surrounding countryside though, in one sense Rose Cottage itself was perhaps the fulfilment of a long-time dream... Cousin Mary's dream in *The Scent of Water* before she too moved to the Chiltern Hills of Oxfordshire: "a house and garden of my own...in the deep country with my dear Jenny Kennedy, just the two of us."[1072]

In those days, Peppard Common could still be said to be in the country. A few houses were grouped around it and to the north the road that crossed the common disappeared towards Henley between tall elm trees, the village pond to the left and the seventeenth-century inn, The Dog, to the right. The entrance to Dog Lane could hardly be seen where it left the road beside the inn, and the two cottages in the lane hiding behind the inn could hardly be seen either.[1073]

Quite certainly, from the point of view of her work the physical seclusion of Rose Cottage was something she did love and fully appreciate:

I have found the home of any writer's dreams...with nothing to be seen from the windows except the garden, fields and woods, and a great sky.[1074]

And it seems that she found in this place too something else of great value to her, which perhaps she had not experienced fully - if at all - for many years: "those quiet times in life when nothing much happens and yet when a great deal happens that cannot be put into words."[1075] The long years of bereavement and war; illness and nursing; worry, hard work and loss had brought her to what Jessie perceived as breakdown. Now, through "the miracle of renewal" their new life had surely provided what she needed most at this time... peace.

"Quiet times are growing times and I think that quietness is helped by living in a house that is very old," she said. "Both Jessie and I are aware of the influence of our small house and garden upon us... It is happy and peaceful."[1076]

The Heart of the Family

"The mind has pits," murmured Sebastian.
"You have to be in a moderate state of normality to control your mind... A haunted mind, a sick mind, or even a mind weakened and bewildered by a sick body, hangs always over a pit of darkness."[1077]

Despite her fears her writing days were not over. *The Heart of the Family* was at last finished and published in 1953 with a dedication to C.I.C., the initials of her aunt Irene – Constance Irene Collenette - who had been with Elizabeth when her mother died. The Eliot trilogy was now complete, its third book centred on faith, acceptance and forgiveness.

Damerosehay's two cornfields maintain their symbolic importance to the end - the everlastingness of Traherne's "orient and immortal wheat" alongside the cultivated field, symbolising the struggle to bring human life to fruition... so often such a hard and harrowing struggle.

The real cornfield was being harrowed, and Hilary drove slowly, that Nadine might feast her eyes upon the sight of the two old horses passing back and forth, with a cloud of gleaming gulls following after.[1078]

Beautiful. But this description from the previous Damerosehay novel, *The Herb of Grace* has also an echo of the harrowing of the human heart in John Masefield's poem *The Everlasting Mercy*.

O wet red swathe of earth laid bare,
O truth, O strength, O gleaming share...
O Christ who holds the open gate,
O Christ who drives the furrow straight,
O Christ, the plough, O Christ, the laughter

Of holy white birds flying after…[1079]

Its message of anguished spiritual struggle (the poem is included in *A Book of Comfort*[1080]) resonates in *The Heart of the Family*. This novel is much darker than the rest of the trilogy, and the central Damerosehay theme of regeneration after war takes on a new intensity. In *The Herb of Grace* David had been feeling close to breakdown after his experiences as a bomber pilot, but in this novel he has to wrestle at an even deeper level, with his guilt over the consequences of his action. He invites to his comfortable family home the Jewish concert pianist Sebastian - a man who, he later comes to realise with horror, lost his own home, wife and children in the bombing of Hamburg. David himself took part in that raid, and he experiences to the full the remorse that Elizabeth says can rot away the very vitals of the soul.

Lo, all my heart's field red and torn…[1081]

It applies to both men, for as perpetrator and victim each is scarred by the same event. But whereas David's metaphorical heartbreak can still be healed, Sebastian's heart is physically broken too and he is close to death. Life, love and loss have been infinitely more harrowing for him than they ever were for the Eliots. However as he arrives at Damerosehay and passes the fields, he sees - not torn-up harrowed earth - but "a cornfield bending beneath the wind."[1082] It is the beginning of his inner healing.

As he then enters the house and takes possession of his room he sees, hanging over his bed, the same image: "Van Gogh's painting of the lark singing and tossing over the wind-blown corn."

> *He remembered the thrill of delight the picture had given him when he had first seen it, and he remembered naturally and easily. That was odd, for he had lived for so long with shutters in his mind closed against all memory of past happiness. He had himself put up the shutters and almost exhausted his will with the effort of holding them shut; yet the memory of the light, and of the lark, had slipped through quite easily and brought no pain.*[1083]

In Masefield's words:

> I did not think, I did not strive,
> The deep peace burnt my me alive;
> The bolted door had broken in,
> I knew that I had done with sin.

> I knew that Christ had given me birth
> To brother all the souls on earth,
> And every bird and every beast
> Should share the crumbs broke at the feast.[1084]

Damerosehay's deep peace, and the loving-kindness of its inhabitants, slowly burn away his hatred. But alongside the peace he is aware of the battle raging within David. He recognises it as a fight in which the sinful inner man is "done to death…by some terrible adversary; terrible and glorious."[1085] His insight is borne out by another great poem, this one overtly quoted in the novel, when he finds in his room and opens at random, the works of Gerard Manley Hopkins.

> But ah, but O thou terrible, why wouldst thou rude on me
> Thy wring-world right foot rock? lay a lionlimb against me? scan
> O in turns of tempest, me heaped there; me frantic to avoid thee and flee?
> Why? That my chaff might fly; my grain lie, sheer and clear…[1086]

Later, lying sleepless in bed, Sebastian remembers the words of an old prayer that he thought he had forgotten.

> *"Take, O Lord, from our hearts all jealousy, indignation, wrath, and contention, and whatsoever may injure charity and lessen brotherly love. Have mercy, O Lord, have mercy on those that crave Thy mercy; give grace to them that stand in need thereof…"*
>
> *O God, the idiocy of jealousy, indignation, wrath and contention. Yet it would be hard to stop hating, when hatred had been the source of his strength for so long. It had been like food to him… It had been life. Without hatred he would feel hideously weak. It might take him a long time to learn to let go of hatred, to learn to endure after some different fashion. "Give grace to them that stand in need thereof." What exactly did Christians mean by grace? Hilary Eliot would know…*[1087]

Hilary does know. This son of Lucilla is another of Elizabeth's wonderfully wise, humble and effective clergymen. Based again on her father no doubt; but in the simplicity of his rural ministry perhaps inspired by some of her favourite priest poets - like Thomas Traherne who Margaret Drabble says "remained, by choice, a poor priest" or George Herbert - "the perfect country minister, careful of his flock, generous, humble, kindly, a Good Samaritan."[1088]

Hilary explains to Sebastian that the hating kind of endurance can break you; the only answer is - like corn bending before the wind - *acceptance*.

> *There is always the Thing…the hidden Thing, some fear or pain or shame, temptation or bit of self-knowledge that you can never explain to another…For it is the essence of it that it is, humanly speaking, a lonely thing…*
> *If you endure it simply because you must, like a boil on the neck, or fret yourself to pieces trying to get rid of it, or cadge sympathy for it, then it can break you. But if you accept it as a secret burden borne secretly for the love of Christ, it can become your hidden treasure. For it is your point of contact with Him, your point of contact with that fountain of refreshment down at the roots of things. 'Oh Lord, thou fountain of living waters.' That fountain of life is what Christians mean by grace… In those deep green pastures where cool waters are there is no separation. Our point of contact with the suffering Christ is our point of contact with every other suffering man and woman, and is the source of our life.*[1089]

In conversation with Lucilla, Hilary reveals a deep understanding of Canon Goudge's way of prayer.

> *I suddenly put into practice and knew as truth what of course I had always known theoretically, that if pain is offered to God as prayer, then pain and prayer are synonymous. A sort of substitution takes place that is like the old story of 'Beauty and the Beast.' The utterly abominable Thing that prevents your prayer becomes your prayer. And you know what prayer is… it is union with God in the deep places where the fountains are. Once you have managed the wrenching effort of substitution, the abominable Thing, while remaining utterly detestable for yourself, becomes the channel of grace for others, and so the dearest treasure that you have.*[1090]

It is a paradox – just as a courageous plunge into darkness leads to light, so pain, accepted, brings one into contact with the freshness. And for both David and Sebastian it does lead them out of their remorse and hatred, so that at the end Sebastian can die in peace.

> *"There was a rightness in his death that makes it seem entirely natural," said Hilary... "Sebastian had finished. The last of the chaff had gone."*[1091]

Chaff. David's final words to Sebastian on the night of his death had been to tell again the story of the cornfield.

> *"[A] ship was wrecked on the marshes a hundred years ago....And you know that old cornfield that you pass on the road through the marshes, not the one on the inland side of the lane that is sown and reaped each year, but the one in the marsh? The ship had a cargo of grain and that queer tough corn has sprung up every year since the ship was wrecked there."*
>
> *'Except a grain of wheat fall into the ground and die', Sebastian remembered. There were so many kinds of death, and probably the one he had chosen tonight was one of the easiest. But it would not be unproductive. Though he knew nothing else about it, he was sure of that.*[1092]

And it is not unproductive. It brings the fruitfulness of a fallen grain of wheat, for on the same day new life springs up at Damerosehay: a baby is born. Hope and regeneration is the book's final message, as David looks down into the face of his newborn child.

> *The sky was flecked all over with gold clouds like feathers, as though wings protected the world. Sunset or sunrise, he had forgotten now which it was. The old house seemed to hold them both, and to hold, too, a welling up of freshness, as though it renewed its youth in the youth of this marvellous child.*[1093]

These final words complete a trilogy about the rebuilding of life and faith after two world wars. They echo the great affirmation of faith and hope at the end of Hopkins' *God's Grandeur*, which Elizabeth placed on the title page of this novel.

> There lives the dearest freshness deep down things;
> And though the last lights off the black West went
> Oh, morning, at the brown brink eastward, springs –
> Because the Holy Ghost over the bent
> World broods with warm breast and with ah! bright wings.[1094]

Peppard

She said,

One of the things in my working life about which I am most thankful is that someone or something prompted me to write three books about…Damerosehay, and that those three seem to be my readers' favourites. As long as the three books are read Damerosehay has not quite vanished from the world and I have not lived in vain.[1095]

※

One other work born of her love for this corner of England is a small guide-book to The Chapel of the Blessed Virgin Mary at Buckler's Hard, Beaulieu: "one of the loveliest chapels in the country." She had already described it in *The Bird in the Tree*:

> *David, his arms outstretched along the back of a seat, sat at the back of the chapel and looked about him at the well-remembered details that yet always touched him afresh with their beauty. He liked the dark panelling, the faint smell of incense, the lamp burning before the altar, and the beautiful old altar-frontal embroidered with roses and carnations. Above all he liked the statue of the Madonna carved out of very dark wood. She was an unusual Madonna for she had the broad plump comfortable face of a country woman, just the sort of face that must have been seen years ago at the Hard, the face of a buxom wife and mother going about her business in the busy town or kneeling Sunday by Sunday, her children clinging to her skirts, saying her prayers... Her homeliness contrasted oddly but delightfully with her crown, with the lily in her hand and the cherubs at her feet.*[1096]

Revised and updated with additional information in 1989 - by then more than 30 years since it was first written – the booklet remained in the chapel for at least fifty years, until it was replaced by a new guide in 2008. This edition however still makes reference to Elizabeth, stating that the Master Builder's House at Buckler's Hard is "almost certainly" the inspiration for The Herb of Grace inn.[1097] It concludes with her sonnet entitled *The Statue of the Virgin at Buckler's Hard*:

> *Homely of form and feature, without charm*
> *Of grace, used to the weight of the pitcher*
> *On the shoulder, counting herself richer*
> *For the weight of the babe upon the arm;*
> *Yoke-fellow to unending toil, the knell*

> *Of grief, seeing in them the stuff of bright*
> *Life, the warp of which the woof is love, light,*
> *And laughter of the children at the well;*
> *About her feet that ached with weariness*
> *Cherubs nestle. Mother of God she stands*
> *Holding a lily in her toil-worn hands,*
> *Royally crowned a Queen in blessedness.*
> *Mother of God, when fails the heart for fear,*
> *Now at this hour, and at our death, be near.*[1098]

Among the handful of Elizabeth's poems published posthumously is *Our Lady* which includes these lines meditating on the nature and appearance of Christ's mother.

> *Mary, our mother, how I wish I knew*
> *What you looked like...*
>
> *I think of two pictures of our Lady*
> *That satisfy.*
>
> *Fra Angelico, friend of the angels,*
> *Painter and saint,*
> *Saw Gabriel and Mary delicate*
> *As flowers, ethereal as rainbows,*
> *Not of this world.*
>
> *The Spaniard Velasquez, lover of men,*
> *Seeking their depths,*
> *Portrayed our Lady as a peasant girl,*
> *Sturdy and strong, with a grave dignity*
> *And courtesy...*
>
> *One can picture this woman and her son*
> *In their dark hour.*
> *His cross, not her hands, holds him now upright*
> *In love and prayer, arms stretched out to the world*
> *He dies to save.*
>
> *She is there, a rock of strength beside him,*
> *Without movement,*
> *Frozen by the agony within her*

Peppard

> *But giving him the last ounce of her strength*
> *To help him through.*
>
> *Mother Mary, how can we reconcile*
> *These two pictures?*
> *How can that fragile flower of a girl*
> *Be the same woman as the rock of grief?*
> *"They are the same…"*
>
> *These two painters, uniting earth and heaven,*
> *Were men of truth.*
> *The woman of toil and grief united*
> *With her delicate spirit is Mary,*
> *Mother of Christ our Lord who is our joy*
> *Now and for ever.*[1099]

A year after *The Heart of the Family*, in 1954 *Woman's Journal* followed *God So Loved the World* with another Christian work: *The Beloved*. Later included in *The Lost Angel* under the simple title *John*, this was the short story imagining the grief and remorse felt by the disciples after the crucifixion. At the end of the story, as John visits the tomb and realises that Christ's death has become life, his own darkness turns to light.

> *Without knowing what he did he fell on his knees too. He wondered why he had thought the tomb so dark, for the light of the sun filled it. He saw no heavenly spirits; for him they were not necessary. He heard no voice speaking, but he heard the birds singing outside in the garden. Was the Master outside in the garden? Mary, perhaps, had seen him. Yet John stayed where he was, for he who had forsaken his Lord did not deserve to see his Lord. But he knew that he would see him again; if not in this life then in another…*
> *John could wait. Length of time no longer mattered. Nothing mattered but the fact of Life.*[1100]

※

The following year William Collins produced their new edition of Robert Louis Stevenson's *A Child's Garden of Verses*. What Elizabeth says in her Introduction about Stevenson's attitude to happiness tells us much about her own, and her determination that the books she wrote should be happy ones. It was her father's attitude too, for he "understood while he was still very young that cheerfulness is one of the first duties of a Christian;"[1101] and so he kept his dark times always well-hidden. One of his fellow students at Oxford remembered his "bright sunny nature"[1102] and Elizabeth said "he was always such fun"[1103] with his inexhaustible "fund of funny stories, not one of which was ever forgotten."[1104] She knew that her father's "gaiety was not altogether natural lightness of heart; it was very largely a spiritual achievement"[1105] and she recognised the same quality of *resolved courageous joy* in Stevenson. She shared his understanding that, whereas sudden joy is a given thing, happiness itself is a *task*. So often, before it can be given away it has first to be willed and deliberately created out of pain.

The spontaneous joy of the happy child expressed in

> *The world is so full of a number of things,*
> *I'm sure we should all be as happy as kings*

leads us to the resolved courageous joy of the man in what must surely be the best beloved of all the adult poems,

> *If I have faltered more or less*
> *In my great task of happiness.*

When we say of a writer that he can capture for us the magic of existence we mean that he is spiritually aware of the joy of existence, and that not in spite of, but because of suffering. R.L.S. suffered. Only a man whose life and work were rooted in suffering could have written The Celestial Surgeon. *He knew happiness to be not just a negative condition of immunity from pain, but a positive thing, a task, a creation of beauty hammered out by the courage of a man on the anvil of his pain. He learned that sensitiveness to beauty which can be taught by the raw nerves of illness, the value of sharp contrast which can make the swing from wretchedness to relief such sheer delight, and that pleasure in small things, "books, and my food, and summer rain," which a restricted life can give to those who refuse to make prison bars of their restrictions.*[1106]

This woman who had herself led such a restricted life in many ways, included *The Celestial Surgeon* in her *Book of Comfort*, in a section headed *The Holy Spirit, the Comforter, and His Gifts*:

> If I have faltered more or less
> In my great task of happiness;
> If I have moved among my race
> And shown no glorious morning face;
> If beams from happy human eyes

> Have moved me not; if morning skies,
> Books, and my food, and summer rain
> Knocked on my sullen heart in vain:
> Lord, Thy most pointed pleasure take
> And stab my spirit broad awake;
> Or, Lord, if too obdurate I,
> Choose Thou, before that spirit die,
> A piercing pain, a killing sin,
> And to my dead heart run them in![1107]

Not all happiness had to be willed, however. Hélène now had two children, and there is a reference in the RLS preface to a visit that must have brought joy to their Aunt Elizabeth.

> *Children of every age are adventurous and their favourite games are always games of adventure, and do not change very much with the passing of the years. Boys climb trees now just as they always did, and march their armies to victory and sail upon voyages of exploration. Our modern cottages, flats and bungalows do not always provide suitable stairs upon which to build ships, but there are other places. I looked out of my window not long ago and saw almost an exact replica of* A Good Play. *The two small boys who were staying with me had climbed to the roof of the wood shed, and with flag flying were going "A-sailing on the billows" there. They had dragged chairs to the top of the wood shed, and provisions from the larder, and it was really a better place than the stairs because there was no way of getting them down.*[1108]

Elizabeth had paid deserving homage to Stevenson's work, but before leaving the Damerosehay novels, it is worth recording the powerful effect her own books could have on their readers. Elizabeth's obituary in the *Daily Telegraph* records that in Bath, in 1954, a magistrate had given two copies of *The Bird in the Tree* to a young married couple seeking separation. Their case was adjourned for a month, during which time they were asked to read the book. They did so, and returned to the Court to announce their reconciliation, "to everyone's pleasure including the author's."[1109]

Similarly, Jessie remembered years later receiving a request for a copy of the Damerosehay books from Louis Bouyer. She said, "As the best preparation for marriage he had given a young couple the Eliot trilogy… and could I get him another copy? So that's what he thought of her books; that was the best present he could give."

Hodders published the trilogy in 1957: *The Bird in the Tree*, *The Herb of Grace* and *The Heart of the Family* collected into one volume entitled *The Eliots of Damerosehay*, for which Elizabeth wrote a preface.

Three years after moving into Rose Cottage, in 1956, she and Jessie went to Keyhaven for a holiday. Jessie sent a postcard from Milford to her mother in Wales; a picture of Harewood House, saying "This is Damerosehay... We are having very restful time and enjoying immensely." And the preface to the Eliots' trilogy begins: "There seems no more suitable place to write a preface to this book...than where I am now, sitting in the window of the drawing-room at Damerosehay, looking out at the ilex tree."

All the work inspired by Keyhaven was now complete, and in the meantime Elizabeth had written another novel.

The Rosemary Tree

After we had settled into Rose Cottage I said goodbye to the old life by finishing a final book about Devon, begun while I still lived there.[1110]

This is the one, nameless reference in *The Joy of the Snow* to *The Rosemary Tree*, a novel that had the critics reaching for all the usual adjectives. "Spring in Devon brings charming solutions to everyone's problems...the Wentworths are another of Miss Goudge's delightful families" said *The Daily Telegraph*, while *The Scotsman* described it as "another of those blends of fairytale grace, human warmth and spiritual feeling which only Elizabeth Goudge can contrive."[1111]

Her great admirer Alan Hull Walton, however, said that "there was only one of her novels I found not quite to my personal taste, and that was *The Rosemary Tree*."[1112] And Jessie Monroe remembered that,

> Whoever was her editor then came to see Elizabeth and said "I didn't know you had it in you to write about such a horrible character as you have in *The Rosemary Tree*!"

Jessie made a joke of it and told the editor, "Oh that's since *I* came, she knew about that sort of thing!!" – but it is true that in the middle of all that fairytale grace, charm and human warmth sits Mrs. Belling, the head of Oaklands school, who is quite unlike any character she had yet created. She is the obvious antithesis of Elizabeth's own headmistress at Grassendale who, she said, "taught us to love God... I think, by the infection of her own love, which so penetrated and illumined all she did." After Miss Amy Lumby died in June 1917, the young Elizabeth had come to understand "the way in which the spirit of the one man or woman at the helm can subtly alter the whole atmosphere of some institution."[1113] And here is Mrs. Belling; outwardly such a sweet old lady, but in reality a poisonous "infection" in the atmosphere of Oaklands with her self-centred, iron control over both pupils and staff.

> *Mary did as she was told... But as she slowly crossed the lawn she realized she was returning to her duty not because it was her duty but because she could not help herself. For the first time she felt frightened by her aunt's compelling power.*[1114]

Mrs. Belling, however, is not the only old lady in this novel. In complete contrast is Harriet at the vicarage, who has a very different kind of power over John and Daphne's household.

> *She had been nanny to John...and his bleak childhood had been redeemed from disaster by her love. He said he could not face life without her. They all said they could not do without her. In the paradoxical nature of things if she could have believed them she would have been a much happier woman, but not the woman whom they could not do without.*[1115]

Harriet is so humbly lacking in self-focus that she cannot see her own worth to them: how the loving wisdom of her faith spills over into the stress of their lives and brings peace. Nor can Daphne identify its source, but she benefits from it nonetheless.

> *Daphne looked at her, dainty and fresh in her snowy shawl and frilled white nightcap, charming and serene. "She's got something," she thought. "I wouldn't know what it was, but something – some sort of wisdom." It struck her suddenly that, in the possession of Harriet, so had she. She leaned back and relaxed and through the uncurtained window saw the first stars above the trees.*[1116]

Like the dark obverse of the same picture, we are also given a glimpse of Mrs. Belling in her bedroom.

> *She was looking extremely comfortable, propped up against a quantity of soft but not over-clean pillows. A torn lace cap hid her white hair and she wore a quilted pink satin dressing-jacket with eggstains down the front... Baba was asleep on her soiled pink satin eiderdown and*

> *the eiderdown smelt of Baba. Mrs. Belling smelt of the scent she used and the cigarette she was smoking... The room was unbearably close and stuffy.*[1117]

Harriet is another of Elizabeth's characters who is not free - confined by crippling arthritis, she never now leaves her room. And when after a slight stroke Mrs. Belling too becomes confined to bed, the contrast between the two women is complete.

> *[John] did not know her, for the mask had gone. The sweetness, the placidity, had vanished, and this was Mrs. Belling. She was speechless with rage, shaking with it, her face purple, her hands plucking at the soiled eiderdown, but what he saw in her eyes was fear...*
>
> *"You'll take a turn for the better now this bright weather has come, Mrs. Belling," he said, and heard his banal words coming as from a great distance. He himself was at a great distance from this woman. Nothing he could do or say would bridge the gulf because there was nothing here to appeal to. There was nothing here but anger and fear, things in themselves entirely sterile. Divorced from the love of righteousness, the fear of God, they were nothing. There was nothing here. He had not realized before the ghastly evil of negation. He had seldom felt such evil. Nothingness was a bottomless pit.*[1118]

Nearly twenty years later, attempting to answer the question "What do I think about hell?" Elizabeth wrote,

I would like to believe that no human soul ever becomes a totally evil spirit... that no human soul is ever destroyed. I want to believe that every single soul reaches God at last. And yet – love cannot compel... I have to believe that the soul may refuse if he wishes.[1119]

And in Mrs. Belling, she imagined the fate of a woman who did refuse. John has found her in this fear, in this bottomless pit of nothingness, because she has already, finally, chosen the path of refusal.

> *Between sleeping and waking she heard Baba whimpering under the bed and felt a momentary stirring of something like compunction. She swung on a dark tide, but not overwhelmed yet, because the compunction bore her up just once more. Suspended between one world and another, she remembered dimly that there had been other times when some weakening*

> *of self-love had lifted her up like this to abide the questioning, the detested probing questioning. 'Whom do men say that I am..?*
>
> *She had always refused even to consider an answer, struggled to get away from the intolerable claim made upon her, fought to get back to her ownership of herself. The questioning now was childishly simple, not the question which had been like the thundering of a great wave along a beach, but a gentle question put to a child… 'Won't you call the little dog out from under the bed?' Swinging in darkness on the dark tide, she saw him quite clearly, shivering on the floor, a paw that had been hurt in his fall doubled under him, blood oozing from the corner of his eye where her ring had cut him, an obese unpleasant little dog who loved her and had tried to lick her hand. But it was too much trouble to drag herself out of sleep and call to him. Why should she? She was just getting warm and comfortable. Let him stay there. 'No,' she said.*[1120]

In *A New Vision of Reality* (1989), Bede Griffiths defines sin as refusing to love; refusing to respond to the Love which is constantly trying to draw us back to itself. We refuse, he says, because we want to stay as we are; and to cling on to what we already have. In this novel Maria Wentworth accepts loss, and learns to value in humility her "empty, dirty hands," but Mrs. Belling's power is rooted in clinging; she has kept such an iron grasp on her possessions that she would not even allow her little dog to be taken into the garden, out of her sphere of control.

> *"Pat, fetch Baba back to me at once," said Mrs. Belling.*
> *She showed no agitation, for it was always too much trouble to be agitated, but she had never at any time allowed any personal possessions to be removed from her against her will, except only that one removal of her husband by death; and when she thought of that she still, after all these years, boiled with resentment deep within her sham serenity…*
>
> *"At once. Do as I tell you, Pat."*
> *She did not raise her soft voice, but the sweetness had gone out of it. Pat had not realized before how entirely they all obeyed Mrs. Belling, but she realized it now. It was as though an iron hand had picked her up and put her by the French window.*[1121]

And if sin is refusing and clinging, says Bede, then grace is its opposite: allowing ourselves to be drawn back into God's love; opening up and letting go. Harriet, we feel, must have said Yes to God long ago, for in contrast to the selfish refusal that has sealed the fate of Mrs. Belling, she accepts the restrictions of her life and lovingly gives what strength remains to her for the good of others. The very opening lines of the novel establish the fact of Harriet's faith - she has begun the day by reading her Bible - and by the third paragraph of Chapter One we are aware of the depth of her prayer life.

> *Since she had had to lead this shut-in invalid life she had found illness involved suffering almost as much from the tyranny of painful thoughts as from physical pain. Outside this lovely valley where she lived the world was a dreadful place and first one misery would possess her mind and then another… She lacked the physical strength to thrust tormenting thought from her even if she had wanted to but she did not want to. The fortunate, she thought, and she counted herself fortunate, should not insulate themselves in their good fortune. If they could do nothing else they could pray…*[1122]

(*A Book of Comfort* includes a quotation from Father Congreve of Cowley: "If I cannot work or rise from my chair or my bed, love remains to me; I can pray.")[1123]

> *…and she prayed as she was able, grieving over the childishness of her prayer but trying to make it real to herself by letting the travail of her mind bring forth one concrete fact at a time to pray about; one child in danger, some particular man in darkness, some particular prisoner facing the world again with fear and shame; God knew who they were even if she did not.*[1124]

❄

Michael is the released prisoner facing the world again with fear and shame; but on the last page of the novel, when he finally meets Harriet, she makes him aware that his is not the only kind of imprisonment.

> "That's a cruel thing men do to God, making a prisoner of Him."
> "I don't think I know what you mean," said Michael.
> "The grey clouds, they are like men's unbelief," said Harriet. "And men live frozen and afraid, when a touch of the sun would change all that. But they imprison the sun."[1125]

The same message appears in one of Elizabeth's poems, *Old Age*:

Peppard

> *Oh the agony in God's heart*
> *When we choose our selfish evil*
> *And mock and deny his goodness.*
> *With his sunlight on our faces*
> *We turn into the cold darkness*
> *Of our own shadow; and blame him*
> *For our chosen desolation.*[1126]

As Michael talks to Harriet - this man whose childhood was scarred by his mother's death - there comes a dawning realization of the depth of her faith, and the power for good that it gives her. Nevertheless he feels her advice is hard to take.

> *"Many who would like to believe, can't, Harriet," said Michael.*
> *"That's a lie," said Harriet calmly. "If you want a good thing badly enough you get it. Not overnight, maybe. But you get it..."*
> *"Perhaps faith is hard to come by when you're alone, Harriet," he said.*
> *"Until now I've been alone."*
> *"We're never alone," said Harriet. "That's the mistake so many make. There'd be less fear if folk knew how little alone they are..."*

The last words of their conversation are the final words of the book:

> *"You've forgotten your mother, maybe?"*
> *"No, I never forget her," said Michael.*
> *"Then it's an odd thing you thought yourself alone," said Harriet.*[1127]

The novel is named after the herb of remembrance, rosemary, which in the old tradition was thrown upon a coffin by sorrowing mourners as their last farewell. Is it perhaps no coincidence therefore, that she should write with such depths of spirituality about Harriet and Mrs. Belling: these two, completely contrasting, white-haired old ladies? Elizabeth had already written her last book about Lucilla Eliot, the character who had so much of Ida Goudge in her, but maybe in this "final book about Devon" she was also remembering those painful final months of her illness.

> *If a patient remains mentally himself, however bad the physical distress may be the person you know is still there with you, but in mental illness the beloved personality seems lost and you appear to be living with a stranger; at times a frightening stranger, talking (and perhaps with truth) of the nearness of the powers of darkness... You feel you have lost the person you love...*

But…a few days before her death my mother returned, weak and dying but entirely herself. And much more than herself… She came back peaceful and spiritualised.[1128]

❄

The relationship between the two teachers at Oaklands must have been, at least in part, inspired by her new friendship with Jessie, for Mary O'Hara's appearance, with her "curly red hair" and "very white skin"[1129] is very like the description of Jessie Monroe. And Jessie's humorous description of herself: "My mother was pure Welsh, and my father was pure Scots, which makes me a pure mongrel!" ties in with what we are told of Mary: "upon both sides she was pure unadulterated Celt."[1130]

The description of Miss Giles is much less flattering. She's "turned fifty" with "chronic nervous dyspepsia"[1131] and on one occasion has "such an appalling migraine that she was unaware of anything but the necessity of controlling her pain sufficiently to do her duty."[1132] Ill and lonely, Miss Giles looks back on her life and concludes morbidly that she "had been left to sink or swim, marry or die. And she had died. For what had her life been but death?"[1133]

However, the younger woman's kind and caring friendship gradually lifts her out of her depression and changes her life.

> *Giles had a look at her skirt in the long glass and pulled it up to hang evenly. Then she sat down before her dressing-table and looked with terror at the rows of bottles upon it. She had had a birthday two days ago, and Mary had given her a complete set of all that was necessary for presenting to the world the sort of face that Mary thought should be presented to it. Miss Giles had not dared to use any of the bottles yet, but she had read all the little booklets enclosed with them, had mastered their contents and now had a clear working hypothesis for future procedure. Yet she remained terrified. "I must, to please O'Hara," she said to herself, took a deep breath and shook the first bottle.*
>
> *Yet, as she applied the contents with her finger-tips, apprehension was lost in a wave of sheer delight as she realized that there was more than liking, there was love, between herself and Mary. Until this moment she had not fully known it. She…remembered the day she had had migraine and Mary had brought her tea. It had begun that day. Half blind with pain as she had been then, she had thought Mary's curly hair looked like the feathers of a bird, and remembered the poem about patience.*

> *And where is he who more and more distils*
> *Delicious kindness? – He is patient. Patience fills*
> *His crisp combs, and that comes those ways we know.*

> "If we wait for it, in such simple ways," she thought, "through a bird's song, a cup of tea, a child with a bunch of flowers, through men and women of goodwill. Why did I despair? Could I not have emulated, just for a moment or two, the eternal patience?"[1134]

The quotation is once again from Gerard Manley Hopkins – "the ending of the sonnet on Patience" which of all his poems linking Christ with the symbol of a bird was, Elizabeth said, "best of all to me."[1135]

❉

In 1956 *Woman's Journal* "proudly" announced that the serialisation of *The Rosemary Tree* would begin in the March issue: "Her new novel of charm and distinction starts next month." Alongside the announcement and under the heading *…by Elizabeth Goudge* the February issue also carried an autobiographical article, revised from the one already published in *The Elizabeth Goudge Reader*, with photographs of Rose Cottage and its inhabitants.

Some years later, Elizabeth wrote a humorous article: *On Being Photographed – A True Story* that tells the tale of these illustrations.

> Have you ever turned the pages of a glossy magazine and seen the photos of lovely rooms in a beautiful house and wondered if they could be <u>real</u>? They always look unreal to me because of their tidiness. Does anyone live in rooms where all the books stand upright in the shelves, where the flowers are arranged as for a royal wedding and nothing is where it ought not to be? No papers strewn on the floor, no dog's bones buried behind sofa cushions? And the gardens beyond the polished windows! Shaven lawns, tidy beds, no weeds, no fallen leaves. These are utopian homes. People can't live in them.
>
> But they do, I discovered. On a day in early autumn, some years ago, I was visited by a lovely lady who was on the staff of one of the glossy magazines. She had come to discuss stories and articles, but every now and then, as we sat talking in my much-loved, much-lived-in sitting room, her attention wandered. She kept looking about her. "A lovely old cottage," she said at last. "I think it <u>could</u> be photographed." For a moment I felt cold with dismay, but she said no more, and I forgot about it until a few days later when a letter came from the magazine. They would like to send Mr. Ionescu (that is not his real name but he came from Eastern Europe) to take photographs of my cottage and garden. Would Tuesday October the 14th be suitable?

In one's wilder moments one accepts a desperate challenge, and I said yes. Oh, how we worked! On the Monday our Mrs Wells put off her wash day to come and clean the house down. The friend who lives with me concentrated on the garden and the floral decorations. My task was to tidy the books and clear up my mess. Now our cottage has a saving grace. A little room, once the old washhouse, leads out of the sitting room and no one notices the door in a dark corner. I can open the door, pick up my typewriter, manuscripts, overflowing waste paper basket, piles of unanswered letters and the dog's bones, fling the whole lot inside and shut the door again. I did that. I also prepared a lunch for Mr. Ionescu.

Tuesday morning saw us exhausted but triumphant. We'd done it. We were as tidy as any of those utopian homes. The garden looked like the Chelsea flower show and indoors the floral decorations were worthy of Constance Spry. There was not a dog's bone to be seen, and we'd brushed her. It was St. Luke's summer and the day was glorious. The omens seemed propitious.

Mr. Ionescu was to come at ten o'clock. We waited. The clock struck eleven o'clock. We waited again. At twelve o'clock I rang up the magazine. It said it would ring Mr. Ionescu's home and ring back to me again. It did that. He had mistaken the day and gone to Brighton. The magazine was very apologetic and it made another appointment for a week later.

During the week we watched St. Luke's summer anxiously. Would it last out? We implored St. Luke to be good to us. On the Monday there was a chill in the air and the sunshine was strangely misted. Once more Mrs. Wells put off her wash day and the whole process of preparation was gone through again. But somehow we had lost heart. When we went to bed that night we heard the first rush of the wind over the roof and the first spatter of rain against the windows.

When we got up in the morning the gale had blown itself out but rain fell monotonously from low dark clouds upon a ruined garden. The chrysanthemums were blown flat and the leaves lay on the lawn in sodden drifts. Indoors the fire would not burn and one could scarcely see the flowers. Mr. Ionescu and his camera and arc lamps arrived at ten 'clock. He had great charm and exquisite manners, bowing over my hand in a way that made me feel twice the woman I look. But he did not smile as he looked through the windows at the wet fields and the mournful cows sheltering by the dripping hedge and in a deep sad voice he marvelled greatly that anyone should live in the country from choice. Then he turned with resignation to the business of the photographs.

Two lamps were necessary to illumine the indoor shadows. The rooms were taken, and the dog and myself. The dog knows how to behave when her likeness is required. She drops dejectedly to my feet and gazes mournfully at the photographer. She knows that the only way to get out the other end of this is to submit and get it over. Then we went out into the garden and the sky was so dark that one of the arc lamps had to come too. I had recently written a book called The Rosemary Tree *and Mr. Ionescu asked, "Is there one?" I explained that rosemary does not like our soil. As soon as we coax a cutting to a small bush it dies on us, but there was at the moment a little creature of twelve inches high still struggling for life. "Then I'd better photograph it," said Mr. Ionescu sadly. So he photographed me kneeling on the wet leaves and bending solicitously over the poor little rosemary bush. The dog was not in this one. She had given up and gone indoors...*[1136]

Unlike Elizabeth and Jessie, Froniga, the fictional seventeenth-century inhabitant of Rose Cottage in her next novel, would have no problems with growing rosemary in its soil.

She stood and looked at her rosemary tree. It had grown here ever since she could remember and she suspected that it had been planted when the cottage was built, for of all the trees of divine power rosemary is the most potent in driving away evil, and few gardens were planted without it. Upon the journey to Egypt, Mary threw her blue cloak over a rosemary bush, turning the white flowers to the blue of her mantle, and when she returned to Nazareth she would spread her son's little garments to dry on a rosemary bush after she had washed them. Rosemary, dew of the sea, the freshest and sweetest-smelling plant in the world, is steeped in the mercy of Christ...
She greeted her tree and curtseyed to it. That it was a living personality she was convinced.[1137]

The largest of the photographs illustrating the article is of Elizabeth apparently seated gracefully in her bedroom and smiling down at the mournful Tiki. Jessie laughingly recalled, however, that as part of the day's general mayhem "she was taken in my room and not hers at all – hopeless!"

❋

One thing the photographs do clearly show is the beauty of the old cottage and the ancient black timbers in its walls, as described in *The Joy of the Snow* and fictionalised in *The White Witch*:

Solid old tree trunks, heavy and hard as stone, hold the cottage together, with lesser beams that seem to be ships' timbers, since they have bolt holes in them. Old ships used to be brought up the Thames to just below Henley and broken up there, and ships' timbers are to be found in houses and cottages within easy reach of Henley. On a very hot day an aromatic scent comes from the beams. Spices? Were these beams once part of a spice ship?[1138]

She did not know...what ship had built her home, but she had her ideas about it... A small stout rivercraft that had plied up and down the Thames from the Port of London with treasure from the East – tea, cinnamon, pepper, cloves and green ginger... When her room was warm, as now, she could fancy she smelt the cinnamon and ginger, and they gave a sharp, racy tang to the cool scents of the English herbs that hung from the beams.[1139]

Soon after our arrival Jessie called my bedroom 'the captain's cabin' merely from the look and shape of it, and great was my joy when the same friend who had brought Jessie into my life gave me a copy of a poem she had seen framed and hanging on the wall of an old house in Devon.[1140]

The poem, describing her room as a "square and candle-lighted boat" was *The Country Bedroom* by Frances Cornford, a granddaughter of Charles Darwin who was awarded the Queen's Medal for Poetry in 1959. Originally part of her *Autumn Midnight* collection of 1923, it was published again shortly after the move to Rose Cottage, in the *Collected Poems* of 1954. Incidentally when Duckworth reprinted *The Bird in the Tree* around this time – in 1954 and '56 – the woodcut dust-wrapper illustrations were by another Darwin granddaughter: Cornford's cousin (and Mervyn Horder's friend) Gwen Raverat. Her preferred method of illuminating her work-table was to place a light behind a glass globe filled with water, like Isaac Peabody in *The Dean's Watch*.[1141]

The poem's description of an owl in the darkness beyond her window, and an old horse beneath, sleeping "among drowned daisies," chimed with some of the delights of Rose Cottage.

At night the open country beyond us seems to hold such a great depth of darkness; and...an old white horse, put out to grass in the fields below our windows, was one of the joys of our early years... There used to be a big old hawthorn tree in the centre of the field, where he would shelter from sun or rain. I have a clear picture in my mind of the hawthorn tree white with blossom and the old horse standing beneath it knee-deep in buttercups; and another picture of hares dancing near the tree. In an apple tree in the farm orchard at the bottom of our garden owls nested and brought up their families year after year. The hawthorn and the orchard are cut down now, and the old horse is dead, but the owls have found another tree and are with us still.[1142]

Protected

The new tone of peace and tranquillity which comes through in Elizabeth's descriptions of life at Rose Cottage must have been the result, at least in part, of the way in which Jessie set out to protect her, and to lessen some of the pressures she had previously been under. (Is it perhaps no coincidence that she finally managed to conquer her stammer around this time - in "late middle life"?)[1143] Seeing her new friend initially so white-faced and ill, Jessie must have realised how unprotected she had been thus far, and how exhausted by the twin demands of her career and her domestic life.

No doubt a best-selling author would have been regarded as something of a celebrity in their new locality - like Mary Montague in *The Dean's Watch* perhaps, who was "vastly amused to find herself a personage."[1144] This could have caused problems had it not been for Jessie's protection, one manifestation of which was to erect a physical barrier behind which she could shelter - Elizabeth records how her friend, "prizing privacy beyond rubies" added trees and "innumerable tall flowering shrubs" to their garden.[1145]

What she does not say – and perhaps may not even have fully realised - is that Jessie deliberately restricted her own involvement in the village life in order to protect her. "Actually I don't know a lot of people here," Jessie admitted in late 1991, "because there were so many fans that wanted to latch on when we came, that I thought it was far better to keep out…"

> It *is* a very scattered kind of place… But that's the real reason you see - anybody who knew me would want to come in, and the creation time would have been eroded so badly with all these people wanting to meet "the eminent," that I wasn't going to be responsible for anything like that… Affable, but not friendly!

Jessie even made herself rather unpopular it seems, with at least one person. Audrey, Elizabeth's long-time friend from Oxford, introduced her into our conversation with the question, "You've met what's-her-name Monroe..?" and said,

> One used to find that one was not going to be allowed to go and see Elizabeth very often, and it was rather sad, because she might have asked me to go and see her, and I'd arrange

a time, and then find that I was told she wasn't up to it. It was...rather galling.

Nonetheless, with Jessie so solicitous for her well-being Elizabeth did not have to cope with visitors at times when she wasn't up to it, and this was surely to the good. Yet they did not live in any kind of isolation, far from it; for over the years Elizabeth did make friends close by, of course – like the Carnegie Medal-winning children's novelist and illustrator, Cynthia Harnett - "my great friend at Peppard."[1146] There was the poet Ruth Pitter "that dear and funny and great poet whom I see sometimes, because she lives in the Chilterns;"[1147] and her "dearest Madeau" - the BBC producer Madeau Stewart at Burford. And she had family nearby too: her "very special cousin"[1148] Janet Parmiter lived only a few miles away.

Another cousin, Sybil Harton ("I love her very dearly"[1149]] had temporarily left the area not long before they arrived at Peppard, when her husband, the Vicar of Baulking was made Dean of Wells. After her husband's death in 1958 she returned to the Wantage area, although Jessie said she and Elizabeth did not meet until 1963. Their grandmothers were sisters: the daughters of the Mr. Ozanne who had sold his home to Victor Hugo. (Sybil was the granddaughter of "Rosalie, the youngest [who] sat on the great man's knee. Sybil and I boast about this," Elizabeth said jokingly to Madeau.[1150]) Herself the author of Christian works, Sybil Harton undertook a lecture tour of America in 1959. During an interview there[1151] she produced a musical instrument – her recorder - saying that she and her late husband had been very keen on English folk music and dancing. Indeed in their early years together she taught folk dancing in the parish for which he would play the accompaniment… which explains their friend John Betjeman's nickname for her – Mrs. Folky.

Many others, not just friends and family, were 'allowed' to visit Rose Cottage: for Elizabeth had an army of fans worldwide, many of whom made great efforts to meet her. (According to one newspaper interview, this steady stream of visitors was exacerbated by her close proximity to Henley – high on the 'must-see' list for overseas tourists.)[1152] Despite Elizabeth's own admission that "the great and Christian virtue of hospitality is a rather weakly plant in myself and Jessie; it needs a lot of nurturing"[1153] the fans were frequently successful – most likely because she did regard it as a great and Christian virtue. As she said of the manor-house in *The Rosemary Tree*,

> *Hospitality, here was…sacramental… His guests had always been the objects of his reverence.*[1154]

Elizabeth had not always found it easy to extend this reverence to reporters, however. Their determined efforts had overwhelmed her in the days of *Green Dolphin Country*, when the MGM prize had first made big news.

Reporters and interviewers, mortal men and women who are persecutors only because they must earn a living like the rest of us, appeared to me at that time in the guise of vultures. On one desperate day I cast myself on my bed and vowed that anyone attacking the front-door bell that afternoon should go unanswered. But reporters are enterprising people, especially if female; that particular girl, that afternoon, came in through the window.[1155]

Nevertheless according to Jessie, Elizabeth's mother had always instilled into her that she must simply cope with it: telling her that, "If you're famous, that's the price you have to pay; you *owe* it." But Jessie set out to curb this idea to a certain extent: looking back, she described some of the visitors as mere "fawners" who took Elizabeth away from her work and correspondence, and exhausted her – as she observed, with no real benefit to anyone. (This was Jessie's opinion of course; just as Ida's directives on the responsibilities of fame had been her own.) She remembered,

> We were rung up one lunchtime, by two people who said, Could we come, and we said Yes. And they sat there and talked about absolutely nothing and then said, "Well isn't it marvellous, we never thought we'd be here and see you!" And there we were – she was worn out by the time they'd gone, and that was her 'afternoon off' gone entirely, with no real reason.

The visitors did not always ring and ask. Jessie had kept one fan-letter sent to Elizabeth which said "I broke in on your Sunday nap" – but still went on to describe the 'magical' intrusion, from their point of view, as full of grace. Sometimes the fans were an even greater trial, arriving in coach-loads and peering in at her windows. Elizabeth did once try setting up a hut in the garden, where she could find the peace and solitude to write, but during a 1968 interview she "pointed out the somewhat derelict summer house where once she planned to work. 'There were too many interruptions – telephone and so on,' she said, 'it wasn't really practical.'"[1156]

Perhaps Elizabeth's own attitude to visitors can be found in the fiction: Miss Montague in *The Dean's Watch* simply accepts the inevitable.

> *Even now [the Dean] came only seldom to see her, afraid to trespass on her hospitality and afraid to tire her. She wished he would come oftener*

but like all the old and infirm she had accepted with rueful humour the fact that she must be visited oftenest by those she least wished to see. It was the sensitive, the gentle and humble who feared to come too often lest they tire her. The coarse-fibred had no such inhibitions.[1157]

Miss Montague's attitude to the droppers-in, too, sounds as if it may have been Elizabeth's own: "She was pleased to see them, but always very tired."[1158]

Added to this inevitable consequence of celebrity was her awareness of the fans' high expectations, before they finally met the real Elizabeth Goudge. As she had said of Jessie's friendship: "To be loved as the faulty person you actually are, rather than as the pleasing personality that people think you are, is an unspeakable relief."[1159]

Inspiration

Years later, Elizabeth commented to a friend on the weather in Oxfordshire: "It is lovely here in spring. But not in winter. There is nothing between us and the North Pole."[1160] Her biography of Saint Francis too, describing the brothers' missionary journey to England in 1224, says that "Christmas Day found two of them in a wood near Oxford. It was very cold, that penetrating cold of Oxfordshire that enters the very bones."[1161]

True to the vision of her work however, even the winter cold was inspirational, and was to be transmuted into a thing of joy and beauty for her next novel *The White Witch*.

> *After Christmas bitter cold…clamped down upon the country… It did not seem possible that spring would ever come.*
>
> *[But] Froniga found fresh delight in her home. When she got up on fine mornings she would find her window covered with frost flowers, with behind them the fires of the rising sun. She could not see the sun, she could only see the flames that seemed sparkling and crackling just behind her window, and she would stretch out her arms and laugh with joy. The fire on her hearth had never seemed to burn so merrily. The apple logs had blue and yellow flames, the cherry logs smelt like flowers and the burning fir-cones were edged with the same colour that had sparkled behind the frost flowers on her window. She would kneel before*

> her hearth, warming her hands and singing, and Pen, her white cat, would weave round and round her purring and vibrating. But Pen was not so white as the snowflakes that fell outside her window, sometimes singly, like the feathers of a white swan that had passed overhead, sometimes in dense masses of falling light.[1162]

It is obvious, both from the *Woman's Journal* article and *The Joy of the Snow* that the beauties of Froniga's home had been inspired by Rose Cottage itself, and the discoveries Jessie made in its old garden.

Most of our windows look east, and from them we watch flaming sunrises, seen in the cold winters through the frost flowers on the window-panes, vast golden afterglows, storms and rainbows. It is a peaceful place and there are more birds in this garden than in any garden I have known.[1163]

> The doves who lived at the farm beyond the orchard were circling out from their cote, over the garden and back again, in a high silvery curve against the sky…and robins and chaffinches were hopping near her without fear…

> Her garden…was a fragrant and musical place, humming with bees, with grass paths separating the cushions and knots and parterres of colour and scent. Froniga had more than a hundred herbs and knew all their names and just where to find them. She loved them all with passion, but best of all she loved her great rosemary bush, her lavender hedge and beds of mint geranium…her germander and marjoram…

> Her rose garden…in June was one of the loveliest in the neighbourhood. She grew her roses chiefly for medicinal purposes but for their beauty too; apothecary and rosa-mundi, velvet and village maid, damask roses for making melrosette, the musk rose for its scent that drifted on every breeze, maiden's blush and incarnation because she loved them. Of sweetbrier roses she grew a quantity…They hedged her whole domain as well as the herb garden and the cottage was named after them.[1164]

In the wilderness at the bottom of the garden Jessie found remnants of very old roses, Apothecary and Rosamundi, Maiden's-Blush and Moss rose. Transplanted they have flourished. They bloom only once a year, but they are worth all the modern roses put together, they are so lovely and their scent is so exquisite. Sports of the old primroses have appeared, jack in-the-green, hose-in-hose and galligaskin, but though we bought plants of the old species and tried to grow them again we failed. Jessie tried to bring back to the garden plants it *might have held originally, collecting all the herbs she could and planting rosemary and lavender. The place is now very green, shady and bird-haunted, with climbing roses and clematis trained to grow up the old trees.*[1165]

Inspirational indeed; although around the time The White Witch was published the reality of the garden was a little different; as she told Audrey in an October letter, written shortly after she had "finished Saint Francis and sent him off to my agent..."

The summer has been appalling. Just a solid weight of water falling from the sky. We have begun fires rather too early, but we found we had green mould growing even over the floor of the sitting room, as well as over all the books, so we felt we had to – and Tiki thinks it is marvellous! The poor garden is beaten and battered into a pulp.[1166]

She had rounded off the recent *Woman's Journal* article self-mockingly, saying: "As I get older I write worse and worse and more and more slowly, and people sometimes say to me hopefully, 'Aren't you going to stop writing now?' But writers, though they may grouse and grumble over the fatigue of their work, and break their hearts over its poor quality, can no more stop writing than they can stop breathing..."[1167]

In fact, despite the comments on her failing powers, she now went on to write some of her greatest books. The dedicatee of the first of them was Jessie, to whom she owed so much of her returning health and happiness: "*The White Witch* is Jessie's book, commemorating the spells she wove over the garden,"[1168] she said. It commemorates too Rose Cottage, which "took charge of me and made me write about itself."[1169]

The White Witch

> *I was looking out at the garden, and over the sweetbrier hedge to the field beyond, and feeling the first twinges of love for the place, when a woman came down the narrow path in front of the window. She came from the place where the path ended abruptly in the hedge and I was told later that there used to be a gate there leading to the lane. Her name was Froniga.*[1170]

"Whether I saw a ghost or whether I imagined the whole thing I don't know," she added; but she said in an interview that one of the characters, Madona, was definitely not imaginary.

> *The first year we were here the gypsies were camping on the field. I had never met any real gypsies before, and twenty years ago they had the painted caravans and the camp fires and they used to sing round them. There was an amazing old grandmother and I would look up and see this marvellous old face smiling at me through the kitchen window while I was doing the washing up — she went into my book just as she was.*[1171]

> *Outside in the windy dusk stood a thin, stooped old woman wrapped in a worn brown cloak, a diklo over her head, wisps of white hair straggling about her brown wrinkled face. She looked frail as a cobweb. Then suddenly she smiled, and her face lighted up with an inexpressible tenderness as she spoke the words of…greeting, "O boro Duvel atch' pa leste, Tshai." [The great Lord be on you.] She spoke the last word over again, tenderly, "Tshai. My daughter."*[1172]

The story is set in the English Civil War, although the critic at *The Times* saw the book as "less an authoritative historical novel of the civil war than…a compassionate enquiry into the minds of men and women."[1173] Parson Hawthyn, the village clergyman, is nothing if not compassionate. He has his own political sympathies in the conflict, but nevertheless does not allow them to interfere with his basic Christian love and broad tolerance for humankind in all its diversity of belief.

> *He was no bigot. He believed that truth is a great globe and that men see only that part of it upon which for them the light shines. He believed that through any creed held in sincerity the finger of God can reach and touch a man. He believed that if men struggled to find the light, they*

would reach the light, not only in spite of but through their mistakes and limitations.[1174]

As *The White Witch* was published in 1958 and her biography of St. Francis the following year, it is more than likely that Elizabeth was writing the one while researching the other. Certainly Parson Hawthyn is a Franciscan figure, a little man of deep faith and "great simplicity" who is "very poor."[1175] In defiance of his village Squire, a Puritan, he creates a Christmas crib for the children of the village, and in this too he is like Francis. The saint is believed to have made the first recreation of the Bethlehem stable scene at Christmas - motivated, she says in *Saint Francis of Assisi* by the fact that the villagers "were a simple and childlike people, even as he was himself, and to behold with their bodily eyes the stable and the manger, and the gentle beasts, would help them to see the Babe."[1176]

Parson Hawthyn's Squire, however, desecrates the village church in an act of anger and violence, throwing out and burning the crib in a fire that also sets light to the Parson's tiny cottage. Elizabeth had already described a similar scene in *The Three Grey Men*, and she may well have had in mind the fate of Little Gidding in the diocese of Ely, immortalised in T.S. Eliot's *Four Quartets*. Although recent research suggests that this may not now be the case, it has always been thought that during the Civil War, after the community there had given refuge to Charles I, Cromwell's soldiers ransacked Little Gidding church in the winter of 1646; that they threw many of its fittings, including the font and lectern, into a nearby pond, and ripped out the organ and pulpit which they then burnt outside the church.

For a man of prayer like Parson Hawthyn all things work for good, and so with his home burnt down, he takes the opportunity to visit the black witch, Mother Skipton, and ask her for shelter. Even such a good man as the Parson, however, finds that it is no easy task to do the will of God when it involves confronting evil.

> *Every step forward now was exhausting him, and not only because of the wind, but because of his own desperate inner reluctance. To go to that evil house and live there pressed upon night and day by that woman's wickedness. He groaned as he bent forward into the wind and then stopped altogether, so overwhelming was the temptation to turn back. Surely he was guilty of presumption in going on? What could he, a weak sinner, do against that evil? He would himself be lost...*
>
> *That he might have a little rest from his conflict with the wind, he turned round. Facing south it seemed almost balmy, and there was a*

> *line of light in the sky behind the village and the church. Unconsciously he took a few steps back towards the light, and then stopped, checked by the very ease of what he was doing. Ease and the will of God were seldom synonymous. He turned round again and struggled on.*[1177]

His own inner battle is won; but the woman must face a similar struggle when he arrives and asks her for shelter, adding after a pause, "I ask you in the name of God."

> *He waited, aware of the struggle that was going on in her. He gave no sign of his own anxiety as he waited for her answer. His reluctance to be here was now a thing of the past. If she yielded to that plea he believed she might be saved.*
>
> *She spoke at last, her voice low and hoarse. "You saved my life. You may lodge here."*
> *"In the name of God," he said. "Repeat it after me, in the name of God."*
> *She was silent.*
> *"In the name of God," he repeated.*
> *She struggled again and then gave in. "In the name of God," she said, and suddenly reached breaking point. Her arms upon the table, her face hidden, she wept long and wildly.*[1178]

This battle of wills is only one of many instances of division and conflict in the novel, although because the Parson gives everything he has and is, in order to do God's will, this one ultimately ends in good. Elsewhere, the evil complexities of civil war create a world that is the very opposite of the Franciscan ideal of simplicity and brotherly love. It is a world where people are separated by race, class and gender, as well as – even within families – the barriers of politics and religion.

In one particular battle scene she describes, it is not just soldiers who are destroyed as the two armies clash.

> *His trumpet rang out for the charge. There was a shout from the rebels, and they too charged. Rupert set his horse at the hedge, leapt it and came riding down upon them. The two forces met each other, crashed and reeled, trampling the young green corn beneath the feet of their struggling horses. Overhead the larks continued to sing as they had sung all the morning.*[1179]

A critic might well find it incongruous that in the face of such terrible death and destruction, the author finds it necessary to describe the trampled corn. Why, in the middle of such bloody fighting would she make mention of the birds, and the plants in the battlefield? Well partly perhaps because she had seen for herself, during the war years, that War and Nature were two different worlds:

Nature herself was quite indifferent to our danger. The cuckoos and the air-raid sirens shouted together and once, just after the sound of a distant bomb explosion had died away, I remember that I heard a hen in the next-door garden cackling with satisfaction because she had just laid an egg. I found that extremely comforting. Whatever happened nest-building and egg-laying would go on and the earth would continue to pass through all the seasonal changes of her beauty. "While the earth remaineth, seed time and harvest, and cold and heat, and summer and winter and day and night shall not cease."[1180]

But this scene of battle has strong echoes, too, of Damerosehay's corn and larks imagery, as well as that hidden three-word quotation from John Masefield's poem which resonates in *The Heart of the Family*. There is symbolic as well as literal meaning in the trampling of the 'young green corn'.

> And Thou wilt bring the young green corn
> The young green corn divinely springing,
> The young green corn for ever singing;
> And when the field is fresh and fair
> Thy blessed feet shall glitter there.[1181]

As with Damerosehay in the two World Wars, it is the things of Christ that are being destroyed as the soldiers fight. Nevertheless, the destruction is not permanent: the corn may be trampled but its singing is "for ever." The evil in humankind is powerless to destroy the eternal music; and so as the battle rages, overhead the larks maintain their song.

Elizabeth said, "I like the book, it is one I actually enjoyed writing."[1182]

❋

In the same year Rosemary Sutcliff also produced a novel about the Civil War. Entitled *The Rider of the White Horse*, it was published with an introduction by Elizabeth Goudge.

A friendship had begun between the two women in 1950. Rosemary Sutcliff remembered that when her first novel came out its illustrator, Walter Hodges, showed the proofs to Elizabeth; whereupon she sent its author a letter, wishing her luck and enclosing a tiny jade elephant as a gift. They exchanged letters and met maybe half a dozen times. Although Sutcliff was twenty years Elizabeth's junior, travel was not easy for her as at the age of two she had been diagnosed with Still's disease, a rare form of juvenile arthritis which eventually confined her to a wheelchair. Jessie remembered at least one visit with her father, when she was "carried in by Commander Sutcliff."

They were both single women with a background of art-school training; each acknowledging the influence of similar childhood reading like *The Wind in the Willows*, the *Just So Stories* and *Puck of Pook's Hill*. Sutcliff also became a Carnegie Medal winner, and in recent years a film has been made of perhaps her most famous children's novel, too: *The Eagle of the Ninth*. According to Jessie, "Rosemary Sutcliff modelled herself on Elizabeth and then went from strength to strength." Certainly some of the beautiful imagery in *The Rider of the White Horse* – for example, a scene where the heroine takes a sprig of rosemary from a silver bowl, and tosses it into a fire made of old ship's timbers - does seem to suggest Elizabeth's influence.

In a generous and fitting tribute to her friend's work: "I can only say, baldly and inadequately, that I love this book," wrote Elizabeth in her preface… "It has qualities of poignancy and gentleness that make it unforgettable."[1183]

Rosemary Sutcliff was, deservedly, among the authors included in a National Portrait Gallery exhibition in 2002, entitled: *Beatrix Potter to Harry Potter – Portraits of children's writers*. It featured images of fifty-four twentieth-century writers with a resumé of their achievements. One, as the title suggests, was J.K. Rowling, and the exhibition catalogue records that she grew up in a house full of books, including *The Wind in the Willows*, but that her favourite book from childhood was Elizabeth Goudge's *The Little White Horse*. Kenneth Graham of course, the creator of Mole, Rat and Mr. Toad, also featured in the exhibition, as did Tolkien and C.S. Lewis. Elizabeth herself curiously did not, despite her Carnegie Medal and the fact that, like these other celebrated authors, her books for children have a universal appeal for readers of all ages. As Alan Hull Walton pointed out, "whether adult or for children didn't matter. *Sister of the Angels* and *Linnets and Valerians* bedazzled me as much as *Green Dolphin Country*."[1184]

Saint Francis of Assisi

1959 marked the twenty-fifth anniversary of Elizabeth's career, and a Prospectus of her work was produced: "designed to help her thousands of admirers to find their way among the various published titles." Under five headings, Novels, Religious, For Children, Short Stories and Miscellaneous, it lists twenty-five titles and their publishers. (In fact her total output was a little greater than this, as *The Fairies' Baby* and *Three Plays* are not listed.) "Nearly 10,000,000 copies of Elizabeth Goudge's books," it says, "have been sold since she first began to write over twenty-five years ago."[1185] The back page lists some Press opinions, including this rhetorical questioning from the *Aberdeen Press and Journal*:

> Quality of writing, breadth of vision, humanity, characters redolent of life in many aspects – what more could you ask in a novel? What else would you expect from Elizabeth Goudge?[1186]

Her new book that year, *Saint Francis of Assisi* generated a glowing tribute from a fellow novelist, Frances Parkinson Keyes. Her critique of *My God and My All* – its American title - in the U.S. *Saturday Review*[1187] begins by quoting Elizabeth's own words about St. Francis:

> *There are a few saints whose light sends such a beam through the darkness of this world that the darkness not only cannot extinguish it but is forced to recognize it and cannot forget it. Francis of Assisi is one of these.'*[1188]

It continues with the observation that every lover of St. Francis should be thankful that Elizabeth Goudge has produced this "tender, wise and moving" biography. For it makes the saint's beam in the darkness "brighter and more far-reaching" than anything Ms Parkinson Keyes has read about him before. She admits that she has, in fact, read everything about St. Francis on which she could lay her hands, but "never has any of it been presented... in such a way as to throw such significance and radiance on the "beam" that it becomes a blazing light."[1189]

Peppard

Reading what Elizabeth says of Francis further reveals his influence on her own work. There is his reverence for trees and woodland: for in the old chronicles about the first Franciscans, she says, "the phrase 'into the wood' comes again and again…"

> *It was their cathedral and they went there to pray. In the aisles of the wood each man could find his own solitude and be undisturbed in his prayer.*[1190]

One thinks of the Eliot family and their guests, for whom Knyghtwood is a place of peaceful retreat, almost of pilgrimage. Individual trees too could have great significance for Elizabeth (surely she named the wood at The Herb of Grace after the Knightwood Oak – at five hundred years old, the largest tree in the New Forest?) "Some trees seem to have an added depth in their living, just as saints have"[1191] she says, and this is John Wentworth's experience in *The Rosemary Tree*:

> *What in the name of wonder had happened to the apple-tree? He knew its fantastic beauty of old, and he thought by heart, but he had never seen it quite like this…The apple-tree was a personality, older than the house, tall and twisted and encrusted with lichen, its widely spread roots clutching the earth with the splayed feet of a giant, its trunk knobbly with knot-holes, its branches flung crazily skyward like the arms of a madman praying. In spite of its fantastic skeleton it was always beautiful…*
>
> *But though the leaves had not come yet, John had never seen it quite so amazingly lovely as today. The whole tree was blazing with light, sparkling, yet so gentle that it did not blind his eyes. Its clean, clear silveriness washed into the dark smelly old kitchen like a wave of sea-water washing into a cave, in and out again, cleansing it. Yet the light had never left the tree and was composed of the myriad minute globes of water with which the mist had spangled every twig. The sun had come out for a moment and been born, a microcosm of itself, in the heart of each globe.*
>
> *"My God," ejaculated John. It was not a profane exclamation but an acknowledgment of a miracle and a revelation.*[1192]

Through Elizabeth's eyes an apple tree becomes a minutely detailed revelation of miracle. This is the 'transfigured commonplace' of which

Michael Mayne writes in *This Sunrise of Wonder*. It is a way of seeing that is not granted to all, he says, quoting William Blake's observation, that "the tree which moves some to tears of joy is in the eyes of others only a green thing which stands in the way."[1193] Beethoven too was aware of the holiness of trees and, in *A Diary of Prayer* praises God for them:

> Almighty One, in the woods I am blessed. Happy everyone in the woods. Every tree speaks through Thee. O God! What glory in the woodland![1194]

Edward Elgar, during the year he spent composing his great sacred work *The Dream of Gerontius* – the year Elizabeth was born - said in a letter, "This is what I hear all day… the trees are singing my music – or have I sung theirs?"[1195]

To St. Francis, "birds and flowers, trees, sunlight and water, were…the Word of God." Within their strict vow of poverty, the first Franciscans "never turned their backs on anything that spoke to them of God's love and care and beauty." And so Saint Clare too, when the Poor Clares were established, did not deny herself "the one Franciscan luxury, flowers…"

> *Her little garden was only a terrace four paces long, but creepers grew over it and in it she planted lilies, roses and violets that they should speak to her of the purity, love and humility of Christ.*[1196]

This then is the key to the symbolism behind the flowers, implicit in so many of Elizabeth's novels. Sometimes, like the lilies of the valley in *The Scent of Water* they are symbolically "nearly strangled by weeds but smelling like heaven."[1197] Sometimes, as in *The Dean's Watch* they are a more mysterious and elusive presence… that "strange scent of violets that comes sometimes in a mild midwinter after shed rain, though there are no violets."[1198]

※

Elizabeth herself had at least one link with a Franciscan order, for in 1972 she would write the foreword to *Daffodils in Ice*, a collection of poems written by an enclosed nun of the Poor Clares.

And another, very personal connection with the monastic life was her lay membership of the Companions of The Society of the Precious Blood, a contemplative Augustinian order at Burnham Abbey. The Sisters there remember that Elizabeth stayed at the Abbey and shortly afterwards took the decision to become a Companion, because she had felt spiritually at home there. Membership of this third Order is for those who "identify with the values of the consecrated life" and "seek to deepen their spiritual life within their daily circumstances." It involves praying for the Sisters, and helping them "in any way that is appropriate for the person concerned; keeping in touch with one Sister who forms the link between the Society and the Companions."[1199]

These Sisters, too, published a small volume of poems entitled *The Mercy of Leaves*, for which again Elizabeth wrote a preface. She pointed out that "the writers of the poems share a common outlook...."

> *Because they see all life and creation irradiated by the love of God they see in depth; a sunrise means more than itself and pain has purpose. Yet the unity of outlook cannot dim the individuality of each separate poem. When love is the creating power it seems impossible for two sparrows' feathers, or even two snowflakes, ever to be the same. The stronger the microscope, the less are they alike. That is the way God likes it.*[1200]

Study Always to Have Joy

One element of the Franciscan life that Elizabeth tried to follow mirrored the resolve she had admired in Robert Louis Stevenson - the determination to create joy.

> *Joy...was a gift to them, the resurrection gift of Christ who said, "Your heart shall rejoice, and your joy no man taketh from you," but in the thought of Francis to be joyful was also a command, as much so as the command to be poor and humble and to walk in love. It was their business to see that their joy was not taken from them. It was a flame to be tended and, if it went out, to be immediately lit again... He would allow no gloomy faces. To a grieving brother he said, "Why dost thou make an outward show of sorrow and sadness for thy offences? Keep thou this sadness between thee and thy God, but before me and others, study always to have joy, for it befits not a servant of God to show... sadness or a troubled face."*[1201]

It seems that Elizabeth took to heart this command to keep these things between herself and God for, although quite a number of her own prayers would be published a few years later, her Prayer When in a Bad

Mood remained firmly within the pages of her notebook. There is no way of knowing when it was written; although it is in the same notebook that contains, among other things, the diary entries of her mother's last illness, and so maybe it was written at that time of great strain, when she was worn out with nursing. It includes these words:

> *Lord, I know I am in a shocking state of mind. In a way I feel perhaps I ought not to be praying at all: I am far too disgruntled for recollection and generosity and good resolutions and all those things which are necessary to Your service. But I know at the same time that it is better to try to pray than merely to give in and indulge any poisonous humour. Possibly if I prayed more, I should be less at the mercy of these glooms.*
>
> *Give me the strength to break myself in as I would a rebellious colt. Show me that the remedy lies in submission to You and not in wallowing in self.*
>
> *Lord, I accept...*[1202]

And she used her prayer's "breaking-in" imagery to describe Francis:

> *When a man is determined to break himself in for God he takes every opportunity for self-conquest that offers itself. No matter how small it is, it brings its added strength...*[1203]
>
> *The serenity of the saints is not necessarily something they are born with, but the fruit of struggle. Robert Bridges says of them, "Their apparent grace is won by discipline of deadly strife." The control is hardly held and can break when a man is tested beyond his strength... It is a comfort to think that even the saints can at times be betrayed by the weakness of the body.'*[1204]

She was too self-deprecating to describe her own struggles as deadly strife – in fact typically suggests "laughable" as a possible adjective in the following paragraph - but we do know that her struggle involved more than simply conquering a bad mood.

> *That there is nothing so therapeutic as work I have proved over and over again, but for many years I had another reason for always fighting to get back to work. I had a perhaps laughable conviction that I had a visiting demon (I saw him once and he was horrible) who brought darkness and was determined that I should not write books.*[1205]

> *[St. Francis] was always acutely aware of the strength and horror of evil, not only the evil of wicked men but that diabolical unseen evil which in the spiritual world is arrayed with such power against the powers of light. He felt often in his own body and mind and soul the tides of the*

> *eternal conflict, and sometimes he would feel himself almost swept away by evil. Like all men of his time he personified in an almost human way the powers that are above and below us, their conflict interpenetrating ours. The angels and the demons were very real to him. In some dark and lonely place he would think he heard a footfall behind him, or the beat of dark wings, and he would be terrified. Yet he never ran away from the terror but stayed and faced it out, for he knew that the power of God is always mightier than any evil that can assail us, and he believed also that God can use even the demons for a good purpose.*[1206]

This terror is reminiscent of Elizabeth's experience on the lonely moorland of Skye - the "loud, shattering, double-rap behind me...like two mighty blows of a door-knocker in quick succession, but much louder. I have sometimes been wakened from sleep at night into a state of momentary fear by this same double rap, but this was infinitely more terrifying and it came from exactly behind me." She did jump to her feet and turn round, but on that occasion did not, like St. Francis, stay and face it out.

> *I was not brave enough to stay, and left the lovely place more precipitately than I have ever left anywhere. I did not actually run but the pace was good and steady and did not slacken until I reached the homely little hotel beside the harbour down below.*[1207]

She always faced and fought down her "visiting demon" however.

> *When I had once more disentangled myself from him and the sun showed signs of coming out again I would write as hard as I could, determined that I would write books and that they should be happy ones. And I think they were, for a dark background to one's life tends to make the happier times happier still...*
>
> *I had been living [at Rose Cottage] for some years when standing in the garden one day, looking across the fields to the woods in the distance and thinking of nothing except their beauty, I had a sudden conviction that my demon had left me for good; torn off me finally by my father. I left the garden and went back into the house full of grateful thanks to my father. All sheer fantasy, probably. The mind is capable of playing any number of tricks upon one; especially a horrifically imaginative mind. Fantasy or not, from that day my demon seemed to retreat.*[1208]

> *[Francis] knew there was no better armour against sin than joy and would say to the brothers, "If the servant of God would study to preserve within and without the spiritual joy which comes of cleanness of heart, and is acquired by devoutness of prayer, the demons would not be able to harm him, for they would say: 'since this servant of God has joy in*

tribulation as in prosperity, we can find no way of entering to him nor of hurting him."[1209]

She describes how even at the end of his life, in the days of his blindness, Francis was able to turn his darkness into joy.

> *Francis lay still in worship. He heard the first flutings of the birds and knew that the sky was lightening. It was no longer a grief to him that he could not see the sun, and would not again see clearly the beauty of earth that he loved so well, for like his suffering it had been given to him as a pledge of heaven. It was passing from him now, for it had done its work, preparing him by its reflections and shadows of blessedness for the heaven of God's love that was to come, encompassing him about with songs of deliverance. Yet in its passing he felt he loved it more dearly than ever, adored God in it and for it as never before and was infinitely grateful for all that God through the beauty of the world had given him and taught him. He had loved his brothers and sisters the birds and animals and flowers but now with heaven so near his thoughts turned not so much to them as to those greater creatures of God, the sun and moon, the stars and winds and waters, and mother earth herself. Joy mounted in him, up and up with the song of the lark as she sprang towards the sun. When the warmth of the new day was on his face... Francis rose from his bed and began to sing.*[1210]

The song Francis composed after his night of suffering was the *Canticle of the Sun*.

Elizabeth's own poem inspired by this - *Spring Song* in *The Little White Horse* - was reprinted in *Woman's Journal* in February 1960 under the title *Thanksgiving for the Earth*.

> *Praised be our Lord for our brother the sun,*
> *Most comely is he, and bright.*
> *Praised be our Lord for our sister the moon,*
> *With her pure and lovely light.*
> *Praised be our Lord for the sparkling bright stars*
> *Encircling the dome of night.*
>
> *Praised be our Lord for the wind and the rain,*
> *For clouds, for dew and the air;*
> *For the rainbow set in the sky above*
> *Most precious and kind and fair.*

Peppard

For all these things tell the love of our Lord,
The love that is everywhere.

Praised be our Lord for our mother the earth,
Most gracious is she, and good,
With her gifts of flowers and nuts and fruit,
Of grass and corn and wood,
For she it is who upholds us in life
And gives us our daily food.

Praised be our Lord for the turn of the year,
For new-born life upspringing;
For buds and for blossoms, for lambs and babes,
For thrush and blackbird singing.
May praise, like the lark, leap up from our hearts,
To Heaven's gate upwinging.[1211]

❉

Her book about Francis complete, and her mind no doubt still full of his love and childlike humility, she then wrote what was surely her greatest novel, *The Dean's Watch*, about the loving Mary Montague, the childlike watchmaker, Isaac Peabody, and the great yet humble Dean.

The Dean's Watch

By the time I came to write The Dean's Watch *I had written about all the places where I had lived except Ely, the best loved, but the Ely book had always been at the back of my mind, waiting... At a time of special quietness at Rose Cottage I knew I was now ready to write that book.*[1212]

"Quiet times are growing times," she said... and her new life had given her more than just the physical peace and quiet of Rose Cottage. As she gradually emerged from the tunnel of war, hard nursing and bereavement, she must have found too, the peace that comes after a time of great anguish, when the stress and strain is finally over. There is a beautiful image in *The Dean's Watch* of calm after storm:

> *The storm had passed and the whole fen lay bathed in spent sunlight. Every stream and stretch of water among the rushes, that had been whipped and tormented by the storm, lay quiet now, reflecting the piled masses of white and silver clouds that floated like swans on the far deep pools of the sky. Every twig was strung with sparkling crystal drops, and every drop had a rainbow caught in its heart.*[1213]

And was this special quietness connected in any way with the sense of her 'demon' being lifted? She does not say, but that experience had left her full of gratitude to her father, and this novel is a wonderful tribute to him. Although the Dean was based on the man she had seen some forty years ago at the Gray's Inn Ball, by the time she came to write about him he had "possessed himself of much of my father's character" she says[1214] – and Adam Ayscough is arguably the greatest of all the great and humble men of God she ever created. She takes a text for the book, from Psalm 68 - as a clergyman would for a sermon - and at the end of the story it becomes the Dean's epitaph: "God is the Lord by whom we escape death."[1215] It is surely no coincidence that Canon Goudge had preached a sermon at Ely based on the same psalm.

So it is a very Christian book, in which many of the characters have some kind of battle to fight; but at the same time, it has elements almost of fairytale. The crooked houses and bulging, lighted shop windows of the Market Square; Isaac Peabody the clockmaker, and little Bella in her bonnet and muff and muslin frock – all of them would be equally at home in Mrs. Molesworth's Victorian fairy-tale (in fact Isaac meets little Bella for the first time when she goes in to buy a cuckoo-clock.) And yet the disparate elements come together in one seamless whole. One delightful theme, yet again, is that of a little child coming into the joyless lives of old people and turning them upside-down with love. In the final book about Damerosehay, David Eliot's little daughter Meg had thus helped Sebastian. And here now is Bella with the childless Dean, and his bachelor man-servant, Garland, who has failed to stop the little girl running unannounced into the Study:

> *"Sir," he panted, "I beg pardon. I tried to stop the young lady, sir, I did indeed but –"*
>
> *He paused, shocked and horrified by what he saw, for Bella was sitting upon the Dean's knee with the umbrella up. From beneath its silken beech-green shade she looked out triumphantly at Garland, her blue*

> *eyes sparkling and her yellow head a froth of dancing curls... The Dean smiled at him and hardly knowing what he was doing he returned the smile, standing stupidly by the door. He was very tired. The past weeks had told on him considerably.*
>
> *"There is no need for you to distress yourself, Garland," said the Dean. "I shall be much obliged if you will ask Cook if there is a sugar biscuit in the house. A glass of milk perhaps. She will know what would be suitable..."*
>
> *******
>
> *Garland entered with a round silver tray scarcely bigger than a water lily leaf. Cook had known what would be suitable. On a small plate, with rosebuds on it, lay an equally small queen cake iced in pink. In a rosebud cup with a gold handle was some warm sugary milk. Having assured himself with a quick glance that the Dean was none the worse for Bella, Garland placed this on the writing table, piled cushions on a chair and lifted her to their summit. His movements as he turned to go were not as precise as usual. The Dean was aware of a slight hesitancy.*
>
> *"Wait, Garland," he said. "Then you can take the tray away." Garland waited. He was a bachelor, having been jilted in youth by a barmaid who had eloped with a sergeant-major in the marines. Devotion to the Dean had largely filled the gap, but watching a young thing eat a sugar cake is one of the major pleasures of life.*[1216]

We know that on occasion, as she had with St. Francis, Elizabeth would use similar material for both short stories and her novels. Thus her children's story *The Easter Bunny*, although it had been published at least twelve years before *The Dean's Watch*, also features an elderly gentleman who transforms the lives of two orphans – and is himself transformed by the joy of their sudden appearance in his hitherto dull world. (And in this tale it is, again, the animals who have the wisdom, for the little girls are led to him when they chase a dancing, mad March hare, very like Serena in *The Little White Horse*.) The gentleman's manservant, like Garland, brings refreshments and piles the chairs with cushions; and he too is loath to depart, "hovering outside the door, waiting to come in and feast his lightened eyes upon them once again." Such is the stupefying effect upon the two elderly men - shaken out of their, until now, unchanging routine – that Mrs. Mason the housekeeper – "a roundabout, white-haired old lady, as kind as they are made" - is "obliged to force them to bestir themselves."[1217]

Let God Arise

> Study this sixty-eighth Psalm for yourselves…and see how, as in Ely Cathedral, the styles of different periods are blended. There is a noble faith from the first; but what shall we say of the savagery…? We are far as yet from the mind of Christ.
>
> But soon there is a change; the arches begin to soar; grace and beauty and tenderness appear. God, while losing nothing of His majesty, is seen to be a God of love to His own people. He sets the solitary in families; He brings the prisoners out of captivity; He refreshes the weary; best of all, He Himself daily bears our burden.[1218]
>
> Henry Leighton Goudge

The Dean's Watch had been inspired, long ago, by the sight of two people very much in love. But when it finally came to be written it was about, not just lovers but love itself: the healing that it brings; the damage done by its lack; the beauty wrought by the creative love of craftsmen. Above all, the love of God. Both the Dean and Mary Montague know that love is "the only indestructible thing. The only wealth and the only reality. The only survival. At the end of it all there [is] nothing else."[1219] It is a reiteration of her father's last words to Elizabeth - "Dear one, it is loving that matters."[1220]

The novel's dedicatee is Mildred Woodgate whose book, *Father Congreve of Cowley*, also has a message about love. "It is not years that make souls grow old," says Father Congreve, "but having nothing to love, nothing to hope for."[1221] And to his great grief, the Dean is a lonely man. His love is rejected even by his wife Elaine, and his elevated social position keeps him aloof from those he would like to love.

> *All his life he had loved children and poor people, and such child-like trusting little oddities as the extraordinary little man sitting opposite to him, all those whom Christ had called "the little ones." But he never knew what to say to them and his unfortunate appearance always frightened them.*[1222]

His forbidding façade, however, is broken open and he finds new friends who bring him great joy – amongst them, little Bella and the young orphaned lovers, Job and Polly. He discovers the truth of Father Congreve's words in *A Book of Comfort* - that "the kindness of youth to old age is an unlooked for delight."[1223]

The novel revolves around two central images, of hiddenness and brokenness. The hiddenness of things is symbolised by the Dean's watch – a beautiful precision instrument made by a great craftsman, and yet the Dean has never looked beyond its exterior; never opened up the gold case to find the working machine at its heart. Seeing only its exterior he takes insufficient care of it, and its consequent brokenness brings it into the grateful hands of that "extraordinary little man" Isaac Peabody, for repair. It is he who fully appreciates the watch, and later reveals to the Dean its hidden beauty.

It becomes a metaphor for the Dean's ministry in the City. The more he looks beyond its façade - looks within to appreciate its intricate workings, and learns from its humbler inhabitants - the more he reveres, loves and cares for them all.

> *Who could have believed that they were there beneath the crust of things? Life had taken on a strange richness since Mr. Peabody had sidled like a terrified crab into his study, had lifted the thin gold shell of his watch and shown him the hidden watchcock.*[1224]

This watchcock is in the form of "a man carrying a burden on his shoulders" just as the Dean, in his hidden prayer life, carries the burden of the city's evil to God.

> *He carried the evil on his own shoulders to the place of prayer, carried it up a long hill in darkness, but willingly. Each time he felt himself alone, yet each time when the weight became too much for him it was shared, then lifted, as though he had never been alone. Yet if there had been no hope of help he would still have been just as willing.*[1225]

Revealing hidden things is not always as simple as opening the pair-cases of a watch, however. Sometimes the process involves the pain of brokenness and yet, when Love is involved, the breaking is always ultimately creative. Evil too has the power to break, of course, but as the Dean reassures Miss Montague, "Evil has hard work to get its hands on what it really wants to destroy... Which has eternal value, this watch or the love that made it?"[1226]

At the climax of the story is the breaking of the exquisite celestial clock, Isaac's masterpiece. It is a tragedy for the old man after all his long and painstaking work, but the Dean tries to console him, too, with his own understanding of the holy mystery of brokenness:

> "Mr. Peabody, I beg that you will listen to me and endeavour to believe what I say. The love that created and gave the clock is of more value because the clock is broken. It has entered into eternity, as does the soul when the body fails and dies."[1227]

The Dean's death at the end of the novel proves the truth of his words; dying, he brings to fruition so much of what he had tried and failed to achieve in his lifetime. In his will he leaves to his new friend Isaac Peabody "my watch and my faith in God," and for the old clockmaker there is only one response to the Dean's bequest; he must overcome his life-long fear, and go into the Cathedral.

In Elizabeth's own memory of Ely, "The cathedral dominated everything, always. Wherever you went in the Fen country you had only to look up and see it there. Towering up above the scared yet exultant ants of human creatures it sucked into its dark porches it was always, in all weathers, whether its mood was terrible or beautiful, a symbol of eternal life."[1228] This towering church that Isaac must enter is, then, the symbol of eternal life; of the God by whom we escape death. He wrestles with real fear as he finally approaches its doors for the first time.

> *Suddenly he was terrified… The Cathedral soared like a towering black wave that would presently crash down on him and knock him into the abyss. Unable to move he stood there sweating with terror.*[1229]

But love for his friend is leading him, broken by grief, to open the door and find what lies within - just as he had opened the watchcase for the Dean to reveal its hidden heart. Isaac must go in, but like the plunge into black waters in *Henrietta's House*, he has to go through terrifying darkness in order to find peace and light.

> *The Porch of the Angels…looked like the threshold of a great pit… He plunged into the darkness…stumbled through it and fumbled at the great iron-bound door. It had a handle but in his fear he did not see it… He was in a panic now because the great door would not yield when he pushed it, and he beat on it with his fists. It was opened quietly from within by the bedesman, and he passed in.*

> *The splendour seemed to fall upon him like a vast weight, but the door had closed behind him and he could not go back. He began to creep up the nave, seeing nothing, for after the first glance he had kept his eyes on the ground. He saw only the ancient paving stones, worn into hills and valleys by the tread of many feet. They were stained with colour because the midday sun was shining through the south windows... [He] sat down, his head on his chest and his hands between his knees. He noticed that the colour that lay upon the paving stones was lapping over his old cracked boots. Now and then a small cloud passed over the sun and it faded but a moment later it was back again. His breathing grew a little easier and his sight cleared.*
> *Beyond the toes of his boots was...a flat black marble slab let into the floor. Words were cut upon it, "God is the Lord by whom we escape death", and above that the name of his friend, and the date, and that he had been Dean. The colour was lying on the dark slab just as it was lying on Isaac's boots. Just that, he thought, only that. He liked the simplicity but he could not understand why they had put those words. The Dean had not escaped death. His grave was under that stone.*
>
> *He did not move on any further for he was tired, and still he did not look up, but he began to feel less frightened... Beyond the sunlit patch was the terror of the Cathedral but here there was a homeliness. And something more. He had been bitterly cold when he climbed up the steps to the porch but now he was glowing with warmth. He felt as though someone had wrapped him about with a comfortable old coat...*[1230]

It is the beginning of his inheritance.

> *Faith in God. God. A word he had always refused. But the Dean had said, put the word love in its place. He did just that, speaking to this warmth... "Bring us, O Love, at our last awakening, into the house and gate of heaven."*[1231] *The words had slipped as gently into his mind as the colour came and went over his boots. Just lately so many things that the Dean had said to him were coming back to his memory. He had scarcely attended to them at the time but they must have sunk down below the surface of his mind to its deeps, because now they were slowly being given back to him. Sentence by sentence he quietly remembered the whole prayer. Though it said, "at our last awakening" he felt himself to be already in the house. It wasn't any different anywhere else to what it was here. If he moved on through the Cathedral all of it would be as homely as it was here because of this warmth, and when the house*

lights went up the great darkness would be full of friendly faces... He was at home.[1232]

❄

Towering above the novel's trinity of protagonists - the Dean, Isaac Peabody and Mary Montague - is this even greater character of the Cathedral itself. It not only dominates the landscape but has a central role in all their lives.

The powerful impact of a great church was nothing new in Elizabeth's work of course. As early as 1939, in *Sister of the Angels* Henrietta had already experienced something of Isaac's fear – "an unaccustomed feeling of panic" – within the cathedral.

Everywhere was this sense of space and height and a reaching out to an end that was never found... The place in its eternal greatness and grandeur seemed to her as frightening as life itself.[1233]

And she too had been very aware of the mystery of the fractured sunlight which "came through the stained glass windows curiously changed, split up into reds and blues and greens, robbed of its brightness and subdued to the colours of mystery."[1234]

Evelyn Underhill, whose words had inspired the central trinity of *Green Dolphin Country*, used similar images in her *Light of Christ* – a collection of Retreat addresses on prayer that were given at Pleshey in 1932, although not published until after her death in 1941, two years after *Sister of the Angels*. Underhill says metaphorically that to go inside ourselves to the hidden place of contemplative prayer is like entering a great church which one has been told has magnificent windows –although seen from outside they have no beauty. It is only when we open the door and Go In, that we are bathed in the light that streams through them. Just as the colours of stained-glass break up the white light, which might otherwise dazzle us; so in contemplative prayer "the windows of Christ's Mysteries [are] split it up into many-coloured loveliness..."[1235]

Mary Montague

If the Dean is the greatest of all Elizabeth's fictional clergymen then Mary, this great woman of prayer, is arguably his equal. So important is she to this novel that almost an entire chapter is devoted to her life story… which is also her journey of faith. It begins with brokenness. As a small child she suffers a broken leg; and then comes the hard realisation that her consequent lameness has broken all her youthful dreams too - of marriage, wonderful adventures, a successful career. If all her dreams will never now come true, then what is she to do with her life?

> *She never knew what put it into her head that she, unloved, should love.*[1236]

Mary's faith journey has begun, and in its detailed depiction one can hear again occasional echoes of Underhill's *Light of Christ*, which states, for example, that contemplation is not a thing of the emotions, nor some kind of "pious daydream," but a selfless concentration on the mysteries of Christ.

> *She took a vow to love. Millions before her had taken the same simple vow but she was different from the majority because she kept her vow, kept it even after she had discovered the cost of simplicity. Until now she had only read her Bible as a pious exercise, but now she read it as an engineer reads a blueprint and a traveller a map, unemotionally because she was not emotional, but with a profound concentration because her life depended on it.*[1237]

It means, too, putting aside any idea of an "easy-going religion"[1238] and being prepared to put oneself totally into God's hands, without reserve of love, or fear of suffering.

> *Bit by bit over a period of years, that seemed to her long, she began to get her scaffolding into place. She saw that all her powers, even those which had seemed to mitigate against love, such as her shrewdness which had always been quick to see the faults of others, her ambition and self-will, could by a change of direction be bound over in service to the one overmastering purpose. She saw that she must turn from herself, and began to see something of the discipline that that entailed, and found too*

as she struggled that no one and nothing by themselves seemed to have the power to entirely hold her when she turned to them.

It was then that the central figure of the gospels, a historical figure whom she deeply revered and sought to imitate, began at rare intervals to flash out at her like live lightning from their pages, frightening her, turning the grave blueprint into a dazzle of reflected fire. Gradually she learned to see that her fear was not of the lightning itself but what it showed her of the nature of love, for it dazzled behind the stark horror of Calvary.

At this point, where so many vowed lovers faint and fail, Mary Montague went doggedly on over another period of years that seemed if possible longer and harder than the former period. At some point along the way, she did not know where because the change came so slowly and gradually, she realised that he had got her and got everything. His love held and illumined every human being for whom she was concerned, and whom she served with the profound compassion which was their need and right, held the Cathedral, the city, every flower and leaf and creature, giving it reality and beauty. She could not take her eyes from the incredible glory of his love. As far as it was possible for a human being in this world she had turned from herself. She could say, "I have been turned," and did not know how very few can speak these words with truth.[1239]

❄

Perhaps in this story there is an echo of Elizabeth's own lived experience too, for in mid-life Mary's old and ailing parents prop their whole weight upon her ("*How exhausted she was by…her mother's asthmatic heart and querulous temper*") and she finds herself in a muddle of exhaustion and depression that all but destroys her faith.

> *She was used to feeling exhausted and paid no attention to it, for it was her normal state, but this abysmal fatigue both of body and mind was not her normal state. She was in darkness.*[1240]

It is during a rare chance to escape from her duties for an hour ("*like a truant from school…and the air seemed fresh and sweet after her mother's overheated bedroom*") that she too, like Isaac, finds peace and rest in the Cathedral. Underhill talked about the dim vault above the great pillars of the Cathedral where the Christ is to be found: "the Figure…the Son, so far above us and yet so divinely near"[1241] - and for Mary Montague it is not the light from the windows, but an experience of being alone in the Cathedral's darkness that restores her faith in the Man on the rood.

> *It was very dark in the Cathedral, except for the glow of the large charcoal braziers that were lit here and there... Vast curtains of shadow fell from the invisible roof and they seemed to move like a tide of dark water...*
>
> *And high up in the darkness that her sight could not penetrate he was there upon the rood. Her hands folded in her lap Miss Montague shut her eyes, for she was very tired. She ceased to feel lonely...*
>
> *The man on the rood [was there], sharing the same darkness with her and with a vast multitude of people whom she seemed to know and love.*[1242]

She begins to understand the darkness and unbelief. And still there are echoes of Evelyn Underhill, who says that Christ's mysteries reveal to us the "reality of beauty and holiness" and the "messy unreality of most of our own lives."[1243]

> *How much more friendly it is when you cannot see, thought Miss Montague, and how much closer we are to him. Why should we always want a light? He chose darkness for us, darkness of the womb and of the stable, darkness in the garden, darkness on the cross and in the grave. Why do I demand certainty? That is not faith. Why do I want to understand? How can I understand this great web of sin and ugliness and love and suffering and joy and life and death when I don't understand the little tangle of good and evil that is myself?*
> *I've enough to understand. I understand that he gave me light that I might turn to him, for without light I could not have seen to turn. I have seen creation in his light. He shared his light with me that I, turned, might share with him the darkness of his redemption. Why did I despair? What do I want? If it is him I want he is here, not only love in light illumining all that he has made but love in darkness dying for it...*[1244]

The similarities with Evelyn Underhill were perhaps not deliberate - as Elizabeth said, personal belief came into her books apparently without her knowledge or contriving - but it would be more than appropriate if this novel about hidden things should itself have a hidden meaning. Looked at in the light of Underhill's words, *The Dean's Watch* acquires a whole new level of significance. The invitation to go in to the cathedral becomes metaphorically an invitation to the life of contemplative prayer. It is surely no coincidence that what Miss Montague finds there, in the darkness, is paradoxically a way out of her darkness, as she makes the vow:

> *I will learn to pray.*

It is a promise that changes her life and the focus of her work.

❋

Had Elizabeth, too, made just such a promise at this new stage in her life? Even though she had had a lifetime of faith, and many years of praying as her father had taught her, with an intention?[1245] (Miss Montague had come to understand "however dimly, that to draw some tiny fraction of the sin of the world into her own being with this darkness was to do away with it."[1246])

A prayer life requires self-discipline, but contemplative prayer needs stillness and quiet, and despite the inspiration of her father's spiritual direction it cannot have been easy for Elizabeth to undertake the work of prayer in the years following his death, with her mother to care for and the constant commitment to write. Those years in the dark tunnel, particularly towards the end, may have been too demanding for her to take time out really to pray as she might wish (she actually says in her Bad Mood prayer: *perhaps if I prayed more...*) But now she had discovered 'certain things' that could only grow out of the kind of peace and quiet she found at Rose Cottage... a deepening prayer-life, surely, was one of these. It is more than likely, too, that she was by now a Companion of the contemplative Order at nearby Burnham Abbey, whose work involves "reaching out on behalf of others to the source of all love and goodness, and holding before Christ the pain and suffering of the world."[1247]

And yet she seems to say in *The Joy of the Snow* that the contemplative way of prayer was still something she herself had not experienced.

> *I could never understand why [my mother] turned away from the prayer of silence and of contemplation. When she was praying, as soon as the prayer of silence began gently to take her, she would break off. The thing which so many of us, myself for instance, so desperately long for, and are too self-centred to receive, she could have had, and she refused it.*[1248]

So perhaps Elizabeth's books describe a way of prayer she had only read about, or more recently observed at Burnham Abbey? And yet it is difficult to believe that she is not, at least in part, writing of her own experience, for it is a feature of all the books so far created at Rose Cottage. In *Saint Francis of Assisi* she tells of

that threshold of heaven that is always there for us, like an old church porch in a street where the traffic thunders by, if only we can manage to forget ourselves and our busyness for long enough to become conscious of it, to get out of the traffic and go in.[1249]

And in *The Rosemary Tree* this deepening prayer was something Harriet experienced in her later years.

The birds' voices woke her that morning, and she lay listening to them while she watched the changing sky. What did the voices mean? The longer she lived the more deeply aware did she become of profundities of meaning in everything about her. To grow old was to become less aware of the normal aspect of things, which hitherto you had taken for granted as all that there was, and to sink more deeply into the darkness of their meaning. As she watched and listened, the bright clouds and the birds' voices became as a growing darkness. She fought against it for a moment, not wanting to waste the colour and the sound, then yielded, for the darkness was a better thing than either.[1250]

Froniga, too, had

come back full-circle to a loneliness that could scarcely be called loneliness any longer, so deeply had she found union with the source and end of her being and so companionable did she find the Way that led from one to the other... This companionship contained within itself all that she longed for.[1251]

Elizabeth said she was unable to receive the prayer of silence that she so desperately longed for. Nonetheless, that period of exhaustion after her mother's death had surely brought the same benefit to her faith-life as it did to Miss Montague's – that although she had appeared to be breaking up, in fact 'the enforced lengthening of the tired intervals between one thing and another meant more time to learn the work of prayer.' Perhaps this is what she meant by 'those quiet times in life when nothing much happens and yet when a great deal happens that cannot be put into words.'

Peace of Mind

There was no peace at the launching of a new book, however; *The Dean's Watch* generated the usual round of magazine serialisation, critical review and interviews. One journalist who beat a path to her door was Kenneth Allsop, and certain things about this book and its author seem to have intrigued him. Not least that such a book, written by someone with the label of Romantic Novelist should be so popular in 1960. (Allsop, as the author of *The Angry Decade: A survey of the Cultural Revolt of the 1950s*, knew much about current trends in literature and theatre.) Perhaps most intriguing of all was the fact that its author should prove to be, on acquaintance, not at all the stereotypical writer of romantic novels he had been expecting.

In fact his opening sentences for the Book Page of the *Daily Mail* suggest that what Allsop experienced at Rose Cottage was - not the usual promotional author-interview - but an encounter with a woman who made a profound effect upon him. He begins by telling his readers that when he met Elizabeth Goudge he discovered in her that "rarest human condition," peace of mind.[1252]

And over and above her fame as a romantic novelist she was also, he concluded, a "successful person" - not just because her novels sold "an effortless 50,000 copies each" but "in a sense that is both profounder and simpler – in her attainment of serenity and self-abnegation." By the standards of the rat-race, he says, she is "probably a mouse." And by those of the "literary pace-makers and fashion-setters she is perhaps quaintly archaic," in that her books are about goodness, kindness, virtue, charity, piety and spirituality.

> Yet Miss Goudge does not regard these old-fashioned values that are her material as marketable commodities. They are her own experience and her own beliefs.[1253]

He cannot resist one mocking reference to the sterotypical romantic novel – a reference that bears no recognisable resemblance to any of Elizabeth's books, incidentally, and certainly not to *The Dean's Watch* - and yet he concludes his article with words almost of homage, saying that although in peaceful Rose Cottage she is living "geographically a far cry from the heat and broil of life," curiously, Miss Goudge, the gentlewoman writer, seemed to me to be at its still centre.[1254]

Elizabeth said in this interview,

I believe that peace of mind is the most precious thing you can have. It is also the most difficult thing to find. You have to win it. How? I suppose only by courage and patience, and not going under. As a deeply religious woman, I believe that peace of mind can be found only in God. That is not a widely held view today. It isn't one I consciously try to propagate in my books, but perhaps those ideas do come through.

It was not a widely held view. Describing the life and times of her near contemporary R.S. Thomas, his biographer Byron Rogers said he was writing about religious faith at a time when, "for many, this seemed little more than whimsy."[1255] And Thomas of course was a clergyman, and a highly respected poet: what level of whimsy, then, would some critics condemn in a writer of popular fiction? More than sufficient for her to be dismissed as a lightweight writer of facile happy endings, whenever they encountered the faith that "came through" in her books. Little wonder, therefore, that she told Kenneth Allsop, "It rather hurts my feelings to be labelled a romantic novelist."

Then she laughed.

No, I take that back. I suppose I do write romantic novels. They are escape stories. Everyone should be concerned with the events and troubles in the world around, but there must be escape from them at times...I know that the accusation against the romantic novel is that it simplifies human problems and conflicts. Still I don't think there is anything wrong in making a fairy story of life. There are many happy moments, many good and worthwhile things.[1256]

Beneath the almost fairytale setting of *The Dean's Watch* there are indeed human problems and conflicts. There is the apprentice Job, running away from the beatings of his drunken master; the Dean's struggle to rid the city of its slums; the pain of his unhappy marriage; the psychological damage inflicted on Isaac by his tyrannical father, which drives him at times to drink; Miss Montague's unhappy childhood; Emma's spiteful jealousy of the young lovers that causes the precious clock to be broken... And although Elizabeth was an outsider in the Angry Decade, there is even anger in this novel - the Dean's, as he campaigns against social evils:

His terrible anger uncovered the deplorable state of the workhouse, and revealed to a horrified city the conditions under which women and girls worked in the labour gangs in the fens. He exposed graft, exploitation of children and the weak, hypocrisy and greed wherever he found them.[1257]

The *Times'* obituary said that Elizabeth "followed Jane Austen's advice 'to let other pens dwell on guilt and misery.'"[1258] Certainly her pen did not *dwell*; but neither did it ignore.

Despite the underlying conflicts in this novel, however, it was definitely not in the contemporary realist genre; and the book's success in 1960 is the more remarkable because of this change in the way of looking at the world. It affected a whole generation of authors; like Daphne du Maurier, whose career spanned roughly the same years as Elizabeth: 1931 to 1977. Margaret Forster's biography says that after the publication of her novel, *The Scapegoat* in 1957, she realized that the style of her work was not now "in sympathy with the trend towards the realistic fiction she hated," and although she "had it in her" to alter her style, she did not want to; her desire was to remain "true to an older tradition."[1259]

As Kenneth Allsop points out in some wonderment, in staying true to her own vision Elizabeth did *not* sacrifice her popularity in a changing world. She herself confirmed that the new tradition was at odds with her own view:

I don't read many contemporary novels. That isn't because I object to authors dealing with social problems. I think perhaps some of them rather deliberately dwell on the grim aspects of life, make the whole world seem ugly and squalid.[1260]

This was a view she still held to in 1972, when writing her article on Historical Novels for the *RNA News*.

It is easier to be a realist than a romantic. And by a realist I do not mean someone who has the courage to confront pain and tragedy steadily, to seek it out in order to stay with it and try to be of use, even be torn in pieces by it if necessary rather than hide or run away. This is a different sort of creature altogether, this is a saint, and I can't recollect that any saint I ever heard of was ever a writer...

No, the sort of realist I am thinking of wears not rose-coloured spectacles but telescopic lenses and concentrates upon the filth in the gutter, and the spots and wrinkles of the human face, and describes what he sees with the greatest possible exactitude. Anyone can do it with a little practice, and if you stand in your own light it does not matter because what you are looking at is mostly darkness, and we live in a dark and evil age.[1261]

Nearly thirty-five years on, it is the same message as *Towers in the Mist*: that the descent into darkness represents the *easy* option. Her father had expressed his own concern about contemporary literature, in his 1935 book,

The Apocalypse and the Present Age. (Dr. Goudge considered the theatre "of the greatest importance in national life and he liked to study it."[1262]) He said,

> The world's standard of purity has never been high, and Christian standards are often today openly repudiated. It is not merely that in novels and plays the old Victorian reticence is cast aside; for this there may be an arguable case; there is also a great deal that is gross and immoral with the trail of the serpent plainly seen upon it. Few of us are people to whom this is harmless. Immoral books and plays affect us as detective stories of burglary and murder do not. There are novels, like those of Dostoieffsky [sic] which have much of the spirit of Christ; and novels like those, for the most part of the Victorians which are wholesome and often instructive. The same is true of plays. But there has surely been a marked change for the worse; and, if at our places of entertainment Jezebel looks out of the window, we ought not to go in till Jezebel has been thrown out.[1263]

Michael in *The Rosemary Tree* too, had been aware of the potential for harm – the power of our dark thoughts to infect the lives of others.

> *It was a small library entirely lined with books. Michael gave an exclamation of pleasure. They'd have Cervantes there. They'd have Chaucer and Malory, Trollope and Jane, and all the writers in whom he delighted because they wrote of a world in which men did not live on the edge of a volcano, counting out the last minutes before the flames… Their laughter while they did it set one's teeth on edge and drove one to do rotten things.*[1264]

The actress Joan Plowright was a part of the angry decade, achieving some of her most acclaimed successes in the realist style of theatre, and acknowledging in her autobiography how exciting it was to be part of that new movement. Nevertheless, an experience of *Romeo and Juliet* at the Aldwych Theatre brought her to a similar conclusion about the spiritual importance of literature. Shakespeare is always so "strengthening…beautiful and timeless" she says, whereas in the aftermath of the Angry Brigade there seemed "so little new inspiration." Indeed far from being strengthening like Shakespeare, after a time these "ordinary, domestic plays about ordinary domestic life" seemed "a bit deadening."[1265]

Beyond the Snow

Elizabeth's belief in the importance of concentrating upon the light was shared by Ruth Pitter. In the preface to her *Collected Poems* of 1968 Pitter said,

> I have not ignored the aches and pains; but neither have I wished to propagate them. They will be heard now and then, but our private sorrows, at least, can be largely consumed by a sort of internal combustion…
>
> To vary the metaphor, I think it is a pity, when even a few drops of the wine of delight are to be had, to let too much of the waters of affliction get into them; so that we must, as it were, be always baling.[1266]

Not all contemporary novelists focused upon the gutter, however: fortunately there were still writers of vision – notably one of the great academics of her Oxford years.

In our hearts every one of us would like to create a new world, less terrible than this one, a world where there is at least a possibility that things may work out right. The greatest writers are able to do this. In The Lord of the Rings *Professor Tolkien has created a world that is entirely new and if the book ends in haunting sadness, Frodo and Sam do at least throw the ring in the fire.*[1267]

Love of Creation

Tolkien's fictional world was the source of the collective nickname Elizabeth and Jessie gave to their first three dogs: The Hobbits. For they had discovered that Dandie-Dinmonts, like Hobbits, love to live in tunnels and holes; and are adept at 'disappearing swiftly and silently' on their large furry feet.[1268] By now their beloved Tiki had died and a new Dandie puppy had arrived at Rose Cottage. In an April letter to Audrey she tells her "I am at last struggling along towards the end of my new book" [*The Scent of Water*] and "I would love to dedicate it to you if you wouldn't mind." She adds, "Miranda – our dog – is now seven months old and an absolute darling."[1269] Unlike the first of the Hobbits, the ragamuffin Tiki, Miranda is described in

The Joy of the Snow as "our beautiful filmstar dog… a fine lady who liked to pose on silken cushions."[1270]

❋

The December edition of *Woman's Journal* in 1961 carried the short story that would later appear in her Christmas anthology as *Christmas on the Moor*. Its title in the magazine however was Shakespeare's phrase, *The Bird of Dawning* [1271]- very appropriate for Elizabeth, with her great love of birds. In a 1960s letter she told Audrey,

I feel very bird-minded just now for I feed them every day and in this bitter cold weather they get so tame. Fieldfares came yesterday. I hate the cold but I do enjoy the birds.[1272]

There is so much in Elizabeth's work that betrays her love of birds, from gulls and larks, through thrush and woodpecker – which she would call by their old country names of stormcock and yaffingale - to the cockcrow at dawn, and the symbolic blue bird in the ilex tree at Damerosehay. She loved their colours, the patterns and freedom of their flight and the joy of their song. Even as a small child, one of the things that struck her most forcibly about visits to Uncle James and Aunt Emma's country house was that "at night in the deep stillness of the Sussex countryside the nightingales sang."[1273] (Although there was always darkness mixed in with the light of course. She told a friend how in order to attract butterflies to the garden, she and Jessie had planted two buddleias: "but we cannot enjoy the butterflies because the gangs of sparrows who afflict us kill them. It is heartbreaking to see the lovely wings torn off and lying on the grass."[1274])

Several of her books have images of swans in flight – flying upriver at Damerosehay with a rhythmic beating of their great wings; or in *The Dean's Watch* Isaac's vision after the Dean's death, of two flying swans with "the golden light touching their wings and breasts."[1275] In line with the book's text, this has an echo of Psalm 68: of the dove with its wings "covered with silver, and her feathers with yellow gold."[1276] But it surely also borrows from a legend recorded by an old friend of her father's, the author Edith Olivier, that whenever a Bishop of Salisbury dies, two white birds are seen in the sky. Miss Olivier had herself seen two such birds flying over the Wiltshire water-meadows when Bishop Wordsworth died in 1911.[1277]

When Elizabeth compiled her *Diary of Prayer* - published in 1966 - she introduced each of the twelve sections with a poem. The one she chose for her birth-month is a translation of the fourteenth-century Welsh poet Dafydd

Beyond the Snow

ap Gwilym: his description of a sacramental experience of early morning birdsong.

> While it was yet neither quite bright nor dark,
> I heard a new and wonderful High Mass.
> The Chief Priest was the nightingale: the lark
> And thrush assisted him: and some small bird
> (I do not weet his name) acted as Clerk.
> My spirit was lapped in ecstasy…
>
> Heaven is a state wherein bliss and devotion mingle,
> And such was mine this morn : I could have died
> Of rapture…[1278]

Rapture for the music of the dawn birds, and - in that same letter to Audrey - for "the marvellous sunrises I see from my window across the snowy fields," and the morning stars.

This morning there was a marvellous sky of stars. I have a queer sort of sight – if I don't have my spectacles on any point of light becomes a brilliant five-pointed star. A marvellous star arose in the east and moved slowly across the sky until it stood over the church, then it vanished into some trees. As it was Epiphany morning, until I heard the hum of the plane's engine, I could think it was the star of Bethlehem. It really was lovely to see.[1279]

The same mediaeval Welsh poet praises the stars too, in *A Book of Peace*:

> Blessed be the Maker's name
> By whose craft stars were fashioned,
> For there is nothing brighter
> Than the small, round, pure-white star.
> The high heaven's light it is,
> A clear and steady candle…[1280]

❄

Elizabeth's books always reflect the two worlds - not only the sublime, but the way life can, and so often does, plummet to its opposite. And so after rapturous birdsong and Epiphany starlight comes the unintentional irony in the title of her next novel. For just before publication of *The Scent of Water* she and Jessie were without water in the cottage for six weeks. As the *RNA News* reported,

Rural living was described as considerably less than ideal in such winters as 1962/3 when they were completely frozen up in Dog Lane, The water from the well proved brackish, and snow-melting unsatisfactory.[1281]

It was a worse winter even than 1947, when she had written parts of *The Herb of Grace* wrapped in her eiderdown. *The Daily Telegraph* called it the most severe season in living memory. Elizabeth told Audrey on 4th January that "the snow blizzards did not start with us until the 27th. Since then we have been buried in snow. The lane is full of drifts but the tradesmen can get down to us on foot, so we are luckier than many people."[1282] And as far as the water supply was concerned humour saved the day, for Elizabeth told the RNA:

Fortunately the farm at the bottom of my garden has a piggery and the pigs seem to have generated sufficient heat to keep one pipe unfrozen. We ran a hosepipe from this into the tank in my bathroom and so Jessie and I were able to have baths on alternate days![1283]

Appleshaw

For the setting of the new book she had returned again to Oxfordshire and the Chilterns, but not this time to Rose Cottage. Mary Lindsay's home in *The Scent of Water* is surely yet another house from her childhood: Nanny's parents' home in Bath. As ever Elizabeth could recall it in detail, even though she only visited infrequently - "if there was an aunt handy to be with my mother" - and then stayed only "for a short while." It had all the fascination for a child of a house hidden away within a walled garden.

On arrival, having got out of the cab and paid the cabby, the traveller faced the high stone wall that surrounded the house and garden... There was a strong door in the wall, an iron chain with a ring on it hanging to one side. This, one pulled and a bell sounded far away in the depths of the house.[1284]

Beyond the garden door was discovered "a short stone-paved path arched over by a curved iron roof green with age, supported by iron posts on each side." And then Mary, Nanny's older sister (who had borne the brunt of Elizabeth's bad behaviour when her mother was away in Bath) "appeared in the wide darkness at the open front door, smiling a welcome." On stepping over the threshold, one discovered that

> *The hall was stone-floored, large and dark as a cave. Worn stone steps led up to the kitchen upon one side and upon the other was the large dining-room... Beyond the dining room was an exquisite little parlour which was only used on Sundays.*[1285]

Her fictional evocation of this remembered house is indicative of Elizabeth's deep sense of place in childhood; and of her ability to use and combine her own memories to create an equally memorable world for her readers. To reach the village in *The Scent of Water* the child Mary had had to pass through an avenue of lime trees; ("Ain't another lime avenue like this in all the county," says the boy driving their pony trap.[1286]) But this is not recorded among Elizabeth's Bath memories; it is more likely, the "double lime avenue nearly a hundred yards wide" that Myfanwy Piper describes in the *Shell Guide to Oxfordshire*.[1287] Elizabeth would surely have seen this: if she made the journey to visit Ruth Pitter at Long Crendon, say; or if, perhaps, Jessie had taken her to the site of the Battle of Chalgrove nearby, as research for *The White Witch*. As she says of the creative process: "A book begins with falling in love. You lose your heart to a place, a house, an avenue of trees..."[1288]

Beyond the fictional limes is "a remote village in the Chilterns" called Appleshaw; and set down within it... surely, Nanny's home in Bath.

> *Opposite the lych-gate of the church lilacs grew in a tangled mass behind a garden wall. In the wall was a green door under a stone archway. It had a round brass handle and beside it was an ancient rusted iron bellpull... The lilacs had grown so tall that their branches hung over the wall and over the arch above the door. Four steps led up to the door and they were very worn in the middle. What could be behind the door Mary couldn't imagine. Not the world she knew. The thicket of purple and white blossom, the door and the steps, were like a picture painted a long time ago, and it horrified her to see the boy dragging the bellpull out of the wall and hanging on to it while a solemn peal sounded far away, muffled and sad, as though it rang at the bottom of the sea. One did not ring the doorbells of painted pictures...*
> *The door opened inwards very slightly... She hung back, then grabbing at her courage she pushed through with her father behind her. The door shut behind them and they were in a scented darkness. At least that was how it seemed to her at first as she stood on worn paving stones with her back to the door... It had seemed dark but now the light was silver. The paving stones were those of a narrow paved passage with four*

> *delicate fluted pillars on each side. The roof was made of wooden beams holding the weight of a great wisteria vine that entirely covered them and hung down in curtains of scent and colour on either side. Beyond the leaves and flowers Mary was dimly aware of birds singing in a garden.*
>
> *At the end of the passage a little old woman in a black dress, with snowy mob cap and apron, stood at an open door smiling and holding out her hand.*[1289]

When Mary next returns to the house as an adult, it is her own – her inheritance from her cousin – and as she explores, the layout of the house is revealed. But first, she must step into darkness.

> *She had forgotten just how dark this hall was. It seemed like a cave, and from the depths of it there came a dank breath of mildew and mice.*
>
> *It was then that Mary had her one moment of panic, frightful panic, as though the earth was suddenly opening under her feet... But it was too late to turn back now...*
>
> *She stepped over the threshold of the house and came into the stone-flagged hall... There were two doors to the left, the dining-room and parlour she supposed, and to the right two stone steps led up to a door which, like the one in the garden wall, was set within a stone arch. It drew her, it was so attractive and she went quickly up the steps, lifted the latch and stepped suddenly into warmth and light.*
>
> *It was a big old-fashioned kitchen...*[1290]

One of Mary's vivid memories of her childhood visit was of a silver tankard of lilies of the valley in the hall. But on her arrival decades later of course, "there were no lilies of the valley in a silver tankard to make light in a dark place." Nevertheless she discovers that the little white flowers are still there, growing just outside the kitchen door.

> *There was a bed of lilies-of-the-valley growing under the window, nearly strangled by weeds but smelling like heaven. She was tired and confused indeed, for the next thing she knew she was outside on her knees grubbing up the weeds to give the lilies light and air. And then she was picking a bunch of them...*[1291]

Like the unearthing of the white deer in *The Herb of Grace*, the finding of the lilies is the first symbolic step towards what is at the heart of her old cousin's legacy – the rediscovery of her faith.

The Scent of Water

> O Father, help us to know that the hiding of Thy face is wise love. Thy love is not fond, doting and reasonless. Thy bairns must often have the frosty cold side of the hill, and set down both their bare feet amongst the thorns: Thy love hath eyes, and in the meantime is looking on. Our pride must have winter weather.[1292]
> George MacDonald in *A Diary of Prayer*

It is somehow fitting that *The Scent of Water* appeared after such a bleak winter because it deals with mental illness, that bleak and hard thing that Elizabeth had had to cope with both in her own life and her mother's.

Like *The Dean's Watch*, the new novel had a Bible text as its epigraph. Appropriately enough, it comes from the Book of Job: for this is a story about the struggle to accept, not rebel; about the need to hold on, even in the darkest times to the belief that through "the scent of water" - God's grace - even a life that is felled and broken can bud again and bring forth fruit.

> For there is hope of a tree, if it be cut down, that it will sprout again, and that the tender branch thereof will not cease. Though the root thereof wax old in the earth, and the stock thereof die in the ground; yet through the scent of water it will bud, and bring forth boughs like a plant.[1293]

Uniquely among her books, this novel starts with a death; but it is right that it should, for old Mary Lindsay's dying brings about a fresh beginning. Like the Dean's death it bears fruit; for her cousin's daughter – her namesake - begins a completely new life when she inherits all that Mary has to give: her cottage, her peaceful village life… and her diaries. Again like the Dean, Mary passes on her faith like a bequest, for through the diaries her story slowly unfolds, revealing to a new generation her struggles with illness, her rebellion against her fate, and her search for God. All this the younger Mary learns, alongside the history of her home and its environs. Thus as the diaries' contents are gradually made known the novel becomes multi-layered - a kind of timeless story of everyman - as the different generations find, through the same, ongoing struggle, acceptance and faith in God.

Just as *The Dean's Watch* had celebrated the value of brokenness, so too in *The Scent of Water* we find characters who are "cracked pitchers."[1294] Cousin Mary's life is blighted by her recurring mental illness; and a legend recorded in her diary reveals that centuries before, William the Hunchback's physical disability had similarly plunged him into despair. The restrictions imposed on their lives seem at first, as for Mary Montague in the previous novel, like a closed door shutting them away from all life's joys; and yet like her, they each find an alternative and deeper joy in a growing awareness of God and an increasing love for Him and all creation.

Like Miss Montague, too, they discover that this finding is dependent upon *acceptance* of their brokenness; acceptance of the lack of those joys that will never be theirs. It is dependent upon a letting-go of the rebellion and resentment that at first afflict Cousin Mary when she realises, as a young woman, how her illness is going to impact on her life. She has yet to learn the truth of Dr. Goudge's advice to his daughter: that "One should accept suffering as peacefully and quietly as one could and try to draw nearer to God through it."[1295]

> *"When God is cruel to you everyone else is cruel too. When he turns his back he turns the whole world with him..."*
>
> *The diary broke off abruptly and began again a few days later. "I oughtn't to have said that about God. I don't know enough about him. I don't even know if he exists. Only if he doesn't exist why did I refuse? When you say, I won't, you refuse somebody and when you say, yes I will, you say it to somebody. I remember now that I did accept, that night when I woke up in the hospital room and...realized that I was sane again. I was so thankful that I said, yes, I'll do it."*[1296]

She has reached a milestone on the faith journey. Dag Hammarskjold records a very similar acceptance in his spiritual diary, *Markings*, which was published in translation, with an introduction by W.H. Auden, in 1964:

> I don't know Who – or what – put the question. I don't know when it was put. I don't even remember answering. But at some moment I did answer Yes to Someone – or Something.[1297]

The result of this Yes, for him, was a certainty that "existence is meaningful" and that his life from then on had a goal.

Mary's diary continues:

> *You might say that wasn't a real acceptance, because what I'd refused had already happened to me. But yet it was. You can go on refusing even after it's happened to you, like the child who screams and kicks the door after it's been shut up in the dark room. Or you can sit quietly down in the dark and watch for the return of light.*[1298]

This recalls a passage from George MacDonald in *A Book of Faith* which C.S. Lewis, too, included in his own MacDonald anthology:

> Troubled soul… God… has an especial tenderness of love towards thee for that thou art in the dark and hast no light, and His heart is glad when thou dost arise and say, "I will go to my Father…" Fold the arms of thy faith, and wait in the quietness until light goes up in thy darkness.[1299]

In fact *The Scent of Water* reflects the insight of many great Christian texts. As in *Green Dolphin Country* there are echoes of *The Practice of the Presence of God*; for William the Hunchback, like Brother Lawrence, owed his conversion experience to the vision of a leafless winter tree. Gazing at it, and realising that given time its leaves would return again, followed by blossom and fruit, Brother Lawrence "received a lofty view of the providence and power of God" which remained with him forever.[1300] And William's vision comes when, determined in his despair to commit suicide he finds himself - as in the imagery of George MacDonald's prayer - literally among the thorns. But he finds that God is there with him also.

> *He looked hard at the tree, seeing it already as his gallows, and then found that he could not look away. There were no green leaves yet to veil the starkness of it, it was still a winter tree, and the thorns looked long and sharp. He looked deeper and deeper into the tree, into the heart of it, trying to see himself hanging on the tree, and presently, with horror, he did. And then, staring as though nothing of him now existed except his straining eyes and thundering heart, he knew it was not himself but another. And he knew who it was. He would never, afterwards, attempt to describe what he saw. He could not. But he did say that he believed the fair Lord of life had accepted a death so shameful of deliberate intent*

> *of love, so that nothing that can happen to the body should cause any man to feel himself separated from God…*
>
> *Then did Brother William get upon his feet right joyously, and going to the thorn tree he plucked therefrom a curved and thorny branch and set it about his neck as though it were the halter from which his Lord had saved him. Yet he plucked it from the tree not as a halter but as a yoke, for now was he the thrall of Christ, yoke fellow with his Lord in the bearing of the cross. And he went forth singing into the wood…*[1301]

The former Dean of St. Paul's, W.R. Inge (whose work on the book of Hebrews[1302] had been published with an accompanying chapter by Dr. Goudge) said in his *Mysticism in Religion*, that mystical enlightenment brings about "a real change in the personality."[1303] William had been consumed with unhappiness and self-loathing, but after this experience he is completely transformed.

> *With changed and smiling countenance…quite changed from the man he had been, he presented himself before the Abbot and asked that he might be accepted as a lay brother.*[1304]

There are echoes of Dame Julian's words, too – as well as of Elizabeth's own lived experience - in the account of Cousin Mary's journey of faith. Julian described sin as "so vile and so horrible"[1305] and Cousin Mary realises that "It may take me my lifetime to know the vileness of my own sin…but until I do know I will not know God."[1306] And in Mary's dream of stifling darkness, a sword of light had kept a channel open that led her into the cave where the Christchild lay: "and I fled down it… I ran and ran and came out into the light. I had escaped."[1307] Julian says: "Flee we to our Lord and we shall be comforted…and safe from all manner of peril."[1308]

St. Augustine, too. The old clergyman tells Cousin Mary not to be afraid of losing her mind, because "you lose it into the hands of God."[1309] Augustine's much-loved prayer, concluding with the acknowledgment that "my heart is restless until it rests in Thee," has the same message on the subject of loss:

> To Thee will I entrust whatsoever I have received from Thee; so shall I lose nothing.[1310]

And Cousin Mary's acceptance, her "Yes I will" is, of course, akin to another great Yes from the supreme Mary: "Behold the handmaid of the Lord; be it unto me according to Thy word."[1311]

❄

When light does go up in her darkness, fearful as the struggle has been, Cousin Mary discovers that it has been worth waiting for.

> *When respite came could there be anything more marvellous than the sunburst of light? What was life like, Cousin Mary wondered, for those who seem to live more or less always on an even keel? For them too there must be the swing of the pendulum, for nothing living could escape it, but the self-pity of her youth began to leave her as she considered their relative joys, only so far up because it had been only so far down, in comparison to her sunbursts. They would never reconcile her to the abyss, nor was it right that they should since the abyss was evil, but the sombre backcloth increased joy to the point where wonder and thankfulness merged into a clarity of sight that transfigured every greeting of her day. She opened her window in the morning and saw a spider's web sparkling with light and was aware of miracle. Sitting in the conservatory with her sewing she knew suddenly that the sun was out behind the vine leaves and that she was enclosed within green-gold light as in a seashell. She dropped her sewing in her lap and was motionless for an hour while the light lay on her eyelids and her gratitude knew no bounds. Standing inside the willow tree she looked up and a thrush was there, so close to her that she could learn by heart the gleaming diapason of his breast, the sleek folding of the wing feathers, the piercing bright glance going through her like lightning…Once she held up her finger to a butterfly and it alighted there, and though it soon flew away again her finger wore the sensation of airy lightness like a jewel until nightfall. She grudged herself to sleep on the moonlit nights for she could not bear to lose a moment of the moon's serene companionship. These and other greetings she recorded in her diary. "They are more than themselves," she wrote, "and when the wonder grows in me I am more than myself… If any words come to me then they are those of the old man's second prayer, 'Thee I adore'.[1312]*

It is, however, a fearful struggle. The light is not simply given to her; it has been hard-won by a deliberate act of the will, by "hope…deliberately opposed to despair."[1313] By what Hilary had called, in *The Heart of the Family* "the wrenching effort of substitution."[1314] Since that novel, both Miss Giles and Miss Montague had won through into the light too, whereupon each asked of themselves the same question: "Why did I despair?"[1315]

※

In previous books, several of Elizabeth's characters had been driven to the brink of breakdown by the horrors of war; but in this novel she has the courage to write about mental illness which has no obvious cause. Cousin Mary simply has to confront the fact of her own difference.

> *When did I begin to realise that other people don't wake up every morning in unexplainable misery, don't, as soon as they are ill or exhausted, become sleepless and desperate?*[1316]

Jean Anderson, too, knows herself to be different:

> *The dread of meeting someone who did not know about her was one of her worst fears. They would try and talk to her, and she would not know what they were talking about, or if she did know, and she knew more often than people realized, and the answers were lucid in her mind, she would not be able to find the words to give them form. She would see the surprise in the face of the newcomer, the embarrassment, and then the relief with which he effected his escape.*[1317]

No wonder, then, that *The Scent of Water* had such a huge impact and generated so much correspondence from readers. It looked squarely at one of life's winter experiences, and yet with a message of hope. Cousin Mary does not have the freedom to live a 'normal' life, and yet as she discovers, to accept it all with courage and prayer can bring one out onto the other side of imprisoning darkness, even to "the Lord of glory."

> *I remembered the sword of light that had split the rock of sin, making for me the way of escape to where he was at the heart of it. At my heart. At the heart of everything that happened to me, everything I did, everything I endured... He had a sword in his hand and all evil at last would go reeling back before it. He had entered the prison house of his own will. And so he was not trapped and nor was I. There was always the way of escape so long as it was to the heart of it, whatever it was, that one went to find him.*[1318]

A New Kind of Heroine

For the first twenty years or so of her working life, Elizabeth's female protagonists had been in the main either adorable little girls, or adult women who were beautiful and loved: married (or about to be) and the mothers of children. Indeed even some of the girls, like Maria and Stella, were already loved in childhood by the boys who would grow up to be their husbands. The few single women on the whole - having no home of their own - were to be found doing the hard work in someone else's house : Margaret Eliot for example; or the toiling Miss Brown in *The Castle on the Hill*. Could this mean that Elizabeth saw her unmarried self as something of a cipher, not worthy of centre-stage? She had, after all, grown up in a world where single women were superfluous and had no power; where even Virginia Woolf had written to her sister, in 1911:

> Did you feel horribly depressed? I did. I could not write, and all the devils came out – hairy black ones. To be 29 and unmarried – to be a failure – childless – insane too, no writer. I went off to the Museum to try and subdue them.[1319]

Opportunities for women, and society's attitudes towards them, had changed since then ... but not so much, as yet, within the pages of an Elizabeth Goudge novel. The one real exception is Marguerite in *Green Dolphin Country*: who represents the ascetic in the trinity of "deep cravings of the self." She is still beautiful and loved – and in fact she is only, as it were, "accidentally" single since she retains the lifelong adoration of the man who has loved her since childhood, and who mistakenly proposed to her sister instead. And yet for Marguerite it is the life of prayer – not marriage – that brings deep peace, joy and fulfilment. When still living at home with her parents, she is aware that in the Victorian eyes of the outside world she is a superfluous woman; that her life must seem to be

> *just a passing of the time somehow by a woman whose first youth had passed away without her having been able to lay hands upon the blessed employment that the care of husband and children would have given her.*[1320]

But she knows, too, that "what the world sees of the life of any human creature is not the real life: that life is lived in secret, a reality that moves behind the façade of appearance, like wind behind a painted curtain." And Marguerite believes that her real life is "of value, besides being an immense joy to herself."[1321]

After Mrs. Goudge's death, once Elizabeth had said goodbye to the matriarch Lucilla as protagonist, there comes a change. There is still a lingering sneer in *The Rosemary Tree* at the unmarried girl, for Margary's (beautiful) mother fears that she will

> *develop into one of those old maids who sit forlornly in draughty cottages, surrounded by mementoes of the past, and talk incessantly about the old home. Daphne disliked old maids and felt that to be the mother of one would be the final humiliation of her life of humiliations.*[1322]

But this is only Daphne's opinion, for John Wentworth "felt differently" about his little daughter. "He did not fear eventual loneliness for her, for he knew the preciousness of the single state... The cell, and the sunlight moving on the bare wall."[1323]

There is a pivotal change in this novel, in that the ageing, worn-out spinsters in the background are brought forward, out of the shadows. Unattractive Miss Giles, over fifty, with her migraines and dyspepsia and sagging skirts, blossoms through the kindness of a child and the care of a younger woman, and her life is transformed. Harriet, too. Crippled with arthritis, unmarried, childless - she has none of the old 'essentials' of a heroine, and yet she is not in the background either. She has been a servant in the household, and yet her life is about so much more than domestic toil. She is absolutely central to the plot; her wisdom and prayers, in fact, central to all their happiness.

Then in *The White Witch* comes Froniga. Like the earlier heroines she is again beautiful and loved - by not one, but two men – and she becomes the adoptive mother of a brood of children. But by the end of the novel, all this has passed away. She remains single and independent, and she finds "great happiness in solitude." Though she is still pursuing her useful and worthwhile work as a herbalist, it is her deepening life of prayer – "the companionship of the Way" - that brings the greatest peace and fulfilment. "Though she toiled for the sick more selflessly than she had ever done, yet at the same time this companionship contained within itself all that she longed for."[1324]

And now in Miss Montague and Cousin Mary the new kind of heroine is complete. Neither of these plain and unreservedly single women has ever had – or will have - a love-life, a career, or children. Both have been barred from the life of a "normal" woman by their imperfections of body and mind - and yet as Cousin Mary discovers, the restricted life offers a very special kind of blessing.

Though I am able to do nothing else in this life, except only seek, my life seeming to others a vie manquée, yet it will not be so, because what I seek is the goodness of God that waters the dry places. And water overflows from one dry patch to another, and so you cannot be selfish in digging for it.[1325]

Neither woman has to settle for a vie manquée. On the contrary, each discovers an inner life which is a source of deep peace and fulfilment. Cracked pitchers, both of them; insignificant by worldly standards: they are yet on the road to spiritual greatness - which Elizabeth said in *The Joy of the Snow* "is, I believe, largely a matter of slow, hard, slogging discipline."[1326] She describes Mary Montague in particular as a woman who "had for years led an extremely disciplined life," and in fact there is something of the nun about Mary - not only in her intense prayer life and enforced single state, but in the vocational "vow" she takes to love.[1327] Also in her lack of freedom; for both of the two new heroines are in a sense confined by their restricted lives. Yet as Elizabeth said of another woman of prayer - the author of *Daffodils in Ice*:

There is no sense of imprisonment… This is not a confined woman, but one who has attained to the liberation of spirit that is born from the trinity in unity of discipline, sacrifice and selflessness and from nothing else at all.[1328]

❉

It seems that in the writing of these two novels, in her early sixties, the old attitude to the unmarried woman was vanquished at last. No longer the humiliation of being an old maid, or even the *mother* of one; no longer the one, unattainable ambition of love, marriage and children: but a single life bringing great fulfilment of a very different kind. She had dared to bring these single women – so like herself - Out into the Open.

Move into the clear.
Keep still, take your stand
Out in the place of fear
On the bare sand;

Where you have never been,
Where the small heart is chilled;
Where a small thing is seen,
And can be killed.

> Peppard
>
> Under the open day,
> So weak and so appalled,
> Look up and try to say,
> Here I am, for you called.
>
> You must haunt the thin cover
> By that awful place,
> Till you can get it over
> And look up into that face.[1329]

It is interesting that this poem by Ruth Pitter is to be found in Elizabeth's *Book of Peace* – placed in the section entitled *Final Peace*.

Progress

In echoes of many poets and mystics, Elizabeth's work always celebrates the sacred relationship between God, humankind, and the natural world; and laments too, the destruction brought about by mechanisation and progress.

A Book of Comfort includes part of D.H. Lawrence's poem, *Work* with its at-one-with-Nature ideal of creating artefacts organically, "as a bird that leans/its breast against its nest, to make it round.../putting them forth, not manufacturing them."[1330] Mr. Baker in *The Scent of Water* is just such an artisan – he is the last of the bodgers, the men who had worked outdoors in the beech-woods of the Chiltern Hills since the eighteenth century, making parts for the famous Windsor chair industry at High Wycombe. He is a marvellously colourful character, tall and "cadaverous as Don Quixote. He had ginger hair, a walrus moustache, a sad thin mouth and receding chin. He wore corduroy trousers tied below the knee with string." Mary asks him if he will continue to help with the gardening at The Laurels…

> *There was a long pause and his Adam's apple began to work in his long thin throat. His voice, when it came, was that of a bronchitic corncrake. "Might do," he said at last…*[1331]

But in the woods he is "in his proper milieu…the woods that were his home and his life, his kingdom and his world. Technically this wood probably belonged to Mr. Hepplewhite; in any other sense Mr. Baker held it in direct tenure from his God."[1332] His workshop in a ruined farmhouse is as much a part of nature as Lawrence could desire. His workbench is the farmhouse's ancient door, "a solid slab of oak supported upon sawn tree trunks."

> *Mr. Baker stood before it shaping a chair leg that was revolving in a primitive lathe, the power supplied by a bent ash sapling fixed beneath the bench... The stone floor was littered as deep with wood shavings as the floor of the wood beyond with beechmast. Through the narrow window the honey-coloured sunbeams slanted down, and a couple of butterflies. Birdsong rang in the place, rising to the great roof and echoing there. The wood had so quickly taken the place to itself that Mary found it hard to visualize the busy farmhouse life...*
>
> *He was already deeply absorbed, deftly shaping a chair leg... Yet she dared to ask him a few questions.*
> *"Do you send them to a factory, Mr. Baker?"*
> *He answered, though without looking up. "Aye. There's still a small factory that takes 'em. When that closes down that's the end."*[1333]

His air of sadness is thus explained, for his noble way of life is coming to an end. And in this sense Mr. Baker was a very topical character, for the bodgers' work for the chair industry did cease in the 1960s. In recent years however there has been a revival of interest in the ancient woodland craft of greenwood turning on pole-lathes: and happily, there are still a few bodgers at work in the woods.

Similarly, Jean Anderson regrets the advent of machines, and tells Mary during an outing in her car that it was Eve eating the apple "that led to motors..."

> *"James says that the internal combustion engine is the root of all evil."*
> *"Aren't you enjoying my car?"*
> *"I'd enjoy it more if it was a dogcart."*
>
> *Mary laughed and drove on. When they reached Thornton they found the narrow High Street packed with traffic. There was an aerodrome not far away and jets screamed overhead. Mary was inclined to think that the Andersons were right. Of all the evil things that man had plucked from the tree of the knowledge of good and evil, machinery was possibly the worst. It had destroyed bodgers, with all that meant in terms of human dignity, and without these ghastly planes bombs could not be dropped.*[1334]

Elizabeth had already, twenty years before, written a comical scene in *Henrietta's House* featuring one of the very first motor-cars, "smelling dreadfully and roaring like a lion, with steam coming out of its front [and] smoke pouring from its tail."[1335] By the end of the novel, it has mysteriously disappeared.

> *It just vanished from the lane where Felicity and Jocelyn had left it. Felicity said the fairies had removed it because they just wouldn't have such a horrible contraption about the place, but Grandmother pooh-poohed the idea and said that human thieves had taken it. Anyway, it was gone, and Felicity and Jocelyn weren't sorry, for when they had seen their motor car in the streets of Torminster, and in the lanes among the blue hills, they had come to the conclusion that it was not suitable there.*

But Elizabeth understood the liberating value of machines as well. When she wrote to Audrey, telling her that *The Scent of Water* was finished and posted off to the publishers, she added,

> *Jessie and I are very thrilled at the thought of the new car which will be on the market in about a year's time. It is cushioned on air in some way so that one does not feel the jolts. We hope to get one and think it will make motoring much easier for me.*[1336]

And as far as progress was concerned, in *The Joy of the Snow* she readily acknowledged her own "criminal" part in the destruction of the English countryside.

> *I think I even believed that Marldon would wear forever the beauty it had already worn for centuries. Tidal waves come in very quickly and no one realised then how soon a flood of bungalows and holiday camps, caravans and petrol pumps, shops and motor roads and roaring traffic would wash away most of the beauty that looked so eternal. And of course it never occurred to me that I myself was a criminal, for here, as at Barton, our bungalow was one of the first of the flood.*[1337]

The Sixties

The Scent of Water was quickly followed by her children's book, *Linnets and Valerians* which she set in the hills of Devon: according to a *New York*

Times book review, "blending fantasy and fact with the sure touch of the born storyteller."[1338] It has some marvellously colourful characters: peg-legged Ezra who talks to the bees; Lady Alicia's majestic black manservant, Moses Glory Glory Alleluja; and a family of young children who make an unexpected appearance at the home of their elderly bachelor uncle, and transform his hitherto quiet and donnish life for the better.

Her delightful blending of fantasy and fact mixes among other things the Church of England, magic spells and the great god Pan who, as Uncle Ambrose explains is "the spirit of nature. Men worshipped him in ancient Greece."

> *'Don't they now?' asked Timothy.*
> *'No,' said Uncle Ambrose. 'They don't believe in him now.'*
> *'Is he real?' asked Timothy eagerly.*
> *'Not now.'*
> *'Was he ever real?'*
> *'When men believed in him he was real to them.'*
>
> *'Not now?'*
> *'Not now.'*
> *'Not now,' echoed Timothy sadly, and the echoes were like a bell tolling. There was a long sad silence and then...*
> *'Shall we believe in him?' suggested Timothy.*
>
> *Uncle Ambrose's eyes twinkled. 'That, Timothy' he said, 'is a most unsuitable suggestion to make to a clergyman of the Church of England. I am no longer permitted to believe in the ancient gods. You, of course, can do as you wish.'*
>
> *Timothy, with shining eyes, closed the book. 'I wish,' he said.*[1339]

The twins in *The Herb of Grace* had already discovered in Knyghtwood "the Person...who plays the pipes" - and in this novel the children are watched over by "the spirit of Nature" – in the form of a trinity of bees – whenever they leave the protection of their uncle's house.

As part of his household, and therefore as children of the Vicarage, they must be sure to behave well in church: "I trust you will set a good example to the congregation," says Uncle Ambrose as he leaves them at the vestry door. Seated in the Vicarage pew beneath the pulpit however, Timothy so far forgets himself as to speak - telling Nan he wishes "animals and birds could come to church" - just as his uncle begins to preach.

> "Sh!" whispered Nan in anguish, and Timothy was aware of a chasm of icy silence opening between text and sermon, and of Uncle Ambrose's terrible eyes fixing them over the top of his spectacles. He blushed crimson and straightened himself. All four sat as though they had swallowed pokers, hands folded in their laps and eyes fixed on their prayer-books on the shelf in front of them, and so they remained for thirty-five minutes, while Uncle Ambrose's incomprehensible sermon rolled out like thunder over their heads. When it was over and he gave out the last hymn Betsy was so stiff that she nearly fell over when she tried to stand upright.[1340]

Wonderful humour – with a reflection of Elizabeth's remark that the children of the clergy "are not generally fond of sermons, for they have had to sit through too many."[1341] This seems not to have affected her church-going however: she and her mother are remembered as "a regular part of the congregation"[1342] at Marldon; and an Easter letter to Audrey from Peppard says "I think I have never seen our little church look so lovely as it did this year. There were no primroses, but masses of forsythia and wild daffodils, so that it was all gold."[1343] Both of these churches would have provided what she said was her favourite form of worship: "a completely simple early-morning Communion service at any village church."[1344]

Four other children's tales with a Devon connection came out in 1964 – all published by the Parnassus Gallery, Moretonhampstead. These were *Arabella or The Bad Little Girl*, *Maria or The Good Little Girl*, *Serena the Hen*, and *The Shufflewing*. Short stories presented in the form of a small, eight-page booklet with an illustrated cover, they were a kind of storybook greetings card: the first page printed with the decorated message "To wish you … … … …" Each carries a list of all the stories in the series, adding that there are "other titles in preparation" but according to Jessie only the four were produced:

> She had an artist friend who said, I've drawn these pictures, will you write stories to them? So between them they brought out four little booklets.

The artist friend was Isobel Morton-Sale, co-founder of the Parnassus Gallery with her husband John, who had illustrated the dust-wrappers for several of Elizabeth's novels, including *Green Dolphin Country*, *Gentian Hill*, *The Herb of Grace*, and *The Heart of the Family*.

The content of these little stories is very light – except for '*Maria*' which is quite startlingly spiritual. Almost certainly written at the same time as she was working on *The Child from the Sea*, it tells the story of a little girl who wants to know "where had she come from and where was she going?" The answer comes through a visit to an old lady, who gives her a box of sea shells.

> *Lifting the lid with her trembling old hands she showed the little girl the lovely rainbow-tinted fluted shapes inside. "They come from foreign parts, my love," she said. "And this one – look, this big one – holds a great treasure – a Voice – it has a Voice inside it. When you get home hide yourself in a quiet place and put it to your ear, and you will hear the sea talking."*
>
> *Maria took the box and said thank you very prettily, but in her heart she thought that she did not want to hear the sea talking because he talked too loud.*
> *"Not that sea," said the old lady, just as though Maria had spoken aloud, "the other one."*
> *Maria asked, "What other one?" but she got no answer because the old lady had fallen asleep.*
>
> *So she ran home and sat in the little stone gazebo at the bottom of the garden, where it was quiet, and put the shell to her ear. At first she did not hear anything, but with her inside eyes, not the mortal ones but the other ones, she saw a great illimitable sea, very calm and safe, and upon it a little boat travelling along in absolute security. Then she heard. For it was true, there was a Voice inside the shell, the Voice of the other sea, and it told her where she had come from and where she was going, and her eyes sparkled and her cheeks went rosy with her joy. The earthquake had not helped her much, nor the wind, nor the fire, but the still small Voice was one that a child could understand. But the sad thing was that she could never, as long as she lived, make other people understand what it was that she knew.*[1345]

The earthquake, wind and fire, and the still small voice are of course a direct reference to the Old Testament story of Elijah listening for the voice of God.[1346] The inspiration for the seashell, it would seem, was Wordsworth in *A Book of Peace*.

> I have seen
> A curious child, who dwelt upon a tract
> Of inland ground, applying to his ear
> The convolutions of a smooth-lipped shell;
> To which, in silence hushed, his very soul

> Listened intensely; and his countenance soon
> Brightened with joy; for murmurings from within
> Were heard, sonorous cadences! whereby
> To his belief, the monitor expressed
> Mysterious union with his native sea.
> Even in such a shell the Universe itself
> Is to the ear of Faith: and there are times,
> I doubt not, when to you it doth impart
> Authentic tidings of invisible things;
> Of ebb and flow and ever-during power;
> And central peace, subsisting at the heart
> Of endless agitation.[1347]

The final publication for 1964 was the first of what would become a trilogy of anthologies: *A Book of Comfort*. Jessie said that of the three it was the one Elizabeth liked best, because it was full of her personal favourites; it was "the things she'd collected all her life." In its preface she says,

> *The collecion and hoarding of bits and pieces is basic to all animals, from the squirrel with his nuts laid by in a hollow tree for comfort in the dark days to the anthologist with his oddments stored up in his memory for a similar purpose. Anthology-making is therefore essentially selfish, like self-preservation. Indeed it is self-preservation, for where should we be in our bad times without the treasure stored up in our minds?*[1348]

It is interesting that the things she had squirreled away all her life were needed to bring *comfort*. But having mentioned the bad times, as always she was quick to balance them with gratitude for the good: "Our existence is as light with comfort as it is weighted with weariness," she says. Nonetheless, the value of these "bits and pieces" for the relief of life's dark days did not escape the *Times Literary Supplement's* reviewer, who deemed it "a quiet anthology to sustain the human spirit."[1349]

A second omnibus edition of her work was produced the following year, when *A City of Bells, Towers in the Mist* and *The Dean's Watch* were published collectively under the title *Three Cities of Bells...* Wells, Oxford and Ely, of course. Writing of *The Dean's Watch* in its preface, she said:

> *All that I experienced while writing it I still remember vividly. No writer can ever truly be said to like a book he or she has made because the book written down falls so tragically short of the book in the mind before it was written, but there is always one we care for more than another and in the (unlikely) event of our being remembered after our death we would like it to be for this book. The Dean's Watch is for me this special book.*[1350]

She was still of the same mind six years later, telling an interviewer that although she really preferred her children's books to her adult work,

Of all the novels, I got most satisfaction out of The Dean's Watch *and if I were only to be remembered for one book, that is the one I would like it to be.*[1351]

Despite the changing world of the Sixties her short stories were still to be found in women's magazines, and *Dogs of Peking*, first published in *The Ikon on the Wall* in 1943, was not considered too old-fashioned for inclusion in the July edition of *Woman's Journal* in 1965. In another look back to the forties, *Green Dolphin Country* too was still of sufficient interest to warrant a ten-minute radio interview (recorded by the BBC in July for the series *Home this Afternoon*) some twenty-one years after its publication.

While all this was going on she was putting together *A Diary of Prayer* which came out in 1966. Its preface says,

These prayers, a mixture of old and new, were not collected for literary merit, though some of the great prayers of the world are among them, but as practical help for a Christian still in the kindergarten of prayer.[1352]

"A proportion of them," she added, had been "collected over the years, with no thought of an eventual anthology;" which means that they had been collected for her own use – she herself is the Christian in the kindergarten of prayer. She used the same expression years later in a letter to Louis Bouyer, to describe her prayer life in relation to his. The book also copyrights "new material" by Elizabeth Goudge, presumably indicating that all of the twenty-three unattributed prayers are her own work.

A year later yet another anthology was published: the second in her trilogy, this time on the subject of peace.

Never have we longed for peace as we do now, when war has become an obscene horror worse than any imaginable storm, and noise and confusion so invade cities and homes that we are in danger of having our very minds and souls battered to a uniform pulp. But in our much greater need we turn to the same sources of peace as our forefathers did; to Janus-faced nature when it is her tranquil smile she turns to us, and not her frown, to painting or gardening or whatever creative work brings us self-forgetfulness, to fire-lit homes and all the human love and friendship they stand for. And to the peace of the eternal mystery.[1353]

A Book of Peace had, according to Jessie, involved a lot more work than its predecessor, because both this and the third in the trilogy, *A Book of Faith* necessitated much reading and research.

Alongside all this other work, Elizabeth had been trying for some years now to get on with the book that was to be her last novel, *The Child from the Sea*. When it was finally published in 1970 she said it had begun ten years ago, and according to Jessie's recollections she must indeed have been working on it in the early Sixties. It took so long to write, Jessie said "because she had to abandon it twice, because of these requests to do the two anthologies. She had to drop everything and then pick it all up again." Elizabeth herself said that it "took years to write."

Another anthology of her own work came out in 1967 too, but presumably without adding to her workload for she later told a friend that Hodders had compiled this themselves.[1354] It was *A Christmas Book*, made up of three of her short stories, plus extracts from *God So Loved the World* and five of the novels.

Extracts from her work continued to be used worldwide in anthologies and children's storybooks. In America, for instance, *The Well of the Star* featured in Edward Wagenknecht's *Stories of Christ and Christmas*; and Macmillan Canada published *Into Wonderland*, where the Franciscan *Spring Song*, together with an illustration from *The Little White Horse*, rubbed shoulders with the work of Robert Louis Stevenson, Edward Lear, Rudyard Kipling and Walter de la Mare.

The Little White Horse itself was read on BBC Television early in 1967, in their children's story-telling programme, *Jackanory*. This came hot on the heels of *The Dean's Watch* as *A Book at Bedtime*, which had been broadcast in fifteen radio instalments in the run-up to Christmas 1966. It was not - as Jessie recalled - an exact re-telling of the story:

> They had *The Deans Watch* on *A Book at Bedtime* and they altered the ending – I suppose they bought the rights and that's it. I didn't hear much of it but I think it was fairly true until the end, and then I know I sort of leapt about in outrage.

In the autumn of 1967 BBC Radio itself radically changed, from the old Home Service / Light Programme format to the new Radios One, Two, Three and Four. But it seems that this new-look BBC was as keen as ever to use Elizabeth's work, for another *Book at Bedtime* followed in June 1968 – this time, the now thirty-two-year-old *A City of Bells*. She herself was not so keen, telling the editor of *RNA News* "I tried to listen to it but it sounded so dreadful. Such an old book. I can't think how I came to write it."[1355]

It was not just the novels that were of interest to the BBC. Having systematically rejected her plays earlier in her career, they were now to find Elizabeth herself of value to them as a broadcaster. She was contracted to write, and read on air, a talk entitled *In the Beginning was the Word*, to be broadcast in the five-minute morning religious slot *Five to Ten* on Radio Two, in July 1969. Inspired by the Peace anthology, it quoted from some of the poems and also the Elijah story she had used in *Maria or The Good Little Girl*. Her subject was the prayer of silence: the "journey within ourselves."

She began by quoting from the preface to *A Book of Comfort*: that "we are all anthologists" in that we keep a collection of oddments in our memory "for comfort in the dark days."

I find that the ones I take out most often speak of peace and silence. The world today is violent and noisy, and my mind, echoing the outward confusion, in such a turmoil that silence seems the deepest need. Yet I believe that men have always felt like this, for they have always gone on lonely journeys, to deserts or the eternal snows, and God has always had to say to our minds, "Peace, be still" before he can call us to journey within ourselves to find him in the quiet place at the centre of our being.

The kingdom of God is within you ...[1356]
Enter into thy closet, and when thou hast shut thy door, pray to thy Father which is in secret.[1357]

A story of Elijah, a poem on two levels, illustrates these two journeys. Worn out and deeply depressed Elijah climbed a mountain to find peace in a cave in the rock, but his mind as well as the mountain was in turmoil and he had to pass through noise to find the peace.

A great and strong wind rent the mountains ... but the Lord was not in the wind: and after the wind an earthquake; but the Lord was not in the earthquake: and after the earthquake a fire; but the Lord was not in the fire: and after the fire a still small voice. And it was so, when Elijah heard it, that he wrapped his face in his mantle.[1358]

This takes us to a mysterious saying of St. John of the Cross.

The Father uttered one Word; that Word is his Son, and he utters him forever in everlasting silence; and in silence the soul has to hear it.[1359]

And so silence is an attribute of God, the ground of our being, and if the journey to find it is hard it is not a selfish journey, because from that ground grow the qualities of love and joy and peace that give value to our service to other people.

She admitted she sometimes felt that "It's all very well for the saints and poets to talk, but this journey into silence is too hard. I shall never get there."

But some people get there, and if the rest of us were at least to start out on the journey the world might be a less violent and noisy place.

To illustrate the journey she made reference to one of the poems in *A Book of Peace*... and to an image she had used again and again in her own work:

The journey, and the finding, are wonderfully described in a poem by James Kirkup called A Cave.[1360] *Like the story of Elijah it is on two levels, but James Kirkup's Cave is not in a mountain but deep in the earth. The journey through unknown darkness is terrifying, but he finds what he wanted, and feels much as Elijah did when he covered his face.*[1361]

❋

Also in 1969 came yet another anthology - *The Ten Gifts* compiled by Mary Baldwin, showing how Elizabeth's work celebrates the gifts of Love, Wonder, Beauty, Delight, Compassion, Understanding, Faith, Tranquillity, Truth and Courage.

And the last of her children's books was published too: *I Saw Three Ships*. A novella that had appeared in *Woman's Journal* back in December 1954, it is a delightful Christmas story set in the West Country, and based on the visit of the Three Wise Men.

'The Wise Men might come,' said Polly. 'Why not? Susan at the sweet-shop told me that Christ Himself came to the West Country when He was a little boy.'

'That's only a legend, dear,' said Dorcas.
'What's a legend, Aunt?' asked Polly.
'A story whose truth cannot be proved,' said Dorcas.

'You can't prove God,' said Polly. 'Where did they land, Aunt Constantia?'
'My love!' ejaculated Constantia in distress.

'It might have been here,' said Polly. 'I expect he sailed into our harbour just when the cocks were crowing. There He was, walking up and down the streets of our town very early in the morning, and the doors were locked and no one rang the bells. Wasn't that odd?'[1362]

He was in the world... and the world knew him not.[1363] Once again, a child shocks the grown-ups with her apprehension of Mystery, and willingness to believe the unbelievable.

Just as the story *The Canticle of the Sun* had been punctuated throughout by the words of St. Francis' hymn of praise, this tale is woven around the nine verses of the old Christmas carol. Its final verse is the book's last word to the reader:

> *...Then let us all rejoice amain,*
> *On Christmas day, on Christmas day;*
> *Then let us all rejoice amain,*
> *On Christmas day in the morning.*

Pembrokeshire

Despite this very respectable output of new books, Elizabeth told the *RNA News* in 1968 that she was "getting very slow." She added, "The historical novel I'm working on does not progress very fast."[1364] Nevertheless, two years later *The Child from the Sea* finally made it into the bookshops.

Its inspiration had come during a holiday at Jessie's cottage in Wales, "a part of the world I would never have seen had she not taken me one spring to stay for two months in her cottage on the coast." As such, she says, the book is "as much Jessie's as *The White Witch* since it has its roots in the beauty of Pembrokeshire..."

Another place to grip the heart. Not in the least like Keyhaven, not like the Island, yet bringing back memories of both. Another old cottage possessed of its own particular peace, a fisherman's cottage this time, with stone steps leading up to the front door; a half-door upon which, having opened the top half, you can lean your elbow as upon a window-sill, and look out across the estuary to the bay, with the sea wind in your face... Birds... You go to sleep, listening to the eerie cry of the oyster-catchers, a fluting just heard above the wash of the sea. Looking out early in the morning you may be in time to see the herons standing in meditation beside the estuary, perhaps the swans and ducks, certainly every kind of gull and comic cormorant. For the fortunate the seals may appear; but you have to be fortunate for they do not appear for everyone. They do not appear for me. Behind the cottage the small garden slopes up to the apple trees, and when you look up there is the mountain; and 'up the mountain' (a phrase used by the people of the place) mountain joy is to be found; the smell of wet moss, the sound of the streams coming down, the keening of the wind, the curlews crying, and behind it all the great silence that is always waiting behind the murmuring of these things. The sea is glorious but the mountain is better still.[1365]

This two-month visit was presumably the one she described in an interview as "the most lovely holiday."[1366] It was one of at least three trips she made to this beautiful part of Wales, the first probably in the late fifties or early sixties, for she used it as the setting for *The Silver Horse* and this had appeared as a magazine story, at least as early as 1962. She told a friend that it described Jessie's cottage "and the lovely country round."[1367]

Though she had scarcely slept all night Delia was wide awake with the first gleam of day. The sun saw to that, flooding the window with light, gently touching her... She pushed the window wide open. Sitting up she leaned her elbows on the sill, her chin in her hands. The air, cool from the sea and from the night, did not come in this morning upon wings, for there was no wind, but lapped in over the sill as gently as the ripples upon the crescent of gleaming sand beyond the river. Though the sky was already luminous, wreaths of mist hung over the river and Mynydd Melin rose up out of a billowing whiteness that hid the rocks and the caves along the shore...

The tide was going out and the boats in the harbour lay sprawling on the sand, the little river threading its way beside them to the sea. Delia looked for the herons. They were sometimes here in the early morning when the mists still lay over the river and before the harbour had woken to life. They were shy birds and with the first banging door, the first echo of a voice, they would be gone. Leaning far out of the small window she looked for them and found them, first one and then another. They stood upright by the river on the far side, delicate dream-shapes half hidden and half revealed by the mist. They stood as though charmed into stillness, meditative, creatures of another world as well as of this one. Delia had always been aware of the herons' world but she did not know what it was. Certain creatures, certain sounds and scenes, belonged to it, and in dreams she fancied she sometimes breathed its air, but it had no tangible reality...

Once, Delia and Dewi had...walked to the Lion Rock above the Bay of the Seals, where the waves moved in the great caves, and where in the spring the white seal calves lay on the beach of coloured stones basking in the sun. They had lain on the rock and watched the seals but they had not dared to go down and creep close... the seals, like the herons, were denizens of two worlds.[1368]

Her love for the place is manifest in this detailed account of its beauty. Perhaps it was the embodiment of a poem she loved too: for amongst all the bits and pieces she squirreled away in *A Book of Comfort* is Dylan Thomas's *Poem in October*, evoking the sights and sounds of just such a landscape in Wales - herons and gulls, sea and boats and harbour. Much as she loved the place however, because of her poor health the long journey to Jessie's cottage was "a nightmare" for her, said one of her friends.[1369] Had the travelling been easier she might have spent much more time in the landscape of this favourite poem, her heart gripped by Dylan Thomas's "heron priested" shore.[1370]

The Child from the Sea

Further along the coast is St. David's Cathedral, one of the great shrines of the world, and further along still is Roch castle, where Lucy Walter, the secret wife of Charles II, was probably born and where she spent her early childhood. It was on my first visit to Pembrokeshire that I read a book about her written by one of her descendants. It is a rare book, now out of print, and giving a very different account of her from those given by the history books... I had not got far with my reading before I was longing to write about this new Lucy... And I wanted, too, to express the pent-up joy of the birds and the sea and the holiness of the Cathedral.[1371]

Many of Elizabeth's short stories are set in a past age, and some of them incorporate real historical figures within their cast of characters: she wrote, among others, about Jane Austen and Shelley, Shakespeare and Keats.[1372] But *The Child from the Sea* is the only novel in which the protagonist is a real person, whose story has to be woven within the confines of historical fact. "I didn't draw this from my own life at all," she said in an interview, "and I think it was almost the first book that wasn't influenced by the homes I have had."[1373] Because of this, *The Times* reported, the book involved a good deal of research and Elizabeth drew on the services of the London Library in order to re-create seventeenth century Covent Garden, The Hague, Paris and Rotterdam.

The interviewer also mentioned that Jessie helped to research the Welsh background at Roch Castle. Looking back from the perspective of the 1990s however, Jessie was quick to play down the idea that she had had any role to play in Elizabeth's work, describing how once,

> We had a French couple come from *Femmes d'Aujourd'hui* – they couldn't speak English and we couldn't speak French - and I came out as her *collaboratrice*, which is the LAST thing I was!

Indeed Jessie herself paid tribute to Elizabeth's meticulous research, citing a particular review of *The Dean's Watch* she had kept, on the art of clockmaking. *The Horological Journal* had pointed out the pitfalls of even attempting to delineate Isaac's horological background: so many novelists come to grief over this kind of technical detail, it concluded; but "Miss Goudge," on the other hand, had "succeeded in being remarkably correct."[1374]

❉

Although Elizabeth may not have drawn from her own life for *The Child from the Sea*, she did still write about her faith - as she had never failed to do throughout her entire career. Edward Wagenknecht was one of the discerning critics who recognised her worth in this respect. From the first, he said, Elizabeth had shared with her readers her own "sensitive and far from superficial reading of life." Reviewing *The Child from the Sea* in *The News-Tribune*, he acknowledged the book's "mystical awareness," and how this added to her characters a dimension that was not to be found in other contemporary novels. As to Lucy Walter herself, she is one of the most "enchanting heroines in English fiction," he decided. A "completely convincing combination of hoyden, rebel and saint," she "captures the reader's heart in the first chapter and never lets it go again."[1375]

There is indeed an added dimension to Lucy. Here is a Goudge heroine who has not only a prayer life but, even as a child, a mystic's awareness. Lucy's whole life is coloured by a few significant childhood moments – her mystical experiences of oneness with Nature, and ultimately with the God at its heart. And surely, the inspiration behind this dimension was once again Thomas Traherne, in these words which were soon to be included in *A Book of Faith*.

> Your enjoyment of the world is never right till every morning you awake in Heaven; see yourself in your Father's palace, and look upon the skies, the earth and the air as celestial joys; having such a reverend esteem of all, as if you were

among the Angels. The bride of a monarch, in her husband's chamber, hath no such causes of delight as you.[1376]

In this novel, as in the old book Elizabeth read in Wales, Lucy becomes not the mistress but the bride of the monarch, Charles II. Traherne's observation that the world is "none other than the House of God and the Gate of Heaven" continues:

> You never enjoy the world aright till the sea itself floweth in your veins.[1377]

Lucy's first real knowledge of union, of being "married" to the natural world, comes – like the butterfly that alighted on Cousin Mary's finger in *The Scent of Water* - through the clasp of a tiny bird's claw.

> *It was then she became aware of the birds. They were coming down from the sky like drifting autumn leaves, martins, chaffinches, goldfinches and linnets, finding their way to the bracken-sheltered hollows and the warm dry hedges and the safe crannies of the rocks. Lucy had watched the bird migrations before but she had never seen one halted like this, halted as the warning sounded along the shore. She stood still, scarcely breathing, her arms out and her face turned up to the darkening sky, and they had no fear of her. A wing brushed her cheek and just for a moment some tired little being alighted on her hand, putting on one finger for ever the memory of a tiny claw that clung like a wedding ring. It was for her a moment of ecstasy, of marriage with all living creatures, of unity with life itself, and she whispered in Welsh, "Dear God, this happiness is too great for me!"*[1378]

Her first truly mystical experience occurs as she looks deep into the heart of a rose.

> *The marble seat was white as the last rose blossom, opening unexpectedly in this late glow of warmth. She felt the cool petals against her cheek and turning her head she saw the leaves like lifted hands holding it out to her. She lifted her hands too and then dropped them, afraid to touch the flower lest she bruise it. Instead she looked deep into its heart, that glowed golden at the centre of the exquisite whiteness. The very faint perfume came to her. She looked and time ceased. The world went away too…only she and the flower existed. Then she too stole away from herself, though sight remained that could look upon the flower, and song remained, for*

> *she was singing to it. When she first began to hear the song she did not know it was herself that was singing, she thought it was a seraph behind her in the tree; or the tree itself. Yes, the tree was certainly singing. They sang together for a while, and the trees in the park sang; looking up she saw the gold and crimson leaves like tongues of singing fire drifting through the air. The terrace was carpeted with fallen leaves and when she stretched her toes down and touched them gently they sang too. The sharp sweetness of a robin's song chimed in and the world was full of praise.*[1379]

When she later finds herself trapped in a cave, the memory of this experience has the power to rescue her from fear; as she comes to realise the *source* of its power.

> *Chancellor Pritchard had told Old Parson that the mercy of God was in his heart. She put her hand over her heart and it was jumping about more like a frightened bird than God. Yet she could not think of anywhere else inside her where God could be; unless he was inside this agitation. She put both hands now over her bumping heart and shut her eyes, trying to see him there. She could not. She saw instead the damask rose...and it glowed at its heart and was still. She was exceedingly surprised. "God?" she asked. Then she spoke again, but a little afraid to hear her own voice saying the tremendous word out loud in this stony place. "God."*[1380]

Lucy becomes better able to understand these experiences through the spiritual guidance of the clergyman who in later life becomes her friend: another figure from history, Dr. Jeremy Taylor.

> *She told him she thought she had come from the sea and he agreed that indeed she had. "The sea is a picture of the divine mystery from which we came and that laps for ever on the shores of our being, and sounds about us when the storms come. The mystery is within us also and in all that lives, even in the bodies of the small fishes in the sea-pools, the mystery of the being of God. There is no creature that breathes but the breathing is the rhythm of his love, no flower that glows with any other light but his, no voice that speaks in kindness but the cadence of the compassion is his own.*
>
> *Shyly she told him about...how she had seen the golden-hearted rose and how it had seemed to glow inside her in the cave. "There the small child touched the deeps of prayer," he said. "The adoration, and then the experience of divine rescue."*

> *"But I am not a religious kind of person," she told him, "and I do not know how to pray."*
> *"You will know when the storms come. It is then that God goes out of his way to meet his children. Until that time comes keep in memory that which you have found to be within you, and without you in the world's glow."*[1381]

He then instructs Lucy in the importance of being regularly in the presence of God.

> *"When the clock strikes, or however else you shall measure the day, it is good to turn to God, that the returns of devotion may be the measure of your time. And do so also in the breaches of your sleep. You do not even need to speak. To turn is enough…*
>
> *To grow in holiness is to grow in the power of turning from yourself to God and his children. When there is no more turning back to yourself, that wounding of the soul of the world, then you are whole…."*
>
> *"Thank you sir,"* she said. *"It will be a secret thing, this life of turning."*
> *"Secret and yet shared,"* he told her. *"You will share this with every man and woman who has ever tried, however feebly, to love God and his neighbour."*[1382]

Dr. Taylor is right, for Lucy later becomes aware of what it is she shares with other men and women:

> *"Waiting near a crowd of people what do you hear and see?" [Charles] asked her in a low voice.*
>
> *Her answer surprised him. "I try to hear the echo of a song they have brought from far and sing within themselves all the while they chatter nonsense, and to catch on their faces a glimpse of what they will be at their journey's end. Sometimes on first waking I have found myself with a singing rising up all round me but before I have understood the words the thread has broken and it has vanished. And that glimpse, it comes like light on a face and then is gone, but if you have once seen it I do not think you could ever dislike the face it visited; not even if that face afterwards became evil. I think that evil is not immortal but that the light is."*[1383]

And the memory of the rose and the cave do sustain her when the storms come.

> *She lay down on her bed for a while and with all the resolution she could summon drove her frantic mind away from the scaffold to the bridge above the stream...and up the steps to the terrace where the damask rose grew. She looked for it in vain among the green leaves, but just as her thoughts grew frantic once more the leaves murmured to her of the cave where she had found it within herself.*
>
> *"Go in. Go down the stony passage that leads to the cave at the heart of the world that is also your own heart. He is there, as well as at the heart of all earth's flowers, and he is the peace of the world, and the joy of the world, and all that is. The love of lovers is one of the reflections, and there are many trembling in the troubled waters of our living, trembling for a moment and then broken and lost. But he is not lost. And what he is no man knows."*
>
> *She opened her eyes. The murmur of leaves had become another voice. There had been no words that her physical ears could hear yet she knew what had been said to her.*[1384]

Here, spelt out as a command in the final novel, is a call to the journey referred to so often in earlier books: to that Going In. Going in, despite all fear, to the darkness at the heart of the mystery, where will be found peace, holiness, light... God. For he is in the stony cave, as well as at the golden heart of all earth's flowers... the cave and the rose are one.

At the end of her life, Lucy meets an old man who has travelled even deeper into prayer.

> *He had travelled within himself, she realized, a journey of enquiry into the deeps. What image had he placed within himself? Perhaps none. Perhaps his prayer was imageless. Where he had gone was no golden hearted rose, only the silence.*[1385]

❋

George MacDonald had once linked the image of the sea with forgiveness.

> I prayed to God that He would make me... into a rock which swallowed up the waves of wrong in its great caverns

and never threw them back to swell the commotion of the angry sea whence they came. Ah, what it would be actually to annihilate wrong in this way – to be able to say, "It shall not be wrong against me, so utterly do I forgive it!"[1386]

And Elizabeth said of *The Child from the Sea*:

I doubt if it is a good book, nevertheless I love it because its theme is forgiveness, the grace that seems to me divine above all others, and the most desperate need of all us tormented and tormenting human beings…and also because I seemed to give to it all I have to give; very little, heaven knows. And so I know I can never write another novel, for I do not think there is anything else to say.[1387]

The Inward Eye

The Child from the Sea was dedicated to Freda Green, the friend who had brought Jessie into Elizabeth's life; and coincidentally it introduced her to yet another new friend: the BBC Producer Madeau Stewart. As its preface says, Elizabeth's inspiration for the book's depiction of seals on the Pembrokeshire coast had come from a radio programme she had heard, when Miss Stewart had described how she played her flute to the seals on the Isle of Inch Kenneth. By the end of 1970 the two women had met at Rose Cottage, and six months later were rehearsing for an unscripted, thirty-minute interview for radio transmission in September. It must have been well received for Elizabeth told her, "I am so pleased to have the cutting from the *Church Times*. I think it is most encouraging for us both, and so are all the letters I have been receiving."[1388]

The same year, 1971, saw the publication of the collection of short stories entitled *The Lost Angel*. Giovanni - the final story in this, her final book of fiction - is about St. Francis.

Brother Francis…loved light, and loved it so much that when Giovanni had asked him once what God was like he had said he was like light. He had said that the glorious sun in the sky is like God the Father, and the sunshine coming down from the sun and warming us through and through is like Christ our Saviour, and that both of them dwell within the hearts of all men as a gift of light that is God the Holy Spirit.

> *Giovanni had taken this quite literally and when his heart jumped for joy he would see with his inside eyes the leap of a bright flame. And when it had jumped it would die down again and he would see a round, glowing ball lying still like a coal in the fire…*
> *But his outside eyes could not see it, and this grieved him.*[1389]

This was not the first time she had referred in her stories to the "inside eyes" - and they were not a fiction. Elizabeth had this ability to translate ideas and words into pictures she could actually see. Although she rather deprecated this, saying "even in old age I cannot manage to grow up sufficiently either to listen to music, to think or pray without seeing pictures in my mind,"[1390] yet it was perhaps akin to what William Blake too called the 'inward' eye. Not always a welcome gift, maybe – as on the occasion when she 'saw' her demon - yet it seems a rather wonderful one. This is from a letter she wrote in old age in admiration of a phrase Madeau Stewart had written: "Intersecting haloes of harmonies that embellish the music…"

> *It is a glorious sentence! [and] makes for me a picture that I can see with my inside eyes. The haloes are not solid, like one sees sometimes in pictures of the saints, but very delicately coloured hoops. They weave in and out of each other in a gentle kind of dance which itself forms a circle about the golden glory in the centre. What that is I don't know but the gold is that special glowing and strong, yet soft to the eyes gold that is the colour of love, and so of God.*[1391]

In her Franciscan story, Giovanni does not remain in grief, for St. Francis ensures that he does eventually see God's light with his outside eyes too. With echoes of John Clare's prose-poem *Dewdrops*[1392] and of the apple-tree-after-rain which brought John Wentworth figuratively to his knees in *The Rosemary Tree*, this is the little boy's vision:

> *The whole meadow, stretching from his feet to the sun, was sparkling as though it were on fire, as though every wet flower and blade of grass was carrying a tongue of flame. The light was so brilliant that it dazzled the eyes. Blinking, Giovanni bent down and picked a small blue flower with rayed petals that grew at his feet. He looked at it and saw that it held in its heart a globe of light shining and sparkling like the sun. It was the sun. And the light of the sun. And so, thought Giovanni, all the flowers and the grasses must have the light of the Holy Spirit inside them just like I have. Perhaps everything has. And then he thought, I'll take it to Brother Francis…*[1393]

But by the time he reaches Francis, of course, "the raindrop that had looked like the sun had vanished" and tears come to Giovanni's eyes.

> *"God the Holy Spirit has gone out," he said. "I was bringing him to you and he's gone out."*
> *"He never goes out," said Brother Francis…*
>
> *[He] looked at Giovanni and he thought how lustrous are the tears of children, lustrous as their love. He stretched out his little finger and with infinite care touched first Giovanni's eyelashes and then the heart of the flower.*
>
> *"I was mistaken," said Brother Francis. "And you were mistaken when you thought you had not brought him to me in the heart of this flower. Look!"*
>
> *Giovanni looked, and at the centre of the flower that Brother Francis was holding up towards the sun was the flame once more, sparkling and brilliant as ever. It was the sun, and the light of the sun.*
>
> *"I don't understand," said Giovanni.*
> *"Nor do I," said Brother Francis, and then he suddenly began to laugh, and Giovanni began to laugh. They laughed and laughed, and then…they sang…*
>
> *They sang more and more joyously, and so did the birds. The singing ran through the woods, and it was Whitsunday.*[1394]

Perhaps it was no coincidence that this story of St. Francis affirmed the presence of the Holy Spirit in human tears, for this was a time of great sadness in Elizabeth's life. Her beloved cousin Hélène, her 'adopted sister' had died while still only in her fifties.

In September 1971 Elizabeth wrote to Madeau enclosing "two exquisite little leaflets called *Letters from our Daughters* by Cynthia Sandys and Rosamond Lehmann." The leaflets told how "their young daughters died and communicated with them – not through a medium but mind to mind."[1395] She followed this up with another letter at the end of the month saying "I do hope you won't find the letters disturbing. I found them very comforting, having lost a beloved cousin (she lived with us as a child and so was like a daughter) about two months ago, and I find my thoughts of her are helped along by the letters."[1396]

Jessie explained the duality of the close relationship between Elizabeth and Hélène… because of Mrs. Goudge's illness, she said, it had been "Elizabeth who did the bringing-up" and Hélène in consequence had been "as near as makes no matter either her sister or her child."

※

The same letter to Madeau said that they would be going to Wales on the 14th October, although Elizabeth sent a postcard in early November saying "I have not been able to get out much since we came." She added, "We go home slowly next week by way of Ross on Wye and get home a fortnight today."[1397] Despite this slow journey, her next letter reported that she had been unable to get her Christmas letters sent out in time, because: "Though I loved Wales, it and the long journey were rather too much for me."[1398]

Writing About Herself

Elizabeth had now published the last of her fiction, but she still had much more to say on the subject of her own life and faith. Alan Hull Walton recalled how horrified he and others had been to hear her announce that *The Child from the Sea* would be her last book and, "I'm not going to write any more." He insisted that for the sake of all her millions of readers worldwide, she must write her autobiography – she owed it to them:

> And she smiled that calm, delightful, wonderful smile which I've never seen on any other face, and said: 'Yes, I'll do it.'"[1399]

Although Elizabeth's dedication in *The Joy of the Snow* is "For Alan Walton and the other friends who wanted me to write this book," she herself gave a slightly different version of the story to Ruth Martin for *Trade News*.

> *Hodder and Stoughton asked me to write my autobiography. I didn't think I could do that, but I have promised to try and write about my childhood. If you're as old as I am, you go right back to the Edwardian age, and life then was so different it might almost have been lived on another planet. I've made several false starts on this book, but I'm not going*

to be beaten by it – I hope! I'm so used to writing a story that when I've got to tell the truth, it really is quite difficult.[1400]

Two years later, when Rosemary March interviewed her for *The Daily Telegraph* she recounted a similar tale, saying that it was her publishers who had begged for a memoire of her childhood. Although Elizabeth complied with the request, she reported that "having to re-live those days is proving a painful experience."

I've been filled with remorse and frustration. Looking back on experiences from this new perspective can be quite harrowing. Yet I'm glad I've started writing like this, some of it is even self-indulgent. I like describing people I've loved.[1401]

She was then, at the age of seventy-two, only halfway through the book, and she admitted it was becoming "increasingly difficult" to find the right words. Although you can drive yourself physically and mentally, she said, you can't force the creative faculty… "Sometimes I get so dissatisfied with my day's efforts, I wonder if the book will ever reach the publisher."[1402]

This book that she was initially so reluctant to write evolved into something much more than simply a memoire of childhood. After its publication, Elizabeth explained the process to Philippa Toomey, for *The Times*.

I didn't want to write it at all. I thought that to look deeply into myself like that would be absolutely terrible, and I felt my life so uneventful, but friends asked me to do it, and I really was bullied, bullied by my publishers into writing it! So I said I will write about my childhood, but I went on after that – childhood wasn't quite long enough, so there was nothing for it but to go on. I found it extremely difficult, much more difficult than writing a novel. I have done no exciting things, like going to India or trying to climb Everest, or any of the wonderful things that some people do.

The passing of years brings a static quality to one's memories, even though they are living things in a living past. They can be looked at objectively as one looks at a picture. Even one's past selves can be looked at in this way, so different are the past selves to the self one now is. I acknowledge that in all of us the basic temperament, formed by inheritance and upbringing and early experience, cannot be changed, however desperately we may long to change it. But what is built upon the unchanging foundation by our own seeking and struggling, by what happens to us and by the profound influence exerted over us by the people we meet and live with, or whose books we read, creates an ever-growing and changing personality. One looks back at almost a stranger: "Knowing myself, yet being some-one other."[1403]

As Alan Walton said, no-one but herself could have written *The Joy of the Snow* – but her friends too, had their own memories.

Kathleen Millington said that Elizabeth *loved* her father, and "she was very like him – those deep set eyes…" Many of her characteristics too, were shared with her father. Not least, of course, that they were both writers - although Elizabeth was quick to point out that her father's books were "works of scholarship" and so "the single likeness between us was an inability to compose on a typewriter; neither of us could think without actually holding a pen in the hand."[1404] Perhaps Adam Ayscough owes something to them both:

> *A wave of self-loathing, of self-distrust, would go over him at first. Who was he that he should dare to take a pen into his hand? And how puerile was the result when he had done it. He would struggle wearily through a page or two and then forget himself, coming to the surface an hour later knowing that his book was his artefact, and whatever the result he could no more not make it than fail to breathe.*[1405]

Jessie well remembered the hard work writing entailed for Elizabeth.

> She did all these books in longhand – crossed them out and rewrote and so on, then a *tidy* longhand… and some of them she did *three times* in longhand – wrote, remedied, and then remedied again for the typist to get the finished copy.

In her younger days she could do the typing herself, but as the *RNA News* said in 1968, "she now finds this too tiring for reason of [a] back complaint."[1406] Two years later she confirmed this, telling Ruth Martin that her books began life in "an appalling sort of shorthand, which I wouldn't let anyone see for the world." She used to then type up the second draft herself "before having it finally prepared for the publishers," but the article reported that she had now "adopted the sensible procedure of reading from this manuscript into a tape recorder, for transcription by an audio-typist."[1407] This interview also revealed that she had resisted all requests for her manuscripts from American universities, and according to Kathleen, "She made Jessie burn all her manuscripts before she died – Jessie was very reluctant to do it."[1408] But she set no store by such things. When Muriel Grainger was preparing her anthology *A Pattern of People*, Elizabeth told her,

> *Please don't bother to post on the MS from Coward McCann. Put it on your next bonfire in the garden! I don't think it is really worth keeping these things.*[1409]

Perhaps there was a deeper reasoning behind this; beyond the reluctance to let people see her appalling shorthand. Way back in the forties, a description of Mr. Birley in *The Castle on the Hill* reveals a horror of self-glorification:

> *A lifelong devotion to the writer's craft had not succeeded in making him think that the life of his own mind and spirit, out of whose reactions to external events he fashioned his books, was the most important life there was.*[1410]

She added approvingly that Mr. Birley "remained utterly free of the taint of self-absorption and most deeply and sensitively aware of the life about him." These qualities seem to reflect what one of his friends said of her father: "He was so entirely free from any form of egoism, whether self-indulgence or self-assertion or self-righteousness."[1411]

Father and daughter shared a commitment to both writing and prayer, which involved hard work and discipline. Elizabeth said Canon Goudge's days were "an austere fixed routine of work and prayer, beginning at six in the morning and finishing at midnight.[1412] [He] knew how to slog. He worked harder than anyone I have ever known."[1413] And Jessie described a similarly full and disciplined life for Elizabeth - an "ordered life of prayer, reading, writing, rest and charitable listening and giving." Elizabeth said once, "I like to write in the early morning, before anything much has a chance to happen"[1414] – which means perhaps that her days were pretty full of happenings, for she added "I envy people who can write at night, when all is quiet and peaceful." And yet she coped with it all. Jessie said she had the ability to work "in deep concentration, and yet break off to time" and she particularly mentioned her ability to keep up the creative process even "though nursing a terminally ill mother who was a bit demanding."

> She was the most amazing person. She got up in the morning and answered the most important correspondence. If she was lucky she got on to her writing...But whatever she was doing, she could get up and put the vegetables on at the right time and have the lunch ready. (Having cooked for her mother...she HAD to get up from her creative things and get the lunch for Mother.) And her research for her work was meticulous and thorough.

An extract from *The Rosemary Tree* – which cites the monastic life of prayer as an illustration of the hardness of discipline - suggests that this may not have been a natural facility but something learnt slowly, over years.

> *The apportioning of different activities to appropriate moments was one of the disciplines of life. It must be hard even for the holiest and most disciplined of nuns to leave off praying when the dinner-bell rang, and harder still to start praying again after dinner when they didn't feel that way, but [she] must learn.*[1415]

Father and daughter were both "great dreamers" who sometimes told each other their dreams. They were alike too, she said, in that he "loved the beauty of the world perhaps even more than I do… But," she was quick to add,

> *His love for human beings equalled it,*[1416] *[whereas] I realise that together with the beauty of the world that holds them I have loved places too much and people not enough.*[1417]

Nevertheless Canon Goudge was "essentially a shy and reserved man"[1418] and Rosemary Sutcliff remembered his daughter too as "a very private person" and "a lovely person." Muriel Grainger also said she was "very modest…so humble…very shy," and this – as Sonia Harwood's memories of their meeting show - could be quite an obstacle for a writer so sought-after by her readers.

> Elizabeth said, I feel very shy about meeting you because I'm awkward with people and I'm always afraid of being a disappointment to them. They like my books and then they find me very shy.

Sonia had written a fan-letter after reading *The White Witch*, and after that,

> We continued writing to each other, about once a month I suppose, for several years. One day Elizabeth said, How about having phone chats? So I rang her up and after that I rang her about once a month… Eventually she said, "I would like to meet you…"
> I met her for the first time in 1967… She opened the door and flung her arms round me. After that I went to visit her at least once a year…until she became so ill that she really couldn't cope with visitors. We still went on writing, and I had a letter just a few months before she died.

There is no evidence that Elizabeth ever allowed her shyness to separate her from others; quite the contrary. Despite being in Lord Horder's opinion, "As far as possible from the stereotype of the romantic lady novelist," Elizabeth had been one of the original members of the Romantic Novelists'

Association and in later life became its Vice-President (having been "bullied" into the job, according to Jessie, by Barbara Cartland herself!) At the age of seventy-seven Elizabeth wrote to Muriel,

> *Being so old and crocky I don't get to their functions, but I know some of them and what dear people they are.*[1419]

One function that she missed was their Awards Presentation at the Park Lane Hotel in 1972, for which she had "donated a charming silver cup, a modern copy of an Elizabethan porringer" as the prize for the Historical Award, "re-introduced this year."[1420] (It is still being presented annually.) The RNA Chairman had been to lunch at Rose Cottage to show Elizabeth the new trophy, and reported that it "greatly pleased the donor." She added, incidentally, that

> A boisterous welcome was given by the new Dandie-Dinmont – successor to the late Miranda – called "Froda" after *Lord of the Rings*, one of Miss Goudge's favourite books.[1421]

Froda was the third of the "magical" Hobbits - Randa having died, like Tiki, at ten years old. Elizabeth described her as "a fairy creature who darts lightly about her kingdom of the garden, appearing and disappearing like a gleam of sunshine, aloof and mysterious in her fantasy world."[1422]

Visits like that of the RNA Chairman were by no means unusual, despite what Elizabeth said about hospitality being a rather weakly plant. In fact unlike herself and Jessie, she said, Rose Cottage itself thrived on company.

> *The moment the front door is opened to a guest I can feel the delight that rises up from its hospitable old heart. I once entertained thirty writers in our sitting room and even above the noise of the thirty all talking at once I imagined I was aware of the contented cat-like purring of the cottage.*[1423]

This - despite the admission that "a party looming on the horizon cast over [my father] the same shadow of impending doom as it still does over me"[1424] - was a gathering of the romantic novelists themselves, with their Vice-President as hostess. So she was more hospitable than she would admit; and this was certainly true where her readers were concerned. Like Sonia Harwood, Kathleen Millington's friendship with Elizabeth began when she wrote a fan letter in appreciation of her books, and as the friendship progressed she was invited to visit. She went twice, she said, and each time stayed for a couple of nights.

> It was wonderful of her to ask me – a nobody – but somehow we just fitted in. And they made me have breakfast in bed, and she came and sat on my bed and chatted to me.

Sonia remembered particularly, at a time of difficulty in her own life, Elizabeth's "tremendous sympathy with anyone in trouble."

> She was absolutely marvellous because she had that sort of listening quality about her, and her sympathy just came through… it was like PEACE. It was quite marvellous the way it happened. I'd never known anyone else respond in quite the same way, because we had a tragedy in our lives and Elizabeth was such a help to me – and to many other people. She had a quality about her…she just seemed to *know* all about it somehow.[1425]

Yet a remark of Sonia's is perhaps indicative of how much helping others tired Elizabeth at times, and how she coped with it: "She always went to bed early; she liked to be in bed when I rang so she could just relax."

She would respond to need in other ways too, for more than one among her friends and family members used the word *generous* to describe her, and remembered specific examples of her generosity. (Again like her father: who practised his economies even into old age to ensure that he had more money to give away.) And there are letters to friends that tell how she also gave *practical* help to those in need. She writes to Muriel about looking after someone "after a severe operation."[1426] And to Audrey too, telling how she and Jessie had had "four friends in trouble staying with us one after the other and needing a lot of looking after, and it was lovely to be able to give it."[1427] From the evidence of these letters she was still caring for others in her seventies, when she was not in the best of health herself.

Her health problems were ongoing… Lord Horder said she was "always in pain, which she triumphed over." In answer to an enquiry about her health, Elizabeth told Madeau that "the arthritis is osteo, not rheumatoid, crippling but not too painful, except that it dislikes motoring. I am very lucky."[1428] And in *The Joy of the Snow* she again counted herself lucky.

> *I am lucky enough to be able to say that I have never experienced great pain, but I do know from the minor pain of migraine headaches how confused one can be. It wakes you in the middle of the night and you hunt for the appropriate pills. An hour later, when the pain has reached its height, you are so confused that you cannot remember if you took them or not.*[1429]

Sonia said "she suffered a lot from migraines and often her eyes were very dark. We always booked two dates when I was going to see her, so that if she had a migraine we could fall back on the second date." Elizabeth's eyesight had deteriorated too, certainly by the time she was seventy for she told Muriel that the "proof-reading of *The Child from the Sea* floored me! My sight was getting bad by that time."[1430]

Audrey – despite finding it galling that she too was 'not allowed' to visit at times – nevertheless acknowledged that Elizabeth "had very poor health."

> She really had an awful lot to contend with, and she never complained. She had this awful softening of the spine which must have been agony and that I think affected the whole of her body. She was in a lot of pain…I don't know when it came on, because one never heard much about it until it got rather bad. She'd never been strong.

Travel had been difficult for years. Even in her early sixties, a letter to Audrey says, "Thank you for saying you'd like me to come and stay. But until I can overcome this nerve pain…I'd only be a nuisance because journeys finish me off entirely."[1431] (This would have been no short journey, however; for since her marriage in the late 1950s to the sculptor Charles d'Orville Pilkington Jackson, Audrey's home had been in Scotland.) Despite her optimism over the new type of car being designed in the early Sixties, according to the *RNA News* her back complaint was still making travel exhausting in 1968. Jessie confirmed that despite "all this lovely country round here I couldn't run her to see anything because it would take too much out of her for days and days afterwards – travelling was always awkward for her after I knew her." Kathleen confirmed that when she first got to know Elizabeth in the Sixties, the extent of her travelling was when "Jessie took her for short runs in the car." Although there was an exception, of course: the occasional "nightmare" journey to Jessie's cottage in Wales. But she did not become housebound until in her eighties: a letter at the end of 1973 describes a short drive whose sole object was to contemplate the beauty of autumn, her favourite season.

> *[Jessie] took me for a drive through the Nettlebed beechwoods just at sunset. We did not do much driving – mostly sat and gazed. The woods seemed on fire with every gorgeous colour you can think of and, when the sun was nearly down, three low straight belts of gold lying on the beech leaves.*[1432]

And this seems to have been an annual treat for the duration of her Oxford years; only coming to an end in 1982. She told Madeau then, in a spirit of counting her blessings: "I am the most fortunate old woman I know, and if I can't see the Nettlebed beech woods this year, it will be the first time for 30 years that I haven't seen them."[1433]

Nevertheless short journeys only were possible, like the planned visit to her cousin Sybil at the end of 1978, when she told Madeau regretfully:

I had hoped I would be able to combine a glimpse of you on my way to pay a visit to my 80 year old cousin in her lovely hidden cottage in the Wantage Hills. But Jessie says it is not en-route at all and can't be done. My arthritic back doesn't like motoring. (I don't know why it should be so bad-tempered about it; the backs of other osteo-ancients don't seem to mind much.)[1434]

She had also been to see another cousin in the spring of that year, in the Oxfordshire village of Goring, when Jessie "drove by the side roads, and the woods were full of bluebells."[1435]

Although travel became more and more restricted, radio and television could bring beauty into her life. Having told Audrey in 1965, "We have not got TV" by 1978 it was a part of their lives and she was able to describe for Muriel how "Jessie and I have watched Tortelier's Master Classes on TV. He is marvellous to watch... that mobile sensitive face." While on the subject of music she added, "Yes I love Vivaldi and Albinoni. Today, in the Sunday morning radio programme *Vivaldi's Venice* there was a heavenly piece of music, a setting of the eighth Psalm by Benedetto Marcello."[1436]

Kathleen said, "She loved beauty and beautiful things; she didn't like ugliness, but was very aware of it in the world and never shrank from writing about it... And she could describe it so *livingly*." Some people might think her writing was "rather pretty-pretty," she added, "but of course she wasn't like that."

Elizabeth was variously remembered as very loving, very sweet and kind-hearted, gentle (and yet strong-willed – there was nothing weak about her) and of great faith... everything you would expect her to be from her books, according to one friend. And Jessie agreed: "Elizabeth was exactly like her books." Alan Hull Walton too described how, when he moved from London, he became friendly with Elizabeth. It was the "most wonderful surprise" of his life, he said, to discover that Elizabeth was "exactly like her books– kind, quiet, charming." Even, he thought, to the point of "self-depreciation"[1437] - and perhaps, having to cope with the adoration of so many fans, it was this latter quality which prompted her to write with such wry humour about Miss Montague.

She was happy in old age and vastly amused to find herself a personage in the city, almost an institution, beloved, revered, and apparently the hostess of a salon. Shrewd as she was she could not but be aware that her chair by the fire had become a throne, and that when she went to the cathedral in her bath-chair, it was a queen's progress. When she looked back on the unloved girl she had been, on the toiling drone of her middle years, on the shabby prayerful recluse of her elderly years, it was all beyond her comprehension. But she enjoyed it and with a slightly mocking amusement dressed up for the part with velvet shoes on her feet and lace about her shoulders and over her head. She knew her own worthlessness and so did God, though he loved her none the less, and this false idea of her that the city had got into its head was a private joke between them.[1438]

Walton added that although Elizabeth herself denied it she was "extremely intelligent and well-read." Audrey too said that she was "*extraordinarily* well read" – adding that although not "conventionally good looking," she was "very attractive...very vivacious."

> Even when she wasn't well there was a vivacity about her which was always attractive, and although she was shy she could be very interesting when you got her talking about the things she wanted to talk about.

Although Elizabeth had long ago abandoned the idea of art and handicrafts as a career she still enjoyed both as hobbies. She told Ruth Martin that although her college studies included drawing, "it wasn't an artist's course as such" and she had since "tried and tried to paint. If I live to be older than I am, and really don't do any more novels, I would like to be like Grandma Moses, only working in watercolours!"[1439] Her love of painting and the creative process in general, is apparent in descriptions of Henrietta in *Sister of the Angels*.

The painter, as he mixed his water colours and began his portrait, had upon his face that set, almost locked look that she had seen upon her father's face when he was writing...

She expected that she had it when she was drawing. She always thought she felt a sort of click in her head when she concentrated her attention upon this work that of all others meant most to her; as though her mind

> *and her work locked together and a key had actually turned.... It was a good feeling...*[1440]
>
> *Ferranti brought her every day to the studio, and then, with amazing understanding, went away and left her; and she would paint on and on regardless of time, undisturbed by anyone except old Martha bringing her lollipops, until he fetched her again. She thought that she had never been so happy; that she never again would be so happy. Here, she thought, was all she would ever ask of life; an empty room under the sky, a sheet of blank paper, a paint brush and a box of paints. This was her kingdom.*[1441]

Her love of art complemented her love of nature for Elizabeth said that during her college days, she was "never so happy as in the greenhouse making studies of flowers that would later be used for embroidery and leather-work designs."[1442] Kathleen remembered that "she did beautiful needlework" and Jessie, pointing out the sitting room chairs at Rose Cottage, said: "That was the sort of embroidery she did – she put the design round it herself. She continued to do embroidery...almost to the end, until her sight began to go." She cited the chairs as a further example of Elizabeth's self-discipline in apportioning time to different tasks: "She could take up the embroidery," she said, "and embroider a little bit, and put it down just like that." She also remarked on her ability to inspire creativity in others:

> She was a tremendous person for inspiring other people to do things— people who'd compose music to her verses, or make plays. We've got quite a lot of things like that... excerpts from her books done as illuminated manuscripts, a painting of a broken stump, still growing - inspired by *The Scent of Water* - a song called *The Joy of the Snow*...

She loved poetry too, of course, "and her knowledge of it was great," said Kathleen. "She was a friend of John Betjeman and Ruth Pitter."

Neighbours

Ruth Pitter lived directly north of Peppard at Long Crendon in the Chilterns, on the Oxfordshire / Buckinghamshire border. Like Elizabeth and Jessie, she too had moved to her final home there in 1953. A letter marking the occasion from her friend C.S. Lewis[1443] – his first to be informally addressed to Dear Ruth and signed Jack Lewis – observed that her new home was in a lovely village, and extended a warm welcome to the Oxford area from himself and his brother Warnie. As to Pitter's friendship with John Betjeman, she described him in a letter as a man she "knew a little and loved a lot."[1444] While house-hunting in Oxfordshire she had been taken to visit him by their mutual friend Lord David Cecil, and later she and Betjeman shared more than one appearance in the television discussion programme, *The Brains Trust*, in the late Fifties.

Elizabeth's cousin Sybil and her husband had for years lived near the Betjemans and were their friends. The Reverend F.P. Harton, indeed, was their spiritual adviser, and author of *Elements of the Spiritual Life*, a book which John Betjeman recommended to T.S. Eliot in a letter of 1936. Also on his recommendation, the Reverend Harton had prepared Betjeman's great friends John and Myfanwy Piper for their confirmation in 1940. The Pipers lived just a few miles from Peppard at Fawley Bottom (re-named by Betjeman, Fawley Bum) and the Betjemans themselves were only a little further afield at historic Wantage, birthplace of King Alfred, in the Vale of the White Horse.

Alan Hull Walton, too, lived "not so very far away."[1445] It was he and David Reid, the musician friend who had introduced him to Elizabeth's books, who were with her when she announced her intention to stop writing, and begged her for an autobiography.

Travel was difficult for Elizabeth, but just how wide was her social circle during the thirty years at Peppard? There were so many links, so many possible friendships within the environs of Oxfordshire. She and Betjeman shared the same agent, David Higham, and Betjeman had a large circle of friends, including Christopher Hollis (one of the 'distinguished sons' of Mrs. Hollis at Wells, who Elizabeth used to play with) and her own 'friend of a publisher' Mervyn Horder… although he said he only met with her face to face about eight times in all. And did she ever make the short journey to visit those great friends of both Horder and Betjeman, the Pipers? If she did - although Fawley Bottom was an old flint farmhouse, not architecturally

Peppard

"contemporary" like theirs – could they even have been the inspiration behind the artistic Roger and Joanna in *The Scent of Water*?

Who knows… apart from a few eminent divines, Elizabeth's memoires name no names.

The Little Things

There was a family heirloom Elizabeth loved - a collection of miniatures that she called the Little Things, which had been passed down to her through the Collenette family in Guernsey. Kathleen obviously sent her a birthday card once with the picture of a similar collection, for Elizabeth wrote back,

> *Thank you so very very much for the lovely birthday card. How I do love it. The glass case was exactly like that, when I saw it first in my great-aunt's parlour in the Channel Islands. (She left the "little things" to my mother, and I have them now, but not the case, which I think was broken…)*[1446]

She must have loved them very much, for she included them in more than one of her novels. First of all, in *A City of Bells*:

> *On the stand stood every kind of miniature object that Mary had been able to collect throughout her life. There were tiny chairs carved out of ivory, a Bible the size of your thumb-nail which could be actually read with a magnifying glass, a silk purse with tiny coins inside, a tea-set of Bristol china, a bottle of shells the size of pins' heads, a little telescope through which you could look and see a picture of Brighton, and many other treasures, thirty of them altogether, all of them works of art and not a single one of them bigger than an acorn. Martha lifted off the shade and the children gloated, as they had gloated many times before and would gloat again, kneeling reverently on their knees and not daring to touch until Mary gave them leave.*[1447]

Nearly thirty years later they appeared again in *The Scent of Water*.

> *She lifted the glass case off the stand and they sat down together on the floor and began slowly to undo the tissue paper and cotton wool in which Mrs. Baker had wrapped the little things. It was hard to tell which of*

them was the more excited. One by one they appeared, the treasures of silver and gold, of jade, pinchbeck, glass, ebony and ivory, and Edith greeted each of them with delighted recognition. "Here's the mandarin who nods his head. Here's the peacock and the ivory mouse. Here's the little thimble and scissors in the silver basket. Here's the bluebird in the cage of golden wire. The lantern with the ruby glass. The dwarf with the red cap. The telescope with Brighton Pier at the end when you look through it. The elephant with a house on his back."[1448]

Elizabeth was not the only writer of the age to have a special feeling for little things. Joyce Grenfell recorded how Walter de la Mare also loved them, and had a cupboard full of "miniature furniture, shells, cups and dishes."[1449] Henrietta's reaction to the Little Things in *A City of Bells* perhaps gives an insight into why Elizabeth loved them so much. She was "uplifted…"

The thought of so much patience and skill poured out upon the making of things so tiny gave her a feeling of liberation. The sight of perfection was like a gate that let one out into freedom, and if one could make small things so lovely then it seemed that one had not got to go very far or own very much to be free.[1450]

Not just miniature work, but hidden work too features in many of the novels – things more hidden, even, than the workings of the Dean's watch. In the cathedral at Torminster, for instance:

So passionately had the sculptor enjoyed himself that he had taken as much trouble with the parts that did not show as the parts that did; you could put your finger round behind a grinning imp and find he had an unseen tail lashing away in the dark.[1451]

Elizabeth's joy in the self-effacing humility of such hidden work perhaps began in childhood with the influence of *Puck of Pook's Hill*, where Hal o' the Draft tells the children sadly of his youthful pride: regretting that his aim at that time had been, "not to serve God as a craftsman should, but to show my people how great a craftsman I was."[1452]

Little things and hidden things have a symbolic role too, particularly in *The Scent of Water*. Little acts of kindness, done to little people whom the world tends to think do not matter – the shy, the lonely, the mentally ill… They are of immense importance and have great results, like the brief conversation with a retired clergyman which triggers Cousin Mary's lifelong faith journey; and her own legacy to a little girl of the next generation, whom again she has met only once. And symbolically Mary too finds hidden beauty in the carved tracery of the church. She puts her fingers through a "lattice work of thorns" and discovers within, bunches of little flowers which "haven't been seen since the carving was put in its place...They will never be seen."[1453] Hidden beauty, at the heart of painful thorns...

Even the Three-Fold Prayer which is given to her, and which transforms her life, is a little thing - a tiny trinity – three little prayers of only three words each. And symbolically implicit at the heart of all this littleness is that tiniest of things underlying all, the mustard-seed of faith.

In *The Savage and Beautiful Country*, Alan McGlashan too writes of the symbolic significance of small things - the paradox of the almighty contained in the tiny. Of how the paradoxical phrase *smaller than small, yet bigger than big* seems to make no sense, and yet perfectly expresses humanity's "earliest concepts of the Divine." He cites as examples, the Little Copper Man of the Finnish *Kalevala*; and the Babe lying in a manger, in whose praise - in the words of the Book of Job: "the morning stars sang together and all the sons of God shouted for joy."[1454]

Evelyn Underhill's poem *Immanence* says

> I come in the little things,
> Saith the Lord.[1455]

And to repeat the words of Dame Julian of Norwich that Elizabeth loved so much: "He shewed me a little thing, the quantity of an hazel-nut, in the palm of my hand... I looked thereupon...and thought: *What may this be?* And it was answered... *It is all that is made...*"

> *I took the lid off the little box...Under the cotton wool was something small and white and delicate. I picked it up and my breath caught in my throat so that I could not speak. It was a carved ivory coach, about the size of a hazel nut, and inside was Queen Mab. There are no words to describe the loveliness of that coach, like a sea shell, or the beauty of the little queen's face half-smiling beneath her tiny crown.*
>
> *I held it in the palm of my hand and it seemed to be all that there is.*[1456]

So says Cousin Mary in *The Scent of Water*. Julian of Norwich concludes:

> In this Little Thing I saw three properties. The first is that God made it, the second is that God loveth it, the third, that God keepeth it. But what is to me verily the Maker, the Keeper, and the Lover, - I cannot tell; for till I am

Substantially oned to Him, I may never have full rest nor very bliss: that is to say, till I be so fastened to Him, that there is right nought that is made betwixt my God and me.[1457]

※

Jessie contrasted Elizabeth's love of small things, and the narrowing physical restrictions of her life, with the breadth of her inner life and faith:

> Despite her physical inability to travel she delighted in the minute and near-at-hand, and if she couldn't experience much of the middle distance in all her latter years, like us, she was judged to be ahead of us in wider, loftier vision, and the best of newly-emergent ideas.

As an illustration of this, she recalled a visit from Kenneth Preston, the friend to whom Elizabeth dedicated *A Book of Faith*:

> Canon Preston was one of the last of her father's pupils and knew them in Christ Church, and was a fan as well as a friend. I remember him coming once and he was giving her an earnest report of some tremendous gathering that he'd been to there, of divines. They'd been thrashing through a new idea that had come up.
>
> And he said to her, "We've been working hard at this - and you've got it already!"
>
> She'd received it from her own thinking. That was impressive I thought…She had been thinking along her own lines and got to the same point, which was rather marvellous.

Hélène's second son Hugh, a priest, wrote with respect of Elizabeth's theological insight.

> I…discovered on reflection that usually whenever Elizabeth did say something different or express something in her Anglican way, which at the time I thought clashed with my more RC way of looking at things, that she was invariably right and that thanks to her I was learning… Elizabeth

always had a thought or an insight which I found helpful and formative in my own faith journey…

Elizabeth was quintessentially Anglican…with a broadness of view and a willingness to patiently listen to and consider other points of view which one wouldn't normally associate with the Anglican communion. As you know from her autobiography, Elizabeth was interested in ESP and saw this as one of the many ways of God revealing himself. Her faith was deep and quiet, totally unostentatious, open and accepting, certainly compassionate and undoubtedly the centre, the hub, and I think the main motivation behind all that she did and wrote; certainly fed by prayer and reflection and also by the Eucharist which she attended every Sunday when she could and which, when she wasn't well enough to go to church towards the end of her life, was brought to her.[1458]

Heavenly Music

He added,

Undoubtedly in my view, music was an essential part of Elizabeth's faith experience; she saw it as a way of praying and of being in communion with God.

Indeed she said in *The Joy of the Snow*, that "the Word speaks perhaps more clearly through music than through any other medium known to men, even the beauty of the world itself."[1459] For Elizabeth to rank anything above the beauty of the natural world is surely the highest praise. She even seems to include music as one of the Little Things in *The Child from the Sea* - in her reference to "that small scale of notes that is one of the ladders to heaven."[1460] She wrote to Madeau too in 1976: "Sometimes I think music is our one hope. Evil can't get hold of it. It is entirely spiritual and is truly the voice of God."[1461] Three years later she found an affirmation of this in Neville Ward's book *The Following Plough*, telling Madeau, "He says this:

> 'Devotion has found its most satisfying expression not in formal prayer but in art, in the building of the great cathedrals and innumerable churches, in much painting and sculpture, and in such an outflowing of heavenly music that must often have stopped evil in its headlong course.'[1462]

Hugh Dutton also remembered that 'Whenever I stayed with her, after tea and before supper Elizabeth would say, "Now it's time to listen to some glorious music,"

> whereupon she would recline on the settee and I was the one who had to choose the concert for the evening from her collection of records; and there we would be just the two of us – Jessie was usually in the kitchen preparing the supper, but with the door open so that she could listen also – listening to an hour and a half of "glorious music." And we listened; just the music, no reading and no conversation. It was not just to be listened to but also to be prayed, of that I am certain.

They listened to "classical and sacred music of course":

> Thomas Tallis' *Spem in Alium*, Mozart's 21st piano concerto and the Beethoven late quartets immediately come to mind. Until I really knew Elizabeth I could never cope with the late quartets but now solely thanks to her I love them. The 131 was her absolute favourite.[1463]

❄

Bede Griffiths remembered the impact of the Late Quartets in his youth at Oxford: how inspired he and his friends had been by the concept of a transcendent beauty that could grow out of suffering and struggle. For at the end of his life Beethoven had passed beyond his strife and anguish, into a peaceful reconciling of the two worlds of darkness and light, pain and joy. Much of Beethoven's anguish had been centred on the tragic loss of his hearing. Alec Harman and Wilfrid Mellers, in *Man and his Music*, record how he lived through a period of nervous breakdown and "terrible mental suffering;"[1464] but at the end of his life found a new understanding: pain and joy were reconciled, and he came to understand the meaning of William Blake's words, that "without Contraries is no progression. Attraction and

Repulsion, Reason and Energy, Love and Hate, are necessary to Human existence."[1465]

Many of Elizabeth's characters, too, grapple with the problem of life's contraries. In *The Bird in the Tree* David Eliot, looking at "the squares of moonlight lying on the floor" had remembered

> *the time when he had first realised that pain is a thing that we must face and come to terms with if life is to be lived with dignity and not merely muddled through like an evil dream.*
>
> *It had been when his father was dying. His mother had not troubled over much to keep him out of sight and sound of his father's pain; she had thought he was too little to understand. But he had understood... Terrified by it he had fled one evening to the dark attic, slammed the door and flung himself down sobbing upon the floor. He had sobbed for an hour, sobbed himself sick and exhausted until at last, childlike, he had forgotten what it was he was crying about and had become instead absorbed by the moonlight on the floor. It had been like a pool of silver, enclosed and divided up into neat squares by the bars of the window. He had counted the squares and the lines, dark and light, and had been delighted with them. He had touched each with his finger, this way and that, and had been utterly comforted...*
>
> *Later, in bed, he had been comforted once more by the thought of that pattern. In some vague way he had understood that dark things are necessary; without them the silver moonlight would just stream away into nothingness, but with them it can be held and arranged into beautiful squares.*[1466]

At the end of the Second World War *Green Dolphin Country* stated the belief with even greater conviction.

> *Could you understand the meaning of light if there were no darkness to point the contrast? Day and night, life and death, love and hatred, since none of these things can have any being at all apart from the existence of the other, you can no more separate them than you can separate the two sides of a coin. To possess one is to possess the other...*[1467]

The Three-fold Life

Neville Ward's *The Following Plough* discusses the concept of spiritual growth as a thing of three phases, separated from each other by the "crisis of reluctance" which St. John of the Cross called the dark night of the soul. In the first stage, the self must be liberated from "misunderstanding of the truth about God and life." Thus freed, it can grow into a "recognizable confidence," which comes from deeper knowledge of itself and of God, and a commitment to God. For those who can attain to the third stage, this is when one's life is "integrated and simplified in the love of God and openness to him."

Ward observes that it is a visibly recognisable pattern in the life and work of many great artists, citing as examples Shakespeare, Schubert, Rembrandt and Monet. And it is "marvellously shown" he says, in Beethoven's "spiritual pilgrimage, as his thought and feeling deepen through their well-defined three periods."

> The 'Hammerklavier' sonata was written between his second and third periods, in an extraordinary depth of anguish before he entered the reconciliation and serenity of his 'unitive' way.[1468]

The self-effacing Elizabeth would not want to hear herself linked in any way to these great names of music, art and literature – and yet surely her work had something of a three-phase pattern, too. In the early days, when she was still trying to formulate her ideas about good and evil, God and pain, she had watched her father at prayer and wished that she too could pray. She wrote her first novel about the young Michelle, frustrated by the contrasts of the two worlds; and soon afterwards she plunged into the darkness of nervous breakdown. As she gradually recovered she entered into a new phase, always supported by the teaching on prayer that she had received from her father. Against a background of war she wrote a series of books in which the dark tide of evil is challenged by the power of prayer, unselfishness and love. Her own life at this time was in many ways hard and it culminated in another kind of breakdown after her mother's death, this time apparently compounded of bereavement, remorse and sheer physical exhaustion. But she was able to write down, at the end of it all, Hilary's advice in the last Eliot novel - not to fight against the Thing, not to just grimly endure it, but to accept it, and use it. It can become, in this way, one's greatest treasure.

In the quietness of Rose Cottage a third phase began slowly to evolve, and she placed centre-stage in her final novels characters who have acquired, through acceptance of suffering, an inner peace. Almost thirty years after Michelle's anguish, Cousin Mary learns not to fight against her hard fate, but to say *Yes I will: Into Thy Hands*. And there has been through the years, too, a slowly growing awareness that the contraries represent not a battle, but a balance; as one character after another overcomes a crisis of reluctance and fear in order to plunge into the darkness… and then discover that paradoxically it leads to Light.

Beethoven's last works marked the end of his own struggle against the blows of Fate. A question and answer are written on the score of his last quartet, the Opus 135, which sum up his new attitude. "Muss es sein? Es Muss sein!" he writes – "Must it be? It must be." In this final work, say Harman and Mellers, "question and answer have become one."[1469] It is akin to Cousin Mary's acceptance of her mental illness: it must be, and she will go through life thereafter saying *Yes, I will* to whatever God asks.

At the end of his life Beethoven could let go of his struggles with fate and the world, because he had "fought and won a more important battle in his own spirit." Previously he had wanted to conquer life, saying "even with the frailties of my body, my spirit shall dominate." But he learnt instead to pray, "O God give me strength to conquer myself, for nothing must bind me to this life."[1470]

Perhaps T.S. Eliot's greatest poetry was that inspired by Beethoven's Late Quartets. He wrote to Stephen Spender in March 1931, telling him that he was listening to the A minor Quartet on his gramophone and finding it worthy of inexhaustible study, and that he would like to try and capture its spirit in verse: that heavenly joy that he found in some of Beethoven's later work, which he thought the human spirit might attain as the *fruit of reconciliation and relief* after great suffering.[1471]

Man and his Music concludes that in the last lines of *Little Gidding* Eliot comes "about as close to describing in words what Beethoven's last quartets are about as is humanly possible."

> And all shall be well and
> All manner of thing shall be well
> When the tongues of flame are in-folded
> Into the crowned knot of fire
> And the fire and the rose are one.[1472]

Elizabeth said, "Of all the great poems I have loved and learned by heart, and that have come through life with me as much loved as human friends, I think one of the greatest is T.S. Eliot's *Little Gidding*. So much spiritual experience is held in such a small compass and yet is so perfectly described."[1473] And Elizabeth's friend Sister Raphael Mary said in a letter to Jessie: "She loved Beethoven's quartets. They express so much of what her prayer was like. Don't you think?"[1474]

Credo

In the spring of 1972 Elizabeth told Madeau that "Joanne Scott Montcrieff of the BBC (who lives near me here) asked me if I would do one of the Holy Week talks – the ones they have before the daily service in the morning – and encouraged by the confidence you gave me and egged on by Jessie, I said yes. I've just managed to come out the other end of writing the script, with awful struggles, but speaking it will be worse, so please keep your fingers crossed for me."[1475]

It was broadcast on the morning of Good Friday.[1476]

Every year at this time, when the birds begin to sing and the crocuses are coming up like flames out of the earth, we come face to face with the astonishment of spring. There was not a trace of all this a short time ago; then there was darkness and cold and now there is singing and light. What has happened? Death has turned himself around, as the year has turned around, and shows us life, and this week we remember that God in the person of his son has also lived and died and risen again.

I believe that God who made the world of nature has made it as the reflection of what he does and is. St. John of the Cross saw the soul in her longing for God searching for him through the woods, and asking, "Has he passed your way?" And the trees reply, yes,

> *...through these woods and groves he passed apace,*
> *Turning, as on he sped,*
> *And clothing every place*
> *With loveliest reflection of his face.*

We see something of what God is in nature, that he is beauty and strength, life and light, and I myself see in the passing seasons the work of his incarnation, when he leaped down to us and caught us up to be with him in his life and death, even as he is with us in ours, and to be swept up with him to the new life of his resurrection.

I see the same process echoed in the course of history when some civilization grows to a peak of beauty and then decays and appears to die. Yet the death is only that of the body. If we take as an example Greek culture at its purest and strongest, at that moment when it reflected something of the beauty of God, we can see that the soul of it is with us still. I think this is the way God works in history. This is what he does as he slowly brings mankind to his ultimate (and inconceivable) purpose for us.

The same rhythmic process is echoed in our own lives. They glow and then darken, love turns to loss and life seems over. But if we keep the ways of God in memory our darkness does not turn to despair, for we realize that nothing too terrible can be happening to us, since we are echoing the pattern that love himself devised. Yet love our God cannot have intended that death should be the dreadful thing it so often is. Surely he wanted it to be a natural process of linking one mode of life to another. Is it our sin, we wonder, that has made it so hard? And here we see the nature of the love of God, for when he came to die he did not choose a gentle ending but one of the worst deaths that the sin of man has yet been able to devise, that men might see in the dreadfulness of his death the measure of his love. His life shows us the nearness of his love, his death its greatness and his resurrection its eternity. And since as a man he is one of us we can see in his resurrection of love an experience that could be ours too.

And so I have come to think that the only eternity there can be is that of love. God is love and only as things exist in him are they eternal. And this brings us to what for human beings is a most vital question; what exactly is love?

I cannot find a true answer to this question, since the being of God is beyond comprehension, but for practical purposes here and now I would say that our earthly loving is a pitiful attempt to turn towards the world some reflection of the face of God. And if we ask how, then three words come to my mind; selflessness, giving and forgiving. Our own attempts at loving are like flowers struggling to push their way through poisonous weeds, jealousy and lust and possessiveness that grow up out of the mud of our self-love. Only in Christ do I find what I am looking for. Looking at his earthly life I see that because he was rooted in selflessness he could bring every good quality to perfection. His strength, courage, honesty, his wisdom and compassion, peace and forgiveness, have the clearness of light, and like light they poured from the sun of his being in a ceaseless giving that was life to all who could receive it. Crowds followed him wherever he went. They had not known that giving could be like this.

But I doubt if the self-giving of his life alone would have been enough to make us lift our eyes from our own mud and look up. It took his death to do that, as he had known it would. "I shall draw all men to myself when I am lifted up from the earth." But in looking up at the cross I do not think he would want us to think too much of the details of his dying. Could it be that his death by torture shows us not only the greatness of God's love, but also that his presence is with every man, woman and child who must suffer agony and degradation? He would rather we thought of them, for the reflection of his face is seen in their faces even more clearly than in the world of nature. But at the crucifix, which has been a symbol of love for two thousand years, we can hardly look enough. I do not know who it was who first pointed out that the cross with its upright and cross piece is the I crossed out. And the figure on the cross, with arms stretched out to God and man, pictures all the generosity of giving.

The third word, forgiving, is shown too in the outstretched arms. What mother, when a child in tears runs to her saying, "I am sorry", does not hold out her arms? The crucifixion began with a prayer of forgiveness, "Father, forgive them, for they do not know what they are doing." And then comes forgiveness in action. The penitent thief had cursed Christ with the rest until something silenced him. Perhaps it was meeting the eyes of Christ, but it may simply have been the awareness of silence beside him, the silence in which so many find God.

I think the beginning of forgiveness, its birth, is stillness and silence. The records of Christ's life and passion show him as a man who did not retaliate. When the poor whom he loved suffered injustice he was roused to anger in their defence, but when he was the victim he did not defend himself. Then thinking of him, and the dignity of his silence, I seem to pass within it to a great depth and feel that he opened himself, almost in the way a flower opens its heart to the sun, to receive not the sun but all the evil done to him, that it might be ended. If that is true then forgiveness in its fullness is letting the evil done to you end in you. I think this is the way Christ forgave the thief. His silence received the abuse and let it drop into the depths of his love, like a stone dropping into deep water, and as his love is bottomless that was the end of it.

Did the thief feel the evil drawn out of his heart, its place taken by the love of God flowing back to its home? I think he must have understood something of what was happening to him because of what he said. "Jesus, remember me when you come to your throne." And Christ replied, "I tell you this: today thou shalt be with me in Paradise." The gospels do not record any words of penitence or forgiveness. Perhaps Christ and the thief had no need of these because they had passed so quickly to what lies beyond them, to the coming together of two people in love and their desire to be always together. There had been a death, the death of sin, and now there was this new birth. And so the pattern of birth and death and life again is seen once more in this total forgiving of Christ upon the cross. It was fore-giving. Almost before the sinner had had time to turn to him Christ had destroyed his evil and taken possession of his broken heart.

For there is that condition of the broken heart, since even the love of God cannot take possession of a closed heart. Something must predispose it to break open from within. In the case of Mary Magdalen Christ said it was because she had loved much. With the penitent thief it was perhaps the bearing of much pain. In others it can be the sight of beauty or the experience of loneliness. I believe love can make use of almost anything to break our hearts, and some of us, looking back on our lives, can see the exact moment when it happened. For me it was the experience of forgiveness. Someone forgave me much unkindness, quickly, freely, simply, in the true Christ-like manner, and it broke me.

But we ourselves cannot forgive in this total way, this divine way that if only we could practise it would rid the world of all its evil. Christ's love was bottomless, but I know only too well that the bottom of my loving is reached rather quickly. So what can we do?

It sounds almost absurd to say that as a minute beginning we can learn not to increase the evil in the world by nursing a grievance. It is easy to see how evil builds up from the chain reaction of retaliation, but it is not so easy to see how it builds up also from nursing a grievance. Someone injures us in some way, or we think they do. We do not retaliate but we brood over our sense of injury until it becomes a thorn in the mind, and poisons form round the thorn, anger and resentment and criticism. And poison is a thing that can spread from mind to mind without a word spoken. But how do you get rid of a thorn when it is actually there?

Well, if we resent things done to ourselves I have found it can be very helpful to spend twenty minutes remembering all the hurting things I myself have done and thought and said, and the shame of this exercise brings me to Christ that he may tell me what to do. He said, "Pray for your persecutors." I believe praying and loving are the same, and that in the end prayer always wins. If only evil could die in this way, in the depths of forgiveness within each one of us, there would be such a new birth and flowering of love as the old world has never seen before.

That is the objective side of forgiving, that is what we have to do, but there is also the subjective side, how we ourselves should receive forgiveness. I think it is only now that I am old that I see forgiveness as so supremely important, and this is because of something which happens to us in old age. It is the coming round full circle to face your beginnings. Memory of the distant past wakes up in an extraordinary way and you find yourself meeting again not only the joys and sorrows of the past but the sins too. Forgotten cruelties confront you, forgotten lovelessness and cowardice. It may be that you were sorry for these things at the time, but if so you see how poor and inadequate was the sorrow because you so little understood the depths of your own vileness. (And our conception of sin can change as we grow old. What seemed nothing at the time seems hideous now.) But I have been taught that despair is a sin and not to be able to accept the forgiveness of Christ is sacrilege. He told those he healed that their faith would set them free, and as with illness so with sin that is sometimes the root of illness. If we can believe that the sins of broken-hearted sinners are lifted away from us by Christ, then we are set free to rejoice in our freedom with the simplicity of children. Forgiveness is like spring. Flowing so freely to us from our Lord and God it is like sunshine and a west wind. It can make even our old age green and fresh.[1477]

※

Again she reiterates the importance of Forgiveness - and alongside it, an awareness of life as a circle, and old age a journey towards renewal. Both had been themes in *The Child from the Sea*, and the same message is in the penultimate chapter of *The Joy of the Snow* with its reference to *Little Gidding*, in which Eliot "follows up his eerie meeting with the stranger who is his past selves with a description of the remorse that the end of life cannot fail to bring..."

But he does not leave our old age stuck in the remorse, he brings 'the exasperated spirit' round through growth and purgation to the memories of childhood, to where the circle is complete, with the fragmented selves becoming the whole person, whole as the child who came into the world and ready for the renewal for which the other springs of our lives have been no more than prophecy.[1478]

The Joy of the Snow

Her autobiography asks a question: "What do we all feel, at the end of our work? Near the end perhaps, of our life?" But Elizabeth was not yet at the end of her work. Although she was in her seventies and they had been at Rose Cottage for over twenty years now, it seems that she was still as busy as ever. The fact that she had been involved in radio broadcasting at the same time as toiling at her autobiography, is perhaps the source of one humorous remark in *The Joy of the Snow*. Looking back to the older gentlewomen of Edwardian days, she says that having reached a certain age they "dressed for the part [in] a lace cap" and then "sat down" for the rest of their lives.

Very little was expected of these ageing ladies. They had done their work, were revered for it and might now sit down. I suppose it is on balance a happy thing that old people are put on the shelf less early now; but I do have days when I hanker for a lace cap.[1479]

After all the "bullying" and hard work involved in its production, she finally came to wondering if *The Joy of the Snow* would ever make it to the booksellers, because publishing, as she said in a letter to Muriel Grainger, was "in such a state."[1480] Britain was in the grip of industrial troubles - the 'three-day week' - and because of this the book was published first in America. However, an article in her local newspaper, the *Oxford Mail*, on Thursday 22nd August 1974 recorded that Hodder and Stoughton were publishing the book, at a price of £3.25, "today."

Their reporter, Anthony Wood, said that critics in the USA had already complained that she did not "write much about the string of successes she has penned" except to explain why three of them were her own favourites.[1481]

Why had she not? Probably because of the dislike of self-glorification described in Mr. Birley: that had, perhaps, motivated her to put her own manuscripts on the bonfire. But she had already described the writing of a memoire as looking back at "almost a stranger – 'knowing myself, yet being someone other.'"[1482] Could it be that, looking back at her fictional heroines from the viewpoint of her hard-won peace of mind, they too were in a sense unrecognisable? Had she in some sense simply *outgrown* most of her books? Except for those three: which were about the Bridge world, Forgiveness, and Ely… and its great Dean who was so very like her father.

Whatever the complaints however, or the reasons for them, *The Joy of the Snow* was a success. In addition to the newspaper articles, the BBC interviewed her for an August broadcast[1483] entitled Do you know Elizabeth Goudge? and she wrote to Madeau to tell her "that there were more telephone calls and a big post this morning from people who had enjoyed our programme."[1484] Later, extracts from the book were included in Radio Four's *Pick of the Week*, and it was also abridged for broadcast in twelve instalments on *Woman's Hour*. It was very well reviewed, not least by its dedicatee Alan Walton, who stated categorically that it was "the best of her books, the most well-written, and the most enlightening – in every conceivable way."[1485]

He was only one of many critics who were favourably impressed. Marjorie Kunz, writing for *The Church Times*, said that the book not only had the

> grace, sincerity and imaginative intensity of the best of her novels, but it also throws a fascinating light on the process by which the author has transmuted the experiences and impressions of her childhood and youth in particular into the material for her stories… She must have been an unusually observant child, capable of deep attachments and with a passion for the English countryside, and for the lovely old houses and gardens where she lived and to which her novels were later to bear eloquent witness.[1486]

William Barclay, reviewing it for *The Expository Times*, called it a "beautifully written record of a beautiful life. If poetry is 'emotion recollected in tranquillity', though it is written in prose, this book is a poem."[1487] And in the opinion of the *Sunday Times*' critic, it "traces a satisfying full circle from a childhood in, literally, holy places to a maturity reached by real philosophical progression."[1488]

Lord Horder, now retired as Chairman of Duckworth, wrote a long review for *The Bookseller* and like Kenneth Allsop fourteen years earlier, compared the style and content of her work with contemporary literature; concluding it was old-fashioned by the standards of a media world where *Last Tango in Paris* "persistently drowns" *The Sound of Music*. His target audience, the booksellers, however would know how "unreal" such a film was compared with the majority of ordinary people's lives, and would welcome this autobiography of

> an author who has unshamedly and undeflectibly pursued her own brand of sweetness and light for forty years... who has stood quietly apart from the fever of the literary establishment [and] whose books have sold in millions.[1489]

Jessie said that Elizabeth "almost never kept criticism – her mother kept one or two, I think. There should have been sheaves of them, but she threw those all away. But one or two from people she valued very much, she kept." Jessie produced copies of Mervyn Horder's review, and those of William Barclay and Alan Walton, who said,

> Not only is she gifted with an extremely beautiful English style; not only are her novels, essays and children's stories veritable treasures of perfect construction – but she has preserved in print, for all time, descriptions of a sane, sober, considerate and healthy way of life, which is fast disappearing; and absent from most novels today... There is nobody like her...

> The importance of Elizabeth Goudge's books can be judged, not only from the number of times she is mentioned on radio, and her fan mail...but also from the fact that on Sunday 4th August this year, the Reverend David Staple broadcast from Cardiff a sermon devoted almost entirely to her magnificent novel, *A City of Bells*. This was a tribute if ever there was one. And yet her writings never strike us as being 'religious' or 'moralistic'. Anyone can read them with pleasure and delight... She is unique in a very special way.[1490]

※

The final chapter of this book which William Barclay described as "a poem" is entitled *The End of our Exploring* - a quotation from Eliot's *Little Gidding*. It is both a discussion of the nature of 'the last things' and a statement of Elizabeth's own faith.

What do we all feel, at the end of our work? Near the end perhaps, of our life? Much the same, I expect. If like myself we are one of the lucky ones, overwhelming gratitude. And mixed with the gratitude, shame; for living and working should all be done in obedience to whatever vision of God may have been given to us; and how we do fail our vision of him.

What do I believe about the vision of God, and about judgment? Our ancestors believed that all souls would stand before the judgment seat of God, and that many would be sent to a hell of lasting torment. Today our ideas are less concrete but more merciful. What do I believe myself about judgment? My own picture of these things is clear in my mind. It is only my own picture but I expect I share it with many others. With me it is, literally, a picture, for even in old age I cannot manage to grow up sufficiently either to listen to music, to think or pray without seeing pictures in my mind.

I believe that we are created by love and that sooner or later the persuasion of love will draw us up out of our darkness to stand in its exquisite light and see ourselves at last as we really are. The picture I see is of a seed deep in the earth. Somewhere, far up above the weight of darkness pressing upon the pitiful little seed, is the drawing and the calling of the sun. It seems an impossible journey towards something that has never been seen and cannot be known, but half unconsciously the blind seed puts out roots to steady itself, pushes an imploring hand upwards and starts the struggle. The poor mad poet Christopher Smart said, "the flower glorifies God and the root parries the adversary." The struggling plant knows as little about the flower he will presently be as he knows about the God he will glorify, but the flower calls to him too as he pushes up through thick darkness with the adversary clinging to his feet.

The picture of the soul now turns in my mind from that of a plant to a little animal, like a mole, scrabbling with his forepaws to make an upward tunnel, kicking out with his hindlegs at the adversary who tries ceaselessly to drag him back and down. Often he is dragged down, but he recovers himself and goes on and with each fresh beginning he is a little higher up; and always the pull of the sun is far more powerful than that of the adversary.

He is through at last and stands in the sun, and sometimes in my picture he is a little animal with trembling paws covering his face, and sometimes he is a shivering spike of a flower with a closed bud. The sun must woo the opened eyes to peep between the chinks of the paws, or persuade the closed petals to open a little way. It is enough. A little warmth, a little light, and the creature can know for whom, and for what he was made. For love, that he may love perfectly, and perfected be useful to the love that has loved him from the beginning and will love him to the end.

But meanwhile, what is he? It is the judgment. There is no judgment seat for the sun does not judge him; merely warms him and gives him light. He is his own judge and strengthened by the warmth he looks at himself in the light. What has he made of himself in the dark tunnel? What is he like? A dirty little animal. A shaky bit of stalk holding up a crumpled bud that has no beauty in it. The knowledge is agony, for with blind eyes down in the dark he had thought a good deal of himself, and the agony is both his judgment and his inspiration. He cannot stand in the light like this. The paws go out in supplication in my picture, or the petals push away the calyx and take on the shape of praying hands. Do what you like with me. Whatever the cost, wash me and make me clean that I may be with you.[1491]

If one believes in a God of love what can one think about hell..? As reported in the gospels Christ said some frightening things about hell and I have spent miserable moments with them, for I was taught that we must not pick out from the teaching of Christ the things we happen to like and repudiate the rest. But I cannot see that anywhere in what are called 'the hard sayings' Christ says that any human soul will live eternally in hell….

In the parable of the sheep and the goats it appears that the latter have finally rejected love, for they hear dreadful words, "Depart from me, ye wicked, into everlasting fire." This surely does not mean the eternal torment of a soul in the eternal fire but its destruction. This, Christ thinks, is fearful enough since Saint Matthew's gospel reports him as saying, "Fear him who is able to destroy both soul and body in hell." And indeed it is fearful that any soul that God made for total love should be totally destroyed, but I cannot think that the destruction contradicts those greatest of all words, "I, if I be lifted up, will draw all men unto me." That sentence almost gives the definition of a man; a creature still capable of wrenching his eyes off himself and looking up, a creature (unknown to himself, perhaps) secretly longing for love and capable of it. If there should ever be a creature who had lost even the capability he would be no longer a man but a devil…[1492]

I would like to believe that no human soul ever becomes a totally evil spirit – a devil – that no human soul is ever destroyed. I want to believe that every single soul reaches God at last. And yet – love cannot compel. Love can draw the little animal up and up, perhaps fighting all the way, to the point where he is aware of the presence of the sun and feels its warmth embrace him. He cries out like Jacob, "What is your name?" and he knows the answer and what it means. But he has to be asked a question himself. "Now you know what I am, do you want me?" As it is almost inconceivable to me that love should have to ask such a question of any soul he has created, so it seems equally inconceivable that he would ever receive any answer except, "Wash me and make me clean that I may be with you." Yet I have to believe that the soul may refuse if he wishes. And what then? Not eternal torment since the sun is fire, but eternal death… And yet, Christ conquered death.

One struggles with thoughts and words, and then suddenly they all fall down like the cards with which a child has laboriously tried to build a house, and lie there in chaos at one's feet. For we know nothing. The mystery of the universe and of our tiny breath of being is too great for us… In this state it comforts me to remember that the great religions of the world have been called "Traditions of response." Certainly all true living all down the ages has been a condition of response; to mountains and trees and great waters, to music, poetry, to each other, to loveliness without end, and always it is the response of as much love as we are capable. And as response grows we are capable of more and more love. Growth is not sterile. Out beyond all these things must be the reality that speaks through them, and when our own thoughts and words crumble it helps to turn to the mystics who are lifted above our confusions, and to the old myths of the world, some of them almost as old as time…

This leads her to quote from "a poem I love, taken from the Bhagavad-Gita," remarking that Christians "would agree with nearly all of it, delighting in the way in which the great religions echo each other as the chimes of the church bells used to do on Christmas night."

But for us, though we believe great sons of God walk the world in every age, only one of them is the supreme Son of God who fulfils all longing because he is "everything God asks of man, and everything man asks of God."[1493]

❋

She published just one more book. It was the final anthology – very appropriately about faith - which was already in the making when *The Joy of the Snow* came out. She had told Philippa Toomey in 1974,

I love making anthologies...and I'm doing a third one now. After A Book of Comfort *and* A Book of Peace *I've been asked to do* A Book of Faith. *I start by putting in everything I love very much myself. I'm rather inclined to stick to the old favourites, and making anthologies has made me read more of the modern poets, and to find them very good, even to my old fashioned tastes.*[1494]

Like *The Joy of the Snow* the anthology was published first in America, for in August 1976 she sent a friend "the American copy... It has not been published in England yet, though I go on hoping that it will be. In time for Christmas perhaps...." In fact, the British edition did come out in 1976. The recipient of the gift was Father Louis Bouyer, and she told him "I am so very glad you think the *Book of Faith* might be useful. I hoped perhaps it could be enjoyed by some of those many people who long for faith but can't seem to understand how all that is lovely and lovable leads on to God."[1495] She talked about these lovely and lovable things in her foreword, an extract from which was used by BBC Radio for a Christmas Eve broadcast entitled *In Praise of God*.

We live in a maze of symbols, all of them from the sun to a bird's feather, from the Bach B minor Mass down to the echo of a bell, uniting to give us this multi-coloured treasure that starts us off on the journey that has been described down the centuries in so many myths and stories, but is always the same journey...

Faith, it seems, is in part a readiness to receive the symbols not only as gifts of immeasurable value in themselves but as far more; echoes, gleams, reflections, intimations of what George MacDonald calls "the secret too great to be told." The symbols cannot tell us what it is, but if we are ready and willing to watch and listen and receive, they breathe out to us the knowledge that it is there. To breathe in this breath, to catch its perfume or the echo of its music, is to experience the faith that Christ likened to a grain of mustard seed, a simple thing, yet hiding within itself the possibility of miraculous transformation. What the essence of our faith can be, I still do not really know, but I do know the words that come to me when I hear great music or see the sun lighting up the spiders' webs on a morning when the garden is spangled with dew. "I bring you good tidings of great joy."[1496]

They were her last published words.

Correspondence

She was now seventy-six and it was forty-two years since *Island Magic*—"forty years of a job I <u>loved</u>," she told a friend some years later, "How many people have had that joy?"[1497] Although there were to be no more books she had by no means put away her pen, for books had never comprised the full extent of her writing. The 1974 article in *The Oxford Mail* had said that she was currently at work on an anthology, but that "most of her time is taken up answering letters. She still gets about fifty a week from devoted fans and likes to reply to each one personally." She told their interviewer,

Some don't need much answering, of course. But if they come from people who are ill or old I try to say something helpful or encouraging. And children must always be answered in detail.[1498]

She had told Kenneth Allsop in 1960, "I get many letters from people who are ill saying that they have found support or encouragement from something I have written. That gives me great happiness."[1499] And as early as 1952, she had written in the preface to *White Wings* that one of the joys of the story-teller's profession is "that correspondence with readers who tell him that the thoughts of his mind have given them pleasure." *The Dictionary of National Biography* records that such letters meant more to her than any of the rewards of fame, giving instances of letters received from grateful readers who had been "inspired to paint and compose and regain the ability to write creatively,"[1500] or were helped to acceptance of life's troubles and problems.

Jessie recalled:

> People would ask on really deep things, like "I have five children and when the last one came I nearly went off the

> deep end. I'm torn – I'm a Roman Catholic…should I use contraception?"
> [Q: So people really did look upon her as a spiritual adviser?]
> Oh rather, I've got quite a lot of letters written to me after the event to say how much they were helped through and how they turned their lives about, and managed to endure their marriage or make it better, or whatever. It's so amazing because she had what I'd call a quiet life.

The Joy of the Snow however records only Elizabeth's own gratitude.

> *Often readers of my books tell me how much I have taught them about human nature. That is what they think. Actually it is the other way round. If I have any knowledge of human beings it is largely a reflection of themselves. So many people coming to see me over so many years, so many letters, often written in times of difficulty, or sorrow, all so revealing of their writers. If that cannot teach me something of human beings nothing can. I only realise now how grateful I am to them all, how much they have taught me, how much I owe to them.*[1501]

Canon Goudge too had had a worldwide correspondence. She said in her preface to *Glorying in the Cross* that "letter-writing played a very large part in my father's life… his personal correspondence, from all over the world, was enormous." Like his daughter, he responded to the letters personally and made his correspondents "most truly his friends." As one of them said, "One never appealed to him without getting an immediate response."[1502] They each maintained a lifetime of contact with friends and readers alike.

Perhaps father and daughter, while equally grateful for their correspondents, would on occasion have been equally wearied by their task - like John Wentworth in *The Rosemary Tree*:

> *Patiently, as best he could, he answered these letters, writing sometimes long into the night, covering many pages with his small neat handwriting,* [Dr. Goudge's handwriting, "although its illegibility was the despair of his correspondents, was precise and dainty"] *pegging away at it until his neck ached and his fingers cramped, and then doggedly praying for the whole lot of them until he was too bemused with headache and sleep to know what he was doing. Then he would have to give up and go to bed.*[1503]

Nevertheless Elizabeth felt regret that she had not been able to give these people even more of her time:

About this I have one big regret, and this is a regret that I believe other writers feel too. For those who cannot work at all without periods of quietness there is not the time or strength for the people brought to us by our books.[1504]

It was the books that had brought Father Louis into her life. The friendship of this distinguished French theologian meant a great deal to Elizabeth, and Jessie remembered that like many of her friendships it had begun with a letter from him in praise of her work, after which they corresponded for years. "He thought she was marvellous in the ideas behind her stories," Jessie said. Elizabeth admitted in *The Joy of the Snow* that "some of my readers have intellects that make me tremble with awe," and could only imagine that it was "likemindedness, that has nothing to do with intellect"[1505] which attracted them to her books. At the end of 1975, Father Louis wrote to say that he was sending Elizabeth the gift of an ikon, to which she replied,

Your letter came yesterday and I do not know how to thank you for it, and for the wonderful gift that is on its way to me…it has arrived already in my soul…I have always longed for an Ikon… Whenever I look at it I will remember what you said: "An embodiment of my prayer in communion with you and for you." And also of my prayer for you (though I don't feel worthy of praying for you). Thank you for it more than I can tell you.[1506]

The following year he had a book published which, to her joy, he dedicated to Elizabeth:

I feel overwhelmed, and so honoured and happy that you should want to dedicate your book to me. Only I must tell you that I am not like you. I have not kept pace, as you have, with all that men and women think now. I am just about as behind the times as I can be.[1507]

This typical humility does not accord with what Jessie had said of her advanced theological insight, and she certainly knew enough of Teilhard de Chardin, for example, to quote from his *Le Milieu Divin* in *The Joy of the Snow*. She added a self-effacing comment, of course: that she had "read Teilhard de Chardin, tried desperately to understand him, failed completely, yet found my life immeasurably enriched by the mere failure."[1508] However she read more than this one book, for in July 1978 she wrote to Muriel:

I am so glad you have Hymn of the Universe *and* Mass on the World. *I love them and you will too. I see there is a new book on him just out. What a hard time he had. He was ahead of his time.*[1509]

The English translation of *Hymn of the Universe* was published in 1965, and so she may well have been reading it as she worked on *The Child from the Sea*. Père Teilhard exhorts the reader to "bathe…in the ocean of matter…"

> For it cradled you long ago in your preconscious existence;
> and it is that ocean that will raise you up to God.[1510]

Father Louis sent her a copy of his own book,[1511] and then again in early 1980, a copy of its English translation. She wrote back,

It was thrilling when the French copy came, even more so now that the English translation is published and I am <u>reading</u> it! I wonder if you realise what an honour it is to have a book by one of the greatest scholars and theologians of our generation dedicated to an ignoramus like me. To have the honour of your friendship all these years of course means more to me than I can tell you, and to know that I have the strength of your prayers to hold me up. My prayers are so childish still and I [am] ashamed of this, but they are yours every day… It is an added joy to have a bit of C.S. Lewis included. I learned so much from his books as they came out one by one when I was young.[1512]

By then within weeks of her eightieth birthday and in failing health, she added, "I hope I may be allowed to see you in the life to come – only among the "many mansions" your place will be so much higher than mine."[1513]

She carried on with her correspondence even when it was almost physically impossible. The eye trouble that had caused her to be "floored"[1514] by proof-reading *The Child from the Sea* had got worse. A 1977 letter said she had "cataracts in both eyes – not quite ready for operation yet… It takes me so long even with spectacles and magnifying glass to read or write a letter."[1515] In this she was like C.S. Lewis who struggled to continue with his correspondence at the end of his life, "sometimes with an arm so rheumatic" that he could "hardly push the pen," says Clyde S. Kilby in *Letters to an American Lady*. And why? Because for him, taking the time to advise or encourage another Christian was both a "humbling of one's talents before the Lord" and "as much the work of the Holy Spirit" as writing books.[1516]

❋

It was through a fan letter that Elizabeth had become friendly with the poet Muriel Grainger, who first wrote to her in the spring of 1977. Three months later they were in discussion about Muriel's idea for a possible anthology. Although Elizabeth confessed in one letter, "I could not [read your poems] before because my cataracty eyes had given out,"[1517] by

Christmas - that is, within the course of nine months - Elizabeth had written sixteen letters to Muriel alone.

Muriel sent Elizabeth an article she had written in praise of her work. Entitled *Religion and Romance*, it was published that year in the November edition of *Reform*, the magazine of the United Reformed Church. It is a perceptive critique which goes straight to the heart of her achievement.

> She is unique in being a writer of extremely popular romances which are at the same time fundamentally religious. Not that Miss Goudge sets out to 'put Christianity across'... The love of God; the power of prayer; the reality of the Kingdom of the Spirit – these things are woven into the fabric of her plots with a naturalness and inevitability that come from Miss Goudge's own convictions and experience, and it is this factor that makes them so acceptable, and so telling... Behind the everyday and absorbing events in the novels, one senses the eternal world of spirit that holds their true meaning...
>
> The Spirit blows where it wills, and chooses its own channels, and one of them is surely Elizabeth Goudge's romantic fiction.[1518]

Elizabeth, predictably, was uncomfortable when she read the pre-publication copy.

> *Your article is very kind indeed, but I felt very uncomfortable reading it. I stand out in it as such a paragon of a woman. When I am writing, something beyond me seems in control. But oh, if only I could practise what it is given me to say. As a Christian I am a failure.*[1519]

As Muriel's anthology, *A Pattern of People* was prepared for publication Elizabeth reached her seventy-eighth birthday, and a month later the two women met for the first time. Muriel had perhaps brought as a gift a copy of her *Music at Midnight*, for in her next letter Elizabeth said she was reading it "with quiet joy." She said, "You are a true poet – what a heavenly thing to be," and added, "Being a lover of Esdras I especially love *Uriel and Esdras*.[1520] It is a poem that chimes with some of Elizabeth's own imagery – in this extract, of harrowed fields, and waiting in the dark.

> Uriel came to Esdras in the night
> ...holding in the hollow of his hands

> The seed of truth that seeks a furrowed mind
> For its fruition.
>
> Esdras had lacerated his red field
> With murmuring rebellion, tossing the stubborn clods
> And beating them for meaning – but in vain.
> There was no answer there to all his questioning
> Only the tilled soil, and the waiting in the dark.[1521]

Walter de la Mare had written to Miss Grainger in 1950, praising the newly-published *Music at Midnight* and selecting phrases he particularly liked. He made no selection from page nine however – on which two poems were printed: *Paradox* and *The Single Eye*. He simply said, this whole page was "the real thing."[1522] In *Paradox* there is again a similarity of vision: specifically, in the image of the fearful dark water in which we almost drown and yet which is, at the same time, the fount of life.

> Rise from the dark, the depths, the dead,
> And shake from your triumphant head
> The fearful flood that would have drowned –
> There too the fount of life is found.
>
> Sing, shriven, resurrected spirit
> Of this new earth that you inherit;
> Breathe in the once-familiar air –
> And find yourself a stranger there.
>
> This was your home. Now home must lie
> Beyond the orbit of the eye,
> Nor in your own house shall you be
> Till you put off mortality.[1523]

Music at Midnight was the first of five published books of Muriel's poems, and in her first letter Elizabeth had said, "How lovely that you write poetry. I try sometimes but the result is terrible!"[1524] It seems, nonetheless, that Muriel must have asked if there were any poems that could be included in her anthology, for she had replied:

> *My verses are pretty poor – dreadful when I compare them with yours – but I am wondering if I could manage a few that might be not too bad. I could try if Hodders decide to go ahead with the anthology and if you think it would be a good idea.*[1525]

And were there any new short stories to include, Muriel wondered?

I am very much afraid I have no unpublished stories that are any good. Only verses – but those would probably not be wanted.[1526]

And it seems that they were not, for the finished anthology was all prose: a mixture of short stories and extracts from the novels, designed to illustrate Elizabeth's "unforgettable characters." Muriel wrote in its foreword, that here was

> A pattern of people – a pattern woven in true colours with an extra strand of gold that is Elizabeth Goudge's unique contribution. It shines through all her work.[1527]

Elizabeth's poems were eventually published – posthumously - as an appendix to the 1990 anthology *A Vision of God*. Jessie sent a copy of the book to Kathleen Millington in 1991, telling her: "The nest, I brought back from Costa Rica, having been handed it by my cousin." It was a souvenir of a long holiday she had had in March 1978. As Elizabeth told Muriel at the time:

My Jessie…is going to Costa Rica for the whole of March, to visit a cousin… I have friends coming to keep me company, but how I shall miss her! I have been going downhill these last few months (only to be expected at nearly 78!) and she is a great strength to me.[1528]

She may have been going downhill, but she was inspired by Jessie's gift to write a fourteen-stanza poem, *The Hummingbirds' Nest* telling how the gift made its way across the world into her collection of Little Things.

> *Travelling over the curve of the world,*
> *The leagues of the sea, it came home at last,*
> *As a gift of love for an old woman,*
> *To a glass cabinet holding treasures*
> *Of a lifetime; small things, cups and saucers,*
> *Shells, birds and beasts of ivory and glass.*
>
> *Bigger than these, the nest upon its twig*
> *Watched over them with kindliness. Empty*
> *Only to the eye but full of living*
> *Memories of light and warmth and colour,*
> *Crimson and azure, purple and soft gold,*
> *The whisper of leaves spelling out blessing.*

> *The children, when the nest was shown to them,*
> *Were speechless with wonder as their fingers*
> *Explored carefully the rounded softness*
> *Of the white cotton lining, and their eyes*
> *Were wide and bright as imagination*
> *Saw birds like jewels flashing through the air.*
>
> *There is an eternity in beauty*
> *That death is never able to destroy.*
> *The gentlest things, the frailest, are not lost...*[1529]

※

At the height of all the correspondence about *Pattern of People*, in August 1977 a letter to Muriel said,

Please forgive for not having written before. My nephew has been staying with me, and so many people have been coming and going, that I was too tired to do anything but cook.[1530]

The tiredness was worth it, however, because the coming and going had been the result of what she called "a great occasion for us." Her nephew Hugh was to be ordained. She wrote a month later to tell Muriel that it had been "a lovely sunny day and a glorious service. Reduced me nearly to tears several times. They were all so young."[1531]

But not all of 1977 had been so glorious. She had already confided:

You tell me you have had a very bad year. Since you have told me that, I can tell you I have too, one of the worst, and I am so neurotic that bereavements and tragedies make my old-age aches and pains worse.[1532]

And now in September: "I think I have been feeling half stunned with tiredness through the troubles of this summer but am "coming to" now, with the prospect of a holiday in a fortnight."[1533] She was going to spend the month of October at Jessie's cottage, but the holiday did not turn out quite as planned. Her next letter reported that she had returned from Wales "wonderfully refreshed in mind after my time in Jessie's dear little fisherman's cottage…"

But physically I was unlucky as the second time I went out I fell down the flight of old stone steps leading to the back door. Yet I was incredibly lucky - I did not break a single bone! My arthritic back and hip were very angry with me and so I could not leave the

cottage again… Getting home was a bit grim but I am getting better now, and getting up for a part of every day.[1534]

But some weeks later she was still not well. On 30th December, after some discussion about the anthology, she asked:

Did I write for Christmas? I do hope I did, but I was ill before Christmas and over it, and I am in such confusion that I do not know what I am doing – though I know I have not yet packed up the gifts I am giving let alone thanked anyone for those I have had!! But Epiphany is coming. I love Epiphany. I can remember then that Christ was born.[1535]

She had told Father Louis, too,

I keep my Christmas at Epiphany. Being so old I get so tired and harassed packing up all the parcels for all the children, and cooking and washing up (with wonderful help from Jessie) that I can hardly remember about the Incarnation. But at Epiphany there is peace. Also it was my parents' wedding day, and as their marriage was so happy it was always a special day when I was a child.[1536]

There came another great occasion for the family in 1978 – Hugh's second ordination – and despite all, as he records, Elizabeth was again well enough to attend.

> Elizabeth made the effort, which was not easy for her, to come to both of my ordinations, my deaconal in 1977 and my priestly in 1978. I remember that she and other members of my family were seated opposite me – the chapel benches were arranged in choir form and not in the usual way – and before the ceremony started – this is my priestly ordination – I looked over to her and smiled. She was already looking at me, not at me so much but into me, through my eyes; she didn't smile back, my smile did not interrupt that intense look, and the expression on her face was unforgettable, it was intensely one of deep love and I think concern; I can see that look now as clearly as I saw it then… of deep, deep love and concern; it was as if she and I were the only ones in the chapel at that moment and all was silence and peace. That is probably the one sure time when Elizabeth – unconsciously I imagine – communicated to me her profound and firm spirituality.[1537]

She told Muriel that "Hugh's ordination on Saturday was a very great experience."

> *I had never been to an RC ordination before and the centuries-old ceremony was so beautiful (a lot of young men singing for joy at the tops of their voices is a glorious sound!) The ritual movements for the anointing, the blessing of the young priest by his brother priests, the bishop kneeling humbly to kiss the hands he has anointed, and much else, with the sun shining down on the simple primrose-coloured plain vestments and the lighted candles, looked at times like some medieval holy picture. The ordination was followed by the Eucharist and…my godson Mark and his wife Elizabeth read the lessons.*[1538]

Hugh remembered how she "brought my chalice up to the altar during the presentation of the gifts…"

> a chalice which was her ordination present to me, which of course I still have and treasure. She told me afterwards that she was terrified of dropping it, but she managed everything splendidly with my brother firmly holding her by the arm and she completed everything with grace and dignity.[1539]

※

It was a great blessing that she had been able to attend such a special service, for Jessie said that churchgoing in general became much more difficult for her in the latter years.

> She wasn't capable of doing more than one service, say, every other fortnight here, because of getting into the car. And we went to the early one as it was shorter – because she couldn't sit; she was so thin you see that the pews ate into her bones, or in the winter it was perhaps too cold. But otherwise she had the communion brought quite frequently, by different people.

Her health was failing too. A letter to Muriel in July, just a month after the ordination, said, "There is not much time. At least not for me, at 78. A 'turn' I had (my second lately)… made me realise that."[1540] And it seems that in August she was still not well; for she made a half-humorous reference in another letter to Muriel, to the fact that both of them had been suffering from the body's "tantrums".[1541] That year, Jessie went to Pembrokeshire alone.

[Jessie] is having three weeks holiday but comes home next Monday. I hope Wales, where she is, is having this glorious sunshine. I have an RC friend staying with me, so we were more or less glued to the TV last Sunday morning. I shall never forget it. One almost felt that that man had a greatness that could save the world.[1542]

As this was October 1978, "that man" was the new Pope, John Paul II.

※

By now she and Jessie had another dog, their fourth. Such is the pain of losing beloved pets that Elizabeth had said in *The Joy of the Snow*, "heartbreak every ten years is hard to face when the years go by so quickly… Froda, happily, is only three years old and so I have every hope that she will outlive me."[1543] But in June 1978, in a letter to Madeau Stewart, came the news that

Froda, our darling dog, died. We wondered if we could bear ever to have another and then we were asked if we knew of anyone who would give "a good home" to a little Shih-Tzu (Tibetan dog) at the dogs' rescue centre. We hoped we were a good home and so now we are ruled by Tashi. When he came he was a pitiful little terrified bag of bones after three years ill treatment, but now he is a lovely dog with a great character.[1544]

Madeau was hoping to get a Dandie-Dinmont, and Elizabeth agreed. "You must have a Dandie… A friend who breeds them said I did wrong in *The Joy of the Snow* to say they are not long-lived. They often are. It was just that we were unlucky with ours."[1545] Both Tiki and Randa had lived to ten years old; Froda must have died when she was about seven.

As well as the lovely little dog, her home too was still a source of joy.

Jessie and I are still in our Rose Cottage – not so quiet as it used to be, with Concorde backwards and forwards overhead, and motorcycles up and down the lane, but still lovely. Now and then we look half-heartedly for a bungalow, for the garden is too large for Jessie now she is 65, and the stairs a trial for me in my 79th year – but we don't find our bungalow – I rather think at the bottom of our hearts we don't want to![1546]

And still, there was the joy of *people*. She told Muriel in February 1979, "I have lately been adopted as "Mother" by two daughters, and they are young and lovely and having a dreadful time and seem to need me, so how lucky I am."[1547]

Old age had brought her a kind of freedom too.

Peppard

Nobody laughs at an old lady... You can fling your arms round somebody, just as a child can, and there's no misinterpretation. You can express your love for other people in a way far easier than it used to be... I'm a very shy person, and have never been able to conquer it.

But nowadays I'm not nearly so anxious. Worry is no longer as cruel as it was and I feel truly able to say, 'It's done, life's over with' – and be content.[1548]

ONE DOES GET OLD AT LAST

Long light is over at last, evening is here,
Companion of the day:
We go slowly under branches getting bare
Just as the books say.

Fancy, it's true, then – stiff about the knees,
Mind and eyes a bit dim;
While we can still see, under the thinning trees,
It's time we turned to Him.

For there is something in us willing to go,
Something that knows its time;
We do not need to feel a feather of snow
Or see the first white rime

To know that our long day, so short, is nearly
Spent, and it is the season
To use the little wisdom we bought so dearly
And stored, while we could reason.

Easier far now than it was at first, love,
No more to be possessed,
Or to possess ourselves, or things; the worst, love,
Is over, not the best.[1549]

Ruth Pitter
In *A Book of Faith*

Willing to Go

Frightened person though I am I do not know yet what people mean when they say they fear death. Injury, disease, pain, these things that meet us on the way to death and test our courage to the utmost, yes, but not death itself. Yet I believe that the fear of death must come at some moment to every soul, and that it is right that it should. A sense of immunity is a bad thing, a separating thing. At the end of it all, perhaps at the end of many lives, there should be no human experience that we have not, all of us, shared with each other. How can we hope for union with God until we have come to regard unity with each other as the greatest treasure that we have as we journey to him?[1550]

Jessie remembered that on the 1st April, 1979,

> She was sitting in that chair there… I'd brought half the dinner in and while I went to get the vegetables she got out of her chair and just dropped, so whether it was a small stroke or not, I don't know… Her bones were so brittle that she broke her femur – not the hip; that would have been all right.

> That was one o'clock; and we got the ambulance and she was in the hospital by two, but she didn't get a bed till six – I think a doctor saw her very late, and then they set it badly. So then she had to have the Head of Department to break her leg and set it again, and they were so long in coming to do it, that she suffered a great deal then. She wouldn't go into a nursing home – she said 'No, I must be like other people' and she went into the public ward.

> It was a particularly bad ward – absolutely appalling, appalling. I'd heard about this ward before…

> I didn't pick it up then, when I was going to visit her – she was bearing it stoically. But they wouldn't let you ring the bell for anything; they'd leap at you. When people were beside her in dire need, she rang the bell and they said "We've told you, you *must not* ring the bell." She shouted out the first night, when she wasn't through the anaesthetic - she

thought we were in danger - and they came and were terrible again. So it really was… not just being in hospital, it was a terrible ward.

Elizabeth wrote a long poem about the experience, *Easter in the Ward*. Typically, she tries to find good things to be thankful for:

Sister competent, serenely kind.
Young nurses, mostly kind, sometimes not,
But good to look at, full of laughter.
Pots of bright flowers, shafts of sunlight,
Small children visiting Mum or Gran.[1551]

Nevertheless it was a place that "held much pain [and] many uncomforted tragedies" – and for her, being shut away from nature made the misery even worse.

There must be a freshness in the world,
Trees unfurling their dear April green,
The doves calling, kingcups by the stream,
White violets scenting the hedgerows.

The windows showed only stark chimneys…
Cars and lorries passed but no birds sang.[1552]

The poem records how she spent Easter Sunday in this "hot and crowded ward." That was 15th April, but by the time she wrote to Muriel on 6th May things were a little better: she had been moved to the local hospital at "peaceful Peppard" and here she made some "dear friends among the patients and nurses." She wrote again on the 23rd however - this time from yet a third hospital:

Things were not going right with my leg – the surgeon found that owing to my age the bone had crumbled and the pin had slipped, so I came here to this Clinic and he did it all over again. Next week I go to a Nursing Home for physiotherapy which is run by a friend of mine, and I expect I shall be there for about a month in Oxford. I still find letter-writing difficult so I have dictated this to Jessie.[1553]

Writing to Louis Bouyer on 29th May, the day before she was to be moved to the nursing home, she told him that it was "a good place with a nice garden, and best of all a chapel and resident chaplain."

I shall be there about five weeks and Jessie will be able to take a good holiday. She is very tired after the long strain.[1554]

Elizabeth knew only too well what it was like to be worn out by nursing, and she was very solicitous for Jessie and insistent that she take regular breaks. But just how much of a trauma it had been for the patient herself is obvious from her comments to Father Louis when she explained to him too, how "the operation had to be done all over again…"

It was a worse one than the first, and has been very painful, and the coward in me hoped I should not come through. But I did and they tell me I am a very tough old lady! But I was glad for my surgeon's sake – he was so distressed over the first failure, which was not in the least his fault. I have been in a very good clinic, and have been beautifully looked after. The surgeon hopes and believes that all will go well now.[1555]

In a later letter she admitted to Muriel, too, that she had at one point been hoping for death.

When I had my second operation I prayed to die, and when I heard that I nearly had, saved only by the last blood transfusion, I found it hard to forgive them. Very wicked and very ungrateful of me![1556]

As might be expected prayer had helped her to come through, and she prayed using the rosary that had been Father Louis' gift to her: "The rosary you gave me is with me of course and [I am] using it daily – well – I need not tell you what a help it is. You know."[1557] Later, in August she wrote again, "What a comfort my rosary is! Especially on wakeful nights."[1558] But happily these were wakeful nights in her own bed, for by then she was home again. Having written to Madeau from the nursing home on 1st July that "I have to be taken off my walking aid and put on to two sticks, and shown how to manage steps before I can go home"[1559] she was able to write to Muriel on the 25th,

It is lovely to be at home with Jessie and Tashi. Jessie has made me a lovely little bedroom out of our downstairs spare room. I crawl about on two sticks and have a lot of pain but the whole experience has been very good for me. I have seen and shared so much suffering…and I'm glad. My life had been too sheltered.[1560]

She had been hoping to be home by July in time for a planned visit from Father Louis, and it seems her wish was fulfilled, for in November she told him, "It seems a long time ago that we were sitting out in the garden in warm sunshine, and I was enjoying being with you (but oh, what a dull hostess I was that day!)" By now she was feeling much better however:

I am slowly improving. I can now manage the stairs and sleep upstairs in my own room – a great joy. And I can do the cooking again – another joy![1561]

In this "lovely" November of "very cold sunshine" she had also had her first outing, when Jessie drove her the few miles to her cousin's home.

I have never in my life seen such glorious autumn colouring. It was a little misty and the gold and orange and flame-colour of the leaves seemed to burn out through the mist. And when we stopped the car for a while and let the windows down we could hear the birds singing. In these heartbreaking days of violence and cruelty and sorrow the glory of nature, and of music, seem our greatest refuge and comfort, don't they. God's voice speaking comfort…
I still have a good deal of pain but on my last monthly visit to the surgeon he said that by January he thought the bone would be sufficiently mended for him to take out a bit of 'ironmongery' that is pressing on a nerve and causing the pain. So that is something to look forward to.[1562]

But 1980 came, and she was still at home on 11th February, and describing for him a corner of her room that held special treasures – which included his own books and the ikon that had been his gift to her. "I am finishing this letter upstairs in my bedroom. The ikon of Our Lady and her Babe stands beside my crucifix on top of a small bookcase which holds your books, and the Confessions of St. Augustine and Dame Julian of Norwich and a few more of the great ones." She confided that "moving about on crutches is painful but I have no pain when I keep still, and am lucky enough to sleep well. Jessie is so very good to me." She added,

My broken leg is not mending well and I am waiting now for a bed in the Reading Clinic so that I can have another operation. It seems I was too old to have quite such a bad fracture. But this is not a major operation like the other two, only minor, to relieve the pain of the support I must always have inside, a sort of second thigh bone. I shall be home again in a week or so.[1563]

Her optimism was unfounded, for in early August she told Madeau,

My last operation on my smashed-up old leg, which was supposed to be a slight one, turned out to be the worst of the three and landed me with three months in bed in hospital on traction. I pointed out to God that being eighty I should now be allowed to die but for some reason or other he did not agree with me. And I have pointed out to Jessie that I ought to go into an old ladies home, but she thinks we ought to stay together, so for the time being at any rate we are together... As I am very crippled she is very tied to me and I think it is wrong. But I am improving and hope I shall improve more.[1564]

The following Spring – 1981 - she said again,

Just for the moment we are sticking together in this cottage we love so much – though I have a very nice home for senile old ladies in my eye and my name on the list. My surgeon and our doctor said we should go into a bungalow but we hated those we looked at and I am going downhill so fast that it did not seem worth the agonising struggle of a move, so Jessie has made a dear little bedroom for me out of our tiny downstairs room, and the district nurse comes in to help me and we manage.[1565]

In September 1980 she had told Muriel she had the support of a zimmer and could "manage to get out and sit in the sun in the garden in good weather. I am very crippled after the last disaster of an operation but hope I shall improve."[1566] And she did improve, for she was able to write, nine months later:

I am very much better now. At the moment sitting in my chair in the sitting room with a big pot of the first June roses beside me, and I can see the print of Wells Cathedral from where I sit...The surgeon in the hospital told me no old person of my age should have lived through the three big hip and thigh operations I had – yet here I am! Channel Islanders are very tough and I take after my mother.[1567]

The broken leg was not now her only problem however, for "arterial sclerosis (grand medical name for hardening of the arteries) is a very up-and-down illness," she said. "The bad and good times alternate. This is a good time..." As always, she was full of gratitude and thanks.

I have a very good vicar who brings me my Communion, and an old friend, a retired priest who lives near, hears my confession and in bad times has given me anointing. I also have a very kind doctor, so I am well looked after.[1568]

Nevertheless, she wrote in October of that year, 1981, "With so many different complaints I am never very well now and have to spend much of the day lying on my bed." But she had the joy of another visit from Father Louis to look forward to - in the same letter she said, "How good to think of seeing you next Wednesday! I am looking forward to it so much." And to double her joy, he would not be the only visitor: "I am hoping it will be Hugh who will meet you from the station."[1569]

However Christmas brought a reversal, for she had to say goodbye to Hugh, who left for South America to begin his work as a missionary priest. Louis Bouyer sent her a gift of books, and she replied in the new year,

How good God is to us all, in the small things as well as the great ones! With Hugh gone from me, and the snow deep and the wind bitter, I must confess to feeling a very miserable old woman – and the two lovely books have arrived to comfort me, and also a letter.[1570]

Death was very much on her mind.

I am feeling much more peaceful in my mind, more able to leave my dying in God's hands, and also Jessie's welfare and strength, wanting only his will for us both...
How grateful I am to God for your friendship and all you have taught me, and all your generosity. If I do not see you again in this world I hope I may be allowed to be with you in the next – but I am afraid my unworthiness will put a barrier between me and so many who mean much to me. There is a poem I put, I think, in my last anthology. It begins "Study to deserve death." So that must be my task now.[1571]

❋

O Saviour of the world, lifted upon the cross that all men might be drawn to your love, dying for the salvation of us all, we beseech Thee to make that love and that salvation a growing reality of glory to those who face their death. Grant to them, O Lord, Thy gift of a perfect repentance, and then may the heaven of Thy forgiveness banish all fears from them forever.

Elizabeth's prayer For the Dying[1572]

The Last Two Years

She did survive the hard winter however, despite all, and wrote more cheerfully in March,

Jessie and I are very happy to see the spring. It has been a hard winter, with so much snow and bitterly cold; especially hard for Jessie with me to look after. But with all her care here I am still in this world, and grateful to God that I am seeing one more earthly spring.

I hope I have learnt some patience, and peace in resting in the will of God... It is lovely to see the sun again, and flowers coming out in the garden.[1573]

A month later,

We are having day after day of glorious sunshine. The garden is very beautiful, and covered with scented white wild violets. I wish I could send you some...this beautiful spring lifts up our hearts...[1574]

But she and Jessie also had a battle on their hands that spring, for a potential buyer had a plan for development of the field opposite their cottage. It was the same field - "what we call 'our field' (though it isn't)" – that she had described for Madeau two years earlier, when "this morning every sheep was outlined in silver."[1575] Now there were plans to build a house on it, as "a money-making business" just over their garden hedge - "It will not only rob [us] of our view and privacy, but will destroy useful agricultural land – it is the sheep field, and the last bit of unspoiled seventeenth-century Peppard left."[1576] She wrote later in the year, however, to say that they, and others in the village who joined the fight, had won their case and the field was saved... "Joy of joys!"[1577]

Another source of stress was the disappointment over what she called "a TV picture of my books, life and homes." The idea had been mooted in early 1981, after which the project was planned, then abandoned and finally resurrected. By the time the go-ahead came, however, she felt incapable of coping with it. She told Madeau, "I have so many things the matter with me now, and I could not do it... You know what it's like. It is not only just at the time but all the things that happen to you afterwards. Multitudes of letters and people coming to see you etc..." She explained that the arterial sclerosis was "making me quite barmy. I can write letters, taking a long time to do it, but I cannot talk, move about or remember things. I get up for a short while every day, and love seeing my friends, but I felt I could not cooperate in the picture without ruining it, so I thought – and still think – it was a duty to say no. But was I disappointed!"[1578]

Not surprisingly, by now she could no longer cope with a huge correspondence and, apart from letters to close friends, had begun to send out a duplicated response to much of her mail: "Thank you so much for your kind letter. I am sorry that owing to illness and failing sight I can no longer answer letters." She was still very aware of what was happening in the world however and wrote to friends, with concern, about current events.

Books were still a part of her life, despite her failing eyesight. A 1982 letter to Madeau says "My talking book machine is a great joy, and of all the books I have heard so far, I loved best Yehudi Menuhin's autobiography."[1579] She had other things to cheer her too, not least, the prospect of yet another visit from Father Louis that autumn.

I am not very well but then I can't expect to be with all the queer things I have the matter with me, but though I long for the next world I hope I will still be in this world when you come in the Autumn. My Jessie still continues to be wonderfully good to me. Her garden is beautiful and I manage to sit out in it for a bit every day…

It is August now and we are having our annual Promenade Concerts in the Albert Hall, a great deal of beautiful music.[1580]

It was not just her own pleasure in the music that gave her joy each year. She had told Madeau three years earlier:

How I love the roar of applause that breaks out from all those young people when they have been listening to something they have loved. It is truly heartening.[1581]

Father Louis came in September:

How lovely it is to think of seeing you…Yes I am free on Monday 13th. If you could take a taxi from the station Jessie would take you back to the station after tea. I shall have her home then. She was very tired and went away for a fortnight's rest, but returns on Sunday evening. I have not been at all well but there must be no grumbles, for I never expected to have the joy of seeing you again, and I shall be a new woman at sight of Jessie. Of all my many blessings she is the greatest God has given me.[1582]

By the end of '82 she was telling Madeau that she was housebound. "I don't go out now because all the work the surgeon did…has come undone, because my bones crumble. I need operation four but the doctor says I can't have it at my age."[1583] And in the winter edition of *RNA News* she said she was "half blind with cataracts, so no more writing, and very crippled with crumbling bones."[1584] It was a bad winter, and Jessie herself became ill. Elizabeth told Father Louis, in February 1983,

It has been, and is being (February is always our worst month) a very nasty winter. I have never known a winter when there was so much illness. A lot of it illnesses doctors have not encountered before. Jessie was very ill before Christmas with bronchitis and something else added on. The second doctor we called in did not know what it was. We were very anxious about her but she pulled through and though she is not her old self again she is improving. Before the present snow and cold we had a patch of warm weather that brought out all the spring flowers much too soon. The garden looked lovely, and now we are longing for the flowers and warmth to come back.[1585]

Elizabeth must by now have been very tired after the years of pain and illness, for a month later she added,

You are quite right, I must not long for death quite as much as I do. I must try harder to leave it all in God's hands. I must trust Him for Jessie too. If I love her so much how infinitely more must He love her. She is determined that we stick together, and He brought her safely through her bad illness at Christmas as though He wanted that too. She knows there is a nursing home ready to have me if she gets too tired.[1586]

But Sonia Harwood said,

> Jessie nursed Elizabeth to the very end. I had a letter [one of the last I had] saying "I feel I should go into a home, but Jessie won't hear of it."

Sadly, several years after Elizabeth's death Jessie, after all her care, had to leave Rose Cottage and go into a home herself for the last years of her life... but it was in her beloved Wales.

❄

It seems to have been pretty much a winter of gloom, but although on March 1st she grumbled a little to Madeau about the effects on the brain of her hardening arteries, she could still go on to tell her "What a lot extreme old age has taught me. And pain even more."

I've got to know [Christ] as never before, and never was there anyone more worth knowing. I can't read now, owing to cataracts, or write much either, but that gives me more opportunity to think. I think I could put my faith into one sentence, "There is a glory somewhere, and life goes on, and Christ is a reality."[1587]

She told Louis Bouyer, too,

I find more and more joy in intercession, and I find nothing in my life has brought me nearer to our dear Lord Christ as has suffering. I wouldn't have missed it, and it can become a part of prayer, as I know it has for you. It still amazes me that you have honoured me with your friendship. I am still only in the kindergarten and you so very far above me. When I try to count my blessings – so many that I cannot possibly make a list of them, friendship is very near the top. Though with me it is a case of "They are all gone into the world of light and I sit lingering here."[1588]

By June she was telling Madeau that she was "going slowly downhill… (though I call it uphill, because I am longing to get out of my painful old body) but I can manage to be glad that I am seeing the roses coming out for another summer."[1589] C.S. Lewis gives his own very similar idea of going uphill in a letter to his American Lady correspondent, describing death in the same image - of simply taking off clothes - that Elizabeth had been taught in childhood.[1590] There is nothing to be afraid of, he tells her: for in death we are simply divested of the body and its sufferings, like "taking off a hairshirt." Indeed he adds, death is our deliverer and our friend: because the things ahead of us are so much better than "any we leave behind."[1591]

In *The Rosemary Tree* Winkle's visits to her other country had given her an understanding of the things ahead.

> *When her life out there was over she would come back here again, like a tired bird returning full circle to its nest. All that she seemed to lose she would find again; only she would be even richer than she had been, because she would bring back with her the gathered treasure of her flight to add to the treasure of this heavenly country. But she wouldn't keep it, for one kept nothing here. One gave it.*[1592]

There were other joys that summer, alongside the roses; including a visit from her great friend at Burnham Abbey. As she told Madeau in October, "Enclosed though she is, she is allowed to spend one day of her yearly "rest" with me. She came not long ago and Tashi was overcome with joy. She is one of the few truly holy people I know and Tashi knows she is holy."[1593]

In the same letter too, she records that "Yesterday a lovely thing happened":

> *We had the piano tuned and the man who came to do it was a musician. When he had tuned the piano he sat and played it and I have never heard anyone play so exquisitely… [He] was elderly and retired and only tuning pianos occasionally to help friends who own a music shop. I shall remember his playing until I die. His touch was as gentle and light as an autumn leaf drifting down.*[1594]

Audrey visited too: she was now living near Oxford again, having been widowed in 1973 and a decade later remarried. Despite her comment about not always being "allowed" to see Elizabeth she said, "I saw her quite often when she was lying on a couch in the sitting-room. I last saw her not very long before she died – a matter of months... She was in a lot of pain."

Despite all, Elizabeth never lost the love for her work. "Can you explain this?" she asked Madeau. "On days when I can't speak I can – even if very slowly and with difficulty – *write*. Is it because words mean so much to me? They have always been my life."[1595] And she could still appreciate the interweaving of darkness and light, for although it was "horrid to feel winter is coming" it was also "lovely that Jessie has the Welsh woman's passion for an open fire."[1596]

Sadly, the pain of her last days was not only physical. A very great grief, just a few months before she died, was the death of little Tashi. In January she wrote to Madeau, as "the only friend really able to understand what we feel..."

Tashi, our dog, has died after suffering more than we should have allowed him to suffer, in the hope that we should be able to keep him with us for just a little longer. But it would have been cruel to let it go on and the vet had to end it. He was the dearest dog we ever had and we loved him more than any other – which is saying a great deal. He had endured so much cruelty but it had not been able to injure his gentleness and holy dignity, nor his powers of love. So there is one more little grave in our garden and one more grief.[1597]

There was, too, the grief of being no longer able to do the work she loved. Jessie said she was still trying to write until the end - she had told Madeau, "Writing is the greatest joy life gives, isn't it?"[1598] But, said Jessie, "the flow of blood to the brain was so slow:"

> She was writing a novel, but she couldn't get the words out. She'd got the whole plan in her mind, and the title [*The Spirit of the Wood*]. But the pages of agony, where she wrote what would come into her mind and then crossed it out because it wasn't good enough, or the right words... That gave her great grief.
>
> As she says, a writer dies with a pen in her hand. It wasn't *actually* in her hand, but it was up to two or three days before.

Like her father before her, Elizabeth died after a fall. An early Easter card for Madeau, dictated to Jessie and dated Sunday 25th March 1984 says, "I've been so long in replying because I've only just returned from hospital after a bad fall – Nothing broken but a bad shake-up, so that I'm mostly in bed and can't do much." Then in her own hand, much distorted, "from

Peppard

Elizabeth." She died on the following Sunday - three weeks before her eighty-fourth birthday – in the presence of loved ones, in her own little downstairs bedroom at Rose Cottage.

※

GOUDGE. On April 1, gracefully at home, ELIZABETH, beloved author, aunt and friend...

The Times

THE HOUSE AND GATE OF HEAVEN

"To Die into Your Resurrection"

It was five years to the day since Elizabeth had been taken to hospital with the broken femur, and her poem *Easter in the Ward* tells how in all the pain and sadness of that experience she had prayed to die on Easter Day.

A clock struck. Midnight. A new day born.
Easter morning and I prayed for death.
'To die into your resurrection.'
Could one ask for any greater gift?
I asked for it again and again.
'To die into your resurrection.'

The hours passed and there was no answer.
Dawn came and with it a line of verse.
'The shining silence of the scorn of God.'
But the poet was mistaken there,
Our courteous Lord was never scornful
And silence can be love's still small voice,

Asking that we should wait a moment,
Accepting from him the proffered gift
Of his own everlasting patience...[1599]

She had waited in patience: not only a moment, but for five years; and now in the year of her dying it was still not yet Easter Day.

And yet in a sense, it was. For April 1st was the date she had selected, eighteen years earlier, to represent Easter Sunday in *A Diary of Prayer*. Her chosen prayer for that day is a poem by Edmund Spenser, which she had listed in one of her notebooks under "Resurrection": "Most glorious Lord of life, that on this day / didst make thy triumph over death and sin..."[1600] Canon Goudge's last words to his daughter, on love, echo in its final couplet:

So let us love, dear love, like as we ought,
love is the lesson which the Lord us taught.

❋

The Dean's Last Sermon

He took his text from Dean Rollard's psalm, the sixty-eighth, "God is the Lord by whom we escape death." He spoke of love, and a child could have understood him. He said that only in the manger and upon the cross is love seen in its maturity, for upon earth the mighty strength of love has been unveiled once only. On earth, among men, it is seldom more than a seed in the hearts of those who choose it. If it grows at all it is no more than a stunted and sometimes harmful thing, for its true growth and purging are beyond death. There it learns to pour itself out until it has no self left to pour. Then, in the hollow of God's hand into which it has emptied itself, it is his own to all eternity. If there were no life beyond death, argued the Dean, there could be no perfecting of love, and no God, since he is himself that life and love. It is by love alone that we escape death, and love alone is our surety for eternal life. If there were no springtime there would be no seeds. The small brown shell, the seed of an apple tree in bloom, is evidence for the sunshine and the singing of the birds.[1601]

The Dean's Watch

Dreams of Heaven

I was walking through a great forest in a strange country. There was blue water not far away, for I saw the gleam of it through the trees, and all around me there shone that glorious especial light of dream and dawn. Yet in spite of the familiar light the country seemed strange to me because the great trees that soared upwards, and the flowers that carpeted the ground, were quite different from the trees and flowers of earth. They were different because they were more intensely alive, so alive that I felt their life not only through the medium of sight but as music sounding in my ears and thrilling through my body. The soaring upwards of the great branches was a movement of adoration that could literally be heard, though there was no wind and they were utterly still, and the ground was singing—bright with the flowers. And it was the same with the birds singing in the trees, who did not fly away when I came near, and the brown furry beasts in the undergrowth whose peeping bright eyes welcomed me as a sister; they were alive with that intense aliveness that leaves no room for fear.

... Or else it was not they but I who was more intensely alive... I seemed to have a new sort of body and mind. I felt astonishingly light and clear and airy, as though my whole being had been set free from every sort of grossness. And that hateful unseen barrier, that in our waking hours seems to slip between the beauty of the natural world and our straining selves

just at the moment of the longed-for union, was gone. I felt that the flowers were singing with my voice and that the sap of those mighty trees ran tingling in my veins. This sense of shared strength, of an at-one-ment that like wind or water swept away the stagnancy of sin, leaving one clean right through, was so glorious that it seemed to catch up out of my being a burning flame of praise that was tossed like a bird into the air.

The music that was all about me seemed suddenly to be concentrated into a single voice and looking up I saw a blue bird just above and in front of me, singing and tossing with delight, not flinging me snatches of song as I passed like the birds in the trees but accompanying me upon my way. I did not know who or what he was – only that if I followed him all would be well with me – and that if you follow the way of praise whatever happens you can't go far wrong.

Then I suddenly knew something else – this glorious one-ness with trees and flowers and creatures was only the beginning of wonders. Effortlessly, easily, as though my wonder and expectancy were wings that carried me, I began to run after the blue bird...[1602]

Dreams

❄

Then, oh then, I felt the Presence with me
At my left, but at some little distance,
A cloaked figure, the hood hiding his face,
Stood motionless, a figure of still peace
And gentle dignity. Yet how alive
He was! The glory of the rising sun
Was his, the colours of the morning sky,
The life of the unfolding flower buds.
...I thought, 'If only I could see his face.'

How could I? Such a glory must be earned.
A saint, beholding his glory unveiled,
Fell at his feet as one dead. Seeing him
Clothed in light upon the mountain his friends
Trembled and were exceedingly afraid
Until he came himself to comfort them.
Even in dream I could not go to him,
But even in dream he could come to me.

How can I tell of it? There are no words
Except his own words spoken long ago,
When he spoke of his longing to gather

The House and Gate of Heaven

His chickens under his wings. How often
Have I tried to do just what he wanted,
To run and run and hide under his wings
And nestle close to his warm heart of love.
But, a sinner, I could not find the way.

'Come unto me,' he said, but now he came
To me...

And so I thought that a fold of his cloak
Came round me with exquisite tenderness,

Soft as a cloud, as light as air, until
A gleam of sunshine like happy laughter
Lit the transparent feathers to rainbow
Loveliness. I felt their delicate touch
And a joy too great for a dream to hold...

Only a dream, but never forgotten
It shines in the dark like the morning star.

The Dream[1603]

The Last Dream of All

Sometimes in her dreams at night she stood beneath the branches of a mysterious wood, and looked down a moonlit glade, her eyes straining after something that she could not see. And when she woke up, there would be tears on her cheeks because her longing had been unsatisfied. Yet she was not unhappy because of this dream. She knew that one day, when she was a very old woman, she would dream this dream for the last time, and in this last dream of all she would see the little white horse, and he would not go away from her. He would come towards her and she would run towards him, and he would carry her upon his back away and away, she did not quite know where, but to a good place, a place where she wanted to be.

Final paragraph of *The Little White Horse*

❄

APPENDIX I

A SERVICE OF THANKSGIVING
Friday 6 April, 1984

A service was held for Elizabeth in the village church at Peppard, which had once been part of an unforgettable dream. She wrote of it in *The Joy of the Snow* in 1974.

I was a ghost in my dream... not visiting an old house but Peppard Church, whose spire I can see from my bedroom window and whose bell sounds across the fields to tell us the time...

[I was] that simple creature, the hart, coming to the water springs... The place where they spring can become as beloved as one's home, and those who are with you there are no longer the congregation but the family. I was one with them in my dream, loving them, and yet because they could not see me I experienced at the same time that happiness which reprehensible solitaries like myself feel when they can slip into an empty church and be alone there. When they went up to the altar I went with them and knelt at the far end of the line, the last of them.[1604]

❄

"No flowers at Elizabeth's request, but she asked for any donations in lieu to be sent to Invalid Children's Aid Association."[1605]

She had said, writing about her career choices all those years ago, that she had "always been obsessed with the thought of suffering, especially the suffering of children." And now she had chosen that her death should benefit a charity founded in 1888 to help poor children who were either seriously ill or disabled. Its clergyman founder said that poverty alone is "bad enough, God knows," but that for those both poor and handicapped existence must be unbearable, and "It's up to us to do something about it."[1606]

For *A Diary of Prayer* she had written these words "For sick and crippled children":

O most loving Lord, you who know all things know that nothing weighs more heavily on our hearts and minds than the suffering of sick or crippled children...

Lord, strengthen, bless and direct all the labour, all the prayer, and all the love that is poured out upon children who suffer, and grant that there may be no heart left that is unconcerned for them, and no mind unresolved to make of this sinful world a safer and happier home for them.[1607]

❋

Jessie wrote to tell Madeau that Elizabeth had wanted a "service of thanksgiving for Christ our Lord with as little mention of me as possible."[1608] In fact Elizabeth had made plans for it herself, telling Madeau in 1982:

I was writing out instructions for my funeral service the other day. Sounds gloomy but isn't. I am longing for the day when I shall be allowed to leave my painful old body, for Jessie's sake even more than my own. She is very tired.[1609]

Jessie too was thinking first of her friend's release from suffering, when she added: "At her end we could only feel joy and thanksgiving for E's setting out on her 'journey' as she called it – freed from all the pain and disabilities of the last years."[1610]

After the opening sentences, the service began with Psalm 138: "I will praise thee with my whole heart." Then came the Old Testament Lesson… something Elizabeth had chosen for *A Book of Faith*. It is a passage from the Book of Esdras in the Apocrypha, and a note from Jessie says "Elizabeth had this passage marked in her New English Bible."

> 'Look forward to the coming of your shepherd, and he will give you everlasting rest; for he who is to come at the end of the world is close at hand. Be ready to receive the rewards of the kingdom; for light perpetual will shine upon you for ever and ever. Flee from the shadow of this world, and receive the joy and splendour that await you. I bear witness openly to my Saviour. It is he whom the Lord has appointed, receive him and be joyful, giving thanks to the One who has summoned you to the heavenly realms. Rise, stand up, and see the whole company of those who bear the Lord's mark and sit at his table. They have moved out of the shadow of this world and have received shining robes from the Lord. Receive, O Zion, your full number, and close the roll of those arrayed in white who have faithfully kept the law of the Lord. The number of your sons whom you so long desired is now complete. Pray that the Lord's kingdom may

come, so that your people, whom he summoned when the world began, may be set apart as his own.'

I, Ezra, saw on Mount Zion a crowd too large to count, all singing hymns of praise to the Lord. In the middle stood a very tall young man, taller than all the rest, who was setting a crown on the head of each one of them; he stood out above them all. I was enthralled at the sight, and asked the angel, 'Sir, who are these?' He replied, 'They are those who have laid aside their mortal dress and put on the immortal, those who acknowledged the name of God. Now they are being given crowns and palms.' And I asked again, 'Who is the young man setting crowns on their heads and giving them palms?' and the angel replied, 'He is the Son of God, whom they acknowledged in this mortal life.' I began to praise those who had stood so valiantly for the Lord's name. Then the angel said to me: 'Go and tell my people all the great and wonderful acts of the Lord God that you have seen.'[1611]

The first hymn was "All my hope on God is founded" – she had told Madeau that it was her favourite.[1612] The second was a setting of one of the poems of Henry Vaughan. In its affirmation that 'there is another country,' she had placed this in *A Book of Comfort* under the title "The Peace of Heaven."

> My soul, there is a country
> Far beyond the stars,
> Where stands a winged sentry
> All skilful in the wars:
> There, above noise and danger,
> Sweet Peace sits crown'd with smiles,
> And One born in a manger
> Commands the beauteous files.
> He is thy gracious Friend,
> And – O my soul, awake! –
> Did in pure love descend
> To die here for thy sake.
> If thou canst get but thither,
> There grows the flower of Peace,
> The Rose that cannot wither,
> Thy fortress, and thy ease.
> Leave then thy foolish ranges;

> For none can thee secure
> But One who never changes –
> Thy God, thy life, thy cure.[1613]

In between the singing of the hymns, prayers were said and the New Testament lesson read. It was one of the Bible passages included in *A Book of Comfort* - from Paul's letter to the Ephesians –and on the draft Order of Service Jessie wrote, "E. asked for this."

> For this cause I bow my knees unto the Father of our Lord Jesus Christ, Of whom the whole family in heaven and on earth is named, That he would grant you, according to the riches of his glory, to be strengthened with might by his Spirit in the inner man; That Christ may dwell in your hearts by faith; that ye, being rooted and grounded in love, May be able to comprehend with all saints what is the breadth, and length, and depth, and height; And to know the love of Christ, which passeth knowledge, that ye may be filled with all the fulness of God.
>
> Now unto him that is able to do exceeding abundantly above all that we ask or think, according to the power that worketh in us, Unto him be glory in the church by Christ Jesus throughout all ages, world without end. Amen.[1614]

After an Address and prayers, the final hymn was John Henry Newman's "Praise to the Holiest in the Height" from *The Dream of Gerontius* – the same that had been sung at her father's funeral in 1939. The coffin was then taken to the crematorium for the singing of Bishop Cosin's great seventeenth-century hymn to the Holy Spirit based on Veni, Creator Spiritus – again, a poem chosen by Elizabeth for inclusion in *A Book of Comfort*. It concludes with a great affirmation of trust in God:

> When Thou art guide, no ill can come.[1615]

Commemorative cards were printed to mark the occasion, containing two prayers: her own three-fold prayer from *The Scent of Water*,

> Lord have mercy…
> Thee I adore…
> Into thy hands…[1616]

and the prayer of Thomas Traherne that she had set as the closing words of her autobiography, and which she described as "rejoicing in the glory of love."

> O God, who by love alone art great and glorious, that art present and livest with us by love alone: Grant us likewise by love to attain another self, by love to live in others, and by love to come to our glory, to see and accompany Thy love throughout all eternity.[1617]

At the close of the service two Special Prayers had been said, immediately before the Grace: this one by Thomas Traherne, rejoicing in love, and Elizabeth's beloved words of John Donne… again, part of her personal collection in *A Book of Comfort*; and the comfort also of Isaac Peabody when at last he found the courage to go in to the cathedral after the Dean's death:

> Bring us, O Lord God, at our last awakening, into the house and gate of heaven, to enter into that gate and dwell in that house where there shall be no darkness or dazzling, but one equal light; no noise nor silence, but one equal music; no fears nor hopes, but one equal possession; no ends nor beginnings, but one equal eternity; in the habitations of Thy glory and dominion, world without end. Amen.[1618]

APPENDIX II

ELIZABETH GOUDGE – COMPLETE WORKS

1919
The Fairies' Baby and Other Stories
Morland, Amersham, Bucks and London, W & G Foyle
Contents:
    The Fairies' Baby
    Josephine
    The Fairy Queen's Jewels
    Winky and the Fairy Snapdragon
    The Flower of Happiness

1934
Island Magic
London, Duckworth

1935
The Middle Window
London, Duckworth

1936
A City of Bells
London, Duckworth

1937
A Pedlar's Pack and other Stories
London, Duckworth
Contents:
    A Shepherd and a Shepherdess
    Doing Good
    A Pedlar's Pack
    Sweet Herbs
    Cloud-capped Towers
    Picnic with Albert
    Escape for Jane

Rabbits in a Hat
Punch and Judy
Rescue on the Island
The Bee and the Bonnet
The Luck of the Cat
The Roman Road
At the Sign of the Cat and Fiddle
The Hour Before Dawn
Something Turns Up

1938
Towers in the Mist
London, Duckworth

1939
Three Plays: *Suomi, The Brontes of Haworth, Fanny Burney*
London, Duckworth

Sister of the Angels. A Christmas Story
London, Duckworth

Foreword to *The Rider of Mendip and other poems* by Alan C. Tarbat
Bristol, J.W. Arrowsmith Ltd.

1940
The Bird in the Tree
London, Duckworth

Smoky-House
London, Duckworth

My Father : preface to **Glorying in the Cross** by H.L. Goudge
London, Hodder and Stoughton

1941
The Golden Skylark and other stories
London, Duckworth
Contents:
    The Golden Skylark
    The Cat and the Sailing Ship
    Madame Ysabeau

From Whence?
A Crock of Gold
The Dark Lady
The Well of the Star
Made from a Hazelnut
The Patience and Good Hope
The Well of St. George
Midnight in the Stable

The Well of the Star
New York, Coward McCann
Abridged as **David, The Shepherd Boy:** Undated advent calendar, illustrated by B. Biro
London, Hamish Hamilton

1942
The Castle on the Hill
London, Duckworth

Henrietta's House
London, University of London Press and Hodder & Stoughton
[as **The Blue Hills**
New York, Coward McCann]

1943
The Ikon on the Wall and other stories
London, Duckworth
Contents:
The Ikon on the Wall
Dogs of Peking
Make-Believe
Son of David
White Wings
The Strength in the Stone
The Foresters' Ride
The Hospitality of Mr. Pettigrew
The King's Servant
The Answer
The New Moon
By the Waters of Babylon

1944
Green Dolphin Country
London, Hodder & Stoughton
[as *Green Dolphin Street*
New York, Coward-McCann]
Filmed [1947] as *Green Dolphin Street*
[Metro-Goldwyn-Mayer]

1946
The Little White Horse
London, University of London Press
Filmed [2009] as *The Secret of Moonacre*
[Warner Brothers Pictures/Velvet Octopus/UK Film Council]

The Elizabeth Goudge Reader
Compiled and arranged by Rose Dobbs
New York, Coward McCann
[as *At the Sign of the Dolphin*
London, Hodder & Stoughton: 1947]

Songs and Verses
London, Duckworth
Contents:
    The White Owl
    The Statue of the Virgin at Buckler's Hard
    February
    The Heron
    The Nightingale
    Turn to your Rest
    Bury Pomeroy Castle, 1941
    Christmas Party
    In the Stable
    Trains
    Guardian Angel
    Amen
    Spring Song
    Lullaby
    The Frog
    Nannie
    The Good People
    The Little Red Fox

    Apple Trees
    Free Trade
    Courtesy
    The Little White Horse
    Lady of Mine
    Bell Song
    Thanksgiving for the Earth
    Cock Song
    Streams
    Waiting
    Memory
    The Sea
    Return
    Betrothal

1948
The Herb of Grace
London, Hodder & Stoughton
[as **Pilgrim's Inn**
New York, Coward McCann]

Christmas at the Herb of Grace
London, St. Hugh's Press, undated

1949
Make-Believe
London, Duckworth
Contents:
    Make-Believe
    The Well of Saint George
    Rescue on the Island
    The New Moon
    Picnic with Albert
    Doing Good
    The Foresters' Ride
    Midnight in the Stable

Gentian Hill
London, Hodder & Stoughton

c.1949
Foreword to *Haunted Borley* by A.C. Henning
Printed by E.N. Mason & Sons Limited, Colchester

1950
The Reward of Faith and other stories
London, Duckworth
Contents:
    The Canticle of the Sun
    The Reward of Faith
    The Three Grey Men
    The Legend of the First Christmas Tree
    Son of David
    The Ikon on the Wall
    The Well of the Star
    By the Waters of Babylon

1951
God So Loved the World, A Life of Christ
London, Hodder & Stoughton

The Valley of Song
London, University of London Press

1952
White Wings - Collected Short Stories
London, Duckworth
With ***Foreword*** by Elizabeth Goudge : *The Entertainment of Story-telling*
Contents:
    Dogs of Peking
    White Wings
    The Strength in the Stone
    The Hospitality of Mr. Pettigrew
    The King's Servant
    A Pedlar's Pack
    A Shepherd and a Shepherdess
    Sweet Herbs
    Cloud-Capped Towers
    Escape for Jane
    Rabbits in a Hat
    Punch and Judy

The Hour Before Dawn
The Golden Skylark
The Cat and the Sailing Ship
Madame Ysabeau
From Whence?
A Crock of Gold
The Dark Lady
Made from a Hazel Nut
The Patience and Good Hope
The Soldiers of the Queen
The Gap in the Hedge

1953
The Heart of the Family
London, Hodder & Stoughton

1955
Introduction to *A Child's Garden of Verses* by Robert Louis Stevenson
William Collins

1956
The Rosemary Tree
London, Hodder & Stoughton

1957
The Eliots of Damerosehay
London, Hodder & Stoughton:
Omnibus edition of *The Bird in the Tree, The Herb of Grace, The Heart of the Family*
With **Preface** by Elizabeth Goudge

1958
The White Witch
London, Hodder & Stoughton

c.1958
The Chapel of the Blessed Virgin Mary, Buckler's Hard, Beaulieu
Printed by Kings of Lymington Limited / Lyndhurst Printing Company Limited

1959
Saint Francis of Assisi
London, Duckworth

[as *My God and My All: The Life of St. Francis of Assisi*
New York, Coward McCann]

Introduction to *The Rider of the White Horse* by Rosemary Sutcliff
London, Hodder & Stoughton

1960
The Dean's Watch
London, Hodder & Stoughton

1963
The Scent of Water
London, Hodder & Stoughton

1964
Linnets and Valerians
Leicester, Brockhampton Press
[as ***The Runaways***
Hodder Children's Books, 1996]

A Book of Comfort: An Anthology
London, Michael Joseph
With ***Preface*** by Elizabeth Goudge [editor]

Arabella or The Bad Little Girl
Maria or The Good Little Girl
Serena the Hen
The Shufflewing
Moretonhampstead, Devon, Parnassus Books/Parnassus Gallery

1965
Three Cities of Bells
London, Hodder & Stoughton
Omnibus edition of *A City of Bells, Towers in the Mist, The Dean's Watch*
With ***Preface*** by Elizabeth Goudge

1966
A Diary of Prayer
London, Hodder & Stoughton
With ***Prayers*** and ***Preface*** by Elizabeth Goudge [editor]

1967
A Book of Peace: An Anthology
London, Michael Joseph
With *Preface* by Elizabeth Goudge [editor]

A Christmas Book
London, Hodder & Stoughton
With *Preface* by Elizabeth Goudge
Contents:
    Christmas in the Cathedral [*The Dean's Watch*]
    Christmas on the Moor
    Christmas on the Island [*Island Magic*]
    Christmas at the Inn [*The Herb of Grace*]
    Christmas with the Elizabethans [*Towers in the Mist*]
    Christmas with the Children [*A City of Bells*]
    Christmas with the Three Grey Men [*At the Sign of the Dolphin*]
    Christmas in the Village
    Christmas with the Angels [*God So Loved the World*]

1969
I Saw Three Ships
Leicester, Bockhampton Press

The Ten Gifts, An Elizabeth Goudge Anthology
Selected by Mary Baldwin
London, Hodder and Stoughton

1970
The Child from the Sea
London, Hodder & Stoughton

1971
The Lost Angel
London, Hodder & Stoughton
Contents:
    The Two Caves
    The Silver Horse
    Three Men
    Lost – One Angel
    Saint Nicholas
    John

Giovanni

<u>Undated</u> **Foreword** to *The Mercy of Leaves* : S.P.B.

1972
Foreword to *Daffodils in Ice* by Sister Mary Agnes
London, Workshop Press

1974
The Joy of the Snow: An Autobiography
London, Hodder & Stoughton

1976
A Book of Faith
London, Hodder & Stoughton
With **Foreword** by Elizabeth Goudge [editor]

1978
Pattern of People: An Elizabeth Goudge Anthology
Edited by Muriel Grainger
London, Hodder & Stoughton

<u>All above USA editions published by Coward McCann, New York</u>

[In addition to the above UK/US publications are the many translations into other languages; serialisations in magazines; stories and extracts reprinted in anthologies etc., worldwide. The few selections from these works, referenced in the text, are purely representative.]

1990
A Vision of God: A Selection from the writings of Elizabeth Goudge
Edited by Christine Rawlins
London, Hodder & Stoughton
With previously unpublished ***poems*** by Elizabeth Goudge:
    Our Lady
    Rainbow in Wales
    To our Plum Trees in Winter
    Old Age
    Easter in the Ward
    The Hummingbirds' Nest
    The Dream

ACKNOWLEDGMENTS and BIBLIOGRAPHY

My grateful thanks to the many people and publications who have helped with the making of this book.

To David Higham Associates and The Estate of Elizabeth Goudge for permission to quote from the work of Elizabeth Goudge and from her unpublished correspondence.

To all who contributed by the sharing of memories, photographs and archive material:
Father Louis Bouyer; Father Hugh Dutton; Mrs. Mary Gale; Mrs. Freda Green; Dr. Anthea Sherliker; Miss Rosemary Sutcliff; and The Society of the Precious Blood, Burnham Abbey.
For their welcoming kindness, too: Mr. and Mrs. Mark Dutton; Miss Muriel Grainger; Mrs. Sonia Harwood; Lord Horder; Mrs. Audrey Macbeth, née Clark; Miss Kathleen Millington; and Miss Jessie Monroe, both at Rose Cottage and in Wales.

To Mr. & Mrs. Michael Cansdale and Mrs. Pamela Egan for their generous hospitality in allowing me to see Elizabeth's homes in Wells; and to Mrs. Maureen Johnstone at Providence Cottage.

My thanks also to the helpful staff at the BBC Written Archives Centre, Caversham; at IPC Magazines, for access to the Woman's Journal archive; at the Bodleian Library, Oxford, custodians of EG's letters to Mrs. Audrey Macbeth; and at the Oxfordshire History Centre, custodians of EG's letters to Miss Madeau Stewart.

And my grateful thanks to Mr. Christopher Rowan Grainger for EG's letters to Miss Muriel Grainger, now in the author's archive.

Acknowledgment is gratefully made for permission to include the following works or extracts from them:

Kenneth Allsop: *Kenneth Allsop's Book Page: September 23, 1960*
© The Daily Mail. Reproduced by permission

Humphrey Carpenter: *The Inklings*
Reprinted by permission of HarperCollins Publishers Ltd
Copyright © 1978 Humphrey Carpenter

Mark Davis: *Glimpses of the Carmelite Way*
Copyright © 2007 Mark Davis. Reproduced by permission

Excerpt from "Little Gidding" from FOUR QUARTETS by T.S. Eliot. Copyright © 1943 by T.S. Eliot. Copyright © renewed by Esme Valerie Eliot. Reprinted by permission of Houghton Mifflin Harcourt Publishing Company. All rights reserved

Muriel Grainger: *Music at Midnight*
The Fortune Press, undated. By kind permission of Mr. Christopher Rowan Grainger

Alan Hull Walton: *Sharing Happy Memories. Books and Bookmen: December 1974*
By kind permission of Publishing News and the Kingston University Archive

Marjorie Kunz: *Writer's Story. September 20, 1974*
By kind permission of The Church Times

Ann Lewin: 'Dark Moments' from *Watching for the Kingfisher*
Published by Canterbury Press. © Ann Lewin 2004, 2006 and 2009. Used by permission

C.S. Lewis: *The Lion, the Witch and the Wardrobe*
© C.S. Lewis Pte. Ltd. 1950. Extract reprinted by permission

Alexander McCall Smith: *Interview with Rebecca Franks*
By kind permission of BBC Music Magazine

John Masefield: *The Everlasting Mercy*
Reproduced by permission of The Society of Authors as the Literary Representative of the Estate of John Masefield

Ruth Pitter: *Poems 1926-1966*
The Cresset Press 1968. By kind permission of Mr. Mark Pitter

J. Neville Ward: *The Following Plough* : Epworth Press, 1978
reproduced by permission of The Trustees for Methodist Church Purposes

Memories of Wartime Marldon
Reproduced with the kind assistance of Marldon Local History Group

New English Bible
© Cambridge University Press and Oxford University Press 1961, 1970
Used by permission

RNA News
By kind permission of The Romantic Novelists' Association, and with grateful thanks to Ms. Pia Fenton and Mrs. Jenny Haddon

Speeches of King George VI and Sir Winston Churchill
Contain public sector information licensed under the Open Government Licence v2.0
<u>Excerpts from speeches by King George VI</u> dated 1939, 1945, 1946 and 1947 re-used under the terms and conditions of the Open Government Licence v2.0
<u>Wartime Speech of Sir Winston Churchill</u> reproduced with permission of Curtis Brown, London on behalf of the Estate of Sir Winston Churchill. Copyright © Winston S. Churchill

Bibliography

Albery, Nicholas [ed.] *Poem for the Day*. Sinclair-Stevenson 1994.
Blagg, Helen M. *Statistical Analysis of Infant Mortality and its causes in the United Kingdom*. P.S. King & Son, 1910
Bridges, Robert [ed.] *The Spirit of Man*. Longmans, Green & Co. 1916.
Bridges, Lieutenant-General Sir Tom. *Word from England*. English Universities Press, 1940
Brooke Little, J.P. *The University City of Oxford*. Pitkin, undated.
Burnett, Frances Hodgson. *The Secret Garden*. Heinemann, 1911.
Carey, John. *The Unexpected Professor: An Oxford Life in Books*. Faber and Faber, 2014.
Carpenter, Humphrey. *W.H. Auden, A biography*. George Allen & Unwin, 1981
The Inklings. George Allen & Unwin, 1978.
Cook, K.M. *Grassendale-St. Mary's Gate 1886-1986*. John Catt Limited, 1986.
Cropper, Margaret. *Evelyn Underhill*. Longmans, Green & Co, 1958.

Davidson, Norman J. *Things Seen in Oxford.* Seeley, Service & Co Limited, 1927.
Davis, Mark. *Glimpses of the Carmelite Way.* Rockpool Publishing Ltd, 2007.
Delafield, E.M. *Thank Heaven Fasting.* Virago Press, 1988.
De Waal, Esther. *Seeking God.* Fount / Faith Press, 1984.
Dowling, Alfred E.P. Raymund. *The Flora of the Sacred Nativity.* Kegan Paul, Trench, Trubner & Co, 1900.
Drabble, Margaret. *A Writer's Britain.* Thames and Hudson, 1979.
Duane, O.B. *Mysticism.* Brockhampton Press, 1997.
Duncan, Anthony. *The Elements of Celtic Christianity.* Element Books, 1997.
Eccleshare, Julia. *Beatrix Potter to Harry Potter,* National Portrait Gallery, 2002.
Eliot, T.S. *Four Quartets.* Faber and Faber, 1944; *The Waste Land and other poems.* Faber & Faber, 1940.
Engen, Rodney. *The Age of Enchantment: Beardsley, Dulac and their Contemporaries 1890-1930.* Dulwich Picture Gallery, 2007.
Foot, Michael. *H.G. The History of Mr. Wells.* Doubleday, 1995.
Forster, Margaret. *Daphne du Maurier.* Chatto and Windus, 1993.
Gordon, Lyndall. *Eliot's New Life.* OUP, 1988.
Goudge, H.L. *Addresses for Lent and Good Friday:* Skeffington and Son [undated]; *The Apocalypse and the Present Age:* Mowbrays, 1935; *The Case Against Pacifism:* A.R. Mowbray, 1938; *The Church of England and Reunion:* SPCK 1938; *Sermons for the Christian Year:* Skeffington and Son [undated]. *The Study Bible: Hebrews.* Cassell and Company, 1926
Grainger, Muriel. *Music at Midnight.* The Fortune Press, undated.
Grenfell, Joyce. *Joyce Grenfell Requests the Pleasure.* Macmillan, 1976.
Griffiths, Bede. *The Golden String:* The Harvill Press, 1954; *A New Vision of Reality:* William Collins, 1989.
Haddon, Jenny & Pearson, Diane: *Fabulous at Fifty.* RNA, 2010
Hamilton, James. *Arthur Rackham, A Life with Illustration.* Pavilion Books, 1990.
Hamilton, William. *The Quest for the Post-Historical Jesus.* SCM Press, 1993.
Hammarskjold, Dag. *Markings.* Faber & Faber 1964.
Hankey, C.P: *The Pictorial History of Ely Cathedral.* Pitkin, 1962.
Harman, Alec and Mellers, Wilfrid. *Man and his Music.* Barrie and Jenkins. 1962.
Hastings, Adrian. *A History of English Christianity 1920-1985.* William Collins, 1986.
Havell, H.L. *Stories from The Aeneid.* George G. Harrap & Co, 1913.
Huxley, Aldous [Ed.] *The Letters of D.H. Lawrence.* William Heinemann Ltd. 1932.

Inge, W.R. *Mysticism in Religion*. Hutchinson's University Library, undated; *The Study Bible: Hebrews*. Cassell and Company, 1926.
Kilby, Clyde S. [Ed.] *C.S. Lewis - Letters to an American Lady*. Hodder & Stoughton, 1969.
King, Don W. *Hunting the Unicorn: A Critical Biography of Ruth Pitter*. Kent State University Press, 2008.
Lawrence, Brother. *The Practice of the Presence of God*. Hodder & Stoughton, 1981.
Lewin, Ann. *Watching for the Kingfisher*. Inspire, 2004.
Lewis, C.S. [Ed.] *George MacDonald, An Anthology:* Geoffrey Bles, 1946; *The Lion the Witch and the Wardrobe*: Geoffrey Bles, 1950.
Lewis, W.H. [Ed.] *Letters of C.S. Lewis*. Geoffrey Bles, 1966.
Lycett Green, Candida. *John Betjeman, Letters Volume Two*. Methuen, 1995.
Marnham, Patrick. *Wild Mary – A Life of Mary Wesley*. Chatto & Windus, 2006.
Mayne, Michael. *This Sunrise of Wonder*. Harper Collins, 1995.
MacCarthy, Fiona. *William Morris*. Faber & Faber, 1994.
McCall Smith, Alexander. Interview with Rebecca Franks. BBC Music Magazine, April 2011.
McGlashan, Alan. *The Savage and Beautiful Country*. Houghton Mifflin, 1967.
Molesworth, Mrs. *The Cuckoo Clock*, 1877. Reprinted in the C.I.C. Series: J.M. Dent, 1954.
Olivier, Edith. *Without Knowing Mr. Walkley*. Faber and Faber, London 1939.
Piper, John. *Oxfordshire, A Shell Guide*. Faber and Faber, new edition 1953.
Pitter, Ruth. *Poems 1926-1966*. Barrie & Rockliff, The Cresset Press, 1968.
Plowright, Joan. *And That's Not All*. Weidenfeld & Nicolson, 2001.
Roberts, Roger L. *Treasures from the Spiritual Classics – Light of Christ: Evelyn Underhill*. A.R. Mowbray, 1981.
Rogers, Byron. *The Man who went into the West: The Life of R.S. Thomas*. Aurum Press, 2006.
Sayer, George. *Jack, A Life of C.S. Lewis*. Hodder & Stoughton 1997.
Silf, Margaret. *Sacred Spaces*. Lion, 2005.
Shattock, Joanne [Ed.] *The Oxford Guide to British Women Writers*. Oxford University Press, 1993.
Spalding, Frances. *Gwen Raverat: Friends, Family and Affections:* The Harvill Press, 2001; *John Piper, Myfanwy Piper: Lives in Art:* Oxford University Press, 2009; *Virginia Woolf: Paper Darts:* Collins & Brown, 1991.
Stevenson, R.L. *A Child's Garden of Verses*. William Collins [introduction by EG] 1955 and [introduction by Laurence Alma Tadema] 1946.
Sutcliff, Rosemary. *Blue Remembered Hills*. The Bodley Head, 1983.
Underhill, Evelyn. *Light of Christ*. Longmans, Green and Company, 1944; *Practical Mysticism*. J.M. Dent & Sons, 1914.

[Unnamed Editor] *Modern Gift Book for Children, The*. Odhams Press Limited. 1948
Ward, J. Neville. *The Following Plough*. Epworth Press, 1978.
Wildiers, N.M. *An Introduction to Teilhard de Chardin*. Fontana, 1968.
Williams, Charles [Ed.] *The Letters of Evelyn Underhill*. Longmans, Green and Company, 1943.

FILM

Her Majesty the Queen Mother in Public
British Movietone News/C21C co-production

Elgar by Ken Russell
British Film Institute *Archive Television:* BBC Worldwide 2002

ENDNOTES

Works by Elizabeth Goudge are listed by initials as follows:

ACB	A Christmas Book © 1967
ADP	The All-Day Prayer in *Guideposts* June/July 1973
AS	Autobiographical Sketch in EGR 1946 [later amended as *byEG*]
ASD	At the Sign of the Dolphin © 1947 [UK title of EGR]
BC	A Book of Comfort © 1964
BF	A Book of Faith © 1976
BP	A Book of Peace © 1967
BT	The Bird in the Tree © 1940
byEG	…by Elizabeth Goudge in *Woman's Journal* Feb.1956 [AS, slightly amended]
CB	A City of Bells © 1936
CGV	Preface © 1955 to Stevenson, R.L: *A Child's Garden of Verses*, first published 1885
CH	The Castle on the Hill © 1942
CS	The Child from the Sea © 1970
DP	A Diary of Prayer © 1966
DW	The Dean's Watch © 1960
EGR	The Elizabeth Goudge Reader: Dobbs, Rose [ed] © 1947
FB	The Fairies' Baby and other stories © 1919
GDC	Green Dolphin Country © 1944
GH	Gentian Hill © 1949
GS	The Golden Skylark © 1941
GSLW	God So Loved the World © 1951
HF	The Heart of the Family © 1953
HG	The Herb of Grace © 1948
HH	Henrietta's House © 1942
IM	Island Magic © 1934
ISTS	I Saw Three Ships © 1969
IW	The Ikon on the Wall © 1943
JS	The Joy of the Snow © 1974
LV	Linnets & Valerians © 1964
LWH	The Little White Horse © 1946
MB	Make-Believe © 1949

MF   My Father in *Glorying in the Cross* © 1940
MW   The Middle Window © 1935
RF   The Reward of Faith © 1950
PP   A Pedlar's Pack © 1937
RT   The Rosemary Tree © 1956
SA   Sister of the Angels © 1939
SFA   Saint Francis of Assisi © 1959
SH   Smoky-House © 1940
SV   Songs and Verses © 1947
SW   The Scent of Water © 1963
TCB   Three Cities of Bells © 1965
TLA   The Lost Angel © 1971
TM   Towers in the Mist © 1938
TP   Three Plays © 1939
TWW   The White Witch © 1958
VG   A Vision of God: Rawlins, Christine [ed] © 1990
VS   The Valley of Song © 1951
WS   The Well of the Star © 1941
WW   White Wings © 1952

For uniformity, all chapter numbers are shown in Roman numerals.

Dates of letters are as accurate as research will allow – EG almost never dated her letters with the year.

Quotations from EG's friends refer to author interviews with: Jessie Monroe, Audrey Clark [Mrs. Audrey Pilkington Jackson / Mrs. Audrey Macbeth], Sonia Harwood, Kathleen Millington, Lord Horder. Quotations from Freda Green and Sister Raphael Mary are taken from their letters to Jessie Monroe. Letters are identified by recipient's initials: Louis Bouyer [LB]; Audrey Clark [AC]; Muriel Grainger [MG] and Madeau Stewart [MS]

Critical opinion / Interviews:
BJ   Book Jacket publicity, undated, as selected by publishers
RM   Ruth Martin: *Trade News*, 29 August 1970
PT   Philippa Toomey: *The Times*, 21 August 1974
AHW   Alan Hull Walton: *Books and Bookmen*, December 1974
RNA68   *Romantic Novelists' Association News*: No.60 August/September 1968
RNA72   *Romantic Novelists' Association News*: No.75 Spring 1972

Bible quotations are from the King James Version, unless otherwise indicated

1. Ward, J. Neville: *The Following Plough*, ch.I © 1978
2. Lewin, Ann: *Watching for the Kingfisher* © 2004

TWO STRANDS TWISTED TOGETHER, OF BLACK AND GOLD

3. SW VII.III
4. Julian of Norwich [c.1342-c.1416]: *Revelations of Divine Love*. In BC Part IV.V.
5. JS ch.XVI.I
6. Goudge, H.L: 'National Danger' in *Addresses for Lent and Good Friday* [undated]
7. JS ch.XIV.III
8. JS ch.II.I
9. SW ch.IV.II
10. TWW Part One ch.VI.II

THE FIRST CITY OF BELLS

11. JS ch.I.I
12. CGV
13. Ibid.
14. Reprinted in 1956 edition: Wm. Collins and Co. Ltd
15. JS ch.I.II
16. by EG
17. HH ch.III
18. In *The Modern Gift Book for Children* © 1948
19. Ibid.
20. SA ch.II
21. AS
22. JS ch.I.III
23. Ibid.II
24. TCB Preface
25. CB ch.I.IV
26. MF p.21
27. JS ch.I.III
28. JS ch.VI.I
29. MF p.21
30. CB ch.I.IV
31. JS ch.I.II
32. JS ch.I.III
33. HH ch.IV
34. TCB preface
35. JS ch.I.III
36. CB ch.VI.IV
37. CGV
38. AS
39. Ibid.
40. CB ch.XIV.V
41. AS
42. Sonia Harwood
43. JS ch.VI.IV
44. MF p.15
45. JS ch.VI.IV
46. MF p.20
47. AS
48. CB ch.III.I
49. AS
50. CB ch.XII.II
51. CB ch.II.I
52. CB ch.III.I
53. AS
54. Ibid.
55. JS ch.II.I

AN EDWARDIAN FAMILY

56. ch.IV.III
57. JS ch.V.II
58. JS ch.VI.II
59. FB: *The Flower of Happiness* p.106
60. JS ch.XII.III
61. JS ch.III.II
62. JS ch.IV.IV
63. JS ch.V.I
64. Ibid.
65. JS ch.V.III
66. Ibid.
67. byEG
68. JS ch.IV.IV

69	JS ch.II.II	107	JS ch.III.IV
70	JS ch.I.I	108	JS ch.I.II
		109	IM ch.IV.III

MOTHER AND CHILD

		110	JS ch.IV.I
71	Bible: Ecclesiastes 4, vv. 12 and 10	111	CGV
72	JS ch.IV.IV	112	JS ch.II.III
73	ADP		
74	MF p.18		

THE DISTRESSED HOUSEHOLD

75	JS ch.I.III	113	JS ch.V.V
76	ADP	114	CB ch.I.IV
77	JS ch.V.I	115	JS ch.V.V
78	JS ch.II.III	116	JS ch.IV.II
79	FB: *The Fairies' Baby* p.3	117	Ibid.I
80	JS ch.IV.IV	118	Blagg, Helen M: *A Statistical Analysis of Infant Mortality and its causes in the UK.* 1910
81	DW ch.3.I		
82	JS ch.IV.IV		
		119	JS ch.IV.I

TWO WORLDS

		120	Ibid.
83	ch.II.II	121	CB ch.IX.VI
84	Ibid.	122	JS ch.IV.I
85	RT ch.VI.II	123	MB ch.VI
86	CGV	124	JS ch.IV.I
87	Ibid.	125	JS ch.IV.II
88	JS ch.IV.III		
89	Ibid.IV		

GUERNSEY

90	SH	126	JS ch.III.I
91	Stevenson, R.L: *A Child's Garden of Verses*, first published 1885	127	Ibid.
		128	GDC Book One, Part I.II
92	CGV	129	JS ch.III.I
93	IM ch.V.II	130	IM ch.I.II
94	BT ch. VIII	131	JS ch.III.I
95	MF p.7	132	IM Ch.I.II
96	JS ch.IV.IV	133	JS ch.III.I
97	CS Book One ch.I.I	134	Ibid.IV
98	JS ch.IV.IV	135	IM ch.II.I
99	TM ch.II.II	136	JS ch.III.I
100	MF p.18	137	Ibid.II
101	TM ch.II.II	138	Ibid.I
102	JS ch.IV.II	139	Ibid.
103	DW ch.3.I	140	To LB: 11 February 1980
104	JS ch.IV.II	141	JS ch.II.III
		142	JS ch.III.II

IN THE KITCHEN

		143	Ibid.
105	JS ch.II.II	144	Ibid.
106	HF ch.XVII.I	145	Ibid.

146 Ibid.I
147 Ibid.III
148 Ibid.IV

BATH
149 JS ch.IV.III
150 Ibid.
151 LWH ch.11.III
152 JS ch.IV.IV

LONDON AND SUSSEX
153 JS ch.V.III
154 GH ch.VI.I
155 JS ch.V.III
156 Ibid.
157 BT ch.IV.I
158 JS ch.V.III
159 Ibid.
160 Ibid.
161 CB ch.X.VII
162 CB ch.X.VIII
163 JS ch.V.III
164 LV ch.XIII
165 JS ch.V.III
166 RT ch.V.II
167 CB ch.XII.I

UPPINGHAM
168 JS ch.V.IV
169 1992: Letter to Jessie Monroe / telephone call to the author
170 GH ch.II.III
171 JS ch.V.IV
172 Ibid.
173 FB: *The Fairy Queen's Jewels* p.40-44
174 HH ch.XIV
175 JS ch.V.IV

THE UNSEEN PLAYMATE
176 AS
177 AS
178 JS ch.VI.IV
179 LWH ch.II.III
180 AS
181 CGV

182 JS ch.V.IV
183 BT ch.V.I
184 JS ch.V.IV
185 LWH ch.I.IV
186 LV ch.XI
187 LWH ch.I.IV
188 CGV
189 Ibid.

THE HIDDEN THINGS
190 Ibid.
191 JS ch.V.IV
192 CGV
193 RT ch.III.III
194 Thomas, R.S: *Children's Song* in BC Part II.II
195 Vaughan, Henry [1621-1695]: *The Retreat* in BC Part II.I
196 IM ch.V.III
197 Vaughan, Henry[1621-1695]: *The World* in Silex Scintillans, first published 1650.
198 Wordsworth, William [1770-1850]: *Intimations of Mortality* in BC Part II.I
199 RT ch.III.II

CHILDHOOD FAITH
200 JS ch.IV.IV
201 Ibid.I
202 Ibid.III
203 Ibid
204 JS ch.IV.IV
205 Ibid.III
206 Ibid.
207 BT ch.II.I
208 BT ch.IV.I
209 JS ch.II.II
210 JS ch.IV.IV
211 Ibid.
212 Ibid.
213 Dreams in EGR/ASD
214 IM ch.II.II
215 JS ch.IV.IV
216 LWH ch.II.II

497

217 CB ch.III.II
218 CB ch.VII.v

THE SECOND CITY OF BELLS
219 MF p.21
220 JS ch.VI.I
221 JS ch.IV.II
222 SA ch.I
223 Later given to Sonia Harwood
224 JS ch.IV.II
225 MF p.21
226 JS ch.VI.I
227 Ibid.
228 MF p.22
229 JS ch.IX.I
230 JS ch.VI.I
231 RT ch.XVII.III
232 JS ch.VI.III
233 Hopkins, Gerard Manley[1844-1889]: in BF Part Two.II
234 JS ch.XII.III
235 JS ch.VI.I
236 Ibid.
237 JS ch.V.III
238 Ibid.
239 JS ch.IV.IV
240 JS ch.VI.I
241 JS ch.VII.I
242 JS ch.VI.I
243 Ibid.II
244 Ibid.
245 Bede [672-735]. Quoted in Hankey, C.P: *The Pictorial History of Ely Cathedral* © 1962
246 JS ch.VI.IV
247 MF p.20
248 JS ch.VI.IV
249 Ibid
250 DW ch.11.IV
251 DW ch.12.1
252 JS ch.VI.I
253 Ibid.IV
254 Ibid.
255 Ibid.
256 MF p.23
257 JS ch.VI.III
258 Ibid.II
259 Ibid.III
260 CB ch.VII.III
261 JS ch.VI.III
262 Ibid.II
263 To MS: 30 November 1978
264 JS ch.VI.IV
265 AS
266 JS ch.XV.I
267 JS ch.VI.I
268 JS ch.XV.II
269 JS ch.VI.II

LOSS
270 Ibid.
271 LWH ch.I.I
272 JS ch.IV.II
273 JS ch.VI.II
274 Ibid.
275 Ibid.
276 Ibid.

BOOKS
277 JS ch.VI.III
278 HH ch.II
279 JS ch.II.III
280 Ibid.
281 In *The Guardian*, 21 December 2002: Wilson, Jacqueline, 'Griselda's Big Adventure'
282 Molesworth, M.L: *The Cuckoo Clock*, first published 1877
283 DW ch.1.I
284 DW ch.15.I
285 AS
286 JS ch.VI.III
287 MF p.14
288 FB: *The Fairy Queen's Jewels* p.44
289 JS ch.VI.III
290 Ibid.III
291 RT ch.VIII.I
292 To MS: January 1980

SCHOOL
293 byEG
294 JS ch.VI.V
295 JS ch.VIII.III
296 JS ch.VIII.I
297 CH ch. XII.II
298 JS ch.VIII.I
299 Ibid.
300 AS
301 JS ch.VI.V
302 JS ch.VIII.II
303 HG ch.II.II
304 JS ch.VIII.II
305 JS ch.VIII.I
306 AS
307 JS ch.VIII.I
308 Ibid.II
309 IM ch.III.IV
310 AS
311 JS ch.VIII.I
312 SH ch.I
313 JS.ch.VIII.I

FATHER AND CHILD
314 JS ch.VIII.V
315 HG ch.XIV.I
316 JS ch.VIII.V
317 Ibid.
318 Ibid.
319 Ibid.

FEAR AND DARKNESS
320 JS ch.VI.III
321 JS ch.I.II
322 JS ch.VI.III
323 JS ch.VII.I
324 Ibid.
325 Ibid.
326 Ibid.
327 Ibid.
328 JS ch.VIII.III
329 JS ch.XI.I
330 JS ch.VII.IV
331 RT ch.IX.I
332 Ibid.
333 JS ch.VII.IV
334 JS ch.VI.V
335 MF
336 JS ch.VI.V
337 CB ch. IX.VI
338 JS ch.VI.V
339 RT ch.VI.I
340 JS ch.VI.V
341 In VG
342 JS ch.VI.V
343 LV ch.VII

THE GREAT WAR
344 JS ch.VIII.I
345 JS ch.VI.V
346 JS ch.VIII.IV
347 Goudge, H.L: Lecture I *The Apocalypse and the Present Age*, © 1935

CHOICES
348 JS ch.VIII.IV
349 Ibid.VI
350 Ibid.IV
351 AS
352 Ibid
353 Ibid. p.103

PAINTING PICTURES
354 AS
355 JS ch.VIII.V
356 Ibid.
357 JS ch.VIII.VI
358 Ibid.
359 Ibid.
360 AS
361 *Sweet Herbs* in WW and PP
362 JS ch.I.II
363 IM ch.I.I
364 JS ch.VIII.VI
365 JS ch.VI.III
366 BT ch.Two.IV
367 SA ch.V
368 In MacCarthy, Fiona: *William Morris* © 1994

FIRST LOVE
369 MF p.25
370 JS ch.VIII.IV
371 MF p.26
372 JS ch.VIII.IV
373 AS
374 MF p.26
375 JS ch.XV.II
376 Kathleen Millington

FAITH AND UNBELIEF
377 JS ch.IX.II
378 Ibid.
379 Donne, John [1572-1631]: *Sermon*s, in BC Part III.II
380 Tennyson, Alfred : *The Higher Pantheism* [1870] in BP Part XV
381 Freud, Sigmund: *The Future of an Illusion* © 1927
382 JS ch.III.II
383 JS ch.VIII.III
384 Hopkins, Gerard Manley [1844-1889]: *God's Grandeur.* BC Part III.IV
385 Boros, Ladislaus [1927-1981] in BF Part 7.I
386 JS ch.VIII.III

SISTERS
387 Ibid.
388 Ibid.
389 Ibid.
390 JS ch.III.I
391 JS ch.VIII.III
392 Ibid.
393 Ibid.
394 Ibid.

TEACHING
395 JS ch.VIII.VI
396 JS ch.III.II
397 AS
398 JS ch.VIII.VI
399 byEG
400 AS

401 JS ch.V.I
402 JS ch.VIII.VI
403 Ibid.IV
404 Ibid.VI
405 MF p.27
406 JS ch.VI.I
407 JS ch.VIII.VI

THE WASTE LAND
408 Bible: Psalm 63 v.I
409 Carpenter, Humphrey: *W.H. Auden, a biography* Part I ch.IV © 1981
410 Griffiths, Bede: *The Golden String* ch.II © 1954
411 JS ch.VIII.III
412 JS ch.XI.III
413 MF p.30
414 ADP
415 JS ch.XI.III
416 Ibid.

TOM QUAD
417 JS ch.VIII.VI
418 TP *The Brontes of Haworth* Act I Scene II
419 JS ch.VIII.VI
420 JS ch.IX.I
421 TM ch.II.II
422 TCB preface
423 JS ch.IX.III
424 Ibid.
425 TM ch.VIII.I
426 JS ch.IX.I
427 LWH ch.II.II
428 MW ch.II.II
429 JS ch.IX.I
430 TWW Part Three ch.II.I
431 JS ch.IX.I
432 TCB preface
433 byEG
434 JS ch.IX.III
435 JS ch.VIII.VI
436 JS ch.XII.III
437 JS ch.III.II

500

OXFORD LIFE
438 Delafield, E.M: *Thank Heaven Fasting* © 1932
439 JS ch.IX.III
440 Davidson, Norman J: *Things Seen in Oxford* © 1927
441 JS ch.IX.III
442 TWW Part Three ch.II.I
443 JS ch.IX.I
444 TWW Part Three ch.V.II
445 Ibid.III
446 JS ch.IX.I
447 Griffiths, Bede: *The Golden String* ch.II ©1954

BARTON
448 JS.ch.X.I
449 Griffiths, Bede: *The Golden String* ch.I © 1954
450 JS ch.X.I
451 BC Part V.VI
452 JS ch.X.I
453 Ibid.
454 JS ch.X.II
455 Ibid.I
456 MF p.28
457 JS ch.IX.II
458 byEG
459 SW ch.IV.II
460 JS ch.I.III
461 ADP

ACADEMIA
462 byEG
463 MF p.14
464 Carpenter, Humphrey: *The Inklings* ch.4 © 1978
465 Carpenter, Humphrey: *The Inklings* ch.4 © 1978
466 9 July 1927. Lewis, W.H. [ed] *Letters of C.S. Lewis* ©1966
467 All JS ch.III.III
468 RT ch.III.I
469 Ibid.
470 Carpenter, Humphrey: *The Inklings* ch.4 © 1978
471 Ibid.
472 SW ch.III.IV
473 Brooke Little, J.P: *The University City of Oxford* [undated, post-1955]
474 JS ch.IX.III
475 CB ch.I.IV
476 JS ch.IX.III
477 DW ch.XI.IV
478 Carey, John: *The Unexpected Professor* ch.6 © 2014
479 MF p.27
480 MF p.29
481 MF p.16
482 JS ch.XII.III
483 JS ch.IX.II
484 MF p.18
485 MF p.16

TIME TO WRITE
486 JS ch.X.1
487 JS ch.X.III
488 Ibid.
489 JS ch.IX.I
490 JS ch.VIII.VI
491 SW ch.II.I
492 AS

ISLAND MAGIC
493 JS ch.X.III
494 Ibid.
495 byEG
496 AS
497 JS ch.II.I
498 JS ch.X.III
499 IM ch.I.V
500 S
501 6 March 1912. Huxley, Aldous [ed]: *The Letters of D.H. Lawrence* © 1932
502 Horder, Mervyn: 'A Joyous Biography' in *The Bookseller*, 3 August 1974
503 All BJ
504 IM ch.I.V

505 Ibid.
506 Carpenter, Humphrey: *The Inklings* Part Three ch.2 © 1978
507 JS ch.VIII.VI
508 TM ch.VII.III
509 JS ch.I.I
510 JS ch.VIII.VI
511 MF p.27
512 IM ch.I.V
513 IM ch.II.I
514 IM ch.IX.III
515 CH ch.VII.III
516 IM ch.II.I
517 IM ch.IX.III
518 BP Part XV
519 ADP
520 IM ch.IV.V
521 Underhill, Evelyn: *Practical Mysticism*. First published 1914
522 Ibid.
523 IM ch.IX.III
524 Underhill, Evelyn: *Practical Mysticism*. First published 1914
525 TP *The Brontes of Haworth* Act I Scene III
526 Mary Agnes, Sister: *Daffodils in Ice* © 1972
527 IM ch.I.VII

SUCCESS
528 JS ch.X.III
529 Ibid.
530 *RNA News*, New Year 1970
531 byEG
532 JS ch.X.III
533 Coward McCann edn. © 1939
534 AS
535 All BJ
536 Rogers, Byron: *The Man who went into the West*. P.113 © 2006
537 Griffiths, Bede: *The Golden String* ch.IV © 1954
538 MW ch.I
539 MW ch.V.V

GETTING AWAY
540 JS ch.X.IV
541 Ibid.
542 JS ch.III.III
543 Ibid.
544 In PP and WW
545 In *Woman's Journal* June 1946
546 JS ch.X.IV
547 MW ch.II.II
548 MW ch.IV.III
549 JS ch.VII.IV
550 JS ch.XV.II
551 MW ch.IV.III
552 In GS and WW
553 JS ch.X.IV
554 In IW and WW
555 JS ch.X.IV
556 JS ch.V.III
557 To MG: 4 February 1979
558 JS ch.X.III
559 Ibid.
560 HG ch.XIX.II

INNER VISION
561 McGlashan, A: *The Savage and Beautiful Country* © 1988
562 To MG: Spring 1978
563 Bible: Luke 17:21 / McGlashan, A: *The Savage and Beautiful Country* © 1988
564 Carpenter, Humphrey: *The Inklings* ch.3 © 1978
565 CB ch.VII.III
566 TWW Part One ch.VII.I
567 LV ch.IX
568 JS ch.VII.II
569 AS
570 SW ch.XIII.II

A CITY OF BELLS
571 BJ
572 MF p.14
573 JS ch.III.III
574 Ibid.
575 JS ch.VI.II

502

576 CB ch.II.II
577 BJ
578 CB ch.I.VI
579 Ibid.
580 CB ch.XIII.IV
581 CB ch.I.VI
582 JS ch.XI.I
583 TP: *Fanny Burney* Act I Sc,II
584 BJ

BREAKDOWN
585 JS ch.XI.I / Shakespeare: *King Lear* Act I sc.V
586 SW ch.V.II
587 Newman, John Henry [1801-1890] *The Dream of Gerontius*
588 JS ch.XI.II
589 DW ch.VII.II
590 Sister Raphael Mary to Jessie Monroe c.1991
591 MW Book II.II
592 JS ch.V.I
593 JS ch.XI.II
594 JS ch.I.I
595 CB ch.II.III
596 TM ch.II.II
597 RT ch.III.I
598 SW ch.V.II
599 Woolf, Virginia [1882-1941]: To Violet Dickinson, 30 October 1904
600 JS ch.IV.III
601 IM ch.II.I
602 CB ch.VII.II
603 RT ch.III.I
604 JS ch.X.I
605 JS ch.II.II
606 In Nicholson, Virginia: *Singled Out* p.23 © 2007
607 Ibid.

CHILDLESSNESS
608 MW Book II ch.V.III
609 JS ch.VIII.IV
610 TP *Fanny Burney* [*Joy Will Come Back*] Act II Scene II
611 JS ch.I.III
612 JS ch.VIII.IV
613 TWW Part One ch.IX
614 Letter to the author from Dr. A. Sherliker 1992
615 *Woman's Journal* April 1940
616 SA ch.VI
617 CH ch.IV.III

LOST LOVE
618 CB ch.IV.I
619 CB ch.V.IV
620 HG ch.XVI.I
621 TP *The Brontes of Haworth* Act I Scene II
622 BT ch.XI.I
623 MW Book II ch.V.II
624 BT ch.X.III
625 TWW Part Three ch.IV.III
626 RT ch.XIII
627 Ibid.
628 Ibid.
629 Rosemary March: *The Daily Telegraph* August 1972
630 JS ch.VIII.IV

FEARS AND BURDENS
631 JS ch.VI.V
632 Carpenter, Humphrey: *The Inklings* ch.5 © 1978
633 CB ch.VIII.V
634 CB ch.V.IV
635 SW ch.IV.II
636 IM ch.I.V
637 CB ch.XIV.II
638 Ibid.III
639 CB ch.VIII.V
640 In BC Part IV.III
641 MW Book II ch.V.III
642 CB ch.XIV.III
643 Ibid.VII

GETTING THROUGH
644 Cowper, William [1731-1800]: *The Task* in BC Part IV.I

645 JS ch.XI.I
646 HG ch.IX.III
647 CH ch.II.I
648 CH ch.VI.I
649 HG ch.VIII.II
650 *Irving Penn Portraits*: National Portrait Gallery exhibition, 2010
651 SA ch.VI
652 JS ch.I.I
653 JS ch.XII.I
654 MF p.17
655 SW ch.V.II
656 JS ch.V.I
657 SW ch.V.II
658 Ibid.
659 JS ch.V.II
660 Ibid.
661 Ibid.
662 Attenborough, John: *Dictionary of National Biography 1982-1985* © 1986
663 SW ch.V.II
664 DP February 14
665 JS ch.VIII.IV
666 CH ch.X.I
667 CH ch.VIII.VI
668 BT ch.VIII
669 HG ch.XVI.I
670 JS ch.VIII.IV
671 SA ch.V
672 BF Part IX.II

TOWERS IN THE MIST
673 BJ
674 RNA72
675 BJ
676 MF p.30
677 Hardy, Thomas: *Jude the Obscure* Part Sixth.II. First published 1895
678 JS ch.VIII.III
679 TM ch.XI.III
680 Hardy, Thomas: *Jude the Obscure*, Part First.III. First published 1895
681 Ibid.
682 TM ch.I.I

683 Foxe, John: *The Actes and Monuments*. 1563
684 Havell, H.L. *Stories from The Aeneid*. 1913
685 The Bible: Psalm 121:1
686 TM ch.I.IV
687 Ibid.
688 TM ch.XVII.IV
689 JS ch.XI.III
690 MacDonald, George [1824-1905] in BF Part IX.2
691 TM ch.I.IV
692 JS ch.X.I
693 MF p.18
694 JS ch.X.I
695 Sidney, Philip [1554-1586] *Arcadia*
696 Goudge, H.L: Introduction to *The Church of England and Reunion* ©1938
697 30 April 1941. In Williams, Charles [ed]: *The Letters of Evelyn Underhill* © 1943
698 JS ch.II.II
699 TP
700 byEG
701 AS

THE DARK TUNNEL
702 MF p.21
703 MF p.31
704 Ibid.
705 JS ch.XII.I
706 DP 24 April: *Hickes' Devotions* [18th century]
707 MF p.33
708 DP November 13
709 JS ch.XII.I
710 JS ch.I.I
711 Benson, E. [1829-1896] DP November 14

THE SECRET DISCIPLINE – HER FATHER'S SPIRITUAL LEGACY
712 JS ch.XII.I
713 MF p.17

714 Ibid.
715 BT ch.IX.I
716 ADP
717 Ibid.
718 RT ch.III.I
719 Eliot, T.S: *The Family Reunion* © 1939
720 RT ch.XIV.II
721 RT ch.III.I

LEARNING TO COPE
722 JS ch.XII.II
723 S ch.X.I
724 JS ch.XII.III
725 Ibid.II
726 Ibid.III
727 CH ch.I.I
728 CH ch.I.II
729 To BBC, December 1939
730 SA ch.V
731 Ibid.
732 GH Book III ch.III.I
733 Foreword to Tarbat, Alan C: *The Rider of Mendip and other poems* © 1939
734 GH Book III, ch.IV.IV

DEVON
735 JS ch.XII.II
736 Ibid.
737 'West Country Magic' in *The Horn Book Magazine,* March 1947
738 JS ch.XIII.I
739 'West Country Magic' in *The Horn Book Magazine,* March 1947
740 LV Knight Books edn. First published 1967
741 JS ch.VII.IV
742 Ibid.
743 JS ch.XII.II

PROVIDENCE COTTAGE
744 JS ch.XII.III
745 Ibid.
746 BT ch.II.IV
747 Ibid.V
748 JS ch.XII.III
749 Ibid.
750 JS ch.XII.IV
751 Ibid.
752 JS ch.XIV.III

REBUILDING THE WASTE LAND – THE BIRD IN THE TREE
753 BT ch.II.IV
754 BT ch.II.V
755 Wells, H.G: *Love and Mr. Lewisham,* first published 1899
756 BT ch.III
757 BT ch.IV.I
758 BT ch.IX.I
759 King Edward VIII
760 BT ch.VIII
761 SW ch.VII.III
762 BT ch.VIII
763 BT ch.IV.I
764 HG ch.II.II
765 BT ch.I.IV
766 Bible: Gospel according to John 12:24
767 BT ch.I.IV
768 Bible: Gospel according to Mark 4:28
769 BT ch.I.IV
770 HG ch.II.II
771 Traherne, Thomas [c.1636-1674]: *Centuries of Meditation* in BC Part II.I
772 Finzi, Gerald : *Dies Natalis* Op.8
773 Traherne, Thomas [c.1636-1674]: *Centuries of Meditation* in BC Part II.I
774 Ibid.
775 BT ch.II.IV
776 *There is no rose of such virtue as is the rose that bare Jesu.* Anonymous c.1420
777 Bible: Song of Solomon 4:12
778 BT ch.II.IV
779 Ibid.
780 Rosemary Sutcliff: telephone call to the author

781 DP November 14

WORK AND WAR
782 JS ch.XIII.I
783 JS ch.XII.I
784 JS ch.XII.IV
785 JS ch.XIII.I
786 AS
787 CH ch.VIII.I
788 JS ch.VIII.VI
789 JS ch.IX.II
790 *Dreams* in EGR/ASD
791 Ibid.
792 RT ch.I.I
793 JS ch. XII.IV
794 EGR/ASD
795 Kipling, Rudyard: 'Hal o' the Draft' in *Puck of Pook's Hill*, first published 1906
796 SH ch.I
797 *Richard II* Act II Sc.I
798 SH
799 Churchill, Winston: wartime broadcast
800 CH ch.I.I
801 JS ch.III.I
802 Bridges, Robert: Preface to *The Spirit of Man*, first published 1916
803 Hay, Ian: Foreword to *Word from England*, Bridges, Tom [ed] © 1940
804 MF p.20
805 CH ch.III.II
806 In *The Horn Book Magazine*, March 1947

THE CASTLE ON THE HILL
807 CH ch.V.I
808 Wolfe, Humbert: *The Uncelestial City* © 1930
809 CH ch.V.I
810 CH ch.I.II
811 CH ch.V.I
812 CH ch.XIV.II
813 Ibid.
814 CH ch.II.I

815 To Lady Cynthia Asquith, 2.Nov.1915 in Huxley, Aldous: *The Letters of D.H. Lawrence* © 1932
816 CH ch.XV.II
817 Ibid.III
818 Goudge, H.L: *The Case Against Pacifism*. 1938
819 MF
820 BJ
821 CH ch.I.II
822 JS ch.XIII.I
823 To AC: 7 August 1942
824 JS ch.XIII.I
825 CH ch.XII.I
826 Ibid.
827 JS ch.XIII.I
828 JS ch.II.III
829 JS ch.III.III
830 JS ch.XIII.I
831 JS ch.III.III
832 JS ch.IV.III
833 To AC: 7 August 1942
834 Ibid.
835 Ibid.
836 JS ch.XIII.I
837 ADP
838 DP August 30
839 SH dedication

HENRIETTA'S HOUSE
840 Ellis, Richard: *The Saturday Review*, 5 October 1942
841 SA ch.VI
842 *Dreams* in ASD/EGR
843 HH ch.X
844 Ibid.
845 SA ch.I
846 HH ch.XI
847 SH ch.XVI
848 HH ch.XII
849 HH ch.XI
850 Hastings, Adrian: *A History of English Christianity 1920-1985* ch.27 ©1986

FAITH, MYTH AND FAIRYTALES
851 JS ch.VII.IV
852 Ibid.
853 PT
854 *Victorian Fairy Painting.* The Royal Academy of Arts exhibition, London: 1998
855 Ibid.
856 Hamilton, James: *Arthur Rackham, A Life with Illustration.* P.10 ©1990
857 Kilby, Clyde S.[ed]: *C.S. Lewis, Letters to an American Lady,* 9 October 1954 © 1967
858 Lewis, C.S [ed]: Preface to *George MacDonald, An Anthology* © 1946
859 MacDonald, George [1824-1905] *Phantastes* ch.III. First published 1858.
860 Blake, William [1757-1827] 'Night' from *Songs of Innocence* in BC Part V.II
861 Smart, Christopher [1722-1771]: *Jubilate Agno*
862 Britten, Benjamin: Festival cantata *Rejoice in the Lamb,* first performed 21 September 1943
863 Quoted in Albery, Nicholas (ed): *Poem for the Day* © 1994
864 Duncan, Anthony: *The Elements of Celtic Christianity* p.103 ©1992
865 Griffiths, Bede: *A New Vision of Reality* ch.11 ©1989
866 Bible: Epistle of Paul to the Ephesians 6:12
867 Griffiths, Bede: *A New Vision of Reality* ch.9 © 1989
868 HH ch.XI
869 BC Part V.V
870 HH ch.XI

THE JOY TO COME
871 To MG: 10 September 1977 [The other story was 'Dogs of Peking']
872 JS ch.XIII.II
873 To AC: 7 August 1942
874 SV
875 JS ch.XIII.II
876 Ibid.

GREEN DOLPHIN COUNTRY
877 JS ch.XIII.II
878 Attenborough, John: in *DNB 1981-1985* © 1986
879 AS
880 TP: *The Brontes of Haworth* Act II. Sc.III
881 PT
882 RNA68
883 JS ch.X,III
884 BJ
885 JS ch.XIII.III
886 To AC: undated fragment
887 JS ch.XIII.III
888 JS ch.XIII.IV
889 Best, David: *Memories of Wartime Marldon* [Marldon Local History Group 2008]
890 JS ch.XIII.IV

THE FILM
891 To AC: undated fragment
892 Ibid. 2 October 1947[?]
893 RNA68

THE PRACTICE OF THE PRESENCE OF GOD
894 To AC: undated fragment
895 To AC: 7 August 1942
896 GDC Book Four, Part II ch.Two.II
897 GDC Book Two, Part II Ch.One.I
898 To MG: 21 June 1977
899 GDC Book One, Part II ch. Two.II
900 GDC Book Two, Part IV ch.One.I
901 GDC Book Two, Part III ch.One.IV
902 AS
903 *The Spectator,* 10 November 1944
904 JS ch.XIII.III
905 *The Spectator,* 10 November 1944

906 To AC: 13 December 1944
907 Ibid. 2 October 1947[?]
908 JS ch.V.I
909 Ibid.
910 JS ch.XIII.III
911 Ibid.

AFTER THE WAR
912 JS ch.VII.II
913 Ibid.
914 Henning, A.C: *Haunted Borley* [undated]
915 'West Country Magic' in *The Horn Book Magazine*, March 1947
916 SFA Part Four ch.V.1
917 *Our Brother the Sun:* In RF as *The Canticle of the Sun*
918 BC Part I.II
919 LWH ch.IX.III

THE LITTLE WHITE HORSE
920 Bible: Revelation 19:11
921 LWH ch.XI.III
922 LWH ch.IX.II
923 LWH ch.III.II
924 LWH ch.VIII.I
925 BC Part I.2 and SFA Part Four ch.V.1
926 BC Part III.V
927 LWH ch.XI.I
928 'Of Pilgrim's Inn' in *Wings*, April 1948
929 Ibid.
930 AC from Ida Goudge: 15 November 1946
931 Ibid.

A BLEAK WINTER
932 EGR/ASD/RF
933 HG ch.III.IV
934 WW
935 *About Elizabeth Goudge*. Omnibook Magazine September 1948
936 LWH/SV

937 Sayer, George: *Jack, A Life of C.S. Lewis* ch.17 © 1997
938 LWH ch.I.II
939 LWH ch.X.II
940 Lewis, C.S: *The Lion, the Witch and the Wardrobe* ch.12 © 1950
941 LWH ch.XI.I
942 Ibid.II
943 Lewis, C.S: *The Lion, the Witch and the Wardrobe* ch.15 © 1950
944 To LB: 11 February 1980
945 Sayer, George: *Jack, A Life of C.S. Lewis*, ch.13 © 1997
946 JS ch.II.I

THE WHITE DEER
947 Lewis, C.S: *No Beauty we could Desire* in BP Part XVI
948 'Of Pilgrim's Inn' in *Wings: The Literary Guild Review*, April 1948
949 HG ch.XII.III
950 'Of Pilgrim's Inn' in *Wings: The Literary Guild Review*, April 1948
951 McCall Smith, Alexander: *Music that Changed Me*. BBC Music Magazine, April 2011
952 'Grown-up Fairy Tale' in *Saturday Review*, April 1948
953 HG ch.I.IV
954 HG ch.IX.III
955 King George VI: Christmas Broadcast 1945. National Archives
956 Ibid. 1947
957 MW Book One ch.I
958 King George VI: Christmas Broadcast 1946. National Archives.
959 HG ch.III.II
960 Foss, Hannen [ed]: *Christmas Lasts For Ever* 1947[?] and *And so we got Married* © 1951

GENTIAN HILL
961 *Woman's Journal*. November 1949
962 BJ
963 JS ch.II.I

964 AHW
965 Julian of Norwich [c.1342-c.1416]: *Revelations of Divine Love* in BC Part I.7
966 Bible: Deuteronomy 33:13
967 GH Book One ch.VI.IV
968 Plato: *The Banquet* in BC Part III..IV
969 GH ch.V.I
970 DP November 12
971 GH Book One ch.VI.I
972 GH Book One ch.XI.II
973 MF p.8
974 De Waal, Esther: *Seeking God*, ch. IV. © 1984
975 BJ

MOTHER'S LAST ILLNESS

976 JS ch.XIV.I
977 JS ch.XIV.1
978 Apocrypha: Wisdom of Solomon 3:5
979 Ibid.
980 JS ch.XIV.1
981 GSLW ch.XII.V
982 JS ch.XIV.I
983 SFA ch.V.III
984 RT ch.XV.III

GOD SO LOVED THE WORLD

985 GSLW ch.X.IV
986 GSLW ch.X.III
987 Lewin, Ann: 'Dark Moments' - *Watching for the Kingfisher* © 2004
988 byEG
989 All BJ
990 Loades, Ann: *Dorothy L. Sayers Spiritual Writings* p.17 © 1993
991 MF p.27
992 GSLW ch.X.II
993 BJ
994 Hamilton, William: *A Quest for the Post-Historical Jesus* ©1993
995 MF p.7
996 JS ch.V.I
997 MF p.9
998 Goudge, H.L: *The Church of England and Reunion*, Introduction. ©1938
999 MF p.11
1000 MF p.28
1001 Typescript in Dr. Mark Dutton's archive

THE VALLEY OF SONG

1002 BF Part X.III
1003 JS ch.XV.II
1004 VS ch.XI.I
1005 Ibid.II
1006 Bible: Gospel according to Luke 18:17
1007 VS ch.III.II
1008 Traherne, Thomas [1636-1674]: *Shadows in the Water*. BF Part 6.3
1009 Ibid.
1010 VS ch.IV.II
1011 JS ch.VII.V
1012 Ibid.
1013 DW ch.12.II
1014 VS ch.VI.I
1015 Davis, Mark: *Glimpses of the Carmelite Way* p.64 © 2007
1016 Ibid.

ALONE

1017 TWW Part Three ch.IV.II
1018 JS ch.XIV.II
1019 TWW Part Two ch.X
1020 Lewis, C.S. *The Day with a White Mark* in BP Part XIV
1021 JS ch.XIV.II
1022 JS ch.XIV.III
1023 John in TLA
1024 JS ch.XIV.III
1025 Pilcher, Rosamunde: *Under Gemini* ©1976
1026 JS ch.III.I
1027 JS ch.X.I
1028 JS ch.III.I
1029 JS ch.X.I
1030 JS ch.V.III

1031 JS ch.IV.III
1032 JS ch.IV.I
1033 JS ch.VI.II
1034 JS ch.X.I
1035 JS ch.IV.I
1036 JS ch.X.I
1037 JS ch.XIV.III
1038 TWW Part Three ch.IX.II

TO MAKE AN END IS TO MAKE A BEGINNING

1039 Julian of Norwich [c.1342-c.1416]: *Revelations of Divine Love*. BC Part IV.V
1040 JS ch.XIV.III
1041 TWW Part One ch.VIII
1042 JS ch.XIV.III
1043 Ibid.
1044 Ibid.
1045 AHW
1046 BJ
1047 Foreword to WW
1048 Ibid.
1049 To AC: 2 October 1947
1050 In Dr. Mark Dutton's archive
1051 JS ch.XIV.III
1052 JS ch. XIV.III
1053 *Dreams* ASD/EGR
1054 JS ch.X.II
1055 Goudge, H.L: 'The Future Life' in *Addresses for Lent and Good Friday*. [undated]
1056 JS ch.X.II
1057 Ibid.
1058 JS ch.XIV.V
1059 JS ch.XIV.IV
1060 JS ch.XII.II
1061 JS ch.V.I
1062 JS ch.XIV.IV

ROSE COTTAGE

1063 RT ch.XVII.IV
1064 JS ch.XIV.IV
1065 RT ch.XVIII.I
1066 AHW
1067 JS ch.XIV.I
1068 JS ch.XV.I
1069 PT
1070 JS ch.XV.I
1071 Piper, John: *Oxfordshire, A Shell Guide* © 1938, new edition 1953
1072 SW ch.V.II
1073 JS ch.XIV.IV
1074 byEG
1075 JS ch.XV.I
1076 Ibid.

THE HEART OF THE FAMILY

1077 HF ch.VI.I
1078 HG ch.II.II
1079 Masefield, John: *The Everlasting Mercy* © 1911
1080 BC Part III.II
1081 Masefield, John: *The Everlasting Mercy* © 1911
1082 HF ch.I
1083 Ibid.
1084 Masefield, John: *The Everlasting Mercy* © 1911
1085 HF ch.VI.III
1086 Also in BC Part IV.IV
1087 HF ch.VI.III
1088 Drabble, Margaret: *A Writer's Britain* © 1979
1089 HF ch.VII.II
1090 HF ch.XV.I
1091 HF ch.XIX.III
1092 HF ch.XVIII
1093 HF ch.XX.II
1094 Also in BC Part III.IV
1095 JS ch. XIV.II
1096 BT ch.IX.I
1097 *St. Mary's Chapel, Buckler's Hard*. The Beaulieu Estate, 2008
1098 SV
1099 In VG
1100 TLA
1101 MF p.13
1102 MF p.11: Professor de Burgh
1103 MF p.14

1104 MF p.26
1105 MF p.9
1106 CGV
1107 BC Part III.IV
1108 CGV
1109 *The Daily Telegraph* 3 April 1984
1110 JS ch.XV.II

THE ROSEMARY TREE
1111 BJ
1112 AHW
1113 JS ch.VIII.I
1114 RT ch.IV.I
1115 RT ch.I.I
1116 RT ch.XIII
1117 RT ch.X.II
1118 RT ch.XVI.II
1119 JS ch.XVI.III
1120 RT ch.X.III
1121 RT ch.IV.I
1122 RT ch.I.I
1123 BC Part IV.II
1124 RT ch.I.I
1125 RT ch.XVIII.II
1126 In VG
1127 RT ch.XVIII.II
1128 JS ch.XIV.I
1129 RT ch.III.III
1130 RT ch.X.I
1131 RT ch.III.I
1132 RT ch.IV.II
1133 RT ch.III.I
1134 RT ch.XVII.I
1135 JS ch.IV.IV
1136 Typescript in Dr. Mark Dutton's archive
1137 TWW Part One ch.VII.I
1138 JS ch.XIV.VI
1139 TWW Part One ch.X.I
1140 JS ch.XIV.VI
1141 Spalding, Frances: *Gwen Raverat: Friends, Family & Affections* © 2001
1142 JS ch.XIV.VI

PROTECTED
1143 JS ch.VIII.III
1144 W ch.VII.II
1145 JS ch.XIV.IV
1146 To MG: 16 July 1978
1147 To MS: 30 January 1976
1148 To MS: 18 November 1982
1149 To MS: 6 November 1979
1150 Ibid.
1151 *Milwaukee Journal* 19 November 1959
1152 RM
1153 JS ch.XV.I
1154 RT ch.I.III
1155 JS ch.XIII.III
1156 RNA68
1157 DW ch.VII.III
1158 DW ch.IX.I
1159 JS ch.XIV.III

INSPIRATION
1160 To MG: 30 December 1977
1161 SFA Part Two ch.I.I
1162 TWW Part Two ch.X.I
1163 byEG
1164 TWW Part One ch.VII.I
1165 JS ch.XIV.IV
1166 To AC: 4 October 1958
1167 byEG
1168 JS ch.XV.II
1169 Ibid.

THE WHITE WITCH
1170 JS ch.II.I
1171 PT
1172 TWW Part Three ch.VIII
1173 BJ
1174 TWW Part Two ch.IV.II
1175 TWW Part One ch.VI.II
1176 SFA Part Four ch.III
1177 TWW Part Two ch.VIII.III
1178 Ibid.
1179 TWW Part Three chII.I
1180 JS ch.XIII.I [Bible: Genesis 8:22]

1181 Masefield, John: *The Everlasting Mercy* © 1911
1182 JS ch.XV.II
1183 EG Preface to Sutcliff, Rosemary: *The Rider of the White Horse* © 1959
1184 AHW

SAINT FRANCIS OF ASSISI

1185 *A complete list of the works of Elizabeth Goudge.* Unattributed. 1959
1186 BJ
1187 *The Saturday Review of Literature*, 6 June 1959
1188 SFA Part One ch.I.I
1189 Parkinson Keyes, Frances: *The Saturday Review of Literature*, 6 June 1959
1190 SFA Part Two ch.I.I
1191 JS ch.IX.I
1192 RT ch.I.II
1193 Mayne, Michael: *This Sunrise of Wonder* ch.VII © 1995
1194 DP April 14
1195 Quoted in *Elgar*, Ken Russell's 1962 documentary for BBC Monitor series
1196 SFA Part Two ch.II.II
1197 SW ch.II.III
1198 DW ch.II.III
1199 Burnham Abbey website / SPB Letter to the author
1200 Foreword to *The Mercy of Leaves*. SPB [undated]

STUDY ALWAYS TO HAVE JOY

1201 SFA Part Two ch.I.I
1202 Manuscript in Dr. Mark Dutton's archive
1203 SFA Part One ch.IV.II
1204 SFA Part Four ch.I.I
1205 JS ch.XIV.III
1206 SFA Part Two ch.I.II
1207 JS ch.VII.IV
1208 JS ch.XIV.III
1209 SFA Part Two.I
1210 SFA Part Four ch.V.I
1211 LWH ch.IX.III

THE DEAN'S WATCH

1212 JS ch.XV.II
1213 DW ch.12.I
1214 JS ch.XV.II
1215 Book of Common Prayer 1662: The Psalter
1216 DW ch.14.III
1217 'The Easter Bunny' in *The Modern Gift Book for Children* © 1948

LET GOD ARISE

1218 Goudge, H.L: 'The Transcendence of God' in *Sermons for the Christian Year* [undated]
1219 DW ch.7.III
1220 JS ch.XII.I
1221 Woodgate, Mildred: *Father Congreve of Cowley* © 1956. BC Part IV.2
1222 DW ch.5.II
1223 Woodgate, Mildred: *Father Congreve of Cowley* © 1956. BC Part IV.2
1224 DW ch.12.II
1225 DW ch.IX.I
1226 DW ch.7.III
1227 DW ch.XVI.II
1228 TCB Preface
1229 DW ch.3.I
1230 DW ch.ch.18.IV
1231 Donne, John [1572-1631]: In BC Part Five I.I
1232 DW ch.18.IV
1233 SA ch.II
1234 Ibid.
1235 Underhill, Evelyn: *Light of Christ* © 1944

MARY MONTAGUE

1236 DW ch.7.II
1237 Ibid.
1238 Underhill, Evelyn: *Light of Christ* © 1944
1239 DW ch.7.II

1240 Ibid.
1241 Underhill, Evelyn: *Light of Christ* © 1944
1242 DW ch.7.II
1243 Underhill, Evelyn: *Light of Christ* © 1944
1244 DW ch.7.II
1245 ADP 1973: "50 years of living 'with intention' since that day."
1246 DW ch.VII.II
1247 SPB
1248 JS ch.VII.I
1249 SFA Part Four ch.IV
1250 RT ch.VIII.I
1251 TWW Part Three ch.X

PEACE OF MIND

1252 Allsop, Kenneth: *I Meet the Queen of Green Dolphin Country*. Daily Mail 23 September 1960
1253 All Ibid.
1254 Ibid.
1255 Rogers, Byron: *The Man Who Went into the West*. © 2006
1256 EG to Kenneth Allsop: Daily Mail 23 September 1960
1257 DW ch.II.IV
1258 *The Times*: 3rd April 1984
1259 Forster, Margaret: *Daphne du Maurier*, © 1993
1260 EG to Kenneth Allsop: Daily Mail 23 September 1960
1261 RNA72
1262 MF p.30
1263 Goudge, H.L: Lecture II, *The Apocalypse and the Present Age* © 1935
1264 RT ch.V.II
1265 Plowright, Joan: *And That's Not All*, chapter 22. © 2001
1266 Pitter, Ruth: *Collected Poems 1926-1966* © 1968
1267 JS ch.I.II

LOVE OF CREATION

1268 JS ch.XIV.V
1269 To AC: 1 April 1962
1270 JS ch.XIV.V
1271 *Hamlet*, Act I, sc.I
1272 To AC: 6th January. Possibly 1969
1273 JS ch,V.III
1274 To MS: 12 November 1973
1275 DW ch.18.I
1276 Bible: Psalm 68:13
1277 Olivier, Edith: *Without Knowing Mr. Walkley* ch.XVII © 1939
1278 DP April
1279 To AC: 6th January. Possibly 1969
1280 Ap Gwilym, Dafydd: *The Stars*, in BP Part V. 14th century
1281 RNA68
1282 To AC: 4 January 1963
1283 Ibid.

APPLESHAW

1284 JS ch.IV.III
1285 Ibid.
1286 SW xh.I.II
1287 Piper, John: *Oxfordshire, A Shell Guide* © 1938, new edition 1953
1288 JS ch.II.I
1289 SW ch.I.II
1290 SW ch.II.III
1291 Ibid.

THE SCENT OF WATER

1292 DP 27 January
1293 Bible: Job 14 vv.7-9
1294 SW ch.XIII.II
1295 MF
1296 SW ch.V.II
1297 Hammarskjold, Dag: *Markings*. © 1964
1298 SW ch.V.II
1299 BF Part 9.II
1300 Lawrence, Brother: *The Practice of the Presence of God*. 17th century © E.M. Blaiklock 1981
1301 SW ch.XIII.II

[1302] Inge, W.R. and Goudge, H.L.:*The Study Bible – Hebrews* © 1926
[1303] Inge, W.R [1860-1954]: *Mysticism in Religion* [undated] : ch.XI
[1304] SW ch.XIII.II
[1305] BC Part IV.V
[1306] SW ch.VII.III
[1307] Ibid.
[1308] BC Part III.VI
[1309] SW ch.V.II
[1310] DP November 12
[1311] Bible: Gospel according to Luke 1:38
[1312] SW ch.X.IV
[1313] Ibid.
[1314] HF ch.XV.I
[1315] RT ch.XVII.I and DW ch.VII.II
[1316] SW ch.V.II
[1317] SW ch.IV.II
[1318] SW ch.VII.III

A NEW KIND OF HEROINE
[1319] Virginia Woolf [1882-1941] to Vanessa Bell, June 1911
[1320] GDC Book Two part II ch.I.I
[1321] Ibid.
[1322] RT ch.III.I
[1323] Ibid.
[1324] TWW Part III ch.X
[1325] SW ch.V.II
[1326] JS ch.X.I
[1327] DW ch.VII.II
[1328] Sister Mary Agnes, The Poor Clares.
[1329] Pitter, Ruth [1897-1992]: *In the Open.* BP Part XIII

PROGRESS
[1330] Lawrence, D.H [1885-11930]: *Work.* BC Part V.3
[1331] SW ch.II.III
[1332] SW ch.IX.I
[1333] Ibid.
[1334] SW ch.X.III
[1335] HH ch.III

[1336] To AC: 30 August 1962
[1337] JS ch.XII.IV

THE SIXTIES
[1338] BJ
[1339] LV ch.VII
[1340] LV ch.VIII
[1341] JS ch.IX.II
[1342] Marldon Local History Group website
[1343] To AC: 5 May 1963[?]
[1344] JS ch.VII.III
[1345] *Maria or The Good Little Girl* © 1964
[1346] Bible: I Kings ch.19
[1347] BP Part V
[1348] BP preface
[1349] BJ
[1350] TCB preface
[1351] RM
[1352] DP preface
[1353] BP preface
[1354] To MG: 21 June 1977
[1355] RNA68
[1356] Bible: Gospel according to Luke 17:21
[1357] Bible: Gospel according to Matthew 6:6
[1358] Bible: 1 Kings 19:11
[1359] St. John of the Cross [1542-1591]
[1360] Kirkup, James [1918-2009]: *The Cave*. BP Part I
[1361] *In the beginning was the Word:* radio broadcast 1969
[1362] ISTS ch.I
[1363] Bible: Gospel according to John 1:10

PEMBROKESHIRE
[1364] RNA68
[1365] JS ch.XV.II
[1366] PT
[1367] To MG: 10 September 1977
[1368] LA
[1369] Kathleen Millington

1370 Thomas, Dylan [1914-1953]: *Poem in October*. BC Part I.V

THE CHILD FROM THE SEA
1371 JS ch.XV.II
1372 *Escape for Jane; The Golden Skylark; The Dark Lady; Made from a Hazel-Nut*. All in WW.
1373 PT
1374 *Horological Journal:* January 1961
1375 Wagenknacht, Edward in *News-Tribune* 24 September 1970
1376 Traherne, Thomas [1636-1674]: in BF Part X.III
1377 Ibid.
1378 CS Book I ch.V.I
1379 CS Book I ch.VI.III
1380 CS Book I ch.VI.IV
1381 CS Book III ch.II.I
1382 Ibid.
1383 CS Book III ch.7.III
1384 CS Book III ch.V.IV
1385 CS Book III ch.17.I
1386 MacDonald, George: *Annals of a Quiet Neighbourhood*. In Lewis, C.S: *G. MacDonald, an Anthology*
1387 JS ch.XV.II

THE INWARD EYE
1388 To MS: 14 September 1971
1389 TLA:*Giovanni*
1390 JS ch.XVI.I
1391 Reply to a March letter from Madeau Stewart, 1982
1392 John Clare [1793-1864]: BP Part V
1393 TLA: *Giovanni*
1394 Ibid.
1395 To MS: 14 September 1971
1396 Ibid. 30 September 1971
1397 Ibid. 8 November 1971
1398 Ibid. 14 February 1972

WRITING ABOUT HERSELF
1399 AHW
1400 RM
1401 Rosemary March: *The Daily Telegraph* August 1972
1402 Ibid.
1403 PT
1404 JS ch.II.II
1405 DW ch.XIV.II
1406 RNA68
1407 RM
1408 KM
1409 To MG: 24 October 1978
1410 CH ch.I.II
1411 MF p.12: Professor de Burgh
1412 JS ch.IV.IV
1413 JS ch.X.I
1414 RM
1415 RT ch.III.III
1416 JS VII.V
1417 JS ch.I.II
1418 JS ch.II.II
1419 To MG: 12 June 1977
1420 RNA72
1421 Ibid.
1422 JS XIV.V
1423 JS ch.XV.I
1424 JS ch.II.II
1425 SH
1426 To MG: 9 August 1977
1427 To AC: 6 February 1979
1428 To MS: 14 October 1978
1429 JS ch.XI.I
1430 To MG: 3 July 1978
1431 To AC:1 April 1962
1432 To MS: 12 November 1973
1433 To MS: 16 November 1982
1434 To MS: 4 November 1978
1435 To MG: April/May 1978
1436 To MG 16 July 1978
1437 AHW
1438 DW ch.VII.II
1439 RM
1440 SA ch.VI
1441 SA ch.VII
1442 JS ch.VIII.VI

NEIGHBOURS
[1443] King, Don.W: *Hunting the Unicorn* P.192 © 2008
[1444] Ibid. p.235
[1445] AHW

THE LITTLE THINGS
[1446] To KM: 1st May, year unknown
[1447] CB ch.XII.III
[1448] SW ch.V.I
[1449] Grenfell, Joyce: *Joyce Grenfell Requests the Pleasure.* Ch.XVIII © 1976
[1450] CB ch.XII.III
[1451] Ibid.
[1452] Kipling, Rudyard: *Puck of Pook's Hill.* First published 1906
[1453] SW ch.XI.I
[1454] Bible: Book of Job 38:7
[1455] Underhill, Evelyn: *Immanence, A Book of Verses.* First published 1912
[1456] SW ch.XIII.II
[1457] Julian of Norwich [c.1342-c.1416]: *Revelations of Divine Love* in BC Part I.V II
[1458] Father Hugh Dutton: letter to the author, 21 December 2001

HEAVENLY MUSIC
[1459] JS ch.III.II
[1460] CS ch.I.I
[1461] To MS: 30 January 1976
[1462] Ward, J. Neville: *The Following Plough* ch.VI © 1978.
[1463] Father Hugh Dutton: letter to the author, 21 December 2001
[1464] Harman, Alec and Mellers, Wilfrid: *Man and his Music* © 1962
[1465] Blake, William [1757-1827]: *The Marriage of Heaven and Hell*, 1790
[1466] BT ch.IV.I
[1467] GDC Book Two, Part III ch.I.IV

THE THREE-FOLD LIFE
[1468] Ward, J.N: *The Following Plough* ch.IV © 1978

[1469] Harman, Alec and Mellers, Wilfrid: *Man and his Music* © 1962
[1470] Ibid.
[1471] In Gordon, Lyndall: *Eliot's New Life* © 1988
[1472] Eliot, T.S: *Four Quartets* [1944] in Harman, Alec and Mellers, Wilfrid: *Man and his Music* © 1962
[1473] JS ch.XV.I
[1474] Sister Raphael Mary to Jessie Monroe c.1991

CREDO
[1475] To MS: 14 February 1972
[1476] BBC Radio Four. 31st March 1972
[1477] Typescript in Dr. Mark Dutton's archive
[1478] JS ch.XV.I

THE JOY OF THE SNOW
[1479] JS ch.IV.II
[1480] To MG: 6 October 1977
[1481] Anthony Wood: *Elizabeth Goudge.* Oxford Mail, 22 August 1974
[1482] PT
[1483] 14th August 1974
[1484] To MS: 16 August 1974
[1485] AHW
[1486] Kunz, Marjorie: *Writer's Story.* Church Times, 20 September 1974
[1487] Barclay, William: *Men and Affairs..* The Expository Times, September 1974
[1488] Jennings, Paul: *The Sunday Times*, 29 September 1974
[1489] Horder, Mervyn: *A Joyous Autobiography.* The Bookseller, 3 August 1974
[1490] AHW
[1491] JS ch.XVI.I
[1492] JS ch.XVI.II
[1493] JS ch.XVI.III
[1494] PT
[1495] To LB: 21 August 1976
[1496] *Faith:* EG Foreword to BF

CORRESPONDENCE

1497 To MS: 4 November 1978
1498 Anthony Wood: *Oxford Mail*, 22 August 1974
1499 Kenneth Allsop: *Daily Mail*, 23 September 1960
1500 John Attenborough in *DNB* 1981-1985
1501 JS ch.XV.I
1502 MF pp.29/30
1503 RT ch.VIII.V
1504 JS ch.XV.I
1505 JS ch.II.I
1506 To LB: 31 December 1975
1507 Ibid. 21 August 1976
1508 JS ch.XI.III
1509 To MG: 3 July 1978
1510 Teilhard de Chardin, Pierre: *Hymn of the Universe* p.65 © in English translation 1965
1511 Bouyer, Louis: *Woman in the Church* [incl. essay by C.S. Lewis] © 1979
1512 To LB: 11 February 1980
1513 Ibid.
1514 To MG: 3 July 1978
1515 Ibid. 14 August 1977
1516 Kilby, Clyde S. [ed]: Preface, *Letters to an American Lady* © 1967
1517 To MG: 9 August 1977
1518 Grainger, Muriel: 'Religion and Romance'. *Reform*, November 1977
1519 To MG: 11 July 1977
1520 Ibid. 31 May 1978
1521 Grainger, Muriel: in *Music at Midnight* © 1949
1522 Letter in the possession of Mr. Christopher Rowan Grainger
1523 Grainger, Muriel: in *Music at Midnight* © 1949
1524 To MG: 23 March 1977
1525 Ibid. 29 July 1977
1526 Ibid. 27 August 1977
1527 Grainger, Muriel [ed]: *Pattern of People* © 1978
1528 To MG: 1 February 1978
1529 In VG
1530 To MG: 27 August 1977
1531 Ibid. 10 September 1977
1532 Ibid. 14 August 1977
1533 Ibid. 10 September 1977
1534 Ibid. 6 October 1977
1535 Ibid. 30 December 1977
1536 To LB: 4 January 1977
1537 Letter to the author from Father Hugh Dutton: 21 December 2001
1538 To MG: 20 June 1978
1539 Letter to the author from Father Hugh Dutton: 21 December 2001
1540 To MG: 3 July 1978
1541 Ibid. 9 August 1978
1542 Ibid. 24 October 1978
1543 JS ch.XIV.V
1544 To MS: 5 June 1978
1545 Ibid. 16 August 1978
1546 Ibid. 5 June 1978
1547 To MG: 4 February 1979
1548 Rosemary March: *The Daily Telegraph* August 1972
1549 BF Part X.I

WILLING TO GO

1550 JS ch.V.V
1551 *Easter in the Ward:* in VG
1552 Ibid.
1553 To MG: 23 May 1979
1554 To LB: 29 May 1979
1555 Ibid.
1556 To MG: 25 July 1979
1557 To LB: 29 May 1979
1558 To LB: 16 August 1979
1559 To MS: 1 July 1979
1560 To MG: 25 July 1979
1561 To LB: 14 November 1979
1562 Ibid.
1563 To LB: 13 February 1980
1564 To MS: 5 August, 1980
1565 To MS: 4 March 1981
1566 To MG: 30 September 1980
1567 To LB: 8 June 1981
1568 Ibid.

1569 To LB: 22 October 1981
1570 To LB: 8 January 1982
1571 Ibid.
1572 DP February 17

THE LAST TWO YEARS
1573 To LB: 29 March 1982
1574 To LB: 27 April 1982
1575 To MS: 7 January 1980
1576 To MS, 25 March 1982
1577 To MS: April 1982?
1578 To MS: 19 August, probably 1982
1579 To MS: undated, in reply to a March letter.
1580 To LB: 1 August 1982
1581 To MS: 11 September 1979
1582 Ibid. 9 September 1982
1583 To MS: 18 November 1982
1584 *RNA News* Winter 1983
1585 To LB: 8 February 1983
1586 Ibid. 21 March 1983
1587 To MS: 1 March 1983
1588 To LB: 21 March 1983
1589 To MS: 28 June 1983
1590 JS ch.V.V
1591 17 June 1963 in Kilby, Clyde S. [ed] *C.S. Lewis: Letters to an American Lady.* © 1967
1592 RT ch.III.II
1593 To MS: 23 October 1983
1594 Ibid.
1595 To MS: 23 October [1983?]
1596 To MS: 7 September [1983?]
1597 To MS: 5 January [1984?]
1598 TO MS: 25 March 1982

TO DIE INTO YOUR RESURRECTION
1599 In VG
1600 Spenser, Edmund [1552-1599]: Amoretti LXVIII
1601 DW ch.17.III

DREAMS OF HEAVEN
1602 In ASD
1603 In VG

APPENDIX I
1604 JS ch.VII.III
1605 Renamed 1986 as Invalid Children's Aid Nationwide (I CAN)
1606 Rev. Allen Dowdeswell Graham: in London Metropolitan Archives.
1607 DP February 16
1608 Jessie Monroe to Madeau Stewart: 4 May 1984
1609 To MS: 6 July 1982
1610 Jessie Monroe to Madeau Stewart: 4 May 1984
1611 Apocrypha: 2 Esdras 2:34-48. New English Bible © 1961, 1970
1612 To MS: 6 July 1982
1613 BC Part V.I
1614 Bible: Ephesians 3, vv.14-21
1615 BC Part III.IV
1616 SW ch.V.II
1617 DP 21 August
1618 BC Part V.1 *Heaven*

Index

A

Aberdeen Press and Journal 347
Albinoni, Tomaso 416
All-Day Prayer, The *[EG]* 204
Allsop, Kenneth 367, 368, 369, 434, 439
Alma Tadema, Laurence 5
ap Gwilym, Dafydd 373
Apocalypse and the Present Age, The [HLG] 99, 370
Apocrypha, The
    Book of Wisdom 289
    Esdras 443, 472
Arabella or The Bad Little Girl *[EG]* 390
Argosy 151
Arts and Crafts 103
At the Sign of the Dolphin 228, 252, 272, 467
Atwood, Margaret 194
Auden, W.H. 121, 378
Augustine, St. 285, 380, 454
Aunts
    Beatrice 33, 207
    Emily 33, 34, 44, 111, 155
    Emma Goodhart 19, 20, 46, 372
    Eva 33, 34, 57, 164, 208
    Irene 33, 34, 238, 289, 290, 315
    Marie 33, 34, 44, 113, 114, 137, 157, 164, 238, 287, 303, 308
    Rosalie Ozanne 115
Austen, Jane 83, 87, 369, 370, 399

B

Bach 438
Baldwin, Mary 396
Baldwin, Stanley 140, 246
Barclay, William 434, 435
Barker, Cecily Mary 101
Barton-on-Sea 132, 133, 141, 142, 143, 155, 167, 207, 213, 215, 225, 228, 237, 308, 388
Bassano Studio 186
Bates, H.E. 255
Bath, Somerset 19, 20, 45, 61, 75, 228, 324, 374, 375
BBC
    Book at Bedtime, A 394
    Children's Hour 237, 268, 282
    Do you know Elizabeth Goudge? 434
    first radio broadcast 124
    Five to Ten 395
    Holy Week Talks 429
    Home This Afternoon 393
    In Praise of God 438
    Jackanory 268, 394
    Pick of the Week 434
    Woman's Hour 434
BBC Music Magazine 279
Bede, Venerable 76
Beethoven 308, 349, 425, 427, 428, 429
Belloc, Hilaire 281
Benedictines 286
Bennett, Arnold 151
Benson, Archbishop 203, 224
Betjeman, John 337, 418, 419
Bhagavad-Gita 438
Bible, The
    Book of Job 377, 422
    Ecclesiastes 20
    Elijah 395
    Ephesians 474
    Psalms 121, 202, 355, 357, 372, 416, 466, 472

Revelation 264
Song of Songs 223
Bird in the Tree, The [EG] 28, 47, 54, 62, 64, 84, 106, 179, 191, 200, 204, 216, 217, 222, 228, 320, 324, 335, 426
Birthday Party, The [EG] 229
Blagg, Helen M. 36
Blake, William 246, 247, 276, 349, 406, 425
Blessed Virgin Mary 223, 320, 381
Bloch, Carl 293
Blue Hills, The [EG] 13, 240
bodgers 386
Book of Comfort, A [EG] 58, 110, 121, 185, 222, 246, 248, 264, 267, 284, 303, 316, 323, 329, 358, 386, 392, 399, 438, 473, 474, 475
Book of Faith, A [EG] 192, 247, 296, 298, 379, 393, 400, 423, 438, 450, 472
Book of Peace, A [EG] 110, 276, 301, 373, 386, 391, 393, 395, 396, 438
Books and Bookmen 283
Bookseller, The 144, 434
Boros, Ladislaus 112
Bouyer, Louis 264, 275, 324, 393, 438, 441, 442, 447, 452, 453, 455, 456, 458, 459
Bowes-Lyon, Lady Elizabeth [Queen Elizabeth, the Queen Mother] 124
Bridges, Lt.Gen. Sir Tom 231
Bridges, Robert 163, 231, 351
Britten, Benjamin 247
Brontë, Emily 149
Brontës of Haworth, The [EG] 143, 159, 208, 252, 295
Brontës, The 83
Buckler's Hard 269, 296, 320
Burne-Jones, Edward 126, 246
Burney, Fanny 167, 174, 182, 208, 282
Burnham Abbey 349, 350, 365, 460
by Elizabeth Goudge [EG] 332

C

Cain and Abel 186
Canticle of the Sun, The [EG] 287, 397
Carmelites 300
Carnegie Medal 273, 346
Carpenter, Humphrey 136, 137, 145, 161, 182
Carroll, Lewis 245, 246
Cartland, Barbara 413
Castle on the Hill, The [EG] 87, 146, 176, 186, 191, 208, 227, 228, 231, 232, 234, 237, 239, 240, 253, 411
Cecil, Lord David 419
Cervantes 370
Chaucer 370
Cheltenham Ladies College 137
Child from the Sea, The [EG] 28, 390, 394, 397, 399, 400, 405, 408, 415, 424, 432, 442
Child's Garden of Verses, A 322
Child's Garden of Verses, A [EG Preface] 3, 25, 34, 84
Christian Science Monitor, The 168, 295
Christmas at the Herb of Grace [EG] 281
Christmas Book, A [EG] 270, 394
Christmas on the Moor/Bird of Dawning, The [EG] 372
Churchill, Winston 230
Church of England and Reunion, The [HLG] 199, 295
Church Times, The 293, 294, 295, 405, 434
City of Bells, A [EG] 9, 10, 11, 12, 35, 37, 48, 66, 78, 96, 139, 162, 164, 167, 170, 172, 177, 179, 193, 208, 392, 394, 420, 421, 435
Civil War, English 342, 343, 345
Clare, John 406
Clark, Audrey
  attitude to Jessie Monroe 336
  Commem Balls 130
  first met EG 128

outings with EG 160
theatre with EG 159
widow of C.d'O.P. Jackson 460
Cockiolly Bird, The 83
Collenette, Adolphus [grandfather] 18, 39, 42, 43, 44, 110, 111, 112, 113, 114, 195, 260
Collenette, Marie-Louise Ozanne [grandmother] 44, 113, 164, 302
Coming of the King, The [EG] 295
Conan Doyle, Arthur 151, 245
Congreve, Father 329, 357, 358
Conrad, Joseph 151
Constant Heart, The / Sister of the Angels [EG] 208
contemplative prayer 148, 259, 349, 361, 365, 395
Cornford, Frances 335
Cosin, Bishop 474
Cotswolds, Aunts' house 155
Coward McCann 154, 252, 270, 410
Cowper, William 185
Crock of Gold, A [EG] 200
Csupo, Gabor 268
Cuckoo Clock, The 84

D

Daffodils in Ice 149, 349, 385
Daily Mail, The 152, 174
Daily Telegraph, The 144, 252, 254, 324, 325, 374, 409
Damerosehay trilogy, book I 217
Damerosehay trilogy, book II 277
Damerosehay trilogy, book III 315
dark night of the soul 427
Darwin, Charles 335
David the Shepherd Boy advent calendar [EG] 151
Davis, Miles 257
Dean's Watch, The [EG] xiii, 23, 30, 76, 77, 84, 101, 169, 226, 299, 335, 336, 338, 349, 354, 355, 356, 357, 365, 367, 368, 372, 377, 378, 392, 393, 394, 400, 466, 484

de Burgh, Professor 103, 295
de Chardin, Pierre Teilhard 247, 441
Delafield, E.M. 129, 151
de la Mare, Walter 273, 394, 421, 444
Devon
    Ark, the 225, 228
    Marldon 225, 236, 250, 251, 255, 256, 282, 288, 289, 295, 390
    Providence Cottage 225, 228, 230, 251, 270, 288, 309
    Torquay 237, 239, 295, 307
de Waal, Esther 286
Diary of Prayer, A [EG] 190, 202, 224, 240, 349, 372, 377, 393, 456, 465, 471
Dickens, Charles 83, 245
Dictionary of National Biography, The 252, 439
Dior, Christian 261
Dobbs, Rose 270, 272
Dogs
    Brownie 134, 141, 142, 164, 308
    Froda 413, 449
    Max 308
    Randa 371, 413, 449
    Tashi 449, 453, 460, 461
    Tiki 308, 309, 310, 334, 341, 371, 413, 449
Dogs of Peking [EG] 393
Doing Good [EG] 37
Donne, John 109, 110, 111, 112, 475
Doyle, Richard 245
Drabble, Margaret 317
Dream of Gerontius, The 169, 349, 474
Dreams [EG] 228, 241, 467
Dream, The [EG] 468
Duckworth 144, 150, 154, 208, 253, 272, 287, 306, 335, 434
Dulac, Edmund 105
du Maurier, Daphne 281, 293, 369
Duncan, Anthony 247
Dutton, Hélène née Collenette 33, 113, 114, 115, 132, 133, 155, 207, 234, 239, 250, 251, 255, 324, 407, 408

Dutton, Hugh 423, 424, 425, 446, 447, 448, 456
Dutton, Mark 239, 250, 448

E

Easter Bunny, The *[EG]* 6, 7, 101, 281, 356
Easter in the Ward *[EG]* 98, 452, 465
Eckhart, Meister 284
Elgar, Edward 169, 349
Elijah 31, 32, 391, 395, 396
Eliots of Damerosehay, The *[EG]* 324
Eliot, T.S. 58, 121, 206, 244, 281, 343, 419, 428, 429, 433
Elizabeth Goudge Reader, The 270, 282, 332
Ely
    cathedral 76
    fen countryside 76
    ghost 94
    house 72
Entertainment of Story-telling, The *[EG]* 306
Etheldreda, St. 76, 78, 79
Euphan Todd, Barbara 248
Everlasting Mercy, The 315, 316, 345
Expository Times, The 434
extra-sensory perception 94, 238, 262

F

Fairies' Baby and Other Stories, The *[EG]* 18, 101
Fairies' Baby, The *[EG]* 23
Fairy Queen's Jewels, The *[EG]* 51, 86
Faulks, Sebastian 257
Fauré's *Requiem* 279
Femmes d'Aujourd'hui magazine 400
Finzi, Gerald 222
First World War 38, 87, 100, 102, 223, 232, 235
Flower Fairies of the Spring 102
Flower of Happiness, The *[EG]* 18, 101
Forster, Margaret 369

Foss, Hannen 281, 294
Foxe's Book of Martyrs 196, 308
Francis of Assisi, St. 115, 264, 265, 266, 267, 287, 343, 347, 348, 349, 351, 352, 353, 354, 356, 405, 407
Freud, Sigmund 110
From Whence? *[EG]* 157

G

Gap in the Hedge, The *[EG]* 271
Garnett, Eve 273
Gentian Hill *[EG]* 46, 50, 209, 210, 229, 282, 283, 284, 286, 287, 301, 390
Gielgud, John 159
Giovanni *[EG]* 405
Girls' Diocesan Association 128, 158
Glimpses of the Carmelite Way 300
Glorying in the Cross [HLG] 229
God So Loved the World *[EG]* 290, 291, 293, 322, 394
Golden Skylark, The *[EG]* 151, 228, 232, 282, 306
Gone with the Wind 256
Goodall, John S. 282
Good Housekeeping 151
Gore, Bishop 109, 110, 117, 134, 308
Goudge, Elizabeth de Beauchamp
    arterial sclerosis 455, 457, 459
    aunts and uncles 33
    awareness of evil 181
    birth 3
    career choices 100
    Carnegie medal 273
    cats 308
    childhood discipline 27
    childhood games 12
    childhood loneliness 53
    childhood terrors 47
    childhood theophany 60
    childlessness/empathy with children 174
    Christmas radio broadcast 438

churchgoing 11, 79, 87, 93, 109,
    307, 390, 424, 448, 455
College days 103
contemplative prayer 148
correspondence with readers 439
Court curtsey 89, 128
crabs and lobsters 32
death 462
decorating the cathedral 78
depression 169, 292
disciplined life 411
dreams 49, 64, 227, 241, 264, 273,
    299, 412, 466, 471
earliest memories 3
early writing 15
enjoyment of radio and
    television 416
Epiphany 373, 447
exactly lke her books 416
eye trouble 415, 442, 459
fairy houses 51, 57
faith nearly shattered 169
fans and reporters 338
father's hostess 133
films of her novels 256, 268, 287
first love 108
first novel 143
first published book 101
first theatre 91
FRSL 286
funeral service 471
generosity 414
giving away toys 36
going to the drawing-room 24
Gray's Inn Ball 108, 128, 355
Guernsey holidays 38
guilt 22, 181, 253, 292
health problems 414
Holy Week broadcast 429
hospitality 413
Hugh's ordinations 446, 447
inspiring others 418
leaving Devon 309
leaving Ely 124
Little Things 420, 445

lost love 179
Louis B. Mayer award 254
love for Nanny 28
love of birds 372
love of dawn sky 86, 373
love of music 424, 458, 460
manuscripts 410
moor terror 95, 157, 352
mountain joy 157, 397
move to Devon 213
needlework 418
nervous breakdown 168
nose-bleeds 89
operation I [Peppard] 451
operation II [Peppard] 453
operation III [Peppard] 454
operation [Oxford/Barton] 167
Oxfordshire countryside 314
painting 417
poems 98, 250, 272, 273, 320, 321,
    329, 445, 452, 465, 468
prayers written by 188, 190, 240,
    350, 393, 422, 456, 471, 475
restrictions on young females 129
romantic novelist 367, 368, 412
sacked from teaching 142
school days 87
school uniform 92
selling Providence Cottage 309
shyness 136, 412
smile 408
socialist politics 10, 121, 262
stammer 87, 95, 102, 103, 109, 115,
    135, 336
sympathy 414
taught to ride 53
teaching 115
temptation to suicide 185
theatre-going 38, 92, 102, 143, 151,
    158, 159, 160, 263, 307
three phases to life 427
travel 154
travel difficulties 415
unseen playmate 54
very like her father 410

visiting demon 351
visits to Uppingham 50
well read 417
writing in longhand 410
Goudge, Henry Leighton 7
   Adam Ayscough's character 355
   advice to EG on prayer and
      suffering 204, 365
   attitude to money and taxes 309
   attitude to the scriptures 293
   bullying at school 286
   canonry at Ely 71
   cheerfulness and fun 323
   country walks 14
   courageous optimism 189
   Curate at St. Mark's, Leicester 164
   death 201
   depression 188
   Doctor of Divinity 71
   Ely sermon 357
   Evangelical background 19, 295
   family prayers 29
   generosity 207
   last days 201
   last words to EG 201, 357, 465
   love for the whole church 295
   love of nature 14, 76, 201, 232, 412
   love of theatre 19, 370
   meeting EG after school 90
   operation 167
   Oxford slum districts 139
   parcelling last book with EG 200
   parents 46, 309
   parish work in WW1 96
   playtimes with EG 19
   Principal, Wells College 8
   reading RC missal 295
   Regius Professor of Divinity 116
   sermon on pacifism 236
   supporting EG in trouble 187
   teaching at King's College,
      London 107
   the Study 16
   worldwide correspondence 440

   would have made a happy
      monk 199
Goudge, Ida de Beauchamp
   accident 21
   a queenly extravagance 140
   as Peronelle 143
   better health at Ely 74
   choosing Devon home 215
   death 289
   illness at Marldon 225, 239
   illness at Oxford 133
   illness at Wells 75
   last illness 287
   letter to Audrey 270
   living at Barton 132
   operation at Wells 75
   operations at Oxford 167
   psychic powers 94
   reaction to Nanny's death 238
   receiving polite calls 128
   story-telling 20
   victim of snobbery 128
Grainger, Muriel 259, 410, 412,
      433, 442
Grassendale School 87, 88, 89, 99, 100,
      114, 142, 325
Green Dolphin Country *[EG]* 39, 228,
      250, 252, 253, 258, 292, 338,
      361, 379, 383, 390, 393, 426
Green Dolphin Street [film] 256, 268
   Oscar 257
Green, Freda 177, 288, 290, 295, 304,
      309, 405
Grenfell, Joyce 421
Griffiths, Bede 65, 122, 131, 132, 152,
      218, 248, 328, 425

H

Hamilton, William 294
Hamlet 45, 159, 184, 192, 247
Hammarskjold, Dag 378
Handel's *Messiah* 79
Hardy, Thomas 194
Harewood House 217, 223, 269,
      301, 325

Harman, Alec 425
Harnett, Cynthia 337
Harton, F.P. 419
Harton, Sybil 337, 419
Hart, Richard 256
Harwood, Sonia 412, 413, 459
Hastings, Adrian 244
Haunted Borley [EG preface] 263, 269
Heart of the Family, The [EG] 31, 217, 302, 315, 316, 324, 345, 381, 390
Heflin, Van 256
Henrietta's House [EG] 5, 10, 13, 52, 83, 228, 240, 241, 253, 266, 282, 359, 388
Hepburn, Katharine 256
Herbert, George 318
Herb of Grace, The [EG] 88, 91, 159, 178, 186, 192, 217, 220, 228, 271, 276, 280, 292, 315, 316, 320, 324, 374, 377, 390
Hereward the Wake 76
Hickes' Devotions 202
Higham, David 150, 419
Historical Novels [EG] 369
Hodder and Stoughton 253, 270, 272, 324, 409
Hodges, C. Walter 208, 209, 263, 345
Hollis Family 12, 15, 22, 23, 53, 84, 419
Holme, Thea 208, 282
Hopkins, Gerard Manley 45, 111, 317, 319, 332
Horder, first Baron 253
Horder, Mervyn 144, 253, 287, 302, 305, 306, 335, 412, 414, 419, 434, 435
Horological Journal, The 400
Howard, Elizabeth Jane 151
Howells, Herbert 223
Hugo, Victor 41, 337
Hummingbirds' Nest, The [EG] 445
Huxley, Aldous 151

I

Ikon on the Wall, The [EG] 228, 249, 282, 306, 393
Inge, W.R. 380
Inklings, The 136
In the Beginning was the Word [EG] 395
Invalid Children's Aid Association 471
I Saw Three Ships [EG] 396
Island Magic [EG] 27, 32, 33, 37, 39, 40, 41, 44, 64, 89, 105, 143, 144, 145, 148, 167, 171, 182, 193, 206, 253, 439

J

Jerome, Jerome K. 151
John of the Cross, St. 267, 395, 427, 429
Johnson, Samuel 167, 247
John /The Beloved [EG] 322
Joy of the Snow, The [EG] xiii
   critical acclaim 434
   final chapter on faith 435
   published 433
   reluctance to write 409
   requests for autobiography 408
Joy Will Come Back [EG] 167, 208
Joy, William 8
Jude the Obscure 194, 195
Julian of Norwich 284, 303, 380, 422, 454
Just So Stories, The 346

K

Kaper, Bronislau 257
Keats, John 163, 399
Keyes, Frances Parkinson 347
Keyhaven 88, 90, 106, 116, 142, 200, 217, 269, 296, 325, 397
King Charles I 343
King Charles II 399, 401
King Edward VII 47
King Edward VIII 164

King George V 47, 140
King George VI 124, 135, 164, 225, 280
King Henry VIII 140
Kingsley, Charles 245
King's Servant, The [EG] 282
King's Speech, The 135
Kipling, Rudyard 229, 246, 394
Kirkup, James 396

L

Lake Isle of Innisfree, The 133, 152
Lang, Andrew 83
Lawrence, Brother 258, 259, 261, 379
Lawrence, D.H. 144, 150, 151, 235, 386
Lear, Edward 394
Lehmann, Rosamond 407
Leicester Mail, The 283
Letters from our Daughters 407
Letters to an American Lady 246, 442, 460
Lewin, Ann xi
Lewis, C.S. 122, 123, 136, 161, 182, 244, 246, 258, 273, 275, 301, 379, 419, 442, 460
Liberty magazine 257
Linnets and Valerians [EG] 48, 55, 98, 101, 162, 214, 388
Lion, the Witch and the Wardrobe, The 273, 276
Little Gidding 58, 244, 429, 432, 435
Little Gidding, diocese of Ely 343
Little Island Set in a Silver Sea [EG] 176, 229
Little White Horse, The [EG] 45, 53, 55, 66, 81, 127, 228, 263, 264, 265, 268, 270, 273, 346, 353, 356, 394, 468
Little White Horse, The [film of] 268
Little White Horse, The (Poem) [EG] 272
Littlewood, Joan 282
London School of Medicine for Women 21
Lost Angel, The [EG] 322, 405
Lyra Innocentium 71

M

MacDonald, George 192, 198, 245, 246, 377, 379, 404, 438
Magic Isles [EG] 155
Make-Believe [EG] 37, 39, 228, 253, 282, 306
Malory 370
Manchester Guardian, The 144
Manicheism 122
Marcello, Benedetto 416
March, Rosemary 409
Margolyes, Miriam 268
Maria or The Good Little Girl [EG] 390, 395
Martin, Ruth 408, 410, 417
Mary Agnes, Sister 149
Masefield, John 315, 345
Mayne, Michael 349
McCall Smith, Alexander 279
McGlashan, Alan 160, 422
Mellers, Wilfrid 425
Methodist Recorder, The 164
Middle Window, The [EG] 127, 151, 152, 153, 154, 156, 157, 159, 167, 169, 174, 179, 183, 193, 209, 218, 280
Midnight in the Stable [EG] 200
Millington, Kathleen 306, 410, 413, 415, 416, 418, 420, 445
Molesworth, Mrs. 84, 355
Monet 427
Monroe, Jessie 22, 133, 134, 151, 178, 253, 275, 287, 288, 302, 305, 306, 325
  Celtic Presbyterian 308
  characteristics 306
  cottage in Wales 397
  dedicatee of The White Witch 341
  description of herself 331
  EG books 307
  EG's greatest blessing 458
  first meeting with EG 305
  illness 458
  inspiration for Mary O'Hara 331

love of open fire 461
nursing EG 459
protecting EG 336
Rose Cottage Garden 340
visit to Costa Rica 445
More, Thomas 282
Morning Post, The 156
Morris, William 103, 104, 107, 126
Morton-Sale, Isobel and John 261, 390
Mozart 425
Mutiny on the Bounty 256
My Father [EG] 187, 229, 236, 440
My God and My All [EG] 347
myth and imagination 160, 161

N

Nanny [Ellen Jolliffe] 26
death 237
EG's love for 28
help after Dr. Goudge's death 207
kindness 26
leaving Ely 80
nurse to Mrs. Goudge 61, 154
parents' home in Bath 61
poem dedicated to 26, 229
National Portrait Gallery 186, 346
Nelson, Thomas 154, 287
New Forest 88, 229, 314, 348
Newman, John Henry 169, 474
News-Tribune, The 400
New York Times, The 193, 389
Nice Man, St. George [EG] 200
Norland College 26

O

Observer, The 293
Old Age [EG] 329
Olivier, Edith 372
Omnibook 253, 257, 271, 283
On Being Photographed – A True Story [EG] 332
Origen 248
Our Brother the Sun [EG] 264
Our Lady [EG] 321

Oxford
attitude to females 136
Christ Church Cathedral 126
Christ Church Meadows 127
glories 130
Magdalen cloisters 131, 146, 214
Tom Quad 117, 124, 127, 142, 193, 245
Oxford Group 294
Oxford Guide to British Women Writers, The 193
Oxford Mail, The 433, 439
Oxford University Dramatic Society 159
Ozanne, William [great-grandfather] 41

P

Palmer, Samuel 142, 152
Parmiter family 50, 176, 337
Parnassus Gallery, Moretonhampstead 390
Passing Show, The 151
Patey, Bob 251
Paton, Joseph Noel 245
Pattern of People, A 410, 443, 446
Pearn, Nancy 150
Peck, Gregory 256
Pedlar's Pack, A [EG] 151, 168, 193, 306
Penn, Irving 186
Peppard 314, 336, 337, 419
church 390, 471
proposed development 457
Rose Cottage 309, 310, 313, 314, 325, 332, 334, 335, 336, 337, 340, 341, 352, 354, 365, 366, 367, 371, 374, 405, 413, 418, 428, 433, 449, 459, 462
Philips, J.B. 293
Pilcher, Rosamunde 302
Piper, John and Myfanwy 314, 375, 419
Pitter, Ruth 337, 371, 375, 386, 418, 419, 450
Placidus 276, 277, 278

Plato 284
Plowright, Joan 370
Pollinger, L.E. 150
Pope John Paul II 449
Poynter, Edward 246
Practical Mysticism 148
Practice of the Presence of God, The 258, 379, 513
Pre-Raphaelites 104, 108, 126
Preston, Kenneth 423
Prince Albert 245
Prince Albert [King George VI] 124
Princesses Elizabeth and Margaret Rose 237
Public Opinion 144
Puck of Pook's Hill 229, 245, 346, 421

Q

Queen Elizabeth the First 194
Queen Elizabeth, the Queen mother [Lady Elizabeth Bowes-Lyon] 124
Queen Mary 140
Queen Victoria 3, 19, 245

R

Rackham, Arthur 105, 246
Ransome, Arthur 273
Raphael Mary, Sister 429, 460
Raphael Tuck and Sons 9
Raverat, Gwen 335
Reading College 103
Reed, Donna 256
Reform Magazine 295, 443
Reid, David 419
reincarnation 123, 153
Rembrandt 427
Reward of Faith, The [EG] 253, 270, 287, 306
Richard II 229
Richards, Dakota Blue 268
Rider of the White Horse, The [EG preface] 345

RNA News 253, 257, 369, 373, 394, 397, 410, 415, 458
Romantic Novelists' Association 253, 374, 412, 413
Rosemary Tree, The [EG] 25, 49, 58, 59, 73, 86, 97, 137, 173, 206, 228, 291, 310, 313, 325, 332, 333, 337, 348, 370, 406, 411, 440, 460
Rowling, J.K. 268, 346
Royal Academy 245
Ruskin, John 103, 106, 155, 245, 246

S

Sackville-West, Vita 260
Saint Francis of Assisi [EG] 253, 339, 341, 343, 347, 366
Sandys, Cynthia 407
Sayers, Dorothy L. 100, 244, 293
Scent of Water, The [EG] xv, 50, 135, 138, 142, 163, 168, 182, 187, 189, 220, 314, 349, 371, 373, 375, 377, 378, 379, 382, 386, 388, 401, 418, 420, 421, 422, 475
Schofield, Paul 151
Schubert 427
Scotsman, The 325
Scott, Walter 83, 281
Seaby, Professor 105, 106
Second World War 5, 151
  Battle of Britain 230
  bombs in Marldon parish 239
  Christian literary creativity 244
  evacuees 236
  fall of Greece 249
  invasion of Guernsey 231
  Marldon and D-Day 255
  phoney war 215
  the Blitz 231
Secret of Moonacre, The 268
Serena the Hen [EG] 390
servants 226
  disappearance of, postwar 226
  Ely 81
  Ely/Oxford 227
  Wells 30

528

Sex Disqualification Removal Act 102
Shakespeare 89, 91, 92, 93, 102, 116, 159, 229, 245, 246, 247, 263, 370, 372, 399, 427
Shaw, George Bernard 307
Shelley, Norman 282
Shelley, Percy Bysshe 183, 399
Shepherd and a Shepherdess, A [EG] 150, 155
Shufflewing, The [EG] 390
Sidney, Philip 199
Silver Horse, The [EG] 398
Sister of the Angels [EG] 7, 71, 106, 176, 187, 192, 193, 208, 241, 242, 263, 361, 417
Smart, Christopher 247, 436
Smoky-House [EG] 27, 90, 228, 229, 242, 263, 266, 296
Socrates 114
Songs and Verses [EG] 228, 250, 253, 272
Spender, Stephen 428
Spenser, Edmund 465
Spirit of the Wood, The [EG] 461
spiritual greatness 385
Spring Song [EG] 264, 353, 394
Statue of the Virgin at Buckler's Hard, The [EG] 320
Stevenson, Juliet 268
Stevenson, Robert Louis xiv, 3, 4, 12, 27, 54, 57, 322, 323, 324, 350, 394
Stewart, Madeau 337, 405, 406, 407, 408, 414, 416, 424, 429, 434, 449, 454, 457, 458, 459, 460, 461, 472
St. Hugh's Press 281
Strand Magazine 150, 151, 174
Streatfield, Noel 273
Strength in the Stone, The [EG] 158, 249
suicidal characters 183
Sunday Times, The 236, 434
Suomi [EG] 200, 208
superfluous women 174

Sutcliff, Rosemary 224, 345, 346, 412
Swinburne, Algernon 84

T

Tallis, Thomas 425
Tarbat, Alan C. 209
Taylor, Jeremy 402
Teachers
  Ely governess 85
  Miss Bartlett 89, 91, 142
  Miss Lavington 14
  Miss Lumby 87, 325
Temple, William 244
Ten Gifts, The 396
Tennyson, Alfred 110
Teresa of Avila, St. 123
Thackeray, William Makepeace 83, 245
Theatres 167
  Aldwych 370
  Arts 167
  Court 93, 159
  Globe 263
  Hampstead Embassy 151
  Mermaid 263
  Oldham Coliseum 282
  Old Vic 159
  Oxford Playhouse 159
Theologia Germanica 147
Things Seen in Oxford 129
Thomas, Dylan 399
Thomas, R.S. 58, 152, 368
Thoreau, Henry David 152
Thorndike, Dame Sybil 151
Thorndike, Eileen 151
Three Cities of Bells [EG] 11, 392
Three-Fold Prayer, the 422
Three Grey Men, The [EG] 270, 343
Three Plays [EG] 193, 208, 347
Time magazine 283
Times Literary Supplement 392
Times, The 295, 314, 342, 369, 399, 409, 462
Tolkien, J.R.R. 145, 161, 162, 371
To Nannie [EG] 27
Toomey, Philippa 409, 438

Tortelier, Paul 416
Tortoise stove 82
Towers in the Mist [EG] 28, 29, 125, 126, 145, 170, 173, 193, 194, 195, 196, 199, 209, 229, 233, 369, 392
Trade News 408
Traherne, Thomas 64, 65, 221, 222, 296, 298, 315, 317, 400, 401, 475
Trollope, Anthony 10, 83, 370
Turner, Lana 256

U

Uncles
    Clavel Parmiter 34, 50
    Great-Uncle William 260
    James Goodhart 20, 34, 46, 75, 253, 372
    William Collenette 33, 113, 207
Underhill, Evelyn 148, 257, 261, 361, 362, 363, 364, 365, 422
University of London Press 253, 296
U.S. Saturday Review of Literature 144, 240, 279, 347

V

Valley of Song, The [EG] 296, 298, 300
Van Gogh 220, 316
Vaughan, Henry 58, 473
Victoria and Albert Museum 103
Virgil 196
Vision of God, A 445
Vivaldi, Antonio 416

W

Wagenknecht, Edward 394, 400
Wales, Pembrokeshire 397, 399, 405, 448, 459
    Roch Castle 399
    St. David's Cathedral 399
Walton, Alan Hull 283, 306, 325, 408, 410, 416, 417, 419, 434, 435
Ward, J. Neville ix, 424, 427
Washington, Ned 257

Waste Land, The 121, 122, 123, 222
Weatherhead, Leslie 189
Weekly Scotsman, The 152
Well of the Star, The [EG] 151, 200, 228, 294, 394
Wells
    Bishop's Palace 8, 11, 223
    Cathedral Church of St. Andrew 7
    Principal's House 8, 9, 16
    Principal's House shrubbery 93
    Tower House 3, 7, 8, 9, 12, 22, 84
    Vicars' Close 9
    Wells today 74
Wells, H.G. 151, 218
West Country Magic [EG] 213, 232, 264
White Deer, the 276
White Wings [EG] 151, 249, 253, 282, 306, 439
White Witch, The [EG] xv, 110, 116, 127, 130, 162, 175, 179, 300, 301, 303, 304, 334, 339, 341, 343, 375, 397, 412
Williams, Charles 136, 145
Wind in the Willows, The 83, 240, 346
Wings, the Literary Guild Review 276
Winn, Godfrey 293
Wodehouse, P.G. 151
Wolfe, Humbert 233
Wolsey, Cardinal 125, 139, 140
Woman's Home Companion 151
Woman's Journal 151, 200, 208, 229, 253, 257, 264, 271, 283, 287, 293, 322, 332, 340, 341, 353, 372, 393, 396
Woodgate, Mildred 357
Woolf, Virginia 144, 171, 383
Wordsworth, William 58, 60, 64, 65, 155, 391

Y

Yeats, William Butler 132, 152